MATZPEN
A History of Israeli Dissidence

Lutz Fiedler
Translated by Jake Schneider

EDINBURGH
University Press

Edinburgh University Press is one of the leading university presses in the UK. We publish academic books and journals in our selected subject areas across the humanities and social sciences, combining cutting-edge scholarship with high editorial and production values to produce academic works of lasting importance. For more information visit our website: edinburghuniversitypress.com

Original version © Vandenhoeck & Ruprecht GmbH & Co. KG, 2017, 2022
English translation © Jake Schneider, 2020, 2022

Edinburgh University Press Ltd
The Tun – Holyrood Road
12 (2f) Jackson's Entry
Edinburgh EH8 8PJ

First published in hardback by Endinburgh University Press 2017

Typeset in 11/15 Adobe Garamond by
IDSUK (DataConnection) Ltd

A CIP record for this book is available from the British Library

ISBN 978 1 4744 5116 1 (hardback)
ISBN 978 1 4744 5117 8 (paperback)
ISBN 978 1 4744 5118 5 (webready PDF)
ISBN 978 1 4744 5119 2 (epub)

The right of Lutz Fiedler to be identified as author of this work has been asserted in accordance with the Copyright, Designs and Patents Act 1988 and the Copyright and Related Rights Regulations 2003 (SI No. 2498).

Originally published in German as *Matzpen. Eine andere israelische Geschichte* (Göttingen, Germany: Vandenhoeck & Ruprecht, 2017)

The translation of this work was funded by Geisteswissenschaften International – Translation Funding for Work in the Humanities and Social Sciences from Germany, a joint initiative of the Fritz Thyssen Foundation, the German Federal Foreign Office, the collecting society VG WORT and the Börsenverein des Deutschen Buchhandels (German Publishers & Booksellers Association).

Published with the support of the University of Edinburgh Scholarly Publishing Initiatives Fund.

Contents

List of Figures	v
Acknowledgements	vii
Introduction: Cohn-Bendit on the Roof in Gan Shmuel	1
1 Communist Dissidents	29
De-Stalinisation in Israel	29
Revolt Against the Histadrut	43
Shalom, Shalom ve-Eyn Shalom – Peace, Peace, When There is No Peace	54
2 The Israel–Palestine Question	78
'Al-Ard and Us': In Support of Israeli Arabs' Protest	78
Traditions of Dissent: Bygone Utopias of Jewish–Arab Coexistence	86
From the Algerian War to the Palestine Question	102
'Foreign Natives': Prospects of Recognition	114
3 The Invention of a Hebrew Nation	139
'One Day, Two Declarations'	139
'. . . and the Canaanite Was Then In the Land'	150
Profaning the Language: The Emergence of Israeli Hebrew	161
Hebrew Pornography	172
From Hebrew Nation to Semitic Action	180
After 1967: Hostilities and Contradictions	188

4	*Hal'a HaKibush!* – Down with the Occupation	213
	The Six-Day War and the Return of the Palestine Question	213
	Parting Ways: Utopias in Conflict	226
	Border-Crossings: From Gan Shmuel to Damascus	240
	State or Revolution	251
5	*Khamsin*: A New Vision for the Middle East	281
	London–Paris–Beirut	281
	Eli Lobel: 'A Foreign Minister without a State'	287
	Arab Self-Criticism and Palestinian Revolution	297
	Journal of Revolutionary Socialists of the Middle East	306
6	Beyond the Holocaust: Jewish Past, Hebrew Present, Socialist Future	325
	Cohn-Bendit's Departure: Israel and the Holocaust	325
	Jewish and Hebrew Memories Juxtaposed	336
	Socialism or Barbarism	352
	Lebanon 1982: 'The Real War and the Imaginary War'	366

Bibliography	405
Index of Persons	455

Figures

I.1	A group photo of the revolution	5
1.1	Cover of the first issue of *Matzpen*, 21 November 1962	31
1.2	Akiva Orr as a seaman, early 1950s	45
1.3	Oded Pilavsky in the early 1960s	52
2.1	Moshé Machover and Jabra Nicola	102
3.1	Advertisement in *Haaretz*, 22 September 1967	144
3.2	Dan Omer outside his protest tent in Jerusalem, 1966	179
3.3	Uri Avnery and Haim Hanegbi, shortly after the war of June 1967	191
3.4	The Hebrew writer Shimon Tzabar during his London period, 1974	195
4.1	Michel Warschawski and Sylvia Klingberg at a demonstration in Tel Aviv	219
4.2	Haim Hanegbi and Ilan Halevi on the campus of the Hebrew University of Jerusalem, Givat Ram, 1969	236
4.3	The defendants in the courtroom, Haifa, 1973	249
5.1	Cover image of the first issue of *Khamsin*	283
5.2	Eli Lobel in the 1960s	291
6.1	Daniel Cohn-Bendit and Dan Ben-Amotz at the Hebrew University of Jerusalem, 1970	326

The author would like to thank Meir Wigoder, Haim Hanegbi, Jonathan Lobel, Sharon Orr, Dan Hadani, Ehud Ein-Gil, Moshé Machover and Amos Ben-Shachar for granting permission to reprint their photographs.

Figs I.1 and 3.3: © Private collection of Haim Hanegbi

Figs 1.1 and 5.1: © Lutz Fiedler

Fig. 1.2: © Estate of Akiva Orr (held by Sharon Orr)

Fig. 1.3: © Estate of Oded Pilavsky/www.matzpen.org

Fig. 2.1: © Private collection of Moshé Machover

Fig. 3.1: © Haim Hanegbi, Shimon Tzabar

Fig. 3.2: © Amos Ben-Shachar

Figs 3.4, 4.1, 4.2 and 6.1: © Photographs by Meir Wigoder

Fig. 4.3: © From the collection of the National Library of Israel, courtesy of Oscar Tauber (Dan Hadani collection)

Fig. 5.2: © Private collection of Jonathan Lobel

Acknowledgements

This book is a translated and updated version of a German-language book that was originally published with Vandenhoeck & Ruprecht in 2017. Its publication was preceded by a long personal journey, and the book has multiple origin stories. One of them began in December 2004 with a screening at a Jerusalem cultural centre. The film was the documentary *Matzpen: Anti-Zionist Israelis*, whose director Eran Torbiner hoped to save the story of these Israeli leftists from oblivion. The film resonated with earlier conversations in which Dan Diner had called my attention to Matzpen and pointed out that the group had yet to be historically interpreted in the context of Jewish and Israeli history. His suggestions began to prompt questions of my own. It is thanks to him, my academic teacher and doctoral supervisor, that this initial mixture of political curiosity and intellectual fascination was translated into a scholarly interest and then developed into a dissertation project. For his intellectual guidance, for his help with this project's conception and implementation and for his personal trust, I owe him a permanent debt of gratitude.

The work on this monograph had its institutional home at the Simon Dubnow Institute for Jewish History and Culture at Leipzig University in Germany directed then by Dan Diner. I am particularly grateful to him and to his former deputy, Susanne Zepp, for the support and the opportunity to participate in an exciting intellectual environment. My appreciation also goes to my former colleagues, who contributed to this book's completion with their support, friendship and openness to dialogue, in particular Nicolas Berg, Hans-Joachim Hahn and Omar Kamil, as well as Mohammed Ahmed, Judith Ciminski, Arndt Engelhardt, Mandy Fitzpatrick, Walid Abd El Gawad, Jan Gerber, Natasha Gordinsky, Philipp Graf, Marion Hammer, Yaron Jean, David Jünger, Klaus Kempter, Carolin Kosuch, David Kowalski, Ulrike Kramme, Felix Pankonin, Nicole Petermann, Anna Pollmann, Regina Randhofer, Carina Roell, Grit Scheffer, Momme Schwarz, Alexandra Tyrolf, Sebastian Voigt and Robert Zwarg. My conversations with Haim Be'er (Ramat Gan), Yaakov Ariel (Chapel Hill) and Sadik J. Al-Azm (Berlin) led me to ask new questions about my subject.

I owe special thanks to the German Academic Exchange Service (DAAD) for funding a one-year research stay at the Koebner Minerva Center for German History at the Hebrew University of Jerusalem. In addition to intensive research, I had the opportunity to conduct numerous interviews with Matzpen members and others whose willingness to share information was indispensable to this project. Among them were Uri Avnery, Ehud and Aviva Ein-Gil, Ilan Halevi, Haim Hanegbi, Oded Pilavsky, Udi Adiv and Khalil Toama. I am extremely grateful for their support and commitment to my project. In London, Moshé Machover opened up his private archive to me. I warmly thank him and Michael Warschawski, Leila Kadi, Kristin Couper-Lobel, Gabriel Lachmann, Ruth and Klaus Rürup, Menachem Carmi and Alexander Flores, who shared their vast knowledge, as well as important personal documents, with me.

Without the support of friends and family in Leipzig, Berlin and Jerusalem, the often-challenging work on this book would not have been possible. For this, I thank my parents Monika and Wolfram, my brothers Falk and Jörg, as well as my father-in-law Andreas Gallas, who sadly did not live to see the realisation of the English publication. I also thank my friends for their solidarity, encouragement and patience, specifically Friederike Ankele, Netanel Anor, Irene Aue-Ben-David, Martin Eichler, Hannes Giessler-Furlan, Gero and Michael Götschenberg, Corry Guttstadt, Negar Habibi, Carsten Ilius, Grit Jilek, Laura Jockusch and Omer Offen, all the Lindstrots, Irit Lourie, Katrin Reimer-Gordinskaya and Jenny Tillmanns. No one accompanied the evolution of this book – the German original and the English translation – more extensively than Elisabeth Gallas. As my partner and closest confidant, she shared in my enthusiasm and sustained me in the face of a laborious abyss. For her company and stamina during the process of putting together this book, I am more indebted to her than I can express in these few short lines.

It gives me great pleasure and fills me with gratitude that the book is now available in English, and I owe a great deal of thanks to the many people who have made this publication possible. First and foremost, I would like to thank Edinburgh University Press for including the book in their programme. Nicola Ramsey, Adela Rauchova, Emma Rees and Kirsty Woods have carefully guided the development of this English-language publication from the very beginning.

The translation of the German-language book was generously funded by the Börsenverein des Deutschen Buchhandels, the Fritz Thyssen Stiftung, VG Wort and the Federal Foreign Office, who awarded the book with the 'Geisteswissenschaften International' prize and enabled me to take on the challenge of returning to and revising it. I am very thankful for this opportunity.

I could not have found anyone better than Jake Schneider, who without hesitation was ready to embark on the adventure of translating this book. He did a tremendous job in transforming the German version of this book into English, demonstrated sensitivity for the topic, was always patient and sympathetic regarding all my enquiries and has done more than anyone else to ensure that the book found the right tone. I also owe a lot of thanks to Elizabeth Welsh, who patiently took over the copy-editing and gave the book its final touches. Ella Shechter has checked all my translations from the Hebrew with patience and accuracy, and I am most grateful to her. Tizian Raschpichler was so kind to assist with the compilation of the index.

My warm thanks also go to Petra Gamke-Breitschopf, head of the editorial department at Dubnow-Institute, who aided me tirelessly in turning the German manuscript into a book and was extremely helpful in ensuring that there would be an English-language translation.

When the book was published in German, Hannes Giessler-Furlan, Andrea Kirchner and Jan-Eike Dunkhase provided vital assistance with their readings and critical comments. For the English version, I relied on the support of my friends Kobi Kabalek (State College), Yaakov Ariel (Chapel Hill), Debby Farber (Be'er-Sheva/Berlin) and Adi Gordon (Amherst), whose critical readings and comments on some chapters on some chapters were of tremendous help. I dearly thank them all. For all remaining mistakes, I alone bear responsibility.

Finally, I wish to thank my colleagues and friends from the Selma Stern Center for Jewish Studies Berlin-Brandenburg and at the Department of Cultural History and Theory at Humboldt University Berlin, in particular Liliana R. Feierstein, in the framework of which I was able to prepare this version of the book for publication.

More than a year before I completed the work on my dissertation from which this book resulted, I received word of the death of Akiva Orr (1931–2013). For many years, he had allowed me deep insights into his own life story and the story of Matzpen. His life was guided by his faith in historical progress: hope that humans would take fate into their own hands and coalesce into a united humanity. This book is dedicated to his memory.

Lutz Fiedler
Berlin, Summer 2020

Introduction: Cohn-Bendit on the Roof in Gan Shmuel

High hopes accompanied the arrival of the twenty-five-year-old Daniel Cohn-Bendit to Israel in the spring of 1970, but he wasted no time in unceremoniously dashing them. Following the events of May 1968 in Paris, Israeli newspapers had run numerous articles about the leader of the French student protests, mainly highlighting his Jewish ancestry. 'Danny the Red Calls for Overthrowing De Gaulle's "Police State"', ran the headline of a feature report in *Maariv* in May 1968, which pointed out that of all people, 'Cohn[-Bendit], a Jew and a German citizen born in France' was on the warpath against De Gaulle, the same general who had imposed an arms embargo against the Jewish state the previous year.[1] Photographs of the May upheavals in Paris had also sparked memories among members of the leftist Kibbutz HaZorea, where Cohn-Bendit, years before making his name, had spent several weeks back in the summer of 1963 discussing socialism, communism, Zionism and the State of Israel. Now, a year after the Six-Day War, his friends from that visit were convinced that he was 'by no means anti-Israel', and that 'if we could explain our situation to him, he surely would agree with our stance'.[2] Two years later, in May 1970, when Cohn-Bendit finally accepted an invitation from the Hebrew University Student Union to attend their annual Students' Day, various factions awaited the international celebrity with great anticipation. *Maariv* printed an article titled '"Danny the Red" Arrives in Israel', the first of many varied reports on his visit. Later, Cohn-Bendit recalled and summarised the subtext of the early vivid press coverage welcoming him back to Israel: 'He is coming. It is up to us to convince him to stay.'[3]

However, Daniel Cohn-Bendit's two visits – first as a youth in 1963 and then as the reborn 'Danny the Red' of 1970 – were divided by more than the Six-Day War, which had prompted the resurfacing of the long-neglected Palestine question after Israel occupied the Gaza Strip and the West Bank. As those two iconic moments, June 1967 and May 1968, were juxtaposed, the conflict over Israel and Palestine had drawn the attention of the global New Left and become a battleground of the movement's self-declared internationalism. As one of the leading lights of the New Left in France, Cohn-Bendit had naturally reached out to the New Left's Israeli contingent ahead of his visit, whose vocal dissent over the Palestine question had placed it in the spotlight of the worldwide political movement. Meeting them, therefore, was Cohn-Bendit's top priority: 'From the very first day, I had a discussion with my friends from Matzpen', he recalled in his memoirs, referring to the Israeli Socialist Organization by its nickname. Together, he and its members had decided that he 'should represent the traditional internationalist position: "I am against a Jewish state, against an Arab state. I am for a socialist and free Middle East, open to everyone who wants to live in a society governed by workers' and farmers' councils."'[4] Even though the young celebrity had come to Israel at the invitation of the student union, upon his arrival, he decided to serve as a spokesperson for the New Leftists of Matzpen.

The first affront came as soon as Cohn-Bendit arrived at Lod International Airport (now Ben-Gurion Airport, Tel Aviv). When the face of the Paris Student Rebellion landed on the evening of 24 May 1970, he was greeted at the airport by the press's camera flashes and the official delegation of the student union. Cohn-Bendit greeted its chair with no more than a ceremonial handshake before turning affectionately to Haim Hanegbi (1935–2018) of Matzpen, who was standing at the margins of the group, and proclaiming that his friends in Matzpen were 'the sole few revolutionaries this country has'.[5] On Students' Day, when he delivered his speech at the Hebrew University of Jerusalem's expansive Weiss Auditorium, his audience listened intently to his remarks about the events of May 1968 in Paris, the student rebellions and his thoughts about prospects for a social revolution. But the more he voiced the political demands of the Israeli Radical Left – loudly opposing the Israeli occupation and calling, just as stridently, for mutual recognition between Israelis and Palestinians – the more outraged heckles erupted from the crowd, coalescing finally into a chant of 'Danny, go home!' A few days later, members of the right-wing Gurei Ze'ev (Wolf Boys) group tried to disrupt another evening discussion at a student residence hall in Jerusalem.[6] The situation reached a further dramatic climax during a visit to Gan Shmuel, a left-wing kibbutz in the north, where the ideals of collective equality and socialist revolution had been pursued in the name of Zionism and internationalism alike.[7] The images of Paris in May '68 had made their mark there too. An official event with the leader of the student rebellions was scheduled to be held in the kibbutz's large cultural hall. However, when Cohn-Bendit arrived at the gates of Gan Shmuel escorted by a delegation of Matzpen members, the mood soured. The kibbutz leadership declined to permit the speeches, which they feared would denounce the Jewish state, to be given at their community centre.

In the end, the event did take place, drawing even more attention as an impromptu private gathering on the flat roof of a building in the kibbutz. 'The audience was nearly in danger of collapsing the roof', Haim Hanegbi later recalled of the crowded event, which was held under the proviso that Cohn-Bendit's Matzpen escorts were banned from speaking.[8] In addition, to keep Cohn-Bendit in his place, Benyamin 'Benio' Gruenbaum (1907–72), the kibbutz's unchallenged authority, joined him as his discussion partner on the rooftop stage. More than anyone else, as an admired teacher of the kibbutz's children, Gruenbaum had imparted left-wing Zionist values to multiple generations of Gan Shmuel.[9] Now he wanted to defend his kibbutz to Cohn-Bendit as a fulfilment of the socialist utopia and the Zionist dream. But the recalcitrant leader of the student movement was only mildly impressed. In a provocative mood, he asked Gruenbaum point-blank whether the country's Arabs were also included in this paradise of freedom and equality.[10] 'Can socialism be for Jews only? If it is socialism, then it should be for everyone. [. . .] The road of Zionism has already been a road of conquest',[11] he is reported to have said, summarising his core stance on the fundamentals of the Palestine question: 'My basic view rests on the idea that all people are equal, with equal rights, and that every nation has the right to self-determination.'[12] Soon some of the audience members were so incensed that they repeatedly cut the power supply, leaving all the participants in the dark.[13]

The scene on the roof in Gan Shmuel was more than just a political confrontation – that is, a clash of opposing views on the Israel–Palestine conflict. In fact, the figures of Gruenbaum and Cohn-Bendit represented two different sets of experiences in Jewish history that were now colliding by way of the Palestine question. To a degree, they embodied the dramas of Jewish and Israeli existence in the twentieth century. Benyamin Gruenbaum may have been the educator who shaped the kibbutz, and whose political notion of the unity of socialism and Zionism drew on the experiences of turn-of-the-century Polish Jewry.[14] But as the firstborn son of the Polish politician Yitzhak Gruenbaum, he also bore the scars of the catastrophic collapse of Polish Jewry. His father's advocacy for minority rights at the Polish Sejm had won him the nickname 'King of the Jews'; after immigrating to Palestine in 1933, the elder Gruenbaum became head of the Jewish Agency's Rescue Committee (the Vaad Hatzalah), tasked with rescuing European Jews.[15] Benyamin Gruenbaum's younger brother Eliezer had opted to remain loyal to communism over the family's decision to move to Palestine. In Europe, he fought the communist fight for universal liberty, first in Spain and then as part of the French Resistance, before he was eventually captured by the Nazis. In the final years of the war, Eliezer was forced to serve at Auschwitz as a Kapo. After liberation, he died in uncertain circumstances during Israel's War of Independence.[16] In the end, Kibbutz Gan Shmuel itself was testimony both to Zionists' ultimate hopes and to the failure of the alternatives in Europe. After 1945, the kibbutz became home to a growing number of Holocaust survivors.[17] The day after his night-time discussion on the roof, the young Cohn-Bendit was also scheduled to meet with those survivors, who would leave a lasting impression on him.[18]

Thinking back to his visit to Israel, he reflected: 'I, for example, have never been personally or directly oppressed; I repressed the fact that my parents were forced to leave Germany.'[19] Born in 1945 to exiled parents in France, Cohn-Bendit was shaped tangibly by D-Day: 'When the Allies landed, they said, "now we can make a child of freedom".' Cohn-Bendit recalled his parents' stories from their youth and his own path from 'a child of freedom' to the figurehead of the New Left in France.[20] The statelessness of the young French-born German Jew played another part in his decision to identify with internationalist principles and socialist utopias. 'My ideology is a strange blend, because I am not deeply rooted anywhere and am therefore especially receptive to all experiences', he wrote, before concluding: 'One must overcome one's own emotional ties to the national past.'[21] This self-proclaimed internationalism had found vivid expression in Cohn-Bendit's political biography. Far beyond France and Germany, he had become a symbolic figure of the New Left, whose agenda for social change ranged from a universalistic anticolonialism to protests against the Vietnam War and support for dissident movements in the Eastern Bloc.[22]

Cohn-Bendit was less occupied with his own Jewishness or the State of Israel. When asked at Gan Shmuel how he saw himself, his reply was ironic: 'The first time I felt like a Jew was when a hundred thousand students were demonstrating in Paris, chanting "We are all German Jews!"' Even Algerian Arabs had joined in the calls against his deportation from France, a memorable gesture of transnational solidarity.[23] Since 1967, when the Six-Day War

Figure I.1 A group photo of the revolution. A meeting between Daniel Cohn-Bendit, Matzpen members and members of the Israeli–Arab organisation Abnaa el-Balad, 1970. Standing (left to right): Haim Hanegbi, Marius Schattner, Ilan Halevi, unidentified, Daniel Cohn-Bendit, Mohammed Kiwan, Udi Aviv. Lower row: unidentified.

placed the Israel–Palestine conflict at the centre of debate for the European Left, it was, in fact, the tragic fate of the Palestinians that began to spark Cohn-Bendit's internationalism. But it was not until the spring of 1970, when he revisited Israel and became acquainted with the local left-wing activists of Matzpen, that he joined the Israeli dissidents' position on this issue. This became apparent on the rooftop in Gan Shmuel, where he proclaimed to his audience: 'The solution [to the conflict] is a socialist Israel in which Israeli Jews and Arabs – Christians and Moslems – can live together.'[24] Eventually, only fifteen miles from the left-wing kibbutz, near the Arab town of Umm al-Fahm, Cohn-Bendit came another step closer to this internationalist vision. Together with his Matzpen escorts, he met with members of the Arab group Abnaa el-Balad (Sons of the Village), who had already been envisioning a common future together with members of the Israeli New Left.[25]

By then, Israel's excitement in the run-up to Cohn-Bendit's visit had flipped against him. The terror attack on an Israeli school bus on 22 May, directly ahead of Cohn-Bendit's visit, shook the country and significantly influenced his concluding press conference. By neutrally condemning the deaths of any children, Jewish and Arab alike, he significantly distanced himself from the immediacy of the terror. 'Don't you ever show your face here again!' a reporter shouted at him, demanding a clear statement of solidarity.[26] The *Jerusalem Post* dubbed Cohn-Bendit's visit 'Danny's "Eight-Day-War"'.[27] Even Israel's prime minister, Golda Meir, entered the fray. 'Cohn-Bendit had nothing interesting to report to us', she later said. To her mind, he had simply been given 'an opportunity [. . .] to rebuke Israel and the Jewish people'.[28] And the left-wing Zionist newspaper *Al HaMishmar* concluded that even if Cohn-Bendit had failed 'to suppress his feelings of enmity against Israel and its justified struggle', the source of those feelings lay in Israel itself. The journalists were convinced that Cohn-Bendit had been exposed to almost a week of 'brainwashing' and to the 'demagogical anti-Israel spirit' of the notorious Matzpen group.[29] They were not entirely mistaken: in the end, what Cohn-Bendit remembered most vividly about his visit to Israel was his formative encounter with his political allies in the Israeli New Left. 'Matzpen redeems the "honour" of the Jews', he remarked later in his memoir. And he came to the conclusion that '[t]hirty or forty years from now, when people examine the question of Israel, it will be highly important for young people who are becoming political to be able to identify with Matzpen'.[30]

Matzpen, the Hebrew word for compass, was the name of the magazine of the Israeli Socialist Organization, whose story this book will recount. Matzpen also became the nickname of that organisation as it developed a disproportional reputation as the country's greatest domestic threat and became a codeword for radical dissent in Israel in the years following the Six-Day War, 'a name the majority of Israelis loved to hate'.[31] The roots of the Israeli Socialist Organization and the beginnings of its political deviation trace back to the autumn of 1962, when a small group of communist dissidents gathered around Akiva Orr (1931–2013), Moshé Machover (b. 1936), Oded Pilavsky (1932–2011) and Yirmiyahu Kaplan just after breaking off from the Communist Party, known by its Hebrew abbreviation Maki (Miflaga Kommunistit Isra'elit). The birth of Matzpen was a manifestation of the New Left's secession from the ideological hegemony of a party-communism loyal to Moscow. Its 'second birth', which finally made Matzpen a household name in Israel, revolved around the war of June 1967 and Israel's conflict-laden existence in the Middle East. Society accorded this small group of just a few dozen members a prominence utterly out of proportion with its actual size or its true political influence. On the eve of the war, when Arab threats of annihilation united domestic Israeli society across party lines, Matzpen broke with this consensus. Even during the war, the London *Times* released a 'Joint Israeli–Arab Statement on the Middle East Crisis', co-authored by the Israeli leftists and a Palestinian group on 3 June, which opposed the escalation and called for a socialist solution to the Israeli–Arab conflict.[32] Just when the national euphoria over the military victory was being further fuelled by Israelis' newfound access to Jewish holy places, renewing Israel's confidence, Matzpen was demanding an immediate withdrawal to the borders of 4 June 1967. Shouting the rallying cry *Hal'a HaKibush!* – Down with the Occupation! – the small group of young leftists paraded down the streets of the Jewish state and through the university campuses of Tel Aviv and Jerusalem. At a time when Israel's prime minister, Golda Meir, was openly questioning the very existence of a Palestinian people,[33] Matzpen was proclaiming the rights of this same people: both to exercise self-determination and to resist the Israeli occupation. Given the guerrilla activities and recurrent violence by Palestinians, Matzpen was accused of making common cause with Israel's enemies, betraying the national interest and harbouring disloyalty towards Israeli Jewry. Members of the group were physically beaten on several occasions on university campuses and during their many demonstrations.[34] Newspaper articles accused Matzpen of 'psychopathy', 'treason' and a 'collective lack of integrity', resurrecting the old trope of the 'self-hating Jew'.[35]

The resentment, rejection and even hatred that Matzpen inspired after the Six-Day War were not short-term responses to their provocative protests against the Israeli occupation or to their solidarity with the Palestinians. Indeed, the group had inflamed deep-seated sensitivities – in fact, it had asked questions that touched upon the very existence of the Jewish state. Just as the Six-Day War had unearthed Israel's conflict with the Palestinians but was by no means the conflict's original cause or trigger, Matzpen's public protests did not solely centre on the events of 1967. 'Identifying with Israel's enemies has been Matzpen's party [sic] line since its very establishment', wrote the journalist Avraham Wolfensohn in the pages of *Davar*, a Hebrew-language daily newspaper, in May 1970.[36] His contemptuous judgement, though, also expressed a truth. Long before the war, Matzpen had stressed that the national dispute between Israeli Jews and Palestinian Arabs was almost deadlocked because it was not a conventional territorial conflict, but a collision between pioneering settler–immigrants and a resident population. As a conflict over the foundation and preservation of a Jewish nation-state in a majority-Arab environment, these New Leftists saw this quarrel as irreconcilable: the establishment of the Jewish state and the Palestinian national catastrophe were irrevocably linked, tainting the legitimacy of the state itself.[37] In the era after Auschwitz, when the Jewish world stood in almost unanimous solidarity with Israel on the territory of historical Palestine, such a radical perspective towards the Israel–Palestine conflict must have violated the collective notion that a Jewish state was the essential prerequisite for Jews' safety and survival after the Holocaust.

Yet these radical leftists were neither the first nor the only group in Israel to address the state's founding conflict. Concurrent with Daniel Cohn-Bendit's visit to Israel, issue 54 of *Matzpen* reprinted excerpts from the short story 'Khirbet Khizeh' by the Israeli writer S. Yizhar (Yizhar Smilansky), a canonical masterpiece from 'the most important author of the Palmah generation'.[38] Narrated from the perspective of a participating soldier, the story openly describes the forced displacement of the Arab populace and the destruction of Arab villages during the Israeli War of Independence.[39] And yet the moral shock that the author was expressing at the time had different motives from those of Matzpen's reprinting. As an intelligence officer in the Giv'ati Brigade, Smilansky had participated in the war himself, and as a Ben-Gurion loyalist and Member of Knesset for his Mapai party (Mifleget Poalei Eretz Yisrael; the Workers' Party of the Land of Israel), he had remained silent in public about the military government and the measures against the Arab minority in the Jewish state.[40] Matzpen's intentions were different. By printing Smilanky's story under the headline 'History of Zionism', they set out to transform his literary work into a critical, political manifesto that confronted Israeli society with its historical responsibility and compelled it to action.[41] In relation to Israel's ongoing conflict with the Palestinians and the Arab world, their future-oriented internationalism based on socialism and revolution laid the groundwork for untangling the basic questions surrounding Israel's founding conflict and for negotiating its long-term transformation. The political agenda of Matzpen was determined by the idea of a 'de-Zionisation of Israel and its integration in a socialist Middle Eastern union', which would facilitate a new existence for Israeli Jews within their Arab region.[42]

These transformative ambitions, indeed, the reinvention of Israeli society itself – in order to resolve the Israel–Palestine conflict and seek a common future for Israeli Jews and Palestinian Arabs – are the subject of this book. Facing ominous scenarios for the outcome of the Israeli–Palestinian conflict, Matzpen sought to be no less than a compass and to orient Israeli Jews towards establishing a lasting, secure existence in the Middle East. In the timeline of history, this compass pointed straight at the future and drew on utopian ideas. Matzpen's hopes for change were radically informed by the universalistic expectations that the New Left had resurrected upon its secession from the old party-communism: the renewal of past utopian visions of progress, and of a united humanity. In view of the historic 'Palestine question', and given the irreconcilability of the conflict over a Jewish state within its Arab surroundings, the compass needle of the New Left turned away from the Zionist notion that the Jews had an historical right to Palestine. Rather, they were convinced that a new direction towards de-Zionisation and socialism would give Israeli Jewry fresh legitimacy. The members of Matzpen hoped that by decoupling themselves from the Zionist project – a nationalist movement that had entered the scene as outsiders in an Arab region – they could forge a new beginning for an Israeli collectivity that had since been born in that region. In developing this notion, they looked beyond the realm of politics and entered the sphere of culture. After the varied groups of diasporic Jews began to undergo a collective transformation during their national territorialisation, Matzpen belonged to a milieu that sought to radicalise this process by emphasising the existence of an all-new emergent Hebrew nation. Hence, their advocacy of a political breakaway from the project of a establishing and asserting a Jewish nation-state also embodied a complete secularisation of the Israeli present and a retreat from the religiously grounded bond between a unified Jewish people and Eretz Israel.[43]

Ultimately, the visionary redefinition of Israeli existence by the Israeli Left also pointed outward: to the Palestinian Arabs and the Arab world at large. The invention of another Israel – apart from its Zionist history – simultaneously heralded the transformation of the Arab societies through comprehensive modernisation and secularisation, a development linked to the hope that the Arab world would be willing to recognise a non-Arab nation in their midst and accept its belonging in the region. And yet, as sweeping as these ideas for reinventing Israel may have been, they also revealed a giant blind spot: their creators disregarded the Jewish experience of the Holocaust and the genocide's ramifications for the Jewish collectivity. The directional needle of their compass wavered when the Israeli leftists were not just confronted with the Zionist claim to a Jewish state in Palestine, but challenged by Jews' existential retreat into their own collectivity and their own state – based on nothing but the experience of annihilation. This made the Jewish past, the Israeli–Hebrew present and the socialist future mutually irreconcilable.

The radical vision of reinventing Israel was not merely grounded in hopeful expectations or in a conviction that the region could be transformed. What makes these ideas particularly interesting is their links to various historical experiences beyond Zionism that had been largely buried by the founding of the state. Within Matzpen's political programme of reinventing Israeli existence, Haim Hanegbi played an emblematic role in rediscovering and revering archives of those historical experiences from pre-state eras. In 1970, Hanegbi had eagerly met Daniel Cohn-Bendit at Lod Airport and shown him around the country. After two of Matzpen's founders, Akiva Orr and Moshé Machover, moved to London before the Six-Day War, the charismatic bohemian Hanegbi rose to become a spokesperson for the Israeli Radical Left.[44]

In April 1968, when a group of religious Jews, who were intending to settle in Hebron to enforce the Jewish presence there, celebrated Passover with the governing Labour Party's approval,[45] Hanegbi's denunciation was guided by political convictions and personal memories alike. He placed the full weight of his family's history into his public protest. 'Anyone pretending to speak on behalf of the entire Hebronite community is misleading the public', he wrote in an indignant letter that was printed in the *Haaretz* daily newspaper on 20 May 1968.[46] Negating the settlers' claims to be resuming the tradition of Hebron's Jewish community, which had existed until the riots of 1929, Hanegbi signed the letter as Haim Bajaio-Hanegbi, referring to his 'family which has inhabited Hebron continuously for the last four centuries' and identifying himself as the 'sole heir of the famous Rabbi of Hebron, Haim Bajaio'. In that capacity, he demanded that the state recognise the 'sanctity of [his] private property' in Hebron and decried the Jewish settlers' request for legal establishment. 'I shall demand the realisation of my ownership rights when the ownership rights of the Palestinian Arabs over their property in Israel are realised', the letter concluded. 'Until such a day arrives, I herewith permit those who inhabited my land before the Israeli occupation on 5th June, 1967, to go on doing so.'[47]

Immediate political relevance was only one aspect of this public protest. Hanegbi's reference to his grandfather also pointed to the history of Jewish–Arabic coexistence in Hebron under the Ottoman Empire and the British Mandate.[48] His grandfather, Haim Bajaio, had lived in Hebron as an Arab Jew. Apart from Hebrew and Ladino (Judeo-Spanish), he spoke fluent Arabic, and was held in equal esteem by both Jews and Arabs. Even after the riots of summer 1929, Haim Bajaio returned to Hebron and resettled there, before eventually moving to Jerusalem in the mid-1930s. His grandson, Haim Hanegbi, had likewise grown up in a Jerusalem shared by Jews and Arabs, before the war of 1947–9 divided the country along ethnic lines. Hanegbi brought this set of experiences to Matzpen. 'So, in the 1960s, when we talked about the principle of equality in Matzpen, I wasn't just thinking in terms of socialism or a universal concept', Hanegbi recalled many years later. 'With me it was *baladi*, my country, the scents and memories of my childhood.'[49] The period of pre-state coexistence between Jews and Arabs in Palestine took on an almost mythical status. He remembered obsessively 'collecting [. . .] Mandate period maps to locate the villages that had been erased, the life that ceased to be. And the feeling that without them this is a barren country, a disabled country, a country that caused an entire nation to disappear'.[50]

Some of that bygone commonality was revived and revised in Matzpen when the group became a gathering place for both Jews and Arabs. In that light, the story of Matzpen is also the story of a Jewish–Arab relationship that, under the banner of socialist internationalism, claimed to be paving the way towards a common future for the whole region. This relationship grew out of the involvement of members such as Ahmad Masrawa, who was born in 1939 and raised in the Arab village of Ar'ara in the north. He joined shortly after his role in the 1966 documentary *My Name is Ahmad* lent him prominence in the public debate on the situation of Israeli Arabs.[51] The film depicted more than Masrawa's personal story. Rather, using him as a case study, it illustrated the history of an Arab in the Jewish state who had experienced harsh social exclusion while seeking work and housing in Tel Aviv. By joining Matzpen, Masrawa received recognition as an equal within a state that was inconsistent about the equality of its Arab citizens. 'In Matzpen, we Palestinian members were not there as token Palestinians to be pampered and indulged', recounted Khalil Toama, who had joined in 1963, a year after the group was established. 'We were valued equally and had equal rights.'[52] Toama was born in 1944 in Rama, in the north of the British Mandate's territory on the land of the future Jewish state; his Christian Arab family had returned home after the displacements of 1948. The Israel–Palestine conflict and the harried circumstances of Arabs inside the Jewish state became his lifelong cause. Indeed, it contributed to his decision to study law at the Hebrew University of Jerusalem in 1963. He soon rose to become secretary of the Arab Student Council, but he did not find an outlet for his hopes of Jewish–Arab coexistence until he joined Matzpen.

Toama's political activism quickly placed him in the crosshairs of the Israeli security apparatus, and he was repeatedly summoned to court appearances.[53] In early 1968, Toama finally came into open conflict with the state institutions when he allowed Ahmed Khalifa, a member of the Palestinian political group Kaumiun Al Arab, to stay in his home. Under charges of collaborating with the enemy, he was taken into administrative detention on 8 January and prosecuted in short order. The case outraged Toama's political allies: there was no clear evidence of a crime, and his trial was held in a military rather than civil court.[54] Besides releasing their own statement, the members of Matzpen organised a broad-based international campaign for his release, which prompted shows of solidarity in many countries and drew renewed attention to the general situation of Arabs in Israel. The initiative was backed by such intellectuals and literati as Erich Fried, Bertrand Russell and Jean-Paul Sartre.[55] At home in Israel, Matzpen attracted major media attention with its protests.[56] In July 1968, Haim Hanegbi and his fellow activists stood outside the Military Court of Appeal wearing T-shirts reading 'We are all Khalil Toama' and 'We are all Palestinian Arabs', an echo of the slogan 'We are all German Jews' that Parisians were chanting that year in solidarity with Daniel Cohn-Bendit.[57] But it was all in vain. Although Toama's eighteenth-month prison sentence was suspended and he was released early on parole, the conditions of that parole confined him to his native village and thus prevented him from continuing his studies. Disheartened, he accepted an invitation from the Socialist German Student Union (SDS) to take up residence in Frankfurt am Main. The news of this internationalist connection trickled home: 'He now lives in Frankfurt, where he shares a flat with Danny Cohn-Bendit.'[58]

The campaign for Khalil Toama's release was only one of Matzpen's public initiatives. Soon afterward, when Ilan Shalif (b. 1937) signed a statement against Israel's occupation policy, the community of his left-wing kibbutz, Negba, first demanded a retraction and then decided to expel him – to the vocal objections of Matzpen.[59] The demonstrators outside the kibbutz gates carried placards decrying 'McCarthyism in Negba'. And yet, the campaign to free Khalil Toama was mostly an unprecedented success outside Israel and beyond the Jewish community. 'Matzpen's drive to mobilise world opinion against the Jewish state was an ordeal Israelis had never experienced', the Israeli political scientist Ehud Sprinzak later wrote, looking back. '[N]one of the anti-Zionist movements active *in* Israel had ever dared to oppose the Jewish state among the Gentiles'.[60] On that basis, contemporary commentators such as the foreign correspondent of the *Maariv* daily newspaper stressed that of all Matzpen's tactics, nothing alienated Israeli society more than the group's willingness 'to wage its battle among *goyim* [Gentiles] in a forum where Israelis confront their enemies'.[61] Indeed, Matzpen had rapidly made a name for itself abroad. In particular, the New Left in Europe and the United States provided a forum for the group and raised its international profile.[62] In Paris, London, Washington and Frankfurt, the representatives of the Israeli Left were treated as experts on the Palestine question; this gave the Matzpen story a transnational dimension.[63] The Matzpen members also attracted attention when they directly confronted Israeli politicians. This took place in June 1969, when Eli Lobel (1926–79) of Matzpen was invited by the SDS chapter in Frankfurt to deliver a rebuttal to a talk by Asher Ben-Nathan, the Israeli Ambassador to Germany, and again during a joint Israeli–Palestinian protest coinciding with Golda Meir's visit to London that same year. After the Six-Day War, when Palestinian organisations began recruiting international support in the face of the Israeli occupation and could count on a solidarity speech from the dissidents at their rallies, the public outrage against Matzpen in Israel became almost limitless.

Even so, shortly after Daniel Cohn-Bendit arrived in Israel, the government-friendly newspaper *Davar* wrote: 'Despite the anguish and the harm that Matzpen's international activities cause for Israeli PR, [. . .] [t]he damage that Matzpen inflicts domestically is much more grievous.'[64] Cohn-Bendit's visit occurred during a time when latent tensions within Israel were coming to a head; tensions that had been submerged by the wave of national euphoria after the Six-Day War.[65] In autumn 1968, the Israeli journalist Amos Elon had investigated the student protests in Europe and concluded that Israeli society demonstrated all signs of stability, at least on the surface, and that the country had long since outgrown its own youthful rebellion: the Zionist revolution. Scarcely two years later, this conclusion would prove deceptive.[66] An ongoing process of segregation and individuation was beginning to crack open the social homogeneity of the immediate post-war period. Certainly, these early shifts could not be attributed solely to Matzpen's own activities. Especially in the cultural realm, various scandals were gesturing towards a transformation in the social consciousness. For example, in April and May 1970, the play *Queen of the Bathtub*, by prominent playwright and director

Hanoch Levin, caused a scandal that spread far beyond the lobby of Tel Aviv's Cameri Theatre.[67] Its open criticism of Israel's militarised society, its charge of societal hubris after the war and its laments of the Arab population's treatment under Israeli occupation unleashed a tempest of indignation, violent attacks and a bomb threat before the play's run was finally cut short under pressure from the Tel Aviv authorities.[68]

'McCarthy is alive and hiding in Israel!' ran a feature in *Haaretz* in May 1970, criticising the culture of public debate, which was stirred up by the ongoing Goldmann Affair.[69] The previous month, the Israeli government had put an end to the efforts by Nahum Goldmann, president of the World Jewish Congress, to broker a direct meeting with the Egyptian president and pave the way to peace talks.[70] Yet the 'Give Goldmann a Chance' demonstrations, which were organised by various groups on the left fringe of Israeli society, were only one side of the Israeli domestic response. The other response was to denounce Goldmann publicly. 'Dr. Goldmann no longer believes in the Zionist solution', said Aryeh Dolchin, a minister from the right-wing Gahal party, turning against him, 'He is becoming a standard-bearer for Matzpen and Rakach [the Communist Party].' At a gathering of students in Tel Aviv where Goldmann was scheduled to speak, he was greeted with fierce opposition, with shouts of 'Goldmann is a traitor! A destroyer of Israel! A foreign agent! Matzpen! Go to Moscow!'[71] Before long, the Goldmann Affair provoked the next social upheaval. A group of graduating high school students wrote an open letter to Golda Meir expressing their doubts about reporting for their military service in view of the ban on Goldmann's initiative.[72] The 'Michtav HaShministim' (Letter by Sixth-Formers) first raised concerns when it became evident that the signatories were students attending elite Jerusalem high schools and the main author, Shmuel Shem-Tov, was the son of a leading cabinet member.[73] In the wake of the letter, a legitimate concern began to spread that Matzpen's influence on Israeli youth was clearly on the rise, a concern some of the letter's co-authors did not contest.[74] This was half a year after the school newspaper *Gashush* had sparked an initial debate over the influence of the Israeli New Left on the country's schools.[75] *Haaretz* then ran an article titled 'Matzpen and the Educational Gap', alleging and bemoaning the Israeli youth's waning connection to Jewish history and the alarming rise of Matzpen's influence at Israeli schools.[76] Yet, not until the summer of 1972 would Israel witness its first real post-1967 conscientious objector, Giora Neumann, whose affiliation with Matzpen provided ample fodder for the daily newspapers.[77] By spring 1970, Matzpen already seemed to have become the scapegoat; all purportedly critical or dissident views were ascribed to the group's ultimate influence, regardless of its members' true involvement. Unsurprisingly, that spring witnessed the first public proposals to take the Israeli leftists to court. But the suggestion of revoking the Israeli passports of Matzpen members living abroad did not lead anywhere, and nor did Member of Knesset Mathilda Guez's call for banning the organisation outright.[78] 'The first cracks within Israeli society [. . .] were already revealing themselves', wrote Cohn-Bendit retrospectively about the situation in Israel at the time, adding that the attacks on Matzpen were 'attempts [. . .] to stave off this development'.[79] After all, Daniel Cohn-Bendit's visit single-handedly attested to Matzpen's significance and its lasting impact on Israeli society. With its utopia of a reinvented Israel, Matzpen took on the role of Israel's internal 'other' and kept confronting Israeli society with itself.

* * *

Amidst the turbulent spring of 1970, during which Daniel Cohn-Bendit arrived in Israel, the first accounts of Matzpen's history began to appear. There had already been reports on the group's activities in Israel and abroad since the end of the war of June 1967, and a few even earlier – reports on which this book draws as sources.[80] Yet those months were the first time the Israeli press produced detailed explanations of this social phenomenon – Matzpen – that kept the whole country in suspense. In May 1970, Haviv Canaan (in *Haaretz*) and Avraham Wolfenson (in Davar) each published a four-part series of articles;[81] meanwhile, *Yediot Aharonot* published a multi-page feature article by Aaron Bachar profiling the group.[82] Whereas Canaan's report made a point of objectivity, Wolfensohn accused Matzpen of lacking any scruples in their struggle against Zionism and for the Palestinians' cause. Bachar's reaction was polemical: 'No one could have anticipated [. . .] that in the course of time this small circle would grow into the most repulsive ulcer that has ever existed in the Israeli political landscape.'[83] The tone of coverage changed by 1992, the thirtieth anniversary of Matzpen's founding, when several in-depth articles in the Hebrew press reviewed the group's history. The pluralisation of Israeli society and the historical distance from the phenomenon took some of the venom out of the language.[84]

Perhaps owing to the ongoing, pressing questions of the conflict and the embattled political and cultural self-definition of Israeli Jews, academic research about Matzpen still has not lost its political edge, decades after the fact. Beginning with the very first attempts to describe the group within its historical context, there is a palpable tension between the requisite academic distance and the authors' own political leanings. This holds true, for example, of Nira Yuval-Davis's master's thesis, 'The Left in Israel: Matzpen, the Israeli Socialist Organisation', which was submitted to the sociology department at the Hebrew University of Jerusalem in 1970 and published there seven years later.[85] Not only was Yuval-Davis's thesis the very first academic volume about Matzpen to give a sociological overview of the group's history and activities, but it also signals its author's political evolution; before long, she found herself moving among the same circles as Matzpen. Another example of intermingling political perspectives and academic research was the master's thesis of Ehud Sprinzak, completed in 1973 at Hebrew University's Levi Eshkol Institute for Economic, Social and Political Research. Until 1970, as the chair of the Union of Israeli Students in North America, he had tried to contain Matzpen's influence at American universities. Three years later, these experiences animated his academic thesis, 'The Emergence of the Politics of Delegitimization in Israel, 1967–72', which devoted two chapters to the Israeli Left, one of them specifically on the impact of Matzpen.[86] More than two decades later, as a distinguished professor, Sprinzak based his findings on the broader history of extremism inside Israel on his earlier research and political judgements.[87] And even in the recent past, following the failure of peacemaking efforts in Israel in the 1990s, research into Matzpen has continued to pursue a political cause. The prime example is the groundbreaking 2003 documentary *Matzpen: Anti-Zionist Israelis* by Israeli filmmaker Eran Torbiner.[88] In many respects, this film paved the way for future involvement with Matzpen, its genesis, protagonists and vision. The work of Tikva Honig-Parnass and Ran Greenstein, who were both Matzpen members or allies in the 1970s, served a similar function. While Honig-Parnass's descriptions are embedded in a critique of the

Zionist Left in Israel, in which she all but recapitulates Matzpen's role in her own disconnection from socialist Zionism,[89] Greenstein endeavours to catalogue the various critical voices on the issue of Palestine, including the Israeli leftists of Matzpen. A collection of his enlightening essays appeared in late 2014 under the title *Zionism and its Discontents*.[90] Its claim to be a guide for people seeking societal alternatives in the Israel–Palestine conflict testifies to the book's political nature.[91] In parallel, a body of historical research into the history of the Israeli Left went beyond immediate political aims. Its origins stretch back to Charlie Glass's essay, 'Jews Against Zion' from 1975, which explored Matzpen's political identity as part of a broader discussion on Jewish dissidence in the Israeli–Palestinian conflict.[92] His study established a research tradition that was carried on by the books of David N. Schnall (*Radical Dissent in Contemporary Israeli Politics: Cracks in the Wall*) and Laurence J. Silberstein (*The Postzionism Debates: Knowledge and Power in Israeli Culture*).[93] Their comprehensive research situates the history of Matzpen in the framework of dissident currents in the Jewish state and within the depiction of an Israeli community beyond Zionist principles. August Grabski's article 'Matzpen and the State of Israel (1962–1973)' from 2006 instead compares and contrasts Matzpen's political outlook with that of the United States Socialist Workers Party (SWP).[94] In 2010, the Israeli historian Nitza Erel published the first thorough monograph on the history of Matzpen. Erel's study provides a comprehensive portrait incorporating an extensive corpus of published sources.[95]

This book's approach departs from Erel's portrayal of the group, which restricts itself mainly to the organisation's history. Placing a stronger focus on the history of concepts and memory, I will situate Matzpen in the broader context of the divergent notions of Israeli community and identity. Building on past research, this book probes the development and ideas of Matzpen, treating the group as a fisheye lens that focuses basic questions of Israeli Jewish existence within a single story. The invention of another Israel, as Matzpen intended, is thus also fertile ground for another history of Israel, a history from the margins. For that very reason, this book avoids taking a purely organisational history approach or centring its discussion on the group's immediate political allure, although I will devote ample space to these topics, citing both the group's Hebrew publications and existing translations into German and English.[96] Rather, I will tell the story of Matzpen as the narrative of its protagonists, reconstructing their lives in each chapter alongside key events of Israeli history. This approach may defuse political perspectives, but, more importantly, it will decode them as expressions of experience and memory that take effect in various distinct historical constellations. Partly for this reason, the book draws extensively on biographical writings and autobiographical memories that were in some cases written down and in others recounted orally in interviews.[97] Although this book is intended to provide a new perspective on the history of Israeli dissent in the 1950s, '60s and '70s, it is certainly not all-embracing. For example, it does not delve into the relationship between Matzpen and the Israeli Black Panthers movement, which stirred up Israeli society from 1972 onwards. Sami Shalom Chetrit, Nitza Erel, Tali Lev and Yehuda Shenhav have examined this collaboration from different perspectives and with profound understanding.[98]

The first chapter, 'Communist Dissidents', sets out the origin story of the Israeli Socialist Organization as the outcome of a split from the Communist Party. Building on the work of Sondra Rubenstein and Joel Beinin, I show that this split resulted from more than mere ideological frictions in the communist movement.[99] The chapter delves beneath the superficial ideological fault lines to expose opposing perspectives towards the Jewish state's interior structures and exterior relationships. I examine two early political positions held by future representatives of Matzpen – their radical critique of Israel's Histadrut trade-union movement and their divergent interpretation of the war of 1948 – and consider the extent to which these stances influenced the later emergence of a New Left in Israel.

The second chapter, 'The Israel–Palestine Question', discusses Matzpen's independent engagement with, and analysis of, the Palestine problem. It elaborates on how they came to interpret it as a colonial-type conflict between nationalities: a clash between a European population aiming to establish a state and a native population, residing there since before the foundation of Israel. This is analysed, first, in view of the Trotskyist traditions of dissidence that already existed in Palestine before the establishment of the State of Israel.[100] Second, it is situated in the context of Algerian decolonisation, as the dramatic fate of the

French Algerians gave the Israeli Left a new conception of their own circumstances in the Israel–Palestine conflict. Applying Albert Memmi's writings on the coloniser and the colonised and comparing them to Albert Camus's stance on the Algerian question, I will lay out Matzpen's programme to cut ties with the legacy of Zionism, and thus recognise Israeli Jews' transformation into a new Hebrew nation: 'foreign natives' (Dan Diner) who belong to the region.[101]

The third chapter, 'The Invention of a Hebrew Nation', examines the enormous cultural foundation underpinning Matzpen's political vision of a post-colonial existence for Israeli Jews. Matzpen built on a process of transformation that had worked to turn Diaspora Jews into new Hebrews, or Israelis. Drawing on the research of Yaacov Shavit and James Diamond into the movement of the Young Hebrews, or 'Canaanites', the chapter outlines an emerging Hebrew-language culture that blossomed in the young Israeli state of the 1950s and '60s and defied the discourse of a unified Jewish people.[102] This exposes a cultural context that had its roots in the Zionist Right, but grew far beyond its political origins. Culturally, it centred on the magazine *Haolam Hazeh*, which was published by Uri Avnery (1923–2018), and extended as far as Matzpen on its far-left fringe. Finally, I will also highlight the internal political differences within this milieu, gaps that the Six-Day War ultimately rendered unbridgeable.[103]

Although the Six-Day War of 1967 sounded the death knell for this secular Hebrew–Israeli identity, the interplay of June '67 and May '68 brought about a turning point for Matzpen with the incursion of currents and trends from the European New Left. Expanding upon the research of Ran Greenstein and Nitza Erel, the fourth chapter, '*Hal'a HaKibush*', reconstructs Matzpen's split as a history of clashing perspectives on the solution to the Israel–Palestine conflict.[104] In view of the Palestinian Liberation Organisation's (PLO) turn towards diplomacy after the Yom Kippur or October 1973 War, I will read the internal quarrels among Israeli leftists as a confrontation between distinct temporal imaginaries: on the one hand, a stubborn devotion to the utopic timeline of revolution, and on the other, a shift towards realpolitik, territorial compromise and the prospect of a transitional two-state solution.

Considering the example of *Khamsin* magazine, the fifth chapter analyses how the language of progress, socialism and revolution remained the basis for cooperation between Jewish, Israeli and Arab intellectuals throughout the Middle East in the 1970s. To that end, the chapter begins by unearthing the story of the magazine's driving force, Eli Lobel and his internationalist efforts, as kind of a 'foreign minister without a state', to further the interests of post-colonial communities. Building on the research of Fouad Ajami into the history of the Arab Left, I portray a group of Arab dissidents that formed around Sadik Al-Azm (1934–2016) and Lafif Lakhdar (1934–2013), a circle whose efforts for mutual recognition in the Israel–Palestine conflict were linked to their advocacy for the modernisation and secularisation of the Arab world.[105] Hence, *Khamsin* was the 'Journal of Revolutionary Socialists of the Middle East' whose shared vision transcended the political and national fault lines of the era.

The final chapter, 'Beyond the Holocaust: Jewish Past, Hebrew Present, Socialist Future', can be read as laterally linked to this chronology. This section analyses the story of Matzpen using concepts proposed by Hannah Arendt and advanced by Dan Diner, which frame 1940s Palestine as a spatial realm that enabled the preservation and continuity of self-conceptions and political visions from the pre-Holocaust era.[106] It explores the degree to which Israeli leftists' social and national utopias of socialist revolution and Hebrew nationhood, mutually reinforcing each other, contributed to their avoidance of the significance of the Holocaust and its impacts on Jewish consciousness.[107] Drawing on the work of Anita Shapira, among others, I will show that, from the outset, the notion of a new Hebrew nation was insulated from the Jewish historical experiences in Europe.[108] As the group clung to its faith in progress, rooted in the socialist teleology of history and referring to the political struggles of previous generations, Matzpen's alienation from the consequences of mass extermination only increased. Its members remained unaware of the new Jewish collective self-image that had originated in Auschwitz, as a result of which the majority of Jews had transferred their shared identity to the Jewish state. Thus, this book concludes with an historical aporia: the conflict between the perpetual effects of the Holocaust, on the one hand, and the unresolved Israel–Palestine conflict, on the other. The quest for a road out of that aporia – for a way to cut that Gordian knot – is also part and parcel of Matzpen's history and legacy.[109]

Notes

1. Uri Dan, 'Danny the Red Calls for Overthrowing De Gaulle's "Police State"', *Ma'ariv* (17 May 1968), p. 2 [Hebrew]. All Hebrew- and German-language sources below will be cited using original English translations of their titles without the inclusion of transliterations.

2. Schraga Har-Gil, '"Danny the Red" Travelled Israel', *Ma'ariv* (7 June 1968), p. 13 [Hebrew].
3. Daniel Cohn-Bendit, *Der grosse Basar: Gespräche mit Michel Lévy, Jean-Marc Salmon, Maren Sell, Reihe Romane, Reportagen, Autobiographien* (München: Trikont-Verlag, 1975), p. 12.
4. Ibid.
5. Haim Hanegbi, 'A Royal Visit', *Koteret Rashit* (25 May 1988), p. 23 [Hebrew].
6. Helen Epstein, 'New Arrivals on the Israeli Left', *Midstream* 16: 8 (1970), pp. 10–19, at p. 13; Gabi Baron, 'Attempt to Disrupt Cohn-Bendit's Gathering was a Failure', *Yediot Aharonot* (1 June 1970) [Hebrew].
7. Dominique Vidal, 'If I Forget Thee, O Zion. Could Israel's Kibbutz Experiment Finally Fail?', *Le Monde Diplomatique* (August 2000).
8. Hanegbi, 'A Royal Visit'.
9. Ibid.
10. Ibid.
11. Schraga Har-Gil, '"Danny the Red" Gives Advice to Israel', *Ma'ariv* (31 May 1970), pp. 12 and 16, at p. 13 [Hebrew].
12. Schraga Har-Gil, 'Der rote Danny im Kibbuz', *Jedioth Chadashot* (4 June 1970), p. 3.
13. Hanegbi, 'A Royal Visit'.
14. Aryeh Dayan, 'We Were "Stalin's Children" and We Have Nothing to Be Ashamed Of', *Haaretz* (25 April 2000), pp. 4ב–5ב [Hebrew].
15. Nahum Barnea, 'The King of the Jews and His Son', *Koteret Rashit* 209 (3 December 1986), pp. 24–31 [Hebrew].
16. Galia Glasner-Heled, 'Displaced. The Memoir of Eliezer Gruenbaum, Kapo at Birkenau – Translation and Commentary', *Shofar* 27: 2 (2009), pp. 1–23, at pp. 2–4.
17. Vidal, 'If I Forget Thee, O Zion'.
18. Jonathan Yavin, 'Danny the Red in the Land of White and Blue', *Haaretz* (3 December 2000).
19. Cohn-Bendit, *Der grosse Basar*, p. 17.
20. Thomas Mayer, 'Daniel Cohn-Bendit im Interview', *Der Standard* (23 April 2014); Sebastian Voigt, *Der jüdische Mai '68: Pierre Goldman, Daniel Cohn-Bendit und André Glucksmann im Nachkriegsfrankreich* (Göttingen: Vandenhoeck & Ruprecht, 2015), p. 140.
21. Cohn-Bendit, *Der grosse Basar*, pp. 10–11.
22. Daniel Cohn-Bendit, *Wir haben sie so geliebt, die Revolution, Dt. Erstausg* (Frankfurt am Main: Athenäum, 1987).

23. Har-Gil, 'Der rote Danny im Kibbuz'.
24. Har-Gil, '"Danny the Red" Gives Advice to Israel'; Har-Gil, 'Der rote Danny im Kibbuz'.
25. Ygal Sarneh, 'Olive Grove Ploughed the Final Time by Lawyer Mohammed Kiwan', *Yediot Aharonot* (16 February 1996), pp. 10–11 [Hebrew].
26. Cohn-Bendit, *Der grosse Basar*, p. 16.
27. Helen Epstein, 'Danny's "Eight-Day-War"', *The Jerusalem Post* (3 June 1970).
28. 'Golda Meir gegen Verbot von Rakach und Matzpen', *Jedioth Chadashot* (7 June 1970), p. 4.
29. 'The Week of "Danny the Red"', *Al Hamishmar* (7 June 1970) [Hebrew].
30. Cohn-Bendit, *Der grosse Basar*, p. 17.
31. Ehud Sprinzak, *Brother Against Brother: Violence and Extremism in Israeli Politics from Altalena to the Rabin Assassination* (New York: Free Press, 1999), p. 119.
32. 'Joint Israeli-Arab Statement on the Middle East Crisis', *The Times* (8 June 1967), p. 5.
33. 'There were no such things as Palestinians. When was there an independent Palestinian people with a Palestinian state? It was either southern Syria before the First World War, and then it was a Palestine including Jordan. It was not as though there was a Palestinian people in Palestine considering itself as a Palestinian people and we came and threw them out and took their country away from them. They did not exist.' Golda Meir, *The Sunday Times* (15 June 1969).
34. Michel Warschawski, *On the Border* (London: Pluto, 2005), pp. 25–6.
35. Avraham Wolfensohn, 'The Conscience of Matzpen: Part I', *Davar* (27 May 1970), p. 3 [Hebrew].
36. Ibid.
37. See Lutz Fiedler, 'Akiva Orr (1931–2013)', *inamo (Informationsprojekt Naher und Mittlerer Osten)* 73 (2013), pp. 82–5.
38. Anita Shapira, 'Hirbet Hizah. Between Remembrance and Forgetting', in Benny Morris (ed.), *Making Israel* (Ann Arbor: University of Michigan Press, 2007), pp. 81–123, at p. 97.
39. S. Yizhar, *Khirbet Khizeh* (New York: Farrar, Straus and Giroux, 2014).
40. Shapira, 'Hirbet Hizah', p. 87.
41. 'History of Zionism', *Matzpen* 54 (1970), pp. 6–7 [Hebrew].
42. Israeli Socialist Organization (Matzpen), 'The Palestine-Problem and the Israeli-Arab Dispute, 18 May 1967', in Arie Bober (ed.), *The Other Israel: The Radical Case Against Zionism* (Garden City: Doubleday, 1972), pp. 208–13, at p. 212. First published in: *World Outlook* 22: 5 (2 June 1967); *Matzpen* 36 (1967) [Hebrew]].

43. It is unsurprising that Shlomo Sand, a former Matzpen member, has carried forward this cultural–political project to this day. See Shlomo Sand, *The Invention of the Jewish People* (London: Verso, 2009); Shlomo Sand, *The Invention of the Land of Israel* (London: Verso, 2012); Shlomo Sand, *How I Stopped Being a Jew* (London: Verso, 2014).
44. Epstein, 'New Arrivals on the Israeli Left', p. 14.
45. See Gershom Gorenberg, *The Accidental Empire: Israel and the Birth of Settlements, 1967-1977* (New York, Godalming: Owl, 2007), pp. 138–52.
46. Quoted from the English translation: Haim Bajajo-Hanegbi, 'Sanctity of Private Property', *Israel Imperial News* 2: 6 ([October] 1968), p. 7.
47. Ibid.
48. Haim Hanegbi, 'My Hebron. A Story of a Different Love', *Koteret Rashit* (20 July 1983), pp. 20–3 [Hebrew]; E. Torbiner, *Hebron in my Heart*, 2012, Israel, 21 min, film, https://www.youtube.com/watch?v=8HVz4YtHkJA (accessed 19 April 2020).
49. Ari Shavit, 'Cry, the Beloved Two-State Solution', *Haaretz* (6 August 2003).
50. Ibid.
51. Tom Segev, *1967: Israel, the War, and the Year that Transformed the Middle East* (New York: Metropolitan Books, 2007), p. 70.
52. Khalil Toama, 'Zusammenleben in Würde, Gleichheit und Gleichberechtigung. Gespräch von Sophia Deeg mit Khalil Toama', https://www.neuerispverlag.de/aushang/deeg_id124_toama.pdf (accessed 15 April 2020), p. 7.
53. Nissim Bajaja (Haim Hanegbi), 'The Khalil Toama Affair', *Matzpen* 41 (1968), pp. 2–4 [Hebrew].
54. 'Arab Student Detained for Sheltering a Leader of the Terror Groups in the West Bank', *Israel Imperial News* 1: 9 (1968), pp. 9–10 and 14.
55. Bajaja (Hanegbi), 'The Khalil Toama Affair'.
56. Sprinzak, *Brother Against Brother*, p. 119.
57. *Matzpen* 43 (1968), p. 3.
58. Epstein, 'New Arrivals on the Israeli Left', p. 14.
59. Warschawski, On the Border, pp. 22–3. Another reason the statement caused unease was its international syndication in both France's *Le Monde* and the USSR's *Pravda*. Soon the 'Pravda declaration' was the talk of the town. An English translation was printed in: Uri Davis, *Crossing the Border: An Autobiography of an Anti-Zionist Palestinian of the Hebrew Language Group* (London: Books and Books, 1995), pp. 362–5.
60. Sprinzak, *Brother Against Brother*, p. 122 (emphasis in original).
61. Gabriel Strassman, 'The "New Left" and its "War on the Jews"', *Ma'ariv* (5 December 1969), p. 18 [Hebrew]; see also Nitza Erel, *Matzpen: Conscience and Fantasy* (Tel Aviv: Resling, 2010), p. 218 [Hebrew].

62. Warschawski, *On the Border*, p. 56; Benjamin Ferron, 'La transnationalisation de "Matzpen". L'organisation socialiste israélienne (1962-2006)', *Pôle Sud* 30 (2009), pp. 67–84.
63. Tariq Ali, *Street Fighting Years: An Autobiography of the Sixties*, 1st Citadel Underground edn (New York: Citadel Press, 1991), p. 43; Ferron, 'La transnationalisation de "Matzpen"'.
64. Avraham Wolfensohn, 'The Conscience of Matzpen: Part IV. The Slanderers of the Land', *Davar* (2 June 1970), p. 6 [Hebrew].
65. Galit Margalit, 'Israel. 1968 and the "67 Generation"', *Bulletin of the German Historical Institute* 6 (Supplement) (2009), pp. 111–17.
66. Amos Elon, 'Our Youth Rebellion Lies Behind Us', *New Outlook* 11: 7 (1968), pp. 46–9.
67. Mendel Kohansky, 'The Case of the Dispossessed Queen', *Midstream* 16: 7 (August/September 1970), pp. 75–8.
68. Shimon Levy, 'Queen of a Bathtub. Hanoch Levin's Political, Aesthetic and Ethical Metatheatricality', in Gerhard Fischer and Bernhard Greiner (eds), *The Play Within the Play: The Performance of Meta-Theatre and Self-Reflection* (Kenilworth: Rodopi, 2007), pp. 145–65.
69. Sylvie Keshet, 'Spring 1970. Or: McCarthy is Alive and Hiding in Israel!', *Haaretz* (15 May 1970), p. 10 [Hebrew].
70. Meir Chazan, 'Goldmann's Initiative to Meet With Nasser', in Mark A. Raider (ed.), *Nahum Goldmann: Statesman Without a State*, SUNY Series in Israeli Studies (Albany [Tel Aviv]: SUNY Press; Chaim Rosenberg School of Jewish Studies, the Chaim Weizmann Institute for the Study of Zionism and Israel, Tel Aviv University, 2009), pp. 297–324.
71. Keshet, 'Spring 1970'.
72. The letter is reprinted in: Uzi Benziman, 'Security is the Quest of Peace (Interview with the Sixth-Formers)', *Haaretz* (1 May 1970), p. 17 [Hebrew].
73. Epstein, 'New Arrivals on the Israeli Left', p. 11.
74. Benziman, 'Security is the Quest of Peace (Interview with the Sixth-Formers)'.
75. See Erel, *Matzpen*, p. 200.
76. Uzi Benziman, 'Matzpen and the Educational Gap', *Haaretz* (8 May 1970) [Hebrew].
77. Eric Marsden, 'The Plight of Israel's Young Pacifists', *The Times* (16 June 1972), p. 16; Ilan Kfir, 'The Conscientious Objector Continues to Play the Role of a Martyr', *Yediot Aharonot* (12 June 1972), p. 15 [Hebrew]; Erel, *Matzpen*, pp. 203–5.
78. 'Golda Meir gegen Verbot von Rakach und Matzpen'; Arie Bober, 'Introduction', in Arie Bober (ed.), *The Other Israel: The Radical Case Against Zionism* (Garden City: Doubleday, 1972), pp. 1–34, at p. 5.

79. Cohn-Bendit, *Der grosse Basar*, p. 13.
80. Moshe Meisels, 'No Room in Maki for Critical Voices', *Ma'ariv* (9 October 1962), p. 3 [Hebrew].
81. Haviv Canaan, 'Disgust at the Fossilisation of Communism', *Haaretz* (15 May 1970), p. 17 [Hebrew]; Haviv Canaan, 'Matzpen's Aspiration. A State for Everyone', *Haaretz* (18 May 1970), p. 12 [Hebrew]; Haviv Canaan, 'The Differences between the Stances of Matzpen and Al-Fatah', *Haaretz* (19 May 1970), p. 12 [Hebrew]; Haviv Canaan, 'The Heads of Matzpen and their Careers', *Haaretz* (20 May 1970), p. 18 [Hebrew]; Wolfensohn, 'The Conscience of Matzpen: Part I'; Avraham Wolfensohn, 'The Conscience of Matzpen: Part II. The Fate of the Jewish People', *Davar* (28 May 1970), p. 4 [Hebrew]; Avraham Wolfensohn, 'The Conscience of Matzpen: Part III. The Objective. The Extermination of Israel', *Davar* (31 May 1970) [Hebrew]; Wolfensohn, 'The Conscience of Matzpen: Part IV'.
82. Aaron Bacher, 'All the Secrets About Matzpen', *Yediot Aharonot* (22 May 1970), pp. 5–7 [Hebrew].
83. Ibid., p. 5.
84. Sara Leibovitz-Dar, 'The Days of Matzpen', *Hadashot* (20 November 1992), pp. 23–26, 60 [Hebrew]; Yaron Sahish, 'The Myth of Matzpen', *Iton Yerushalayim* (20 November 1992), pp. 10–14 [Hebrew].
85. Nira Yuval-Davis, 'Matzpen. The Israeli Socialist Organisation' (Master's thesis, Hebrew University of Jerusalem, 1977) [Hebrew].
86. Ehud Sprinzak, 'The Emergence of the Politics of Delegitimization in Israel, 1967–72' (Doctoral dissertation, Hebrew University of Jerusalem, 1973) [Hebrew].
87. Sprinzak, *Brother Against Brother*.
88. Eran Torbiner, *Matzpen. Anti-Zionist Israelis*, 2003, Tel Aviv, Israel, 54 min, film.
89. Tikva Honig-Parnass, *False Prophets of Peace: Liberal Zionism and the Struggle for Palestine* (Chicago: Haymarket Books, 2011).
90. Ran Greenstein, *Zionism and its Discontents: A Century of Radical Dissent in Israel/Palestine* (London: Pluto Press, 2014).
91. Ibid., p. vi.
92. Charlie Glass, 'Jews Against Zion. Israeli Jewish Anti-Zionism', *Journal of Palestine Studies* 5: 1/2 (1975/6), pp. 56–81.
93. David J. Schnall, *Radical Dissent in Contemporary Israeli Politics: Cracks in the Wall*, Praeger Special Studies (New York: Praeger, 1979); Laurence J. Silberstein, *The Postzionism Debates: Knowledge and Power in Israeli Culture* (New York: Routledge, 1999).

94. August Grabski, '"Matzpen" and the State of Israel (1962–1973)', *Kwartalnik Historii Żydów* 219 (2006), pp. 354–65.
95. Erel, *Matzpen*.
96. A compilation of important sources by Matzpen in English translation is Arie Bober (ed.), The Other Israel: The Radical Case Against Zionism (Garden City: Doubleday, 1972). Moshé Machover, a founding member of Matzpen, also compiled his most important writings into one volume: Moshé Machover, Israelis and Palestinians: Conflict and Resolutions (Chicago: Haymarket Books, 2012).
97. Alongside autobiographical texts by individual Matzpen members and sympathisers, the cultural supplements of Hebrew-language newspapers proved to be a treasure trove of biographical writings and interviews. Also, interviews lasting multiple hours were conducted with many of the group's leading figures.
98. Sami S. Chetrit, *The Mizrahi Struggle in Israel: Between Oppression and Liberation, Identification and Alternative, 1948–2003* (Tel Aviv: Am Oved, 2004), pp. 119–97; Erel, *Matzpen*, pp. 183–93; Tali Lev and Yehouda Shenhav, 'Don't Call a Worker – But a Panther. Israeli Black Panthers and the Politics of Identity in Israel in the 1970s', *Theory & Criticism* 35 (2009), pp. 141–64 [Hebrew].
99. Joel Beinin, *Was the Red Flag Flying There?: Marxist Politics and the Arab-Israeli Conflict in Egypt and Israel, 1948–1965* (Berkeley: University of California Press, 1990); Sondra M. Rubenstein, *The Communist Movement in Palestine and Israel, 1919–1984*, Westview Special Studies (Boulder: Westview Press, 1985).
100. John Bunzl, *Israel im Nahen Osten: Eine Einführung* (Wien: UTB/Böhlau, 2008), pp. 93–106; Ian H. Birchall, *Tony Cliff: A Marxist For His Time* (London: Bookmarks Publications, 2011), pp. 18–84.
101. Albert Memmi, *The Colonizer and the Colonized* (London: Earthscan, [1957] 2003); Dan Diner, 'Post-postkoloniale Flaschenpost', in Dan Diner, *Zeitenschwelle: Gegenwartsfragen an die Geschichte* (München: Pantheon, 2010), pp. 233–40 [first: *Die Welt*, 19 July 2008]; David Carroll, 'Camus's Algeria. Birthrights, Colonial Injustice, and the Fiction of a French-Algerian People', *MLN* 112: 4 (1997), pp. 517–49.
102. Yaacov Shavit, *The New Hebrew Nation: A Study in Israeli Heresy and Fantasy* (Totowa: F. Cass, 1987); James S. Diamond, *Homeland or Holy Land?: The "Canaanite" Critique of Israel* (Bloomington: Indiana University Press, 1986).
103. Nitza Erel, *Without Fear and Prejudice: Uri Avnery and Haolam Hazeh* (Jerusalem: Magnes Press, 2006) [Hebrew].
104. Greenstein, *Zionism and its Discontents*, pp. 154–94; Erel, *Matzpen*, pp. 145–80.

105. Sadik J. Al-Azm, *Self-Criticism After the Defeat* (London: Saqi, 2011); Ehud Ein-Gil, 'The Roots of Jihad', *Haaretz* (16 March 2006); Fouad Ajami, *The Arab Predicament: Arab Political Thought and Practice since 1967* (Cambridge: Cambridge University Press, [reprint] 1985).
106. Hannah Arendt, 'Zionism Reconsidered', in Jerome Kohn (ed.), *The Jewish Writings* (New York: Schocken Books, [1944] 2007), pp. 343–74; Dan Diner, 'Ambiguous Semantics. Reflections on Jewish Political Concepts', *The Jewish Quarterly Review* 98: 1 (2008), pp. 89–102; Dan Diner, 'Bolschewismus ohne Kommunismus – Ben Gurion und der Holocaust. Zu dem Buch von Dina Porat über Yischuv und Holocaust', *Babylon. Beiträge zur jüdischen Gegenwart* 2 (1987), pp. 127–31.
107. Dan Diner, 'Täuschungen. Israel, die Linke und das Dilemma der Kritik', in Wolfgang Kraushaar (ed.), *Frankfurter Schule und Studentenbewegung: Von der Flaschenpost zum Molotowcocktail 1946–1995*, 3 vols (Hamburg: Rogner und Bernhard bei Zweitausendeins, 1998), vol. 3, pp. 187–94.
108. Anita Shapira, 'Whatever Became of "Negating Exile"?', in Anita Shapira (ed.), *Israeli Identity in Transition* (Westport: Praeger, 2004), pp. 69–108.
109. Dan Diner, 'Israel and the Trauma of the Mass Extermination', *Telos. A Quarterly Journal of Critical Thought* 57 (1983), pp. 41–52.

1

Communist Dissidents

De-Stalinisation in Israel

An unobtrusive notice on the final page of the 28 September 1962 edition of *Kol Ha'am*, the Israeli Communist Party's official newspaper, publicised a rupture in the party's ranks that would leave a lasting impact: 'The Communist Party of Israel announces that Moshé Machover and Akiva Orr (of Jerusalem) as well as Oded Pilavsky and Yirmiyahu Kaplan (of Tel Aviv) have been expelled from the Party for betraying its principles and for organising into factional groups.'[1] There was not much else to be said on the matter, the notice seemed to suggest. But before long, the party leadership was circulating a memorandum for the party's eyes only, titled 'Educational Material about the Machover-Pilavsky Anti-Party Group', that characterised the expulsion as an outgrowth of ongoing conflicts.[2] The memo culminated in an accusation that the expelled members had been agitating against their own party, the Soviet Union and even communism altogether. Whatever the leadership's reasons, this expulsion from the party marked the end of a conflict that had been mounting among the rank and file for some time prior to September 1962. Before the party finally showed them the door, the four dissidents had sent a joint letter to its Central Committee, requesting an opportunity for a long-thwarted internal discussion:

> Comrades, the 20th and 22nd Congresses of the Communist Party of the USSR have indicated a shift in the path of the worldwide communist movement. These congresses have sparked an argument over a whole series of

problems, both in the communist movement as a whole and in each specific party [. . .] An in-depth discussion of these problems is likewise necessary in our own party.³

The letter's four signatories blamed the party leadership for blocking all their attempts to initiate an intra-party discussion. Again and again, they wrote, efforts at open dialogue at party meetings had been suppressed on the basis of flimsy arguments with transparent motives. 'In light of the above', they therefore concluded, 'we appeal to the Central Committee of our party with the proposal of establishing a party bulletin as a forum for future discussions of political and ideological issues on a Marxist-Leninist foundation'.⁴ Yet this final attempt to foment discussion remained fruitless, and the actual reasons behind the party's internal quarrel still remained obscure.

Notwithstanding, these events had already been the subject of coverage by the Israeli media. Several weeks earlier, the independent weekly newspaper *Haolam Hazeh* had reported on the likelihood of communists forming a new party in Israel in the near future: 'The initiative for this idea came from several Maki activists, some of whom have already declared their independence from the party, while others remain members. The essence of the dissidents' complaints is that the party is insufficiently democratic and incapable of adapting to new circumstances.'⁵ Similar predictions were soon made in the prestigious daily newspaper *Haaretz*.⁶ But the matter received the most attention in the non-partisan daily *Maariv*, where an article headlined 'No Room in Maki for Critical Voices' devoted almost a page to the strife among the communists and reported in depth on the four expelled members.⁷ A month later, the magazine *Al HaMishmar*, the official publication of the left-wing Zionist Mapam party, reported on a further development: 'The group that was thrown out of Maki is preparing to publish its own monthly magazine.'⁸ Nine days later, on 21 November 1962, the Israeli Socialist Organization published the first issue of its magazine, *Matzpen*, edited by Oded Pilvasky and Moshé Machover. An Israeli New Left was born (Figure 1.1).

This marginal development would probably not have garnered so much attention were it not part of a much larger upheaval throughout the communist world that had been gathering steam ever since Nikita Sergeyevich Khrushchev gave his secret speech, 'On the Cult of Personality and its Consequences', in February 1956. 'What the notice about the party expulsion describes as a

Figure 1.1 'There is an address!' Cover of the first issue of *Matzpen*, released on 21 November 1962.

surprising instance of "factional organisation" that "undermined Party principles"', commented *Maariv*, soon after the brief announcement in *Kol Haam*, 'did not emerge yesterday, nor the day before. These are the products of unrest within Maki ranks and particularly within the party's younger intellectual circles since the 20th congress of the Soviet Communist Party.'[9] Khrushchev's official condemnation of the Stalinist purges and other crimes perpetrated under Stalin, along with his allegations of a cult of personality, were not intended for public consumption, but the speech's audience was as uncontainable as its impact. Throughout the communist world, which – with few exceptions – had pledged unconditional allegiance to Moscow and Stalin, news of the crimes that had been committed under the leadership of the erstwhile 'idol of the global communist movement' would cause a veritable 'crisis of faith', especially in the Soviet satellite states of Eastern and Eastern–Central Europe.[10] The revelations of Stalinist crimes brought entire governments in those regions to the brink; most of them had risen to power with Stalin's backing, and the installation of communist regimes had been perceived in many places as suppressing national interests.[11] Nowhere were these developments as dramatic as in Hungary, where a popular uprising ushered in the government's collapse and the country's withdrawal from the Warsaw Pact – until Soviet forces brutally suppressed the insurrection. In Poland, where Władysław Gomułka's appointment as prime minister had stirred hopes of a 'Polish way to socialism', the tension between domestic pressure to liberalise and the threat of Soviet intervention had been defused by the removal of the old party leadership.[12] Crucially, though, the era's political watchword came from Italy. Palmiro Togliatti, the chair of that country's Communist Party (CP), had coined the word 'polycentrism' to describe the Soviets' gradual loss of leadership and the idea of specific national roads to socialism.[13]

These ruptures had left traces in Israel, too, even as the leadership of the national CP made every attempt to deny the secret speech's existence and to prevent any discussion of the matter. In his autobiography, the future historian Walter Grab (1919–2000), a member of the party's Tel Aviv chapter at the time, wrote that he had attended a meeting with party secretary Meir Vilner. Fresh from Moscow, Vilner reported in detail on the party conference, but did not breathe a word about the secret speech.[14] The party members were eager to discuss these developments, but this was initially suppressed with the claim that they had been taken in by Western propaganda. At the next party assembly, under the leadership of Politburo member Adolf Abraham Berman, some of the comrades finally vented their frustration and demanded an open discussion. They wanted to talk about not just the content of Khrushchev's speech, but also about the murder of Yiddish-language poets and the wide-scale repression of Yiddish culture in the Soviet Union, as well as the Soviets' arms shipments to Egypt, Israel's neighbour and enemy. Berman, whose brother Jakob was one of the Polish party leaders who had taken the fall, flatly rejected all criticism, pronouncing that the party had no room for 'petty bourgeois, chauvinistic, Zionist elements'. 'That was the expulsion!' wrote Walter Grab retrospectively. 'We were labelled a "faction" that had defied the party line!'[15]

After the speech became public knowledge, some 400 members were either banished from the party or left of their own accord. Only a few of these were long-serving comrades, such as Hanoch Bzozah, who had become a card-carrying member of the Palestine Communist Party in 1930, just a year after immigrating. Bzozah held a critical view of the Soviet Union for years. But later, when his condemnations – of the Soviet line on the Slansky trial and then of the antisemitic eruptions in Eastern Bloc countries – turned him against his own party and its inadequate response to Khrushchev's secret speech, his immediate expulsion for 'Jewish national deviations' was announced on 4 April 1956.[16] This did not keep him from further rebellious outcries. Once expelled, Bzozah co-initiated a campaign that demanded a re-examination of the Stalinist purges that had spread even so far as his own party's ranks in the 1930s.[17]

This first wave of criticism was not successful in bringing about any changes within the CP, however. As early as 1962, *Maariv* asserted that Maki was 'practically the only communist party that has stayed the course. At a time when every communist party, foremost that of the USSR, has seen a personnel shift and rid itself of adherents to the old Stalinist line, the Maki party leadership has persevered as if nothing happened.'[18] The paper was even more curious about the identities of the dissidents of autumn 1962, who were now challenging entrenched party structures afresh. Oded Pilavsky, Yirmiyahu Kaplan, Akiva Orr and Moshé Machover were not names the general public would have readily recognised. These figures, *Maariv* explained, also shared a trajectory that connected them to the turbulent history of the young state's left-wing parties: 'They began their party-political path in Mapam, then switched to Dr. Sneh's "Left Party" and ultimately found themselves in the ranks of Maki.'[19] Hence, to a certain extent, the political contentions within the Israeli Left over relations with the Soviet Union had already marked the young dissidents' path into the Communist Party. Likewise, the establishment of Moshe Sneh's (1909–72) Left Socialist Party (Mifleget HaSmol HaSotzialisti) in 1953 was in response to disputes of the same kind. This short-lived party formed as a breakaway from the left-wing Zionist Mapam in the wake of the Slansky trial. Sneh, the former Haganah leader, had pledged unconditional allegiance to the USSR, breaking ranks with the party majority. He remained persuaded of the Soviet Union's long-term victory in the Cold War and therefore considered Israeli ties to the communist empire to be an existential necessity.[20] But even though Moshé Machover, Akiva Orr and Oded Pilavsky accompanied Sneh on his political trajectory for a time and – along with the entire Left Socialist Party – joined the Communists as early as 1954, when the next controversy over Soviet policies followed a few years later, they were no longer prepared to take his lead unquestioningly. Now, they were doubling down on the previous rebellion in their party, and they came to a point where they were essentially asking to be expelled from Maki.

This young generation of dissidents had not simply joined the Communist Party's ranks and pursued a direct political route; neither had they particularly conformed to the party line. In fact, Akiva Orr had first been politicised by the legendary sailors' strike (better known as the 'seamen's strike') that kept the whole country on its toes in the autumn of 1951. The leftists' solidarity with the strikers had paved Orr's way into Moshe Sneh's Left Socialist Party. Moshé Machover, for his part, had joined the same party after being ejected from the left-wing Zionist youth movement, Hashomer Hatzair (the Young Guard). Machover, the son of a well-known Tel Aviv ice cream manufacturer, was too individualistic to adopt the collective thought patterns of the organisation. Along with his friends Meir Smorodinsky and Shaul Ginzburg, he got caught up on the discrepancy between socialist internationalism and Zionist particularism, which he saw as a kind of 'squared circle'. Initially, he made attempts to resolve these contradictions by recalling the writings of the socialist Zionist Ber Borochov, but this resulted in further conflict, which eventually led to his exclusion from the youth movement..[21] On the other hand, none of the future dissidents took a more direct path into Sneh's party than Oded Pilavsky, born in 1932 in Jerusalem. Pilavsky had been raised in the traditions of the Jewish labour movement; his father was a factory worker and a member of Poalei Zion Smol. As a member of Mashabei Sadeh, a left-wing kibbutz, the younger Pilavsky had first joined the left-wing Zionist Mapam party, before following Moshe Sneh into the Socialist Left and later into the Israeli CP.[22] There, he quickly met a circle of critics dominated by Moshe Levin and Theodor Sheni, but they soon left the party in disappointment. After their departure, Pilavsky carried on the same disputes within the party.[23] As information on the fates of Soviet Jews, the 'night of the murdered poets' and the destruction of Yiddish culture gradually became public, it was Pilavsky who sought an open discussion and wound up in the crosshairs of the party leadership:

> When we heard the news about the destruction of Jewish culture and the murder of Jewish writers, I insisted at an editorial meeting for *Kol Haam*, that we needed to demand that the Soviet Union reopen all Jewish cultural institutions that had been wiped out under Stalin.[24]

Moshe Sneh dismissed this suggestion as a 'bourgeois demand', causing Pilavsky to feel bitterly rejected. When Pilavsky spoke up again, demanding the floor as his democratic right, his former comrade Sneh shut him down a second time. The only new ally he would find was Yirmiyahu Kaplan, who was born in Tel Aviv in 1936 and had been in the Communist Party youth movement for years.

Questions about the crimes of Stalinism, especially in the context of their own party's history, had been raised in Jerusalem as well. Despite the CP's attempts to cloak its past in silence, since their initial arguments in 1956, Akiva Orr and Moshé Machover had harboured their suspicions – in other words, long before they met like-minded counterparts in Tel Aviv. As Akiva Orr wrote, reflecting on the conflicts of that period: 'We began to ask: Who were the founders of the Israeli CP? What happened to them? Why are their names never mentioned? Why did the party never write its own history?'[25]

Nonetheless, they would eventually uncover this history, although the first answers to their probing questions came from outside Israel. By 1960,

Moshé Machover had lived in Poland for a year (working on his dissertation about mathematical logic) and was already disturbed by the impression 'that that was no socialism at all' in this Eastern Bloc country.[26] While there, he also met a generation of young communist dissidents, evolving around Jacek Kuroń and Karol Modzelewski, who demanded a democratisation of the state, the party and society and had begun to dig up the history of Poland's old interwar Communist Party, which Stalin had liquidated in 1938.[27] That Machover's stay in Poland became a confrontation with his own party's past was, however, a result of meeting the widows of former members of the Palestine Communist Party (PKP) who had been detained and murdered under Stalin. During the de-Stalinisation process, the widows were permitted to travel back to their native Poland, where they told Machover about their own bitter experiences and the tragic fates of many communists from Palestine who had died in Stalin's detention camps.[28]

Yet the most famous person Machover met in Warsaw was the Jewish communist and anti-fascist Leopold Trepper (1904–82). Trepper gave him new insights into this forgotten and neglected history.[29] Born in Nowy Targ, Poland, in 1904 under the name Leib Domb, Trepper rose to become the leader of the Belgian underground group 'Red Orchestra', which organised a network of spies against Nazi Germany.[30] Its origins lay in 1920s Palestine, when Trepper was one of the leading members of the Palestine Communist Party (PCP). But his conversion from socialist Zionism to the universalist utopia of a Moscow-led global revolution, which took precedence over the Palestine question, was just one facet of Trepper's story of Jewish communism in Mandatory Palestine.[31] Another aspect was the grim end that met most of his former party comrades at Stalin's hands after the PCP leadership clashed with the Comintern following the violent Jewish–Arab escalation of August 1929.[32] Publicly, the Jewish communists had adopted Moscow's line that the Arab violence was an anti-imperialist uprising; amongst themselves, they saw the events as more like a pogrom. Still, they did not escape the long arm of Moscow. The Comintern had already tried to Arabise the Palestine Communist Party and now found a pretext for summoning its Jewish leaders to Moscow: 'Since the party leaders were Jewish, they were all called back to Moscow', Trepper wrote in his memoir. 'One after another my old friends Birman, Lechtsinski, Ben-Yehuda, and Meier-Kuperman were liquidated.'[33]

Very few of Trepper's friends returned alive from the camps, like his comrade of many years Joseph Berger-Barzilai (1904–78), or escaped the party purges, like Trepper.[34] But when Trepper, after years of working as a spy, fled Nazi persecution and made his way to Moscow, he too was detained there – for nine years. He was only rehabilitated in 1953, after Stalin's death, and was able to leave the USSR for Poland, his birthplace. Unlike 'thaw'-era Poland, where initial steps were made to re-examine the Communist Party's history and rehabilitate its former leaders, such discussions were still suppressed in the Communist Party of Israel. Many years later, in his memoir, Trepper wrote: 'It was not until 1968, more than ten years after Khrushchev denounced Stalin and exposed his crimes at the twentieth congress of the Soviet Communist Party, that the Israeli Communist Party, the Maki, rendered homage to the leaders assassinated during the Stalinist purges.'[35] It was this reluctance to revisit history that triggered Akiva Orr and Moshé Machover's dissent and rebellion after Machover told his comrades about the former Palestine Communist Party members' experiences under Stalinism. Based on those accounts, the two of them drifted farther and farther away from the leadership of their own national party, which had failed to de-Stalinise. 'The leaders of the Israeli [Communist Party] accepted Khrushchev's criticism of Stalin', wrote Orr, summing up their dawning insight from that time, but they refused to accept 'criticism of themselves for having supported Stalin uncritically for decades'.[36]

The communist dissidents' alienation from the party was not entirely caused by its refusal to face the past. The dissidents were driven to a far greater degree by disagreements over the political present and by the revelation that Maki had abandoned its old revolutionary and universalist ambitions in favour of pledging allegiance to the Soviet Union. 'We felt that the CP (in Israel as in other countries) was not a revolutionary party but a club of the friends of the Soviet Union. The policy of this party was determined not by any revolutionary strategy, but by the needs of the foreign policy of the Soviet Union', recalled Moshé Machover, summing up the frictions in the parent party.[37] As they contended with this unconditional loyalty, the young renegades began not only to doubt their own party's behaviour, but to wonder if this loyalty to the USSR was passé: if by now, in the age of the Cold War and peaceful coexistence, the Soviet Union had lost its significance as the birthplace of the revolution and an indicator of social progress. These questions were partly prompted by the writings of former communist dissenters, such as Leon Trotsky's autobiography *My Life* and his theory of permanent revolution as opposed to Stalin's 'socialism in one country'.[38] However, their impact took hold in the context of present-day political shifts, when in Cuba 'a non-communist party had become the driving force of the revolution, while the Communist Party in Iraq had squandered its historical opportunity [for a revolution] – and this was no happenstance'.[39]

Indeed, the late 1950s presented Iraq's communists with an historic opportunity for a political takeover. Although Abd al-Karim Qasim and 'Abd al-Salam 'Arif and their Free Officers and Civilians Movement had been the ones to topple the monarchy on 14 July 1958, Qasim's chief supporters in his struggle against their domestic political rivals (the Baathists and Nasserites) were in the Communist Party, which was 'the largest political force in Iraq'.[40] The communists, who had persisted since their party's establishment in 1934 despite being banned, had a genuine popular base ranging from labour unions and associations of farmers, women and youth to the army and air force. 'The CP had tremendous and virtually undisputed influence' in Iraq, Machover explained. The young communists in Israel were also following the news out of Iraq with bated breath. 'Objectively, it would have been much easier for them to make their own "October" than it had been for Lenin in 1917. But here came the other difference: there was no Lenin, no April Theses, no revolutionary will at all.'[41]

From the Israeli dissidents' perspective, even worse than the Iraqi communists' failure to declare a revolution was that they had been ordered not to by Moscow, which forbade placing political pressure on Qasim.[42] Such a directive overlooked the facts of the situation on the ground in Iraq, where the communists represented the final hope for a secular state inclusive of national and religious minorities. Instead, the order was based on Soviet Cold War strategy and a policy of peaceful coexistence. A communist revolution seemed undesirable in light of Khrushchev's upcoming visit to Washington, the prospect of sparking enmity with neighbouring Arab states and even the risk of provoking an American intervention.[43] 'The chance for an Iraqi October was missed', Machover wrote, remembering their disappointment at the events for which, after the Baath party's takeover, the communists would pay dearly. 'When the revolutionary wave started to recede, when the regime no longer needed the vital support of the CP, the latter was forcibly liquidated and in the end the communists were cruelly massacred en masse', Machover recalled, incensed at the failure of an Iraqi Revolution.[44]

The fate of Iraq's Communist Party testified to a shift in Soviet policy, which placed the possibility of a Mesopotamian revolution second to the Soviets' own foreign policy strategy. Meanwhile, events that took place during the Cuban Revolution pointed in the opposite direction and left a strong impression on the communist dissidents in Israel. The successful revolution of 1959 signified more to them than a mere affirmation of Trotsky's speech proclaiming the value of underdeveloped countries for the spread of global revolutionary movements.[45] Far more important to the Israeli observers was the insight that the revolution debunked a central myth: that the only players capable of revolutionary power were the Soviet Union and parties loyal to it. The revolutionary uprisings on the Caribbean island were not, in fact, initiated by the local communist party, the Partida Socialista Popular (PSP). It was the independent 26th of July Movement, with Fidel Castro at the helm, that led the coup. Borne by intellectuals and farmers and based on the local traditions of the Cuban independence fighter José Martí (1853–95), this revolution was inherently liberal. Just before the revolution, the Stalinist PSP continued to discredit it as 'Trotskyist' and denounced its uprising as 'adventurous';[46] Communist Party members were latecomers to the revolutionary bandwagon. The Cuban Revolution made a global mark precisely because of its pioneering role in taking a self-sufficient path that was independent of Moscow. 'We were completely in favour of such "adventures"', wrote Moshé Machover of his and Akiva Orr's enthusiastic reaction to the news of the Cuban Revolution. 'And we thought: the Cuban CP is clearly not a revolutionary party; but other CPs are not any better. [. . .] So for us the joint lesson of Cuba and Iraq was that the CP was no longer capable of becoming a revolutionary force even when a revolutionary situation [did] arise.'[47]

Given such dramatic developments in the communist world, Machover and Orr no longer wanted to keep silent within their own party. Instead, they called for public discussions about the past and present of communism and about why the party was still taking 'dictation from Moscow' and holding firm, no matter the changing political winds, to the doctrine that 'the intellectual and political hegemony of the communist movement lays in Soviet hands' alone.⁴⁸ What dismayed the young communists most of all was being denied a chance to discuss the issues. Over and over, proposals for dialogue in the party cells were rejected and all attempts to debate contentious topics in the two party newspapers, *Kol Ha'am* and *Zo Haderekh*, were rejected.⁴⁹ Eventually, they felt compelled to distribute leaflets at party meetings, a move that attracted the attention of the party leadership. Initially, party officials made conciliatory efforts to respond by bringing the surging voices of criticism back into the fold. 'Comrades, why are you making things so hard for yourselves?' asked Esther Vilenska, the party secretary, in a meeting with the two of them, before making a peace offering: 'We propose sending you to Moscow with a scholarship.'⁵⁰ But as it grew apparent that the critics would not pipe down so easily, the tone grew harsher. When Akiva Orr again tried to criticise Soviet foreign policy under Khrushchev, he was met with a cynical retort from Meir Vilner, the party secretary at the time: 'For some of our comrades here in the party, something always stinks.' With an air of menace, Vilner added: 'Maybe they have something wrong with their noses.' Shortly thereafter, Machover and Orr were invited to Moshe Sneh's house for a political discussion, only to be admonished once more. Invoking Lenin and the principle of democratic centralism, the two of them stubbornly insisted on a discussion within the party, but this request fell on deaf ears yet again. 'Leave Lenin to me!' came Sneh's loud riposte, terminating the conversation once and for all.⁵¹

The two dissidents would not find a sympathetic audience within the party until they met Oded Pilavsky and Yirmiyahu Kaplan from Tel Aviv. The four men shared their disappointment about the Soviet Union and their own party, as well as similar experiences of being excluded from discussion or publication in their party's media; Pilavsky had already withdrawn from the editorial team of *Kol Ha'am*. But despite their last joint stand against the party leadership – expressed in their co-signed letter – they did not seem to harbour any hope of genuine change in the party. Independent of the party leadership's decision to expel the four dissidents, Machover and Orr announced their own departure, on 26 September 1962: 'We haven't become [the party's] enemies and will not be joining [their enemies] either', began the two men's statement to the members. Yet the impossibility of public dialogue and the lack of faith in a 'clear conception of a separate Israeli road to socialism' – independent of Moscow's – had forced them to strike out on their own, Machover and Orr contended.[52]

The four of them had already been gathering for a while now with a small, like-minded group, who now constituted the core of this new beginning. This group included Meir Smorodinsky (1931–2012), who had moved from Hashomer Hatzair to the Communist Party with Moshé Machover and likewise studied mathematics at the Hebrew University of Jerusalem. That was also where they met Haim Hanegbi, who was much less engaged in his studies, but was a fixture in Jerusalem's bohemian circles. He, too, had considered joining the Communist Party, but his friends had dissuaded him, saying that membership was not worth the effort.[53] Yet he did not want to give up on the promise of a revolutionary future on that basis. Back then, 'the revolution was at the centre of our lives', Hanegbi said in an interview, recalling the era of the new group's founding. 'It was completely clear to us that it was not an option to sit around twiddling our thumbs.'[54] In this spirit, a new organisation would soon be born. 'The word party for us seemed to have a stink clinging to it, so instead we opted for "organisation", a word [*Irgun*] with a militant connotation that would hearken back to the underground struggle against the British', Hanegbi said. 'We couldn't use the word communist, either, because there already was a Communist Party. So we opted for socialist, which is how the Israeli Socialist Organisation came to be.'[55] Hanegbi was also responsible for naming the periodical *Matzpen* (compass). The name, more discreet than that of most party publications, signalled that the movement was about setting a direction, a compass pointing towards the future.

It would take time for the new group's roughly fifteen members to realise that far from being a marginal phenomenon, their secession from party-communism was part of the global emergence of the New Left. However, the Israeli dissidents did not intend to break with the communist utopia and its imagined horizons for the future of humanity. Rather, the retrospective question of 'what had gone so horribly wrong' was asked in the interest of proposing 'an alternative within the terms of Communism itself'.[56] The very first issue of *Matzpen* magazine was already about finding such a perspective. In it, Meir Smorodinsky constructed a long, derisive structural analogy between communist parties loyal to Moscow and Catholic churches loyal to Rome.[57] For his part, Akiva Orr, referring to Lenin's theses of April 1917 and their impact on the Soviets' October Revolution, attempted to resurrect a tradition of open dispute over revolutionary politics among the Bolsheviks, which was obscured by the historiography of the Communist Party.[58] The quest for political alternatives within the communist movement turned the young dissidents' gaze further east – to China. Still, their interest had been stoked less by the Chinese developments as such than by how vehemently Moscow had condemned China's new directions and how the Israeli party leadership had sought to quash any discussion about the Sino-Soviet split.[59] However, in the long run, they would pay greater attention to the incipient New Left in Western Europe and the communist dissident movement of Eastern Central Europe. The contacts Machover made on his trip to Poland from 1959 to 1960 had an abiding influence. *Matzpen* was one of the international magazines that immediately published the 'Open Letter to the Polish United Workers' Party', in which Jacek Kuroń and Karol Modzelewski lodged an appeal to democratise Poland, a letter than became a symbol of a liberated critique of state socialism in the New Left.[60] When the same New Left took its protest to the streets of major European and American cities in 1968, Matzpen wanted to join its ranks.[61]

Although the birth of the New Left was a global outgrowth of the 1950s de-Stalinisation crisis, the movement also had national variations. Just as the French Left was born of out sentiment against the war in Algeria, the Polish dissidents had chafed against, and ultimately fallen prey to, Poland's national self-image as an increasingly ethnically defined nation-state.[62] Likewise, the Israeli Socialist Organization, as it seceded from the Communist Party, distinguished itself through many aspects regarding how it characterised and criticised its own state. 'In reality, we had three points of conflict with Maki', wrote Akiva Orr, tracing the history of the split:

> We thought that the Histadrut needed to be broken up, we contended that the Soviet Union did not have true socialism [. . .] and we believed that the conflict in the Middle East had its origins in the circumstances of the Palestinans and that it was necessary to reach a compromise and an arrangement with them and not with Nasser or Damascus.[63]

Beneath the surface of their ideological disputes over communism, they also disagreed with their parent party about the inward structure and outward relations of the Jewish state. As they called for a radical change within the General Organisation of Workers in Israel (the Histadrut) and reframed the 'conflict in the Middle East' as the 'Palestine question', these disagreements would flare up frequently after Matzpen's founding, as they already constituted a separate aspect of the split from Maki.

Revolt Against the Histadrut

'This Strike Is Justified!' ran the large-type headline of the leaflet that the members of the Israeli Socialist Organization were carrying on the morning of 25 December 1962 in solidarity with the warning strike that had subsumed Israel.[64] For one hour, from 11am to midday, industrial and agricultural machinery would stand idle.[65] A wave of strikes had kept the country in suspense for over a year, and this latest warning strike was the fourth of its kind. It was triggered by an economic policy change by the government. Import restrictions and subsidies for international investment were to be accompanied by a wage freeze and a devaluation of the Israeli pound to the public's deep dissatisfaction.[66] 'The struggle against the wage freeze is justified', declared Matzpen. With the leaflet, the organisation set out to make the workers' cause their own. From that day forward, *Matzpen* bore the subtitle *Workers' Magazine*.

As a focus of both the strikes and the communist dissidents' support, the wage demands were vastly overshadowed by other factors. For the first time, the strike movement had been organised independently by nationwide action committees of the company's workers' councils, which had thereby circumvented the authority of the Histadrut, the official body representing Israeli workers. Founded in 1920, the Histadrut organisation possessed sole authority for calling a labour strike. But when its leadership ruled out protesting the wage freeze, the local action committees felt inadequately represented by their union, so the autonomous action committees joined together to organise coordinated national strikes for the first time in Israel's history. The Histadrut responded without delay, invoking 'wild-cat strikes' and strenuously opposing the independent action committees' demands – indeed, their very existence.[67] In Matzpen, however, the workers' councils had found a less influential but deeply tenacious advocate in their efforts for independent organising. 'The Action Committees are the Workers' True

Representatives', proclaimed the handbill distributed by the group at strike events. 'Instead of asking the Histadrut leaders to support their demands, the workers' councils should take over running the Histadrut.'[68] This was no less than an incitement to a coup. A union whose leadership was hand-picked by, and therefore accountable to, the country's political parties ought to be radically transformed, according to Matzpen, into an elected lobby group representing Israeli workers. 'This was a completely new approach to the problem of trade unionism in Israel', summarised Moshé Machover, explaining this position, which for years was a persistent demand by Matzpen and was in part responsible for sparking the split from its parent party. 'All the "left" parties (including the CP) merely demanded that the Histadrut should change its policy. The CP regarded the Histadrut as an ordinary right-wing union, which should only be made more militant.'[69]

But even if the call for restructuring the Histadrut – or rather, in practical terms, abolishing it – signified a novel revision to the political topography of Israeli society, it did not come out of nowhere. In some regards, it drew on the biographical experiences of Akiva Orr, who at times wrote for *Matzpen* under the name A. Oved (Worker), placing himself in a proletarian tradition, but also signed an extensive piece about the legendary autumn 1951 sailors' strike using the pseudonym Yamai (sailor).[70] According to his recollection, that first Israeli revolt 'shook for a moment the structure of the Histadrut [. . .] down to its foundations', but the union leadership had also 'stabbed' the striking sailors 'in the back'.[71] More importantly for Orr personally, his role in the revolt would mark a political turning point in his life. Before that, Orr, born in Berlin in 1931 under the name Karl Sebastian Sonnenberg, had mostly kept his distance from Israeli politics.[72] His parents, who fled Germany in 1934, had remained aloof from the politics of the Yishuv and the young Israeli state and had passed on that aloofness to their son Akiva, who cultivated a corresponding distrust of political parties and newspapers, as well as the country's ideologically partisan youth movements.[73] Instead, he made himself at home on the beach. He would later describe his young self as a 'beach boy from Tel Aviv' – the winner of national swimming championships in 1946 and 1947, who had gravitated to his beloved sea by joining a naval unit of the Haganah, the pre-state paramilitary organisation. When he was discharged in summer 1950, it only seemed logical that his first position was in commercial shipping for the Israeli

Figure 1.2   Akiva Orr (centre) as a seaman, early 1950s.

merchant marine. He soon began his career as a deck boy (Figure 1.2) on the *Tel Aviv*, an old American steamship that was now being operated by Shoham Trading Limited. After more than a year of constant voyages between Israel, Africa and the Americas, the ship set sail from New York and arrived at the port of Haifa on 8 December 1951 – at the height of the sailors' strike. That strike, Akiva Orr's first, served as an 'enlightening disillusionment' that paved Orr's way into political activism, which he would henceforth pursue as a dissident.[74]

The sailors' uprising in Haifa was also rooted in a demand for wage increases and improvements to the miserable working conditions aboard ship, which had instigated a variety of smaller conflicts throughout the year.[75] But the sailors' complaints to Moshe Golandsky, the Secretary of Seamen at the Histadrut, were brushed off and neglected, a sobering experience that would soon heighten the crisis. The frustration was compounded by Golandsky's status as a desk worker who had scarce knowledge of the sailors' concerns and needs and had secured his appointment solely on the strength of his loyalty to the ruling Mapai party.[76] Finally, when word got out that the Histadrut itself held shares in the Shoham Trading Limited company and therefore had a financial interest in its prosperity, the sailors lost faith in their representatives once and for all.[77] By the summer, they had elected separate 'provisional delegates' to advocate for their interests to the trading company. Initially, however, Yosef Almogi, the secretary general of the Histadrut in Haifa, relented and accepted the provisional delegates as candidates for a new election within the sailors' union. But when the future strike leader Nimrod Eshel (1925–2015) and his allies won the election, they began demanding rights: to political autonomy, to appointing their own secretary and to a charter distinct from the Histadrut's. In response, the umbrella group refused to recognise the election outcome. Ultimately, it was that disregard for the sailors' interests that escalated and fundamentally transformed the conflict from a confrontation over economic issues into a clash over the political leadership of the Histadrut.[78]

The sailors did not commence strike action 'with demands that the shipping company give them a pay rise and better working conditions', Akiva Orr wrote eleven years later. 'They began the strike against the Histadrut for not recognising their elected councils. The slogan at the time ran: "We have no conflict with the [shipping] company – our conflict is with the Histadrut".'[79] When the sailors' provisional delegates passed a resolution on 12 November 1951 calling for everyone to abandon ship and occupy the headquarters of the sailors' union, the legendary sailors' strike commenced. Within four weeks, the strike had grown into the 'wildest experienced by the state up until that time'.[80] The conflict intensified when the Histadrut withheld its strike fund from the strikers and the company tried to hire strike-breakers.[81] The sailors held multiple demonstrations on shore, whereupon the Histadrut enlisted counter-demonstrators from its so-called 'Worker Squads' (Plugot HaPoel), prompting repeated outbreaks of violence at the port.[82] While sailors from Europe to the United States began sympathising with the strike in Haifa, public opinion in Israel was turning against the strikers.[83] Eventually, the Israeli Prime Minister, David Ben-Gurion, attempted to deflect the course of the conflict by conscripting the sailors into the armed services. When the *Tel Aviv* anchored near the Port of Haifa on 8 December 1951, the clash climaxed. On 14 December, which Israeli history would remember as Black Friday, David Ben-Gurion, who was serving as both prime minister and foreign minister, ordered an end to the strike and commanded that the *Tel Aviv*, the very last striking ship, be cleared of sailors.[84]

The strike would scarcely have taken such a dramatic turn after merely weeks – escalating all the way to an intervention by Ben-Gurion himself – had the conflict between the sailors and the Histadrut not implicated the domestic and foreign affairs of the young state.[85] The Israeli Prime Minister with 'quasi-totalitarian characteristics' saw it as his duty to guarantee the unity of the state and demonstrate the political leadership of his Mapai party.[86] The fact that many members of the former paramilitary elite unit Palmach (an abbreviation for Plugot ha-Mahaz, literally 'strike forces') were now leading a strike, of all things, reminded everyone of the history of the state's founding. In 1948, Ben-Gurion had sunk the *Altalena*, the floating arsenal of the Etzel brigades (an acronym for Irgun Tzva'i Le'umi, or National Military Organisation), in a bid to defeat the paramilitary group and its counterpart Lehi (short for Lohamei Herut Israel, or Fighters for Israel's Freedom) and compel them both to join forces with the state military. Now, 'the seamen's uprising was the third and final stage in the struggle of Mapai and Ben-Gurion to eliminate the opposition', this time targeting the disbanded Palmach units that appeared to be revolting in the sailors' name.[87] Although the Palmach had been disbanded peacefully in October 1948, unlike the Etzel brigades, the Palmach veterans' former affiliation and their political links to the left-wing Zionist Mapam party invited suspicions that their strike was a continuation of their past military particularism, with the aim of undermining Ben-Gurion's governing party's political control over the Histadrut. 'In Haifa we experienced McCarthyism', Nimrod Eshel, the leader of the strike, would later recall. 'To be a Palmach man was a stain. One had to be apologetic for not being a Mapai member.'[88] Nevertheless, the sailors' links to the elite military unit boosted their reputation and sparked sympathy among segments of the Israeli public. Uri Avnery wrote in his magazine *Haolam Hazeh*, for instance, that: 'The Hebrew youth sees this as an opportunity to express its disillusionment towards the state and to revive the camaraderie of the battlefield.'[89] The magazine had recently adopted the character as an explicit voice of opposition to Ben-Gurion's government. The cultural crowd surrounding the publisher took the side of the sailors and issued a call for support on 23 November 1951: 'We know that you are fighting for the basic rights of every sailor worldwide [. . .] that you are fighting for the right to have legally recognised elected representatives and against an "all the king's men" type of regime, which prevails in this country to our great misfortune.'⁹⁰ This extended far beyond efforts to reform the Histadrut. In general, these appeals to democracy stood in opposition to Ben-Gurion's policy of *mamlakhtiut* – a form of Israeli statism he had introduced, which sought to 'identify [the Mapai] with the state, and to view any struggle against its rule as an attack upon the state itself'.⁹¹

Finally, nothing fuelled the conflict more than the sailors' support from the left-wing parties – both the communists and the left-wing Zionist Mapam party – dating back to the start of the strike.⁹² The concurrence of the strike with the Ben-Gurion administration's public departure from its previous policy of non-alignment in the Cold War placed the clashes in Haifa in the context of inter-party disagreements over Israel's allegiance with the Eastern or Western Bloc.⁹³ A few days before the strike, the Israeli Foreign Minister officially announced a turn towards the West and voiced Israel's desire for an alliance with the US.⁹⁴ Yaakov Riftin, whose Mapam party saw the USSR as the 'second homeland of the Jewish people',⁹⁵ responded promptly with an appeal for the Israeli public to disobey orders. 'In this forum, we turn to the officers and the soldiers, we turn to the workers and the intellectuals: don't obey this reactionary policy against the national interest',⁹⁶ he implored in the Knesset at a time when his party was openly supporting the striking sailors in Haifa. Rejecting the leftists' allegiance with the sailors, which he interpreted as a frontal attack on his own policies, Prime Minister Ben-Gurion publicly pronounced that these actions were not a strike at all, but 'an attempt by the enemies of the state to paralyse the Hebrew fleet'.⁹⁷ He railed in polemic terms against both parties, accusing them of having been infiltrated by the long arm of the former Jewish caucus of the Communist Party of the Soviet Union. 'The community of workers [i.e., the Histadrut] determines if this is a strike, and not the Yevsektzia and its agents and partners in other factions.'⁹⁸ Invoking the spectre of the strike being under communist control at a time when Mapam and Maki were openly oriented towards Moscow, Ben-Gurion was able to conjure up the threat of a 'civil war' and treat the situation as a political emergency. Finally, the prime minister used his claim of communist subversion and his treatment of the sailors as a 'fifth column' to justify breaking the strike as a defence of his own foreign policy and even Israeli sovereignty.⁹⁹

The strike's support from the left-wing parties made it one of the few Israeli labour conflicts that resulted in attracting new members to those parties.¹⁰⁰

Moshe Sneh made the greatest splash, mounting polemical accusations of fascism and calling Ben-Gurion 'public enemy number one' after the prime minister summoned the striking sailors to military service.[101] When Sneh founded his Left Socialist Party soon afterwards, Nimrod Eshel, one of the leading strikers, felt as though the new party had practically snatched him into its arms.[102] The strike also sparked Akiva Orr's politicisation. According to his memoir: 'I had not decided to join a political party out of ideological conviction, but because of the strike. I knew nothing about the Soviet Union or Marx.'[103] That may have also been why, after the strike ended, he analysed its progression and character for himself and reached different conclusions from those circulating in his party. In Orr's reading, the frictions over foreign policy and party politics, which had catalysed events as they intensified, were scarcely central compared to other questions: why had a conflict over working conditions started as a clash with the workers' own union and led to state-sponsored violence against the strikers? Why were the domains of economic and political conflict intermingling?[104]

The revelation that the workers had different interests from those of their political representatives in the Histadrut leadership led Orr to dig far beneath the contemporary fault lines into the prehistory of the Jewish state and the 1920 establishment of the General Federation of Hebrew Workers in the Land of Israel. Especially in light of its origins, the Histadrut was clearly not an 'ordinary professional association' and not solely a representative body acting on behalf of the economic and social interests of labour.[105] Pinhas Lavon, the director for many years, admitted this overtly in a speech presented at the federation's fortieth anniversary, stressing that the Histadrut was, in fact, 'not a workers' trade union', but was actually established to serve a national function 'in the process of the rebirth of the Hebrew people in its fatherland'.[106] As a brainchild of the Zionist movement, it was primarily designed to create the conditions for the settlement and organisation of a Jewish workforce in Palestine and thus enable the declaration of a Jewish state. After its foundation, it developed virtually into a 'state in the making', a pre-state organisation intended to consolidate all elements of the future polity within itself.[107] Thus, the Histadrut was equally involved in building a national economy and creating the infrastructure required for the settlement of the prospective population. It founded and owned entire enterprises, such as the major construction firm Soleh Boneh, Bank HaPoalim and – together with the Jewish Agency – the Israeli maritime fleet. It also organised the national healthcare system and sociocultural institutions from the daily newspaper to sporting clubs. Significantly, the various trade organisations and unions only became part of the Histadrut later. Hence, 'from the moment of its birth the Histadrut was as much a capitalist employer and entrepreneur and an organ of state (or a state in the making) as it was a labour movement'.[108]

Orr categorised the Histadrut as an entity less like a British trade union and more along the lines of corporatism, drawing structural parallels to the professional groups founded in Benito Mussolini's Italian corporate state to level out the social divisions of bourgeois society. The Histadrut, he wrote shortly after Matzpen's formation, 'comprises an arm of the government whose aim is to smother any labour struggle'.[109] The primacy of politics over economics, inherent to the Histadrut since its establishment, was to be cemented in the constitution through party control over the trade unions. The proportional quotas of the Histadrut leadership elections had not only guaranteed the political domination of the Labour Party for many years, but essentially turned it into an organisation of the 'bureaucratic-authoritarian type' and a 'ruling power bloc'.[110] 'The Histadrut has stopped representing workers in their labour struggles', Orr wrote, sharpening his criticism. 'Instead, it acts on behalf of the employer and the state.'[111] The exercise of political control and the violent clampdown on social conflict during the sailors' strike attained a paradigmatic significance. For the first time, Orr realised that for a 'public employer like [the] Histadrut [. . .] control of the workers matters far more than profit, and a worker's political loyalty matters to such an employer much more than the worker's professional skill'.[112] This later led him to draw comparisons with the Bolshevist Soviet Union. There, too, the Communist Party had considered itself a representative of the country's workers, yet it sought to impose its own power at the expense of the incipient working class's democratic ambitions.[113] In the Soviet case, this spurred similar conflicts that culminated in an uprising by seamen against the political leadership: the Kronstadt rebellion. If Ben-Gurion's governing style in the young Israeli state amounted to a sort of 'Bolshevism without communism' (Eliezer Livneh), in retrospect Orr called the Haifa sailors' strike 'the Kronstadt of Israel'.[114]

Even if his participation in the uprising politicised Akiva Orr and led him to the Communist Party, his independent analysis of events and the relationship between society and the state in Israel expedited his gradual alienation from Maki in the late 1950s and early 1960s. After all, the communists had refrained from such a radical critique of the Histadrut and restricted their criticism to its Mapai leadership. Maki 'calls on the workers to fight to replace this leadership', wrote Orr under his pen name A. Oved, 'but under one condition: the fight must be within the framework of the Histadrut. In principle, Maki opposes the establishment of a competing union outside the framework of the Histadrut.'[115]

Meanwhile, Oded Pilavsky had voiced this conflict in the party from the late 1950s onward until it amounted to an irreconcilable difference. Personally, his problems with the Histadrut reached back farther than the sailors' strike; they were implicit in his life story. 'I was raised in a family with a proletarian consciousness', his memoir begins.[116] Nachum Pilavski, father of Oded and his brother Meir, who would later make a name for himself as Meir Pail, had modelled a political tradition for his children, and his younger son Oded eagerly followed in his footsteps. When their father was working at a potash plant on the Dead Sea, he had clashed with the local Histadrut representatives over his advocacy for the workers' interests. It was only natural that Oded Pilavsky would begin his political involvement by focusing on social issues. That meant more than merely supervising the corresponding columns of *Smol* (Left), the newspaper of the Left Socialist Party, and later serving on the editorial board of *Kol Ha'am*.[117] In Holon, where Pilavsky lived with his parents after being ejected from Kibbutz Mashabei Sadeh, he became actively involved in local workers' struggles. But soon after he was elected to the Holon Workers' Council of the Histadrut via the Maki list, he hit a wall. 'That was where I came face to face with the full significance of Mapai's total control over the bodies of the Histadrut', wrote Pilavsky years later, still brimming with indignation. 'Not a single organisation under the workers' council functioned as an effective democracy. All local and national institutions of the Histadrut were operated in a centralistic and undemocratic manner where the only bosses were Mapai officials.'[118] Only at the very lowest level – in the elections for the workers' committees for each workplace – did Pilavsky witness democratic decision-making in action.

In the early 1960s, cuts in social services prompted the various workers' committees of Tel Aviv and the surrounding area of Gush Dan to merge into temporary action committees that would agitate for pay rises and better working conditions. This was Oded Pilavksy's moment in the sun (Figure 1.3). In the summer of 1961, after the police broke up the action committees' main demonstration, where Pilavsky had given a speech, he tried to protect the committees' continued work, despite the lack of Histadrut support. At a meeting not long after the demonstration, he proposed that the merged workers' committees justified revising the statutes of the Histadrut itself. He thought that there should be an independent list of candidates from the workers' committees, akin to the party lists for electing the Histadrut's Workers' Council, as a grassroots democratic corrective for the federation's centralised structure. But the Histadrut leadership's pressure on the individual workers' committees was not the only factor that quashed this proposal.

In fact, Pilavsky's proposal alienated his own party, which was unprepared for such a radical change. 'I tried to convince the comrades of Maki's Tel Aviv branch that it was up to the party to create a non-partisan, independent list for a fundamental change of the Histadrut, instead of continuing to run hopelessly on the party list', he recalled years later. 'The reaction from the

Figure 1.3 Workers' committee in action: Oded Pilavsky in the early 1960s.

party leadership was very negative, but [so was the reaction] from most of the party members.'[119] Scarcely a year later, when labour struggles were flaring up across the country, Pilavsky repeated his demands, this time in the pages of *Matzpen*. By then, the Maki leadership had argued to its own members that the creation of a party-independent list recruited from workers' committees for the Histadrut leadership elections would dilute its own party-bound votes. 'That means that even according to the Maki leadership, it is not the administration of the particular union that needs to manage its own affairs, but rather this is done by the elite bosses, the party leaders from the top', wrote Pilavsky, openly censuring his former party.[120]

The communist dissidents' critique of the Histadrut was thus a separate element of their antagonism towards their parent party. Beyond that, by demanding that the Histadrut be radically reorganised, if not dissolved altogether, they were insinuating no less than a reformation of the relationship between the Israeli state and Israeli society. 'We are not arguing at all about the past', wrote Akiva Orr about the Histadrut, the erstwhile 'state in the making', 'but in reference to the present, we ask: How are things these days? These days, there is a nation and independent statehood, yet the interests of the working classes are still intermingled – this time with the interests of the government and employers.' Diagnosing after-effects of the pre-state past in present-day institutions, Matzpen surmised that a clean break was needed to turn the Histadrut into an 'independent class organisation of Israeli workers that would represent and promote the interests of workers exclusively'.[121] Merely democratising its internal workings would not fix the party's outdated structures that intermeshed politics and economics. In particular, the fusion of union-like responsibilities with entrepreneurial activities and public services, such as organising the country's sole health insurance provider, undermined any effective protest and demonstrated the workforce's dependency on Histadrut structures. Any workers who came into conflict with the Histadrut were always risking the loss of social security and jeopardising their job prospects at the numerous companies under its control.[122] Thus, fully breaking up the Histadrut's corporatist structures would require stripping away all the federation's quasi-state functions. 'Health insurance must be transferred into the hands of the state', declared Matzpen's policy platform.[123] They also called for the privatisation of factories and companies that were currently listed as under Histadrut ownership. In essence, all demands for transforming the Histadrut signified a reformation of Israel itself, which would be transformed from a corporatist community into a civil state – one in which the hitherto merged functions of state and economy would be separate and the structures for expressing social opposition or economic conflict would exist outside of political or state control.

The radicality of these demands was most apparent in the declared disagreement with the political objective for which the Histadrut had originally been founded: to create a Jewish state in Palestine. The last two items on the first list of demands that Matzpen addressed to the Histadrut called for the federation to guarantee full equality to Arab workers as members and to change its name from the General Federation of Hebrew Workers in the Land of Israel to the General Federation of Workers in Israel.[124] With that, the communist dissidents were raising constitutional questions bound up with the birth of the Israeli state: the establishment of a Jewish state in an Arab region and the associated Israeli–Arab conflict. This opinion had already provoked quarrels with their former parent party and now marked another milestone in Matzpen's own origin story.

Shalom, Shalom ve-Eyn Shalom – Peace, Peace, When There is No Peace

On 8 May 1962, as every year on that anniversary, the Communist Party of Israel assembled in the Red Army Forest near Abu Gosh to celebrate the victory of the Allies over Nazi Germany and to commemorate the Soviet victims of the war. The members travelled from far and wide to attend the meeting, which was where Akiva Orr and Moshé Machover met Oded Pilavsky and Yirmiyahu Kaplan for the first time. However, that was not Orr and Machover's sole objective. They were also hoping for a chance to talk to Moshe Sneh, whose intellectual authority they recognised, despite widening differences of opinion. Five months prior, they had sent him a freshly printed copy of their book *Shalom, Shalom ve-Eyn Shalom* (Peace, Peace, When There is No Peace), which analysed Israeli–Arab relations since the founding of the Jewish state.[125] When they finally met and asked how his reading was progressing, he responded gruffly: 'It took you five years to write and you want me to read it in five months?'[126]

It is fair to assume that Sneh had perused the book at least enough to form that harsh reaction. The book had certainly disgruntled some communists since its publication. Although the party newspaper *Kol Ha'am* described it in positive terms, the daily *Haaretz* remarked that the nearly 500-page volume, published under the pseudonym N. Israeli, 'stands out for its unusual style for a Maki activist'.[127] *Maariv* and *Al HaMishmar* put it more plainly, directly linking the book to Machover and Orr's banishment from the party. In *Maariv*, Moshe Meisels pointed out that the book did not restrict its criticism to Israeli government policy on Israeli–Arab relations, but in fact proposed new avenues unlike those set forth by the parent party. The columnist wrote that Maki 'questions the book', as it 'neither toes the party line, nor was it printed with prior party approval'.[128] 'In the book, they both dealt with the problem of peace in the Middle East and criticised Maki's approach', *Al HaMishmar* summarised.[129] Beneath the surface of worldviews and ideologies, the book exposed disagreements over national issues and views of Israel's position in its Arab region. Later, the writer Maxim Ghilan (1931–2005) even claimed to remember that Machover and Orr had published their book under a pseudonym in anticipation of the conflicts and 'mostly to prevent their expulsion from the Communist Party'.[130]

But the book was not born out of internal tensions in the party, nor had its authors set out to ignite such tensions. In fact, the book was incited by the 'second round' of military conflicts between the Jewish state and its Arab neighbours after the Israeli Sinai Campaign of November 1956 escalated into the second Arab–Israeli war, which later was revealed to be a coordinated military cooperation between Israel and the waning colonial powers of Britain and France. Like many sailors, Akiva Orr had been mobilised for military reserve duty at his naval unit in Haifa. Yet he was not persuaded by Prime Minister David Ben-Gurion's claims that Israel was fighting a purely 'preventive war' in Egypt or that there had been no advance coordination with the two European powers. Before the outbreak of war, Orr himself had observed French aeroplanes at the military airport in Lod and seen military equipment being unloaded from French ships at the port of Haifa.[131] This gave him reason to doubt the official narrative that the Sinai Campaign was a 'no choice war' – a euphemism that continued to colour the official version of events until 1982.[132] Long before the Protocol of Sèvres was published, exposing the secret agreement between Israel and the major powers, Akiva Orr decided to 'document in writing all the evidence that Israel was conspiring with Britain and France' and eventually to write a 'book on the

Zionist collaboration with colonialism'.[133] To that end, he spent years at the Jewish National and University Library in the Terra Sancta building in Jerusalem attempting to sketch a 'coherent picture' of 'the central problem of the State of Israel: the problem of its relations with the Arabs'[134] – using mostly publicly accessible press clippings and Knesset transcripts. The result was a comprehensively annotated collection of texts that, taken together, accused the Israeli government of talking the talk of peace without pursuing any policies of reconciliation with its Arab neighbours. Orr and his co-author Moshé Machover opened the book with a quote from the prophet Jeremiah, from whom they also took their title: 'and from the prophet even to the priest, everyone deals falsely. They have also healed the hurt of My people slightly, saying, "Peace, peace!" when there is no peace.'[135] Thus, at the very end of the book, there was a call to orient all Israeli policy towards peace with the Arab world and, therefore, to initiate a change in the Israeli government. 'We cannot have peace with the Arab states as long as those leaders hold on to power', the book concluded. 'The time has come to implement changes in Israeli policy and Israeli political consciousness. And the sooner the better.'[136] The extent to which this mixture of conflict analysis and concern regarding the future represented an explicitly Israeli position was finally manifested in their choice of pseudonym: N. Israeli.

In expressing the immediate concern that an alliance with Britain and France would mark Israel as a 'collaborator with colonialism' during the advancing decolonisation process, Machover and Orr were voicing their party's perspective and, in a way, affirming their own loyalty. 'The line taken by the Israeli CP on the Suez war was quite good', wrote Moshé Machover later. 'As a result, our faith in the CP increased in the autumn of '56 and this delayed our critical development against the CP line on other issues.'[137] In fact, the Communist Party was the only parliamentary force in Israel to condemn the war in public. When war broke out, even the left-wing Zionist Mapam party put former hesitations aside, remained part of Ben Gurion's government and declared that 'it is imperative that we stand ready, coiled for action. The people are called to the flag.'[138] The communists disagreed. Unlike all other political groups, on the eve of the war, the party opposed any incursion across Egyptian borders by the Israeli Army, warned of the approaching escalation and, in language typical of the party, unequivocally declared: 'The IDF shall not pass beyond the borders of Israel! We shall not grant the imperialists their wish, we shall oppose war, we shall defend the peace.'[139] When Israel's strategic ties to the colonial powers became obvious during the war, their impression was reinforced that the Jewish state was playing the role of 'servant' for major Western powers as regards its foreign policy and acting as 'an instrument in their hand against the cause of peace, against the national liberation movements of the peoples of the Arab East'.[140] Hence, the communists saw the Suez–Sinai Campaign as virtual confirmation of their theory, laid out two years prior by their chief ideologue Moshe Sneh in his treatise *On the National Question: Conclusions in the Light of Marxism-Leninism*, that the conflict between Israel and its Arab neighbours was actually a local variant of the more significant discrepancy of values in the global conflict between the Eastern and Western Blocs. Israel would continue to come into conflict with its Arab neighbours, Sneh believed, until it ceased its opposition to the Soviet Union and its alliance with Western imperialism.[141]

Several years later, when Machover and Orr began writing their own book on the history of the Israeli–Arab conflict, their approach arose from both the escalating dynamic of the most recent war and their initial desire to corroborate their party's anti-imperialist mantra. But as the two dissidents traced the roots of their big-picture analysis, their investigation took them far from the Suez Crisis itself, and they found less and less support for blaming Israel's conflict with its Arab neighbours solely on its Western ties. Their examination of the Jewish Yishuv's war for statehood from 1947–9 gave them an independent understanding of Israel's circumstances in the Middle East that gradually shifted their perspective away from that of the Communist Party. At the outset, Machover and Orrs continued to fit their account into the Communist Party's paradigm, which interpreted the war as a national independence struggle against the power of the British Mandate and explained that the Arab armies had targeted the new state as an extension of the disintegrating British Empire.[142] But their doubts soon set in when they considered the Suez Crisis eight years later, by which point Israel's foreign policy had almost entirely reversed. Back in 1948, the Jewish state was still receiving military aid from the USSR and using force against Arab armies, including the Arab Legion, which was trained and commanded by British officers.

The authors' divergences from their party line deepened when they turned their attention away from foreign allegiances to focus on the United Nations Partition Plan of 29 November 1947, which called for the establishment of both a Jewish state and an Arab–Palestinian state. They wondered why that plan failed. To be sure, the two young authors had to consider numerous circumstances, not least the attacks by the Arab states, which immediately followed the proclamation of the Jewish state and intended to undermine the Partition Plan from the beginning. Yet, departing from the party's anti-imperialist interpretations, Machover and Orr were drawn to another perspective on the war: that of the Palestine problem and the national antagonism between Israeli Jews and Palestinian Arabs. The more they questioned the contours of Israel's borders and the post-war circumstances of Palestinian refugees, the more vividly they perceived a Jewish state founded 'at the expense of the Palestinian Arab people'[143] – an all-out fundamental conflict over Israeli statehood, which also laid the foundation for their imminent rift with their party. Michel Warschawski later explained the shift their book initiated: 'The organisation [Matzpen] put forward a radical critique of Zionism: breaking with the traditional line of the [Israeli CP], it analysed the war of 1948 as a war of ethnic cleansing rather than as a war of national liberation.'[144]

This modified interpretation of the establishment of Israeli statehood would not have brought about a rift with the party had it not tarnished the national self-image of the Israeli CP itself. After all, its predecessor, the Palestine Communist Party, had until 1947 opposed any partition of Palestine in favour of a joint Jewish–Arab polity; the earlier party did not express support for Jewish statehood until the Soviets themselves did.[145] However, this change in attitude was not solely the result of ideological conformity and loyalty to the Soviet Union, which linked the foundation of a Jewish state to its hopes for an anti-imperialist revolt against the British Empire. It was also the culmination of a process that had begun in 1943 with the division into separate Jewish and Arab splinter parties and was compounded by a shift in the Jewish party members' personal identities due to concurrent events in Europe. Most of them were descended from Eastern European Jewry; now, facing the irreversible destruction of that community, they were forced to rethink some of their reservations against a Jewish state. The breakaway of the Arab members in 1943 primarily resulted from their rejection of the Jewish communists' support of a Histadrut-organised strike against British bases in Palestine. For the Jewish communists, in turn, the split was meant to facilitate their soon-to-come calls for authorising unlimited Jewish immigration to Palestine.[146]

Four years later, in the wake of the UN Partition Plan, the Palestine Communist Party had become the Make'i (Miflagah Kommunistit Eretz Israelit, the Communist Party of the Land of Israel), which by referencing the biblical Eretz Israel now bore the trappings of a Jewish connection to Palestine.[147] In May 1948, when Meir Vilner added his signature to the Israeli Declaration of Independence, Shmuel Mikunis travelled once more to Prague to assist with Ben-Gurion's arms purchases and recruit volunteers to defend the new state. This was the Communist Party's 'patriotic honeymoon' period, which briefly produced a 'programme on the national question' that was 'for the first time almost identical with that of the Zionist movement'.[148]

This mélange of ideological anti-imperialism and national identification with the Jewish state was most evident in the party's chief theorist, Moshe Sneh, born Moshe Kleinbaum, who was a late-blooming communist.[149] He had first proved his mettle as the coordinator of the Haganah before finding his circuitous way to the party, and his conversion to communism was borne primarily out of the conviction that a Jewish state could benefit more from siding with Moscow than with London and Washington.[150] Meanwhile, the ideological flexibility of interpretation offered by Soviet anti-imperialism enabled him to consider the Palestinian tragedy, while immunising himself against the notion of an Israeli statehood conflict. The most significant example might be his theoretical ticket into the Communist Party, *On the National Question: Conclusions in the Light of Marxism-Leninism*, which would become one of the party's foundational theoretical texts. Not only does the book describe the Israeli War of Independence as an anti-imperialist liberation struggle, but he also attributes the Palestinian refugee problem and the Palestinian Arabs' statelessness to a combination of two factors: British efforts to exert influence in the region and the West's role in the incipient Cold War. Sneh's treatise proposes the following explanation for the 'displacement of hundreds of thousands of Arab residents from their homeland' and the 'non-establishment of an independent Arab state':

> In both these cases, British and American imperialism prevented the full implementation of the UN resolution, created the disgraceful issue of Arab refugees, spawned the Israeli-Arab tensions, made a mockery of Israeli independence and transformed Eretz Israel into a hotspot of national enmity and a menace of war.[151]

He increasingly inscribed this decoupling of the circumstances of Palestinians from the foundation of the Jewish state into official Communist Party doctrine. Through the anti-imperialist interpretation of the war, which had been targeted 'not against the Arab nation but against our [colonialist] oppressors', Sneh and the party avoided a link being drawn between the Palestinian catastrophe and the founding of the Jewish state.[152] To be certain, Sneh was a determined advocate of Palestinian–Arab refugees' right to return, just as he declared the recognition of a Palestinian–Arab right to self-determination as a prerequisite for any solution to the Israeli–Arab conflict.[153] Maki's binational character, the party's support of the Palestinian cause and the defence of Israeli Arab rights within the Jewish state made the communists, without doubt, exceptional on the political spectrum in Israel. With his ideologically tinted depiction of Israel's founding war of 1948, however, Sneh avoided placing the conflict over the Israeli state's establishment at the centre of the internal communist debate.[154]

This stance did not go uncontested within the party ranks. Indeed, its two ethnic groups had again merged under the name of Maki after Israel's founding. As early as 1956, when the unifying bond with Stalin and the Soviet Union frayed, national disagreements about the first Israeli–Arab war came to light within the party; disagreements that unanimous loyalty to Soviet communism had hitherto neutralised. This affected more than just the circle of Hanoch Bzozah, who had frequently pointed out the Arab states' refusal to sign a peace treaty with Israel, before being expelled for 'Jewish national deviations'.[155] Meanwhile, the Arab party members Emil Habibi and Tawfiq Tubi began to denounce the communists' consent to the partition of Palestine as false loyalty to Stalin.[156] In the same breath, they also rejected the interpretation of the war as an anti-imperialist revolt and insisted that it had been 'unjust[ly] anti-Arab'.[157] But these differences of opinion did not bear immediate consequences. It would take another nine years and mounting national tensions before the contradictions split the party once again along mostly ethnic lines in 1965.[158] Maki then became known as the Jewish Communist Party, which was led by Sneh, Mikunis and Vilenska. The newly founded Rakah party (Reshima Komunistit Hadasha, New Communist List) served as the predominantly Arab Communist Party under the leadership of Meir Vilner, Emil Habibi and Tawfiq Tubi.[159]

In this context of emerging ethnonational divisions within Israeli party-communism, Moshé Machover and Akiva Orr's 1961 book *Shalom, Shalom, ve-ein Shalom* represented a sort of break from a party that had not yet split apart. Aligning more closely with Palestinian Arabs' experience of history and placing a new emphasis on the Palestine question, the book was doubtless also coloured by their own life stories. Moshé Machover had long ago confronted the inherent contradictions of a Jewish state in former Palestine: his initial consideration that Zionism was incompatible with socialism had been strengthened by his expulsion from Hashomer Hatzair. For his part, Akiva Orr had inherited his parents' doubts regarding the Yishuv's ethnic self-isolation, which ran counter to their ideal of individual equality regardless of heritage: 'It was a mistake that we stayed in Palestine', said Orr's father, who, according to his son Akiva's memoir, repeatedly complained that he had 'not predicted an all-consuming national conflict here'.[160] Machover and Orr now drew on these experiences in their jointly authored book. At variance with their party's ideological interpretations, they began delving into the questions of Israel's borders and Palestinian refugees to expose a previously concealed link between the founding of the Jewish state and the Palestinian catastrophe – the Nakba.

Their new version of the history of the first Israeli–Arab war rested on a re-examination of reports of secret negotiations between Ben-Gurion and King Abdullah I of Jordan. Even before the outbreak of war, the two leaders had set out to divide up the territories that the United Nations had earmarked for a Palestinian state between themselves. However, the meetings ceased at the onset of the war without reaching the hoped-for non-aggression treaty.[161] Nevertheless, when Machover and Orr analysed the later Armistice Agreement between the Jewish state and the Hashemite Kingdom of Jordan, it appeared to them as though the two 'friendly enemies'[162] had already turned the Palestinian Arab state into a 'a chip in [the] bargaining over the conditions of the desired peace' a long time ago.[163] 'Before 1960 we did not know that Israel and Jordan had conspired to rob the Palestinians of their territory',[164] Orr later wrote, reflecting on his own learning curve as they composed the book, which makes clear that, in dividing up the territory with Jordan, the Israeli government had 'contributed to the failure of the creation of an Arab state in the other part of Palestine'.[165]

Far more than their discussion of Israel's borders, Machover and Orr's emphasis on a consecutive link between the founding of the Jewish state and the flight of Palestinians steamrolled over past portrayals of wartime events. Contrary to the official Israeli narrative – that Arab state leaders had encouraged Palestinian Arabs to flee the country – they emphasised the close connection with Jewish troops' paramilitary actions. Although this had already been raised in literary form in S. Yishar's (Yizhar Smilansky's) iconic short story '*Khirbet Khizeh*', soon after the war this narrative was buried under talk of a voluntary departure and by Israel's notion of its own 'purity of arms' (Tohar HaNeshek) – the ideal of an ethically balanced use of military violence for nothing but self-defence.[166] Seeking an historical explanation of Yishar's literary portrayal and building on the post-war Israeli debates, Machover and Orr tried to reconstruct the wartime episodes that had ended in more than 700,000 Palestinian Arabs fleeing the country, particularly the contested Plan Dalet of March 1948, which had been developed by the military leadership of the incipient state.[167] Designed as a strategic concept for 'aggressive defence' of the settlements of the future Jewish state,[168] the plan had eventually entertained the 'destruction of villages (burning, blowing up and mining the ruins) especially in settlements that we are not able to permanently control'.[169] Machover and Orr read this as a 'forceful uprooting of Arabs [. . .] which was not the action of "irregular" forces, but a calculated policy of the authorised Jewish institutions'.[170] In some respects, these plans of the Yishuv's political and military leadership also mirrored the contemporary international acceptance of population transfers on the European continent, which emerged following the upheavals of the Second World War.[171] But the critical element for Machover and Orr's narrative was the significance of the Jewish state's founding history that they situated squarely in the birth of the Palestine problem. Their new interpretation eventually claimed a scope far beyond the events of the first Israeli–Arab war. 'The problem is not only the fact that many of the Arabs of Palestine lost their property, their houses and their lands as a consequence of the 1948 war and became refugees', the co-authors asserted. 'The main point is that they were left without a homeland, without being able to satisfy their national aspirations.'[172] Beyond the conflict between Israel and its Arab neighbours, the Palestine question had risen to the fore as an unredeemed promise of recognition of the Palestinian people's national claims: a sui generis problem that Israel needed to resolve – partly for its own sake.

In the 1950s and early 1960s, when the Palestine question and the existence of a Palestinian people were obscured by the conflict between Israel and neighbouring Arab states, Akiva Orr and Moshé Machover were among the first in Israel to lay bare the state's founding conflict.[173] This was the pioneering role of the book, which supplied the ultimate grounds for their expulsion from the authors' communist parent party. 'Even the Israeli Communist Party, the only party that always claimed that a Palestinian people existed and deserved independence, viewed the Palestinians after 1948 as having ceased to be a political entity', concluded Orr. 'No expert on the "Palestine Problem" considered the Palestinians to be a political factor.'[174]

One factor contributing to the skirmishes with their parent party was that Machover and Orr's deviating interpretation extended far beyond the 1948 War and, indeed, prompted them to rethink their own political perspective on the Israeli–Arab conflict in general. Beginning with the elemental significance of the Palestine question, they now sought to paint a comprehensive picture of Israeli foreign policy, which they entirely reframed around the constraints placed on the state by its founding conflict. Besides recognising the entanglement of the Palestine problem and the declaration of the Israeli state, they came to conclude that the Jewish state's demographic and territorial status quo could only be maintained by denying the refugees a right to return and by enlisting the military to protect the territories seized during the war.[175] At Israel's borders, where Israeli hostility against Palestinian border-crossers was tied to retaliations against Arab neighbours, the communist dissidents also observed how the Palestine question was spreading into the military conflict between Israel and its Arab neighbours.[176] Machover and Orr proceeded to put forward their reinterpretation of Israel's border wars: 'From an objective standpoint, the main problem is that of the Palestinian-Arab people, whose right to self-determination was denied it by force and by subterfuge, and from this stem all the various other problems in the dispute between Israel and the Arabs.'[177]

Yet this new angle did not substantially clash with the stances of their parent party until the authors characterised Israel's foreign policy during the Cold War as an ongoing search for an international guarantee of the status quo post bellum. This is what lead the country into the arms of the West, they reasoned.[178] 'It was not the Zionist foreign policy that dictated the Zionist settlement and military policy (as the Communist Party claimed)', wrote Akiva Orr later, explaining the book's shift in interpretation. 'It was the other way round: Zionist settlement and military policy dictated Zionist foreign policy.'[179] On that basis, they assigned comparatively little importance to the Korean War and Israel's initial declared support for the Americans as a means of averting Israel's long-held policy of neutrality,[180] focusing instead on the preceding Tripartite Declaration of 25 May 1950, in which the United States, France and Britain recognised for the first time the inviolability of the Israeli armistice lines and thereby ratified an international 'guarantee of the status quo'.[181]

Certainly, the major powers of the West were pursuing their own self-interests, which arose from the conflicts of the Cold War and, in the French and British cases, from colonial ambitions in the Arab world.[182] But whereas the Israeli CP lamented Israeli efforts to forge a solid alliance with the United States and later colonial France, describing this as a surrender to the West and calling Israel its 'faithful servant',[183] Machover and Orr's perspective shifted. In light of the conflict with its Arab neighbours, it became apparent to them that Israel's foreign policy affiliation had been guided by the country's own security considerations and by the primary objective 'to establish a military alliance with the West, so the latter would impose the status quo on the Arabs'.[184] This led the Jewish state to spend years angling for a seat at the table of US defence treaty negotiations and pushing for access to American arms – before Israel found its first arms trading partner in France, a country which was likewise fighting Arab nationalism.[185] Machover and Orr's account concluded that in its efforts to push its own political cause, the Jewish state had been forced to adapt to the strategies of the major powers in the region and to present matters 'from the point of view of Western interests'[186] so as to impute mutual interests among unequal partners and secure the political backing of a powerful ally, which would protect Israel's own existence in the Middle Eastern conflict.

One strand of their reinterpretation of Israeli foreign policy departed even farther from their parent party's horizons: they highlighted the historical situations in which Israel attempted to secure major Western powers' protection in the region, even though those powers were already beginning to withdraw from the Middle East. At the twilight of colonialism, Israel's hope for a proviso that would inflict a British and French presence upon Arab independence movements was tantamount to trying to stop decolonisation in its tracks. Ultimately, that placed Israel at odds with the colonial powers, who had already begun the journey to decolonisation. This transformed the Jewish state into a defender of the French colonial presence in Algeria at a time when France had already started to consider loosening its grip on the colony.[187] In 1960, when the Lavon Affair revealed that Israel had been the real orchestrator of the 1954 bombardments on American and British installations in the Nile Valley, which had been erroneously blamed on the Egyptians, this provided another clear example of the great lengths Israel would go to prevent the British military from withdrawing from its Arab neighbour.[188] Ultimately, Machover and Orr concluded, Israel's conflict over Palestine seemed to be situating it as the 'the most conservative actor in the region, the Last of the Mohicans of the lost Western cause'.[189] An article in *Matzpen* later argued that the Israelis in power 'are more concerned with the interests of the imperialists than the imperialists themselves, because they feel that their fate is tied to that of imperialism: but whereas imperialism has somewhere to retreat to, they – they haven't'.[190]

As comprehensive as this new interpretation of Israeli foreign policy may have been, given the perennial disagreements between Israel and Western countries, Machover and Orr's main point was that it was impossible to permanently reconcile Israel's motives – related to the conflicts over the Middle East and Palestine – with the interests of the major powers. Since its founding, the Jewish state had striven for an alliance with the United States – an alliance it did not achieve until the 1960s. Meanwhile, anticipating Algerian independence, France began turning away from Israel and towards the Arab world. Hence, the two authors argued that a 'power that has something to lose in the Middle East is not prepared to overtly support Israel', which was the root cause for the failure of the political strategy of forging strong Western alliances.[191] With this argument, Machover and Orr had pointed out Israel's fragile position in the region, which despite all its foreign support was, in fact, reliant on 'borrowed power' (in the words of Dan Diner).

If emphasising the distinct importance of the Palestine problem had moved the communist dissidents to re-evaluate the driving forces behind Israeli foreign policy, their realisation of its long-term failure led them straight back to the Palestine question. At this point, their insight that it was impossible to permanently circumvent the conflict over Palestine, in terms of both foreign policy and power politics, made them realise that a sustainable Israeli state could scarcely be constructed upon a situation in which the Palestinian Arabs 'were left without a homeland, without being able to satisfy their national aspirations'.[192] 'They will not forget their houses, their fields and their homeland. The Jews did not forget the Land of Israel during two thousand years of exile, so why should the Arabs forget it over thirteen years?'[193] Such was the co-authors' response to the Israeli hope that the national aspirations of the Palestinian Arab people would dissolve with their integration into neighbouring Arab countries. They had similar doubts as to whether it was feasible to maintain the political and demographic circumstances of the Jewish state in the long run while the balance of power in the Middle East experienced major shifts. Over the years, more and more Arab states had achieved independence and taken stances supporting the recognition and the rights of the Palestinians in forums such as the Arab League and the Non-Aligned Movement. 'The time-factor is working for the benefit of the Arabs and against Israeli policy', concluded their geopolitical analysis of the contemporary situation, with this horizon in mind.[194] 'Sooner or later Israel will withdraw from the status quo and will be forced to make certain concessions.'[195]

Building on this historically grounded interpretation, Machover and Orr's book culminated in a list of political proposals. 'Only proposals that involve discussion [of] a certain withdrawal from the status quo on the issues of the refugees and the borders have a chance of moving us closer to the longed-for peace.'[196] This was their opening salvo calling for a new Israeli politics. Perhaps that was why the book displeased not only some of their fellow communists, but also Israeli censors. Machover and Orr initially hand-delivered the book to bookstores around the country before supplying a copy to the Israeli authorities. But even though the censorship authorities placed it on the index of banned books, they took no action against its distribution.[197]

Indeed, it was impossible to prevent the book from becoming a primary source and founding document for the dissident movement within and around Maki, even before the establishment of Matzpen. The Palestine question had been formative in the lives of many future Matzpen members, an omnipresent political backdrop. That was not only true for Haim Hanegbi, who had been a distant witness to the massacre of Deir Yassin and had vivid childhood memories of his Palestinian Arab neighbours disappearing from the Mekor Baruch neighbourhood of Jerusalem.[198] Oded Pilavsky shared similar experiences. In winter 1950–1, a few years after the founding of the state, he witnessed the expulsion of Bedouin tribes across the borders into Egypt and Jordan. It was Yirmiyahu Kaplan, who was to leave Matzpen two years later, who eventually resumed Machover's and Orr's political demands on the pages of the magazine's first issue: the Palestinian refugees right of return should be realised according to the United Nations resolution either by actual return or the payment of compensation.[199]

But even as Machover and Orr, having written the book, began to part ways with the Communist Party and blaze their own trail, while they continued to take the United Nations Partition Plan as the reference point for their portrayal of the Palestine question and made fixing its implementation into a prerequisite for a solution, they were operating within the theoretical framework of their former parent party. They continued to see the failure of the establishment of a Palestinian state as the primary obstacle to solving the conflict and perceived the clash as a specific type of nationality conflict – an antagonism between two nations fighting over the same territory.

Only in a few passages of the book did Machover and Orr hint at another, yet unwritten, narrative of the conflict. Almost in passing, they mentioned that the current Middle Eastern conflict was concealing the old 'problem of Palestine' that had preceded the founding of the Israeli state:[200]

> The Jewish settlers did not come to a deserted area, but rather to a land that was populated by another people – the Palestinian Arab people. Tel Aviv was founded at the beginning of the 20th century next to Jaffa, which had existed for hundreds of years, like old Haifa, Jerusalem, Acre, Baysan [Beit-Shean], Beersheva and hundreds of other towns and villages like them.[201]

Founding Matzpen and recruiting new members from different political traditions would expose them to that backstory. Not until this development had fostered a distinct understanding of the Palestine problem was Matzpen truly born.

Notes

1. 'Announcement', *Kol Ha'am* (28 September 1962), p. 12 [Hebrew]. See also Erel, *Matzpen: Conscience and Fantasy*, p. 19 [Hebrew].
2. 'Educational Material about the Machover-Pilavsky Anti-Party Group', hdl.handle.net/10622/COLL00308%2E568?locatt=view:pdf (accessed 26 March 2020) [Hebrew].

3. 'A "Subversive" Document. Why Four Maki-Members were Expelled?', *Matzpen* 1 (1962), p. 2 [Hebrew].
4. Ibid.
5. 'Possibly a New Communist Party will Emerge in this Country', *Haolam Hazeh* (12 September 1962), p. 4 [Hebrew].
6. 'Maki-Leadership Worries about Intellectual Circles of their Former Members', *Haaretz* (14 September 1962) [Hebrew].
7. Meisels, 'No Room in Maki for Critical Voices'.
8. K. Amnon, 'The Group that was Thrown Out of Maki is Preparing to Publish its Own Monthly Magazine', *Al Hamishmar* (12 November 1962), p. 1 [Hebrew].
9. Meisels, 'No Room in Maki for Critical Voices'.
10. Roger Engelmann, 'Einleitung', in Roger Engelmann, Thomas Grossbölting and Hermann Wentker (eds), *Kommunismus in der Krise: Die Entstalinisierung 1956 und die Folgen*, Analysen und Dokumente (Göttingen: Vandenhoeck & Ruprecht, 2008), pp. 9–34; Reinhard Crusius, 'Einleitung', in Manfred Wilke and Reinhard Crusius (eds), *Entstalinisierung: Der XX. Parteitag der KPdSU und seine Folgen*, Edition Suhrkamp ([S.l.]: [s.n.];Frankfurt am Main: Suhrkamp, 1977), pp. 9–20.
11. Jerzy Holzer, 'Die Geheimrede Chruschtschows und ihre Rezeption in Ostmitteleuropa', in Hans H. Hahn and Heinrich Olschowsky (eds), *Das Jahr 1956 in Ostmitteleuropa* (Berlin: Akademie Vlg, 1996), pp. 13–20.
12. Reinhard Crusius and Manfred Wilke, 'Polen und Ungarn 1956. Eine Dokumentation', in Manfred Wilke and Reinhard Crusius (eds), *Entstalinisierung: Der XX. Parteitag der KPdSU und seine Folgen*, Edition Suhrkamp ([S.l.]: [s.n.]; Frankfurt am Main: Suhrkamp, 1977), pp. 98–164.
13. Thomas Grossbölting, 'Entstalinisierungskrisen im Westen. Die kommunistischen Bewegungen Westeuropas und das Jahr 1956', in Roger Engelmann, Thomas Grossbölting and Hermann Wentker (eds), *Kommunismus in der Krise: Die Entstalinisierung 1956 und die Folgen*, Analysen und Dokumente (Göttingen: Vandenhoeck & Ruprecht, 2008), pp. 233–49.
14. Walter Grab, *Meine vier Leben: Gedächtniskünstler – Emigrant Jakobinerforscher – Demokrat* (Köln: PapyRossa, 1999), pp. 124–5.
15. Ibid., pp. 131–3.
16. Beinin, *Was the Red Flag Flying There?*, p. 192.
17. Moshe Meisels, 'Maki Persons Demand the Rehabilitation of the Names of those Communists who "Disappeared" in Russia', *Ma'ariv* (13 September 1956), p. 2 [Hebrew].
18. Meisels, 'No Room in Maki for Critical Voices'.
19. Ibid.

20. Pinhas Ginossar, 'From Zionism to Communism and Back. The Case of Moshe Sneh (1948–1967)', in Jonathan Frankel and Dan Diner (eds), *Dark Times, Dire Decisions: Jews and Communism*, Studies in Contemporary Jewry: An Annual (Oxford: Oxford University Press, 2004), pp. 236–54.
21. Doron Rosenblum, 'The Exile Option in Paris and London. Part 2: London', *Hadashot* (28 September 1999), pp. 22–9, at p. 24 [Hebrew].
22. Oded Pilavsky, 'How I Arrived at Matzpen', https://matzpen.org/2008-09-29/כיצד-הגעתי-למצפן-עודד-פילבסקי-י/ [Hebrew].
23. Meisels, 'No Room in Maki for Critical Voices'.
24. Sahish, 'The Myth of Matzpen', p. 10.
25. Akiva Orr, 'Peace, Peace, Yet There is No Peace', in Akiva Orr, *Enlightening Disillusionments* (Tel Aviv, 2011), pp. 36–48, at p. 45.
26. Moshé Machover, 'Matzpen. The Israeli Socialist Organisation. Interview with Arturo Schwarz', in Uri Davis, Andrew Mack and Mira Y. Davis (eds), *Israel and the Palestinians* (London: Ithaca Press, 1975), at pp. 302–3.
27. Jacek Kuroń describes his first encounter with this story in his autobiography: 'Around that time I was gradually discovering the Communist Party of Poland (KPP), which had been dissolved by the Comintern in 1938. The life stories of its leaders were not acknowledged in *Trybuna Ludu* (People's Tribune) until 1 May 1956. [. . .] This was the first information about the victims of Stalin that reached me. As a result of all this, I began to identify very strongly and forcefully with this party.' Jacek Kuroń, *Glaube und Schuld: Einmal Kommunismus und zurück* (Berlin: Aufbau-Verlag, 1991), p. 152.
28. Lutz Fiedler, Interview of the Author with Moshé Machover (6 November 2007), London.
29. Ibid.
30. Gilles Perrault, *The Red Orchestra* (London: Barker, 1968).
31. Leopold Trepper, *The Great Game: The Story of the Red Orchestra* (London: M. Joseph, 1977), p. 57. See also: Judith Kafri, *Zosha: From the Jezreel Valley to the Red Orchestra* (Toruń: Wydawn. Adam Marszałek, 2009).
32. Mario Keßler, 'Die Augustereignisse 1929 in Palästina, die KP Palästinas und die Kommunistische Internationale', in Mario Keßler, *Antisemitismus, Zionismus und Sozialismus: Arbeiterbewegung und jüdische Frage im 20. Jahrhundert*, 2. Aufl. (Mainz: Decaton-Verl., 1994), pp. 66–80.
33. Trepper, *The Great Game*, p. 57.
34. Mario Keßler, 'Joseph Berger. Communist Activist in Palestine and Victim of Stalinism (1904-1978)', *Moving the Social. Journal of Social History and the History of Social Movements* 51 (2014), pp. 159–78.

35. Trepper, *The Great Game*, p. 59.
36. Orr, 'Peace, Peace, Yet There is No Peace', p. 45.
37. Machover, 'Matzpen. The Israeli Socialist Organisation', p. 301.
38. Ibid., p. 302.
39. Yuval-Davis, 'Matzpen. The Israeli Socialist Organisation', p. 19.
40. Marion Farouk-Sluglett and Peter Sluglett, *Iraq Since 1958: From Revolution to Dictatorship* (London, New York: I. B. Tauris Publishers, 2001), pp. 55–60.
41. Machover, 'Matzpen. The Israeli Socialist Organisation', pp. 303–4.
42. Yuval-Davis, 'Matzpen. The Israeli Socialist Organisation', p. 19.
43. Hanna Batatu, *The Old Social Classes and the Revolutionary Movements of Iraq: A Study of Iraq's Old Landed and Commercial Classes and of its Communists, Ba'thists, and Free Officers*, Princeton Studies on the Near East (Princeton: Princeton University Press, 1978), pp. 903–4.
44. Machover, 'Matzpen. The Israeli Socialist Organisation', p. 304.
45. Ibid., p. 304.
46. Michael Löwy, *Revolution ohne Grenzen: Die Theorie der permanenten Revolution* (Frankfurt/M.: Isp-Verlag, 1987), pp. 137–52.
47. Machover, 'Matzpen. The Israeli Socialist Organisation', pp. 303–4.
48. 'Educational Material about the Machover-Pilavsky Anti-Party Group'.
49. Moshé Machover and Akiva Orr, Letter to the Members of Maki's Jerusalem Branch (20 September 1962), The Israeli Left Archives.
50. Erel, *Matzpen*, p. 25.
51. A. Orr, Interview with the Author, Tenuvot (10 April 2008) [Hebrew]. See also: Erel, *Matzpen*, pp. 24–5.
52. Machover and Orr, Letter to the Members of Maki's Jerusalem Branch.
53. See also: Erel, *Matzpen*, p. 20.
54. Leibovitz-Dar, 'The Days of Matzpen', p. 23.
55. Quoted in Sahish, 'The Myth of Matzpen', p. 10.
56. Tony Judt, *Postwar: A History of Europe since 1945* (New York: Penguin Books, 2006), p. 426.
57. Meir Smorodinsky (S. Meir), 'On Principles that Became Infertile', *Matzpen* 1 (1962), p. 2 [Hebrew].
58. Akiva Orr, 'The Lesson of October and the "Old Bolsheviks"', *Matzpen* 1 (1962), p. 5 [Hebrew].
59. Moshé Machover (Israel Mor), 'Peking – Moscow: 1926–1962', *Matzpen* 3 (1963), p. 4 [Hebrew].
60. Lutz Fiedler, 'Kommunistische Dissidenz und antisemitische Stimmung. Kuroń, Modzelewski und die Vorgeschichte des polnischen März '68', *Jahrbuch des Simon-Dubnow-Instituts* 9 (2010), pp. 165–85 [ger].

61. Akiva Orr, 'Socialism – What Is It? Clarification on the Events in France and Czechoslovakia', *Matzpen* 45 (1968), p. 7 [Hebrew].
62. On the European New Left, see the biographical interviews in Cohn-Bendit, *Wir haben sie so geliebt, die Revolution*.
63. Quoted in Leibovitz-Dar, 'The Days of Matzpen', p. 23.
64. 'This Strike Is Justified!', *Matzpen* 3 (1963), p. 8 [Hebrew].
65. The statement calling for the strike itself is reprinted in Matzpen 2 (1962), p. 8 [Hebrew].
66. Beinin, *Was the Red Flag Flying There?*, p. 239.
67. Michael Shalev, *Labour and the Political Economy in Israel*, Library of Political Economy (Oxford: Oxford University Press, 1992), p. 212; Moshé Machover, Akiva Orr and Haim Hanegbi, 'The Class Nature of Israeli Society', in Moshé Machover, *Israelis and Palestinians: Conflict and Resolutions* (Chicago: Haymarket Books, 2012), pp. 76–98, at p. 92 [first: *Matzpen* 55 (1970); *New Left Review* 65 (1971)].
68. 'This Strike Is Justified!'.
69. Machover, 'Matzpen. The Israeli Socialist Organisation', p. 307.
70. Akiva Orr, 'The Seamen's Strike', *Matzpen* 3 (1963), p. 5 [Hebrew]. Five years later he published another article on the subject, this time under his own name: Akiva Orr, 'An Unfinished Struggle. Insights from the Seamen's Strike', *Matzpen* 35 (1967), pp. 5–6 [Hebrew].
71. Orr, 'The Seamen's Strike'.
72. On Orr's biography, see Fiedler, 'Akiva Orr (1931–2013)'.
73. Ibid. See also Akiva Orr, 'More Enlightening Disillusionment (Stage 2)', in Akiva Orr, *Enlightening Disillusionments* (Tel Aviv, 2011), pp. 17–29, at p. 20.
74. Akiva Orr, *Enlightening Disillusionments* (Tel Aviv, 2011), pp. 4–29.
75. For a general overview on the sailors' strike, see Nimrod Eshel, *The Seamen's Strike* (Tel Aviv: Am Oved, 1994) [Hebrew]; Judd Ne'eman made an excellent documentary on the topic: Judd Ne'eman, *Ja brechen!: Seamen's Strike*, 1981, Israel, 68 min, documentary [Hebrew]. See also Eyal Kafkafi, 'Turning to the Left as a Justification for Breaking a Strike. The Case of the Seamen's Strike', *Tura* 3 (1994), pp. 221–47.
76. Eshel, *The Seamen's Strike*, pp. 38–43; Ne'eman, *Ja brechen!*
77. Akiva Orr, 'Enlightening Disillusionment (Stage 1)', in Akiva Orr, *Enlightening Disillusionments* (Tel Aviv, 2011), pp. 4–16, at pp. 4–6.
78. Ibid; Eshel, *The Seamen's Strike*.
79. Orr, 'The Seamen's Strike', p. 5.
80. Yosef Almogi, *Total Commitment* (New York: Herzl Press, 1982), p. 130.
81. Orr, 'Enlightening Disillusionment (Stage 1)', p. 7.
82. Ne'eman, *Ja brechen!*, min. 36:20.

83. Ibid., min. 40:20.
84. Kafkafi, 'Turning to the Left as a Justification for Breaking a Strike', p. 221.
85. Sprinzak, *Brother Against Brother*, p. 80.
86. Tom Segev, *1949: The First Israelis* (New York: Henry Holt and Company, Inc. [First Owl Books Edition], 1998), p. 285.
87. Ne'eman, *Ja brechen!*, min. 1:40; see also Sprinzak, *Brother Against Brother*, pp. 78–83.
88. Sprinzak, *Brother Against Brother*, p. 83.
89. Ne'eman, *Ja brechen!*, min. 42:40; see also Erel, *Without Fear and Prejudice*, pp. 193–5.
90. Quoted in Eshel, *The Seamen's Strike*, p. 135.
91. Segev, *1949: The First Israelis*, p. 285.
92. Beinin, *Was the Red Flag Flying There?*, p. 75.
93. Kafkafi, 'Turning to the Left as a Justification for Breaking a Strike'. See also Beinin, *Was the Red Flag Flying There?*, pp. 73–6.
94. '"Voice of America": Israel Officially Joins the West[ern Bloc]', *Ma'ariv* (5 November 1951), p. 1 [Hebrew].
95. Beinin, *Was the Red Flag Flying There?*, p. 75; see also Kafkafi, 'Turning to the Left as a Justification for Breaking a Strike', p. 225.
96. Quoted in Kafkafi, 'Turning to the Left as a Justification for Breaking a Strike', p. 226.
97. Quoted in Beinin, *Was the Red Flag Flying There?*, p. 74.
98. Ibid.
99. Kafkafi, 'Turning to the Left as a Justification for Breaking a Strike'; Beinin, *Was the Red Flag Flying There?*, p. 74.
100. Beinin, *Was the Red Flag Flying There?*, p. 75.
101. Kafkafi, 'Turning to the Left as a Justification for Breaking a Strike', p. 230.
102. Eshel, *The Seamen's Strike*, pp. 201–3.
103. Orr, 'More Enlightening Disillusionment (Stage 2)', p. 22.
104. Orr, 'Enlightening Disillusionment (Stage 1)', p. 11.
105. Akiva Orr, 'Changing the Histadrut: How?', *Matzpen* 2 (1962), p. 4 [Hebrew].
106. Quoted in Machover, Orr and Hanegbi, 'The Class Nature of Israeli Society', p. 89.
107. On the history of the Histadrut, see Zeev Sternhell, *The Founding Myths of Israel: Nationalism, Socialism, and the Making of the Jewish State* (Princeton: Princeton University Press, 1998), pp. 178–216.
108. Michael Shalev, 'The Labor Movement in Israel. Ideology and Political Economy', in Ellis Goldberg (ed.), *The Social History of Labor in the Middle East (The Social History of the Modern Middle East)* (Boulder: Westview Press, 1996), pp. 131–61, at p. 146.

109. Akiva Orr, 'Outside or Inside the Histadrut?', *Matzpen* 8 (1963), p. 4 [Hebrew].
110. Avishai Ehrlich, 'The Crisis in Israel, Danger of Fascism?', *Khamsin. Journal of Revolutionary Socialists of the Middle East* 5 (1978), pp. 81–113, at p. 91; see also Sternhell, *The Founding Myths of Israel*, p. 189.
111. Orr, 'Outside or Inside the Histadrut?', p. 4.
112. Orr, 'Enlightening Disillusionment (Stage 1)', p. 10.
113. Orr, 'An Unfinished Struggle'.
114. Fiedler, 'Akiva Orr (1931–2013)'; Diner, 'Bolschewismus ohne Kommunismus – Ben Gurion und der Holocaust', pp. 127–31.
115. Orr, 'Outside or Inside the Histadrut?'.
116. Pilavsky, 'How I Arrived at Matzpen'.
117. Meisels, 'No Room in Maki for Critical Voices'.
118. Pilavsky, 'How I Arrived at Matzpen'.
119. Ibid.
120. Oded Pilavsky, 'A Front to Promote the Worker in the Histadrut', *Matzpen* 18 (1964), p. 8 [Hebrew].
121. Orr, 'Changing the Histadrut: How?'.
122. Machover, 'Matzpen. The Israeli Socialist Organisation', p. 307.
123. 'To Change the Face of the Histadrut [Program]', *Matzpen* 12 (1963), p. 8 [Hebrew].
124. 'And These are the Demands that One Needs to Struggle For [Program]', *Matzpen* 1 (1962), p. 8; see also Shalev, *Labour and the Political Economy in Israel*, pp. 50–5, who shows that the policy of excluding Arab workers from the Histadrut only ended in the late 1950s.
125. Akiva Orr and Moshé Machover (N. Israeli), *Peace, Peace, When There is No Peace: Israel and the Arabs 1948–1961* (Jerusalem: Bokhan, 1961) [Hebrew].
126. A. Orr, Email Communication with the Author (24 December 2009) [English].
127. Mordechai Caspi, '"Peace, Peace, When There is No Peace"', *Kol Ha'am* (8 December 1961), pp. 2 and 7 [Hebrew]; 'Maki-Leadership Worries about Intellectual Circles of their Former Members'.
128. Meisels, 'No Room in Maki for Critical Voices'.
129. '4 Maki-Activists Ejected From the Party Blamed for "Factional Organization"', *Al Hamishmar* (2 October 1962), p. 1 [Hebrew].
130. Maxim Ghilan, *How Israel Lost its Soul* (Harmondsworth: Penguin, 1974), p. 153. Reuven Avinoam (Reuven Kaminer) had a different view: Reuven Avinoam, *The New Left in Israel* (Jerusalem, 1973), p. 4: 'This critique on the party's conservatism avoided any revision of the basic party tenet that both Jews and Arabs have the right to national self-determination in the area previously designated as Palestine. The trend's initial adhesion to the CP's policies on this issue may be illustrated by

the fact that two of its leading members, A. Orr and M. Machover had themselves authored a popular exposition of the CP's position on the subject, published under the title "Peace, Peace and there is No Peace".'

131. Orr, 'Peace, Peace, Yet There is No Peace', p. 38; for the historical context, see Benny Morris, *Righteous Victims: A History of the Zionist-Arab Conflict, 1881–2001*, 1. Vintage Books edn (New York: Vintage Books, 2001), pp. 272–301, esp. 290–1 [English].
132. S. I. Troen, 'The Sinai Campaign as a "War of No Alternative": Ben Gurion's View of the Israel-Egyptian Conflict', in S. I. Troen and Moshe Shemesh (eds), *The Suez Sinai Crisis 1956: Retrospective and Reappraisal* (London: Cass, 1990), pp. 180–95; Efraim Inbar, 'The "No Choice War" Debate in Israel', *Journal of Strategic Studies* 12: 1 (1989), pp. 22–37.
133. Orr, 'Peace, Peace, Yet There is No Peace', p. 39.
134. All quotations come from the English translation by Mark Marshall (2009). The first page number refers to the English text, as provided on www.akiorrbooks.com. The page number in brackets refers to the Hebrew original from 1961: Akiva Orr and Moshé Machover (N. Israeli), *Peace, Peace, When There is No Peace: Israel and the Arabs 1948–1961* (Toronto, 2009), p. xv (2).
135. Ibid., p. xiv (2); Jeremiah 6:13–15.
136. Ibid., p. 497 (468).
137. Machover, 'Matzpen. The Israeli Socialist Organisation', p. 303.
138. Gad Barzilai, *Wars, Internal Conflicts, and Political Order: A Jewish Democracy in the Middle East*, SUNY Series in Israeli Studies (Albany: State University of New York Press, 1996), p. 40.
139. *Kol Ha'am* (15 October 1956), p. 1, quoted in Ibid., p. 50.
140. Quoted in Beinin, *Was the Red Flag Flying There?*, p. 197.
141. Moshe Sneh, *On the National Question: Conclusions in the Light of Marxism-Leninism* (Tel Aviv: The Left Socialist Party, 1954) [Hebrew]; see also Ginossar, 'From Zionism to Communism and Back'; Amir Locker-Biletzki, 'The Settler, the Native and the Communist. Nationalism, Colonialism, and Imperialism in Moshe Sneh's and Emil Touma's Ideology, 1953–1973', in Frank Jacob and Sebastian Kunze (eds), *Jewish Radicalisms: Historical Perspectives on a Phenomenon of Global Modernity*, Europäisch-jüdische Studien – Beiträge (Berlin: De Gruyter Oldenbourg, 2019), pp. 129–52.
142. Orr and Machover (N. Israeli), *Peace, Peace, When There is No Peace*, pp. 1–27 (3–27).
143. Ibid., pp. 57–8 (55).

144. Warschawski, *On the Border*, p. 25.
145. Beinin, *Was the Red Flag Flying There?*, pp. 45–6.
146. Rubenstein, *The Communist Movement in Palestine and Israel, 1919–1984*, pp. 280–2.
147. Beinin, *Was the Red Flag Flying There?*, p. 46.
148. Walter Laqueur, *Communism and Nationalism in the Middle East*, 2nd edn (London: Routledge and Kegan Paul, 1961), pp. 113–14.
149. Ginossar, 'From Zionism to Communism and Back'; Schnall, 'Notes on the Political Thought of Dr. Moshe Sneh'.
150. Martin Ebon, 'Communist Tactics in Palestine', *Middle East Journal* 2: 3 (1948), pp. 255–69, at p. 266.
151. Sneh, *On the National Question: Conclusions in the Light of Marxism-Leninism*, p. 145.
152. Ginossar, 'From Zionism to Communism and Back', p. 252.
153. Ibid., p. 250.
154. Beinin, *Was the Red Flag Flying There?*, pp. 217 and 227.
155. Ibid., pp. 192–3.
156. Ibid., pp. 192 and 227.
157. Ibid., p. 192.
158. Kevin Devlin, 'Communism in Israel. Anatomy of a Split', *Survey* 62: 1 (1967), pp. 141–51; Alain Greilsammer, 'Communism in Israel. 13 Years After the Split', *Survey* 23 (1977–8), pp. 172–92; Martin W. Slann, 'Ideology and Ethnicity in Israel's Two Communist Parties. The Conflict between Maki and Rakah', *Studies in Comparative Communism: An International Interdisciplinary Journal* 7: 4 (1974), pp. 359–74.
159. Greilsammer, 'Communism in Israel', p. 173.
160. Fiedler, 'Akiva Orr (1931–2013)'.
161. Morris, *Righteous Victims*, p. 221.
162. Orr and Machover (N. Israeli), *Peace, Peace, When There is No Peace*, p. 53 (51).
163. Ibid., p. 33 (34).
164. Orr, 'Peace, Peace, Yet There is No Peace', p. 43.
165. Orr and Machover (N. Israeli), *Peace, Peace, When There is No Peace*, p. 55 (53).
166. Meir Chazan, 'The Dispute in Mapai Over "Self-Restraint" and "Purity of Arms" During the Arab Revolt', *Jewish Social Studies: History, Culture and Society* 15: 3 (2009), pp. 89–113, at pp. 99–107.
167. Orr and Machover (N. Israeli), *Peace, Peace, When There is No Peace*, pp. 70–5 (66–72).

168. Benny Morris, *The Birth of the Palestinian Refugee Problem Revisited*, 2nd edn (Cambridge: Cambridge University Press, 2004), p. 75.
169. Orr and Machover (N. Israeli), *Peace, Peace, When There is No Peace*, p. 76 (72); Walid Khalidi, 'Plan Dalet. Master Plan for the Conquest of Palestine', *Journal of Palestine Studies* 18: 1 (1988), pp. 4–33, at p. 29.
170. Orr and Machover (N. Israeli), *Peace, Peace, When There is No Peace*, p. 75 (71).
171. Yfaat Weiss, *A Confiscated Memory: Wadi Salib and Haifa's Lost Heritage* (New York: Columbia University Press, 2011), pp. 36–50; Mark Mazower, *No Enchanted Palace: The End of Empire and the Ideological Origins of the United Nations*, Lawrence Stone Lectures (Princeton, Oxford: Princeton University Press, 2009), pp. 133–42.
172. Orr and Machover (N. Israeli), *Peace, Peace, When There is No Peace*, p. 425 (400).
173. Beinin, *Was the Red Flag Flying There?*, p. 13; Avi Shlaim, 'The Debate about 1948', *International Journal of Middle East Studies* 27: 3 (1995), pp. 287–302, at p. 289; Shimshon Bichler and Jonathen Nitzan, 'To the New Readers Innocent of the Undeconstructed Past. On the Second Edition of "Peace, Peace, and No Peace"', http://bnarchives.yorku.ca/280/1/20100300_bn_to_the_new_readers.pdf (accessed 30 March 2020) [Hebrew].
174. Orr, 'Peace, Peace, Yet There is No Peace', p. 44 (emphasis in original).
175. On the historical context, see Morris, *Righteous Victims*, pp. 259–301, esp. 270–5.
176. Orr and Machover (N. Israeli), *Peace, Peace, When There is No Peace*, pp. 166–224 (153–208).
177. Ibid., p. 44 (43).
178. Ibid., pp. 83–140 (77–128).
179. Orr, 'Peace, Peace, Yet There is No Peace', p. 44.
180. Avi Shlaim, 'Israel Between East and West, 1948–56', *International Journal of Middle East Studies* 36: 4 (2004), pp. 657–73, at pp. 660–1.
181. Orr and Machover (N. Israeli), *Peace, Peace, When There is No Peace*, p. 115 (106); on the historical context, see Shlomo Slonim, 'Origins of the 1950 Tripartite Declaration on the Middle East', *Middle Eastern Studies* 23: 2 (1987), pp. 135–49.
182. Richard L. Jasse, 'The Baghdad Pact. Cold War or Colonialism?', *Middle Eastern Studies* 27: 1 (1991), pp. 140–56; Pinar Bilgin, *Regional Security in the Middle East: A Critical Perspective* (London, New York: Routledge, 2005).
183. Beinin, *Was the Red Flag Flying There?*, p. 171; Ginossar, 'From Zionism to Communism and Back', p. 250.

184. Orr and Machover (N. Israeli), *Peace, Peace, When There is No Peace*, p. 457 (430).
185. David Tal, 'The American-Israeli Security Treaty. Sequel or Means to the Relief of Israeli-Arab Tension', *Middle Eastern Studies* 31: 4 (1995), pp. 828–48, at pp. 829–33.
186. Orr and Machover (N. Israeli), *Peace, Peace, When There is No Peace*, p. 127 (117).
187. Ibid., pp. 157–62 (145–50); see also Michael M. Laskier, 'Israel and Algeria amid French Colonialism and the Arab-Conflict. 1954-1978', *Israel Studies* 6: 2 (2001), pp. 1–31.
188. Orr and Machover (N. Israeli), *Peace, Peace, When There is No Peace*, pp. 138 (127) and 183–5 (170–2); see also Mark Tessler, *A History of the Israeli-Palestinian Conflict* (Bloomington: Indiana University Press, 1994), pp. 341–3.
189. Orr and Machover (N. Israeli), *Peace, Peace, When There is No Peace*, p. 102 (95).
190. Jabra Nicola (A. Said), 'Aden, Great Britain and Israel', *Matzpen* 19 (1964), p. 5 [Hebrew].
191. Ibid., p. 132 (121).
192. Orr and Machover (N. Israeli), *Peace, Peace, When There is No Peace*, p. 425 (400).
193. Ibid., p. 80 (75).
194. Ibid., p. 491 (463).
195. Ibid., p. 490 (462).
196. Ibid., p. 436 (410).
197. Orr, 'Peace, Peace, Yet There is No Peace', p. 47.
198. Haim Hanegbi, 'The Honey We Stole. Memories from the Naqba in Jerusalem', *Mita'am* 13 (2008) [Hebrew].
199. Yirmiyahu Kaplan (Y. Kfir), 'Concerning the Debate of the Refugee Question', *Matzpen* 1 (1962), p. 4 [Hebrew].
200. Orr and Machover (N. Israeli), *Peace, Peace, When There is No Peace*, pp. 30 (30) and 423 (397).
201. Ibid., p. 30 (30).

2

The Israel–Palestine Question

'Al-Ard and Us': In Support of Israeli Arabs' Protest

The public debate was already well underway by August 1964, when the Israeli Socialist Organization took a stance on the Arab Al-Ard group. 'Are the People of Al-Ard [Really] Traitors? [. . .] The Full Al-Ard Memorandum to the UN', ran the bold headline on the cover of *Matzpen*, intended as a critical intervention in the heated debate.[1] The political leanings of the five-year-old group of Israeli Arabs were undoubtedly a pressing issue. Although the Middle Eastern conflict and Israel's clashes with its Arab neighbours had gradually abated, at least on the surface, since the Suez Crisis of autumn 1956, the explosive domestic conflict over the Al-Ard group was attracting international attention.[2] The group had most recently caused a stir on 23 June 1964, when it sent a memorandum to U Thant, the Secretary-General of the United Nations, bemoaning the condition of Israel's domestic Arab community sixteen years after the establishment of the Jewish state. The memo's authors had not pulled any punches. In one of its opening salvos, the extensive document charges: 'The Israeli government keenly hopes to extinguish the Arab national feelings and to liquidate completely the Arab national entity in Israel.'[3] This is followed by a detailed list of policies and legal measures taken by the Jewish state that were deemed to be unilateral violations of the principles of democracy and equal treatment under the law by the Israeli Arabs. They invoke the emergency regulations enforced by the Israeli military administration, which subjected a large part of the Arab population to special monitoring, as well as the domestic confiscations of land that was facilitated by the Absentees' Property Law (1950), a situation referenced in the organisation's very name, Al-Ard (The Soil). The memorandum's authors therefore concluded that, notwithstanding its democratic commitment to the equality of all citizens, the Jewish state was making its Arab residents into 'second-class citizens' and inflaming 'racial discrimination' against them.[4] 'We hereby indict Israel for all her unlawful policies', concludes the text, before calling upon the United Nations to take action:

> [Israel] should bear all the responsibilities and consequences, which are also shared by the United Nations if it shall remain idle and stagnant. [. . .] The peace and stability of the region, as well as the enigmatic future of Israel, depend on the behaviour of Israeli leaders alone.[5]

The Israeli press was not especially fond of the memo or its threatening language. The *Maariv* daily newspaper soon dubbed it a 'memorandum of defamation'.[6] The text sparked further displeasure when the Arab League used it as the basis of a renewed appeal to the international community.[7] Before long, growing numbers of both politicians and civilians were calling for the group to be banned.[8] *Matzpen's* cover headline struck a contrasting tone, calling for a discussion and an independent verdict on the Israeli Arabs' cause. To that end, the magazine reprinted the full text of the Arab group's memorandum. *Matzpen* was the first and only publication in Israel to reprint an unabridged Hebrew version of Al-Ard's report, which it accompanied with a show of solidarity, such as the caption 'Discrimination, Suppression, Persecution'.[9] Just as the idea of Al-Ard – an organisation of exclusively Israeli Arabs – was a political novelty, *Matzpen's* sympathy for their perspective entailed a sea change on the Israeli Left. By running the headline 'Are the Al-Ard Group [Really] Traitors?', *Matzpen* not only rejected public opinion; they simultaneously demonstrated a shift in their own group's reading of the Israel–Palestine conflict, past and present, as well as in the possible options for its future resolution.

The conflict set off by the memorandum to the United Nations was not the initial trigger of the Israeli debate over the Al-Ard group, nor was the group the first to represent the interests of Arabs within the Jewish state.[10] Since the start of statehood, Israeli Arabs' main supporter had been the Israeli Communist Party, which advocated for political equality and opposed the military administration. Al-Ard's emergence changed things. For the first time, a new group of Israeli Arabs self-identified as part of a Palestinian nation and expressed explicit kinship with contemporary Arab nationalism.[11] In parallel to the frictions within the Communist Party that led to the founding of Matzpen, the Al-Ard group (whose full name was Usrat Al-Ard, 'The Family of the Soil') grew out of its members' gradual abandonment of Israeli party-communism in the late 1950s.[12] In the Popular Front, an party-affiliated organisation among the Israeli Arabs, a whole generation of young intellectuals – led by Sabri Jiryis (S. Geries) and including Saleh Baransi, Habib Kahwaji, Mansour Kardush and Fouzi El-Asmar – had dissociated itself from the parent party over disagreements about changes in the Arab world and over the communists' estrangement from Cairo. Like Maki, the Popular Front idealised President Abd al-Karim Qassim's Iraq as the Arab world's contemporary centre of power. Meanwhile, this younger generation of Arab–Israeli intellectuals pinned all their hopes on Gamal Abdel Nasser and the call for pan-Arabism that was emanating from Egypt.[13] The memorandum to the United Nations states, quite early on: 'The al-Arḍ Group believes that the Arabs in Israel are part of the Palestinian Arabs who are an integral part of the whole Arab Nation.'[14] Al-Ard were drawn to Nasser, both for his aspirations of a political union of Arabs and for his nationalist-tinged rhetoric about liberating the Arab world. This notion of liberation pledged new prospects for solving the Palestine question that went far beyond the previous demand for recognition and equality within Israel; indeed, it called into question the very premises of the Jewish state's existence.[15] Apart from contemporary affairs, the group resurrected questions about Israel's borders and the fate of Palestinian refugees; questions that had gone unresolved since the 1948 War. The very first issue of the self-named magazine *Al-Ard* included the following threat: 'The rulers of Israel must understand that the time has come to find a just solution to the refugee problem before another sword comes forth to solve it – and what a sword it will be!' Simultaneously, they called for adjusting Israel's boundaries to match the United Nations Partition Plan of November 1947.[16] Where their self-concept blurs most into Arab nationalism, however, is in their ambition to view Palestine as 'a whole and indivisible unit, in accordance with the wishes of the Palestinian Arab people'. The Al-Ard statement of goals asserts, moreover, that the restoration of its 'political existence' and its 'full legal rights' would be based on its 'right to decide its own fate for itself, within the framework of the supreme wishes of the Arab nation'.[17]

Al-Ard's perspective on the Palestine problem, intoned in the strains of Arab nationalism, had aroused the suspicions of the Israeli authorities since the group's formation. Its first application for a permit to publish a magazine was stalled for months by the responsible district commissioner. With some legal manoeuvring, it released each issue under a different name and masthead. But after thirteen issues, its editors 'were put on trial for publishing a newspaper without a license' and accused of 'incitement against Israel and the Jewish people'.[18] Furthermore, the group's multi-year attempts to obtain the legal status of an Israeli company were condemned to failure. In mid-1962, buoyed by a judgement of the Supreme Court, the group managed to establish a legal entity for publicity and distribution under the name Al Ard Co. Ltd. Notwithstanding, they were again prohibited from publishing an Arabic-language weekly newspaper under the argument that it would pose a threat to the state security.[19] The conflict over Al-Ard's legal status intensified in early 1964 when the group filed for the status of an 'Ottoman association', according to a law dating from 1909. Not surprisingly, one of the purposes of that June's memo to the United Nations was also to call attention to the group's attempts to gain recognition and legal status. But these attempts were made in vain. Al-Ard's admiration for the Egyptian president, their assertion of the Arab nation's unity and, particularly, their repeated challenges to the territorial and demographic integrity of the Jewish state ensured that the perennial waves of protest they inspired would never quite subside. Shortly after the UN memorandum reignited the clash, the daily newspaper *Davar* ran the headline 'Al-Ard: A Small but Dangerous Group'.[20] The cabinet had already unanimously asserted the group's 'subversive nature and [. . .] poisonous nationalist character'; eventually, this led to a motion for an outright ban.[21] In the end, it was Judge Witkin of the Israeli Supreme Court who pronounced the group's aims as 'explicitly at odds with the existence of the State of Israel in general and in today's borders in particular [. . .] Supporters of this association's goals acknowledge neither the State of Israel nor the rights of the Jewish people that resides there'.[22]

Amid this anti-Al-Ard furore, the editors of *Matzpen* did not stop at reprinting the memorandum; they felt the need to take a clear stance on the status of Israeli Arabs. Meir Smorodinsky published such a statement under the headline 'Al-Ard and Us'.[23] Beyond providing a statement in solidarity with the Israeli Arabs' positions, the article provided strong evidence of a shift in Matzpen's perceptions of the Palestine question: a move from depicting it as a conflict of national identities to emphasising a 'colonisation perspective'.[24] Contrary to earlier accounts, which took the 1948 Arab–Israeli war as the starting point of a conflict in which Jewish national claims were achieved at the Palestinians' expense, the young leftists were now delving into a deeper historical dimension. In Meir Smorodinsky's portrayal, the current situation of the Israeli Arabs, as embodied by the Al-Ard group, was wrapped up in the history of the 1948 War and the Zionist settlement in Palestine from a half-century earlier. He introduced his interpretation of the conflict – 'Eretz Israel (Palestine) is part of a region that was under colonial control' – before pointing out its unique demographic configuration:

> The Zionist settlement movement is distinct [from other movements of colonial settlement] because its goal was to dispossess the local population in order to establish a Jewish state. The typical goal of colonial movements was to exploit the country's natural treasures, whereas the goal of the Zionist colonisation movement was the country itself.[25]

This shift in perspective accentuated not only the national opposition between Israeli Jews and Palestinian Arabs, but also its colonial manifestation – as a collision between a native population and a settler population. In other words, it redrew both the conceptual and chronological frameworks of the Palestine question. From this point forward, Matzpen began taking issue with an earlier point of contention: the history of Zionist settlement, with its ambitions of founding a Jewish state. Overnight, the conflict between Israel and Palestine transformed into a conflict over Israel *in* Palestine, over the existence of the Jewish state altogether – insofar as it could only have been established against the will of the native population. 'Thus the story ended with the Arab tragedy of 1948', Smorodinsky concluded, tying up his flashback with a bow:

> A large portion of Palestinian Arabs were displaced and became refugees. The small portion of the Arab people who remained in Israel became a minority. The Palestinians lost their rights both as individuals and as a nation. The problem is how to restore these rights.[26]

In view of the parallel debate over legal efforts against the Al-Ard group, which had reached a fever pitch, this historical deep dive into the roots of the conflict was only the start. The reprinted UN memorandum and Smorodinsky's statement of principles were accompanied by a direct critique of the outcry over the status and legitimacy of this coalition of Israeli Arabs. Challenging the national Supreme Court's justification for seeking to ban Al-Ard – that the group refused to recognise Israel's borders – *Matzpen* decried that it was entirely impossible to expect a group that considers itself part of the Arab nation to 'recognise borders that were drawn at the expense of a Palestinian Arabs' state'. Matzpen went on, in a strenuous protest against the imminent ban: 'The Jewish nation has dispossessed the Arab nation from Eretz Israel. In sorder to reach an agreement, it is therefore up to the Jewish nation to make concessions to them – not vice versa.'[27]

This new perspective on the Israel–Palestine conflict was not only in response to the activities of the Israeli Arabs. Just as the Al-Ard group's self-concept led it out of the Israeli Communist Party's shadow, the decision to classify the Palestine problem as a result of national-minded settlement marked the last step of Matzpen's declaration of independence from its erstwhile parent party's doctrine. The theorist Moshe Sneh, in *On the National Question*, narrowly defined Zionism as a political affiliation with the major Western powers. One of his chapters bore the title 'Aliyah, Colonisation, Security, Independence – None of This Is Zionism'.[28] This perspective negated any historical or practical connection between the establishment of a Jewish state in Palestine and the emergence of the Palestine problem. His former comrades dismissed this understanding of Zionism, arguing that this narrow definition concealed the link between Israel's current conflicts, the politics of pre-state settlement and the foundation of the Jewish state. Their belated retort: 'But everyone knows that immigration and settlement were projects planned and directed by the Zionist movement and that the State of Israel, as it exists today, is only another stage of the Zionist "state in the making".'[29]

In autumn 1963, with the arrival of Jabra Nicola (1912–74) and Jakob Taut (1913–2001) to Matzpen, the group eventually came in contact with a near-forgotten tradition of communist dissent concerning the Palestine question, which had long before stressed the colonial character of that national conflict. Indeed, experiences with the project of Zionist settlement had sparked political criticism from those quarters long before the foundation of the Jewish state. At a time in which the Communist Party of Palestine had split into separate Jewish and Arab offshoots, Taut and Nicola were among a circle of Trotskyite heretics whose deviations from party-communism were more than ideological. Amidst the growing conflict over Palestine and the communist acceptance of partition, they held firm to the utopia of a common binational Jewish–Arab polity into the late 1940s.[30]

This pre-state tradition of a joint Jewish–Arab perspective beyond the nation-state was only one source that informed the emergence of a colonisation perspective in Matzpen. The Israeli Left was also affected by the experiences of spreading decolonisation under the banner of Arab nationalism. The brutal Algerian War – which ended in the spring of 1962, the same year Matzpen was founded – cast a shadow on Israel and the Palestine problem. The impact of eight years of war between the French colonisers and the Algerian National Liberation Front (FLN) extended beyond Algeria's independence.[31] The hasty exodus of around a million French Algerians, former colonists and their descendants who were no longer welcome in post-colonial Algeria, became a lighthouse for the left-wing Israelis of Matzpen, warning of their own rocky waters in the Israel–Palestine conflict:

> From time to time, we tend to forget about the fact that our position is similar to the French settlers in Algeria, with the only difference being that our situation is far less comfortable. While they have the backing of Metropolitan France, we lack precisely this type of support.[32]

Considering the energies at play, it seemed plausible that the power balance in the Palestine problem could cross a similar tipping point. 'Could there be an Israeli "Algeria"?' asked the Israeli journalist Shmuel Segev at the tail end of the debate over Al-Ard.[33] Meanwhile, Matzpen's solidarity with Al-Ard and the group's hope for Arab unity produced several documents from the Israeli Left that grappled with the question of how Israeli Jews could protect themselves from the historic fate of the French Algerians, and how they could instead build new prospects for mutual recognition in the Israel–Palestine conflict. 'A policy that would deny the rights of Jews in Palestine [...] would bring disaster and undermine the Arab national movement', wrote Meir Smorodinsky in a statement that plainly rejected Arab nationalist policies.[34]

The Al-Ard memorandum was not reprinted without contesting commentary – from a Matzpen member, no less. 'Publishing the text does not mean that we identify with its content', remarked Moshé Machover, contrasting the group's Arab nationalism with the Israeli leftists' socialist ambitions. He also dissociated himself from Al-Ard's initial proposal of implementing the 1947 partition plan after the fact. Instead, Machover wrote:

> In our opinion, the only fundamental solution to the problem would involve incorporating Israel in the powerful process throughout the Middle East of moving towards socialism and Arab unity. Naturally, this requires that Israel cease to be a Zionist state embedded in the imperialist system. Our approach also requires recognition of Palestinian Arabs' rights.[35]

As for the memo's claim that dialogue between Israeli Arabs and Jewish Israelis was a lost cause, the communist dissidents firmly disagreed.[36] After all, Al-Ard had found supporters at the democratic/humanist-leaning magazines *Haolam Hazeh* and *Ner* in respect to its demands for instating full legal equality and ending military administration. Mordechai Stein, a lawyer and the publisher of *Halton HaDemokrati* (The Democratic Newspaper), also represented the group multiple times in court.[37] The Israeli Socialist Organization had also previously signed a statement in defence of Israeli Arabs' rights alongside the Al-Ard group.[38] Contrary to the view that any cooperation between Israeli Jews and Arabs had been for nothing, Matzpen's response to Al-Ard sought to inaugurate a new perspective of common ground that would satisfy both the national-minded aspirations of the Arab group and the socialist expectations of the young leftists. The 'Al-Ard and Us' statement concluded: 'We, the people of the "Israeli Socialist Organisation", Jews and Arabs alike, extend a hand of brotherhood to the people of Al-Ard to fight for a common goal. [. . .] Let us come together, beyond differences of religion, ethnicity or nationality.'[39]

This alliance was not to be. The ban on Al-Ard of 11 November 1964 and the arrest of its leading members eliminated the possibility of any such collaboration. The 1965 attempts to legalise the group as a political party and include it on the ballots for the Knesset election failed as well. Yet these roadblocks could not halt Palestinians' political activism and the momentum of the Israel–Palestine conflict. Spurred on by its existential threats for Jews and Arabs alike, and building on an extinct interwar political tradition, Matzpen proceeded to develop a new, independent perspective on the Palestine problem and went out in search of allies for shaping a new, joint future.

Traditions of Dissent: Bygone Utopias of Jewish–Arab Coexistence

Scarcely a year after publishing the first issue of *Matzpen* in November 1962, the small group of dissidents began to attract more renegades from the Communist Party. After a heated discussion about the implications of the 1960s Sino-Soviet split led to the ejection and resignation of numerous party members, the outcasts first approached *Matzpen* as a place to publish their critique of Maki's bureaucratic dogmatism and their defence of the Chinese position, which they viewed as a part in the history of the proletarian revolution. The same outcasts soon joined the Matzpen organisation.[40] Because the retinue of Alisa Nicola (1912–70) and Daud Turki (1927–2009) were predominantly Arabs, this development transformed the Israeli Socialist Organization into a binational group.[41] Moreover, some members brought with them the experiences of a whole generation of Arab communists from the Mandate era. Farid Farah, another new member who found his own way to Matzpen, was the nephew of Bulus Farah. The elder Farah had been among the most prominent Arab members of the Palestine Communist Party in the 1930s until it split in 1943, whereupon he became a leader of the (Arab) National Liberation League.[42] Farid Farah would later reflect on his personal path:

> I grew up in a communist family, but in the Sixties, I was increasingly disillusioned with the party organisation and left Maki. I joined Matzpen because they held positions that were also my own. The question of Jews versus Arabs made no difference to us. In the socialist movement, there are no nationalities, but only rich and poor.[43]

Yet the greatest influencers of Matzpen's outlook and character were Jabra Nicola and Jakob Taut, who had already joined the group several months earlier and had redirected the dissidents' attention from Haifa to the New Left. Nicola and Taut were more than two decades older than Matzpen's founders and had been politically active many years before Jewish statehood. In the 1940s, together with Jakob Moneta (1914–2012), Yigal Gluckstein (1917–2000), Rudolf Segall (1911–2006) and Gabriel Baer (1919–82), they had also been members of the Revolutionary Communists League (Brit HaKommunistim HaMahapachnim), a tiny Trotskyist group with an outsized intellectual and historical impact in proportion to its minor political role.[44] The communist dissidents of the Israeli New Left were thus joining forces with members of 'a group of oppositionist communists who, since the 1930s, had challenged the whole of Stalinist policy, its crimes and betrayals, and advocated a return to the values of a democratic and truly internationalist socialism', wrote Michael Waschawski, a later friend of Taut.[45] 'The significance of this group derived from a rigorous analysis of Zionism and Arab nationalism, the fruit of experience accumulated over several decades and set out in countless worthy texts – which practically no one had ever read.'[46] The firmest detractors of the Palestinian Communist Party's ethnic split in the 1940s had been these same marginalised Trotskyists who still longed to see Jews and Arabs united under an internationalist banner. When the country's communist parties contemplated the United Nations Partition Plan, it was again these Trotskyists who spoke out against partition and in favour of a joint Jewish–Arab future. To be a Trotskyist became virtually synonymous with clinging to an international vision for the future in an era divided by the antagonisms of nationhood. Taut and Nicola's membership sparked great excitement in Matzpen. 'We showed them a lot of respect', Haim Hanegbi recalled. 'Intermingling – us, Jews from the heart of Israeli society, and them, Palestinian Arabs and German-Jewish workers with a class consciousness – was amazing. We learned a great amount from them, especially from Nicola.'[47] In a way, this encounter with the Trotskyists marked a convergence with their own, obscured history.

Although the latter group had mostly made its mark in British Mandatory Palestine, the backgrounds of several of its members exemplified the transfer of European–Jewish experiences to the Palestinian context and reached back to Germany. 'During the 1930s there was a large immigration to Palestine from Germany. The exiles closely reflected the entire German political spectrum', Taut recalled in the summer of 1972, describing the beginnings of the Trotskyist movement in Palestine. 'Among them were a few comrades from the Brandler opposition in the Communist party, the majority of whom soon developed toward Trotskyist positions.'[48] Although framed in the third person, this account was at least partly autobiographical. Taut was born in Galicia in 1913 to an Orthodox Jewish family, who, along with many of their co-religionists from Eastern Europe, relocated to Berlin after the First World War. Escaping social and ethnic marginalisation in the new nation-states of Eastern Europe, they had settled in Berlin's Scheunenviertel neighbourhood.[49] In the new urban environment, the young Taut rejected his parents' religious tradition. Due to the family's precarious circumstances, he was forced to begin an apprenticeship in a metalworking shop at only fourteen. This environment increasingly embedded him in social conflicts and class struggles that would fuel his politicisation and his rapid personal transformation to an active union organiser, a believer in a future socialist utopia and a member of the Communist Party's youth wing. But before long, Taut was drifting away from his new party. He rejected the ultra-left shift of the late 1920s, when Ernst Thälmann and the party leadership adopted the theory of 'social fascism' and targeted the centre–left Social Democrats as their chief political opponents. Instead, Taut found himself joining the Communist Party of Germany (Opposition) (KP-O), led by Heinrich Brandler, and cultivating sympathies with Leon Trotsky.[50]

Taut's main focus on social issues and a socialist utopia automatically placed him at a remove from the national project of the Zionist movement. This was a fork in the road, forcing a choice between two divergent and competing paths of modern Judaism. 'From the very beginning we rejected Zionism in every respect', Taut later said, describing the political stance he had taken even before being exposed to the Palestine problem. 'Zionism, we said, not only would be incapable of solving the problems of world Jewry, but would also create a new Jewish problem in the Arab East.'[51] Casting aside the Zionist dream of territorialising the disparate groups of European Jews, he looked to a socialist horizon. According to this view, the 'Jewish problem under modern capitalism' had arisen partly from 'the crisis-ridden development of capitalism itself' and partly 'because of the failure of the international revolution to spread after 1917. [. . .] Because of the rise of Stalinism, the revolutionary-socialist perspective on the Jewish question was never put into practice'.[52] The Nazis' power grab left no dent in Taut's quasi-canonical optimism and his unwavering faith in progress that accompanied hope for Jews' emancipation in the places where they already lived. And yet this transfer of power would have lifelong dramatic implications for Taut. His politics and his Jewish heritage had made his circumstances ever more precarious, and not only in Germany. Denmark, where he had taken refuge in 1934, denied him the status of political refugee or even a longer-term residency permit because of his Polish nationality. Trotskyist friends managed to convince him to go into exile in Palestine. He had no intention of settling permanently in the country that promised protection from

Nazi persecution, however. For one thing, Taut's romantic and political companion Ruth (Trude) Milo did not share his Jewish heritage. As a communist from a family of Social Democrats, she had also considered leaving Germany, but Palestine must have struck her as a peculiar option, one that 'was simply an accidental and temporary place of refuge'.[53]

Not all of the exiles whom Taut befriended in Mandatory Palestine had come ashore sceptical of Zionism. For example, Jakob Moneta had been sympathetic with the Zionist project in Germany and would only break ties with it after arriving in Palestine in November 1933. Nonetheless, Taut and Moneta drew on various common experiences. Like Taut, Moneta originally came from eastern Galicia. He was born on 11 November 1914 in a shtetl called Błażowa, where his father, a textiles manufacturer from Frankfurt am Main, had met his mother.[54] But the rise in antisemitism in Poland after the war, including several pogroms, led Moneta's family back to Germany. By 1919, the family had resettled in Cologne, where the five-year-old Jakob received religious schooling at a traditional *cheder*. His experiences of antisemitism, which was also spreading throughout Germany, later led him to Hashomer Hatzair, the left-wing Zionist youth movement; urgent social issues led him to the workers' movement. Essentially, this political trajectory was collective rather than personal. Moneta had initially sympathised with the Social Democratic Party (SPD), before he and a whole group of Hashomer Hatzair members joined the youth wing of the Socialist Workers Party (SAP), which itself had split off from the SPD in 1931.[55] So it was that the young Moneta's biography paired Zionist socialism with the proletarian internationalism of the workers' movement; after the Nazis took power, Palestine was his obvious destination. Shortly after arriving, he joined Kibbutz BaMifne ('At the Turning Point'), which he perceived as the realisation of a free and equal society. But witnessing the political realities of Palestine in action led him to conclude, later on, that proletarian internationalism was incompatible with the project of Jewish statehood.[56]

Moneta was not alone in this perception. Besides collaborating to resurrect the German Socialist Workers Party (SAPD) while in exile in Palestine,[57] he met a small group of Trotskyist dissidents at the kibbutz, centring on Ali Fröhlich and Paul (Meir) Ehrlich, who also wanted to resume their prior political work after arriving in Palestine. Another member of the group was

Rudolf Segall, who had fled from Berlin to Palestine in 1934 with the aid of Hashomer Hatzair and now shared a room in the kibbutz with Moneta. From then on, he would accompany Moneta through each step of his political evolution.[58] Although the small group, which numbered fewer than ten, mostly discussed developments in Europe, the Palestine question gained significance for them. Even if Moneta was impressed by the experiment of social equality in the kibbutz, the reaction of its members to the Arab general strike in Mandatory Palestine from April to October 1936 demonstrated the ethnonational exclusivity of socialist Zionism as well. BaMifne was affiliated with the left-wing Zionist Hashomer Hatzair party, which had advocated a binational polity in Palestine.[59] Nevertheless, when the kibbutz members took arms and were drawn into the violent escalation, he saw this as potent evidence of the conflicts inherent in the Zionist settlement project. Jakob Moneta would later describe the kibbutz's fortification efforts: 'We ran barbed wire around the area that served as living quarters, bought a searchlight that swept around the camp at night and constructed lookouts and shooting blinds out of rocks and wood.' The kibbutzniks also received basic military training from the Haganah paramilitary. 'Some of us in the kibbutz were beginning to ask questions about our "enemies"', wrote Moneta about the debates in BaMifne that followed the revolt. These questions went far beyond the escalations of the general strike and the Arab revolt and sought to clarify the political substance of the leftist–Zionist settlement principles, as encapsulated in the twin slogans 'Conquest of Labour' and 'Conquest of the Land'; principles aimed at establishing a separate Jewish community to the exclusion of established Arab residents:

> We came to the conclusion that these people are enduring injustice. We, who are ourselves victims of Hitler, are inflicting injustice on them. If we take our internationalism seriously, we must find a way to those Arab masses.[60]

Within the kibbutz, such positions were unwelcome and rapidly led to open conflict. As the Trotskyists began seeking ways to create a joint Jewish–Arab union, the kibbutz voted against their continued residence and shut them out of the community.[61] The group was forced to start from scratch politically and relocated 50 kilometres to 'Red Haifa', which had become, in the 1930s, a gathering place for German-speaking leftist political exiles.[62] Moneta and

Segall's group sought contact with fellow Trotskyites, and eventually made the acquaintance of Jakob Taut and an extended circle of like-minded allies in the city. 'Some of us had gone to Haifa and found work on the harbour', recalled Moneta, describing their split with the kibbutz and their new political encounters. There, they had linked up 'with a group that was "Trotskyising" [. . .] which went by the name "Marxist Circles" [and] was led by Jigal Glickstein [sic]'.[63]

In many respects, the young Yigal Gluckstein was an outlier among the Palestinian Trotskyists. Unlike most of his fellow travellers, he was not a refugee from Europe; he was born in Zikhron Yaakov, Palestine, on 20 May 1917. As a child of Russian Jews who had arrived in the country in 1902, Gluckstein was born at the centre of the Zionist elite, into a childhood home in Haifa that received regular visits from the future Prime Minister Moshe 'Shertok' Sharett, a friend of the family. Yigal, the youngest of Akiva and Esther Gluckstein's four children, was rather wedded to that legacy, and it took him a while to move on from the tradition that had even led him to join Ben-Gurion's Mapai at the age of fourteen.[64] That eventual parting of ways may have been influenced by Gluckstein's uncle Haim Kalvarinsky, who occasionally visited the young Gluckstein in the Jerusalem neighbourhood of Rehavia. There, Kalvarisky had joined Brith Shalom (the Peace League, est. 1925), which advocated a binational Jewish–Arab existence in Palestine and had even established a school for both Jewish and Arab pupils.[65] His uncle's activism made a significant impression on him and provoked his first act of political dissent from the Zionist mainstream. When he handed in an essay titled 'It is so sad there are no Arab kids in the school' at his school in Haifa, his teacher accused him of being a communist, causing the political-minded teenager to wonder.[66] Soon he was greedily reading the *Communist Manifesto* and *Das Kapital*. His reading led him to pose new questions about the ethnonational specificity of the Yishuv and the compatibility of the Zionist movement's particularist self-definition with the universalist principle of proletarian internationalism. However, the conflicts that grew out of such an accusation were not always easily resolved with a mild, if condemnatory, comment. When Gluckstein, now seventeen, attended another Mapai event and expanded on the speaker Abba Khushi's call for 'workers' unity' by loudly shouting the word 'international', his implicit call for unity between Jewish and Arab workers provoked a harsh reaction: the

Haifa Mapai party official first prohibited the word, then instructed his followers to throw the young man out of the room. The guards at the event broke two of his fingers in the process, as Gluckstein and his childhood friend Alon Talmi would later report.[67]

But this aggressive response did not deter Gluckstein; it only contributed to his radicalisation. Several months earlier, he had left the Mapai youth organisation. In late 1933, he joined the much farther left, hard-line internationalist Chugim Marxistim (Marxist Circles). Young Gluckstein never joined the Palestinian Communist Party, and not only because it was outlawed at the time. The knowledge that the communists in Germany had mobilised against the Social Democrats instead of allying with them against the Nazis caused him to turn away from official communism and its doctrinaire loyalty to the Soviet Union.[68] With Chugim Marxistim, he instead began occupying himself with the writings of Trotsky and making contacts in the Trotskyist organisation in London. Proceeding from the theory of permanent revolution, Gluckstein saw the political and economic struggle against the British Empire as the order of the day, but also as an opportunity for Jews and Arabs to unite across lines of nationality.[69] With that in mind, the painter Chana Ben Dov made contacts at the Cairo literary magazine *Al-Majalla al-Jadida* (New Magazine) for Chugim Marxistim.[70] But if the shared social struggle and anti-imperialist fervour against the British Mandate was going to reunite the ethnically and religiously divided region, there were still some dots to connect. Only after meeting Moneta's and Taut's circle did Gluckstein's group independently assess the disparity between the project of Jewish statehood and the larger Arab region.[71] Jakob Taut later recalled his encounter with Gluckstein's group:

> The youth group developed under its own impetus toward Trotskyist conceptions, at first without overcoming completely its Zionist leanings. That happened very rapidly when the second world war broke out. About that time we (the German group) learned of the existence of this group, which in the meantime had left the "Marxist Circles" and had brought out a few issues of the newspaper *Kol Hama'amad* (Voice of the Class).[72]

In addition to their own magazine *Kol HaMa'amad* (Voice of the Class), the group also published an Arabic-language edition under the title *Sawt al-Haq*

(Voice of Rights). This was published by Gabriel Baer, who was born in Berlin in 1919 and had begun studying Arabic after emigrating from Germany to Haifa.[73]

Meanwhile, as the Second World War began, the group was facing problems of an entirely different kind. A leaflet penned by Gluckstein with the heading 'Our enemy is not the aggressor of 1939. Our real enemy is the aggressor of 1917 that occupied the country' had reached the hands of the British Criminal Investigation Department.[74] Its anti-British sentiments placed even the Trotskyists under suspicion of fraternising with the Soviet Union, which in the days of the Hitler–Stalin Pact was considered an enemy of the British Empire. On that basis, the British authorities arrested Yigal Gluckstein and Jakob Moneta and detained them without a trial. After a brief period in the police jail at Haifa, Moneta was transferred to the Acre Citadel and later to the Masra prison camp.[75] The two of them were detained for more than a year, during which time they began organising against the conditions of their detention and making political contacts, including the Arab Trotskyist Jabra Nicola, a future member of the group with whom Taut and Gluckstein had already connected in Haifa.[76] His arrest for allegedly 'sympathising with the enemy' was itself an example of fate playing a 'bitterly ironic' hand:[77] although Nicola was a member of the Palestinian Communist Party, he had defied its loyalty to Moscow and advocated supporting the British fight against Nazi Germany, a fact that clearly had no impact on his arrest. Not until late 1941, when the German attack on the Soviet Union generated a united anti-Hitler coalition, were Nicola and the other Palestinian communists released from imprisonment.[78]

With its twists and turns, Jabra Nicola's life in many ways constituted 'an inseparable part of the history of the Palestinian communist movement'.[79] Born in Jaffa in 1912 to a Christian Arab family, Nicola was forced to leave school after only four years upon the early death of his father. He supported himself as a housepainter, a job that led him to Haifa and Beirut. The talented teenager, who spoke fluent Hebrew, English and French in addition to Arabic, was initially self-educated. Like some of his fellow Christian Arabs, he was soon drawn to the underground Communist Party, which became his intellectual frame of reference.[80] Jabra Nicola joined the party at the young age of seventeen and quickly rose in the ranks. By 1935, at just twenty-three, he was on the Central Committee. He principally attained recognition for his leadership of the Arabic edition of the party newspaper *El-Nur* (The Light), which he edited for several years.[81] This also put him in touch with the lawyer Mordechai Stein (1896–1969), publisher of *Ha-Or*, the corresponding Hebrew edition. Stein was certainly an unusual party member. Having immigrated from Russia in 1913, Stein had voiced fierce criticisms of the Stalinist purges in the 1930s, leaving a major impression on Nicola and the Trotskyist group in Haifa.[82]

Nicola's dissociation from the party was only partly in response to the political purges in the Soviet Union. A stronger factor was Moscow's decree calling for the Arabisation of the Palestine Communist Party, which, Nicola warned, could cast the party's criticisms of the British Mandate and the Zionist project in a nationalist light.[83] His commitment to socialist internationalism, by contrast, was clearly rooted in his own life story. Since the mid-1930s, he had been married to Alisa Novick, a daughter of Polish–Jewish parents who had discovered communism at a kibbutz in the lower Galilee. He turned his fervent attention to studying Jewish history. In 1935, he published *In the Jewish World*, a book that outlines Zionist and non-Zionist movements in the context of modern European Jewish history.[84] For these reasons, Nicola frequently appeared as an arbitrator in ethnic conflicts within the party and made efforts to integrate the Jewish section and protect it from the pressure of Arab dominance.[85] Soon after his release from British imprisonment, tensions reached a breaking point, and the party split along ethnic lines in 1943. Nicola kept his distance from both sides. Gluckstein, Taut and Moneta had previously succeeded in persuading him to join their group, marking the true birth of the Revolutionary Communist League.

The League could scarcely have begun its work, in 1941, under worse conditions. Although it had welcomed another circle of mostly emigrants from Germany (Susi and Bertold [Dov] Scheller, Moi Katz, Otto Weigler, Sigi Rothschild, Theodor and Hava Blauweiss and Ana Shohat), the League remained isolated and largely irrelevant. 'During the second world war, our political and organisational situation was extremely difficult', Jakob Taut would later conclude. 'We fought (and illegally) against three enemies: Zionists, British imperialists and Stalinists.'[86] The League's critique of the Zionist demand for unlimited Jewish immigration had especially contributed to its isolation:

> Our position was clearly difficult, given that we were a Jewish group with no organised contact with Arab workers, and also because we could not deny the fact that after 1933 many German Jews came to Palestine because they had no choice.[87]

But this marginalisation was only one of the reasons their bulletin, *Kol HaMa'amad*, used pseudonymous bylines and was printed and distributed in secret, as were the group's leaflets. (The bulletin was printed hectographically in Hebrew and Arabic versions and also appeared with somewhat less frequency in German, as *Gegen den Strom*, and in English, as *Against the Stream*.) Even if the British had virtually stopped imprisoning communists after the Soviets joined the war, the Revolutionary Communist League feared the watchful eye of the Mandate – due to the League's contacts in the British Army and its regional and international network.[88]

Additionally, the group had run afoul of both communist parties. The very name of their magazine, *Kol HaMa'amad* (The Class's Voice), was chosen in response to the title of the Communist Party newspaper, *Kol Ha'am* (The People's Voice).[89] But in fact, this title went farther than criticising the communist people's front strategy. The decision to emphasise notions of class over notions of 'the people' or nationality seemed to be tantamount to an insistence on internationalism. Heritage and origins were to be neutralised, and the Jewish–Arab conflict was to be overcome through the common perspective of a socialist revolution. For the same reason, besides politically agitating near the Hebrew University of Jerusalem and searching for contacts in the British military, the group had concentrated on the country's railway and oil refineries – 'on those areas where both Jewish and Arab workers were exploited by imperialist capital'. Jakob Taut would later recall: 'After the war, we decided to continue working in these areas. But our intention, with which our international contacts agreed, could scarcely be realised. After the founding of the Zionist state, very few Arab workers were "tolerated" in the Zionist enterprises.'[90] Following the war, Taut worked as a specialist at Haifa's oil refinery, where he was elected to the works council by Jewish and Arab workers.[91] Dov Shas (1925–2006) was born in Romania and fought in the resistance there against the German occupation. After the war ended, he emigrated to Mandatory Palestine with Hashomer Hatzair and began working at the same refinery. Fresh off the boat from Europe, his exposure to the local Arab population caused him to abandon the Zionist cause and seek out possibilities for Jewish–Arab cooperation.[92] He found like-minded individuals in the small group of Trotskyists. While the numerous mass strikes of 1940s Palestine encouraged dreams of joint Jewish–Arab protest, the announcement of the Partition Plan soon revealed diametric differences and seemingly doomed the idea of a common transnational perspective.

All the Palestinian Trotskyists' political efforts culminated in their rejection of a partition of British Mandatory territory; this stance also brought the group its greatest share of public attention. Although their initial appeal, 'Against Partition!' (September 1947), was solely printed in *Kol HaMa'amad* and left scarcely a ripple, their subsequent manifesto, 'Against the Stream' (May 1948), was syndicated in the *Fourth International*, the English-language publication of the international Trotskyist organisation.[93] By then, the International Secretariat of the Fourth Internationale had already released 'Draft Theses on the Jewish Question Today', its own statement on the issue of Palestine after the Second World War, essentially laying out a party line.[94] Although it acknowledged the murder of European Jews and the resulting rush of survivors to Palestine, its political stance was largely unchanged by this sequence of events, and it built on the socialist expectations of the pre-war period and hopes of a global revolutionary shift. In rather outmoded language, the theses held that a Jewish state could not be expected to solve the Jewish question, nor would such a state serve as a safety net for local or newly immigrating Jews.[95] The Palestinian Trotskyists now aimed to update this assessment. With the Palestine problem intensifying, their manifesto 'Against the Stream' voiced the fear that a 'Hebrew state' in the Arabic East would 'turn out [. . .] a bloody trap for hundreds of thousands of Jews'.[96]

But even though the Palestinian Trotskyists' manifesto resembled their international umbrella organisation's position paper in many respects, their own text testified most prominently to the group's near-isolation in Palestine. Intended primarily as a critique of the prospect of Jewish statehood, the paper simultaneously acted as a reckoning for the two communist parties, both of which, following their own partition, advocated partitioning the country. In any case, their accusations were not solely levelled against the Jewish Communist Party, which had changed its name to the Communist Party of Eretz Israel, prompting the accusation that it had broken off 'the last vestige of contact with the Arab population' and instead 'harnessed [itself] to the Zionist wagon'.[97] They also criticised the Arab communists of the National Liberation League, which by adopting the Soviet stance on the Partition Plan had demonstrated 'that the driving force behind [the League's] policy is not the interest of the Palestinian proletariat, but that of the Kremlin'.[98] The political project of Palestinian communism – to resolve the Palestine question and overcome ethnic differences in a shared socialist utopia – seemed to have foundered. In a passionate appeal against the territorial partition, the Trotskyist dissidents concluded: 'In this burning hell of chauvinism we have to hold up the banner of international brotherhood.'[99] Later, Taut would characterise what that sort of socialist internationalism meant:

> We saw – and see – as our task propagandizing and organizing toward this end among both the Jewish and Arab masses in order to construct a united revolutionary socialist party in the region, which the Stalinists, whose policies always dovetailed with Kremlin diplomacy, were unable to do. In addition, the perspective of a united socialist Arab East was the only one in which we saw the possibility of integrating the Jewish workers into the anti-imperialist and socialist struggle in the region.[100]

Yet that hope did not correspond to real political prospects – and not only due to their political insignificance. Unlike the Trotskyists in Palestine, who were holding high the prewar political ideals of socialist revolution and internationalism, most Jews – after the events in Europe and the Holocaust – were committed to the cause of a state of their own.[101] Meanwhile, Trotsky's writings were inspiring dreams of a socialist revolution in post-war Europe, to which many Trotskyites were therefore eager to return.[102] 'Internationalist political work in Palestine seemed more and more pointless', recalled Jakob Moneta, referring to the period after the Second World War when the road to the first Israeli–Arab war was being paved.[103] Most German–Jewish Trotskyites in Palestine saw themselves as living 'in exile in Palestine' with plans to return 'as soon as possible' to their native countries, where they would 'carry out the work of revolution'.[104] In 1944, wasting no time, Rudolf Segall blazed a trail back to Europe. By securing jobs at the United Nations Relief and Rehabilitation Administration (UNRAA) and the American Jewish Joint Distribution Committee, he managed to return circuitously to Germany by way of Greece and France. Shortly after his return, he began publishing the magazine *Unser Weg* (Our Path) with some other Trotskyist returnees. He later found a job at the Frankfurt-based labour union IG Chemie and co-founded the publishing house ISP Verlag.[105] In Frankfurt am Main, where a network of old Trotskyists formed in the 1950s and 1960s, Segall had a reunion with Jakob Moneta.

Likewise, Moneta, who had arrived in Palestine both as an emigrant and a left-wing Zionist, increasingly saw it as a place of exile while he was living there. His internationalism unfulfilled, he had returned to Germany via France and Belgium with the – later revised – hope that 'history would continue from where it had left off after the 1918 Revolution'.[106] This political optimism would be demonstrated in the later stages of his professional and political career. Straight after his arrival, he worked as an editor for the *Rheinische Zeitung* newspaper and became politically active among the ranks of West Germany's Social Democratic Party. After accepting a position as a social attaché at the West German Embassy to Paris in 1953, he resumed his anticolonial activism, which was further ignited by the outbreak of the Algerian War in November 1954.[107] While Trotskyist groups in Germany publicly advocated Algerian independence, Moneta exploited his diplomatic position in Paris to lend clandestine support to the activities of the Front de Libération Nationale (National Liberation Front, FLN).[108] He invited Algerian FLN activists, who were trying to escape the French authorities, to hide at his flat. He also couriered Algerian aid money from Paris to Geneva in suitcases.[109] Yet Moneta's long-lasting political impact began after he returned to Germany in 1962, when he took over the editorship of two union newspapers, *Der Gewerkschafter* (The Unionist) and *Metall* (Metal). While openly raising social issues in the newspapers, he secretly recommenced his Trotskyist activities as a writer and staff member of Germany's International Marxist Group (GIM).

No former member of the group of Palestinian Trotskyists would leave a greater mark in Europe than Yigal Gluckstein. Although he was born in Palestine, he began to feel increasingly estranged from the country and its political reality. Together with his South African-born wife Chanie Gluckstein, who was a British citizen, Yigal therefore relocated in the summer of 1946, before Israeli statehood, to the seat of the British Empire.[110] Yet only a year later, British intelligence prevented Gluckstein from obtaining a residency permit, forcing the couple to live in Ireland for four years before they could resettle permanently in Britain.[111] Gluckstein's break with Palestine was also reflected in his decision to change his name. He had already published under the name Leo Rock. Now, as Tony Cliff, he had a name that bore an etymological connection to the stone (German: *Stein*) of Gluckstein, but firmly placed him as an Englishman. In Britain, he first joined the Revolutionary Communist Party, the British section of the Fourth International. Then, in 1950, Cliff was among the initiators of the *Socialist Review*. A decade later, he founded the International Socialists and ultimately became the leading representative of its successor organisation, the Socialist Workers Party (SWP). Just as Cliff had cast aside his origin and heritage by changing his name, he moved on from the Palestine question in favour of political engagement in British issues and a deeper exploration of the history and theory of the labour movement. Still, he was never naturalised as a British citizen in his lifetime. The global revolution would remain the only homeland for the stateless Tony Cliff.

Only a handful of the original Trotskyists remained in Israel after statehood, and not all of them continued their political projects of the 1930s and 1940s. For example, Gabriel Baer, who in the 1940s was a leader of the Revolutionary Communist League and continued to publish under his pseudonym S. Munir, gradually withdrew from the political arena after the founding of the Jewish state. Following the Arab mass flight during the battles for Israeli statehood, he observed with resignation that '[t]he barrier between Jewish and Arab workers built by imperialism, Zionism and Arab Reaction, which had been broken from time to time [. . .] has now been fortified by political boundaries between belligerent or at least rival states, excluding the physical contact between Jewish and Arab workers'.[112] Though he still published reviews in *International Socialism* until the early 1960s, against the backdrop of political failure, Gabriel Baer increasingly used his knowledge of Arabic language and culture for his academic work at Hebrew University, where he co-founded the Institute for Asian and African Studies and oversaw the institute's journal, quickly rising to become a formative figure in local Middle Eastern studies.[113] Tony Cliff could not forgive him his move to the ivory tower. In a review of Baer's book *Population and Society in the Arab East* in 1964, Cliff wrote that its portrayal was thoroughly 'informative', but that it sorely lacked a critical analysis of the significance and influence of the major imperial powers in the region. 'Has Dr Baer been muted by Zionist pressure in Israel where he lives?', asked Cliff, mockingly. To remind Baer of his past revolutionary engagement, he signed the review with the byline Y. Sakhry, a name he had once used in the Arabic publications of their common organisation.[114]

Unlike Baer, who had withdrawn into academia, Jakob Taut, Ruth Milo and Jabra and Alisa Nicola remained in close touch with their political allies in Europe and were still politically active within Israel. Taut and Milo had also considered returning to Europe, but had remained in the country, unwillingly at first – as victims of the escalating violence in the Jewish–Arab conflict. In the early hours of 30 December 1947, the Etzel brigades launched a targeted attack on Arab men who had been standing on the bridge outside the gates of the Haifa oil refinery, waiting for work. The explosions killed six Arabs and wounded fifty more. Soon afterward, Arab labourers unleashed their rage in unbridled violence. Shouting 'Kill the Jews', they took revenge on innocent Jewish refinery workers and aimed their weapons at their Jewish colleagues.[115] Within a very short time, thirty-nine labourers were murdered, and ten others injured, some gravely. Jakob Taut was among those with serious injuries. In the midst of the escalation, he had fainted and was later found among the bodies.[116] He regained consciousness in hospital five days later. He could not return to work for quite a while, and not until late 1949 was he able to take up a less onerous job at the refinery. But even as these events inspired Taut's future political commitment to Israel and 'the incident turned him into an Israeli',[117] it did 'not give him any doubts' about his 'unwavering internationalism', according to his friend Jakob Moneta.[118] This is vividly demonstrated by his memories of these horrible experiences, which in retrospect he situated entirely in the context of the first Israeli–Arab war. Although he perceived the Arabs' revenge as the actions of 'socially and culturally retrograde segments of the Arab working class', his experience of Jewish–Arab class solidarity in practice served as the basis for Taut's continued political work.[119] After returning to the oil refinery, he took up a post as a union representative and cooperated with members of the communist Maki and the left-wing Zionist Mapam parties.[120] He also kept in touch with his political associates in Europe and remained close with the Nicolas in Haifa. The war had marked a turning point in their lives, too.

Looking back, it seemed to Jabra Nicola as if both 'my friends and my country' had left him in 1948.[121] Neither did he find a political homeland in the reunited Communist Party of Israel, Maki, which he and his wife had rejoined after statehood for lack of alternatives. The party members knew that the pair were sworn followers of Trotsky, yet they valued Nicola's editorial finesse and so looked past this political allegiance. Thanks to his language skills, he soon made a name for himself as one of the editors of *Al-Ittihad*, the Arabic edition of the party newspaper, and as a translator into Arabic.[122] His linguistic and cultural knowledge of Hebrew and Arabic lent him the role of intermediary, even outside the party.[123] In Tel Aviv in October 1958, he served as a liaison between Jewish and Arab writers in Israel, two groups that, officially, had never come together before.[124]

Despite his party membership, Nicola did not cease his Trotskyist activities. He maintained contact with the Fourth International after the war and soon rose in the ranks of the organisation. Ernest Mandel, the chief political and theoretical mind of post-war Trotskyism, would later remember Nicola as 'the most impressive internationalist I ever met'.[125] Not until the de-Stalinisation crisis of 1956 would Nicola finally come into open conflict with the party and at last be ejected from it. Together with Jakob Taut, he went looking for alternative political allies. The Suez Crisis had given rise to new organisations outside the traditional political spectrum, such as Semitic Action (Peula HaShemit) led by Uri Avnery and Nathan Yellin-Mor. But only when the first edition of *Matzpen* announced the founding of the Israeli Socialist Organization did Nicola, Taut and Dov Shas find their new political home.[126] Ruth Milo and Hava and Theodor Blauweiss also attended its meetings. For the younger Matzpen founders, Jabra Nicola became the formative figure and gave them new insights into the nature of the Palestine problem and prospects for its resolution: 'He had gone through the earlier thirty years of the history of the world revolutionary movement, but was not soiled with all the Stalinist shit', recalled Moshé Machover, reflecting on Nicola's impact (Figure 2.1):

> He remembered from his own experience things we knew only from books. In particular, a vital period of the Zionist colonisation process was for him a living memory. But more important than this: he had exactly what we lacked – a coherent conception of the Zionist colonisation process, and in particular the way it affected the Arab society in Palestine. From him we got a much better and deeper understanding of Israel as an embodiment of Zionist colonisation. Also, he had a conception of the Arab revolution as one [. . .] indivisible process.[127]

Figure 2.1 Two generations, one idea: Moshé Machover (left) and Jabra Nicola (right).

But even as the young Israeli Left to some extent was influenced by the legacy of the pre-statehood Trotskyist dissidents, the old frames of reference were reshaped into an independent understanding of the Israel–Palestine conflict under changed historical circumstances. The era of decolonisation, which peaked during the Algerian War of 1954–62, cast a shadow on Israel, the Palestine problem and, therefore, also Matzpen.

From the Algerian War to the Palestine Question

On 14 June 1960, Israeli–French relations were in crisis, and the Israeli Prime Minister David Ben-Gurion and the French President Charles de Gaulle met in Paris for bilateral talks. Ben-Gurion had travelled there the previous day, after Israel's French ally declared that despite their past assistance with Israel's nuclear research, France would not deliver any uranium for a reactor in the Negev Desert. This prompted Ben-Gurion to seek a meeting to resolve the issue.[128] But the French head of state was preoccupied with very different problems of his own. Since reclaiming the presidency in January 1959, De

Gaulle's most urgent concern had been to end the Algerian War and thus resolve the issue of Algeria, which had absorbed France's rapt attention since the outbreak of the Algerian Revolution on 1 November 1954.[129] In a televised address on 16 September 1959, he had used the word *autodétermination* (self-determination) for the first time in reference to the Algerians, marking a turning point in more than a century of French policy.[130] France had colonised Algeria in 1830 and had since encouraged hundreds of thousands of Europeans – known as *pieds noirs* – to settle there. Ben-Gurion was also interested in discussing France's next moves in the escalating colonial conflict. Indeed, the French presence in Algeria had given the Jewish state a strategic alliance against Arab nationalism. He quickly shared his own perspective with the French leader. The Algerian question could be solved, Ben-Gurion argued, 'by partitioning the country, concentrating the French population along the coast and in the Sahara and, most importantly, by [organising] an immigration ("Aliyah") of a million French people to Algeria'.[131] De Gaulle, having listened calmly to his Israeli counterpart's suggestion, responded with indignation: 'My God, you are trying to establish a new Israel in Africa!' But Ben-Gurion was undeterred. 'Yes, but with one difference: the "new Israel" would have the support of France, with its forty-five million inhabitants and her alliances with the Western countries'.[132] Aside from the Israeli desire to forge a lasting alliance with the French colonial power in the fight against Arab nationalism, the meeting between Ben-Gurion and his French counterpart exposed a structural parallel between Israel's presence in Palestine and that of French colonists in Algeria. Both polities had been established by a minority of newcomers in a majority-Arab region and could only be maintained by military force.

The Israeli Prime Minister's diplomatic overtures may have produced short-term success – De Gaulle essentially declared that Israel's security was France's national interest[133] – but Algerian independence was unstoppable. So was its impact on the Israel–Palestine conflict. With the ink barely dry on the Évian Accords, which were signed on 18 March 1962 and paved the way to Algerian independence, Algeria's future president – not even home yet – told the Cairo-based Middle East News Agency that he was prepared to send 100,000 Algerian soldiers into battle for 'the liberation of Palestine'. In the spirit of his pending sovereignty, the future head of state proclaimed that: 'We do not think in Algeria that our revolution can be complete as long as the liberation of Palestine has not yet been achieved'.[134] This was not merely a show of sabre-rattling from the new Algerian government. For a brief moment, the young country of Algeria was among the chief political supporters of the Palestinian Fatah movement, to which it granted the political recognition and military aid it had hitherto been largely denied.[135]

Faced with these threatening scenarios, the Israeli Prime Minister had already publicly rejected the insinuation of any parallels between the French colony and Jewish Israel a few weeks earlier. In a much-noted interview for the French magazine *Figaro*, Ben-Gurion instead sought to clarify

> that despite apparent superficial analogies between the situations of the French in Algeria and the Jews in Eretz Israel, there is a significant and absolute difference between the two problems. I am not ignoring the tragic problem of the French people who have resided in Algeria for several generations. However, while Eretz Israel has always been an immutable condition for the existence of the Jewish people, the existence and the fate of the French nation are not bound to Algeria, but to Continental France.[136]

Confronted by the threat that the outcome of Algerian decolonisation would be extrapolated to the Israel–Palestine conflict, the Israeli Prime Minister asserted a deeper, divinely ordained legitimacy for the Jewish state in Palestine. By claiming historic rights derived from the Jews' distant past in the biblical Land of Israel, Ben-Gurion sought to justify the nation's present-day existence and thus reframe the political conflict.

While Ben-Gurion was insisting that the differences between the Algerian conflict and the Palestine problem were absolute, Algerian decolonisation was exercising its first belated effects on Matzpen, where it raised a new set of existential questions. There was no place left in post-colonial Algeria for the formerly privileged *pieds noirs*, even though the country was their sole homeland, too – in some cases, going back generations. The more the young leftists of Matzpen saw their fate as a mirror of the position of Israeli Jews in the Israel–Palestine conflict, the more questions this raised about their own position; questions that were scarcely answered by any unilateral proclamation of Israel's legitimacy. In their magazine, Moshé Machover and Akiva Orr instead claimed 'the perspective of a neutral observer', replacing national self-legitimation with historical comparison. To those who could not rationally assess Israeli Jews' precarious position in the Israel–Palestine conflict, whether for 'emotional, national or psychological reasons', they recommended first considering the circumstances of white South Africans.[137] If the latter group perpetuated political inequality between themselves and the black population, clinging to the status quo, their lives would soon be as imperilled as the lives of French Algerians, whose fates Algerian independence had sealed. Machover and Orr concluded by pointing out that, regardless of the differing circumstances and reasons of their settlement, the three historical situations in Algeria, South Africa and Israel were of a piece: 'European settlers arrived – in the course of colonial methods and with their active support – and developed a national, economic, political and independent life' for themselves.[138] No matter how the Jewish polity in Palestine sought to justify itself, the structural set-up was the same: a collision between a resident population and an ethnically and culturally distinct settler population seeking territorial, historical and legal privileges. In all three situations, as the co-authors went on to argue, the origins had been tied to the historical era of colonialism and had resulted in abiding loyalty towards, and dependence upon, the major European powers. Now the colonial powers' collapse posed an existential threat to all three settler groups:

> In the case of Algeria, the situation ended with the emigration of a million French colonists from Algeria to France. [. . .] When it comes to the whites in South Africa, it is near-impossible to predict how the situation will end. And essentially the same situation applies to the Jews in the Arab East. These days, it all depends upon which policies the Israeli government implements towards the Arabs in Israel, towards the Arab world at large and in regard to its domestic issues.[139]

The Algerian War, the significance of which one could scarcely overestimate, opened new realms of insights into the Palestine problem for the young leftists of Matzpen. Against this backdrop, the Trotskyist dissidents' past experiences bore fruit. A new theory of the Zionist settlement project in Palestine discarded, once and for all, the idea of the Palestine problem as a struggle of nationalities that had been caused by the progression and outcome of the first Arab–Israeli war. 'This is not a battle for control of a territory inhabited by a mixed population', declared Meir Smorodinsky, who was one of the first to reject the widely cited parallels to the nationality conflicts of the nineteenth and twentieth centuries.[140] The structure of those earlier conflicts had far more to do with the political landscape of Central Europe and the transition from empires into nation-states. That same region was the birthplace of the Zionist movement, which proposed its own nation-state project along the lines of the nationalist movements of the nineteenth century in response to the failed emancipation of Jews, to modern antisemitism and to the age of pogroms in Eastern and Central Europe. Yet in view of Zionism's distinctive character, which originated in Europe but territorialised in Palestine, Matzpen was less 'concerned with its "legitimacy" or "illegitimacy" as a nationalist movement' than with 'the conditions of its realisation'.[141] As a result of the Zionist movement's spatial shift from Europe to Palestine, inhabited by an indigenous Arab population, the conflict was fated from the outset. Smorodinsky tried to encapsulate both the territorial and demographic structure of the conflict as follows:

> At its core, this is a conflict between the colonial Zionist movement, which has attempted and still is attempting to displace the Arabs out of an ever-growing part of Palestine, and the Arab nationalist movement, which aspires to sovereignty over the full territory inhabited by Arabs.[142]

Although the conflict over Palestine had aspects of a nationality conflict – as a collision between different population groups – it also had a colonial aspect – as a collision between native and settler populations – making it a kind of 'colonial-type conflict between nationalities'.[143] Therefore, such an opposition could no longer be resolved within the same conceptual framework as a European nationality conflict, which would typically come to an end when each group recognised the other's national aspirations or territorial sovereignty. In this case, such a development would amount to this position: '[T]hat the Arabs would be forced to recognise that Zionist Israel aspires – as it did for over 80 years – to displace them, whereas Israel would have to recognise the fact [. . .] that there are already Arabs in the land'. From that point forward, the New Leftists of Matzpen considered the Israel–Palestine conflict – as a clash over the founding and persistence of the Jewish state in an Arab region – to be unyielding and 'irreconcilable'.[144]

This picture of the conflict's origins violated the Herzlian national utopia of Jewish statehood in Arab Palestine, but it also demystified the social utopias of progress and economic justice that were equally innate to the self-image of the Zionist movement. After all, the Zionist immigrants of the first half of the century had arrived with aspirations of statehood, but not with any a priori antipathy towards Palestinian Arabs. The pioneers of the Second and Third Aliyah – who included key originators of the Yishuv's pre-state institutions and many leading politicians of the future Jewish state – had not arrived in Palestine purely in response to modern antisemitism or with the sole aspiration of founding a nation-state. In turning their backs on Europe and the Jewish Diaspora, they simultaneously sought to build a universalistic utopia with socialist features. If the road to Palestine meant a return to Eretz Israel, the first pioneers simultaneously believed that their settlements were 'in utopia' when they 'were actually in Arabia' (Martin Buber).[145] Most of the Zionist pioneers had never laid eyes on the demographic situation in the place they intended to settle or experienced the a priori contrast to the resident Arab population. The socialist horizon of freedom and equality, linked to the settlement project, obscured the role of nationality in the mounting conflict. Instead, it fuelled Theodor Herzl's old dream that the Arabs of Palestine would consent to the project, if only for the simple reason that they would benefit from the country's economic development as much as the Jewish pioneers.[146] This dream of reconciling the project of a Jewish nation-state with the resident Arab population was still being entertained as late as 1964 – for example, in the extensive survey *Israel and the Arab World* by Aharon Cohen, a longstanding expert in Arab issues within the left-wing Zionist Mapam party.[147] Cohen portrayed the Jewish–Arab conflict as a tragic nationality conflict that could be resolved by each side's recognition of the other's claims to nationhood, but Akiva Orr and Moshé Machover identified something in this framing besides an expression of the author's respectable advocacy for Jewish–Arab understanding.[148] Cohen's magnum opus drew their criticism because its efforts to find middle ground relied on Herzl's argument 'that Jewish immigration and settlement had brought great benefit to Palestine',[149] including to Palestinian Arabs, and because Cohen was thus perpetuating the left-wing Zionist conception that socialist utopia and Zionist practice were compatible long after this idea had been debunked by the realities of the conflict.

In contrast to this abiding tendency to mask the ethnonational opposition with the Arab population in social metaphors, *Matzpen* had come to promulgate an historical reckoning with the history of the Zionist settlement movement – and that movement's aims of establishing a state. This pushed back the genesis of the conflict to a time before the founding of the Israeli state. Machover and Orr tried to set Cohen straight: 'The Jewish society that established itself in Palestine after the Balfour Declaration coined the slogans "Kibush Hakarka" [Conquest of the Land], "Avoda Ivrit" [Hebrew Labour] and "Knu Totzeret Ha'aretz" [Buy the Products of the Country]'.[150] These slogans may have been directed inward, by and large, as the Jewish community's conception of its own establishment and stabilisation, but their impact in Palestine projected outwards and became a pretext for excluding the resident Arabs. On this very basis, Machover and Orr emphasised the political nature of Keren Kayemet LeIsrael (the Jewish National Fund, or JNF), the Zionist land-purchasing organisation.[151] The JNF had purchased land from Arabs with large property holdings and immediately banned its resale to create the basis for the territory of the future state. In the force of this proto-state act, Machover and Orr saw the cause of a 'systematic dispossession of Arab *fellahin* from the land they had cultivated for generations'.[152] This conversion of Arab soil into Jewish territory was only realised with the introduction of the principle of 'Jewish labour', enacted by Zionists who, despite their socialist leanings, had built the 'Jewish Yishuv in Palestine in opposition to the Arab proletariat and the rural masses, which were dispossessed of their land'.[153] The exclusive employment of Jewish workers also followed the ideologically guided principle of self-proletarianisation, which had its roots in Leo Tolstoy's utopia of an agrarian socialism.[154] In practice, however, it caused the banishment of Arab workers from a hermetically sealed Jewish economy. Hence, Machover and Orr concluded:

> The crucial fact, which [Aharon] Cohen obscures with an abundance of details, is that the entire interwar Jewish community constituted a closed society that found itself in a rivalry with the local Palestinian-Arab population.[155]

More than a decade before the founding of the Jewish state, this escalating discrepancy had turned into an open conflict overnight; after the riots and massacres of 1921 and 1929, it eventually led to the Arab General Strike in Mandatory Palestine from April to October 1936. However, Cohen's account had not included this collective protest by Palestinian Arabs, which was directed against both the British Mandate and the Zionist settlement. The two authors therefore wrote, clinching their argument: 'This incident, which shook the whole Middle East at the time, is not even mentioned once in A. Cohen's book. [. . .] For a historical book of its kind, that is an unforgiveable sin.'[156]

This angle on the conflict-ridden nature of Zionist settlement in Palestine was by no means novel, nor was it the sole province of left-wing criticism. Since the early days of Jewish settlement, no one had spoken out more clearly against the founding principles of socialist Zionism, which held that its own settlement policy was reconcilable with the interests of Palestinian Arabs, than Vladimir Jabotinsky (1880–1940), the father of the right-wing Zionist Revisionist movement. His dispute with socialist Zionists formed the underlying historical context behind his canonical essay 'The Iron Wall' of 1923. Jabotinsky dismissed it as a 'childish notion' to 'imagine' that the Palestinian–Arab people would 'voluntarily consent to the realisation of Zionism, in return for the moral and material conveniences which the Jewish colonist brings with him' – a notion that 'has at bottom a kind of contempt for the Arab people'.[157] Contrary to his political opponents' hopes of obtaining 'the voluntary consent of the Palestine Arabs for converting "Palestine" from an Arab country into a country with a Jewish majority', Jabotinsky conjured an image of an 'iron wall' and stressed that either the project of Zionist settlement must cease altogether, or it must continue 'against the will of its native population'. Minimising the political differences between 'our "militarists" and our "vegetarians"', Jabotinsky pointed out that both right-wing and left-wing Zionists were engaging 'day after day' in an iron wall of collective self-isolation.[158] Retrospectively examining this period, the critical theorists of Matzpen did not recognise any fundamental, inborn differences between the two wings of the Zionist movement either. They freely admitted the distinctions between the Revisionists, who 'demanded immediate independence for the whole of Palestine under Jewish minority rule', and 'the left-wing Zionists', who presented a less belligerent face and 'wanted to postpone independence until, through increased emigration, the Jews became a majority'.[159] All the same, the tactical approach would not change anything about the underlying fundamental conflict with the Palestinian Arabs. At any rate, the distinctions between various streams of Zionism had faded since the Palestinian general strike of the late 1930s.

It was the head of the Jewish Agency and future Prime Minister David Ben-Gurion himself who maintained the 'iron wall' policy and made it a fixture of his political practice.[160] Since the war of 1947–9, a deliberate emphasis on strength and military intimidation had taken primacy in Ben-Gurion's activist foreign policy towards neighbouring Arab countries. Even as the Israeli Prime Minister repeatedly invoked 'peace and cooperation with the Arabs' as 'our major objective', his trusted friend Nahum Goldman was convinced that he scarcely believed in it and considered diplomatic negotiations with the neighbours to be utopian thinking.[161] 'They only see one thing', he declared to Nahum Goldmann, a proponent of diplomacy, on the eve of the Suez Campaign:

> We have come here and stolen their country. Why should they accept that? They may perhaps forget in one or two generations' time, but for the moment there is no chance. So it's simple: we have to stay strong and maintain a powerful army. Our whole policy is there. Otherwise the Arabs will wipe us out.[162]

Ben-Gurion had hoped that having experienced military force, their Arab neighbours would someday 'realise that it will not be easy to destroy Israel' and eventually accept the country as a reality.[163] His hopes were with 'the next generation' of Arabs, who, in contrast to the generation of Arab leaders who had been defeated by the Jewish state in 1948, 'would probably have forgotten these defeats, and with them the shame and humiliation which a little people had inflicted on Arab armies ten time more numerous than theirs'.[164] Yet the members of Matzpen doubted whether the conflict could ever cool down or the Jewish state ever integrate into the region with the passage of time; doubts that were certainly fuelled by more than the enmity of the Arab states. At any rate, they believed that the heated conflict would never cool down if its origins persisted in the political structures of the Jewish state. Diverging from the thesis of post-Zionism, which viewed the Zionist movement's historical project as consummated – essentially 'complete' – in the establishment of Israel,[165] Moshé Machover contended that 'the state is a Zionist state to this day' and that the objectives of the Zionist movement had been embedded in political structures that aimed to preserve a Jewish majority and to conserve Israel's Jewish character;[166] he certainly hit a nerve: although the new state accorded the same civil rights to all citizens, regardless of their origins, the state's genuinely Jewish character threatened to undermine its democratic nature by giving Arab Israelis a permanently unequal status.[167]

Since Israel was founded – and long before Matzpen – its military rule of the Arab-populated areas and frontiers within its territory had inspired protests: by the Communist Party, Uri Avnery's *Haolam Hazeh*, Ichud's magazine *Ner*, Mordechai Stein's *HaIton HaDemocratie* (Democratic Newspaper) and finally the Al-Ard group. The emergency regulations, which in a sense picked up where the British military left off, officially applied 'to all inhabitants of these areas', but in practice 'mostly affected the Arabs', considerably restricting their freedom to assemble or travel at will.[168] However, this creeping degradation of the Arab population into 'second-class citizens' occupied only one page of discussion in the columns of *Matzpen*.[169] The military government had also become a target of criticism for legalising the confiscation of abandoned Arab lands. For Shimon Peres, the 'use of Regulation 125' (that enabled the declaration of military 'closed areas' to prevent the return to abandoned villages) was the 'direct continuation of the struggle for Jewish settlement and Jewish immigration'.[170] In that spirit, the military government became one tool for the creation of exclusive Jewish settlement areas in the North in the 1950s and 1960s. Under the slogan 'Yehud HaGalil' (Judaization of the Galilee), the campaign aimed to change the demographic balance in an area that had a majority-Arab population. Given this latest incarnation of Zionist land policy within the Jewish state, Oded Pilavsky asked: 'Is it so surprising that the Arab nationalist movement sees Zionism as inseparable from the colonialist movements? Would we see it any differently in their shoes?'[171]

The most telling indication that defining the state as both Jewish and democratic was a contradiction in terms, however, was the Law of Return of 5 July 1950, which, in conjunction with the Nationality Law of April 1952, guaranteed every Jew worldwide the right to immigrate and to obtain Israeli citizenship.[172] Meir Smorodinsky concluded that, because the young state lacked an official constitution, this was the only law that 'takes on a constitutional character' and that 'expresses all governing circles' relationship towards the state'.[173] It practically enshrined in legal form the agenda and perspective of establishing a Jewish nation-state for disparate groups of worldwide Jews.[174] Yet this aspect of 'positive discrimination', which granted diasporic Jews a special legal entitlement to the Jewish state, was not the only motive for Smorodinsky's criticism of this fundamental law. In light of the Palestine problem, he emphazised its 'most negative side': the discrimination of Israel's Arab citizens. Although they had 'ethnic and family ties to the refugees of the 1948 war', the law did not apply to the latter. It also seemd to disadvantage Israel's internal Arab refugees:[175]

> Despite living here for generations, these Arabs are considered 'absentees' and not citizens with equal rights, unlike a Romanian Jew who arrived in Israel yesterday [and] is already considered a citizen today.[176]

The origin-based distinction drawn by the Israeli Citizenship Law therefore extended the state's founding conflict. 'The Arab world will never accept Israel as an equal member of the family of nations in the Middle East', Smorodinsky concluded, 'while [Israel] discriminates against the non-Jewish segment of its population'.[177]

Given the trends in the decolonisation process, Matzpen increasingly dismissed as wishful thinking the notion that a genuinely Jewish state of Israel could last, and worried that if this wishful thinking guided political action, it could even threaten the existence of Israeli Jews themselves. At first, this criticism targeted the official conviction that, for the moment, such a state could be preserved through military posturing and the use of force. 'Tzahal [the Israeli Defence Force] won't solve the problem', declared Oded Pilavsky.[178] His own doubts, like Matzpen's, had reached a new high after Algeria's decolonisation and France's military defeat:

> The FLN's victory in Algeria reinforced and confirmed the assumption that Arabs can overthrow a colonial administration, even a longstanding one. Even if it is backed [. . .] by a major military power like France. In its efforts to subdue the anticolonial forces in the Middle East, supported by American and British aid, Israel is viewed [by the Arabs] in a very similar light as the French in Algeria. It goes without saying that according to this perspective, Israel faces a future like that of the French Algerians.[179]

In contrast with a Zionist temporality, which was borne by the primacy of the Jewish state's legitimacy and by the will to assert it by any means necessary, the members of Matzpen had developed an historical consciousness that it was impossible to sustain a colonial situation's intrinsic inequality during a global era of decolonisation and national independence. In the eyes of the Israeli Left, the dramatic fate of the Algerian *pieds noirs* had recently intensified the debate surrounding Israeli Arabs and the future of Israeli Jews. In his frightening assessment of the historical moment, Meir Smorodinsky concluded:

> Just as the Zionist era is linked to the colonial movement, the end of Zionism is linked to the end of that movement. If the project of settlement in this country does not break ties with that movement, it ought to fear the same [fate] as the French settlement in Algeria, which never disavowed colonialism.[180]

In some respects, this voice of Matzpen was basically that same well-meaning or leftist coloniser whose character traits the Tunisian–French writer Albert Memmi had vividly painted in his dual portrait of the coloniser and the colonised. Memmi had described the moral and political attitudes of a 'coloniser who refuses' amidst a colonial situation marked by formal inequality between a population of natives and a population of settlers from abroad.[181] This coloniser figure is defined in part by his moral doubts about his own privilege, his rejection of the colonial relationship and the resulting rift from his own dominant society. As for the coloniser with anticolonial sympathies, Memmi further asserts:

> If he wants to help [liberate] the colonised, it is exactly because their destiny does concern him, because his destiny and theirs are intertwined and matter to one another, because he hopes to go on living in the colony.[182]

But Memmi did not model the figure of the leftist coloniser after the political structure of the Palestine problem, nor did he intend for it to be applied to that situation. In fact, this figure was modelled on the experience of Memmi's friend, the writer Albert Camus, who had chafed against the French colonial conflict due to his own Algerian upbringing.[183] Following prospective decolonisation, Camus dreamed of the establishment of a new Algeria where Arabs and French-Algerians would treat one another as equals. Such a vision of the future was also implicit in Matzpen's criticism. 'The realisation of the rights of Palestine's Arabs is no less important and advantageous for us than for the Arabs themselves', Oded Pilavsky contended. 'That is the only way we can succeed in obtaining our naturalisation certificate in the Near East.'[184]

But even Memmi, in his reflections on the colonial situation, had emphasised the tragedy of these 'impossible historical situations', in the face of which the 'role of the left-wing coloniser collapses'.[185] With their critique of Israel's Zionist structure and its nature as a Jewish state, the dissidents of Matzpen had crossed a line, and not only within their own society. For all their hopes of overcoming the colonial situation, they could rarely attain recognition in the Arab world either, which would scarcely see them as anything but foreign colonisers. Hence, the universalist critique, with its goal of mutual recognition and equality between colonisers and colonised, was for now subsumed by 'an abstract universality or an ideal to be found in history of the future', an internationalist 'fraternity of peoples'.[186] In light of this position, as so expressed, the story of Matzpen was a story of the criticism of the ongoing Zionist project in the Israel–Palestine conflict as much as it was a narrative of socialist visions for the future, which linked overcoming the conflict to a utopian change for Jews and Arabs in the spirit of mutual recognition. Matzpen hoped for a change in their own society and wished for Palestinian and Arab allies who would be willing to recognise Israelis in a post-Zionist context.

'Foreign Natives': Prospects of Recognition[187]

On 18 May 1967, less than three weeks before the outbreak of the Six-Day War, the General Union of Palestine Students held a large-scale 'Day of Palestine' in Paris. On previous anniversaries of Israeli statehood, this Palestinian group had regularly invited the public to commemorate the corresponding flight and displacement of Palestinians, events that became known in the Arab world as the Nakba (disaster). Perhaps due to the tensions of the moment, that year's gathering far surpassed the dimensions of its predecessors. Even the Israeli daily *Maariv* reported, albeit somewhat tentatively: 'Never before – at least not since Operation Sinai – was there such an organised Arab demonstration in Paris, one that purports to be a show of strength.'[188] The Egyptian Ambassador in Paris was in attendance, as was a former confidant of the Moroccan opposition politician Mehdi Ben Barka, who had been assassinated nearly two years prior. Around 500 Arab university students attended the event. In commemoration of the first Israeli–Arab war, they demanded a right of return for Palestinian refugees, while others agitated more openly for the end of Israel as a Jewish state.[189] Alongside numerous Arab guests of honour, one of the speakers was Nathan Weinstock (b. 1939), a representative of a Belgian Trotskyist organisation, who had not yet reached his thirtieth birthday. But although the invitation rested on the strength of his articles, in which the young man had publicly expressed solidarity with the Palestinian cause, he was there as an emissary to read a text he had not personally composed. Weinstock delivered an address of solidarity by the Israeli Socialist Organization, which aimed – from within Israel – to establish prospects for a common Jewish–Arab future in the Middle East.[190] Moshé Machover and Jabra Nicola had written the short statement only a few days before the event. The group signed off on it as their joint communiqué on the 'Palestine Problem and the Arab–Israeli Dispute'.[191] As the group's first political statement on the Israel–Palestine conflict for an international audience, it distilled the debates of the past few years and would leave a lasting mark beyond the event in Paris; two days later, the Middle East expert at *Le Monde*, Eric Rouleau, would report on the talk in the newspaper.[192]

Matzpen had found an apt spokesperson in Nathan Weinstock, whose political development in parts mirrored that of his Israeli comrades. Born in Antwerp, Belgium, in 1939, he was also first a longstanding member of Hashomer Hatzair, but moved on because of the socialist-Zionist movements' internal ideological contradictions. Whilst studying criminology at the Université Libre de Bruxelles, he joined the Belgian Trotskyist movement, became part of the anticolonial left and centred his political activism on the Palestine problem and his solidarity with the Palestinians.[193] Weinstock gained an international reputation after the Six-Day War, when he began working on a book-length survey of the Israel–Palestine conflict, which would also popularise Matzpen's positions. Just two years later, he published the 600-page volume *Le sionisme contre Israël* (Zionism versus Israel) with France's Maspero publishing house, a central player on the anticolonial left.[194] The book quickly became a sort of 'insider tip among intellectuals who read *Les Temps Modernes* and smoked filterless Gauloises' and a 'handbook for campus anti-Zionists'.[195] Translated into multiple languages, it soon served as a textbook for all leftists who had taken up the Palestinian cause. It was published in German in 1975 under the title *Das Ende Israels?* (The End of Israel?), translated, edited and introduced by Eike Geisel (1945–97) and Mario Offenberg.[196] The English translation, *Zionism: False Messiah*, appeared in 1979 prefaced by a new interview with Moshé Machover.[197] Meanwhile, the book's original French title precluded any unilateral interpretation. In *Le sionisme contre Israël*, Weinstock did not merely offer an historically founded explanation for supporting the Palestinians. His book's chief underlying conviction was that Israel's abiding failure to acknowledge the Palestinians was also a threat to Israeli Jews' existence in the Middle East. Zionism, Weinstock firmly believed, had come to pose a threat to Israel itself.

That view had already been expressed two years earlier in the communiqué that Weinstock read out on behalf of Matzpen at the 'Day of Palestine' in Paris, shortly before the Six-Day War. 'The state of war and hostility between Israel and her Arab neighbors has continued for nineteen years', declared the members of the Israeli Socialist Organization near the beginning of the statement, 'Israel's Zionist leadership has no real prospect of changing this situation.'[198] Since the current policy was a 'cul-de-sac', the Israeli socialists saw it as their 'honourable duty' to present their own independent proposal for a resolution to the Israeli–Arab problem.[199] They seemed to have finally found an international forum in which to discuss political alternatives, mutual recognition and a common future. *Matzpen* optimistically reported that the meeting in Paris had been distinct from similar gatherings in previous years, because, this time, its organisers were not subscribers to Arab nationalism. Instead, it was led by members of the Arab Left who were committed to socialism and internationalism while using the language of revolution, which they directed in no small part against the same autocratic regimes in the region that wished to erase Israel from the map. The Israeli leftists took Weinstock's invitation as evidence that the organisers were moving away from previous 'antisemitic language and demonstrat[ing] an explicitly non-nationalist outlook'.[200] Under the banner of their shared hope for a socialist transformation of the Middle East, the prospect of a common existence appeared to be enabling an anticipatory mutual recognition of Israeli Jews and Palestinian Arabs, disregarding the past and present of the Palestine question. The shared socialist utopia promised to lay the foundation of a new commonality in the future. 'One can therefore sum up the solution which we propose by the [following] formula', Weinstock pronounced in Paris, reading out Matzpen's precise phrasing: 'de-Zionisation of Israel and its integration in a socialist Middle Eastern union'.[201] Hence, Matzpen were seeking a new justification for the Israeli existence in the Middle East, a reinvention that would decouple Israeli Jews from the premises of their Zionist past and liberate them from the abiding burden of their founding conflict – in order to achieve recognition throughout the whole region.

Having thus shored up a foundation for a common future, Weinstock presented proposals for an Israeli metamorphosis in the Israel–Palestine conflict, proposals that had been in the making since Matzpen's establishment and had solidified in a political agenda of 'de-Zionising' Israel. Israel's state and society were to be reconstituted by abolishing all institutionalised structures designed to preserve the state's Jewish character, as these elements accorded unequal status to Arab citizens. Now that the military administration had been formally abolished, this proposal intended to remove the judicial regulations that validated the continued expropriation of the Arab population and the conversion of Arab land into Jewish territory within Israel. Matzpen also advocated the dissolution of all institutions, such as the Jewish National Fund and the Jewish Agency, that had predated Israeli statehood and now served as semi-public entities, contributing to the privileged treatment of the Jewish population.[202] The annulment of Israel's 'Law of Return', the very law that guaranteed every Jew worldwide the right to obtain Israeli citizenship, was central to this metamorphosis. Matzpen's proposal did not, however, mean that they opposed on principle any immigration of Jews to Israel. As Moshé Machover took pains to stress: 'By no means should one give any credence to the racist notion that a person, in matters of immigration to Israel, should be negatively discriminated against for being Jewish.'[203] Instead, repealing the law would halt legal discrimination between immigrants based on their group affiliation. 'Each request to immigrate into Israel will then be decided separately on its own merits, without any discrimination of a racial or religious nature.'[204] Hence, the reinvention of Israel in the spirit of the Israeli Left gave way to an appeal for a 'deep revolutionary change' that would transform the Israeli state 'from a Zionist state (i.e. a state of the Jews all over the world) into a socialist state representing the interests the masses who live in it':[205] a 'zero hour' of Israeli existence with a stance of equal status for both peoples. Significantly, the aspired transformation also implied a rectification of the dramatic demographic shifts that had followed the war over Israeli statehood. When it came to the 'most painful part of the Israeli–Arab dispute'– Palestinian refugees – the Israeli leftists asserted that, therefore, 'every refugee who wants to return to Israel must be enabled to do so'.[206] Any refugees who did not wish to return should be acknowledged and compensated for their property and for their personal and collective suffering. Yet just as the Israeli socialists' manifesto evinced an initial attempt to make amends for Palestinians' suffering due to the founding of the Jewish state, their proposal was equally linked to the objective of creating a new basis for the existence of Israeli Jews. After all, the Zionist settlement of Palestine was unique – and not only because of the colonial manifestation of the conflict with the Palestinian population. 'As a result of Zionist colonisation, a Hebrew nation with its own national characteristics (common language, separate economy, etc.) has been formed in Palestine', explained Weinstock, roughly outlining Matzpen's self-definition for the Arab audience. 'The solution [to] the Palestine problem must not only redress the wrong done to the Palestinian Arabs, but also ensure the national future of the Hebrew masses.'[207]

In some ways, the scenario of Algeria had illustrated the Israelis' own imperilled position to the Matzpen members themselves. This scenario now spawned a vision of an Israeli metamorphosis in the Israel–Palestine conflict – a vision that defied the true shape of history. Still, even in Algeria, the prospect of French Algerians being able to remain in the country did not seem as doomed at first as they would turn out to be. For example, Akiva Orr wrote (with the Palestine problem in mind):

> Despite all that had happened, the FLN [the Algerian liberation movement] asked most of the French settlers to stay in Algeria. The FLN leaders feared the damage that the withdrawal of all Europeans would cause. They fought against the French government and not against the French settlers in Algeria. Only after the French settlers themselves had birthed a movement under the slogan 'L'Algérie française', then clung to it even when the French government was ready to reach an agreement with the FLN, was there no escaping a clash between them and the FLN, which now demanded: 'independence for Algeria'.[208]

In that sense, the Algerian scenario seemed to symbolise more than a tragic example of decolonialisation. It also pointed to the unrealised possibilities for the continued existence of the European population in an Algeria no longer under European rule.[209] That made it especially astonishing that the Israeli socialists took their cue from Jean-Paul Sartre and his political activism regarding the Algerian War, hoping for inspiration when the philosopher travelled to Israel on the eve of the Six-Day War.[210] In choosing him as a reference point, they were blind to the fact that the doyen of the French Left in the Algerian conflict was not occupying middle ground at all. He was clearly taking a side, advocating unbridled anticolonialism and a forceful ejection of the French *colon*. Sartre's preface to Frantz Fanon's epochal *The Wretched of the Earth* testifies to this: 'to shoot down a European is to kill two birds with one stone, to destroy an oppressor and the man he oppresses at the same time: there remain a dead man, and a free man'.[211] The future of the French Algerians was not his cause. In this respect, Sartre differed from his counterpart Albert Camus, on whom Albert Memmi had modelled his portrait of the well-meaning or leftist coloniser.[212] Actually, the two founding fathers of French existentialism were divided by more than their ideological disagreement over the character of the French Communist Party, which Camus had left back in 1937, while Sartre remained in the party of Moscow loyalists until the late 1950s.[213] Their much deeper dispute was over the Algerian question. Born in Mondovi, Algeria, as a *pied noir*, Camus visibly dissociated himself from Sartre's anticolonial 'tabula rasa'. Contrary to Sartre's metropolitan perspective, Camus's sensitivity concerning the colonial dilemma came to a head when the Nobel Prize for Literature was awarded to Camus in 1957. When an Arab student asked Camus at a public event why he did not advocate unconditionally for the just cause of the Algerian struggle for independence, his classic response encapsulated his distinction from Sartre. 'I believe in justice', Camus replied, 'but I will defend my mother before justice'.[214] His mother, the child of Spanish immigrants from Menorca, was born in Algeria, her lifelong and only home, where she remained after her husband's early death and her son's later departure to Paris.

Camus was certainly no defender of the colonial status quo in the Algerian conflict. Rather, he wrote in a 'brief note' reflecting on the war raging in Algeria: 'The Arabs are right, and everyone in France knows they are right, to denounce and reject [the following]'.[215] His list of justifiable grievances includes '[c]olonialism and its abuses, which are institutional'[216] and – here in agreement with Sartre – the martyrdom of torture in France's bloodiest colonial war.[217] Camus was unequivocal that the 'Arab demands' for individual and collective equality, so long denied them by French central authorities, were 'perfectly legitimate'; furthermore, he insisted 'that the Algerian people deserve substantial reparations, both as a means of restoring their dignity and as a matter of justice'.[218] That was his call for an end to discrimination against Arab Algerians, an end to colonial inequality. But with his vision of a post-colonial Algeria, Camus had done more than break ranks with most *pieds noirs*, who showed scarcely any willingness to cede their privileges. As a 'colonial with anti-colonial sentiments', he did not want to imagine the Algeria of his youth without a future for French Algerians.[219] And so he was no less biting in his criticism of the Algerian FLN's anticolonial violence and its indiscriminate terrorist bombings aimed at driving away the *pieds noirs*, who, in his opinion, 'do not have the right to oppress anyone but do have the right not to be oppressed themselves, as well as the right to determine their own future in the land of their birth'.[220]

Camus's vision of a post-colonial Algeria relied on the potency of a new beginning. Hannah Arendt, who appreciated Camus, encapsulated this quality in her concept of 'natality', an anthropological constant whereby human beings are never altogether historically determined, but acquire through birth's new beginning the capacity to initiate something new. And because Arendt saw actions taken towards this horizon as a kind of 'second birth', each new generation bore the possibilities of a 'first man'.[221] *The First Man* was also Camus's title for his posthumous publication, a semi-autobiographical novel set in the Algeria of his childhood. It portrayed a generation of children who were born, through no fault of their own, into the colonial circumstances of a country on which they made no claims other than that of natural belonging by birth. Camus's literary alter ego observes that this generation grew up 'with no father, with no heritage handed down'[222] and only knew metropolitan France as a distant 'abstraction'.[223] Camus's autobiographical self therefore justifies his own existence in Algeria with his sheer presence in this 'country into which he felt he had been tossed, as if he were the first inhabitant', and in which he had put down 'tangled hidden roots that bound him to this magnificent and frightening land'.[224]

At the height of France's 'dirty colonial war', this sense of Algerian belonging allowed him to formulate his political utopia of a post-colonial Algeria. Besides calling for the elimination of inequality, he claimed a kind of birthright for French Algerians who 'have been in Algeria more than a century and number more than a million'.[225] Born into the political constellations of the country, the French of Algeria 'are themselves an indigenous population in the full sense of the word', Camus insisted. Even if they were 'foreign natives' – a neologism Dan Diner used to characterize Camus's existential situation – they, too, should be accorded a right to their Algerian homeland, which 'should not be secondary to that of the native natives'.[226] Thus, Camus's reflections produced a political utopia of a new Algeria shared by Europeans and Arabs, which would become a homeland for both and would recognise them as equals.

> I want to believe with all my heart that peace will dawn on our fields, our mountains, and our shores, and that Arabs and Frenchmen, reconciled in liberty and justice, will try hard to forget the bloodshed that divides them today.

Camus wrote this at the beginning of the Algerian War, concluding his open letter to the Algerian socialist Aziz Kessous. 'On that day, we who are together exiles in hatred and despair will together regain our native land.'[227]

By May 1967, five years after the same war had ended, when Nathan Weinstock read out the declaration by the Israeli Socialist Organization, Albert Camus had already died – in a car accident in 1960. He did not live to see the dreadful outcomes of Algeria's decolonisation, and his moderate voice was forgotten in the post-colonial reality of independent Algeria. Yet it may have seemed as though Weinstock was channelling the voice of an Israeli Albert Camus to the Arab audience: in a Camusian echo, Matzpen's declaration appealed for a public departure from the Zionist definition of the Jewish state, while struggling to obtain a guarantee of a post-Zionist recognition for Israeli Jews in the territory of former Mandatory Palestine. Besides, their situation was even more precarious than that of the Algerian *pieds noirs*, who at least nominally had recourse to a 'mother country', France. In his article engaging with the Palestinian Al-Ard movement, Meir Smorodinsky had previously emphasised that: 'Unlike the white settlers in Kenya, vis-à-vis Britain, [Israeli Jews] have no connection to a metropole'.[228] The Israeli leftists' statement was therefore especially insistent that, although the Zionist movement had sought the creation of a Jewish state for the Jewish people, a new generation of Israeli Jews had since emerged with independent life experiences and characteristics: a new Hebrew nation. The historical perspective of Matzpen members appeared to be revealing a chasm between the Zionist movement's political and ideological self-conceptions – that it was gathering all the groups of world Jewry on the territory of historical Palestine – and the reality of the country, where 'the cultural ties of the Israeli Jews to the Jewish communities in their various countries of origin' had begun to disintegrate.[229] This separation seemed capable of destroying the link between the origins of Zionist colonisation and its de facto outcome. As a result, it would offer Israeli Jews new prospects for recognition – no longer '*because* of Zionism, but *despite it*'.[230] The Paris statement declared, asserting the Israelis' right to self-determination: 'The argument that this nation was created artificially and at the expense of the native population does not change the fact that the Hebrew nation now exists. It would be a disastrous mistake to ignore that.'[231]

This idea of an emergent, breakaway Hebrew nation, in opposition to the concept of the unity of the Jewish people, was neither novel nor unique to Matzpen.[232] This argument reached deep into the history of the pre-state Yishuv and demonstrated how completely once-diasporic groups of Jews had transformed in their newfound territorialised nationhood. However, the novelty in Matzpen's assertion of a distinct Hebrew nation of Israeli Jews was its political renewal in the context of solving the Israel–Palestine conflict. The point of convergence was the emphasis on their cultural distinctness from diasporic Jewish groups, as a way of propelling a political separation from the institutional structures that uphold Israel as a Jewish state. This clean break was endowed with the power to rejustify a post-Zionist Israeli existence. At least outwardly – towards the Arab world – this new conceptual foundation seemed to have much greater legitimacy than all previous efforts to justify Israel as a Jewish state. Before long, Eli Lobel would repackage this founding principle of a new Israeli existence: 'It is only when one envisages continuing the Zionist process that one feels obligated to justify one's past.'[233] However, the turn against the perpetuation of Israel's Zionist history and identity, as revealed in their reference to a new 'Hebrew nation' grown out of the land, did more than liberate the Israeli leftists from the burden of having to justify the inherent violence entailed by the foundation of the Israeli state. Unlike all prior endeavours to legitimise the existence of the Jewish state among its Arab neighbours through either religion or history, the recourse to the reality-on-the-ground of a new Hebrew nation opened up prospects for universal validity.[234] On the mere grounds of their very existence as a distinct national assemblage, which now possessed native and no longer foreign status, Matzpen argued that they deserved recognition – from Palestinians and the Arab world as well.

Willingness to accept Israeli Jews as a distinct nationality became the Israeli leftists' baseline demand from the Arab world. 'If the problem of the existence of this nation is not solved correctly', declared Weinstock in Paris with a note of warning, 'a situation of dangerous and prolonged national conflict will be re-created, which will cause endless bloodshed and suffering'.[235] In light of the ongoing Israel–Palestine conflict and the threat that Arab nationalist movements would want to restore a pre-Zionist status quo ante, this appeal constituted more than an abstract demand. It also meant seeking allies in the Arab world, who, by recognising Israeli Jews proactively, would signal their willingness to coexist on level ground with another national community in the Arabs' midst. This, and only this, would enable the Israeli Jews to 'graduate' from the belief in the necessity of the Jewish state:

> In addition it should be understood that the Israeli masses will not be liberated from the influence of Zionism and will not struggle against it unless the progressive forces in the Arab world present them with a prospect of coexistence without national oppression.[236]

Hence, the manifesto Weinstock presented to his Arab audience in Paris ultimately led to a call for the Arab world to transform itself and transcend its own nationalism.

Confronting incipient Arab nationalism, Albert Camus had already formulated his utopia of a post-colonial Algeria in direct opposition to the demands of an independent Arab Algeria – in which he perceived the threat of a 'new Arab imperialism'.[237] He believed that a common future for Algerians of both French and Arab extraction would only be guaranteed by a larger federation, an 'authentic French Commonwealth', which would rise above both French colonialism and Arab nationalism within a unity of East and West.[238] This was contrary to Camus's unwitting successors among the Israeli Left, who could only imagine a future for Israeli Jewry within an Arab world constructed under the principles of unity and socialism.

> [Only] in such a framework the Hebrew nation will be able to carry on its own national and cultural life without endangering the Arab world and without a threat to its own existence by the Arabs.[239]

For all the superficial affinities, this vision of Arab unity brought together by socialism contrasted starkly with pan-Arab efforts under nationalist banners, such as Nassarism and the Syrian Baath party. Not only did the latter groups' ethno-religious basis for a united Arab world for an Arab people leave no space for the Israeli–Jewish nation, it repeatedly caused conflicts with other non-Arab minorities and nationalities in the region. Unsurprisingly, when contemplating the Arab world, Matzpen also took the side of the Kurdish nationalist movement in its struggle for national self-determination against Arab nationalism. On this point, the Paris declaration argues that it is no coincidence that 'those nationalist Arab leaders who call for a jihad for the liberation of Palestine [. . .] are also not capable of solving the Kurdish problem'.[240] In appealing for Arab unity brought together under socialism, they expressed their quest for a supraregional order that, culturally, would be predominantly Arab, but would recognise the various non-Arab minorities. Within that supranational framework, it seemed less relevant whether Palestinian Arabs' national self-determination and their attainment of recognition would entail establishing a distinct political entity or simply joining forces with a pan-Arabist national movement. Matzpen expressed a similar attitude towards the question concerning where the prospective border of the Israeli state would run. As Moshé Machover remembers:

> We thought (as we do now) in terms of a revolutionary solution, a socialist Israel integrated into a socialist Arab East. Within such a socialist state there would be a Hebrew-speaking autonomous part, whose borders would be internal borders inside the United Socialist Mashreq.[241]

When Nathan Weinstock presented Matzpen's call for 'establishing a socialist union of the Middle East' on 18 May 1967, these dreams were both dazzling and unrealistic. The manifesto concluded: 'The countries that now hold parts of the territory of Palestine – Israel, Jordan and Egypt – should particularly contribute to such a settlement.'[242] But by that day in late May, the next round of Israeli–Arab fighting was already looming and poised to shake the entire region anew. The Egyptian Army had recently begun to concentrate its forces on the Sinai Peninsula, from which UN troops had only recently withdrawn, and was making moves that overtly threatened the Jewish state. On 30 May, earlier threats of annihilation intensified with Nasser's announcement that, after Syria, he had now also gained Jordan as a military ally. Israel's Arab neighbours had joined forces against it, prompting the Israeli military to launch an attack on the morning of 5 June 1967.

The mood at the event in Paris was not unaffected by these impending developments. Many years later, Nathan Weinstock related that his presentation of the Matzpen resolution received scant attention amid the tense circumstances. The participants appear to have paid closer attention to the reports from Radio Cairo about the planned destruction of the Jewish state. 'Very naively, I was convinced that the Palestinian students would be happy to hear my pacifist message', he recalled. 'So I was astonished when not one of them showed the least interest in what I said.'[243] In hindsight, this was the first of many disappointments for Weinstock that would increasingly undermine his trust in Arabs' willingness to integrate the Israelis in the region and would finally usher in a political turn that drew him further and further from his former positions. Eventually, he became an historian with a focus on the displacement of Arab Jews from their longstanding home countries.[244]

Yet the military and political outcome of the Six-Day War would delay Weinstock's consternation by a few decades. More immediately, the effects of the overwhelming Israeli victory would shift the political and military power balance in the Middle East and restore the Palestine question as the focal point of the international debate. For one thing, the occupation of the West Bank and the Gaza Strip placed a much greater number of Palestinians under Israeli control than had been after the war of 1948. In parallel, Israelis' face-to-face exposure to the major Jewish historical and religious landmarks in the newly gained territories began to disrupt the secular, Hebrew definition of their Israeliness in which Matzpen's political vision was ultimately rooted.

Notes

1. Cover page, *Matzpen* 21 (1964).
2. For the historical context, see Morris, *Righteous Victims*, p. 301.
3. 'Discrimination, Suppression, Persecution', *Matzpen* 21 (1964), pp. 3–5 [Hebrew]; quoted from the abridged English translation: 'Al-Ard's Memorandum on the Arabs in Israel', in Jacob M. Landau, *The Arabs in Israel* (London: Oxford University Press, 1969), pp. 228–30 at p. 228.
4. 'Discrimination, Suppression, Persecution', p. 4. This part is not included in the English translation.
5. 'Al-Ard's Memorandum on the Arabs in Israel', p. 230.
6. Shmuel Segev, '"Al-Ard". A Solution to the Palestine Problem in Nasser's Style', *Ma'ariv* (14 July 1964), p. 10 [Hebrew].

7. 'Arab States Plan an Offensive Against Israel at the UN', *Herut* (29 July 1964), p. 1 [Hebrew].
8. Leena Dallasheh, 'Political Mobilization of Palestinians in Israel. The al-'Ard Movement', in Rhoda A. Kanaaneh and Isis Nusair (eds), *Displaced at Home: Ethnicity and Gender Among Palestinians in Israel* (New York: State University of New York Press, 2010), pp. 21–38, at pp. 28–30.
9. 'Discrimination, Suppression, Persecution'.
10. Landau, *The Arabs in Israel*, pp. 69–92.
11. On the history of 'Al-Ard', see Ibid., pp. 92–107; Dallasheh, 'Political Mobilization of Palestinians in Israel'; Ori Stendel, *Arabs in Israel* (Brighton: Sussex Academic, 1996), pp. 109–17.
12. Dallasheh, 'Political Mobilization of Palestinians in Israel', p. 22; Franz Ansprenger, *Juden und Araber in einem Land: Die politischen Beziehungen der beiden Völker im Mandatsgebiet Palästina und im Staat Israel* (München, Mainz: Kaiser; Grünewald, 1978), p. 108.
13. Dallasheh, 'Political Mobilization of Palestinians in Israel', p. 23; Stendel, *Arabs in Israel*, pp. 111–12; Beinin, *Was the Red Flag Flying There?*, p. 207.
14. 'Al-Ard's Memorandum on the Arabs in Israel', p. 229.
15. Dallasheh, 'Political Mobilization of Palestinians in Israel', pp. 26–9.
16. Quoted in Stendel, *Arabs in Israel*, pp. 111–12.
17. Quoted in Dallasheh, 'Political Mobilization of Palestinians in Israel', p. 30; Sabri Geries and Eli Lobel, *Die Araber in Israel* (Munich: Trikont-Verlag, 1970), pp. 171–2.
18. Dallasheh, 'Political Mobilization of Palestinians in Israel', p. 27.
19. Geries and Lobel, *Die Araber in Israel*, p. 170.
20. Yoel Dar, 'Al-Ard: A Small but Dangerous Group', *Davar* (30 July 1964), p. 3 [Hebrew].
21. Quoted in Dallasheh, 'Political Mobilization of Palestinians in Israel', p. 31.
22. Quoted in Geries and Lobel, *Die Araber in Israel*, p. 173.
23. Meir Smorodinsky (S. Meir), 'Al-Ard and Us', *Matzpen* 21 (1964), p. 5 [Hebrew].
24. Uri Ram, 'The Colonization Perspective in Israeli Sociology. Internal and External Comparisons', *Journal of Historical Sociology* 6: 3 (1993), pp. 327–50, at p. 329.
25. Meir Smorodinsky (S. Meir), 'Al-Ard and Us'.
26. Ibid.
27. 'The Suppression of "Al-Ard"', *Matzpen* 23 (1964), p. 8 [Hebrew].
28. Sneh, *On the National Question*, pp. 133–49 [Hebrew].
29. Moshé Machover, 'The Whitewashers', *Matzpen* 41 (1968), pp. 6–9, at p. 7; Eli Lobel, 'Die Juden und Palästina', in Eli Lobel and Sabri Geries, *Die Araber in Israel* (München: Trikont-Verlag, 1970), pp. 4–91, at p. 19.

30. Robert J. Alexander, 'Trotskyism in Israel', in Robert Alexander, *International Trotskyism, 1929-1985: A Documented Analysis of the Movement* (Durham: Duke University Press, 1991), pp. 577–85; Bunzl, *Israel im Nahen Osten*, pp. 93–106.
31. Benjamin Stora, *Algeria, 1830–2000: A Short History* (Ithaca: Cornell University Press, 2004), p. 111.
32. Oded Pilavsky, 'Easternization', *Matzpen* 23 (1964), p. 6 [Hebrew].
33. Shmuel Segev, 'Could There Be an Israeli "Algeria"?', *Ma'ariv* (24 November 1964), p. 7 [Hebrew].
34. Meir Smorodinsky (S. Meir), 'Al-Ard and Us'.
35. Moshé Machover, 'Preface to "Discrimination, Suppression, Persecution"', *Matzpen* 21 (1964), p. 3 [Hebrew].
36. Ibid.
37. Geries and Lobel, *Die Araber in Israel*, p. 130; Erel, *Without Fear and Prejudice*, pp. 221–2; on Mordechai Stein, see also Michael Keren, *Zichroni v. State of Israel: The Biography of a Civil Rights Lawyer* (Lanham, Boulder, New York: Lexington Books, 2002), pp. 55–71; F. El-Manssoury, 'Palestinians and Israelis', *Journal of Palestine Studies* 1/2: 5 (1975/6), pp. 115–26, at pp. 123–4; Dan Miodwonik, 'The Democratic Newspaper and Its Editor Mordechai Stein', *Kesher* 22 (1997), pp. 95–108 [Hebrew].
38. 'To the Jewish Public', *Matzpen* 19 (1964), p. 8 [Hebrew].
39. Meir Smorodinsky (S. Meir), 'Al-Ard and Us'.
40. 'Statement of Banished Maki Members from Haifa', *Matzpen* 14 (1964), p. 7 [Hebrew]; see also Machover, 'Matzpen. The Israeli Socialist Organisation', p. 309 [Hebrew].
41. Erel, *Matzpen*, p. 37; David Schnall, 'Organized Communism in Israel', *Midstream* 24: 7 (1978), pp. 26–36, at p. 29.
42. On Bulus Farah, see his autobiography: Bulus Farah, *From Ottoman Rule to a Hebrew State: The Life Story of a Communist and a Palestinian Patriot* (Haifa: Udi Adiv, 2009) [Hebrew].
43. Quoted in Leibovitz-Dar, 'The Days of Matzpen', p. 24 [Hebrew].
44. Bunzl, *Israel im Nahen Osten*, pp. 93–106.
45. Warschawski, *On the Border*, p. 24.
46. Ibid.
47. Quoted in Leibovitz-Dar, 'The Days of Matzpen', p. 24; see also Akiva Orr, 'He Was No Teacher, But We Learned a Lot From Him', *Matzpen* 73 (1975), pp. 12–13.
48. Jakob Taut, 'On the History of Trotskyism in Palestine. Interview with John Bunzl', *Intercontinental Press* 10: 38 (1972), pp. 1155–7, at p. 1155; the basic text on the history of Trotskyism in the British Mandate of Palestine and Israel is: Birchall, *Tony Cliff*, pp. 18–84; see also Alexander, 'Trotskyism in Israel'.

49. Jakob Moneta, 'Jakob Taut (1913–2001)', *SoZ – Sozialistische Zeitung* (8 November 2001), p. 15.
50. Ibid; for the historical context, see Theodor Bergmann, *"Gegen den Strom": Die Geschichte der KPD (Oppositon)* (Hamburg: VSA-Verlag, 2001).
51. Taut, 'On the History of Trotskyism in Palestine', p. 1155.
52. Ibid.
53. Alain Brossat and Sylvia Klingberg, *Revolutionary Yiddishland: A History of Jewish Radicalism*, 1st edn (London, New York: Verso, 2016), p. 250.
54. Jakob Moneta, 'Mehr Gewalt für die Ohnmächtigen', in Jakob Moneta, *Mehr Macht für die Ohnmächtigen: Reden und Aufsätze*, 1. Aufl. (Frankfurt am Main: ISP-Verl., 1991), pp. 111–26; see also Jan Gerber, *Verborgene Präsenzen: Gedächtnisgeschichte des Holocaust in der deutschsprachigen Arbeiter- und Gewerkschaftsbewegung, Böckler Forschungsmonitoring* (Düsseldorf: Hans-Böckler-Stiftung, 2009), vol. 9, pp. 67–72.
55. Moneta, 'Mehr Gewalt für die Ohnmächtigen', p. 113.
56. Ibid., pp. 115–19.
57. Jan Foitzik, *Zwischen den Fronten: Zur Politik, Organisation und Funktion linker politischer Kleinorganisationen im Widerstand 1933 bis 1939/40 unter besonderer Berücksichtigung des Exils, Politik- und Gesellschaftsgeschichte* (Bonn: Verl. Neue Gesellschaft, 1986), Bd. 16, p. 120.
58. Rudolf Segall, 'Cyrano von Bergerac und die Geduld des Revolutionärs. Ein Gespräch mit Rudolf Segall (II)', *Inprekorr* 416/17 (2006), pp. 23–9, at p. 23.
59. See Susan L. Hattis, *The Bi-National Idea in Palestine During Mandatory Times* (Haïfa: Shikmona Publishing, 1970).
60. Moneta, 'Mehr Gewalt für die Ohnmächtigen', pp. 117–18.
61. Ibid.
62. For the historical context, see Adi Gordon, 'Orient: Exile of the Last Europeans', *Mediterraneans / Méditerranéennes* 14 (2000), pp. 62–8.
63. Jakob Moneta, 'Jakob Moneta wird 85', *Avanti. Zeitung des RSB* 44 (1999), pp. 8–9.
64. Birchall, *Tony Cliff*, p. 5.
65. Ibid., p. 14; on the history of Brith Shalom, see Adi Gordon, *Brith Shalom and Bi-National Zionism: "The Arab Question" as a Jewish Question* (Jerusalem: Carmel, 2008) [Hebrew].
66. Birchall, *Tony Cliff*, pp. 16–17; see also Ygal Sarneh, 'A Revolutionary Life', *International Socialism Journal* 87 (2000).
67. See also his autobiography: Tony Cliff, *A World to Win: Life of a Revolutionary* (London: Bookmarks, 2000), p. 16.

68. Birchall, *Tony Cliff*, p. 23.
69. Ibid..
70. Jakob Moneta, 'Tony Cliff (1917–2000)', *SoZ – Sozialistische Zeitung* (11 May 2000), p. 15.
71. See Birchall, *Tony Cliff*, pp. 69–79.
72. Taut, 'On the History of Trotskyism in Palestine', p. 1155.
73. Moneta, 'Tony Cliff (1917–2000)'.
74. Quoted in Birchall, *Tony Cliff*, p. 51.
75. See Moneta, 'Mehr Gewalt für die Ohnmächtigen'.
76. Moneta, 'Jakob Moneta wird 85'.
77. Moshé Machover, 'Comrade Jabra Nicola (1912-1974)', in Moshé Machover, *Israelis and Palestinians: Conflict and Resolutions* (Chicago: Haymarket Books, 2012), pp. 7–10, at p. 7.
78. Aharon Cohen, 'Portrait of a Helpless Revolutionary', *Emdah* 7 (1975), pp. 20–1, 25; 'Pioneer Palestinian Revolutionist. Jabra Nicola (1912-1974)', *Intercontinental Press* 13: 3 (1975), pp. 95–6.
79. 'Pioneer Palestinian Revolutionist', p. 95; see also Ran Greenstein, 'Palestinian Revolutionary. Jabra Nicola and the Radical Left', *The Jerusalem Quarterly* 46 (2011), pp. 32–48.
80. Merav Mack, 'Orthodox and Communist. A History of a Christian Community in Mandate Palestine and Israel', *British Journal of Middle Eastern Studies* 42: 4 (2015), pp. 384–400.
81. Cohen, 'Portrait of a Helpless Revolutionary', p. 20.
82. Keren, *Zichroni v. State of Israel*, pp. 55–71; Miodwonik, 'The Democratic Newspaper and Its Editor Mordechai Stein'. In 1972, Matzpen dedicated the English-language publication *The Other Israel* to Jabra Nicola and Mordechai Stein, and Akiva Orr also dedicated his later book, *Israel. Politics, Myths and Identity Crisis*, to Nicola and Stein.
83. Birchall, *Tony Cliff*, p. 58; Cohen, 'Portrait of a Helpless Revolutionary', p. 20; see also Greenstein, 'Palestinian Revolutionary', p. 36; Farah, *From Ottoman Rule to a Hebrew State*, pp. 60–2.
84. Musa Budeiri, *The Palestine Communist Party 1919-1948: Arab and Jew in the Struggle for Internationalism* (Chicago: Haymarket Books, 2010), p. 193, note 206; Cohen, 'Portrait of a Helpless Revolutionary', pp. 21 and 25.
85. Greenstein, 'Palestinian Revolutionary', p. 36; Shmuel Dotan, *Reds: The Communist Party in Eretz Yisrael* (Kfar Saba: Shevna Hasofer, 1991), pp. 417–18; 'Pioneer Palestinian Revolutionist', p. 96.
86. Taut, 'On the History of Trotskyism in Palestine', p. 1156.

87. Quoted in Brossat and Klingberg, *Revolutionary Yiddishland*, p. 251.
88. Birchall, *Tony Cliff*, p. 64.
89. Ibid., p. 63.
90. Taut, 'On the History of Trotskyism in Palestine', p. 1156.
91. Moneta, 'Jakob Taut (1913–2001)'.
92. Birchall, *Tony Cliff*, p. 61; 'Dov Shas (1925–2006). Obituary', *Revolutionary History* 10: 1 (2006).
93. Revolutionary Communist League, 'Against Partition!', *Kol Hamaamad* 31 (1947) [Hebrew]; Revolutionary Communist League, 'Against the Stream. The Trotskyist Position in Palestine', *Fourth International* 9: 3 (85) (1948), pp. 86–9.
94. International Secretariat of the Fourth International, 'Draft Theses on the Jewish Question Today', *Fourth International* 9: 1 (83) (1948), pp. 18–24.
95. Ibid.
96. Revolutionary Communist League, 'Against the Stream', p. 87.
97. Ibid., pp. 87–8.
98. Ibid., p. 88.
99. Ibid.
100. Taut, 'On the History of Trotskyism in Palestine', p. 1156.
101. See the chapter 'Socialism or Barbarism'.
102. Gerber, *Verborgene Präsenzen*, vol. 9.
103. Moneta, 'Mehr Gewalt für die Ohnmächtigen', p. 121.
104. Segall, 'Cyrano von Bergerac und die Geduld des Revolutionärs', p. 23; see also Birchall, *Tony Cliff*, p. 82.
105. Segall, 'Cyrano von Bergerac und die Geduld des Revolutionärs'.
106. Moneta, 'Mehr Gewalt für die Ohnmächtigen', p. 122.
107. Jakob Moneta, 'Selbstverfasster Lebenslauf (1977)', in Jakob Moneta, *Mehr Macht für die Ohnmächtigen: Reden und Aufsätze*, 1. Aufl. (Frankfurt am Main: ISP-Verl., 1991), pp. 133–5.
108. Claus Leggewie, *Kofferträger: Das Algerien-Projekt der Linken im Adenauer-Deutschland* (Berlin: Rotbuch-Verl., 1984) [German].
109. Jakob Moneta, 'Erinnerungen an die Algeriensolidarität. Ein Kofferträger', *SoZ – Sozialistische Zeitung* (February 2005), p. 20.
110. Birchall, *Tony Cliff*, p. 84.
111. Ibid., pp. 85–127; Moneta, 'Tony Cliff (1917–2000)'.
112. Gabriel Baer (S. Munier), 'Zionism and the Middle East. The Aftermath of the Jewish-Arab War', *Fourth International* 10: 9 (99) (1949), pp. 277–83, at p. 280; see Greenstein, 'Palestinian Revolutionary', p. 38.

113. Thomas Philipp, 'In Memoriam: Gabriel Baer 1919–1982', *Middle Eastern Studies* 19: 3 (1983), pp. 275–6.
114. Quoted in Birchall, *Tony Cliff*, p. 57.
115. Jakob Taut, *Judenfrage und Zionismus*, 1. Aufl. (Frankfurt/M.: Isp-Verlag, 1986), pp. 122–5; Brossat and Klingberg, *Revolutionary Yiddishland*, pp. 257–8.
116. Brossat and Klingberg, *Revolutionary Yiddishland*, pp. 257–8; Moneta, 'Jakob Taut (1913–2001)'.
117. Michel Warschawski, quoted in Erel, *Matzpen*, p. 35.
118. Moneta, 'Jakob Taut (1913–2001)'.
119. Taut, *Judenfrage und Zionismus*, pp. 122–5.
120. Taut, 'On the History of Trotskyism in Palestine', p. 1156.
121. 'Pioneer Palestinian Revolutionist', p. 96.
122. Cohen, 'Portrait of a Helpless Revolutionary', pp. 21 and 25.
123. Ibid., p. 20.
124. Sasson Somekh, '"Reconciling Two Great Loves". The First Jewish-Arab Literary Encounter in Israel', *Israel Studies* 4: 1 (1999), pp. 1–21, at pp. 3 and 10.
125. Ernest Mandel, *Revolutionary Marxism Today* (London, New York: NLB, 1979), p. XII; quoted in Birchall, *Tony Cliff*, p. 59.
126. Taut, 'On the History of Trotskyism in Palestine', pp. 1156–7.
127. Machover, 'Matzpen. The Israeli Socialist Organisation', pp. 308–9.
128. Michael Bar-Zohar, *Ben-Gurion: A Biography* (Tel Aviv: Magal Books, [1978] 2003), pp. 267–8.
129. Frank Renken, 'Kleine Geschichte des Algerienkriegs', in Christiane Kohser-Spohn and Frank Renken (eds), *Trauma Algerienkrieg: Zur Geschichte und Aufarbeitung eines tabuisierten Konflikts* (Frankfurt am Main, New York: Campus, 2006), pp. 25–50.
130. Ibid., p. 44.
131. Michael Bar-Zohar, *Ben Gurion*, 3 vols (Tel Aviv: Am Oved, 1975), vol. 3, at p. 1382 [Hebrew]; the English translation of Bar-Zohar's biography does not contain this passage. Quoted from Dan Diner, *Israel in Palästina: Über Tausch und Gewalt im Vorderen Orient* (Königstein/Ts.: Athenäum, 1980), p. 259, note 111.
132. Bar-Zohar, *Ben-Gurion*, p. 268.
133. Eric Rouleau, 'Die französische Nahost-Politik', *Europa-Archiv* 23: 5 (1968), pp. 149–70, at pp. 149 and 154.
134. 'Concern over Ahmed Ben Bella's "Declaration of War" Against Israel', *Davar* (12 April 1962), p. 1 [Hebrew]; quoted from Laskier, 'Israel and Algeria amid French Colonialism and the Arab-Conflict. 1954-1978', p. 12.

135. Raphael Danziger, 'Algeria and the Palestinian Organisations', in Gabriel Ben-Dor (ed.), *The Palestinians and the Middle East Conflict: An International Conference Held at the Institute of Middle Eastern Studies, University of Haifa, April 1976* (Ramat Gan: Turtledove Publishing, 1976), pp. 347–73, at p. 352.
136. Here quoted from the Hebrew translation, which appeared two days later in the newspaper *Davar*: Israel Neumann, 'Ben-Gurion Rejects the Comparison Between the Algerian Problem and Eretz Israel', *Davar* (7 January 1962), p. 1 [Hebrew].
137. Moshé Machover and Akiva Orr (Israeli, N.), 'Israel-Arab Peace, How?', *Matzpen* 11 (1963), p. 4 [Hebrew].
138. Moshé Machover and Akiva Orr (Israeli, N.), 'Nationalism and the Israeli-Arab Conflict', *Matzpen* 16 (1964), pp. 6–7, at p. 6 [Hebrew].
139. Ibid.
140. Meir Smorodinsky (Meir, S.), 'The Root of the Conflict. Zionism versus Arab Nationalism', *Matzpen* 23 (1964), p. 6 [Hebrew].
141. Eli Lobel, 'Palestine and the Jews', in Ahmad el Kodsy and Eli Lobel, *The Arab World and Israel* (New York: Monthly Review, 1970), pp. 63–137, at p. 131.
142. Meir Smorodinsky (Meir, S.), 'The Root of the Conflict'.
143. Dan Diner, 'Cumulative Contingency. Historicizing Legitimacy in Israeli Discourse', *History and Memory* 7: 1 (1995), pp. 147–70, at p. 162.
144. Meir Smorodinsky (Meir, S.), 'The Root of the Conflict'.
145. Quoted in Diner, *Israel in Palästina*, p. 48. Hannah Arendt also asserted in 1945 that the 'social revolutionary Jewish national movement' had been 'started half a century ago with ideals so lofty that it overlooked the particular realities of the Near East', mainly referring to the Arab–Jewish conflict. Arendt, 'Zionism Reconsidered', p. 351.
146. Gershon Shafir, *Land, Labor, and the Origins of the Israeli-Palestinian Conflict, 1882-1914* (Berkeley: University of California Press, 1996), p. XI; see also Dan Diner, 'Materialismus, Fortschritt und Utopie. Elemente europäischer Geistesgeschichte im Zionismus', in Karl-Heinz Schneider (ed.), *Der Zionismus und seine europäischen Wurzeln: Dokumentation einer Arbeitstagung in der Evangelischen Akademie Arnoldshain, November 1986*, Schriften / Deutsch-Israelischer Arbeitskreis für Frieden im Nahen Osten (Edenkoben: DIAK, 1987), pp. 37–53.
147. Aharon Cohen, *Israel and the Arab World* (Merhavia: Sifriyat Poalim, 1964); the English translation was published six years later. Aharon Cohen, *Israel and the Arab World* (London: W. H. Allen, 1970).

148. Moshé Machover and Akiva Orr (Israeli, N.), '"Double Misunderstanding". Review of Aharon Cohen's book "Israel and the Arab World"', *Matzpen* 22 (1964), pp. 4–6.
149. Quoted from the English translation: Cohen, *Israel and the Arab World*, p. 235.
150. Machover and Orr (Israeli, N.), '"Double Misunderstanding"', p. 5.
151. See Gershon Shafir, 'Settler Citizenship in the Jewish Colonization of Palestine', in Caroline Elkins and Susan Pedersen (eds), *Settler Colonialism in the Twentieth Century: Projects, Practices, Legacies* (New York: Routledge, 2005), pp. 41–57, at p. 42: 'In 1904 Menachem Ussishkin, one of the central eastern European Zionist leaders, asked rhetorically: "In order to establish autonomous Jewish community life – or, to be more precise, a Jewish state – in Eretz Israel, it is necessary, first of all, that all, or at least most, of Eretz Israel's land will be the property of the Jewish people. Without ownership of the land, Eretz Israel will never become Jewish [. . .] and Jews will remain in the very same abnormal situation which characterises them in the diaspora. They will be without a recognized status. But, as the ways of the world go, how does one acquire landed property? By one of the following three methods: by force – that is, by conquest in war, or in other words, by robbing land of its owner; by forceful acquisition, that is, by expropriation via governmental authority; and by purchase with the owner's consent." Ussishkin ruled out the first method as being "totally ungodly," although significantly he also added that "we are too weak for it." He did not expect Jewish settlers to receive a charter to expropriate land owned by either Arab peasants or landowners. "In sum," he inferred, "the only method to acquire Eretz Israel [Palestine], at any time and under whatever political conditions, is by purchase with money." The dependence of land accumulation for settlement on purchase led to a "low frontierity" in Palestine, resulting in Jewish ownership of only about 7 percent of Palestine by 1948.'
152. Moshé Machover and Akiva Orr (Israeli, N.), 'Hold me. . .', *Matzpen* 25 (1965), p. 2 [Hebrew]. See also Diner, *Israel in Palästina*, pp. 38–64; Baruch Kimmerling, *Zionism and Territory: The Socio-Territorial Dimensions of Zionist Politics* (Berkeley: Institute of International Studies, University of California, 1983).
153. Machover and Orr (Israeli, N.), '"Double Misunderstanding"', p. 5.
154. Anita Shapira, 'The Origins of "Jewish Labor" Ideology', *Studies in Zionism* 3: 1 (1982), pp. 93–112.
155. Machover and Orr (Israeli, N.), '"Double Misunderstanding"', p. 5.
156. Ibid., p. 6.

157. Vladimir (Z.'e.) Jabotinsky, 'The Iron Wall', http://en.jabotinsky.org/media/9747/the-iron-wall.pdf (accessed 30 March 2020) [English translation].
158. Ibid.
159. Israeli Socialist Organization (Matzpen), 'The Palestine Problem. Thesis Submitted for Discussion in August 1966', in Arie Bober (ed.), *The Other Israel: The Radical Case Against Zionism* (Garden City: Doubleday, 1972), pp. 35–53, at p. 47 [first: The Israeli Socialist Organization, *The Other Israel. Israeli Critique of Zionist History and Policy*, Tel Aviv (July 1948), pp. 1–8].
160. Avi Shlaim, 'The Iron Wall Revisited', *Journal of Palestine Studies* 41: 2 (2012), pp. 80–98.
161. Michael Brecher, *The Foreign Policy System of Israel: Setting, Images, Process* (London: Oxford University Press, 1972), p. 284.
162. Nahum Goldmann, *The Jewish Paradox* (New York: Grosset & Dunlap, 1978), pp. 99–100.
163. Quoted in Brecher, *The Foreign Policy System of Israel*, p. 284.
164. Goldmann, *The Jewish Paradox*, p. 99.
165. On the different meanings of post-Zionism, see Tom Segev, *Elvis in Jerusalem: Post-Zionism and the Americanization of Israel*, 1st American edn (New York: Metropolitan Books, 2002).
166. Moshé Machover, 'The Jewish Affinity and the Aliah', *Matzpen* 32 (1967), p. 9 [Hebrew].
167. See Shmuel N. Eisenstadt, *Israeli Society*, The Nature of Human Society Series (London: Weidenfeld and Nicolson, 1967), pp. 394–7.
168. Ibid., p. 396.
169. Israeli Socialist Organization (Matzpen), 'The Palestine Problem', p. 49.
170. Quoted from Emmanuel Dror, 'The Emergency Regulations', in Arie Bober (ed.), *The Other Israel: The Radical Case Against Zionism* (Garden City: Doubleday, 1972), pp. 134–44, at p. 138.
171. Oded Pilavsky, 'Zionism's Most Valuable Fund', *Matzpen* 30 (1966), p. 5 [Hebrew].
172. Eisenstadt, *Israeli Society*, p. 395: 'Nonetheless, a certain asymmetry developed between Jewish and Arab (or any other minority) groups rooted in the very essence of the State of Israel. This was evident from the fact that under the "Law of Return" citizenship was open to all Jews who wanted to come to Israel but was limited to all other groups, to residents or those who obtained special permission to settle.'
173. Meir Smorodinsky (S. Meir), 'The Lesson of Nazareth Illit', *Matzpen* 24 (1965), p. 5 [Hebrew].

174. M. Gouldman, *Israel Nationality Law* (Jerusalem: Institute for Legislative Research and Comparative Law, 1970), pp. 21 and 25.
175. Machover, 'The Jewish Affinity and the Aliah'.
176. Meir Smorodinsky (S. Meir), 'The Lesson of Nazareth Illit'.
177. Ibid.
178. Pilavsky, 'Easternization'.
179. I. Ron, 'Shameful Politics', *Matzpen* 24 (1965), p. 2 [Hebrew].
180. Meir Smorodinsky (Meir, S.), 'The Root of the Conflict'.
181. Memmi, *The Colonizer and the Colonized*, pp. 63–88.
182. Ibid., p. 80.
183. Albert Memmi, 'Camus ou le colonisateur de bonne volonté', *La Nef* (12 December 1957), pp. 95–6.
184. Oded Pilavsky, 'On the Zionist Movement', *Matzpen* 14 (1964), p. 5 [Hebrew].
185. Memmi, *The Colonizer and the Colonized*, p. 83.
186. Ibid., pp. 70 and 84.
187. For the concept of the 'foreign native', see Diner, 'Post-postkoloniale Flaschenpost', p. 237.
188. Uri Dan, '500 Arab Students Held a "Palestine Day" in Paris', *Ma'ariv* (19 May 1967), p. 27 [Hebrew].
189. Ibid.
190. Nathan Weinstock, 'Das Bekenntnis eines ehemaligen Antizionisten', https://www.hagalil.com/archiv/2006/09/weinstock.htm (accessed 9 April 2020). First published in: *L'Arche*, 579–80 (Juli–August 2006).
191. Israeli Socialist Organization (Matzpen), 'The Palestine-Problem and the Israeli-Arab Dispute, 18 May 1967'. First published in: *World Outlook* 22: 5 (2 June 1967); *Matzpen* 36 (1967) [Hebrew].
192. 'Le sionisme et Israël sont dénoncés au cours d'une réunion a la mutualité', *Le Monde* (20 May 1967).
193. Adi Schwartz, 'Point of No Return: Jewish Refugees from Arab and Muslim Countries (Part II)', http://jewishrefugees.blogspot.com/2014/05/weinstock-mass-jewish-flight-was.html (accessed 9 April 2020).
194. Nathan Weinstock, *Le sionisme contre Israël* (Paris: F. Maspero, 1969).
195. Henryk M. Broder, 'Weinstock wird erwachsen', https://www.achgut.com/artikel/weinstock/ (accessed 28 July 2020); Simon Rocker, 'Meet the Trotskyist anti-Zionist Who Saw the Errors of His Ways', *The Jewish Chronicle* (4 December 2014), https://www.thejc.com/news/uk/meet-the-trotskyist-anti-zionist-who-saw-the-errors-of-his-ways-1.62661 (accessed 30 July 2020).

196. Nathan Weinstock, *Das Ende Israels?: Nahostkonflikt und Geschichte des Zionismus*, ed. by Eike Geisel and Mario Offenberg (Berlin: Wagenbach, 1975).
197. Nathan Weinstock, *Zionism: False Messiah* (London: Ink Links Ltd, 1979).
198. Israeli Socialist Organization (Matzpen), 'The Palestine-Problem and the Israeli-Arab Dispute, 18 May 1967', p. 209.
199. Israeli Socialist Organization (Matzpen), 'Preface to the Declaration on the Palestine Problem and the Israeli-Arab Conflict', *Matzpen* 36 (1967), p. 2 [Hebrew].
200. Ibid.
201. Israeli Socialist Organization (Matzpen), 'The Palestine-Problem and the Israeli-Arab Dispute, 18 May 1967', p. 212.
202. Akiva Orr (A. Oved), 'Zionism: Theory and Practice', *Matzpen* 24 (1965), p. 8 [Hebrew].
203. Moshé Machover (Mor, Israel), 'Refugees and Immigrants', *Matzpen* 29 (1966), p. 9 [Hebrew].
204. Israeli Socialist Organization (Matzpen), 'The Palestine-Problem and the Israeli-Arab Dispute, 18 May 1967', p. 210.
205. Ibid.
206. Ibid.
207. Ibid., p. 211.
208. Orr, 'Zionism. Theory and Practice', p. 8 [Hebrew].
209. See also Maxime Rodinson, *Israel: A Colonial-Settler State?* (New York: Monad Press; distributed by Pathfinder Press, 1973), p. 88: 'The colonial origins of the Algerien Pieds Noirs did not prevent the FLN from recognizing their rights, and their departure was not the result of expulsion but of their inability to adapt to the new situation or of their refusal to accept the situation.'
210. 'Editorial: Apropos Sartre', *Matzpen* 34 (1967), pp. 2 and 10, at p. 10 [Hebrew].
211. Jean-Paul Sartre, 'Preface', in Frantz Fanon, *The Wretched of the Earth* (London: Penguin Books, [1961] 2001), pp. 7–26, at p. 19.
212. Memmi, 'Camus ou le colonisateur de bonne volonté'.
213. Detlev Mares, 'Der Bruch zwischen Sartre und Camus. Ein Beitrag zur politischen Kultur Frankreichs zur Zeit des Kalten Krieges', *Französisch heute* 26 (1995), pp. 38–51.
214. Patrick McCarthy, *Camus: A Critical Study of His Life and Work* (London: Hamilton, 1982), p. 294.
215. Albert Camus, 'Algeria 1958', in Albert Camus, *Algerian Chronicles*, 1st Harvard University Press edn (Cambridge, MA: Belknap Press of Harvard University Press, 2014), pp. 175–80, at pp. 175–6.

216. Ibid., p. 176.
217. Albert Camus, 'Preface', in Albert Camus, *Algerian Chronicles*, 1st Harvard University Press edn (Cambridge, MA: Belknap Press of Harvard University Press, 2014), pp. 23–35.
218. Camus, 'Algeria 1958', p. 176.
219. Diner, 'Post-postkoloniale Flaschenpost', p. 235.
220. Camus, 'Preface', p. 35.
221. Hannah Arendt, *The Human Condition*, 2nd edn (Chicago: University of Chicago Press, [1958] 1998), p. 176; see also Seyla Benhabib, *The Reluctant Modernism of Hannah Arendt*, 2 edn (Lanham: Rowman & Littlefield, 2003), pp. 107–13.
222. Albert Camus, *The First Man* (Toronto: Alfred A. Knopf Canada, 1995), p. 278.
223. Ibid., p. 208.
224. Ibid., pp. 279 and 281.
225. Albert Camus, 'Letter to an Algerian Militant', in Albert Camus, *Algerian Chronicles*, 1st Harvard University Press edn (Cambridge, MA: Belknap Press of Harvard University Press, 2014), pp. 113–16, at p. 114.
226. Diner, 'Post-postkoloniale Flaschenpost', p. 237; see also Carroll, 'Camus's Algeria. Birthrights, Colonial Injustice, and the Fiction of a French-Algerian People', pp. 517–49.
227. Camus, 'Letter to an Algerian Militant', p. 116.
228. Meir Smorodinsky (S. Meir), 'Al-Ard and Us'.
229. Jabra Nicola (Said, A.) and Moshé Machover, 'Arab Revolution and National Problems in the Arab East (Summer 1973)', in Moshé Machover, *Israelis and Palestinians: Conflict and Resolutions* (Chicago: Haymarket Books, 2012), pp. 19–25, at p. 23 [first: *Matzpen* 64 (1972)].
230. Dan Diner, 'Israel. Nationalstaatsproblem und Nahostkonflikt', in Wolfgang Benz and Hermann Graml, *Weltprobleme zwischen den Machtblöcken: Das Zwanzigste Jahrhundert III*, Fischer-Weltgeschichte (Frankfurt: Fischer Taschenbuch Verlag, 1981), pp. 165–212, at p. 201 (emphasis in original).
231. Israeli Socialist Organization (Matzpen), 'The Palestine-Problem and the Israeli-Arab Dispute, 18 May 1967', p. 211.
232. See the next chapter, 'The Invention of a Hebrew Nation'.
233. Eli Lobel, 'Military Escalation within Israeli Society', in Arie Bober (ed.), *The Other Israel: The Radical Case Against Zionism* (Garden City: Doubleday, 1972), pp. 65–78, at p. 78 [first: 'L'escalade à l'intérieur de la société israélienne', in: *Partisans* 52 (1970)].

234. Dan Diner, 'Sprachlos am Zaun. Israels Existenz hat drei Begründungen', *Die Zeit* 31 (2002).
235. Israeli Socialist Organization (Matzpen), 'The Palestine-Problem and the Israeli-Arab Dispute, 18 May 1967', p. 211.
236. Ibid.
237. Camus, 'Algeria 1958', p. 178.
238. Albert Camus, 'The New Algeria', in Albert Camus, *Algerian Chronicles*, 1st Harvard University Press edition (Cambridge, MA: Belknap Press of Harvard University Press, 2014), pp. 181–4, at pp. 182–3. See also Neil Foxlee, *Albert Camus's "The New Mediterranean Culture": A Text and its Contexts*, Modern French Identities (Bern: Peter Lang, 2010), v. 38.
239. Israeli Socialist Organization (Matzpen), 'The Palestine-Problem and the Israeli-Arab Dispute, 18 May 1967', p. 212.
240. Ibid., p. 211.
241. Machover, 'Matzpen. The Israeli Socialist Organisation', p. 314.
242. Israeli Socialist Organization (Matzpen), 'The Palestine-Problem and the Israeli-Arab Dispute, 18 May 1967', p. 213.
243. Quoted in Adi Schwartz, 'The Inconvenient Truth about Jews from Arab Lands. Interview with Nathan Weinstock', *Haaretz* (29 May 2014).
244. Weinstock, 'Das Bekenntnis eines ehemaligen Antizionisten'; see also Nathan Weinstock, *Der zerrissene Faden: Wie die arabische Welt ihre Juden verlor: 1947–1967* (Freiburg: ça-ira-Verlag, 2019).

3

The Invention of a Hebrew Nation

'One Day, Two Declarations'[1]

On 20 July 1967, five weeks after the end of the Six-Day War, *Haaretz* printed a letter to the editor by Shimon Tzabar (1926–2007), one of the paper's contributing writers and a well-known figure throughout the country. Long before Tzabar inherited a weekly column in *Haaretz* and began drawing the comic strip *HaKelev va'ani* (The Dog and I), the artist and satirist had made a name for himself in Israel as a children's book author and a columnist for the weekly newspaper *Haolam Hazeh*. He had also drawn some of his satirical cartoons for *Matzpen*.[2] But after the military victory, the subsequent annexation of East Jerusalem and the occupation of the Sinai Peninsula, the Golan Heights, the Gaza Strip and the West Bank, Tzabar confronted the Israeli public with a tone of cynical confrontation. In his letter, with the headline 'Two Questions', he unpicked two Israeli national narratives that had collided during the most recent war and its conquests. Tzabar's first question began: 'For nineteen years now, we've wanted nothing but peace with the neighbours. [. . .] We've only wanted them to recognise our right to exist and to reconcile themselves with it.' But now the Israelis' language and sense of self after their country's military defeat of the Arab armies seemed to be undoing, even debunking, this long-held posture:

> Why else are we suddenly calling territory occupied by our own hands 'liberated territory'? [. . .] Why has the prime minister, on his trip to the Western Wall, announced that we were 'awaiting this for twenty years'? Were our promises before the last war only pretences for the sake of confounding the enemy?[3]

Tzabar's second rhetorical question was another sharp takedown:

> And now I would like to know whether we've truly liberated everything. I would like to know whether there are other territories that belong to us outside and beyond the current borders of the State that have not yet been liberated, or whether with the recent occupations we have taken under our wings everything that we consider our own and we no longer have territorial claims against our neighbours?[4]

Tzabar had no doubts: Israelis' sense of self and their definition of their own territory were also determining factors regarding what future policies to pursue towards their Arab neighbours and whether the country needed to prepare for another war. The question of Israel's identity, he asserted, was directly linked to the country's existence.

Tzabar's letter provoked not a few letters of indignation from *Haaretz* readers. Suggestions aiming at curing the author of his naïveté about the Arab states were soon followed by demands that the paper drop his column.[5] But as polemical as Tzabar's questions might have seemed, in view of the widespread sigh of relief that followed Egypt's threats of destruction, these questions about the shifting idea of Israeliness were essentially responding to Israeli society's collective 'meeting with a deeper, forgotten self' as it came face to face with the newly occupied territories.[6] The conquest of the Old City of Jerusalem and the advance to the ruins of the Second Temple's Western Wall, along with the military occupation of the biblical regions of Judea and Samaria, had an impact on many Israeli Jews, not only those who identified as religious. The Chief Rabbi of the Defence Force, Shlomo Goren, was the first to rush to the Kotel HaMaaravi (Western Wall) with his shofar after the advance into the Old City, sanctifying the return to the Jewish holy places.[7] But the encounter with the newly gained territories prompted what Maurice Samuel called a 'shock of self-identification' for secular Israelis in particular.[8] The new political and territorial circumstances revealed the secularised – but still religious – substance inherent in the Zionist movement's political vocabulary, while adding a new divine justification for Israel's existence on the territory of historical Palestine. In short, Israelis were becoming more Jewish again.

Yet the Israeli government had waged the war as one of self-defence, by no means based on a sacred justification or as a war of conquest. If the government had ever entertained the possibility of territorial expansion in the past, it was only as a potential bargaining chip for post-war negotiations with neighbouring Arab states – a new basis for trading 'land for peace'.[9] However, when such a conquest came to pass, the reality of beholding this historic and religiously significant land unleashed a new dynamic. Only 48 hours after the newly appointed Defence Minister Moshe Dayan had railed against the seizure of East Jerusalem and its historical sites, saying Israel did not need 'that Vatican', Dayan found himself standing at the Western Wall and declaring that the Israeli Army had 'returned to our holiest places [. . .] so as not to abandon them forever'.[10] With a clash looming, Dayan made sure that no Israeli flag was planted on the Temple Mount, thus laying the groundwork for Jordan's future authority over the site.[11] But this detail did not dampen the Jewish holy sites' impact on the Israeli consciousness. When the Israeli cabinet passed its 'land for peace' strategy, Jerusalem, the West Bank and the Gaza Strip were for various reasons excluded from the initial government offer to the Arab states.[12] Apart from all national security considerations, the military victory of 1967 appeared to reignite a sacred ember of Israeli politics that for years had appeared to have been snuffed out by the declaration of statehood. Thus, Shimon Tzabar's letter to the editor was written in response to this flashbulb moment, which had abruptly exposed the religious underpinnings of purportedly secular policies.

This creeping redefinition of the collective self found a prominent trailblazer and radical embodiment in Nathan Alterman, the poet of Israeli Labour Zionism. As a committed advocate of 'rational Zionism', who for years had demanded the acceptance of Israel's 1949 armistice borders, he was thoroughly converted by this encounter with the newly conquered territories.[13] In his columns for *Maariv*, written immediately after the war, the poet emphasised that the military victory had 'erased the division between the State of Israel and the Land of Israel', and that the Jewish people had now returned to their historical roots. Alterman repudiated anyone who called the conquered areas 'occupied territories'. As he saw it, the territories 'occupy us. They embrace us in the arms of the past and future and we are not free men to detach ourselves from them either willingly or through decision.'[14]

The bedrock beneath the Movement for Greater Israel (Ha-Tenu'ah Le-Ma'an Erez Israel Ha-Shelemah) and its mission was, likewise, imbued with sacred meanings. This group was founded only a few weeks after the war to demand that the territories under military occupation be officially annexed, and Alterman became one of its figureheads.[15] On 22 September 1967, it presented the Israeli public with a manifesto complete with fifty-seven signatories who were members of the Israeli popular intellectual elite, including the poets Shmuel Yosef Agnon, Haim Hazaz and Uri Zvi Greenberg, along with numerous representatives of the country's public sector. An important share of the signatures came from disillusioned Labour Zionists, who had once arrived in Palestine from the Diaspora full of sweeping youthful idealism.[16] The group was also supported by some right-wing Zionists, including both Israel Eldad, one of the three leaders of the pre-state Lohamei Herut Israel (Lehi), who had written a paper titled 'Conquering the Land as a Moral Act' the year before the occupation,[17] and Eri Jabotinsky, the son of Zionist Revisionism's founder Vladimir Jabotinsky. United behind a common cause, the signatories began their manifesto with the assertion that the Israeli Army's victory had inaugurated a new era, for '[t]he whole of Eretz Israel is now in the hands of the Jewish people'. Proceeding from this premise, they redefined the Jewish state on the basis of the inextricable link between the Jewish people, the Israeli state and the united Land of Israel: '[J]ust as we are not allowed to give up the State of Israel, so we are ordered to keep what we received there from Eretz Yisrael'.[18] With their commitment to the unity of the land both 'in the past' and 'in the future', they provided a demonstrative example of how a divine temporality can undermine secular history and intrude on contemporary politics. The associated prohibition – that 'no government in Israel is entitled to give up this entirety'[19] – not only revealed an anti-democratic attitude, but testified to their neglect of the simple fact that the newly conquered territory was already populated: by 1.1 million Palestinians.

Seeing this as a threat to both secular Israel and the Palestinian population of the recently occupied territories, Shimon Tzabar felt it was his duty to take further action. Around the time Alterman and his political friends were drafting their manifesto, he was meeting his friend Haim Hanegbi from Matzpen at Tel Aviv's Café Harley. 'We sat and talked about how the state was losing its mind, everyone was talking about the Greater Land of Israel and something had to be done against it', Hanegbi later recalled.[20] He also had experience as a protester. He and his friends Rafi Zichroni and Nathan Zahavi, whom he knew (along with Tzabar) from their work together at *Haolam Hazeh*, walked down the streets of Tel Aviv and Ramat Gan scrawling the slogan *Hal'a HaKibush!* (Down with the Occupation!) in big letters on the walls.[21] The group was sometimes joined by the legendary Tel Aviv diamond trader and millionaire David Ehrenfeld (1929–75), who lived up to a nickname he despised – 'the Red Millionaire' – by donating to Israeli leftists. He was also present at the meeting with Hanegbi and Tzabar at Café Harley.[22] They soon reached a consensus that they would draft a brief letter of protest. Within half an hour, Tzabar and Hanegbi had co-written the several-line declaration. The text began '[o]ur right to defend ourselves from annihilation doesn't give us the right to oppress others' and ended with the demand, in large font, 'Let's leave the occupied territories now' (Figure 3.1).[23] This was not about arguments or clarifications. It was about taking an unmistakable stand against the occupation: 'Occupation leads to foreign rule. Foreign rule leads to resistance. Resistance leads to oppression. Oppression leads to terror, and counter-terror.'[24] These were the slogans that the two co-authors directed towards the jubilant Israeli public. Bucking the trend, they warned: 'The victims of terrorism are usually the innocent. Holding onto the occupied territories will make us a nation of murderers and murder victims.'[25] The initiators first reached out to their friends and political allies for support and permission to include their names in the advertisement as supporters. Then Haim Hanegbi brought a stack of cash to the offices of the daily newspaper *Haaretz* to buy space for the advert.

'I knew it would be much easier with cash', he reported later. As so often, Ehrenfeld had furnished the funds.[26] On 22 September, the same day *Yediot Aharonot* and *Maariv* printed the manifesto of the Movement for Greater Israel, the left-wing Israelis' appeal to principles appeared on page eight of *Haaretz*. Thus, two simultaneous declarations represented two contradictory Israeli self-conceptions and two corresponding stances on the Israeli–Palestinian conflict. But while the Greater Israel Movement gathered a large number of prominent figures behind its manifesto, the nine signatures listed after those of Tzabar, Hanegbi and Ehrenfeld – Dan Omer (1940–84), Rafi Zichroni, Shneur Sherman, Uri Lifshitz, Yehuda Rosenstrauch, Raif Chana

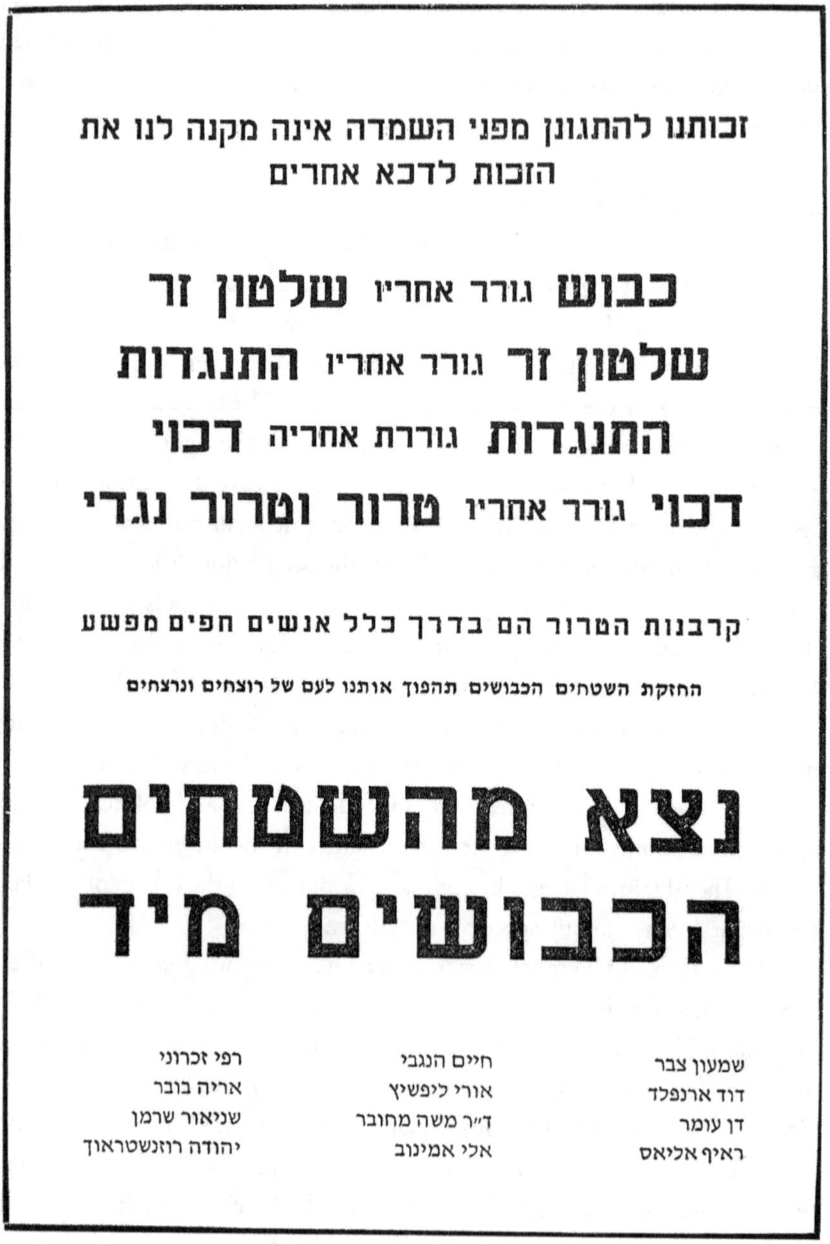

זכותנו להתגונן מפני השמדה אינה מקנה לנו את
הזכות לדכא אחרים

כבוש גורר אחריו שלטון זר
שלטון זר גורר אחריו התנגדות
התנגדות גוררת אחריה דכוי
דכוי גורר אחריו טרור וטרור נגדי

קרבנות הטרור הם בדרך כלל אנשים חפים מפשע

החזקת השטחים הכבושים תהפוך אותנו לעם של רוצחים ונרצחים

נצא מהשטחים
הכבושים מיד

שמעון צבר	חיים הנגבי	רפי זכרוני
דוד ארנפלד	אורי ליפשיץ	אריה בובר
דן עומר	ד״ר משה מחובר	שניאור שרמן
ראיף אליאס	אלי אמינוב	יהודה רוזנשטראוך

Figure 3.1 Advertisement in *Haaretz*, 22 September 1967, p. 8, with the appeal: 'Let's leave the occupied territories now'.

Elias (1936–88), Moshé Machover, Eli Aminov (b. 1939) and Arie Bober (1940–2003) – were names largely unrecognisable to the Israeli public.

It was, of course, no coincidence that in addition to Haim Hanegbi, three signatories – Arie Bober, Eli Aminov and Moshé Machover – were members of Matzpen. Protesting the occupation was the logical next step in the group's long-held stance on the Israel–Palestine conflict. Moshé Machover recalled several years later:

> Well, of course we did not know that such a war was coming. But politically we were prepared, in the sense that our political positions on Zionism, the Palestinian question, the Arab revolution etc. were already adequately formulated and internalised quite some time before the war, and therefore we did not have to grope for new analyses and positions after the war.[27]

In parallel to the advertisement in *Haaretz*, Machover wrote in *Matzpen* that after the war, the Zionist movement had truly carried out a 'resurrection of the dead'.[28] This was only partly a reference to the old intra-Zionist conflicts that were now rearing their heads because of the presence of Palestinians in the recently occupied territories. The war's aftermath also revived the old Zionist reasoning that Jews were divinely entitled to the entire biblical Land of Israel.[29] Long before the war of June 1967, Meir Smorodinsky had fiercely agitated against the secular political theology of the Zionist movement: 'If you ask the Zionists, the road to Israel passes through the synagogue.'[30] Ever since the Uganda debate at the Zionist Congress of 1903, when Zionists finally agreed on 'Eretz Israel', with its sacred meaning, as the prospective site for a Jewish nation-state, the political–theological road to modernity had gone uncontested within Zionism. Along those lines, in the 1930s, Ben-Gurion had defied British Mandate policy in declaring the Hebrew Bible to be the Jewish people's only mandate; during the territorial gains of the Sinai Campaign, he had invoked the emergence of the 'Third Kingdom of Israel'.[31] Smorodinsky therefore made the straightforward assertion that 'Zionism [. . .] cannot help but rely on religion. The Zionists "acquired" the "eternal" and "historic" right to the Palestinian territory from the Tanach and the prayer books'.[32] When Matzpen, in its discussion of the Palestine problem and its resolution, insisted on the existence of a new Hebrew nation of Israeli Jews, their proclamation of its right to self-determination was directed outwards, at the Palestinian Arabs and the Arab world as a whole. But their political claims rested on cultural underpinnings that also offered an alternative to the political theology of Zionism, as the claim of a separate Hebrew nation seriously strained the notion of a trans-territorial unity of the Jewish people that should be gathered in Israel. A new Hebrew nation of Israeli Jews may have emerged from Zionist history, but in Matzpen's view, it had gradually become detached from these historical origins and grown into a distinct and secular national entity in the Middle East.

The declaration of 22 September 1967 was much more than just a Matzpen communiqué, as it would later be perceived. Just as its origins reflected a blend of political and cultural critiques, the circle of supporters represented a scene extending far beyond Matzpen: a small but not insignificant segment of young Israeli bohemia. For example, Haim Hanegbi secured the signature of the painter Uri Lifshitz at Tel Aviv's legendary Café Kassit, where the up-and-coming artist belonged to a larger group of Tel Aviv writers, actors, visual artists and even politicians.[33] At this central meeting place of a flourishing, young Hebrew culture, where poets such as Haim Hefer (1925–2012) and Dan Ben-Amotz (1924–89) would sit and talk alongside such actors as Arik Einstein and Shmulik Kraus, Lifshitz had become close with Shimon Tzabar and Tzabar's childhood best friend, the writer and artist Amos Kenan (1927–2009). Uri Avnery, the publisher of the subcultural weekly newspaper *Haolam Hazeh*, was another Kassit regular and a personification of that scene. Two years earlier, in 1965, when the young Israeli Uri Davis was arrested for protesting the Israeli military administration, the group had jointly agitated for his release. But this time, in the aftermath of the Six-Day War, matters were less cut and dried. Hardly anyone was as enthusiastic about supporting Tzabar and Hanegbi's statement as Uri Lifshitz, who offered his name without even having read the text closely. His friends, the artists Yigal Tumarkin and Itzhak Danziger, abstained. And the text even caused a falling-out between the two old friends, Amos Kenan and Shimon Tzabar.[34]

Greater support came from the heart of bohemian Jerusalem, where most of the signatories were regulars at another café. Before moving to Tel Aviv in 1965, Haim Hanegbi had regularly met friends and engaged in political discussions at the Ta'amon, which was right across the street from the building where the Knesset convened in those years. Café Ta'amon was first frequented by German-born 'Yekkes', before it became a meeting place for former members of the underground Lehi paramilitary, followed by members of Matzpen and the political left in the sixties and the Israeli Black Panthers some years later.[35] Even before the Six-Day War, Hanegbi's visits to Jerusalem often led him to the little café on King George Street, where he would sit with Arie Bober of Matzpen and Eli Aminov, who would enter the organisation in 1967; the circle quickly expanding. Shneur Sherman, who arrived in Jerusalem from the United States in 1965 as a correspondent for the *Jerusalem Post* and a passionate supporter of *Haolam Hazeh*, soon joined their table, as did the writer David Moonshine, who would later chronicle this Jerusalem scene.[36] Café Ta'amon's star and mascot was the young writer Dan Omer. In the autumn of 1966, less than a year before the Six-Day War, he had published the controversial pornographic novel *Ba-Derekh* (On the Way), which was banned as obscene smut.[37] When Omer staged a hunger strike and pitched a protest tent in front of the Knesset, he became an idol of bohemian Jerusalem. He had the support of his friends from Café Ta'amon, as well as its owner Mordechai Kopp, even though Kopp leaned rightward politically. However, this declaration of solidarity was not enough to get the ban on his book overturned.[38]

Omer, Hanegbi, Aminov, Sherman, Bober and their friends often whiled away the daylight hours at the Ta'amon before moving on to nights at Bacchus, a legendary student club based in an old building around the corner on Yavets Street. Bacchus's bartender was Raif Chana Elias, who was part of the group of friends at the Ta'amon and had also signed Tzabar and Hanegbi's newspaper advertisement. The short, skinny Elias, a Maronite Christian Arab, was a longstanding young star of Jerusalem bohemia.[39] He had left his native village of Jish (Gush Halav) in the Galilee to dive into the subcultural life of divided Jerusalem, which was reason alone for special recognition. 'Raif [. . .] was the king of Jerusalem', Amos Kenan later wrote in an 'obituary' for Jerusalem's bohemia. 'He was an Israeli Arab trying to understand us. When he was through with understanding, he moved to San Francisco, where he died.'[40] Kenan had met Elias on a night out at Bacchus, where the latter Jerusalemite was hanging out with his closest friends, Dan Omer, Haim Hanegbi and Eli Kenan (Amos's brother). Elias was the group's beating heart.

His close friend Eli Kenan even wrote an unpublished novel about the man. 'We were like brothers', Haim Hanegbi later recalled; indeed, they were both part of a group of friends who also shared political convictions. When the Six-Day War brought an end to the smaller West Jerusalem of 1948 to 1967, Hanegbi and Tzabar called on many of their comrades from Ta'amon to sign their statement of protest against both the military occupation and the cultural transformation of Israel.

The small Jerusalem bohème and some regulars at Tel Aviv's Café Kassit were the left flank of a new, much broader Hebrew culture that had taken shape after the Zionist settlement in Palestine and was now blossoming in the young Israeli state. As a local Hebrew culture of an Israeli nationality, it was both a 'direct consequence' and 'a failure of Zionism' at once.[41] As the culture drifted farther from its European roots and was shaped by its Middle Eastern environment, it began to define itself primarily as Hebrew, not Jewish. It now drew exclusively on contemporary experiences, no longer traditional sources. Instead of being grounded in religion, it was oriented towards secularism. This newly emergent Hebrew national culture gave rise to a sort of cultural anti-Zionism. Many members of Matzpen also emerged from this new Hebrew community, which constituted the cultural foundation of their political call for the de-Zionisation of the Jewish state. They insisted on their Arab neighbours' recognition of this national collective as an unnegotiable requirement.

In his unpublished autobiography, Shimon Tzabar stressed the seminal impact of this cultural formation on himself and everyone around him. In the introduction, he observed that the accident of his birth in Tel Aviv in the year 1926 placed him among a special generation that would shape the country's culture in a very specific way:

> I was born in a Jewish city, where everyone spoke Hebrew. I did not learn any other language until late in life. The feeling of being a member of a minority group, whether persecuted or not, that Jews feel anywhere else, escaped me. I was one of the first generation of Hebrew speaking natives in a town of Hebrew speakers. I belonged to the majority indigenous population from the outset. As it happened, the culture of my generation shaped the culture of Israel today. To understand the chutzpah, the cruelty and the cynicism of the Israeli society today, one must be familiar with the culture of my generation. As one of my friends, Akiva Orr, once said: Israelis are not Jews. They are gentiles whose native tongue happened to be Hebrew.[42]

Israeli Hebrew was one of the, if not the most, essential features of this new culture. This was no longer the Biblical Hebrew of the Old Testament and the liturgy; this was a Hebrew that had morphed into a profane vernacular language over the course of the Zionist project and had thereby strayed farther and farther from its roots.[43] It was the Hebrew of a new generation of people, who, unlike their parents, were no longer native in a European language or in Arabic: their first language was Hebrew. Thus, it was an open language, no longer limited to a particular sphere of national or religious membership. Indeed, even Raif Elias was remembered as a true master of that new linguistic culture: 'He spoke better Hebrew than Anton Shammas, Nathan Zach or Gabriel Moked', recalled Amos Kenan, who alongside Shimon Tzabar had played a significant part in committing this contemporary Israeli Hebrew to writing. But according to Kenan, Dan Omer was the 'true prophet of that Hebrew culture'.[44]

In the magazine *Haolam Hazeh*, this native Hebrew culture now had its own media outlet. After the twenty-six year old Uri Avnery and his comrade Shalom Cohen bought the weekly from Uri Keisari in 1949, it quickly grew into a symbol of a whole generation. Some of the signatories of the September 1967 declaration also had been involved with *Haolam Hazeh*. Indeed, Haim Hanegbi had joined the magazine's editorial team back in 1960, after Amos Kenan took him to Uri Avnery's office after a party, recommending him with the remark that the man knew a thing or two about whiskey and writing. Before arriving at Matzpen, Arie Bober and Eli Aminov also moved in the magazine's orbit. When a political party grew out of the weekly in 1965, it received the financial backing of David Ehrenfeld, as did many other projects. Rafi Zichroni, another anti-occupation signatory, had also been part of the publication's editorial team. His brother, the well-known lawyer Amnon Zichroni, became the secretary and legal adviser of the freshly founded party. Uri Avnery's magazine thus served as the cultural and political hub of that new Hebrew culture.[45]

Although most of the non-Matzpen members who signed Tzabar and Hanegbi's statement came from the wider *Haolam Hazeh* crowd, this overt show of opposition to the new occupation opened political divisions within that community. The new Hebrew culture had indeed provided a social soil within which Matzpen members came of age and in which they cast down roots. But politically, that culture's contradictions and dichotomies would cause irreconcilable conflict over the Palestine question. This scene's historical origins were not originally left-wing anyway; the phenomenon originated in the Zionist Right, before it swung across the spectrum to the radical left of Matzpen. Amos Kenan, Uri Avnery, Shimon Tzabar, Dan Omer and Haim Hanegbi were the main characters in this narrative of personal friendships and political antagonisms, a story that culminated in a counter-narrative to the Zionist vision of a Jewish people united in Eretz Israel. This is the story of the invention of a Hebrew nation.

'. . . and the Canaanite Was Then In the Land'

The idea of a new Hebrew nation as a contradiction to the Jewish state was by no means an invention of the Israeli Left. Rather, it mirrored a conflict that had existed ever since Jewish settlement began. A specific Hebrew national culture, first evolving under the protection of the British Mandate and established deliberately in opposition to diasporic Jewish existence, was the result of Jewish settlement policy itself. The Jewish diasporic population arriving in Palestine/Israel was transformed into a territorial Hebrew nation with a separate state and its own language.[46]

This concept of a new, yet separate national community reached its most eccentric and spectacular climax even before the declaration of Israeli independence in 1948 with the emergence of the movement known as the 'Young Hebrews'. In the early 1940s, *Epistle to the Hebrew Youth* (*Ktav el ha-no'ar ha-ivri*, 1943) was circulated within the Yishuv.[47] Shortly after, in 1944, an intriguing pamphlet appeared with the enigmatic title *Opening Speech at the Meeting of the Committee with Representatives of the Cells* (*Masa ha-petiha; Be-moshav ha-va'ad im shelihei ha-taim*).[48] Its cover featured a purple flag emblazoned with an Aleph: the first letter of the Hebrew alphabet and the symbol of a radical new beginning.[49] Both publications were disseminated by the Committee for the Formation of Hebrew Youth (Va'ad le-Gibbush ha-No'ar ha-Ivri) and written by the poet Yonathan Ratosh (1908–81). Their titles and designs may have been cryptic, but their message was sweeping in its simplicity. *Epistle to the Hebrew Youth* begins with an appeal to the Yishuv's younger generation 'to reflect on the depth of the chasm and alienation that separates you, the Hebrew youth, from all those Jews in the Diaspora', and reaches the dramatic conclusion that the 'tie that binds the generations of

Judaism cannot be loosened; it can only be severed'.⁵⁰ This Jewish–Hebrew distinction was starkest in the Committee's *Opening Speech*, which laid out a binary that was more black-and-white than ever before:

> [W]hosoever comes from the Jewish Diaspora [. . .] is a Jew and not a Hebrew, and he can be nothing but a Jew. [. . .] Whoever is a Hebrew cannot be a Jew, and whoever is a Jew cannot be a Hebrew.⁵¹

As rock solid as these proclamations were, their frankness obscured the many-year evolution that produced them and followed the tortuous turns of their author's life. Yonatan Ratosh came from the Diaspora himself – specifically, Warsaw.⁵²

Yonatan Ratosh was born Uriel Halperin, to secular Zionist parents, in 1908. His father Yehiel Halperin, who became involved in the Hebrew-language kindergarten movement as a committed Zionist, saw to it that his children were raised with the language that Zionism was reviving. When the family immigrated to Tel Aviv in 1920, Halperin/Ratosh found the country to match his language and began to reinvent himself as a native. The political drive for a sovereign state, which Halperin/Ratosh positioned as a direct challenge to both the British Mandate and the Arab population of Palestine, at first led him into the ranks of the political Revisionists, led by Vladimir Jabotinsky. As an editor of its magazine *Hayarden* (The Jordan), he befriended the future founder of Lehi, Avraham (Yair) Stern. As Halperin/Ratosh's demand for immediate statehood increasingly proved to be too radical, even for Jabotinsky, he began focusing on examining his own group identification and the cultural aspect of the society he envisioned.

When Halperin/Ratosh found an answer to the questions that were troubling him, in 1938 and 1939, he was no longer living in Palestine, but in Paris. He experienced an intellectual 'liberating shock' after attentively reading a small brochure titled *The Canaanites and the Hebrews* by A. G. Horon, a scholar of Ancient Semitic studies.⁵³ In the same city where Eliezer Ben-Yehuda had resolved to revive the Hebrew language in the late nineteenth century, the meeting between Horon and Halperin/Ratosh marked the birth of a new, secular Hebrew nationalism.

Horon, too, had moved in Zionist Revisionist circles and was close friends with Jabotinsky's son Eri. He was born Adolphe (Edya) Gourevitch in

Ukraine, and took the name of the Ugaritic god of vengeance after moving to Paris. His research in Paris into Jewish and Semitic history thus fit into a larger project of equipping the Zionist Right with a new mythology, although that mythology would, in fact, undermine Zionism's basic premises. Building on European Bible scholarship, Horon focused on the Hebrew language and culture of the biblical Land of Canaan, which he saw as one region of an ancient Hebrew civilisation within the Land of Kedem – i.e. the ancient 'East'. This romanticising nostalgia for a pre-Jewish Hebrew history bore more than a passing resemblance to fascist preoccupations of the same period. Likewise, and by no coincidence, the title of the journal that Horon founded soon after, *Shem: Revue d'Action Hebraique* (Shem: Journal of Hebraic Action), was an echo of the far-right *Action Française* (French Action) movement.[54] Horon's views, which would catalyse Halperin/Ratosh's intellectual divorce from his Jewish identity, drew a sharp distinction between a Hebrew nation, united by language and territory, and a diasporic multilingual and multicultural Jewish religious community that had existed outside that national context ever since Babylonian exile. Horon would later famously identify himself as 'a Hebrew from Samaria, not a Jew from Yavneh'.[55] Halperin/Ratosh's next name change made the impact of this abundantly clear: Uriel Halperin now became Yonatan Ratosh.[56] The Paris meeting between Horon and Ratosh would have more lasting effects elsewhere. Whereas the outbreak of the Second World War compelled Ratosh to return to Palestine, Horon moved to the United States. There, his historical theories had a political impact on a group of Revisionists from the Irgun Tzva'i Le'umi (Irgun, for short), led by Rabbi Hillel Kook (Peter Bergson), Shmuel Merlin and Eri Jabotinsky.[57] In Palestine, meanwhile, these Paris-born ideas grew into:

> [A] secular anti-Zionist heresy [. . .] which attempts finally and absolutely to escape from Jewish history and to provide the Jewish national body – at least the portion living in Palestine – with a new 'not Jewish' socio-cultural historical identity.[58]

After returning from Paris, Ratosh tried to influence Lehi politically and dedicated one of his most important poems – 'Ba-Argaman' (In Purple) – to their founder Avraham Stern, who had been killed by the British. However, for the most part, he withdrew noticeably into his writing.[59] He soon gathered around him a small group of poets and sculptors, including Aharon Amir, Benjamin Tammuz and Avraham Rimon, that eventually grew into the Committee for the Formation of Hebrew Youth.[60] Like Ratosh, this group was mostly Diaspora-born and had Hebraicised their surnames from Lipec to Amir or from Kammerstein to Tammuz.[61] One of Ratosh's two brothers, the younger Uziel Halperin, was also in the group. He had been born in Jerusalem, and he took the name Uzzi Ornan. As the committee members discarded their Jewish origins with these acts of renaming, they began delving into their shared interest in the region's culture and history, especially that of the long-lost 'Land of Kedem' or the 'Land of Canaan'. Rejecting the idea that the Jewish migration to Palestine had brought about a Zionist 'resumption' of interrupted history, their *Opening Speech* instead proclaimed:

> We [are] identical to a people with a proud, ancient culture, a member of the primordial human culture. We are identical with the ancient Hebrews in whose country and with whose language we have been raised and whose only full rightful heirs we are.[62]

This new-fangled identity construct was most evident in the Hebrew language, which they saw as the unifying core of the past civilisation. As it was, many of the Young Hebrews were poets who intended to resurrect the Hebrew of the past and build on traditions of the 'Land of Kedem', 'the Land of the Hebrews' or the 'Land of Canaan' in their works.[63] With this context in mind, the literary critic Avraham Shlonsky (pejoratively) labelled the Young Hebrews 'Canaanites'.[64]

The political and cultural references to the 'Land of Canaan', 'the Land of the Hebrews' and the 'Land of Kedem' – these bygone Hebrew civilisations – bore deliberate parallels to the political structure of the United States of America. This Hebrew region, in the Canaanites' eyes, represented a secular, pluralistic space that would incorporate not only the native Hebrews, but also the diverse ethnic and national minorities in the region, such as Maronite Christians and Druze. Contrary to the imagination of America as a space 'with no history', however, the Canaanites had a fixed past in mind, one they now hoped to revive.[65] This evocation of past eras stood in marked contrast to the Arab population of the Middle East and its own nationalist movement. After all, the Young Hebrews had perceived the new unity of the region under the banner of the Hebrew language, lending a sort of 'Hebrew imperialism' to their views. The chief contradiction, however, lay in their opposition to the Zionist movement's aspirations of establishing a Jewish nation-state and territorialising Diaspora Jews within historic Palestine/Eretz Israel. The Canaanites' historical conception, adopted from Horon, viewed Diaspora Jews solely as a religious community, not an ethnic group. Because the Canaanites associated the markers of a common language and territory exclusively with the Hebrew nation that they sought to resurrect, they felt that Zionism – which sought to territorialise and linguistically unify all Jews – could not be a national movement at all. 'The Jews are not a nation and never were', declared the Young Hebrews in their *Opening Speech*, before railing against 'Zionism, as a Jewish phenomenon':

> Zionism, as a Jewish phenomenon, as a phenomenon within a faith-community, can absolutely never, from its beginning to any form it will assume in the future, be a movement of national liberation or a national movement at all.[66]

By locating the Zionist movement squarely in the Jewish Diaspora, the Canaanites aimed to culturally and politically segregate the Yishuv – and draw a definite line (and figurative boundary) between members of the new Hebrew nation and its Zionist rivals. 'The Hebrews in Palestine are in no way the direct result of Zionism', emphasised the Committee for the Formation of Hebrew Youth in no uncertain terms.[67] The Committee perceived the Zionist movement and its revitalisation of Hebrew as merely an attempt to give 'the Hebrew movement a Jewish face' and to tarnish the new nation with the stain of the Jewish Diaspora. 'To the thousand masks of Judaism he [Zionism] is adding yet another – a Hebrew mask', which, the Canaanites implied, must be torn off.[68] The *Opening Speech*, as an oratorical pamphlet, primarily pushed for a shift in consciousness among young Hebrew people, yet, at the same time, Ratosh's group did not shy away from some of the same antisemitic stereotypes that were already making a ghastly mark in Europe. For example, their images of 'cleans[ing]' the 'land of the Hebrews [. . .] of Zionism' and making the 'hearts of the Hebrews [. . .] pure of Judaism' were reminiscent of a founding document of modern antisemitism, the *Protocols of the Elders of Zion*. Ratosh wrote:

> But there is one country in the world and one nation for whom the legend of the Elders of Zion is no legend at all [. . .] over which world Jewry wishes to have control, whom world Judaism wishes to enslave to its approach and

its spirit and to the spiritual needs of the Jewish world, the world of the Diaspora. And this country is the land of the Hebrews, and this nation is the Hebrew nation.[69]

So it was that those who began to dissociate Hebrew and Jewish identities in the territory of the British Mandate took a line that was both anti-Diaspora and anti-Jewish during the unfolding catastrophe of European Jewry.

In essence, the Canaanites were an extreme manifestation of the same revolt against Jewish diasporic existence that was integral to the Zionist movement, whose 'return to history' by nationalising and territorialising modern Jewry implicitly involved 'negating Exile' and premodern religious–Jewish ways of life.[70] Just as the future Prime Minister David Grün became David Ben-Gurion upon arriving in Palestine, Zionist institutions were all emblazoned with the adjective 'Hebrew' to create distance between themselves and Diaspora Jewry.[71] 'If one plays the game of secular nationalism, one must not be affrighted by its consequences', wrote the literary scholar Baruch Kurzweil, the Young Hebrews' first critic.[72] He blamed the Zionist movement itself for dissociating from the sacred core that unifies Jewish existence. In modern Hebrew literature of the nineteenth century, he discerned one strain with tendencies towards a national renewal of Judaism, characterised by an impulse towards a 'return to the national foundations, foundations practically identical with religious roots'.[73] He identified another parallel strain that proceeded from Judah Leib Gordon and Micha Josef Berdyczewski to Josef Chaim Brenner and Shaul Tchernichovsky. These authors represented an 'transvaluation of values' influenced by Nietzsche, and from the start had sought a principled negation of Judaism.[74] In the eyes of Kurzweil, who was an Orthodox Jew, a detachment from Judaism had begun far earlier, during the Jewish Enlightenment and the secularisation process. That was the point at which historicism broke into Judaism, challenging and unravelling the cohesiveness of premodern religious law: 'The real ideological roots of the movement are to be sought in the religious scepticism of the Haskalah and its aftermath', Kurzweil argued.[75] Through that lens, Enlightenment Jews had already taken an axe to the consensus of Jewish collective memory, enabling its pluralisation into competing Jewish histories and even making it possible to renounce Jewish tradition altogether.[76] Nevertheless, Kurzweil perceived a distinct characteristic in the Canaanites. According to the literary critic, 'the break of the Young Hebrews with the Jewish tradition possesses a final, absolute character', which is not easily refuted: 'What they strive for is, as it were, their own self-discovery and the fulfilment of their native spiritual potential, a potential conditioned only by factors whose reality cannot be gainsaid, their own state and their own language.'[77]

In 1970, the philosopher of religion Gershom Scholem also revisited the Young Hebrews and asserted that their decision to cut 'the living tie with the heritage of the generations' was no less than 'educational murder'.[78] As a member of the Zionist movement, he wanted to cling to a Jewish path to modernity as a 'dialectic of continuity and rebellion'.[79] He understood the Zionist project as a rebellion against the old ways of Jewish existence in the Diaspora, but felt that a radical renewal and nationalisation of the Jewish people should be guided by ties to Jewish history and tradition. Thus, he described his own settlement in Palestine, in 1923, as a 'return to our own history' that would have been impossible 'without this *religio*, this "tie to the past"'.[80] When the Young Hebrews went public in 1944 with their *Opening Speech*, Scholem did not dignify them with a direct comment. However, his publications from the time on the science of Judaism (*Wissenschaft des Judentums*) bear a distant resemblance to his later critique of the Canaanites. In the project of Jewish Enlightenment and the science of Judaism, Scholem perceived the beginnings of an historical textual criticism whose historicism would contribute to the destruction of Judaism's sacred foundations, and his response was even more aggressive and polemical than Kurzweil's. Essentially, he wrote, this amounted to a 'tendency toward historical suicide', even the 'destruction and dismantling' of Judaism.[81] Years later, Scholem would proclaim that for similar reasons – the slippery slope from historicism down to a complete renouncement of Judaism – he was a 'downright anti-Caananite'.[82]

If the Young Hebrews had just been a small group of oddballs, it is hard to imagine that they would remain infuriating to Gershom Scholem in the 1970s. But in his early criticism, Baruch Kurzweil had already stressed that the group and its theories were just one eccentric extreme of a much broader cultural shift. Even as they focused on a mythical past, their radical rejection of the Zionist narrative of history spoke, in a way, to an entire generation that had been born in Palestine and felt increasingly estranged from Diaspora Jewry.

This new generation, known as sabras, felt distanced from the once-upon-a-time of Jewish history and were 'placing the accent on the needs of *Now*'.[83] Moreover, the Young Hebrews emerged in a period during which the Yishuv was almost fully isolated from Europe and from Diaspora Jewish life. Under the protective cloak of the British Empire, a prosperous economic and social environment developed with an increasingly autonomous national culture.[84] The Hebrew youth born in Palestine, for whom this sort of nativism resonated most fervently, reached a demographic peak of 35 per cent of the population in the 1940s. 'Time is on its side', cautioned Kurzweil in his critique of the Canaanites. 'It is a movement of youth.'[85]

This fit the experience of the young Uri Avnery.[86] Born Helmut Ostermann in 1923 in the town of Beckum and raised in Hanover, Germany, he and his Zionist-inclined family fled the Nazis to settle in Palestine in 1933. Antipathy towards the British Mandate led him to the Irgun at age fourteen, but its hostility towards the country's Arab population caused him to leave the organisation quickly in 1940.[87] Shortly afterwards, he picked up a copy of Horon and Ratosh's newspaper *Shem*, which he reviewed for a small, right-wing Zionist publication. 'The simple notion that the Land had given birth to a new nation, that was distinct from the Jews and was not expressed in Zionist terms left a big impression on me', he later recalled, describing this first encounter with the Canaanites' ideas.[88] Soon he, too, Hebraicised his name – first going by Josef Ostermann, then Josef Kadmoni and, finally, from his eighteenth birthday onwards, Uri Avnery.[89] Nevertheless, a clandestine meeting between the young Avnery and the much older Ratosh, arranged by Benjamin Tammuz, led to irreconcilable differences, starting with the question of Jewish immigration to Palestine, which Avnery supported and Ratosh flatly rejected.[90] In Ratosh's construct of an unbridgeable divide between Hebrews and Jews, Avnery more readily discerned the man's denial of his own Jewish heritage. While Ratosh drew a principled distinction between Jews and Hebrews, for Avnery this difference was the result of a generational and spatial shift. A Hebrew nation of people who had grown up in Palestine and had moved on from the experiences of their parents' generation would not materialise by resurrecting some distant past either, Avnery believed. This nation reflected a new language, region and culture that were distinct from the lives of the Jewish Diaspora. Like all other settler communities, it was therefore a 'nation without a past', but a nation that naturally fabricated its own myths.[91]

The idea of Canaanism and the emerging generation came to be symbolised by the sculpture *Nimrod*, even though its creator, the German-born sculptor Itzhak Danziger (1916–77), who moved to Palestine in 1923, did not meet Ratosh in person until after he had completed the work.[92] He had taken in early interest in the ancient Middle East while living in London and Paris from 1934 to 1938. After returning to Palestine, he created his best-known sculpture, which manifested its top-to-bottom disengagement from the history of diasporic Jewish experience. Its material was the Nubian sandstone of the Levant, and its subject was Nimrod, the Semitic god of the hunt, a symbol of the ancient Middle East. 'Most of all, [Nimrod] wasn't circumcised!' pointed out Akiva Orr, emphasising the figure's disconnection from Judaism and explaining that for him personally, years before he founded Matzpen, the sculpture had symbolised his own transformation from Karl Sebastian Sonnenberg to Akiva Orr.[93]

Perhaps the most important medium for these negotiations between Jewish and Hebrew identities was the Hebrew literature of the Yishuv. An iconic example is Haim Hazaz's 1943 short story 'The Sermon' (Ha-Derasha). During a conversation with fellow soldiers in the pre-state Haganah, the protagonist Yudka declares – first meekly, then resolutely – 'I object to Jewish history' and proceeds to describe the project of founding a sovereign state in Palestine as 'an act of destruction, a negation of what's come before. [. . .] not *new*, not *renewed*, but *different*.'[94] In saying 'the land of Israel is already not Judaism', Baruch Kurzweil also perceived the story as a potential 'source of all [the Canaanites'] ideas on Judaism'.[95] The fear that the Canaanites would outright infect the military vanguard of Hebrew youth was attested in several other rumours about the tendrils of heretical ideas infiltrating the ranks of the Palmach.[96] Rumours of nocturnal rituals worshiping Ashtoret, the Canaanite fertility goddess, resulted in various military personnel being investigated.[97]

In fact, very few members of the new, native-born generation had joined Yonatan Ratosh's tiny group. The young Amos Kenan, born Amos Levin in Tel Aviv to socialist Zionist parents in 1927, was one of them. He was still a member of Hashomer Hatzair when he encountered the heretics' ideas. What drew him to the group, after reading the *Opening Speech* and especially

Ratosh's poem 'Ba-Argaman', was the Canaanites' love of the land and their sense of belonging in the region. 'That was not about Ashtoret and not about Baal either', wrote Kenan later, explaining his fascination with the Canaanites. 'To the extent that there was a cultural idea, it was an articulation of self-expression. The expression of a new experience.'[98] Others from his generation, such as Boaz Evron (1927–2018) and Yaakov Ashman (1926–74), had felt the same pull and taken a similar path.[99] Yet they also keenly observed that same generational gap that had coloured Uri Avnery and Yonatan Ratosh's affinity-at-arm's-length. Kenan later recounted that in light of Ratosh's radical nativism, he and Yaakov Ashman once analysed the entire group systematically and found that, in fact, only the two of them had been born in the country.[100] More serious was the fact that although Yonatan Ratosh articulated a cultural transformation, the founding of the Committee for the Formation of Hebrew Youth had involved rejecting and harshly criticising all the political groups – anti-British and non-Zionist – from which he himself had sprung. Many years later, Kenan felt that it cast 'a shadow on the Canaanites' that they had not joined any of the underground organisations against the British. He was angry that, instead, Ratosh and his followers chose to move 'like parasites over the backs of the underground movements'.[101]

Kenan himself had found an answer to his pressing questions in the small paramilitary organisation Lohamei Herut Israel (Lehi), which in 1940 split from the right-wing terrorist organisation Irgun Tzva'i Le'umi under the leadership of Avraham (Yair) Stern. After Stern's premature death and under the three-way leadership of Nathan (Gera) Yellin-Mor, Itzhak (Michael) Shamir and Israel (Eldad) Scheib, the terror group was essentially a right-wing nationalist underground, but its anti-imperialism also attracted some individuals with left-wing leanings. In the eyes of its later member Maxim Ghilan, Lehi even appeared to develop into 'Israel's first true anti-imperialist movement for national liberation', partly inspired by the Irish Republican Army.[102] Kenan took a clear side at the time:

> It was no coincidence that my Canaanism led me to Lehi. Lehi was a movement for the liberation of the homeland. And homeland was a native word. The Jewish people, with all due respect, meant nothing to me. Lehi's greatness lay in figuring out who the real foreigners were here. They identified the British, and not the Arabs. [. . .] The enemy was imperialism and the Ben-Gurion state.[103]

Granted, such a judgement would not change the fact that the political terror of Lehi also targeted the Arabs of Palestine, and that Kenan himself was involved in the massacre of Deir Yassin. But it illustrates the extent to which the detachment from Jewish roots and the emergence of a native identity were what inspired Kenan to join Lehi and actively participate in the anti-imperialist underground. The same was true of contemporaries such as Boaz Evron and Shimon Tzabar, who shared an experience of cultural independence and the younger generation's drive for national independence – a drive directed against both the imperial violence of the British mandatory administration and the political leadership of the Yishuv. By proclaiming 'We are not Zionists!', they sought to distance themselves from the Yishuv leaders' deference towards the British, which they dismissed as 'exilic'.[104] Both Evron and Tzabar were recruited by Kenan.[105] Tzabar and Kenan were well acquainted, having grown up together in Tel Aviv and later studying at the same art school. Before Tzabar was recruited to Lehi, he had been a member of the right-wing Irgun Tzva'i Le'umi, but did not see eye to eye with its leadership. Running into Amos Kenan led him to Lehi, from which he was soon ejected when he expressed his support for a binational Jewish–Arab state.[106] Next, he joined the Palmach. Later, Tzabar would often reflect on having been a member of all three of the Yishuv's underground organisations as a young man. Finally, in the midst of the 1948 War, his attentive insights into the Arabs' circumstances led him to join the Hebrew Communist Party, a tiny group that soon merged with Maki, but which Tzabar found too boring to remain in for long.[107]

Uri Avnery was the most independent and productive figure in the ways he 'attempt[ed] to translate the historical platform of Horon and Ratosh into political concepts'.[108] In 1946, four years after his falling out with Ratosh, the group Eretz Israel HaTzeira (Young Eretz Israel) arose from a critical distance towards Ratosh's movement and a perceived need for an independent political intervention.[109] That group, which included Avnery, Ben-Ami Gur, Yaakov Gabay and, again, Shimon Tzabar, was likewise founded in opposition to the British, which is why its short-lived publication bore the title *BaMaavak* (In the Struggle).[110] Instead of focusing on the underground struggle or the elitist concerns of the Canaanites, this group sought to win its own generation's sympathies through the media and publicity as it tried to reinforce their identification with the new Hebrew nation.[111] What set the new group apart, most notably, was its interest in integrating the idea of a nascent Hebrew nation into the dynamism of the Arab independence movement. Unlike the Young Hebrews, whose fantasies of the past had no room for Arab nationalism, the *BaMaavak* group took it as the basis for their own spatial conceptions of the Middle East. In the run-up to the war, Uri Avnery published a leaflet titled *War or Peace in the Semitic Region*, which described the group's political profile. The leaflet's geopolitical perspective moved away from both the Eurocentric terms 'Near/Middle East' and the Canaanites' references to the Land of Kedem.[112] Instead, the coinage of a 'Semitic region' aimed to stave off the conflict between the Hebrew nation and the Arab Nationalist Movement. Drawing on historical myths, Young Eretz Israel claimed to offer a programme for a 'regional liberation struggle' that would unite the Hebrew nationalist movement with the Arab nationalist movements in a joint anticolonial project and pave the way for a regional federation. Thus, the ensuing War of Independence, in which Uri Avnery took part, was to him a war for both a 'Semitic' and 'Eretz–Israeli revolution' in the youths' struggle against the conservatism of the Zionist movements' founding fathers.[113] The war, as he saw it, was to be the vanguard of a regional transformation and part of a generational cultural revolution. But although the young state won its war, the dreams of a Semitic region and a Hebrew cultural revolution were lost – for now. Still, Avnery would work resolutely to Hebraicise the culture. This took place foremost in the journal he published, *Haolam Hazeh* – a magazine that not only would deliver wide-ranging fodder for the country's cultural development, but was also seminal in Matzpen members' cultural positioning.

Profaning the Language: The Emergence of Israeli Hebrew

When Uri Avnery and his former brother-in-arms Shalom Cohen bought the news magazine *Haolam Hazeh* from Uri Keisari in April 1949, it underwent a change of more than ownership. In fact, the publication had found editors who matched its title. Keisari had founded the magazine in 1937 under the name *Tesha Ba'Erev* (Nine in the Evening) and renamed it *Haolam Hazeh* in 1946; the significance of the new, grandiose title – literally, 'This World', contrary to 'Haolam Haba' (The World to Come, or the Hereafter) – would only come to fruition under its new publishers.[114] *Haolam Hazeh* became a symbol of a cultural and political rebellion that advocated democratisation and cultural transformation, rejected the political leadership of the young state and became a pioneer of contemporary Israeli culture.

This development was propelled and enabled by the new generation's self-conceptions and experience of the 1948 War. Avnery and Cohen met as soldiers in an elite unit nicknamed 'Samson's Foxes'. They funded their purchase of the magazine with Avnery's compensation payments for his war injuries; they liked to encourage the legend that they had hatched their scheme to run a publication together in the trenches during the 1948 War.[115] Also, immediately after the armistice, Avnery compiled a series of his articles, publishing them as a bestselling book titled *In the Fields of the Philistines*, which transformed him into a household name across the country. The myth that they, as soldiers, had participated in the country's birth was accompanied by a sense that, as veterans, they had since been betrayed by the newly founded state's political leadership.[116] Their chief target was Prime Minister David Ben-Gurion, who had established the new state in a 'quasi-totalitarian' form and secured its sovereignty after crushing the Etzel and disbanding the Palmach.[117] A few months before Avnery became a co-owner of *Haolam Hazeh*, he published an article within its pages titled 'Ben-Gurion's Victory', which described the disbanding of the Palmach (the army's elite division) as a 'counter-attack of the home front' and 'a charge of yesterday against tomorrow'.[118] The takeover of *Haolam Hazeh* was thus the project of a young editorial team of war veterans, whose vision for their magazine voiced a fresh declaration of war – against David Ben-Gurion – 'from the very first moment'.[119]

Overall, Ben-Gurion and his policy of *mamlakhtiut* (loyalty to the state, statism) appeared to be the opposite of everything Avnery and Cohen's magazine project stood for. 'We wanted a liberal, modern state in which lineage, religion and nationality would be utterly irrelevant', Avnery later recalled, reflecting on their deep-seated, burning antagonism against many things Ben-Gurion stood for, especially his political concessions to Orthodox Judaism and his attitudes towards the Israeli Arabs.[120] But most of all, the magazine repeatedly contested the forceful authority by which the white-haired man led the new state. When Ben-Gurion broke up the sailors' strike in Haifa, *Haolam Hazeh* saw this action as a reprise of the Palmach's disbanding and tried to consolidate public opposition to the statesman. It was in the same spirit that, a few years later, Avnery publicly connected the dots regarding the Lavon Affair, Israel's false flag operation about which the government had kept mum. This, too, further situated the magazine as an overt opponent of Ben-Gurion's policies, and at the same time a pioneer of Israel's civil society that was gradually taking shape. *Haolam Hazeh* rapidly made its rebellion against the political establishment into a trademark when it adopted the motto 'Without Fear, Without Bias'. Unlike most Israeli newspapers, which were affiliated with national political parties, *Haolam Hazeh* insisted on independence and the lack of a party affiliation as indicators of its objectivity and neutrality. On this basis, the publishers hoped to strengthen their readers' feeling of 'being tomorrow's forces of light standing against yesterday's forces of darkness'.[121] The magazine clearly wanted to position itself at the vanguard of a new generation of young and modern Israelis.

These stances soon prompted firm responses, however. An article in which Avnery rejected conscription for women led to a rift with the armed forces, and the magazine lost this invaluable market.[122] Moreover, its ongoing conflict with state officials was one reason the periodical sold 'hardly any' advertisements for nearly twenty years, because the numerous state-managed companies and institutions feared conflict with the government.[123] Ben-Gurion himself studiously avoided mentioning *Haolam Hazeh* by name, instead referring to 'a certain weekly' – a nickname the magazine quickly claimed for itself.[124] The greater burden was the direct physical violence inflicted on the magazine's editorial staff in the early 1950s. Avnery was attacked multiple times, resulting in repeated fractures in his arms and hands; the magazines' newsroom and printing house were the targets of multiple bombings.[125]

But none of this dampened the magazine's social impact. Even if *Haolam Hazeh* was not for sale on army premises, it was read avidly by officers and public servants alike.[126] With a print run of up to 20,000 and several readers per copy, it certainly made a mark on the dominant Israeli society.[127] Beyond the content, this was largely due to the magazine's significance as the vehicle of a veritable media revolution, a form of journalism that was altogether novel in Israel.[128] Unlike the traditional party-affiliated press, which published a mixture of articles on politics and high culture, *Haolam Hazeh* was a type of popular journalism based on Western European and American tabloids. 'Avnery got his ideas for the magazine's design from American magazines that were both critical and populist', co-editor Shalom Cohen recollected. 'Based on the American template, we invented a journalism that was brand new to Israel; *TIME* magazine was our role model.'[129] Despite its genuinely Israeli roots, *Haolam Hazeh* also paved the way for a kind of cultural Americanisation.[130]

This transformation of the media had many faces. Its most visible sign was the introduction of a new form of photography, which had previously played a very marginal role in the Hebrew press. Unlike most newspapers and magazines, *Haolam Hazeh* hired its own photographers, elevating photography to the central medium of journalistic stagecraft and design.[131] This emphasis was due in large part to the sensational style that the magazine cultivated from the beginning, expressed through populistic columns, sensational headlines and, of course, gripping images. Alongside political topics, the magazine covered previously undiscussed aspects of mundane culture from daily life to gossip, their lines often blurring. Reporting shocking revelations often meant invading the privacy of politicians and public figures: another novelty previously unheard of in the Hebrew press.[132]

Perhaps the most important element of this new form of journalism, in terms of its contribution to contemporary Israeli culture, was its novel use of language. This was essentially the result of an inexorable secularisation process and demonstrated the transformation of a formerly sacred language into the medium of an incipient national culture.[133] Looking back on this history of his news magazine, Avnery would later cite the journalist Amnon Dankner:

> We thus introduced a new Hebrew language, a Hebrew that was good but still very clear and simple. An Israeli writer once defined it this way: The language of *Haolam Hazeh* is a muscular but lean language. It has since been emulated by the entire Israeli press.[134]

For this very reason, when Uri Avnery took over the magazine, he brought together an entirely new editorial team made up of young, inexperienced Israelis who represented the country's sabra generation. But as much as *Haolam Hazeh* shaped and cultivated this new Hebrew, it was following another role model: Amos Kenan's weekly column 'Uzi & Co.', which had been running in *Haaretz* since 1950.[135]

Amos Kenan likewise responded to the new state with rage, frustration and disappointment. In an era when nearly everyone felt a sense of duty and connection to the statist collective, his earlier membership in Lehi had made him an outsider in the young society: 'It wasn't just that I came from Lehi; I came from the left flank of Lehi. Essentially, I remained a man without a biography.'[136] All the dreams bound up in his former activism had been squashed by the new state, which he saw merely as a semi-dictatorship by Ben-Gurion. The 'Eretz Israel' of his and Avnery's dreams 'had died in the year 1948'.[137] His rage at the new society – Dan Ben-Amotz quipped that Kenan 'wakes up in the morning and starts hating'[138] – eventually led him back to the Young Hebrews movement, which experienced a resurgence during the first years of statehood and published its own journal, *Aleph*, from 1948 to 1953. Others who did not identify with the new post-war state also found a political and cultural home in the journal. It was there that Yaakov Ashman, who had previously argued with Kenan in Lehi, published his stirring essay 'To Die – But What For?', which articulated an entire 'lost generation's' disconnect from the new state, their sense of having been betrayed by the political leadership.[139] Far from being nostalgic for that lost utopia, the Young Hebrews had also engaged in the debate over the shape of the new state, releasing their own independent policy agenda in the autumn of 1951. They demanded an institutional separation between Israel and international Jewish organisations, a corresponding shift in immigration policy and politico-cultural integration into the region.[140] But their focus was chiefly domestic, in response to the 'status quo' rules that Ben-Gurion had set as early as 1947 within the Agudath Israel party. To uphold the national unity of the state-in-waiting, the future prime minister sacrificed its secularity and guaranteed to the Orthodox party that there would be public adherence to religious stipulations about kosher dietary laws and Sabbath observance. He also ceded jurisdiction over marriage laws to the religious authorities.[141] By contrast, the Young Hebrews' policy agenda issued a battle cry for 'separation of religion and the state' and for 'liberation from all manifestations of theocracy', which would allow a 'secular way of life, and the institution of a completely secular authority in all areas of life'.[142]

In the 'battle for the Sabbath', the advocates of public piety were not just limited to Orthodox and ultra-Orthodox groups on the ground, but even included members of the government.[143] For example, a bill by the Minister of Transport David-Zvi Pinkas proposed a driving ban on the day of rest. In March 1951, a corresponding wave of pro-secular protest was organised as the League Against Religious Coercion. Although Uzzi Ornan was the secretary and Yonatan Ratosh was an active member, the league did not consist exclusively of Young Hebrews. With its focus on the shared conviction 'that matters of religion and faith are the private affairs of each person' and its principled demand for a fundamental division between synagogue and state, the league brought together both left- and right-wing Israeli politicians (such as Yitzhak Gruenbaum and Eri Jabotinsky), while rallying young dissidents behind the cause.[144] The culture wars over the proper role of the Israeli state were also what inspired a young Eli Aminov's entry into politics – long before his confrontation with the Palestine question led him to Matzpen. Amos Kenan, meanwhile, took a much more drastic approach during the heated conflict over forced religious observance as he vented his outrage at Ben-Gurion's regime. Together with Shaaltiel Ben-Yair, whom he had met in the Lehi underground, he aimed to stir up Israeli society with an explosion in front of Transport Minister Pinkas's house as an act of protest against Pinkas's proposed Sabbath driving ban.[145] Although the minister was not directly hurt by the bomb blast – still he died two months later of an heart attack – both men were charged with attempted murder.[146] Yet while Kenan kept mum and was soon acquitted for 'lack of evidence', Gershom Schocken immediately fired him from *Haaretz*. The author had to give up his famous column 'Uzi & Co', which had been widely read across the country since 1950, and went into self-imposed exile in Paris for almost a decade.[147]

Kenan took over the column 'Uzi & Co.' from Benjamin Tammuz, guided it to unparalleled success and made a national name for himself. His column's significance went beyond his sharp criticisms of the Ben-Gurion administration in the astute, witty voice of Kenan's alter ego, Uzi. Its more lasting influence came from its use of a new variety of Israeli Hebrew that intentionally transcribed vernacular language and Israeli slang, a style of prose that slowly (but surely) spread across the magazine landscape.[148] Uzi 'showed people what had been in front of their noses all along', Kenan later reflected. 'He demonstrated that the spoken language is different from the language used in writing. It has a different syntax and a different rhythm. The literary language is fake because you cannot see in it the way people think and speak.'[149] But this transmission of orality to text was not simply an invention of a 'new language'; it was another stage of a historical process, long underway, of 'profaning' the formerly sacred tongue of Hebrew.[150]

This transformation of the Hebrew language, which went beyond all previous attempts to modernise Hebrew – invariably *written* Hebrew, that is – sprang up once more from the Canaanite crowd and its invention of a Hebrew nation. Amos Kenan recollected fierce disputes that erupted between him, Max Fogel and Yaakov Ashman over the nature of the new state's language, soon after the 1948 War:

> We thought that people in this country wrote in a foreign language. A destitute language. A castrated [. . .] language. The language of [Avraham] Shlonsky's Russian-to-Hebrew translations, [. . .] Yiddishisms, and all sorts of things like that.[151]

That was the language of the 'fathers' generation', which bore their diasporic influences and was 'rich in biblical and Mishnaic connotations, a rhetorical repetitive rhythm, and figurative imagery'.[152] Proliferating outward from literature, this register had begun to spread into the magazine landscape of the young state.[153] Against that backdrop, the incursion of the spoken word into written text was about more than simply incorporating individual lexical items. It was about creating an entirely new written language that drew on everyday experience. Kenan was emphatic on this point:

> Each language breathes its own syntax. And spoken Hebrew breathes a different syntax from what came before – that is Canaanism. Perhaps Yonatan Ratosh is a theoretical Canaanite, but I'm a practical Canaanite. I wrote in spoken Hebrew.[154]

This new Hebrew vernacular, which appeared in the writings of Amos Kenan, Yaakov Aschman and Max Fogel in *Aleph*, was partly a rebellion against the diction of the first Canaanite generation. Nevertheless, it was Ratosh who enthusiastically congratulated Kenan for popularising this idiom in 'Uzi & Co.', asserting that it was the 'beginning of a cultural revolution, that once will be a political revolution': the same revolution he, too, had sought.[155]

More than two decades prior, Gershom Scholem perceived the profound significance of this linguistic shift as a phenomenon of secularisation. From the day he arrived in the Jewish Yishuv in Palestine, he had articulated a fear that the development of an oral Hebrew independent from the written language would mean taking a fork in the road and diverging irreversibly from the sacred substance of Jewish tradition. Scholem's bond to Hebrew as the language of revelation and heritage played a critical role in his decision to immigrate to Palestine. As early as 1919, he concluded the following in an essay about learning Hebrew:

> The objective of learning Hebrew is not about gaining abilities, neither to express oneself in that language [...] nor to understand the basic sense of others' expressions. Rather, it is about penetrating Hebrew to a depth at which once can grasp Judaism in its spiritual-intellectual [*geistig*] essence, which is identical to its linguistic component. The vision [*Sicht*] of Hebrew is the objective, not speaking it.[156]

Given his political theology of Zionism, the theorist was deeply disturbed by the aspects of Hebrew's Zionist revival that severed the language from its liturgical and literary roots and transformed it into a day-to-day vernacular. Full of indignation, Scholem wrote to his friend Franz Rosenzweig in 1926: 'The phantasmagoric Volapük spoken in our streets precisely defines the expressionless linguistic space which alone has permitted the "secularisation" of language.' Fundamentally, this was no longer the 'sacred' language whose words had been 'full to bursting with meaning'.[157] They could not be emptied, he postulated, 'unless one sacrifices the language itself'. Scholem drew a radical distinction between spoken Hebrew – which he described as a sort of 'Esperanto' that was 'heavy with impending catastrophe' – and the written language of biblical revelation.[158] Yet precisely because he saw its potential mundane usage as purely 'a manner of speaking', he felt confident that the Hebrew crisis he described posed no immediate threat to the language's Jewish essence. After all, this crisis only applied to spoken, but certainly not written, Hebrew. In 1923, he wrote:

> Hebrew as a language of books, of literature, is alive [...] It has an enormous and astounding vibrancy imbued with an inward glow, and in secularisation it has preserved the reflected light, the eternal resonance of the very revelation to which it owes its everlasting life.[159]

This assessment had already been disproved by some developments in the Yishuv. In parallel to Scholem's theories, efforts had been made to modify the written word, including the first stabs at romanisation, which would have detached written Hebrew from Jewish tradition almost altogether. At the forefront of these proposals was Itamar Ben-Avi – Eliezer Ben-Yehudah's son, who considered himself the first Hebrew child and engaged in an extended dialogue with Mustafa Kemal (Atatürk) about the romanisation of Turkish, which served as his inspiration. Ben-Avi's proposals gained momentum and traction with his 1928 founding of the magazine *Hashavua Hapalestini* (The Palestinian Week), published using the Roman alphabet.[160] Vladimir Jabotinsky, who had already declared that he would by no means mourn the sacredness of Hebrew letters when building a liberal and secular nation in Palestine, also supported these ideas.[161] It was the Revisionist Zionist and communist dissident Arthur Koestler, Jabotinsky's former secretary, who years later continued the assessment that romanising Hebrew was an essential element of a nascent secular Hebrew culture.[162] In a series of articles published shortly after the founding of the Jewish state, he had voiced his conviction that the formative face of this new state would not be the European-born 'Lost Generation', but the new generation born on the territory that was now Israel. Israel, he pronounced in no uncertain terms, would soon be 'an entirely "un-Jewish" country'.[163] Years earlier, he had described this generation in his novel *Thieves in the Night*: 'Hebrew for them was the native tongue, not a precariously acquired art; the Country their country, neither promise nor fulfilment. Europe for them was a legend of glamour and frightfulness [. . .] They were haunted by no memories and had nothing to forget.'[164] Meanwhile, this led him to draw two radical distinctions in his political writings: between a Hebrew nation and the Jewish religion, and between Israel and the Diaspora.[165] In opposition to the 'cultural conservatism' of the Israeli institutions, he now sounded the call for purging the 'rabbinical aura' that still adhered to the Hebrew language.[166] Instead of confining the 'cultural life of the country [. . .] to a medium which has been practically dead for two thousand years', Koestler likewise suggested a radical and modernising shift in the appearance of written Hebrew.[167]

Koestler's ideas were roundly rejected abroad, but were greeted enthusiastically by Uri Avnery's Young Eretz Israel group and its magazine *BaMaavak*.[168] In a letter offering Koestler honorary membership, they agreed to his radical plan 'to cast away the archaic Assyrian alphabet, to which our blind traditionalists cling like frightened bats, and introduce a new alphabet'. The group extolled Koestler's abiding dedication to freedom and democracy, while lamenting that 'far too many of our leaders, who grew up in the ghetto', do not share those values.[169] Eventually, they would abandon the programme of romanising Hebrew. Nevertheless, in founding *Haolam Hazeh* as a magazine for Israeli Hebrew, they carried on the project of linguistic secularisation by wilfully committing speech to the page. Overall, the transcription of the oral vernacular into the written language had made significant progress by the 1950s. Aside from the pioneering efforts of Amos Kenan, a unique linguistic and written culture had developed within the supplements of Hebrew newspapers. Uri Avnery and Shimon Tzabar began working on the *Haaretz* evening supplement *Yom-Yom* (Day by Day) shortly after statehood. It was within these pages that Avnery first reached a national audience, and Tzabar printed his very first weekly columns. Even though the two owed their work to the hands-off management of the editor-in-chief Gershom Schocken, according to Shimon Tzabar, *Yom-Yom* was edited by Benjamin Tammuz, Avraham Rimon and Meidad Schiff, which placed it in the Young Hebrews' cultural sphere of influence. The small group had a broad impact on the culture of the Jewish state in its first decades. And it was within these pages, after all, where Shimon Tzabar eventually Hebraicised his name. 'No such name is going to appear in our tabloid', objected the editors, upon seeing Tzabar's birth name of Hercberg in the byline of the draft of his first article.[170]

Aside from the *Haaretz* cultural supplement, *Maariv*'s newly launched political satire section propelled the spread of this new Hebrew. Ephraim Kishon began writing the column 'Had-Gadia' (One Young Goat) in 1952, only three years after migrating to Israel. Haim Hefer and Dan Ben-Amotz soon followed with the series 'Yalkut Hakesavim' (A Pack of Lies), which rapidly gained traction, partly out of wistful nostalgia for their own generation's lost mythology.[171] The former Palmach member Dan Ben-Amotz made himself the mouthpiece of his cohort's slang. Before long, he became seen as a (self-cultivated) personification of a new species: the native Israeli, the sabra, judging by his books, cultural portraits and textbooks of that generation. *The World Dictionary of Hebrew Slang*, which he co-edited with the former Palmach fighter Netiva Ben-Yehuda and released in 1972, would crown that blend of cultural influence and radical linguistic innovation with a publishing milestone.

Shimon Tzabar, who wrote the satirical series 'Kotzo shel Tzabar' (The Thorn of Tzabar/a Sabra Cactus Fruit) from 1954 onwards, was also part of the same group of language innovators. But he was a step removed from the others, partly because of his membership in the Israeli Communist Party. Unique among his peers, Tzabar also painted, producing works of art imbued with his experiences of the emerging Hebrew–Israeli culture.[172] Together with some fellow alumni of Yehezkel Streichmann and Avigdor Stematzky's Studia Art School, he co-founded an avant-garde art collective, the Group of Ten. The group's paintings were representative of that era's socialist realism, but also set out to establish a school of contemporary Israeli art that would incorporate the locale's culture and people.[173] Yet Tzabar remained a pillar of the satirical scene of the new Israeli linguistic culture described above. In 1964, Amos Kenan and Dan Ben-Amotz began publishing a new satirical publication under the name *Tsipor HaNefesh* (an idiom for something precious, literally 'the bird of the soul'), which was released as a Friday supplement to *Yediot Aharonot*. Of course Kenan and Ben-Amotz insisted on including Tzabar. The editors of the supplement also enjoyed full editorial autonomy, so they did not draw any 'red lines' in the sand.[174] Tzabar expressed himself with an 'obituary' for the Mapai after its party conference – and his stunt had company. The editors' attention-grabbing call for public protests against the expropriation of Arab land in the Galilee even spurred a conflict with Herzl Rosenblum, the editor of *Yediot Aharonot*, who published a fierce attack on the whole editorial board. Dan Ben-Amotz wrote an article criticising Rosenblum, which was blocked from publication; it was Uri Avnery who made space for the piece in the pages of *Haolam Hazeh*. In the end, *Tsipor HaNefesh* was discontinued as a supplement to *Yediot Aharonot* after only one year.

For each of these writers, all roads eventually led to *Haolam Hazeh*, the cultural and political hub of this new Hebrew scene. This held true for Amos Kenan, who was still publicly discredited by late 1952, even though he and Shaaltiel Ben-Yair had been acquitted of the charges against them. After losing his *Haaretz* column, Kenan found work anonymously writing short illustrated Tarzan books for Aharon Amir's Tzohar Press, before Avnery hired him to join the staff of *Haolam Hazeh*, where he published the column 'Knife in the Back', beginning in 1954.[175] The absurdist style with which he panned censorship, the political establishment and the military was ideally matched to that magazine's format. Uri Avnery even called Kenan 'the only real originator our generation has put forth'.[176] Still, Dan Ben-Amotz and Shimon

Tzabar were equal contenders for that title. In the 1950s, *Haolam Hazeh* was already syndicating Hefer and Ben-Amotz's columns from Maariv, as well as publishing both men directly with some frequency. With 'The Thorn of a Sabra', Shimon Tzabar followed in the footsteps of Kenan. He had his journalistic heyday in Avnery's magazine after leaving *Haaretz* temporarily.[177]

Thus, it was thanks to its origin story, owners, profile and slate of authors that *Haolam Hazeh* remained the gathering place and home base for the new Hebrew culture. Although its popular authors also wrote for established publications, the impact of their linguistic revolution was long restricted to satirical newspaper supplements, as the literary scholar Gershon Shaked assessed in hindsight. 'The fiction was slow to seize the opportunities' afforded by spoken Hebrew, which, according to Shaked, 'did not become an integral part of the language of the literary text. [. . .] [Most of] the native generations [still] drew on [. . .] the formulated language of classical Hebrew fiction'.[178] Hence, *Haolam Hazeh* magazine remained the exclusive enclave of this new Hebrew culture and the main habitat of Israeli Hebrew, which spanned all genres and sections there as it did nowhere else. 'A young Israeli who wanted to read his own language, his own newspaper' in the 1950s and 1960s, wrote Avnery later, could 'really only buy *Haolam Hazeh*'.[179] In those first decades of the Jewish state, Hebrew-language culture unleashed its full political impact, which ranged from criticising Israeli society's inadequate secularisation to bemoaning the country's failure to integrate into the larger Arab region. This was also the cultural milieu from which Matzpen emerged.

Hebrew Pornography

In combining political criticism and cultural revolution, *Haolam Hazeh* quickly made a broad base of enemies. It was also accused of distributing 'pornography'.[180] In 1954, when the religious magazine *Haboker* publicly pointed out that the tabloid had 'recently begun presenting images of women partially or completely exposed', *Haolam Hazeh* was not yet publishing such images as a regular feature; they were still outliers in its pages. Rather than levelling an accusation about specific imagery, this indignant complaint referred to a 'pornography without nudity';[181] it was not so much singling out *Haolam Hazeh*'s choice of photographic subjects as its 'revelatory discourse'. The magazine used a new, direct language, but it simultaneously pledged to 'reveal all the facts, and to publish all the facts'[182] – unlike the establishment media. In the spirit of this commitment, Uri Avnery disputed the accusations:

> [A]mong the Israeli publications, every newspaper has already grown accustomed to calling its opponents 'pornographic' newspapers. By now, the word 'pornographic' is applied not only to independent magazines that touch political sore spots, but also to those competing with the party papers at the kiosks.[183]

When it introduced the first version of 'Israeli sex journalism', including real but by no means pornographic nudity, *Haolam Hazeh* became a pioneer of the Israeli press.[184] The first images of scantily clad and later nude women were usually topical, used in reports about Israeli models or prostitution, for example. The introduction of a double cover system in 1959 – with the typically political cover story on the front and images of women in bikinis on the back – made the pairing of sex and politics into a trademark of the tabloid. Soon, *Haolam Hazeh* was called 'the Israeli answer to *Playboy*', based both on the publication's sensationalist style and on its aspirations of mass journalism.[185]

Uri Avnery often described the paper's inclusion of sex and eroticism as part of his 'spaceship method'. Just as a space vehicle carries an independent satellite into orbit, the sensational articles and photographs were intended to draw in a readership who would then encounter the publication's political and subversive themes.[186] Meanwhile, the use of explicitly sexual and vulgar language alongside erotic photography took on its own political message as a 'politically liberating act' and a symbol of social liberalisation.[187] Even if the erotic imagery mostly appealed to a heterosexual male audience, it was also part of the news magazine's general struggle for press freedom and against the compulsory religion that was pervading society. In turn, the combination of sexual and political exposures repeatedly prompted legal action against the magazine. This culminated in the passage of an anti-defamation law in 1965. The editors of *Haolam Hazeh* believed that the law's restrictions on press freedom were designed to take direct aim at its coverage. With the slogans 'Into Prison or into the Knesset' and 'Immunity for *Haolam Hazeh*', they successfully circumvented the new rules by transforming the magazine into a political party, which won seats in the sixth Israeli Knesset.[188] Although the magazine's entry into the political establishment considerably damaged its long-term credibility among its readers, it did guarantee the publishers parliamentary immunity.[189]

The conflict between the Israeli authorities and the magazine *Bul* (Bull's Eye), established in 1965, was not as mild. *Bul* rapidly made a name for itself as 'Israel's first and only sex-magazine' and was predominantly focused on sexuality and eroticism. In fact, it was inspired by *Haolam Hazeh* and sought to expand on its style.[190] *Bul*'s founder, Shmuel Mor, and his co-publisher Maxim Ghilan had been regular contributors to Avnery's magazine in the years prior and were at home in its attendant cultural circles. Mor was a sabra, born in Petach Tikva, and a veteran of the Palmach. Ghilan was born in 1931 in Lille, France, to Sarah and Oscar Goldenhirsch, but his first childhood memories date back to civil-war Spain. Ghilan's father was a socialist millionaire and served as deputy minister of the autonomous Catalonian government. Ghilan only moved to Palestine in 1944 after his father's capture and death sentence.[191] He quickly Hebraicised there and his affinity to a Hebrew nationalism with socialist characteristics led him to the small left-wing fringes of Lehi before the War of Independence.[192] Together with the poets Natan Zach, Yehuda Amichai and Gabriel Moked, he went on to co-found the avant-garde Likrat Group in the early 1950s, which combined criticism of Nathan Alterman's poetics with the adoption of a vernacular, contemporary Hebrew and free-flowing rhythm in Hebrew poetry.[193] In parallel, Ghilan became involved in the influential literary journal *Achshav* and the much less well-known magazine *Kav* and regularly wrote for *Haolam Hazeh* before emerging as *Bul*'s publisher.[194] Ghilan and Mor quickly gathered a small circle of young journalists with dissident Israeli backgrounds. One of them was Rami Livneh, who by then was already a member of Matzpen. 'It was the most daring writing in Hebrew up to then', he later recalled. 'From *Haolam Hazeh* [they] took the necessity of using a flowing, non-convoluted style, with a lead and subhead – the main point at the top.'[195]

Even if *Bul* was modelled on the format and commercial success of *Haolam Hazeh*, the magazine was conceived as a competing project and covered sexual and political subject matter much more assertively. In a manner of speaking, the publishers put the back of *Haolam Hazeh* on the front of their own publication, giving the images of naked women centre stage. The black-and-white photos were no more explicit or pornographic than those in *Haolam Hazeh*, but some readers were offended by the explicit descriptions of sexual acts in a Hebrew that was considered sensational and offensive from the very first issue.[196] Nevertheless, this was not the cause of *Bul*'s first scandal, which was in fact over political exposures. Usually, the magazine only addressed a political issue if other media outlets were not covering it. In late 1966, when the country's journalists heard the rumour that Israeli intelligence had been involved in the disappearance of the Moroccan dissident Mehdi Ben Barka, Mor and Ghilan hoped to land a groundbreaking exclusive with a piece of investigative reporting. All other newspapers held their silence on the topic, as was expected of them. When *Bul* ran the cover story 'Scoop! Israelis in Ben Barka affair?' for its seventy-forth issue on 11 December 1966, the publishers crossed a red line of state censorship.[197] Shmuel Mor was positive that Uri Avnery himself had contacted the Israeli censor about the cover story, which led to the confiscation of all copies, the arrest of its publishers and legal charges of espionage and disseminating false information 'affecting the security of the state'.[198] Yet not only were the two co-publishers spared the most severe punishment for espionage, which was life imprisonment; they did not even serve their one-year prison sentences. President Salman Shazar granted them amnesty, ending Mor and Ghilan's imprisonment only 135 days after it started.[199] That did not mark the end of their conflict with the Israeli state, however. By the autumn of 1967, the paper was once again the subject of legal disputes. This time, prompted by the publication of erotic images and nudity, which led to accusations of obscenity and pornography. The case almost caused a sensation when the acting judge at Tel Aviv Magistrate's Court read out a letter by an anonymous woman proclaiming the magazine a threat to family life and demanding its closure.[200] A decision on the allegations was never made, however, and the case remained pending in the country's courts for several years.[201]

By then, the claims against *Bul* were overshadowed by a much more attention-grabbing trial: that of the Jerusalem writer Dan Omer. His book *Ba-Derekh* (On the Way) had been under investigation by a Jerusalem court since late 1966.[202] More than a decade before Dan Ben-Amotz published what was probably the 'first Sabra pornographic novel', *Ziyunim Ze Lo Hakol* (Screwing Isn't Everything), and popularised Hebrew vulgarisms, it was Dan

Omer's short novel that paved the way.²⁰³ This slim volume, released by the young Jerusalem writer in August 1966, set off a four-year legal battle that made its way from the Jerusalem Magistrate Court all the way to the national Supreme Court. In 1970, on the basis of section 179 of the Criminal Code Ordinance, a legal legacy of the British Mandate, which outlaws 'obscene printed or written matter', the latter court sentenced the author to an eighteen-month suspended imprisonment and a fine of 2,000 Israeli lira. The distribution of his book was henceforth punishable by law.²⁰⁴

The magnum opus by the previously unknown Omer was not shy about breaking taboos. Neither was Golgotha, the small press that published the book. The publisher, an American–Israeli, had founded the press to encourage the circulation of subversive literature.²⁰⁵ Even there, Omer's text stood out, both thematically and formally. It described the six-day journey of a young Israeli man and his companion, a German woman referred to as the 'Teuton', and was provocative not only for its detailed descriptions of various sex acts, but also for the way it dealt with history and politics. On their journey, which also draws the young Israeli and the German woman into memories of the Holocaust, they reach the gates of the Yad Vashem national memorial, which the Israeli protagonist derides as the 'Central Indulgence Fund'. He also criticises the talk of a 'just war' and complains that the generation of sabras in Israel have been preparing for death all their lives.²⁰⁶ Again and again, Omer's Israeli protagonist expresses the sabra's youthful contempt for his own society. Shalom Ben-Chorin, one of the novel's first reviewers, wrote the following shortly after its publication:

> The book's protagonist is disgusted by the phrase-mongers of the State of Israel's ruling class, by the narrow ghetto spirit of an Eastern European petty bourgeoisie, by the religious intolerance of 'God's Cossacks' [Orthodox Jews] and their fanaticism.²⁰⁷

Most of all, Omer was provocative with his language, which, Ben-Chorin believed, 'had, beyond a doubt, never appeared in print in Hebrew literature':

> Dan Omer emphasises that he writes a spoken Hebrew, which is deliberately not the literary written language, but the often very rude jargon of sabra youth [. . .] who do not mince their words.²⁰⁸

His provocations were not limited to his abusive insults of Orthodox Jews; they included sexualised and pornographic vocabulary. 'Until Dan Omer', wrote Shimon Tzabar, Omer's friend of many years, 'Hebrew was a circumcised language, circumcised in the sense that the modern Hebrew words for penis or vagina seldom appeared in print'.[209] The pornographic passages of the book were also the state attorney's grounds for bringing the case. As with the trial over *Bul* magazine, the Jerusalem Magistrate Court denied Omer's motion to call up the poet Haim Gouri as a literary expert witness. Instead, Judge Moshe Landau's decree held that Omer's book had 'not even a spark of literary talent to redeem it' and was 'so obscene that its distribution ought not to be permitted even according to the most liberal and lenient criteria to which we have been accustomed in our days'.[210]

The short novel was neither Omer's first literary work, nor his first act of rebellion. Born in 1940 in Ramat Gan and raised in Jerusalem, Omer had come to blows with Orthodox Judaism multiple times at a young age.[211] After being transferred to a religious nursery school, he developed an aversion to the education he received there, which soon led to his expulsion from another religious school at age seven. He had refused to utter a traditional blessing thanking God for not having been born a woman, arguing that the text was contemptuous towards women. 'That ended the religious part of his life', Omer's father later recalled, linking his son's rejection of Orthodox Judaism to Omer's mother's experiences.[212] Sophia Kagan, a daughter of one of the founders of Hovevei Zion, had been bullied by Orthodox Jews when she attended the Zionist kindergarten in her native Lwów (now Lviv, Ukraine). Omer's father, Oscar Herlinger, had migrated in 1934 from Czechoslovakia to Palestine, where he changed his name to Mareni on the prompting of his good friend Menachem Ussishkin and found a full-time job in the Jerusalem municipal government. His son thought the surname Mareni sounded too Italian, and Hebraicised it to Omer at age sixteen.[213]

From both parents, Dan inherited his love of books and literature, which soon translated into a yearning to write literature of his own. In the early 1960s, after a year in England, he co-founded the literary and arts journal *Kav* with Yona Fisher and Rachel Shapira. The journal published the greats of (subcultural) Hebrew literature, from Yonathan Ratosh and Itzhak Danziger to Amos Kenan, David Avidan and even Yehuda Amichai. Meanwhile, Omer began writing himself. He published his first poems in the collections *Laila Aroch* (Long Night, 1963) and *Elohim baJeans* (God in Jeans, 1966). These products of an Israeli bohemian culture reflected the formative influence of the American Beat movement. When his book *Ba-Derekh* was released, he was already preparing a Hebrew-language anthology of American poetry and prose, which he would later publish as *Howl*, after Allen Ginsberg's scandalous poem.[214] But Omer was most enthusiastic about the novel *On the Road* by Ginsberg's literary comrade Jack Kerouac. *Ba-Derech* was partly an adaptation of this grand example. But he was not at all interested in simply replicating the novel in an Israeli guise.[215]

In sympathy with the Beats' literary and cultural protest against the moral and social conventions of conservative America, Omer saw his own book most of all as a weapon in the abiding conflict over the character of Israeli society and the Hebrew language. Amidst uproar over his book, he contended:

> Hebrew literature has a problem that someone who knows Arabic might understand. In Arabic there is a literary language and a spoken one. We've got a level of beautiful written words that are as exquisite as they are hollow. Today if you're reading Hebrew literature, you need an encyclopedia as well as a dictionary.[216]

Upon completing *Ba-Derekh* in the summer of 1966, he hand-delivered a copy to the chair of the Committee for the Prohibition of Obscene Literature at the Ministry of Education with the intention of provoking a ban and then protesting it.[217] Omer staged a culture war, complete with a public campaign, a hunger strike and brazen sales of the book alongside his protest tent, which was located outside the Israeli Prime Minister's office (Figure 3.2).[218] Omer called himself the 'Columbus of Hebrew literature', a man setting out to explore unknown continents within his own native language:

> They say my novel is obscene for using cheap language and four-letter words. [...] [N]obody has used these words before in writing, although they are used in everyday language.[219]

This trotted-out role as the 'pioneer "pornographer" of Hebrew literature' (in the words of Shimon Tzabar) transformed Omer's trial into another battle of the enduring Israeli culture wars.²²⁰ Just as a whole group of supporters had bought Omer's books and signed a petition for freedom of expression and against literary censorship, his intellectual allies plunged into the public debate. *Haolam Hazeh* – within the pages of which Omer had taken over as a literary critic in the 1970s with the 'Paper Tiger' column – voiced open solidarity with the protest. Shimon Tzabar and Amos Kenan took their friend's side in their columns in *Haaretz* and *Yediot Aharonot*.²²¹ Years after Omer's premature death in 1984, Kenan would refer to him as 'the most important fighter we had in our cultural war'.²²² Yet although the conflict over the character of the Hebrew language was won in the long run – Omer's book was the very last to be banned under section 179 – the associated clash over the state's national and cultural self-definition fell by the wayside. During the trial over the publication of *Ba-Derekh*, the Six-Day War answered the lingering question of the state's Jewish versus Hebrew character and intensified the conflict between Israel and its Arab neighbours. The inventors of a new Hebrew culture, in contrast, sought to advance the State of Israel's secularisation and thus encourage its integration into the region.

Figure 3.2 Writer on a hunger strike: Dan Omer outside his protest tent in Jerusalem, 1966.

From Hebrew Nation to Semitic Action

Only a few days after the Sinai Campaign began in November 1956, Uri Avnery received a surprising phone call from Nathan Yellin-Mor at the *Haolam Hazeh* editorial offices. The two men had parted ways many years earlier and had not crossed paths for quite some time.[223] As the 'political mastermind' of Lehi, Yellin-Mor guided the former underground group into legality and then, as the chair of its successor group, Mifleget HaLohamim (Fighters' List), he occupied a seat in the first Knesset in order to realise the paramilitary group's ends through political means.[224] Lehi's longstanding neutrality on foreign policy matters was upheld in the new party, as was its claim on the entire territory of Mandatory Palestine, a claim it did not renounce after the war's end.[225] Although Avnery was partial to such positions, he had diverged from established party politics upon founding *Haolam Hazeh*. Instead, the magazine became the political outlet of his demands for the separation of synagogue and state, for the equality of Israeli Arabs as citizens and for the new state's integration into the region. By the time the two of them met again in 1951, after Yellin-Mor lost his campaign for re-election to the Knesset and his party fell apart, their opposing viewpoints on the nature of that integration had become irreconcilable. Avnery favoured an alliance between the young state and the Arab nationalist movements, whereas Yellin-Mor wanted a coalition with the region's national minorities: Maronites, Kurds, Druzes and Alawites.[226]

Five years later, the British–French–Israeli military engagement brought the two of them back together. Yellin-Mor's profound concerns about 'Israeli complicity in Britain and France's colonial conspiracy' inspired him to get back in touch with Avnery.[227] Still, it took time to persuade the somewhat younger Avnery that an alliance with colonialism in its waning days would 'now finally vilify Israel as a base of Western imperialism in the region and make prospects of peace and reconciliation with the Arab neighbours even more distant'.[228] First, he had to dissuade Avnery from his patriotic reporting, which initially painted Nasser as the Hebrew state's greatest threat, but went a step further: in the first wartime issue of *Haolam Hazeh*, Avnery reported eagerly on the Israeli Army's territorial conquests in the Sinai Desert and spoke of soldierly courage. Only after Yellin-Mor 'shook him back to his senses did

Avnery understand the gravity of his action and the injustice of defending the imperialist invasion'.²²⁹ Then Avnery, too, became a critic of the military campaign and backtracked from his initial instincts. When the two of them met at Café Ravel in Tel Aviv, they united around this attitude and their ambition for a new political alternative in the country. And that meeting marked the birth of Semitic Action (Peula HaShemit). Boaz Evron, Benjamin Omry and the lawyer Yaakov Yerdor soon joined them. With their common political trajectories, reaching back to pre-state times, the group presented itself as another step in the history of the Hebrew national movement.²³⁰

Within a short time, this initial group grew into a circle of between twenty and twenty-five people who met monthly at Café Herlinger in Tel Aviv. Maxim Ghilan was also involved, and Amos Kenan kept in regular contact from Paris. Although the Herlinger group did not plan any immediate political activities, seeking instead to devise an all-new agenda for the state, it was the involvement of former underground fighters that probably led the press to nickname them the 'Herlinger Underground'.²³¹ In defiance of their public pigeonholing, this group put together a new manifesto that ushered in a sea change in the conflict over Israel's identity, the Palestine question and Israel's role in the Middle East. Later, recalling Nathan Yellin-Mor, Uri Avnery would write that: 'It might be true that only a person with a strong national sentiment can understand the national sentiment beside him'.²³²

Simultaneously, *The Hebrew Manifesto* released by Semitic Action on 1 September 1958 marked a cutting of ties with the Zionist Right – in which many of its key figures had originated – and a transition to a nationalist left, which declared a new Hebrew nation to be the starting point for Israel's integration into the Middle East. *The Hebrew Manifesto* proclaimed the difference between the Hebrew nation and the Jewish Diaspora and sought to decouple Israel's national, political and economic existence from the lives and experiences of Jews outside Israel. Yet it became a 'real Magna Charta [sic] for the rights of both Israelis and Palestinians to their homeland', because it linked Israeli Jews' right to exist to a recognition of Palestinians' right to establish their own state.²³³ The section on 'partnership in the land' asserted: 'The whole Land of Israel is the homeland of two nations – the Hebrew [nation], which gained independence in the framework of the state of Israel, and the Palestinian Arab [nation], which has not gained independence yet.' This section then proceeded to demand that Israeli politicians 'establish a free Palestinian state'.[234] Yet this recognition of Palestinian national ambitions entailed more than just support for the return of Palestinian refugees. It fit into larger plans for a federation, a proposal for the establishment of a 'Jordanian Union' that would unite the entire territory of former Mandatory Palestine. This imperative to preserve the country's unity, if only in some supranational form, was the last gasp of resurgent old right-wing Zionist myths.[235]

Beyond the territory of historical Palestine, such hopes for a 'Jordanian Union' were symptoms of a desire for Israeli involvement in the much larger processes that were transforming the entire Middle East. Although the Sinai Campaign and the Suez Crisis were the direct triggers of Semitic Action's founding, it arose within the broader context of the emerging independence movements of the Arab world. First, British and American military forces intervened to prevent a coup in Jordan shortly before General Qassim's successful revolution in Iraq during summer 1958. The ensuing call for Israel to give up its official alliance with the West and instead to support 'the liberation wars of the region's peoples to crush the remains of colonialism in any form' was not just a product of the group's dreams of a federation of the region's national independence movements.[236] This position paired the past anticolonialist spirit of the Hebrew underground with an awareness of the series of contemporary anticolonial independence movements, in which the former Lehi and *BaMaavak* members saw themselves reflected. At the same time, their hopes of mutual recognition between the Hebrew, Arab and other national movements as a key ingredient of the historic liberation movement in the Semitic-speaking region went hand in hand with the view that such recognition would be the sole guarantee of Israeli existence.[237]

Of all the anticolonial movements at the time, the members of Semitic Action paid the most attention to the Front de Libération Nationale (FLN) and its struggle for independence from France. While the conflict in Algeria had rallied the Israeli government in support of the French colonial power, a statement by the leading FLN representative, Ferhat Abbas, to the effect that Israeli support for Algerian independence would 'help in bridging the abyss separating Israel from the rest of African and Asian nations' had led to some individual Israelis making informal contact with the Algerian side.[238]

Building on initial encounters at Mediterranean conferences organised by the Mayor of Florence Giorgio de la Pira beginning in 1958, Uri Avnery and Shalom Cohen had tried to make *Haolam Hazeh* into a mouthpiece for pro-Algerian Israeli opinion. Alongside critiques of Israeli foreign policy and reportages about the FLN's struggles, they published the 'Manifesto of the 121', in which French intellectuals spoke out against their government's war in Algeria and use of torture there, demanded that France respect conscientious objectors and supported the Algerians' struggle as a legitimate fight against colonialism.[239] A parallel search for a channel for directly supporting the FLN led to semi-official meetings between the dissident Israelis and the UN representatives of the Republic of Algeria's provisional government. These efforts paid off in Paris, where the intermediary Eli Lobel – Matzpen's France-based spokesperson since the Six-Day War – connected Amos Kenan and Uri Avnery with a network of FLN supporters led by Henri Curiel (1914–78).[240] (Curiel had taken over this network from Francis Jeanson's network after Jeanson's imprisonment.)[241] Curiel eventually proposed the establishment of a separate Israeli organisation that would devote itself entirely to supporting the FLN and the Algerian fight for independence. On 28 December 1960, this idea culminated in the Israeli Committee for a Free Algeria, which consisted of Uri Avnery, Amos Kenan, Nathan Yellin-Mor, Maxim Ghilan and Shalom Cohen, who were primarily recruited from Semitic Action.[242]

In Israel, Nathan Yellin-Mor was the main spokesperson communicating the committee's statements of solidarity to the broader public, including the claim that 'all Israeli freedom fighters salute the Algerian people'.[243] Yellin-Mor's dedication to the Algerian cause even reached the notice of the FLN, which delightedly asked Avnery – their temporary middleman in Paris – whether they could draw on the paramilitary experience of the former underground fighter from the notorious 'Stern Gang'.[244] In Avnery's own country, these developments also fed hopes that foreign policy support for the Algerian War of Independence might give a head start to Israeli integration in the Arab region and could defuse the conflict with Israel's Arab neighbours. This prospect lent the committee support that went far beyond the horizon of Semitic Action. Yellin-Mor's media-savvy comment that 'Israel's support for the Algerian struggle for freedom shall contribute to the forming of ties with a most significant Arab population that is not hitched to the Cairo train' made its mark immediately.²⁴⁵ Within a short time, the list of supporters expanded past Dan Omer and Shimon Tzabar to include the magazine editors-in-chief Gabriel Moked (of *Achshav*), Viktor Cygelmann (of the Polish-language magazine *Od Nowa*) and Shimon Shereshevsky (of *Ner*).²⁴⁶ The eventual failure of the Israeli Committee for a Free Algeria's political initiatives resulted from more than just the Israeli government's ongoing alliance with colonial France. More broadly, the implications of the Algerian conflict for the Palestine question, which immediately followed Algerian independence, exposed a yawning gap between the Hebrew anticolonialism of the 1940s and the Algerian aspiration for independence: the anticolonialism of immigrants who had reinvented themselves as natives to oust the British mandatory power in Palestine contrasted with the uprising of an indigenous population against its colonisers.

Even if the Israeli Committee for a Free Algeria failed in its mission, and even if *The Hebrew Manifesto* remained unfulfilled, in the late 1950s and early 1960s, Semitic Action's efforts on behalf of anticolonialism and the Palestinian cause sparked – at least in the estimation of Maxim Ghilan – an 'enormously sympathetic response' from dissident Israeli youth, which eventually gathered around the magazine *Etgar* (Challenge).²⁴⁷ The name traces back to a coinage by Yellin-Mor, who supervised the magazine's editorial work from 1960 to 1967. Shimon Tzabar and Dan Omer contributed their writings and caricatures, joined, most importantly, by Haim Hanegbi, who, years before co-founding Matzpen, had made the rounds of the Hebrew milieu. He began by engaging in editing work at *Haolam Hazeh* and moved from there to *Etgar*, where he spent two years on the editorial board at Yellin-Mor's request. Shortly thereafter, he became secretary of the Israeli Committee for a Free Algeria.

Gabriel 'Gabi' Lachman (b. 1943) and Arie Bober (b. 1940) also had their first political experiences among the *Haolam Hazeh* crowd, together with their friend Aharon Bachar. They would later make up the younger generation of Semitic Action.²⁴⁸ For Lachman, this political stance was a continuation, albeit shifted, of his family's history. If his Berlin-born mother and his Poznań-born father had already familiarised him with the sentiment of not feeling entirely at home in Israel, it was partly through their allegiance to the Communist Party, which their son inherited as an experience of dissent in the Israeli state. Lachman himself later associated this feeling with Avnery's weekly: in the early 1950s, 'it was almost the only [voice of] opposition to the Ben-Gurion government and Mapai, in the struggle against the military administration over the Arab population and in support for struggles like the sailor's strike and the social protests of the Wadi Salib residents.'

Arie Bober brought a different perspective to the table. For the impetuous young man, born in Haifa in 1940 to a strictly religious family, the Hebrew scene represented more of a break with family and tradition. After memberships in various kibbutzim, the charming but self-absorbed chemistry student was so impressed by the aura of the former Lehi leader Yellin-Mor that he joined his newspaper, *Etgar*. It was here he met his future Matzpen comrades, Haim Hanegbi and Gabi Lachman.

With its resolute anticolonialism and the Hebrew-national breach with Zionism, Semitic Action influenced the entire founding generation of Matzpen. Matzpen also grew out of the sabra generation of the Communist Party, and the group's founders were themselves shaped by that cultural transformation.[249] As they seceded from their parent party, Akiva Orr and Moshé Machover, introduced by Haim Hanegbi, several times found themselves in the company of Avnery and Yellin-Mor's group and had considered collaborating. The latter group had returned with an offer of creating a dedicated space for them in the pages of *Etgar*. But because the young dissidents were looking for a revolutionary alternative to the Communist Party, the joint project had no future. 'We discovered at once that they did not have revolutionary intentions at all', Machover later recalled.[250] Still, Matzpen remained part of that Hebrew culture and was perceived as such. Not only did *Etgar* publish Matzpen's mission statement after the rift with its parent Communist Party; Amos Kenan's appeal for a new left in Israel was also printed in *Matzpen*, whose editors insinuated that their own organisation's founding had already answered that call.[251] By making such pledges, Haim Hanegbi – who left Semitic Action upon Matzpen's founding – had also succeeded in convincing its younger members to switch organisations. 'I stole the youth movement from them', he recalled, commenting on the fact that Gabi Lachman, Aharon Bachar and later Arie Bober all moved to Matzpen.[252] He also made a big impression on Eli Aminov, who had been part of the League against Religious Coercion, then *Haolam Hazeh* and finally Semitic Action, before moving to Matzpen in January 1967.

Above all, 'it was clear to us that no solution to the Palestine problem would be possible on the basis of a nationalist ideology', Lachman later wrote, explaining his shift in allegiances.[253] It was not long after the founding of Matzpen that the ideological differences were compounded by disagreements over the history and present status of the Palestine conflict, which flared up in connection with the residual nationalism in Semitic Action's self-image. 'Hebrew nationalism is indeed opposed to Zionism; but it is incapable of confronting Zionism thoroughly and repudiating it radically, root and branch',[254] Moshé Machover argued, stressing Matzpen's distance from *Haolam Hazeh* and Semitic Action.

> For the Hebrew nation has come into being as a result of the Zionist colonization of Palestine, and therefore the nationalist outlook, for which this nation is an absolute and supreme value, cannot radically repudiate Zionism, its progenitor. Hebrew nationalism can only claim that Zionism is outdated, no longer suited to present conditions, and Hebrew nationalism ought to be embraced in its place. Thus Hebrew nationalism gets into a contradiction: on the one hand it repudiates Zionism, and on the other it regards itself as Zionism's legitimate heir.[255]

The Israeli leftists further pointed out that including the Palestinians in a 'Jordanian Union', as Semitic Action proposed, would run counter to Palestinian national aspirations. After all, the Palestinians' discernible greater preference was for participating in the Arab world's process of integration. Even if the Semitic Action's prospect of a 'new unification of the land', including the Palestinians, evoked a supranational idea, this notion would not erase their nationalist heritage. 'The people of the "Semitic Action" took an important step when they gave up Zionism', Akiva Orr and Moshé Machover emphasised in Matzpen, and concluded that they would take a much more important step when they give up "Hebrew" nationalism and establish for themselves, as a supranational ideal, the central ideal of our time – that of socialism'.[256]

Yet, as much as these contrasts were evident in various visions of the future, they had their origins in differing perspectives on the past: that 'the Lehi members who were now in Semitic Action' had inherited the former underground organisation's 'Hebrew nationalism' along with its anti-imperialism reveals the hard-to-reconcile contrast between two different notions of the Hebrew collective's local legitimacy.²⁵⁷ Semitic Action believed that the underground fighting of the late 1940s had targeted the British colonial regime in Palestine, aligning it with the national and anticolonial movements of the region. In light of the Algerian War of Independence, however, the Israeli leftists from Matzpen started to judge their own conflict from the opposite vantage point: the Algerian War restructured Matzpen's view of the Palestine question. With this perspective, the Hebrew nation was not just the child of an anticolonial independence movement, but also the grandchild of a colonial settlement history that placed Hebrews at odds with Palestinian Arabs:

> It is therefore our duty to recognise the fact that whereas for the Jews of Israel, the 1948 War for Independence fulfilled their dreams of national self-determination, for the Arabs of Palestine it signified no more and no less than the replacement of the British *gendarme* with a Jewish one.²⁵⁸

These discrepancies between Semitic Action and *Haolam Hazeh*'s positions and Matzpen's could not be reconciled for long.

Still, these disagreements did not prevent an initial collaboration. In particular, the two groups' efforts on behalf of the legal equality of Israeli Arabs and against the ongoing Israeli military administration united them in protest. Chiefly, the call for support of Uri Avnery's new *Haolam Hazeh-Koach Hadash* party – through which Avnery hoped to protect his publication from a possible ban – led the two groups to work together more closely for the duration of this period. The collaboration was not uncontested within Matzpen, however. Some of Matzpen's Arab members from Haifa, who had joined the group two years earlier, were especially opposed to participating in a party that they felt embodied petty bourgeois and nationalistic concerns. In fact, Daud Turki quit the group over this conflict.²⁵⁹ In the end, only individual members of Matzpen, not the group itself, joined Avnery's list. Still, the predominant view was that the new party remained 'progressive, secular and non-Zionist (though not anti-Zionist)', a position previously absent from Israel's political map.²⁶⁰ In 1965, when the party finally entered the sixth Israeli Knesset with a mandate, the members of Matzpen prided themselves on the fruits of their organisation's support.

The harmony would not last. Soon after that political success, Matzpen accused Avnery of advocating that their group disband and join his party wholesale. In turn, Avnery often suspected Matzpen members of trying to establish a subversive underground within his party. What began as a competition to monopolise this political space was quickly revealed to be a split in perceptions of the Israeli–Palestinian conflict.[261] This was first demonstrated by differing stances towards the Israeli Law of Return: Matzpen demanded its complete repeal, whereas Avnery held reservations and exceptions. For all the confirmed cultural differences, he was much less resolutely opposed to a political link between Israel and diasporic Jewry than the followers of Matzpen, who called for a clear dissolution of Israel's Zionist structure. From the very beginning, however, the conflict centred on the hotly debated question of the contours and validity of Israel's borders. Avnery's essential premise that the Israeli borders of 1949 should be considered binding because they emerged from the Hebrew War of Independence was stridently opposed by his Matzpen allies in the context of the Palestine question and the recurring territorial expansions of the Jewish state. The existing borders of 1949 were 'by no means sacred', they argued.[262]

The conflict finally escalated and came to a head at *Haolam Hazeh-Koach Hadash*'s first party conference to set their policy agenda, in December 1966, when the Israeli leftists of Matzpen refused Avnery's mandatory pledge and his demand for a commitment to specific borders. Moshé Machover voiced the most vocal and indignant disagreement. He pointed out that not only was Avnery committing to a territorial definition that grew out of violating the UN Partition Plan, but he had also publicly advocated annexations in *Haolam Hazeh* during the second Arab–Israeli war of 1956. 'Indeed, suppose the Israeli government will annex Nablus and hold it for a number of years, the status of Nablus at that time will be like that of any territory conquered by the IDF in 1948', Machover's tirade concluded. '[S]o if today we agree to accept, as a matter of *principle*, the border that exists *right now*, why should we not accept in the future any border that would exist then?'[263] The collaboration ended there. Within months, the Six-Day War would shift the country's borders once again and deepen the gulf between the former allies.

After 1967: Hostilities and Contradictions

In the winter of 1973, the philosopher of religion Gershom Scholem gave an in-depth interview about his life and his academic work. Besides revisiting the themes of his Zionist-motivated immigration to Palestine, the conversation became an appeal for a tight link between the Jewish state and Jewish tradition. Since the 1960s, Scholem had repeatedly pointed out the unifying elements between Israel and the Diaspora and stressed 'that the existence of Israel no less than that of the Diaspora, depends on our placing the primacy of our connection with the Jewish people – its history and present state – at the centre of our decisions'.[264] In an aside, he also talked about currents of Israeli politics that, in seeking to unfasten Israel and Israeli Jews' political existence from their ethnic and historical past, agitated for an independent cultural tradition:

> If the Jews try to explain themselves only in a historical dimension, they will of necessity find themselves thinking about self-liquidation and total destruction. If the things Uri Avneri, Yonatan Ratosh, and the Matzpen people say materialise, the Jewish people will find itself without any impulse to continue existing.[265]

It was no accident that Scholem now added Uri Avnery and Matzpen as new targets of his credo – that he was 'downright anti-Canaanite'.[266] He saw both as reincarnations of the same cultural nativists who, rejecting the Zionist narrative of a 'Jewish people' that bridged the Diaspora and Israel, instead sought recognition for a new nation that had emerged from the Israeli present.

But even if the cultural traces of the Canaanite movements, mediated by Uri Avnery and *Haolam Hazeh*, lived on in Matzpen's talk of a new Hebrew nation with a right to self-determination, their political perspectives diverged significantly. The Israel–Palestine conflict had exposed disagreements that would be cast in even sharper relief by the Six-Day War and its accompanying territorial conquests, which, in turn, caused the resurfacing of the Palestine question. These opposing political positions were especially evident when the Canaanite movement briefly revived in an alliance with the incipient Movement for Greater Israel (literally, the Movement for a Whole Israel).[267] Although the politics of radical, secular non-Zionists barely overlapped with the movement's fundamentally religious precepts, the 'Hebrew utopia' of Yonatan Rarosh and Aharon Amir ran parallel to the 'Jewish Messianism' of Nathan Alterman and his movement. Even if the two movements derived their legitimacy from different conceptions of Israel's existence, they shared claims on the unpartitioned country. By founding an action committee for the retention of the newly acquired territories, Aharon Amir laid the groundwork for collaboration with the Movement for Greater Israel. He explained his approach thus:

> With the war, I saw a spontaneous occasion to keep all this, to solve the refugee problem. A chance to integrate the Arabs as far as possible into Israeli society. An opportunity to help achieve the de-Zionisation of the state on a secular, non-denominational basis. Abba Eban said after the war that the choice was to be great or to be Jewish. Eban chooses a Jewish nation, I choose a great one.[268]

There were, indeed, differences between the 'Hebrew imperialism' of Aharon Amir, who sought to unite the region as one territory on the model of the historical 'Land of Kedem', and the Jewish Messianism of the Movement for Greater Israel.[269] However, because both perspectives legitimised the territorial gains of the Six-Day War, they each circumvented the Palestine question and the Palestinians' national and territorial claims.

The various perspectives on the war, the occupation and the Israel–Palestine conflict would also open a rift between the formerly concordant representatives of *Haolam Hazeh*'s cultural and political milieu. The war and the subsequent occupation brought a radicalisation process, during which Shimon Tzabar and Dan Omer moved noticeably closer to the anti-Zionist stance of Matzpen; meanwhile, the founding members of Semitic Action – Uri Avnery, Amos Kenan and Nathan Yellin-Mor – defended the necessity of the war. The disagreements and discrepancies that had already been apparent before the war now turned *Matzpen* and *Haolam Hazeh* into political adversaries.[270]

The first, decisive moment in this new rivalry came when, in the middle of the war, Avnery reported enthusiastically about the Israeli Army's advances. When the troops were deep in the Sinai, had conquered the Old City of Jerusalem and had just made inroads into the Syrian Golan Heights, Avnery defied his partner Shalom Cohen's advice and ran the headline 'The Objective: Damascus!' in *Daf Yomi*, a special daily edition of *Haolam Hazeh*, calling for further advancements into Syrian territory.[271] Fouzi El-Asmar, who edited *Hadha al-Alam* – the Arabic edition of *Haolam Hazeh* – and was a staff member of *Daf Yomi*, was the first to express his bitter disappointment at Avnery's articles. He quit before the war was out.[272] Aggravated by the mood in the wartime newsroom, which increasingly singled him out as an Arab, he found a confidant in his friend Haim Hanegbi.[273] Hanegbi, who was a founding member of Matzpen, a fixture on the *Haolam Hazeh* editorial team and a personal friend of Avnery, was likewise fed up with his militaristic and expansionist attitude. Calling Avnery a 'rabid chauvinist', Hanegbi followed suit and quit *Daf Yomi*. Shortly afterwards, Avnery also dismissed him from the *Haolam Hazeh* editorial team (Figure 3.3).[274]

Uri Avnery was not unconditionally loyal to the Israeli military by any means. The day after the ceasefire, Amos Kenan, who had served as a reservist officer during the war, came into the *Haolam Hazeh* newsroom, shocked. He recounted the military violence that took place during the expulsions of Arab villagers from the area of Beit Nuba, Imwas and Yalu. Avnery encouraged him to write an eyewitness statement. In his role as a Member of Knesset, Avnery hoped to use the statement to protest against the operations, which had already passed a point of no return.[275] Kenan sent his eyewitness statement to Avnery and Moshe Sneh, but also to Levi Eshkol and his Defence Minister

Figure 3.3 In conflict: Uri Avnery (left) and Haim Hanegbi (right), shortly after the war of June 1967.

Moshe Dayan, calling upon politicians and the military to abide by the laws of war and restore the army's moral integrity. Nonetheless, he decided against disseminating it more widely or sharing it with the international public.[276] Kenan was very angry when a translation of his statement appeared in the international press against his wishes. Fouzi El-Asmar had read the statement via Nina Dinur and secretly passed it on to Mordechai Stein, the lawyer and leader of the Third Force Movement, who translated it into English and sent it worldwide. Kenan's enraged personal comments against Stein were only the half of it.[277] In a letter to the editor, printed in *Maariv* under the headline 'The Use of the Report: A Detrimental Service to the Nation', Kenan distanced himself from the statement's dissemination and denounced it as the propaganda equivalent of 'supplying weapons to our enemy' and 'inflat[ing] the real wrongdoing to unrealistic and indecent proportions'.[278] He meant to express strong criticisms in his report, but he had only sought a discussion within Israeli society. 'To the outsider', Kenan's letter to the editor concluded, 'we will stand united as one man'.[279] For Shimon Tzabar, who had been friends with Kenan for years, a friendship affirmed by their joint publication of the satirical magazine *Dapim Zehubim* (Yellow Pages) shortly before the Six-Day War, Kenan's protest against his report's international publication became the first step towards an irreversible estrangement. 'This episode is a good demonstration of what courage means to some intellectuals', he wrote in his autobiography, referring to the incident. 'They would not mind giving up their life for their country, but to sacrifice their popularity is quite a different matter.'[280] Meanwhile, Tzabar said that the 'most courageous thing ever published' in Israel was a small booklet compiled by his friends Dan Omer and Arie Bober shortly after the war ended.[281] Omer and Bober had also served in the Israeli Army during the Six-Day War. The booklet, *Nimas!* (Fed Up!), expressed their displeasure and frustration at the outcome of the war. Like Omer's scandalous book *Ba-Derekh* before it, the booklet was released by Golgatha Books and listed Café Ta'amon as the contact address. Omer and Bober's incensed publication likewise included an eyewitness account of the events of the war. During the war, they were both stationed in the Jordan Valley and had witnessed the Arab residents' hurried escape across the river. With their report, they sought to 'break the conspiracy of silence [. . .] that is so comfortable to the conscience of this nation' and to expose the military force by which the Israeli

Army had prevented the refugees from returning to their homes. The authors drew provocative and polemical parallels to the situation in Nazi Germany and articulated an appeal for Israeli soldiers to refuse combat service:

> Soldier, if you do not [. . .] disobey such orders – you are a murderer! Citizen, if you do not act from this minute on to prevent such orders from being given, you are an accomplice to murder, and, like the German, you will not be able to plead later 'I did not know'.[282]

The booklet positioned itself in firm opposition to the war's territorial conquests and a military occupation, and was accordingly scandalised by any talk of 'liberated', rather than occupied, territories. By including caricatures from Shimon Tzabar and the painter Uri Lifshitz, as well as a text by Haim Hanegbi, the booklet brought together many of the people who had recently signed the advertisement in *Haaretz* calling for an immediate, unconditional withdrawal from the occupied territories.

Apart from expressing their public discomfort with Israel's military actions, this protest against the incipient occupation played a large part in drawing a segment of Hebrew bohemia towards the Israeli Socialist Organization. Unlike Arie Bober, neither Tzabar nor Omer were Matzpen members; they merely moved in the same cultural circles as their political friends. Haim Hanegbi, who moved in both circles equally, had even discouraged Dan Omer from joining Matzpen. The two scenes were too dissimilar, he said, for a rebellious Beat poet from Jerusalem to find his place within a strictly structured New Left group.[283] But a thematic convergence between the two was already evident from the motto on the title page of the newsletter *Shtika: Digest LeBeit HaShlishi* (Silence: Digest of the Third Temple), the self-declared 'second publication of the Israeli anti-annexation movement in Jerusalem'. The motto: 'Hebrew socialist revolution against the nationalistic and fascistic Golgotha'.[284] Omer would later continue compiling articles from the Israeli media, which documented the national and religious discourses about the occupation, in the very pages of *Matzpen*. As it was, the fine distinctions between Matzpen and the subcultural circles of its sympathisers were unimportant to the Israeli public. When Omer and Bober distributed their magazine on the campus of the Hebrew University of Jerusalem, they were cursed at, labelled traitors and self-hating Jews, and beaten.[285]

The exponents of Hebrew culture were now divided by their views on the Israeli occupation and their differing proximity to the positions of Matzpen. This tore apart the friendship between Shimon Tzabar and Amos Kenan once and for all. After a visit to the occupied territories, Kenan, albeit no supporter of the occupation, expressed sentimental feelings about the beauty of the country, which had been divided since 1948. Such sentiments and Kenan's protests against the use of his eyewitness account gave Tzabar doubts about the foundations of their longstanding friendship. So it was that after being rejected by Itzhak Danziger and Yigal Tumarkin, Tzabar did not even approach Kenan when he was searching for people to sign his *Haaretz* advertisement against the occupation.[286] Yet immediately after the war's end, Kenan had promoted his own vision of peace: 'A Palestinian state within the framework of a federation with Israel'. On this, he was in agreement with Uri Avnery, who, moreover, favoured the official phrase 'administrated territories' over the word 'occupation'.[287] Avnery even dismissed the leftists' protest against the Israeli occupation as hyperbole that disregarded the liberal nature of the territory's administration. Far more consequential was his early Knesset vote, in 27 June 1967, authorising the annexation and absorption of East Jerusalem, a vote that prompted harsh accusations in the pages of *Matzpen*.[288] In the eyes of Matzpen, his justification, that Jerusalem should 'become the federal capital [...] of both states', reflected Avnery's stance from 1956: Israel–Palestinian rapprochement only under Israeli military authority.[289] If Avnery wanted peace and even a Palestinian state under Israel's supervision, Matzpen considered 'such a solution' to be merely the 'equivalent to the South African Bantustan "solution" to the problems of relations between whites and Africans'.[290]

The conflict over the occupation would leave friendships in tatters – not only between Tzabar and Kenan, but between *Matzpen* and *Haolam Hazeh*. It was also one reason for the self-imposed political exile of Shimon Tzabar, which in June 1968 led him to Paris and, ultimately, London. Aside from a few visits, he would never return to Israel. Akiva Orr, with whom he stayed for the first few weeks, later remembered Shimon Tzabar having said:

> When I saw that Kenan was enchanted by the landscape but was completely oblivious to the suffering of its inhabitants, I became deeply depressed. If a man like him, who was 'the conscience of the 1948 generation', behaved like this, what could I expect from the rest of this generation? So I decided to exile myself from this colonisatory enterprise.[291]

Such a sweeping dismissal might have been overly harsh, and perhaps also misplaced, given Kenan's eyewitness report after the war and his growing support for the Palestinian independence movement. All the same, it corresponded to Tzabar's personal disappointment and articulated his sense of estrangement from his country and his political and cultural milieu. The same context applies to his satirically exaggerated comment – namely, that he devoted the first half of his life to building Israel, only to spend the second half opposing it.[292] During his journey to Europe, Tzabar was already resolving to produce a satirical magazine fully dedicated to criticising Israel in its reborn, post-1967 form from abroad, and 'decided to hit [the Israeli government] in the place where it hurts most: international public opinion'.[293] Only a few months after Tzabar arrived in London, the first issue of this new magazine appeared. Ironically, he obtained the money to finance it straight from the Israeli government: in the form of compensation payments for a war injury. Its title: *Israel Imperial News*. 'After the victory, the people went completely crazy', Tzabar told the *London Times* (Figure 3.4), explaining his decision to publish the magazine. 'After 2,000 years as a minority, they found themselves in the role of conquerors. I believe our problem is not an Arab

Figure 3.4   The Hebrew writer Shimon Tzabar during his London period, 1974.

problem, but an Israeli problem.'[294] The new English-language publication mostly featured translations of articles that had been previously printed in *Nimas* and *Shtika*, alongside reports on the situation in the occupied territories, which Tzabar gathered from the Hebrew press. Another collaborator was Dan Omer, who began publishing Tzabar's literary journal *Dapim Zehubim* in Jerusalem, but occasionally spent time in London.[295] The new publication reprinted Omer and Arie Bober's joint appeal for military and civil disobedience, as well as the translation of Amos Kenan's eyewitness report – against Kenan's will, of course.[296] As a cry of frustration at the loss of their own country, and as a symbol of political protest by Israelis abroad, *Israel Imperial News* made a splash among British leftists and mainstream dailies alike. Tzabar's only greater success was his satirical book *The White-Flag Principle: How to Lose a War (and Why)*. He had articulated some early thoughts on this subject – the political advantages of a military defeat – even before the war, but these arguments would only take full effect as a critique of the Israeli victory after the Six-Day War.[297]

In Israel, Tzabar quickly became one of the 'most reviled people' for his publications of 1968 and 1969.[298] The daily papers ran articles with such headlines as 'Insults against Israel Abroad' and defamed him as an 'Israeli Lord Haw-Haw', a reference to a British character from 1930's fascist propaganda.[299] Most importantly, however, Uri Avnery continued to condemn Tzabar in the pages of *Haolam Hazeh*. His article 'Wretched Figures' provides vivid testimony to their friendship's descent into enmity. This was compounded when Tzabar joined forces with Moshé Machover and Akiva Orr in London, and that friendship solidified into a political collaboration. After only two issues, Tzabar's biting satirical broadsheet was reborn as *ISRAC*, the magazine of the Israeli Revolutionary Action Committee Abroad (ISRACA), co-published by all three of them. ISRACA served, essentially, as Matzpen's international organisation, and the new magazine conveyed a sharpened political edge. This reinforced Avnery's public verdict on Tzabar's political stance: he was a liar and 'charlatan', a slanderer of the state, who was pretending to suffer political persecution from the comfort of another country, 'betraying the cause of peace' and playing into the hands of Israel's enemies.[300]

Ultimately, Avnery's political turn against Matzpen was what clinched the rift within the Hebrew milieu. If a sense of Hebrew belonging provided the cultural soil in which Matzpen's identity had grown, the kernel of that identity was a socialist vision of the future, according to which Israeli Jews and Palestinian Arabs would achieve mutual and transnational recognition. Soon after the occupation began, the Israeli leftists felt duty-bound to express their unconditional solidarity with the Palestinians. They proclaimed and demanded recognition for the 'right and duty of every conquered and subjugated people to resist and to struggle for its freedom'.[301] At a time when Uri Avnery was not yet prepared to side with the cause of Palestinian Arabs so unreservedly, politics drove a lasting wedge between the two groups and provoked Avnery to agitate pointedly in public against Matzpen, his former allies. Avnery's publication repeatedly accused Matzpen of betraying the nation, supporting Fatah and condoning Palestinian terrorism. Avnery also portrayed the Israeli Left's political utopia of an international unity in the Middle East – a dream that gained new currency after the Six-Day War – as national suicide. Matzpen's agenda, he wrote, was 'not to usher in justice for the Israeli Arabs, not to create a Palestinian state alongside Israel, nor to bring peace between the Palestinian national movement and Israel', but simply 'to destroy Israel'.[302] No matter how fiercely Avnery set out to discredit Matzpen members as enemies of Israel, his political polemics neglected Matzpen's years-long efforts to develop 'their own territorial, national and cultural definitions' of a new Hebrew nation, an idea reinvigorated since the Six-Day War.[303] Especially in light of the nascent Palestinian nationalist movement and its own political constellations, Matzpen had been calling for recognition of the existence of a 'Hebrew nation' and its 'right to national self-determination [. . .] within the context of a socialist federation of the Middle East'.[304] Long before there was any conceivable political prospect of the Palestinians or the Arab world formally recognising the Israeli Jews' right to national self-determination, the New Left of Matzpen was paving the way there.

Notes

1. Meron Rapoport, 'One Day, Two Declarations', *Haaretz* (7 June 2007).
2. Adam Baruch, 'Shimon Tzabar. An Adult Hiding Under a Mushroom', *Ma'ariv* (11 February 1994), p. 19 [Hebrew].
3. Shimon Tzabar, 'Two Questions', *Haaretz* (20 July 1967), p. 2 [Hebrew]; see also Amnon Bierman, 'Where Did Shimon Tzabar Disappear To?', *Yediot Aharonot (7 Days Supplement)* (29 July 1988), pp. 32–3 [Hebrew].
4. Tzabar, 'Two Questions'.

5. Shimon Tzabar, *A Prickly Pear Thorn: Born in Palestine, Growing Up in Israel (An Unauthorised Autobiography)* (London [Private Printing of Shimon Tzabar], n. d.), pp. 213–23. Excerpts of Tzabar's autobiography can be found online: https://www.shimontzabar.com/about/shimons-own-words.html.
6. Harold Fisch, *The Zionist Revolution: A New Perspective* (London: Weidenfeld and Nicolson, 1978), p. 9.
7. Segev, *1967: Israel, the War, and the Year that Transformed the Middle East*, pp. 368 and 546.
8. Fisch, *The Zionist Revolution*, p. 9.
9. See Arye Naor, '"Behold, Rachel, Behold". The Six Day War as a Biblical Experience and its Impact on Israel's Political Mentality', *Journal of Israeli History* 24: 2 (2005), pp. 229–50, at p. 230.
10. Ibid., p. 235.
11. Segev, *1967*, p. 547.
12. Naor, '"Behold, Rachel, Behold"', p. 233; Government of Israel, 'The Land-for-Peace Principle, 19. Juni 1967', in Itamar Rabinovich and Jehudah Reinharz (eds), *Israel in the Middle East: Documents and Readings on Society, Politics, and Foreign Relations, Pre-1948 to the Present*, 2nd edn (Waltham: Brandeis University Press, 2008), pp. 238–9.
13. See Dan Laor, 'The Last Chapter. Nathan Alterman and the Six-Day War', *Israel Studies* 4: 2 (1999), pp. 178–94.
14. Quoted in Ibid., p. 185.
15. Rael J. Isaac, *Israel Divided: Ideological Politics in the Jewish State* (Baltimore: Johns Hopkins University Press, 1976), pp. 45–76; Segev, *1967*, pp. 545–6.
16. Isaac, *Israel Divided*, pp. 45–9.
17. Segev, *1967*, p. 181.
18. 'Manifesto of the Land of Israel Movement' (August 1967), in Isaac, *Israel Divided*, pp. 165–70, at p. 165 (emphasis in original).
19. Ibid., p. 165.
20. Rapoport, 'One Day, Two Declarations'.
21. Natan Zahavi, 'Zahavi on the Ground: Stupid Palestinians', https://www.makorrishon.co.il/nrg/online/1/ART/984/472.html (accessed 29 July 2020).
22. Rapoport, 'One Day, Two Declarations'; on David Ehrenfeld, see Emanuel Bar-Kedma, 'Justice is Money', *Yediot Aharonot. Weekend Supplement* (14 February 1986), pp. 28–30 [Hebrew].
23. The English translation is quoted from Noam Sheizaf, 'Matzpen and the Story of Two Ads', *+972.magazine*, https://www.972mag.com/matzpen-and-the-story-of-two-ads/65842/ (accessed 29 July 2020).

24. It was Moshé Machover who added his own signature to the text during a phone call when he added the words 'and counter-terror' to the sentence 'oppression brings terror'. See Rosenblum, 'The Exile Option in Paris and London', p. 24.
25. Sheizaf, 'Matzpen and the Story of Two Ads'.
26. Quoted in Rapoport, 'One Day, Two Declarations'.
27. Machover, 'Matzpen. The Israeli Socialist Organisation', p. 314.
28. Moshé Machover, 'Resurrection of the Dead (October 1967)', in Moshé Machover, *Israelis and Palestinians: Conflict and Resolutions* (Chicago: Haymarket Books, 2012), pp. 145–50 [first: *Matzpen* 38 (1967)].
29. Ibid.
30. Smorodinsky, Meir (S. Meir), 'Religion. Who Coerces', *Matzpen* 20 (1964), p. 3 [Hebrew].
31. Yona Hadari-Ramage, 'War and Religiosity. The Sinai Campaign in Public Thought', in S. I. Troen and Noah Lucas (eds), *Israel: The First Decade of Independence*, SUNY Series in Israeli Studies (Albany: State University of New York Press, 1995), pp. 355–74, at pp. 361 and 365; see also Anita Shapira, 'Ben-Gurion and the Bible. The Forging of an Historical Narrative?', *Middle Eastern Studies* 33: 4 (1997), pp. 645–74.
32. Smorodinsky, Meir (S. Meir), 'Religion'.
33. Rapoport, 'One Day, Two Declarations'; Daniel Rauchwerger, 'A Life in Painting', *Haaretz* (30 May 2001), http://www.haaretz.com/israel-news/culture/leisure/a-life-in-painting-1.364867 (accessed 11 April 2020).
34. Tzabar, *A Prickly Pear Thorn*, pp. 213–23.
35. Avinoam Bar-Yosef, 'On the Left Leg', *Ma'ariv Weekend Supplement* (6 March 1987), pp. 10–12, 53.
36. David Moonshine, *Moonshines Stories: Short Stories for Young Adults* (Tel Aviv: Modan, 1990).
37. David Ratner, 'A Yesteryear's Tiger', *Haaretz* (3 January 2010), p. 10 [Hebrew].
38. Nitza Ben-Ari, *Suppression of the Erotic in Modern Hebrew Literature* (Ottawa: University of Ottawa Press, 2006), pp. 61–7.
39. Haim Hanegbi, 'Raif Chana Elias', *Chadashot. Shavuot Supplement* (29 May 1990), pp. 8–9 [Hebrew]; David Moonshine, 'The Egg', in David Moonshine, *Moonshines Stories: Short Stories for Young Adults* (Tel Aviv: Modan, 1990), pp. 53–6.
40. Amos Kenan, 'He Was and Existed and Happened', *Yediot Aharonot. Weekend Supplement* (28 October 1988), p. 17 [Hebrew].
41. Benjamin Beit-Hallahmi, *Original Sins: Reflections on the History of Zionism and Israel* (London: Pluto Press, 1992), p. 115.
42. Tzabar, *A Prickly Pear Thorn*, pp. 5–6.

43. For a similar approach, see Ghil'ad Zuckermann, *Israeli, a Beautiful Language: Hebrew as Myth* (Tel Aviv: Am Oved, 2008) [Hebrew].
44. Kenan, 'He Was and Existed and Happened'; see also Adam Baruch, 'Good to See You, Tzabar', *Yediot Aharonot. Weekend Supplement* (30 June 1989), p. 21 [Hebrew].
45. Erel, *Without Fear and Prejudice*.
46. David Ohana, *The Origins of Israeli Mythology: Neither Canaanites nor Crusaders* (Cambridge: Cambridge University Press, 2014); Silberstein, *The Postzionism Debates*, pp. 67–88; Segev, *Elvis in Jerusalem*, pp. 41–6.
47. Yonathan Ratosh, 'Epistle to the Hebrew Youth', in Yonathan Ratosh, *The First Days* (Tel Aviv: Hadar, 1982), pp. 32–8.
48. Yonathan Ratosh, 'Opening Speech at the Meeting of the Committee with Representatives of the Cells', in Yonathan Ratosh, *The First Days* (Tel Aviv: Hadar, 1982), pp. 149–203.
49. Dan Miron, *From Continuity to Contiguity: Toward a New Jewish Literary Thinking* (Stanford, London: Stanford University Press, 2010), p. 189.
50. Quoted from Diamond, *Homeland or Holy Land?*, p. 40.
51. Quoted from Yonathan Shavit, 'The New Hebrew Nation (The Canaanite Outlook). Interview July 1970', in Ehud Ben Ezer (ed.), *Unease in Zion* (New York: Quadrangle/New York Times Book Co., 1974), pp. 61–2.
52. Diamond, *Homeland or Holy Land?*, pp. 24–48.
53. Ibid., p. 34.
54. Shavit, 'The New Hebrew Nation', p. 46.
55. Roman Vater, '"A Hebrew From Samaria, Not a Jew From Yavneh". Adya Gur Horon (1907-1972) and the Articulation of Hebrew Nationalism' (Doctoral dissertation, The University of Manchester, 2015).
56. Diamond, *Homeland or Holy Land?*, p. 37.
57. Shavit, 'The New Hebrew Nation', pp. 68–71; see also Eran Kaplan, 'A Rebel With a Cause. Hillel Kook, Begin and Jabotinsky's Ideological Legacy', *Israel Studies* 10: 3 (2005), pp. 87–103.
58. Shavit, 'The New Hebrew Nation', pp. 5–6.
59. Ibid., pp. 53–8.
60. Ibid., p. 26; Diamond, *Homeland or Holy Land?*, p. 40.
61. Amos Kenan, '. . . and the Canaanite Was Then In the Land. Dan Omer Talks to Amos Kenan', *Proza* 17–18 (1977), pp. 4–11, at p. 5 [Hebrew].
62. Quoted in Shavit, 'The New Hebrew Nation', p. 113.

63. For the distinctions, see Ron Kuzar, *Hebrew and Zionism: A Discourse Analytic Cultural Study* (Berlin: De Gruyter Mouton, 2001), pp. 201–2.
64. Diamond, *Homeland or Holy Land?*, p. 138, note 8. A retrospective summary of the concept of the Young Hebrews was given by Yonatan Ratosh in an interview with Ehud Ben-Ezer: Ratosh, 'The New Hebrew Nation', pp. 201–34.
65. Dan Laor, 'American Literature and Israeli Culture. The Case of the Canaanites', *Israel Studies* 5: 1 (2000), pp. 287–300.
66. Quoted from Diamond, *Homeland or Holy Land?*, p. 56.
67. Ibid.
68. Quoted in Shavit, 'The New Hebrew Nation', p. 8.
69. Quoted from Ibid., p. 63 (emphasis in original).
70. Shapira, 'Whatever Became of "Negating Exile"?', pp. 69–108.
71. 'David Green comes to Jaffa', in Uri Avnery, *Israel Without Zionists: A Plea for Peace in the Middle East* (New York: Macmillan, 1968), pp. 78–100.
72. Baruch Kurzweil, 'The New "Canaanites" in Israel', *Judaism* 2 (1953), pp. 3–15, at pp. 10–11; see also Baruch Kurzweil, 'The Young Hebrews', *Jewish Spectator* (1953), pp. 21–9. Both essays were first published as: Baruch Kurzweil, 'The Nature and Origins of the "Young Hebrew" (Canaanite) Movement', *Luach Haaretz* 1952/3 [Hebrew].
73. Kurzweil, 'The New "Canaanites" in Israel', p. 10.
74. Ibid.
75. Ibid., p. 8.
76. For a later interpretation of this development, see Yosef H. Yerushalmi, *Zakhor: Jewish History and Jewish Memory* (Seattle: University of Washington Press, 1996), pp. 77–102.
77. Kurzweil, 'The New "Canaanites" in Israel', p. 4.
78. Gershom Scholem, 'Zionism – Dialectic of Continuity and Rebellion. Interview, April/Juli 1970', in Ehud Ben Ezer (ed.), *Unease in Zion* (New York: Quadrangle/New York Times Book Co., 1974), pp. 263–96, at p. 277.
79. Ibid.
80. Gershom Scholem, *From Berlin to Jerusalem: Memories of My Youth*, Autobiography Jewish Studies, 1st Paul Dry Books edn (Philadelphia: Paul Dry Books, [1977] 2012), p. 176.
81. Gershom Scholem, 'Reflections on Modern Jewish Studies [1944]', in Gershom Scholem, *On the Possibility of Jewish Mysticism in Our Time & Other Essays*, 1st edn (Philadelphia: Jewish Publ. Soc, 1997), pp. 51–71, at p. 56.

82. Scholem, 'Zionism – Dialectic of Continuity and Rebellion', p. 277.
83. Kurzweil, 'The Young Hebrews', p. 23 (emphasis in original).
84. Itamar Even-Zohar, 'The Emergence of a Native Hebrew Culture in Palestine 1882–1948', in Jehudah Reinharz (ed.), *Essential Papers on Zionism* (New York: New York University Press, 1996), pp. 727–44.
85. Kurzweil, 'The New "Canaanites" in Israel', p. 5.
86. Erel, *Without Fear and Prejudice*, pp. 13–56.
87. See the biographical interview: Uri Avnery, 'Mein Traum, auch heute noch... Uri Avnery: Journalist, Politiker und Friedensaktivist', in Georg Stein and Rudolf Augstein (eds), *Zwei Völker, zwei Staaten: Gespräch über Israel und Palästina* (Heidelberg: Palmyra, 1995), pp. 99–174.
88. Uri Avnery, 'And the Canaanite Was Then in the Land', in Uri Avnery, *The War of the Seventh Day* (Tel Aviv: Daf Hadash, 1969), pp. 145–80, at p. 149; this chapter is not included in the English version of the book: Avnery, *Israel Without Zionists*.
89. Oren Meyers, 'Israeli Journalists as an Interpretive Memory Community. The Case of "Haolam Hazeh"' (PhD Thesis, University of Pennsylvania, 2003), p. 90.
90. Uri Avnery, 'Benjamin's Inn', *Haaretz* (27 December 2007).
91. Avnery, 'And the Canaanite Was Then in the Land', p. 156.
92. Jan E. Dunkhase, 'Nimrod', in Dan Diner (ed.), *Enzyklopädie jüdischer Geschichte und Kultur*, 7 vols (Stuttgart, Weimar: Metzler, 2012–17), vol. 4, pp. 370–5; Ohana, *The Origins of Israeli Mythology*, pp. 13–16; Shavit, 'The New Hebrew Nation', pp. 154–5.
93. A. Orr, Interview with the Author, Tenuvot (10 April 2008) [Hebrew]; for the fact that Nimrod is not circumcised, see also Diamond, *Homeland or Holy Land?*, p. 154, note 31.
94. Haim Hazaz, 'The Sermon', in Haim Hazaz, *The Sermon & Other Stories* (New Milford, Godalming: Toby; Melia [distributor], 2005), pp. 233–49, at pp. 235 and 247 [first: *Luah Haaretz* 5703 [1942/3], pp. 82–96 [Hebrew]] (emphasis in original).
95. Ohana, *The Origins of Israeli Mythology*, p. 86.
96. Shavit, 'The New Hebrew Nation', p. 2; Dunkhase, 'Nimrod', pp. 373–4.
97. Avnery, 'And the Canaanite Was Then in the Land', p. 150; Uri Avnery, 'I'll Never See Anyone Like Him Again. Obituary about Matti Peled', *Ma'ariv* (12 March 1995), pp. 4 and 6 [Hebrew].
98. Kenan, '... and the Canaanite Was Then In the Land', p. 4.

99. Boas Evron, 'Political Ideas and Their Twists. "A Post-Zionist Autobiography"', http://hagada.org.il/2008/09/30/רעיונות-מדיניים-וגלגוליהם-אוטוביוג (accessed 6 September 2019) [Hebrew]; Eli Eshed, 'Yaakov Ashman: A Warrior for Hebrew. The Story of Gidi Geser and its Originator Yaakov Ashman', https://no666.wordpress.com/2006/05/05/לוחם-על-עברי-עלילות-גידי-גזר-ויוצרו-יע/] (accessed 11 April 2020).
100. Kenan, '. . . and the Canaanite Was Then In the Land', p. 5.
101. Ibid., p. 4.
102. Ghilan, *How Israel Lost its Soul*, p. 104.
103. Amos Kenan, 'The Dark Years. Interview', *Koteret Rashit* (26 December 1984), pp. 29–32, at p. 30 [Hebrew].
104. Evron, 'Political Ideas and Their Twists. "A Post-Zionist Autobiography"'.
105. Kenan, '. . . and the Canaanite Was Then In the Land', p. 4.
106. Tzabar, *A Prickly Pear Thorn*, pp. 61–4.
107. Ibid., pp. 78–85; see also Joseph Heller, *Stern Gang: Ideology, Politics and Terror, 1940-49* (London: F. Cass, 1995), pp. 231–4.
108. Shavit, 'The New Hebrew Nation', p. 135.
109. Avnery, 'And the Canaanite Was Then In the Land', pp. 174–7; Ben-Ami Gur (Ben-Ami, G.), 'The Canaanite "Scapegoat"', *BaMaavak* ([May] 1947), pp. 13–14.
110. Erel, *Without Fear and Prejudice*, pp. 36–46.
111. Avnery, 'And the Canaanite Was Then In the Land', pp. 173–80; Erel, *Without Fear and Prejudice*, p. 43; Shavit, 'The New Hebrew Nation', p. 136.
112. Uri Avnery, *War or Peace in the Semitic World* (Tel Aviv: A. Moses, 1947).
113. See also Uri Avnery, 'The Reactionism of the Fathers', *BaMaavak* ([May] 1947), pp. 6–7 [Hebrew].
114. For the history of Haolam Hazeh, see Erel, *Without Fear and Prejudice*; Meyers, 'Israeli Journalists as an Interpretive Memory Community'.
115. Erel, *Without Fear and Prejudice*, pp. 11–13; Meyers, 'Israeli Journalists as an Interpretive Memory Community', pp. 90–3.
116. See Tom Segev, 'Dear Reader', *Koteret Rashit* 232 (1987), pp. 20–5 [Hebrew].
117. Segev, *1949. The First Israelis*, p. 285.
118. Quoted from Meyers, 'Israeli Journalists as an Interpretive Memory Community', p. 109.
119. Avnery, 'Mein Traum, auch heute noch. . .', p. 112.
120. Ibid., p. 113.
121. Quoted in Segev, *Elvis in Jerusalem*, p. 44.

122. Meyers, 'Israeli Journalists as an Interpretive Memory Community', p. 258.
123. Avnery, 'Mein Traum, auch heute noch. . .', p. 132.
124. Ibid; Meyers, 'Israeli Journalists as an Interpretive Memory Community', pp. 1 and 173.
125. Avnery, 'Mein Traum, auch heute noch . . .', p. 132; Uri Avnery, *Optimistic* (Tel Aviv: Yediot Sfarim, 2014), pp. 373–87 [Hebrew].
126. Avnery, 'Mein Traum, auch heute noch. . .', p. 132.
127. Meyers, 'Israeli Journalists as an Interpretive Memory Community', p. 64.
128. Oz Almog, *Farewell to "Srulik": Changing Values Among the Israeli Elite*, 2 vols (Haifa: Zemorah-Bitan, 2004), pp. 56–71 [Hebrew]; Segev, 'Dear Reader'.
129. Almog, *Farewell to "Srulik"*, p. 58.
130. Segev, *Elvis in Jerusalem*, pp. 41–6.
131. Interview with Haim Hanegbi in the movie of Y. Lev, *Uri Avnery: Warrior for Peace*, 2002, Israel, 75 min, film.
132. Almog, *Farewell to "Srulik"*, pp. 56–71.
133. Ibid., p. 58.
134. Avnery, 'Mein Traum, auch heute noch. . .', p. 134.
135. See the collection of Kenan's articles in Amos Kenan, *With Whips and Scorpions* (Tel Aviv: Yisrael, 1952); Gershon Shaked, *Modern Hebrew Fiction* (New Milford: Toby Press, 2008), p. 164: '[T]he spoken language began to appear in print in the 1950s in the journalistic and satirical columns of such writers as Kenan and Kishon.'.
136. Kenan, 'The Dark Years', p. 30.
137. Kenan, '. . . and the Canaanite Was Then In the Land', p. 6.
138. Nurith Gertz, *Unrepentant: Four Chapters in the Life of Amos Kenan* (Tel Aviv: Am Oved, 2009), p. 256.
139. Akiva Orr, *The UnJewish State: The Politics of Jewish Identity in Israel* (London: Ithaca Press, 1983), pp. 208–12 [first: *Aleph* 2 [1950]].
140. Diamond, *Homeland or Holy Land?*, pp. 65–7.
141. Charles S. Liebman and Eliezer Don-Yehiya, 'The "Status-Quo" Agreement', in Charles Liebman and Eliezer Don-Yehiya, *Religion and Politics in Israel*, Jewish Political and Social Studies (Bloomington: Indiana University Press, 1984), pp. 31–40; Segev, *1949. The First Israelis*, pp. 249–51.
142. Diamond, *Homeland or Holy Land?*, p. 65.
143. Segev, *1949. The First Israelis*, pp. 233–62.
144. Ibid., p. 247; Eli Tzur, '"To Be a Free People". The History of the "League for the Prevention of Religious Coercion"', in Anita Shapira (ed.), *A State in the*

Making: Israeli Society in the First Decades (Jerusalem: Zalman Shazar Center, 2001), pp. 205–38 [Hebrew].

145. Amos Kenan, 'These are the Annals of Shaaltiel', in Amos Kenan, *Your Land, Your Country* (Jerusalem: Yediot Aharonot, 1981), pp. 62–78; Gertz, *Unrepentant*, pp. 213–343; Segev, *1949. The First Israelis*, pp. 231–2.
146. Gertz, *Unrepentant*, pp. 342–3.
147. Ibid., pp. 220–1.
148. Almog, *Farewell to "Srulik"*, pp. 63–5.
149. Kenan, 'The Dark Years', p. 31.
150. Jan E. Dunkhase, 'Hebräisch säkularisieren. Anverwandlungen einer heiligen Sprache', *Jahrbuch des Simon-Dubnow-Instituts/Simon Dubnow Institute Yearbook* 12 (2013), pp. 263–386.
151. Kenan, '. . . and the Canaanite Was Then In the Land', p. 7.
152. Shaked, *Modern Hebrew Fiction*, p. 164.
153. Ibid.
154. Kenan, '. . . and the Canaanite Was Then In the Land', p. 7.
155. Ibid.
156. Gershom Scholem, 'Wie soll man Hebräisch lernen?', quoted in Daniel Weidner, *Gershom Scholem: Politisches, esoterisches und historiographisches Schreiben* (München: Fink, 2003), p. 133.
157. Gershom Scholem, 'On Our Language. A Confession [1926]', *History and Memory* 2: 2 (1990), pp. 97–9, at p. 97.
158. Ibid., p. 98.
159. Quoted in Weidner, *Gershom Scholem*, p. 135.
160. Ilker Aytürk, 'Attempts at Romanizing the Hebrew Script and their Failure. Nationalism, Religion and Alphabet Reform in the Yishuv', *Middle Eastern Studies* 43: 4 (2007), pp. 625–45, at pp. 631–5; Yoel Regev, 'Pney Elohim. On Itamar Ben-Avi's Failed Project to Latinize Hebrew', *Mita'am* 22 (2010), pp. 49–61 [Hebrew].
161. Aytürk, 'Attempts at Romanizing the Hebrew Script and their Failure', p. 639; Roman Vater, 'Hebrew as a Political Instrument. Language-Planning by the "Canaanites"', *Journal of Semitic Studies* 62: 2 (2017), pp. 485–511.
162. Christian Buckard, *Arthur Koestler: Ein extremes Leben 1905-1983* (München: C. H. Beck, 2004).
163. Arthur Koestler, 'The Culture of the New State', in Arthur Koestler, *Promise and Fulfilment: Palestine 1917-1949* (New York: Macmillan, 1949), pp. 324–31, at pp. 327 and 331.

164. Arthur Koestler, *Thieves in the Night: Chronicle of an Experiment* (New York: Macmillan, 1946), pp. 9–10.
165. Arthur Koestler, 'Epilogue', in Arthur Koestler, *Promise and Fulfilment: Palestine 1917-1949* (New York: Macmillan, 1949), pp. 332–5.
166. Arthur Koestler, 'The Rebirth of the Hebrew Language', in Arthur Koestler, *Promise and Fulfilment: Palestine 1917-1949* (New York: Macmillan, 1949), pp. 311–15, at pp. 313 and 315.
167. Ibid., p. 312.
168. Buckard, *Arthur Koestler*, pp. 268–70.
169. Yaakov Gabay to Arthur Koestler (22 November 1948), quoted in Ibid., p. 269.
170. Tzabar, *A Prickly Pear Thorn*, p. 91.
171. Shaked, *Modern Hebrew Fiction*, p. 143; Gershon Shaked, 'Fat Haim, Uzi & Co, and Ervinka', *Yediot Aharonot* (13 December 1985), pp. 20–3 [Hebrew].
172. Gideon Efrat, 'The Last Sabra/Tzabar', *Iton 77* 325 ([August] 2007), pp. 18–21 [Hebrew].
173. Gila Ballas (ed.), *Group of Ten, 1951-1960* (Ramat Gan: Museum of Israeli Art, 1992) [Hebrew].
174. Oren Persiko, 'Without Red Lines', https://www.the7eye.org.il/51989 (accessed 13 April 2020) [Hebrew]; Tzabar, *A Prickly Pear Thorn*, pp. 184–5.
175. Erel, *Without Fear and Prejudice*, p. 175; Nitza Ben-Ari, 'Popular Literature in Hebrew as Marker of Anti-Sabra Culture', in Rakefet Sela-Sheffy and Gideon Toury (eds), *Culture Contacts and the Making of Cultures: Papers in Homage to Itamar Even Zohar* (Tel Aviv: Tel Aviv University – Unit of Culture Research, 2011), pp. 219–43, at p. 230.
176. Quoted in Erel, *Without Fear and Prejudice*, p. 176.
177. Ibid.; Tzabar, *A Prickly Pear Thorn*, pp. 175–82.
178. Shaked, *Modern Hebrew Fiction*, p. 164.
179. Avnery, 'Mein Traum, auch heute noch. . .', p. 134.
180. Erel, *Without Fear and Prejudice*, pp. 165–9.
181. Noam Yoran, 'Haolam Hazeh', in Adi Ophir (ed.), *50 to 48: Critical Moments in the History of the State of Israel* (Jerusalem: Hakibbutz Hameuchad, 1999), pp. 137–47, at p. 137.
182. Uri Avnery, 'Some Open Words', *Haolam Hazeh* (12 October 1950), p. 3, quoted in Meyers, 'Israeli Journalists as an Interpretive Memory Community', p. 89.
183. 'Pornography?', *Haolam Hazeh* (11 February 1954), pp. 10–11, quoted in Erel, *Without Fear and Prejudice*, p. 166.

184. 'The first signs of sex journalism appeared (like everything else in Israeli journalism) in *Haolam Hazeh*. Uri Avnery, the founder of modern Israeli journalism in the Holy Land, was the first who dared to insert some erotic moisture into the press.' B. Feldman, 'The Embarrassment Effect', *Iton Tel-Aviv* (5 April 1996), at p. 54 [Hebrew], quoted in Meyers, 'Israeli Journalists as an Interpretive Memory Community', p. 265.
185. Ibid., p. 138.
186. Avnery, 'Mein Traum, auch heute noch. . .', p. 133.
187. Meyers, 'Israeli Journalists as an Interpretive Memory Community', p. 140.
188. Ibid., p. 176.
189. Avnery, 'Mein Traum, auch heute noch. . .', p. 137; Ghilan, *How Israel Lost its Soul*, p. 127.
190. Almog, *Farewell to "Srulik"*, p. 1144; Yotam Feldman, 'Pulp Fiction', *Haaretz* (2 August 2007).
191. Yael Gvirtz, 'Stuck for Already 26 Years', *Yediot Aharonot* (14 August 1992), pp. 12–13 [Hebrew].
192. Adam Baruch, 'Maxim Ghilan Anyway Alone', in Adam Baruch, *How Are Things at Home?* (Kinnereth: Zemorah-Bitan, 2004), pp. 129–55; Yossi Klein, 'Exile in His Country', *Haaretz* (31 July 2003). Considering his late arrival on the Hebrew scene, it is not surprising that Maxim Ghilan's monograph *How Israel Lost its Soul* provides one of the best surveys of the subject.
193. Hagit Grossman, 'Memoir. Writing for the Exiles and the Dispossessed', *Haaretz* (27 May 2010).
194. Gvirtz, 'Stuck for Already 26 Years'.
195. Feldman, 'Pulp Fiction'.
196. Almog, *Farewell to "Srulik"*, p. 1144.
197. Feldman, 'Pulp Fiction'.
198. 'Israeli Editors Given Prison Terms for Security Issue "Fabrication"', *Jewish Telegraphic Agency* 35 (20 February 1967); Gvirtz, 'Stuck for Already 26 Years'.
199. Gvirtz, 'Stuck for Already 26 Years'.
200. 'The Letter from an Anonymous Woman was Read During the Trial of the Editors of "Bul"', *Al Hamishmar* (21 November 1967), p. 5 [Hebrew].
201. Ernst Livneh, 'Das Recht der unzüchtigen Veröffentlichungen in Israel', *Zeitschrift für die gesamte Strafrechtswissenschaft (Auslandsteil)* 83: 1 (1971), pp. 319–31.
202. Ben-Ari, *Suppression of the Erotic in Modern Hebrew Literature*, pp. 61–7.
203. Ibid., p. 319.

204. 'Law Report', *Jerusalem Post* (28 April 1970), p. 6; see also Livneh, 'Das Recht der unzüchtigen Veröffentlichungen in Israel'.
205. Schalom Ben-Chorin, 'Pornografie und Zensur', *Jedioth Chadashot* (2 December 1966).
206. Dan Omer, *On the Way* (Jerusalem: Golgotha, 1966), pp. 124–8 [Hebrew]; Ben-Ari, *Suppression of the Erotic in Modern Hebrew Literature*, pp. 65–6.
207. Ben-Chorin, 'Pornografie und Zensur'.
208. Ibid.
209. Tzabar, *A Prickly Pear Thorn*, p. 243.
210. 'Law Report'. See also Ben-Ari, *Suppression of the Erotic in Modern Hebrew Literature*, p. 64.
211. Ratner, 'A Yesteryear's Tiger'.
212. Ibid.
213. Ibid.
214. Dan Omer (ed. and trans.), *Howl! An Anthology of American Beat Poetry* (Jerusalem: Marcus, 1967) [Hebrew]; see also Yaakov Ariel, 'From a Jewish Communist to a Jewish Buddhist: Allen Ginsberg as a Forerunner of a New American Jew', *Religions* 10: 2 (2019), pp. 1–16.
215. Roy C. Arad, 'Prophet in Jeans. 25 Years Since Dan Omer's Death', https://chicky00.wordpress.com/2010/02/22/נביא-זעם-בגינס--25-שנים-וקצת-למותו-של-דן-ע/ (accessed 13 April 2020) [Hebrew].
216. Dan Omer, 'Quo Vadis Israel?', *The International Times* 3: 39 (1968), p. 17.
217. Ratner, 'A Yesteryear's Tiger'.
218. Ibid.
219. Omer, 'Quo Vadis Israel?'.
220. Tzabar, *A Prickly Pear Thorn*, p. 243.
221. Ben-Ari, *Suppression of the Erotic in Modern Hebrew Literature*, p. 64.
222. Quoted in Ibid.
223. Uri Avnery, 'The Man, Who was Ahead of Everyone', *Haolam Hazeh* (28 January 1990), pp. 18–19 and 41 [Hebrew].
224. Nechemia Ben-Tor, *Torch Bearers of Freedom: Short Biographes of the Leaders of the Fighters for Freedom of Israel (Lechi)* (Tel Aviv: Ya'ir, 2008).
225. Ibid., pp. 334–40.
226. Avnery, 'The Man, Who was Ahead of Everyone', p. 18.
227. Ibid.
228. Uri Avnery, 'Model of a Different Israel. Forty Years to the "Hebrew Manifesto"', *Haaretz Culture and Literature Supplement* (10 January 1997), p. 17 [Hebrew].

229. Ghilan, *How Israel Lost its Soul*, p. 132.
230. 'Conversation Between Etgar and the Founders of Semitic Action', *Etgar* 22 (11 January 1962), pp. 4–6 [Hebrew].
231. 'The Café Herlinger Underground in the Trial of "Haolam Hazeh" Against "Davar HaShavua"', *Davar* (8 May 1958), p. 4 [Hebrew]; Ghilan, *How Israel Lost its Soul*, p. 119.
232. Avnery, 'The Man, Who was Ahead of Everyone', p. 19.
233. Ghilan, *How Israel Lost its Soul*, p. 119.
234. Semitic Action, *The Hebrew Manifesto: Principles of Semitic Action*, 2nd & complete edn (Tel Aviv: Central Committee, Semitic Action, 1959), p. 10 (point 21).
235. Shavit, 'The New Hebrew Nation', pp. 143–6.
236. Semitic Action, *The Hebrew Manifesto*, p. 11 (point 24).
237. Ibid.
238. Ferhat Abbas, quoted in Laskier, 'Israel and Algeria amid French Colonialism and the Arab-Conflict. 1954-1978', p. 3; Mordechai Bar-On, *In Pursuit of Peace: A History of the Israeli Peace Movement* (Washington: United States Institute of Peace Press, 1996), pp. 14–22.
239. Erel, *Without Fear and Prejudice*, pp. 61–4, 98–104.
240. Uri Avnery, *My Friend, the Enemy* (London: Zed Books, 1986), pp. 119–20; Joel Beinin, *The Dispersion of Egyptian Jewry: Culture, Politics, and the Formation of a Modern Diaspora* (Berkeley: University of California Press, 1998), pp. 165–6; Uri Avnery, 'The Silent Idealist', *Le Monde Diplomatique* ([April] 1998).
241. Gilles Perrault, *A Man Apart: The Life of Henri Curiel* (London, Atlantic Highlands: Zed Books, 1987).
242. Laskier, 'Israel and Algeria amid French Colonialism and the Arab-Conflict', pp. 4–6; Beinin, *The Dispersion of Egyptian Jewry*, pp. 165–6.
243. 'Appeal by the Israeli Committee for a Free Algeria', *Etgar* 22 (22 March 1962), p. 3 [Hebrew].
244. Avnery, 'The Man, Who was Ahead of Everyone', p. 19.
245. Nathan Yellin-Mor in *Ha'aartz* (28 December 1960), quoted in Laskier, 'Israel and Algeria amid French Colonialism and the Arab-Conflict', p. 4.
246. Erel, *Without Fear and Prejudice*, p. 102.
247. Ghilan, *How Israel Lost its Soul*, p. 121.
248. On Bober, see Neri Livneh, 'Bober the Second', *Haaretz* (13 May 2003) [Hebrew]; Gideon Ariel and Uri Milstein, *The Oasis of Dreams: The Legend of Hadassim* (Ramat Efal: Survival Publishing, 2006), Chapter 4: Children of Distress.
249. Ariel and Milstein, *The Oasis of Dreams*, Chapter 4: Children of Distress, at p. 19.

250. Moshé Machover, Interview with Arturo Schwarz (April 1972), Private Archive of Moshé Machover, London. This passage is not included in the abridged English version of the interview; Machover, 'Matzpen. The Israeli Socialist Organisation'.
251. Amos Kenan, 'Required in the Country: A Left', *Matzpen* 1 (1962), p. 3 [Hebrew].
252. H. Hanegbi, Interview with the Author, Ramat Aviv (26 August 2008) [Hebrew].
253. Lutz Fiedler, Email Communication with Gabi Lachman (25 June 2012) [Hebrew].
254. Moshé Machover, 'The Social Identity of Haolam Hazeh', *Matzpen* 32 (1967), p. 3 [Hebrew].
255. Ibid.
256. Akiva Orr and Moshé Machover [Israeli, N.], '"The Peula" and the Israeli-Arab Conflict', *Matzpen* 15 (1964), pp. 4 and 7, at p. 7 [Hebrew].
257. Quoted in Erel, *Without Fear and Prejudice*, pp. 112–13.
258. Pilavsky, 'Easternization', p. 6.
259. Akiva Orr, 'A Brutal Revolution', in Akiva Orr, *Enlightening Disillusionments* (Tel Aviv, 2011), pp. 124–9, at p. 125.
260. Machover, 'Matzpen. The Israeli Socialist Organisation', pp. 311–14.
261. Leibovitz-Dar, 'The Days of Matzpen', p. 24.
262. Quoted in Erel, *Without Fear and Prejudice*, p. 114; see also Machover, 'Resurrection of the Dead (October 1967)', p. 150: 'In any case, as far as we – as socialists and enemies of nationalism – are concerned, there is nothing sacred about any border: neither the borders of the [1947 UN] Partition Plan nor the [post-1949] Armistice lines'.
263. Moshé Machover, 'Matzpen and Ha'olam Hazeh–New Force (December 1966)', in Moshé Machover, *Israelis and Palestinians: Conflict and Resolutions* (Chicago: Haymarket Books, 2012), pp. 61–8, at p. 64 (emphasis in original).
264. Gershom Scholem, 'Israel and the Diaspora', in Gershom Scholem, *On Jews and Judaism in Crisis: Selected Essays*, edited by Werner J. Dannhauser (Philadelphia: Paul Dry Books, Inc., 2012), pp. 244–60, at p. 257.
265. Gershom Scholem and Muki Tsur, 'An Interview with Gershom Scholem', in Gershom Scholem, *On Jews and Judaism in Crisis: Selected Essays*, edited by Werner J. Dannhauser (Philadelphia: Paul Dry Books, Inc., 2012), pp. 1–48, at p. 34.
266. Scholem, 'Zionism – Dialectic of Continuity and Rebellion', p. 277.
267. See Isaac, *Israel Divided*, pp. 51–3.

268. Quoted from Ibid., p. 52.
269. Ibid.
270. Ghilan, *How Israel Lost its Soul*, pp. 132–3; Erel, *Without Fear and Prejudice*, p. 114.
271. *Haolam Hazeh – Daf Yomi* 3 (8 June 1967) [Hebrew]; see also Ghilan, *How Israel Lost its Soul*, p. 132.
272. Fouzi El-Asmar, *To Be an Arab in Israel* (Beirut: The Institute for Palestine Studies, 1978), pp. 136–7.
273. Ibid., p. 134.
274. Uri Avnery, 'The Topic of Debate: Uri Avnery', *Ma'ariv* (22 October 1969), p. 34; see also Haim Hanegbi, 'Profil. Who is Uri Avnery', *Israel Imperial News* 2: 6 ([March] 1970), p. 8; Erel, *Without Fear and Prejudice*, p. 296.
275. Uri Avnery, 'Lover of the Country: Obituary to Amos Kenan', https://www.israeli-occupation.org/2009-08-08/uri-avnery-on-amos-kenan-lover-of-the-country/ (accessed 13 April 2020).
276. El-Asmar, *To Be an Arab in Israel*, pp. 140–2.
277. Ibid., p. 139.
278. Amos Kenan, 'The Use of the Report: A Detrimental Service to the Nation', *Ma'ariv* (25 June 1967), p. 19 [Hebrew]; quoted from the English translation in El-Asmar, *To Be an Arab in Israel*, p. 143.
279. El-Asmar, *To Be an Arab in Israel*, p. 143.
280. Tzabar, *A Prickly Pear Thorn*, p. 214.
281. Ibid.
282. 'Editorial', in *Nimas* (September 1967), p. 2, quoted from the English translation in *Israel Imperial News* 1/9 ([March] 1968), p. 9.
283. H. Hanegbi, Interview with the Author (via phone) (20 June 2012) [Hebrew].
284. *Israel Imperial News* 1/9 ([March] 1968), p. 14.
285. Warschawski, *On the Border*, pp. 25–6.
286. Tzabar, *A Prickly Pear Thorn*, p. 216.
287. Avnery, 'The Topic of Debate: Uri Avnery'. For Kenan, see: Amos Kenan, 'At this Moment' and 'Flowers of Peace through the Gun-Barrel', in: Amos Kenan, *Israel: A Wasted Victory* (Tel Aviv: Amikam, 1970), pp. 9–10 [first: *Haaretz* (11 June 1967)] and pp. 10–17 [first: 23 June 1967].
288. Moshé Machover and Haim Hanegbi, 'Letter to All Those "Once-Good" Israelis', *Matzpen* 43 (1968), pp. 8–10.
289. Uri Avnery, *Israel Without Zionists: A Plea for Peace in the Middle East* (New York: Macmillan, 1968), p. 188.

290. Israeli Socialist Organization (Matzpen), 'The Left in Israel', in Arie Bober (ed.), *The Other Israel: The Radical Case Against Zionism* (Garden City: Doubleday, 1972), pp. 102–22, at p. 121.
291. A. Orr, Email Communication with the Author (17 May 2012) [English].
292. Ibid.
293. The Times Diary, 'Tzabar and Israel Imperial News', *The Times* (7 March 1968), p. 8.
294. Ibid.
295. Dan Omer (ed.), *Dapim Zehubim* (Jerusalem: Davka, 1968).
296. *Israel Imperial News* ([March] 1968), pp. 9–12.
297. Shimon Tzabar, *The White Flag Principle: How to Lose a War (and Why)* (New York: Simon & Schuster, 1972).
298. Bierman, 'Where Did Shimon Tzabar Disappear To?', p. 32.
299. Tzabar, *A Prickly Pear Thorn*, p. 226.
300. Uri Avnery, 'Wretched Figures', *Haolam Hazeh* 1627 (6 November 1968), p. 9 [Hebrew].
301. Israeli Socialist Organization (Matzpen), 'General Declaration by the ISO, 22 March 1968', in Arie Bober (ed.), *The Other Israel: The Radical Case Against Zionism* (Garden City: Doubleday, 1972), pp. 226–30, at p. 228.
302. Uri Avnery, 'Caricatures', *Haolam Hazeh* 1657 (4 June 1969), pp. 13–14 [Hebrew].
303. Ghilan, *How Israel Lost its Soul*, p. 156.
304. Moshé Machover, 'The Case for Hebrew Self-Determination', in Arie Bober (ed.), *The Other Israel: The Radical Case Against Zionism* (Garden City: Doubleday, 1972), pp. 176–81.

4

Hal'a HaKibush! – Down with the Occupation

The Six-Day War and the Return of the Palestine Question

By the time the tension of May Day 1969 finally snapped, it was late afternoon. At one end of Dizengoff Boulevard, in central Tel Aviv, demonstrators from the Old Left – the Israeli Communist Party – had just left their International Workers' Day event when they were attacked by a smaller group of teenagers, evidently nationalists, who were shouting 'Down with you!' and 'Communists to Moscow!'. Meanwhile, the demonstrators from the Israeli Socialist Organization were walking north from Jaffa. Seven years after their secession from the Communist Party (Maki), the whole country now knew the latter faction by their periodical's name, *Matzpen*.[1] When the two groups faced off on Dizengoff Boulevard, they were divided by more than the rivalry between Old and New Left. A fresher and deeper wound had materialised in the wake of the Six-Day War, not two years earlier, when the State of Israel annexed East Jerusalem and occupied the Gaza Strip, the West Bank, the Sinai Peninsula and the Golan Heights. The Arab threats of annihilation preceding that war had spread existential anxiety throughout Israel and provoked such vivid fears of a 'new Holocaust' that even Maki had deemed it necessary for the Jewish state to wage a war of self-defence.[2] During their demonstration that afternoon of 1 May, Maki had also expressed their gratitude to the Israeli military forces.[3] An unprecedented domestic consensus prevailed in the country across party lines.

The members of the Israeli Socialist Organization were among the few who had defied that unity. Instead, they turned their gaze elsewhere: first and foremost, to the plight of the Palestinians. While Israeli society was still debating whether the newly acquired territories should be referred to as 'military-occupied', 'administrated' or even 'liberated', the young leftists declared that, from a Palestinian perspective, their status was none of the above, but plainly one of 'foreign occupation' and oppression. Immediately after the 1967 War, Matzpen agitated for an unconditional retreat from the recently conquered territories, a demand they summed up in the slogan *Hal'a HaKibush!* – Down with the Occupation! – which they shouted as they marched down the street that May Day. The partisans of the Communist Party, confronted by the New Leftists and their red flags, were not about to take this provocation lightly. Within seconds, the Communists turned their banners and flagpoles into barriers to block the Matzpen group's way. A loud confrontation began that erupted into a violent brawl. The following day, even the Israeli daily press reported on the turmoil.[4]

If the Six-Day War symbolically repatriated the Communist Party of Israel, so to speak, this third round of Israeli–Arab conflict introduced the Israeli public to the New Left of Matzpen. Its public violation of the new national consensus, visible already in the midst of war, did not fail to turn heads. At a time when all Israel was convinced of the necessity of a preventive war, given the Egyptian president's threats, Akiva Orr met in London (his new home since 1964) with a group of Arabs (who were studying there) to prepare a joint statement against the impending military escalation. On 3 June, two days before the war broke out, they released a 'Joint Israeli–Arab Statement on the Middle East Crisis' under the aegis of the Bertrand Russell Peace Foundation, credited to both the Israeli Socialist Organization and the Palestinian Democratic Front.[5] Hastily, and without the authorisation of the Israeli members of Matzpen, Akiva Orr hand-delivered the document to the offices of the London *Times*, along with a private donation, as an advertisement.[6] On 8 June, when the Six-Day War had already peaked but the fighting was still ongoing, the half-page manifesto appeared in the pages of the well-known London daily. 'The situation in the Middle East is explosive. A cruel war is breaking out', the statement began. 'There is no doubt that this war will destroy many lives, but little hope that it will bring a political solution any nearer.' In their joint credo, which began by summarising the Palestine problem and the Middle Eastern conflict, the signatories simultaneously denounced the surge of Arab nationalism and militarism spouted by everyone from Nasser to Ahmad Shukeiri, while excoriating the hawkish drumbeats on the Israeli side.

> We say to all chauvinist, nationalist and racialist Israeli and Arab leaders: for 19 years you have failed to move one inch towards agreement. You have had two wars, and now you are preparing a third which will bring no salvation but death.

The only alternative, they claimed, was a socialist solution to the Palestine problem and the Middle Eastern conflict, which would imply Israel's de-Zionisation and the re-establishment of the Palestinians' individual and collective rights, but would also guarantee the integration of the Israelis into the Arab region of the Middle East. At least on a symbolic level, they hoped to keep the political alternative of a pluralistic Middle East alive 'so that the bridges of understanding between Jews and Arabs in the Middle East will not be irreparably damaged by the present crisis'.[7]

Once the war was over, when the rest of Israeli society was basking in a victorious sense of optimism, the communist dissidents persisted in their refusal to join the national consensus – even though the territorial gains had strengthened Israel's military security and stoked new hopes of peace. Israel's newfound political control over its adjoining Arab areas had moved the Jewish state out of the Jordanian Army's shooting range and even placed Israel in a position to threaten Amman, Cairo and Damascus.[8] Shortly after the war, these altered circumstances allowed the Israeli Cabinet to use the Sinai and the Golan as bargaining chips in the conflict with Israel's Arab neighbours; an exchange of 'land for peace' could secure the recognition of the Jewish state.[9] At any rate, the hopes of lasting peace were both tangible and improbable. Matzpen's first statement after the war, released in June 1967, declared: 'Despite the present relation of military forces, Israel remains a little island within the Arab world.' Ultimately, they believed, the post-war situation would not alter the fundamentals of the disputes – neither with the neighbouring states, nor, most importantly, with the Palestinians. 'Any "settlement" reached today from a position of strength will only be temporary and therefore illusory', they therefore argued, contrary to all the optimistic anticipation that had issued from Israel's newfound strength.[10] Besides, all hopes of a new diplomatic solution to the conflict were rapidly deflated by the political reality. Israel's new Defence Minister Moshe Dayan, appointed shortly before the war, stated soon after Israel's victory: 'We're waiting for the Arabs to pick up the phone and call.'[11] But the call never came. The Arabs never came to the table with an offer. Instead, when the conference of Arab Heads of State convened on 29 August 1967 in the Sudanese capital of Khartoum, they nailed three 'no's' into diplomacy's coffin – no to peace, no to recognition and no to negotiating with Israel – and thus quashed all hopes of future talks. 'Victory in the war, far from solving the Israeli-Arab problem, has actually intensified it', concluded a statement by Matzpen one year after the war.[12]

At the centre of all post-war disputes, however, was the political situation and military control of the West Bank and Gaza Strip. The Six-Day War had brought the question of Israel's secular character – the internal founding conflict of the Jewish state – back to the surface, but this question was also linked to the return of the Palestine question: the external founding conflict. New problem areas had emerged. In addition to the 400,000 Palestinian Arabs within Israel's borders of 4 June 1967, there were around 1.1 million more Palestinians living in the territories now under Israeli control. Israel now had the largest Palestinian population of any state in the Middle East.[13] Even before the startling advertisement released in the 22 September 1967 edition of *Haaretz*, Matzpen squeezed its way into the public debate with its simple, unconditional and unambiguous slogan '*Hal'a HaKibush*'. 'An Old Story: Rebellion and Resistance against a Foreign Occupation', read the headline of the August edition of *Matzpen*, printed above an image of deserted West Bank streets during a curfew.[14] Alongside articles about the Palestinian situation after the Six-Day War, the issue featured other cases of conflict and military occupation – almost as a warning, which led to Moshé Machover's conclusion 'that nations do not reconcile themselves with any occupation, even less brutal ones'.[15] This argument could not be muddled by the structure of military administration that had already been set up in the West Bank and the Gaza Strip. Moshe Dayan's policy of open bridges may have dubbed itself a socially acceptable or 'enlightened occupation', but on the ground the occupation meant martial law and a state of emergency for the territories in question.[16] 'Whether or not the Israeli occupation is more enlightened or less enlightened than other occupying regimes in the world', Oded Pilavsky contended in *Matzpen*, in the eyes of Palestinians this was still a 'foreign occupation to be condemned and resisted'.[17]

Matzpen's staunch demand for 'immediate withdrawal from all the occupied territories' placed it at odds with most of Israeli society, but the group also attracted numerous young Israelis who had been confronted with the Palestine question for the first time during the Six-Day War.[18] 'Matzpen was the first group to come out against the 1967 War and was at the forefront of the protest movement against the occupation which spread in the first years after the war', Tikva Honig-Parnass would recall many years later.[19] She herself had fought in the War of Independence as a member of the Palmach, joined the left-wing Zionist Mapam and worked as the party's secretary in the Knesset from 1954 to 1955. Beginning in 1959, her experiences of meeting Moshé Machover and Akiva Orr and reading *Peace, Peace, When There is No Peace* led her to question her interpretation of the Israeli War of Independence and its justification. Transfixed by reading the many issues of *Matzpen*, the former socialist Zionist began to understand the Israel–Palestine conflict as a colonial one. Finally, when the Six-Day War placed the spotlight on the Palestine question, it was Matzpen's resolute protest against the occupation and its quest for a common Israeli–Palestinian perspective that 'gained Matzpen support among a rather substantial number of young people'.[20] Many of them were disturbed to find themselves cast indefinitely as the 'occupiers'. With the help of Matzpen, they found an answer to their troubling questions, for they also identified with the group's New Left internationalism. Shlomo Sand, Tamar Selby, Tsvia (Gotsdiener) Glezerman, Meir and Shimshon Wigoder, Aviva Ein-Gil and many others joined the group in the years after the war, each of them on their own paths and transgressing their pre-war political stances in specific personal ways.[21] Years before becoming one of Israel's leading human rights lawyers and legal defenders of the Palestinians, Lea Tsemel was one of these new members of the group. In June 1967, as a talented law student at the Hebrew University of Jerusalem, she volunteered for military service, believing the Six-Day War to be justified. But when the war was over, she brought back not only the memory of having been one of the first Israeli women at the Western Wall, but also her experience of seeing Palestinian refugees streaming down the road from Jerusalem towards Jericho. The urgent questions regarding the tragic fate and future of the Palestinians eventually led her to Matzpen.[22] Indeed, her political passion and captivating personality were also among the reasons that attracted her future husband, Michel Warschawski, who hailed from the French frontier city of Strasbourg, to join Matzpen.

Two years before the Six-Day War, the son of the Chief Rabbi of Strasbourg arrived in Jerusalem as an Orthodox Jew, planning to study at the Merkaz HaRav yeshiva. Although his time at the yeshiva and as part of religious Jerusalem initially distanced Warschawski from everyday Israeli society, the war and the Palestinians' situation plunged him into the conflicts around him and sparked a personal transformation. Like many other Israelis in those days, he had visited the market in Hebron for the first time with the idea of returning to ancestral ground. Yet his encounter with the local Palestinian merchants impressed on him the colonial nature of the occupation. 'As if slapped in the face, I suddenly became aware that [. . .] he was the oppressed, and I was on the other side of the border, with the strong, with the ones in power', Warschawski later recalled.[23] This personal epiphany came with an echo, for he associated the word 'occupation' with his own family's experiences of a hodgepodge of historical events. As a child, he often heard stories set during Germany's occupation of France in the Second World War, against which his parents had fought in the Resistance. As a teenager, he naturally identified with the Algerians in their struggle for independence; this time, the occupiers were French.[24] Now, when the Jewish state became an occupying force, Warschawski had no intention of supporting it. He recapitulated his shift in perception: 'I was unwilling to make the jump from that to being the occupier: I felt a natural compassion for the occupied.'[25] Before long, he left yeshiva and began studying at the Hebrew University of Jerusalem. Soon after hearing the cry of '*Hal'a HaKibush!*' and meeting a few Matzpen members, he joined the group himself (Figure 4.1).

The members of Matzpen were not alone in advocating for a withdrawal from the occupied territories after the war. 'I don't want to be a colonialist!' proclaimed the future peace activist Amnon Kapeliuk in the pages of *New Outlook*, a monthly magazine, describing a feeling larger than himself that, after a justified war, his own state had morphed into an unjust occupier.[26] Only a few weeks after the war's end, the emerging writer Amos Oz summed up the view of a new Zionist Left in the daily *Davar*. He contrasted the

Figure 4.1   Against the war in Vietnam: Michel Warschawski (back row) and Sylvia Klingberg (front left) at a demonstration in Tel Aviv.

'myth of liberation' and the Jewish entitlement to the entirety of historical Palestine against the demographic realities – that is, the completely Palestinian populations of the West Bank and Gaza Strip.[27] The implication was that they, the Palestinians, were, in fact, entitled to a sovereign nation-state of their own. With these shared criticisms, Matzpen now found occasional allies against the Israeli occupation, ranging all the way from Siah (Smol Israeli Hadash; New Israeli Left) to the communists of Rakah.[28] When Rakah stood for election to the seventh Knesset on 28 October 1969, Matzpen led several campaigns in its support.[29] Rakah was the only party in the election that called the newly acquired land 'the occupied territories'. What is more, as it appealed for recognition of a Palestinian right to self-determination and proposed a separate Palestinian state, Rakah was the only parliamentary voice advocating for Israel to withdraw to the borders of 4 June 1967.[30] A vote for Rakah, according to a Matzpen flyer, was both a 'protest vote against the present policy line' and the 'only possible way to vote against the occupation'.[31]

Unlike the new post-'67 leftists, who increasingly viewed the Israeli occupation as the central problem of the Israel–Palestine conflict, Matzpen had scarcely thought of a two-state solution – resolving the Palestine question by establishing both a Jewish state and a Palestinian state – as feasible. To all the opposition voices who feared that an ongoing occupation would transform Israel into a colonial power, Moshé Machover vociferously countered that the 'demographic principle' – 'every people has a right over the territory it inhabits and in which it constitutes a majority' – had held true even before 5 June 1967. Indeed, Palestine had been an Arab country at the start of the Zionist settlement. Historically, the entire Zionist project had been about changing that demographic structure. He concluded:

> [T]hese arguments [by critics of the occupation] are valid not only against the annexations proposed at present, but also against those implemented during and in consequence of the 1948 war, as well as against the initial Zionist claim over Palestine.[32]

The proponents of a territorial annexation of the Gaza Strip and the West Bank had likewise tried to ensnare opponents from the Zionist Left according to this reasoning. Amos Oz's sensational article in *Davar* soon found its retort: 'Indeed, according to a demographic criterion we did not have, at the start of the realisation of Zionism, any right over this country! [. . .] Nevertheless we were not prepared to accept a given demographic situation as the sole criterion.'[33] Once again, the Zionist Right exposed the paradoxes of the Zionist Left and was closer to Matzpen's historical analysis of the Palestine problem. Of course, there remained the fundamental difference that the advocates of a territorial annexation were prepared to continue the practices of historical settlement and the state's foundational conflict into the present, whereas Matzpen lamented that this would only be possible at the expense of both the Palestinian Arabs and the long-term future prospects for Israeli Jews.

Yet no one confronted Israeli society with the political implications of the war and the return to the original conflict between the Zionist project and the country's indigenous Arab population more effectively than the Palestinians themselves. The Six-Day War not only resurrected the Palestine question, it returned the Palestinian people and their plight to public awareness. A few years earlier, they had established a national umbrella organisation, the Palestine Liberation

Organisation (PLO); now, after the defeat of the Arab states, the Palestinians emerged from beneath the shadows of their former advocates in the Arab world. Particularly after Yasser Arafat took over as leader in February 1969, they could no longer be ignored as a distinct political player in the Israel–Palestine conflict.[34] Their newly awakened confidence was expressed in the public rejection of the United Nations Security Council Resolution 242, which sought to enshrine the two-state solution in all future peace talks: 'The Arab Palestinian people, expressing themselves by the armed Palestinian revolution, reject all solutions which are substitutes for the total liberation of Palestine and reject all proposals aiming at the liquidation of the Palestinian problem, or its internationalisation.'[35] A compromise that included a Jewish state in historical Palestine was unthinkable to them, no matter the borders. After the rapid ceasefire between Israel and the Arab states, just two days later on 12 June the Palestinians declared a new form of guerrilla war that would exert force against the Israeli occupation and the Jewish state.[36] Such a 'people's war', inspired by Mao Zedong and Che Guevara, could not be crushed by obliterating the Fatah network in the West Bank, which Moshe Dayan had ordered, despite all negotiation efforts. Between early 1968 and late 1970, a mounting wave of Palestinian violence targeted Israeli society,[37] terrifying the whole country and prompting even the Israeli Communist Party, which had mostly sided with Palestinian national aspirations, to publicly support Israeli retaliations in the autumn of 1968.[38]

Meanwhile, Matzpen's undeterred solidarity with Palestinian organisations, especially its declaration that it was 'both the right and duty of every conquered and subjugated people to resist and to struggle for its freedom', placed the group at the extreme political fringes of Israeli society.[39] In the eyes of these Israeli leftists, the Palestinians' actions were obviously responses to the recent occupations, driving at recognition, freedom and national self-determination; asserting those ends, Matzpen believed, legitimised forceful means. 'The ways, means and methods necessary and appropriate for such struggle must be determined by the people itself', explained the group. 'It would be hypocritical for strangers – especially if they belong to the oppressing nation – to preach to it, saying, "Thus shalt thou do, and thus shalt thou not do".'[40] Against the backdrop of the PLO's nascent bout of guerrilla warfare and its battle cry to 'eliminate Zionism', however, any shows of solidarity within Israeli society were met with nothing but bafflement, hatred and contempt.

Every news outlet from *Davar* to Uri Avnery's *Haolam Hazeh* to the Communists' *Kol Haam* invoked treason and siding with the enemy. 'Terror is a "right"; defending oneself against it is "oppression": that's the Matzpen people's collective conscience', wrote Avraham Wolfensohn in *Davar*, boiling down Matzpen's political agenda to a simple, disreputable formula: 'The objective: the extermination of Israel.'[41]

The members of Matzpen, however, linked their defence of 'the unconditional right of the conquered to resist occupation' with the ineluctable demand for a 'joint struggle of Arabs and Jews in the region for a common future' and mutual recognition, including 'the right of the Israeli people for self-determination'.[42] Their solidarity with the Palestinian's right to organise and to resist the occupation may have been unconditional, but they did not back Palestinian organisations' mission statements unconditionally.[43] 'We distinguish between the resistance to occupation of the Palestinian Arabs as a group and the specific policy of this or that organisation within the resistance movement', explained Moshé Machover and Akiva Orr in an effort to clarify the group's position.[44] The debate regarding what a common future might look like was therefore intensified by related bones of contention: over their respective agendas for changing the situation in the Middle East, and over guaranteed recognition for Israeli Jews' national status. On that basis, Matzpen criticised the PLO, the Palestinian umbrella organisation, both before and after the Six-Day War, when its political leader Ahmad Shukeiri mobilised with the Egyptian president against Israel and threatened to liquidate the state: popularized in the infamous phrase 'throw the Jews into the sea'.[45] Shukeiri's rhetoric eliminated any prospects for the Israeli Jews' collective future; if he had his way, only Jews who had lived in the country before the Balfour Declaration would be granted residency.[46] For the same reason, wrote Oded Pilavsky shortly after the Six-Day War, 'we are principled objectors to [Fatah's] actions', summing up Matzpen's clear rejection of the largest Palestinian organisation's positions:

> For us, the political and military objectives go hand in hand, and Al-Fatah's objective is not to end the occupation of one people by another, but to reverse the outcome: to turn the Arabs into occupiers and the Jews into the oppressed. [. . .] Our support is given in advance to any political movement in the occupied territories that recognises both peoples' right to national self-determination.[47]

Fatah drew further criticism from the Israeli leftists, even after the group began developing a new political agenda and, under the guidance of Yasser Arafat, took over the leadership of the PLO. Certainly, the idea of a secular democratic state on the land of historical Palestine, which Fatah increasingly championed from early 1969, implied fundamental changes: this vision would not only fulfil the national aspirations of Palestinians, but also guarantee Israeli Jews' right to remain.[48] But whereas Fatah's political platform sought 'a progressive, democratic, secular Palestine in which Christian, Muslim and Jew will worship, work, live peacefully and enjoy equal rights', it did not recognise the existence of a Jewish–Israeli nationality;[49] accordingly, Matzpen firmly opposed Fatah's positions that became authoritative for the PLO. In their manifesto 'The Middle East at the Crossroads', Jabra Nicola and Moshé Machover claimed that the Palestinian organisations held 'a misapprehension of the national problem in general and of Israeli reality in particular'.[50] In their view, the notion of a future Palestinian state 'whose members do not differ from one another nationally but only religiously' ignored 'the patent fact' that Israeli Jews constituted 'a national entity', one distinct from either Palestinian Arabs or Jews living elsewhere in the world.[51] Fatah remained unreceptive to the idea that the Jewish settlers had since metamorphosed into a new nation of Hebrew Israelis. But in part, Machover and Nicola's criticism also targeted the brand of Arab nationalism espoused by the PLO, whose 'narrow localist attitude' was neglecting the 'wider struggle for political and social liberation of the Middle East as a whole'.[52] Machover and Nicola's insistence upon a socialist transformation of the Middle East further articulated their awareness that the Israel–Palestine conflict and the question of Israeli Jews' future could only be solved in the context of a modernised and secularised Arab world as part of a resolution of the status of all non-Arab minorities in the region. The recognition of the Jewish–Israeli nation mirrored 'the problem of the various national groups living within the Arab world (Kurds, Israeli Jews, South Sudanese)'.[53] Machover and Nicola viewed a comprehensive guarantee of those groups' right to national self-determination as affirming the conditions for safeguarding, by extension, the existence of Israeli Jews.

As they distanced themselves from Fatah, the members of Matzpen drew closer to another Palestinian organisation, the Popular Democratic Front for the Liberation of Palestine (PDFLP), which in 1969 had split off from George Habash's Popular Front for the Liberation of Palestine. Under its Secretary

General Nayef Hawatmeh, the new group also rejected a local Palestinian nationalism and favoured solving the Israel–Palestine conflict in the context of a pan-Arab revolution. Logically, this went hand in hand with a principled 'rejection of the chauvinistic solutions of some Palestinians and Arabs' prior to the Six-Day War, such as 'slaughtering the Jews' or 'throwing them into the sea'.[54] It was around the same time that they first contemplated recognising Israeli Jews – as a nation, even. Wasting no time, their first manifesto on a democratic solution to the Palestine question invokes the idea of a prospective polity that would grant 'both Arabs and (Israeli) Jews the right to develop their national culture'.[55] Under these stipulations, the group also made efforts to build ties with like-minded Israelis. In 1969, the PDFLP's Khalil Hindi was studying in London and – on behalf of Hawatmeh – reached out to Moshé Machover, hoping to explore both their common ground and their points of disagreement.[56] Soon, the Israeli weekly *Haolam Hazeh* was citing an interview in the PDFLP's Arabic-language newspaper, *Al-Hurriya*, in which Hawatmeh revealed his organisation's connections to the Israeli leftists and announced a future dialogue with Matzpen in a European country.[57] In a subsequent statement of principles for *Al-Hurriya*, which was soon reprinted in France's *Le Monde*, Hawatmeh lodged an appeal for 'dialogue to be initiated with Israeli organisations which follow an anti-Zionist and anti-imperialist line' and urged such organisations to 'organise themselves into an armed popular Palestinian front' and to advance the implementation of a democratic solution to the Israel–Palestine conflict.[58] Although the appeal also extended to the communists of Rakah, Hawatmeh's efforts at dialogue were primarily directed at Matzpen – and, indeed, prompted considerable interest from them. Shortly after its publication, *Matzpen* likewise reprinted a Hebrew translation of the statement alongside a declaration by the PDFLP.[59] Both texts became points of departure for intensive discussions among the group. For the first time, on the basis of the two groups' socialist identifications, a shared perspective between the conflicting parties seemed to be inaugurated, and one that transcended all divisions. Immediately, Oded Pilavsky asserted that PDFLP's establishment and agenda represented 'an important milestone in the development of the Palestinian people's struggle and perhaps the social movements in the Arab world at large'.[60] On the strength of its internationalist worldview and its 'popular struggle against the reactionary and nationalist regimes in the Arab world', Pilavsky asserted that 'we [Matzpen] will accept this challenge – to engage in substantive dialogue with the cited views of Hawatmeh and his people'.[61] By limiting it to a thematic discussion, he was declining to establish an alliance with the Palestinian guerrilla.[62] And even though Pilavsky appreciated 'the stance of the Democratic People's Front towards the Jewish-Israeli people' and their contrast to the Arab nationalist positions of Fatah, he also urged the PDFLP to add the unconditional right of self-determination for Israeli Jews to their programme as a matter of principle.[63] In conclusion, he expressed hope that this conversation would lead to the articulation of a common position and the 'publication of a joint declaration by our two peoples'.[64]

Although each side reached out to the other, a joint declaration never transpired. Instead, the question of how closely to align with the PDFLP exposed fault lines among Matzpen members that would have a lasting impact on the group. Pilavsky's views first encountered palpable opposition from Rami Livneh, who had only recently joined Matzpen in the summer of 1968, a year after the Six-Day War. Livneh, the son of the Communist Member of Knesset Avraham Levenbraun, had previously been a member of Hashomer Hatzair and had written for *Zo HaDerekh*, the paper of his father's party, Rakah. Yet the events of the Prague Spring, combined with the Israeli Communist Party's unconditional support for the Soviet Union, caused him to leave Rakah and join the New Leftists of Matzpen, where he began to identify strongly with the Palestinian cause.[65] 'For a Joint Programme in a Joint Struggle' was the title of his supportive response to Hawatmeh's call. Unlike Pilavsky, Livneh had tabled any disagreements with Hawatmeh's declaration and focused solely on commonalities. In contrast to Pilavski's distanced reaction to Hawatmeh's call for a common struggle – 'individually or with the armed Palestinian movement'[66] – Livneh declared confidently that 'we see ourselves as already having a part in this struggle. We have been already waging this battle for several years, albeit independently, on our front.'[67] This was the first sign of divergent attitudes within Matzpen towards the position of the Palestinians. As the members' views on the critical questions of mutual recognition and the role of violence as a political tool diverged more and more starkly, the crack within Matzpen grew deeper – a crack that, in late 1970, ultimately fissured the organisation and split it twice.

Parting Ways: Utopias in Conflict

Not a week after the heavily attended general meeting of the Israeli Socialist Organization, held on 26 September 1970, Michel Warschawski sent a long letter from Jerusalem to Moshé Machover and Jabra Nicola, who were both currently living in London. At this point, the two founders were only participating from afar in their organisation's latest dramatic developments. 'You have undoubtedly heard about the split in our ranks', began Warschawski's detailed report on what had transpired before and during the general meeting. 'This didn't catch anyone by surprise', he continued. 'Everyone knew that something "significant" was about to happen to the organisation [. . .] that someone would secede.' Certainly, Warschawski's letter affirmed that Machover and Nicola's views remained current as 'the foundation of our work together'.[68] But whereas the London-based founders of Matzpen's perspective on the Israel–Palestine conflict connected the Palestinians' national emancipation with the expectations of a socialist revolution and mutual recognition, some Matzpen members had softened that stance. New voices appeared and tried to tug the group's philosophy in one of two competing directions: either to make Matzpen's positions more socialist and proletarian – the approach sponsored most prominently by Menachem Carmi (b. 1940) – or to reinforce its anticolonial character, as Ilan Halevi (1943–2013) and his followers wished. At the meeting of 26 September 1970, these internal conflicts climaxed. With the founding of Carmi's Brit HaPoalim (Workers' Alliance) and Halevi's HaBrit HaKomunistit HaMahapahnit (Revolutionary Communist Alliance), two factions seceded at once from the already small network of Israeli dissidents, dismissing the priority of a united front in the Israel–Palestine conflict.[69]

But although the conflicts that led to the split had taken place in the political realm of solving the Palestine question, the divorce's context transcended local horizons. The chief secessionists, Ilan Halevi and Menachem Carmi, had joined Matzpen after 1967 and both brought the ideas of a European New Left to the group, which now influenced the intra-Israeli disputes over the Israel–Palestine conflict. These revolutionary leftist ideologies identified the subject of the longed-for revolution as either international workers or the national liberation movements of the 'Third World'. Even before Halevi founded HaBrit HaKomunistit HaMahapahnit, the group's members had already been labelled Fanonists or Maoists for their passionate support of African independence movements, as they sought to transfer European Third-Worldism (*Tiers-mondisme*) to the Israeli context.[70] Menachem Carmi's circle had a similar background. It recruited its followers primarily based on their political identifications with the perspectives of the French Left. Even before the split, they were known in *Matzpen* as 'the Lambertists' – for their devotion to the ideology of the French Trotskyist Pierre Lambert – and quickly became a source of friction internally.[71]

The powerful influence of European New Left movements was an import, and Menachem Carmi was one of its importers. He was, in fact, born in Jerusalem in 1940, and studied economics, first at the Hebrew University of Jerusalem and then at the London School of Economics. But his true political awakening did not come until he lived in Paris from 1967 to 1969, while working for the Organisation for Economic Co-operation and Development (OECD) on a two-year contract. Of course, the Six-Day War and the changes to Israel's map also influenced his departure from his former stance as a leftist with Zionist leanings. Even before joining the group, he had contributed an article to Matzpen: a critique of the traditional Israeli Left and an urgent call for the creation of a new revolutionary party as part of international socialism.[72] However, he would only come of age politically upon joining the Trotskyist movement and its political group surrounding Pierre Lambert in France. His intellectual homeland became the proletarian revolution, with the international worker as the revolutionary subject. Because of its positive references to the workers and its focus on class issues, the Trotskyist group provoked mixed reactions from the start. Shortly before Moshé Machover met Carmi in London in the spring of 1969, Machover received a letter from Eli Lobel criticising the future Matzpen member's activities in Paris. 'All that counts is the struggle guided by the proletariat and the small farmers – that is the only path', wrote Lobel, somewhat pejoratively. Lobel was concerned that in the political lexicon of Carmi's group, social issues took on an extensive role that threatened to upstage colonial and national conflicts. He saw this convergence with the Lambertists as a singular 'catastrophe', mainly because the Lambertists, as part of the Fourth International and as exponents of its policy of 'entryism', epitomised left-wing sectarianism. Lobel was convinced that 'their organisational principle consists mostly of infiltrating any given place with the objective of taking it over'.[73]

He was not entirely wrong on this count. When Carmi returned to Israel in the spring of 1969 and formally joined Matzpen, he did, indeed, plan to persuade the Israeli group to adopt the political views of his international organisation. Matzpen already had one Lambertist member – Yehuda Kupferman, who had arrived in Israel from France in the early 1960s – but Kupferman had not made much of an impact. Carmi's arrival would change that. The two of them rapidly gathered a small band of followers, including Carmi's wife, the future writer Danielle Carmi; Yochanan Yuval; and, importantly, Sylvain Cypel (b. 1947). Cypel had likewise come to Israel from France; he was born in Bordeaux in 1947. His father, Jacques Cypel, published the important Yiddish newspaper *Unszer Wort* (Our Word) in France and had devoted himself to commemorating Europe's obliterated Yiddish culture and to aiding Zionist organisations. In the same spirit, the younger Cypel spent eighteen months in Israel from 1964 to 1965, where he received political and military training in the Nahal programme (Noar Halutzi Lohem, lit. Fighting Pioneer Youth), before completing military service in an elite paratrooper unit. But after the Six-Day War, when he moved to Jerusalem to study for several years, Cypel found himself increasingly opposed to Zionism and the worldview he had grown up with. He became embroiled in deepening discussions with fellow students, whose justifications of the Israeli presence in the Palestinian territories reminded him of the Algerian *pieds noirs*' arguments against a withdrawal from the colony.[74] It was during this period that he met Menachem Carmi, who was seven years his senior. The two of them became friends, and Carmi offered him political guidance. As Cypel later recalled: '[H]e convinced me not so much to become an antizionist – this, I think, would have happened in any case because of the reality of the Palestinian occupation by the Israeli army – but to become a Marxist, and more specifically a Trotskyite'.[75]

The fervour with which the group sought to spread the ideas of its international Trotskyist organisation, even within Matzpen, prompted a quick backlash. 'As "classical" Marxists: we thought that the fall of Zionism and the liberation of the Palestinian people [would] come and mostly [could] only succeed through a revolution lead by the working class', Sylvain Cypel reflected. 'So we were extremely critical towards any "compromise" with "ideological enemies".'[76] As in Cypel's account, this stance of his group had increasingly invited the criticism within Matzpen that the social utopia of an international proletarian revolution was overshadowing the distinct origins and salience of the Israel–Palestine conflict. Hence, Eli Lobel's letter to Moshé Machover ended with disapproval: 'I have been following his developments for a year now and am actually alarmed', he explained, quoting Carmi's harsh reaction to an article by Machover in *Le Monde*, as well as to his co-authored statement in the London *Times*: 'The article in *Le Monde* = petty bourgeois; the letter to the *Times* = petty bourgeois squared; the declaration by Fatah = petty bourgeois nationalism [. . .] etc.'[77] Any demands for the recognition of Palestinian nationalism seemed to give Carmi a whiff of the petty bourgeoisie. While Matzpen was willing to compromise and allow the Palestinian flag, Brit HaPoalim wanted to accept nothing but the red flag. Ilan Halevi later recalled a parallel dispute between Haim Hanegbi and Carmi, in which the latter asserted that he saw no difference between the left-wing Zionists of Mapam and the Palestinians of Fatah. Seen through the lens of his socialist worldview, they equally represented 'bourgeois nationalism'. 'If that's the case', Haim Hanegbi retorted, 'I'm on Fatah's side.'[78]

These differences would not remain compatible for long. The inevitable split occurred at the general meeting in September 1970, followed in short order by the publication of Brit HaPoalim's founding declaration, which centred on the accusation that through all Matzpen's de-Zionisation efforts, the group had lost touch with the Israeli workers' movement and missed its chance to draft its own 'programme of revolutionary socialism'.[79] Instead, according to the new splinter group, Matzpen had courted youth and student protesters too avidly in its activism against the Israeli occupation. It had become a 'petty-bourgeois movement', instead of strengthening the 'role of working-class people as leaders of the socialist revolution' or supporting the struggle to establish an international party of the proletariat.[80] In response to these 'made in France' positions, Moshé Machover and Akiva Orr made strenuous theoretical efforts to demonstrate that Israel was not a normal capitalist state and that its domestic social contradictions had been prefigured by unique factors: the Israel–Palestine conflict, the conflict with its Arab neighbours and its economic dependency on foreign aid.[81] This argument did not help. The new

Brit HaPoalim was gaining members. The first issue of its periodical *Avangard* (Vanguard), dated November 1970, contended that Israel was a, more or less, normal capitalist country that had 'a distinct [. . .] class structure [. . .] and therefore [an] oppressed and exploited class within it'.[82] Brit HaPoalim connected its revolutionary aspirations with domestic social inequalities as well. Consequently, the group abandoned the notion of a specifically Arab revolution, to which Matzpen had attached its dreams of modernisation, secularisation and progress. The group's own hopes were structured around a broader class of Middle Eastern workers that would bring about the de-Zionisation of Israel and a re-establishment of Palestinian rights, and eventually create an 'Israeli soviet republic'.[83] To pave the way, *Avangard* printed analyses of the international proletariat's circumstances and political significance, as well as of global economic developments.

Because the group seemed to downplay the Israel–Palestine conflict in order to focus on other issues, Warschawski saw no real future for Brit HaPoalim in Israel, as he argued in his letter: 'It looks as though [Carmi's group] will not grow any further. [. . .] Gradually, they will stop insisting on Zionist issues, and I don't see any reason people in Israel would rally behind such a sterile programme.'[84] Warschawski's forecast did not bear out. The group remained insignificant in Israel for many years – it only returned to public view in Israeli briefly upon the tragic death of one of its supporters – but the Israel–Palestine conflict would, in fact, rear its head again in the group's internal discussions. At first, the political pressure on the Israeli Lambertists came from outside, from its international parent organisation. After Brit HaPoalim added a call for an 'Israeli socialist revolution' to its programme, in the mid-1970s, the Fourth International accused it of serving Zionism at the expense of the Palestinians, instead of adopting the objective of a binational state in historic Palestine.[85] The issues of the Israel–Palestine conflict also plagued the group from within, causing a U-turn that led to another split. In 1976, the younger generation demanded that the status of the Palestinians should be a greater focus of political advocacy and founded the group Derekh HaNitzotz (The Path of the Spark). The Jewish and Palestinian members of this new group wanted to fully 'join the Palestinian struggle for national liberation' as their contribution to the region's complete emancipation and to the cause of a socialist revolution.[86] Considering the history of their own organisation, which began by prioritising class struggles over national ones, this amounted to a complete reversal.

This prioritisation of the Palestinian struggle was not altogether new, however. In September 1970, it had already caused the second split of Matzpen, with the founding of HaBrit HaKomunistit HaMahapahnit. In a letter to his two friends in London, Michel Warschawski expounded in similar detail on the offensive of Ilan Halevi, who arrived at the general meeting with a draft manifesto proposing a realignment on the Palestine question – essentially, a realignment of the entire group. With his political radicalism and urging for an overtly revolutionary agenda, Halevi's paper invited the same criticisms as Carmi's group. He levelled accusations of 'individual idleness' and of inadequate revolutionary 'discipline', failings that could only be rectified with a proper 'organisational conception'. In short, revolutionary impatience was paired once again with a quest for a new revolutionary avenue.[87] Yet the substance of Halevi's paper, to which he hoped to extract the group's binding commitment, suggested the opposite. Unlike Carmi's group, he did not fault his Matzpen peers for inadequate socialist credentials or for failing to take the workers' perspective. Instead, Halevi felt that the group's approach to the Israel–Palestine conflict was insufficiently anticolonial – and this was the group's central problem. The paper began with the charge that since the Six-Day War, Matzpen had been marked by a growing tendency to 'obscure the roots of the Israeli-Arab conflict [. . .] to overlook the purely colonial character of the contradiction, and to put the stress upon its national dimensions'.[88] In other words, Halevi held that Matzpen members had been devoting too much energy to criticising the Israeli occupation, instead of challenging Israel's internal Zionist structure.

At the same time, Halevi used his paper to articulate a discomfort with what he saw as insufficient support for the Palestinian national movement, which in his eyes had potential as a new revolutionary subject:

> By virtue of its historical situation, the Palestinian movement stands at the front of the struggle, not only against Zionism and pro-imperialist Arab reaction, but also against the force and the ideology of the petty-bourgeoisie, which claims to pass its nationalist reformism for socialism.[89]

Beyond the Palestinian context, this draft manifesto represented the arrival of a much broader current of Third-Worldism that had been radiating from

France: an optimistic belief that the anticolonial liberation movements of the 'Third World' were the pioneers and forerunners of a universal revolutionary transformation.[90] From this perspective, the nationalist movements' political goals seemed congruent with the project of a socialist revolution. Halevi's sworn allegiance to the Palestinian nationalist movement bore strong linguistic traces of this current within the New Left. His statement declared its

> [i]dentification with the Vietnamese people, the Cuban people, the Palestinian people and all the peoples whose heroic resistance to Imperialism not only leads them to the revolutionary way and to partaking in international class struggle, but also constitutes a precious source of lessons and experience for revolutionaries everywhere.[91]

Even before Ilan Halevi submitted his draft programme for discussion within Matzpen, he had travelled to Arab villages in the north of the country in search of more allies for his platform.

In the history of ideas, Ilan Halevi's shift fits into the French-born tradition of Third-Worldism, but the young man had been fascinated by, and had closely identified with, his era's national liberation movements for years, almost since adolescence. Halevi was born Alain Levin in Lyon in October 1943. He was born in a post office building, which his parents' Resistance group was using as both a cache of weapons and a political hideout. 'There were two good reasons for me being born there', he later wrote, reflecting on the traumatic circumstances of his birth:[92]

> In the first place, both my parents were Jews, or considered as such, which didn't make any difference in 1943 Fascist France. A few hours after I was born, and a few minutes after my mother had gone away to some other hiding place, carrying her newborn baby in her arms, the Gestapo came.[93]

Both his parents had already experienced a sense of precarious belonging as Jews, before being drawn into the maelstrom of the catastrophic events of the Second World War, the German occupation and the threat of their extermination for being Jews. His father, Henri Levin, was born in Poland to Russian–Jewish parents and had made his way to France, the land of the universal promise of *liberté, égalité et fraternité*, where he joined the Resistance following the German occupation.[94] That story, which is corroborated by Halevi's brother, is contradicted by another story that Ilan Halevi told to both friends and journalists: the story of a father who was born in Jerusalem into a Yemenite family and immigrated to the United States during the interwar period. After joining the local Communist Party there, he found himself returning to Europe to defend, first, the Republic in the Spanish Civil War and, later, the French Resistance against the German occupation.[95] Halevi's mother, an Istanbul-born Jew with roots in Aleppo, Syria and the Italian–Jewish community, was part of that same underground community. But although the couple shared a belief in the universal promise of the French Revolution while fighting in the Resistance, post-war France would not prove to be a true homeland, neither for them nor for their son. In ethnically homogeneous Normandy, olive-skinned Alain experienced the colonial racism of post-war French society.[96] Even the move to Paris, following his father's death and his mother's remarriage to Emile Albert, a friend from the Resistance who also adopted her children, was not to change this. From a young age, Alain Albert – his new name – felt like a sort of 'boy from nowhere', whose mission it was to keep reinventing himself and building the skills to 'adapt myself anywhere and to anybody'.[97]

Perhaps it was the combination of the traumatic circumstances of his birth, the political legacy of his parents' struggle and his own inborn rootlessness that made the young Alain Albert the 'singular internationalist', as he himself had once described his later friend, the philosopher Félix Guattari.[98] His ability to constantly reinvent himself and to demonstrate solidarity across borders soon made him a passionate defender of national liberation and emancipation movements all over the world. In his youth, he had already sympathised with the Algerians' war for independence and had likened their anticolonial resistance to his parents' activities in the French Resistance.[99] At just fifteen years old, he discovered the theoretical foundation for linking Nazism and colonialism in Aimé Césaire's *Discours sur le colonialisme*. But the father of Négritude had also been a formative influence with his *Cahier d'un retour au pays natal* (Notebook of a Return to Native Land) on Ilan Halevi's first literary writings, published in the pages of *Écrire*.[100] His parallel identification with Fanon's 'wretched of the earth' found its musical expression in his passion for American jazz. Clubs in Paris's Latin Quarter introduced him to African American music and the English language, but also exposed him to musicians who reported on the situation of black Americans and their experiences with racism. Young Halevi (Albert) was just nineteen when he published the paper 'Study in Brown' in Sartre's *Les Temps Modernes* and merged his criticism of French colonialism and American racial segregation.[101] Two years later, his first novel *The Crossing* (1964) delved deeply into the racism of the American South.[102] It remains unclear whether his own encounter with the US Civil Rights Movement in New York and Detroit truly had a formative impact on the text, as Halevi later claimed to his friends, or whether he had solely met James Baldwin, Chester Himes and Malcolm X during their time in Paris.[103] More important is that his biting criticism of white America's racism – written from a black perspective and phrased 'with an acute ear for the colloquial rhythms, pronuncation and syntax' – was an expression of solidarity with Black Nationalism, out of which the Black Power movement would later grow.[104]

His formative encounter with Black Nationalism and the American Civil Rights Movement ultimately took him far beyond the United States: 'His identification with black nationalism led him to Africa', wrote the journalist Arye Dayan, summarising Halevi's path from France to a series of African countries seeking independence in the 1960s.[105] Inspired by the theories of Frantz Fanon and Aimé Césaire, he became a 'travelling activist in the service of Third World struggles'.[106] First, he travelled to Angola in support of its national liberation movement, which had been waging a war of independence against the Portuguese colonial power since 1961. Later, he moved on to Mali, newly independent from France, where he worked as a journalist for a radio station and supported the newly formed socialist-oriented government under Modibo Keita, but also 'considered converting to Islam, in solidarity with African Muslims'.[107] Finally, his journeys took him to freshly independent Algeria, where he undertook translations for the Movimento Popular de Libertação de Angola and the South African African National Congress (ANC) and studied Arabic.[108] Halevi carried over his support for, and identification with, African nationalist movements to Arab anticolonialism. Meanwhile, the question of Palestine became more and more central to his political career. Looking back, he described this development:

> I came to Israel because I'd discovered the importance of the Palestine problem in Algeria. [. . .] I sat in the cafés there, listened to what people were saying, conversed with intellectuals and I understood that the Palestine question is the most decisive question driving people in the Arab world.[109]

His motivations in life so far – in sum, participation in a 'Third World' anticolonial, socialist revolution – had now drawn him into the conflict between Israelis and Palestinians that he had thus far avoided.

Sometime in 1965, he landed at Lod Airport with just one suitcase, bearing the books of Césaire and Fanon under his arm. His first stop was the left-wing kibbutz Gan Shmuel. Alain Albert, still under thirty, had decided to drop his stepfather's surname and to Hebraicise his birth name as Ilan Halevi. Still, his passionate defence of the era's anticolonial revolutions, which attracted enthusiastic supporters among the younger residents of the kibbutz, sparked conflict as it touched increasingly on the Palestine question. Even before the June war of 1967, Halevi caused a dispute with the kibbutz leadership when he compared Menachem Begin with Ahmed Shukeiri in an interview for *Kibbutz HaArtzi* magazine.[110] Finally, in the spring of 1968, his signature under the 'Pravda Declaration' against the destruction of houses in the occupied territories was the final straw. Halevi was forced to leave the kibbutz and move to Jerusalem, where he joined Matzpen (Figure 4.2). Notwithstanding, his membership there was not universally applauded either. No sooner had Halevi joined Matzpen than Eli Lobel sent a letter from Paris to the group's Tel Aviv address, cautiously confiding his doubts about the new member.[111] He had become well-acquainted with Halevi years earlier in Mali and was impressed by his talents and political passions. But Lobel also expressed concerns to his political friends that the young anticolonialist's zeal was at risk of crossing a line into unbridled liberation nationalism.[112] While Halevi was working as a political journalist in Mali, his identification with the black population's nationalist movements had gone so far that even his own colleagues complained he was sometimes indulging in overblown, exuberant propaganda against the country's white residents. Given that revolutionary recklessness, Lobel's letter was presumably rooted in the fear that Halevi's aspired identification with underdogs might carry over to the Israel–Palestine conflict. If he became a categorical supporter of Palestinian nationalism, this would also run contrary to Matzpen's stances to date.

The conflict would not simmer for long. In a matter of months, Halevi had formed a small circle within Matzpen, together with Udi Adiv and Rami Livneh. The three of them were essentially driven by an increased affinity for the Palestinian nationalist movements, aiming at an organisational collaboration. And just

Figure 4.2 Haim Hanegbi (left) and Ilan Halevi (right) on the campus of the Hebrew University of Jerusalem, Givat Ram, 1969. The posters read: 'There is no peace with occupations' (left) and 'MAPAM: Settling in the Golan, seizing land in Latrun and talking peace here' (right).

as they were therefore 'more lenient towards [Arab] nationalism' (in the words of Ilan Halevi) – compared to other Matzpen members, that is – they began reconsidering the group's foundational stipulation requiring Palestinian organisations to recognise the Israeli Jews' right to national self-determination.[113] 'They gravitated towards a "two-stage model" for the Arab revolution', explained Moshé Machover later, as he characterised the development of Halevi's group, which prioritised Arab nationalism over socialism, even though they never stopped criticising the chauvinism of Arab nationalists. 'They envisaged a separate first stage – a "national democratic" one. They tended to think of Arab petty-bourgeois nationalism as still having a revolutionary role to play' and had 'rather exaggerated expectations about the Palestinian resistance movement, and even tended to some extent to tail behind its ideology.'[114] From early on, this stance attracted public criticism from Jabra Nicola, who accused them of 'micro-nationalism' for dissociating themselves from a pan-Arab revolution and contended that even the Baath Movement was more progressive.[115]

The seemingly urgent question of who the revolutionary subject would be, in turn, stoked the conflict with Oded Pilavsky. His family tradition of proletarian internationalism, among other things, made him unsympathetic to the supposed emancipation promised by national liberation movements. In the era of a youth rebellion that was spreading to Israel, the Marxist-trained Pilavsky had also magnetically attracted some teenagers and university students with rebellious and anarchistic leanings. They gave the Israeli New Left reason to hope that the outbreak of a student revolt would usher in a revolutionary and social transformation from within the Jewish state.[116] Yet this perspective was incompatible with Halevi's Third-Worldism and his efforts to align Matzpen with the Palestinian national movement. As Moshé Machover later observed, Halevi's people 'tended to deny the possibility of any revolutionary work among the Israeli Jews [. . .] they did not believe that there was any revolutionary potential at all inside Israeli society [. . .] The practical conclusion of their view was that we should concentrate almost all our activity among the Israeli Arabs.'[117] Consequently, even before the split in the group, Udi Adiv turned his back on Matzpen and focused on direct collaboration with Israeli Arabs. For his part, Ilan Halevi tried to form a solid front against Pilavsky's approach and to win over the majority of the group for his own agenda at the general meeting of autumn 1970. 'He wanted to rally people around his new "platform"', Warschawski later reported to Nicola and Machover, 'because he assumed that Odik [Oded Pilavsky] would not join it. The goal [. . .] was to throw Odik out'.[118]

In the end, Halevi did not succeed in his efforts. After consideration by both himself and his political allies – chiefly Rami Livneh (b. 1945), Dan Vered (b. 1944) and Udi Adiv (b. 1946) – the dispute within Matzpen escalated into a rupture. Within several days, Halevi's statement was repurposed and revised as the founding document of Brit HaKommunistit HaMahapahnit. The programme's deviation from Matzpen's earlier positions was also visible in the language regarding the status of Israeli Jews. True, it also emphasised the 'existence of a Jewish national entity in Palestine–Eretz Israel', from which 'the political question stemming from the existence of that national minority' emerged. But Matzpen's unequivocal demand for the recognition of a right of self-determination for the Hebrew nation was somehow blurred by the demand for a 'clear recognition of their political rights'.[119] 'Wherever Ilan had written the word Israeli, they deleted it and wrote Jewish instead', complained another worried letter that Machover received shortly after the general meeting.[120] A further intensification of the group's ideology was evident in the use of an unconcealed militaristic tone, which had previously been avoided. To shake up Israeli Jews' trust in the Jewish state, Halevi's group had not only hoped for an 'aggravation of the internal economic crisis in Israel', but advocated the 'disappearance of Israeli military superiority'.[121] In that spirit, HaBrit HaKomunistit HaMahapahnit named its new newspaper *Ma'avak* (Struggle); soon, the group itself was known by this name. This tonal shift did not resonate with most Matzpen members, but the new coalition found advocates elsewhere. Marius Schattner, who had arrived in Israel from France merely two years earlier, joined Halevi and his friends. So did Meli and Debby Lerman, who had both come to Israel from Brazil, after obtaining political experience in the struggle against that country's military dictatorship.[122] Most of all, many Arab leftists found a political home in the group, strengthening Ma'avak's resolute binationalism. These included Mahmud Masarwa, Mohammed Ali Halev, Shauki Hatib and Anis Kar'awi.[123]

Considering the political shift inherent in its founding, Ma'avak received no shortage of criticism from the ranks of Matzpen. In London, Moshé Machover had written a strong polemic attack on Ilan Halevi's Third-Worldism and the 'dangerous tendency' of his group's new programme. Machover stressed, in no uncertain terms, that the new group's ideology 'obscures the distinct aspect of the Israeli-Arab conflict, which sets it apart from other colonial conflicts: the fact that the settlers in this conflict represent a nation, not a class or social stratum'.[124] He cannot have more clearly articulated the gap separating a Hebrew anti-Zionist, making the case for his future existence, from anticolonial Third-Worldism, with its stronger identification with national independence movements. Pilavsky also sharply criticised Halevi's group over its reluctance to clearly speak out for Israeli–Jewish national self-determination. They 'stutter about self-determination' in their programme, he wrote, and 'refrain from using this concept at all and instead talk about the political rights of the Jewish national entity in Palestine'. His complaint concluded with the telling question 'What political rights?'[125] Equally harsh was his accusation that they equated the Palestinian movement, a priori, with revolutionary movements taking place in countries like Cuba and Vietnam. Pilavsky pointed out that the other movements were socialist and internationalist movements, but that despite being anticolonial, the Palestinian movement also exhibited traits of 'reactionary nationalism and social chauvinism', and by no means embodied international socialism.[126] He saw Ma'avak's uncritical support as a sign of socialist internationalism surrendering to Palestinian nationalism and therefore labelled their positions 'left-wing slogans' with a 'right-wing meaning'. However, the direct criticisms of the papers did not lead to further condemnation. Looking back, Machover felt that relations had improved over time.[127] Also, the Ma'avak group's considerable activism among Israeli Arabs won Ilan Halevi the epithet 'Abu Nidal' (Father of the Struggle); further, Matzpen members were impressed by the group's many Arab members.[128] The split did not mark the end of collaboration.

Initially though, Michel Warschawski remained sceptical in his letter as to the long-term impact of the new group: 'It doesn't take a prophet to recognise that if they were actually to realise their new ideas and act according to them, they will be silenced by the authorities within six months.'[129] When Ma'avak published its founding document, in short order, it included another text by one of its members. 'Dare to Struggle!' ran the title of the anonymous statement, which dealt with differentiating theoretical positions, but also practical politics. Most of all, the text centred on a new form of political struggle: 'Matzpen must tear itself away from its petty-bourgeois and bohemian roots', the pamphlet concluded. 'Not to do this, to continue along the same lines, will be to offer the Zionist regime the best present it can receive from us: the luxury of a legal – but impotent – revolutionary organisation. [. . .] There is still a possibility of changing.'[130] Half a year and another split later, two of Ma'avak's members had executed that change themselves: Udi Avid and Dan Vered were going underground.

Border-Crossings: From Gan Shmuel to Damascus

On Friday 8 December 1972, the Israeli media released a breaking news story that would have a shocking and enduring impact on Israeli society. First, came the *Haaretz* front-page story:

> Arab-Jewish Spy Ring Uncovered by Security Service, Twenty Arabs and 4 Jews Arrested. One of the 4 Jews – Native of Kibbutz, They Trained in Terrorist Base in Syria, More Arrests Expected.[131]

Davar, Maariv and the evening newspaper *Yediot Aharonot* reported on the story the same day, and the spy ring became an ongoing news story on Israeli radio. Just as quickly as this first story saturated the press, new information about the spies reached the public eye.[132] *Haaretz* had already reported on the arrests of the Israeli Christian Arab Daud Turki, a bookseller living in Haifa, and the Israeli Bedouin Subhi Na'arani from Bosmat Tivon. More attention was devoted to the four Jewish prisoners: Dan Vered and Yehezkel Cohen, from Tel Aviv, and the German-born construction worker David Kupfer, from Bat Yam. But the real outcry centred on one person: Ehud (Udi) Adiv from Kibbutz Gan Shmuel. *Yediot Aharonot* also reported that the spy ring mainly comprised members of the organisation Hazit Aduma (Red Front), a splinter group of HaBrit HaKomunistit HaMahapahnit, which had been founded two years earlier by veterans of Matzpen.[133]

The more details about the prisoner's identities came to light, the more speculations multiplied concerning the spy ring's political objectives and the specifics behind the arrests. Articles revealing that members of the group had had several liaisons with Arab intelligence officers – initially in Athens, but later also in Damascus – were soon supplemented by information about strategic plans for attacks and acts of sabotage. 'The major threat posed by the ring was that of sabotage', *Maariv* reported. 'Such activities [were] to begin in the very near future, the objective being to sow alarm and fear among broad sections of the public and to shatter morale by striking at a number of public targets simultaneously.'[134] There was also talk of kidnapping top-ranking Israeli officials such as Moshe Dayan, and even rumours that the group had planned to assassinate the defence minister. However, few of the early reports that unsettled the country proved to be accurate. That same day, when the news of suspected violent activities seemed to be gaining ground, *Haaretz* and *Maariv* jumped back into the fray, reporting that the prisoners harboured no intention of assassinating public figures or committing any violent acts against them; neither had there been plans for an attack on the defence minister.[135] The spy ring had not been in possession of explosives, *Maariv* reported. The group's recruitment had, indeed, agitated and distressed Israeli society, but it was soon apparent that the state and its citizens were under no immediate threat.[136]

The lasting impact of these events came chiefly from the involvement of Israeli Jews in such a network, not from the fears of a terrorist threat. That Israeli Arabs would organise in this way seemed almost logical. As the *Jerusalem Post* noted: 'It is only human if under one in a thousand of the country's Arabs go to the extreme of trying to help the enemy liquidate a state whose very existence affronts their self-esteem.'[137] Yet the involvement of Jews in the spy network was considered an unprecedented act of treason. 'For the first time in the history of the state, young Jewish leftists, one of whom is a kibbutz member, participated in such a ring', *Haaretz* commented in its first article.[138] In the long run, the involvement of Udi Adiv, hailing from the famous model kibbutz Gan Shmuel, brought the deepest consternation. Indeed, his family heritage represented the traditions and ideals of Zionist socialism. His parents were veterans of Gan Shmuel, and his father was the son of one of the kibbutz' founders. Udi Adiv himself seemed to embody the ideal image of a sabra. After growing up in the kibbutz as a Hashomer Hatzair member with the famed Benyamin Gruenbaum as his schoolteacher, he had proceeded straight to an elite paratrooper unit. 'If there ever was a person who seemed to personify the man on the Jewish National Fund poster', wrote Aharon Bachar in *Yediot Aharonot*, 'Ehud "Udi" Adiv is the man.'[139]

In the public debate, the memory of Uri Ilan became nearly a mirror image of Adiv. Ilan was also born in Gan Shmuel, a decade before Adiv, and likewise grew up there. He received the same education from the same teacher and was taught the same values. Just like Adiv, he had moved from Hashomer Hatzair to an elite army unit, the Golani Brigade. Crucially, he had also crossed the Syrian border twenty years earlier. But unlike Adiv, Ilan had been following the orders of the Israeli Defence Forces. On his mission in the Golan Heights, he was abducted by the Syrian Army and transported into the interior of the country. To avoid revealing any classified information, the young soldier took his own life. When his body was returned to Israel, subsequently, a small note was found tucked under his clothes with the Hebrew words: '*Lo bagadeti. Hitabadeti* – I did not betray. I committed suicide.' From then on, Uri Ilan became a symbol of a sabra's military bravery. And after just two decades, the myth found its antithesis in Udi Adiv. Once again, a kibbutznik from Gan Shmuel had crossed the border into Syria. But this time, his goal was to cooperate with Israel's political and military adversary: 'Uri versus Udi', ran the headlines, 'Children of Gan Shmuel'.[140]

Thus, Israeli society was consumed with the crucial question of why. How could one of their own, born in the bosom of society and raised according to their values, turn on them so drastically? Some, such as Prime Minister Golda Meir, claimed that Adiv was 'mentally ill'.[141] Members of the religious community believed that Adiv represented the downfall of Judaism due to secularisation. And right-wing Israelis exploited Udi Adiv's background as a child of the kibbutz movement to land a sweeping blow against left-wing Zionism. Most importantly, the scandal returned the conversation to Matzpen's influence.[142] Even if only a few of its former members were willing to accept violent means for political ends, it seemed as if Matzpen itself, with its hard-line anti-Zionism, had collectively crossed that Rubicon. The political scientist Ehud Sprinzak wrote shortly thereafter:

> The key to understanding the phenomenon at hand is not the pointless question of whether the members of 'Matzpen' are responsible for the spy ring. [. . .] The aspect of the spy ring that must be emphasised is that the Jewish members extended the ideology and symbolism of Matzpen to its logical conclusion – betrayal of the motherland. Turki, Adiv, Vered and their friends concluded that it was time to put the 'de-Zionisation' into practice.[143]

This analysis was not entirely incorrect. For Udi Adiv, joining Matzpen was, indeed, a crucial step in cutting ties from his kibbutz and its ideology. In the aftermath of the war of June 1967, during which a twenty-one year old Adiv became a witness to the displacement of Palestinian Arabs from East Jerusalem, he personally observed the disintegration of the utopia of socialist Zionism: the marriage between a Jewish state and the universalist ideals of socialist internationalism. Having experienced the success of his own army, he turned his attention instead to the fate of Palestinian Arabs. Writing shortly after Adiv's arrest, the journalist Aaron Bachar surmised: 'It was the battles on the approaches to the Old City in Jerusalem that changed [Udi]'s views on life and the world around him. The sight of the dead and wounded shocked the young kibbutznik, who served in a crack unit. The world that emerged around him after the war was sad, ugly and cruel.'[144] Adiv's friends from the kibbutz also reported a few years later that he had returned from the war completely distraught. The concurrent displacement of Palestinian Arabs from the Old City and nearby villages had also called up memories of forgotten experiences from Gan Shmuel in 1948. Haim Hanegbi of Matzpen would later describe how the 1967 War evoked memories of the first Israeli–Arab war. Udi Adiv, not quite two years old, was sleeping in the kibbutz dormitory with other children when explosions shattered the night-time silence. Their nanny rushed over and explained to the frightened children that the kibbutz members were blowing up the houses of the neighbouring Arab village of Cherkas. When one child asked where their Arab neighbours would live when they returned, the nanny explained that the houses were being demolished to dissuade them from doing so.[145] Nineteen years after that experience, as Adiv perceived the persistent effects of the state's founding conflict in the late 1960s, his doubts about the legitimacy of his own Jewish state evolved into full-throated criticism and an anti-Zionist conversion.[146] 'After everything we'd experienced in the Six-Day War, the exposure to the Palestinians in the territories, I was looking for political direction in my life', he later recalled. 'When I heard about Matzpen, I made efforts to get in touch with them.'[147]

Udi Adiv's short-lived membership in Matzpen was only the first stage of an extended radicalisation process. The young Adiv soon saw the organisation's perspectives on solutions to the Israel–Palestine conflict as inadequate. Rather than placing faith in the progressive dynamics of historical processes, he wanted to take the fate of world history into his own hands. And unlike his comrades, who also critiqued the Palestinian organisations, he wanted to support them unconditionally. When Adiv was still part of Matzpen, he repeatedly proposed the idea of a joint Jewish–Arab struggle in a form modelled on the anticolonial liberation movements of the 'Third World':

> I told them [the Matzpen people]: The Palestinians are sitting in prison and we're sitting in cafés. They replied that I was dangerous, an adventurer. At meetings, whenever I raised the idea of a joint struggle with the PDFLP, people would shout at me.[148]

The criticism came from all directions. 'Ilan Albert [Halevi], Haim Hanegbi, Oded Pilavsky and Jabra Nicola each said that if Udi's opinion is accepted, I will leave the organisation that I helped to build.' Ultimately, the disagreements were too stark:

> In Umm al-Fahm, there was a group of young people known as Abnaa el-Balad. Ilan Shalif and I travelled to them and talked about an armed struggle. I said that the fight had to be directed against the army and police. I returned to a [Matzpen] meeting in Tel Aviv. Ilan Shalif told everyone what I'd said in Umm-el-Fahm. Pilavsky and Shalif scolded me for it. That was my last meeting in Matzpen.[149]

Even before Ilan Halevi's Ma'avak group split from Matzpen, Adiv had left the group and taken his own path. 'He had joined Matzpen but quickly found that our positions were timid or incoherent', Michel Warschawski recalled, reflecting on the arguments that followed. 'Udi and his comrades felt that they had to join up with the Palestinians.'[150] Although Adiv joined Ma'avak shortly thereafter, he would not feel at home there either. Within a year, he left that group as well to co-found *Hazit Aduma* (Red Front) with Dan Vered.

Vered, born in 1944 in Tel Aviv, started his career as a maths teacher. His political radicalisation was not solely a product of the conflict in the Middle East. Some commentators interpreted Vered's participation in the espionage and sabotage ring as a result of the young man never having served in the Israeli armed forces: 'The fact that Dan had not taken part in his generation's shared experiences isolated him [. . .] made him into an exception.'[151] In fact, he was influenced much more directly by his time at the University of Miami, where he studied in 1969 and 1970 and drew attention for his open criticism of the

Israeli occupation.¹⁵² Vered rapidly made connections in left-wing circles there and wound up in the Maoist-leaning Progressive Labour Party. He continued to espouse the party's political convictions after his return.¹⁵³ For example, in an analogy to China's Cultural Revolution, he declared that all pianos in Israel should be destroyed to liberate local society from its bourgeois elements.¹⁵⁴ His ideologically charged Maoist affiliation became the main foundation of his uncritical solidarity with national liberation movements. This vulgar radicalism also characterised the magazine *Hazit Aduma* (Red Front), of which Udi Adiv and Dan Vered published three editions from October 1971 to May 1972, including contributions from David Kupfer, a former member of the communist Rakah party, and Yehezkel Cohen, a former supporter of the Israeli Black Panthers.¹⁵⁵ Instead of conceptually precise historical analysis, the publication was rife with polarising catchphrases. The Red Front moved away from the kinds of questions Matzpen had been historically concerned with, such as how to resolve the colonial situation and how a social revolution in the Arab world, combined with such a post-colonial solution, could permit the recognition of Israeli Jews as a nation within the region. Although they, too, articulated a socialist utopia of a shared future for Jews and Arabs on equal footing, they now attached these egalitarian prospects for the country's Jews to their unconditional support for an Arab liberation struggle.¹⁵⁶ By frivolously equating the transnational struggle of socialism with the programme of national liberation, the group's appeal for 'support for the Arab struggle for national and socialist liberation' (as demanded by Daud Turki) was also 'abandoning the quest for independent analysis and critique of nationalism'.¹⁵⁷ Thus, although they continued to invoke a common proletarian revolution, their tactics and objective seemed to be solely justified by their solidarity with Palestinian nationalist movements. 'With the Red Front, the internationalist programme of the Left ended up being subordinated to militant nationalism', writes Ran Greenstein, summarising the group's singular path, which had been amply illustrated by one of Udi Adiv's political conclusions.¹⁵⁸ 'The task of communists is not to present "proletarian alternatives" or to say that they struggle for socialism', Adiv stressed in the last published issue of Hazit Aduma, 'but to aspire to lead the national liberation struggle, currently led by Fatah. [. . .] Their communist-led national liberation will be their social liberation as well.'¹⁵⁹ Ultimately, Adiv went so far in his support that he proclaimed he was relinquishing his own status as an Israeli and was 'choosing to be [a] Palestinian'.[160] He published his article under the pseudonym Yehuda Palestinai.[161]

In their desire for practical and political action, Adiv and Vered departed from the notion that societal change must come from within. When the two activists left Ma'avak, it was not primarily due to intellectual disagreements. Rather, they did so 'in protest against [the organisation's] failure to implement its revolutionary ideas', as later explained by Habib Kahwaji, who soon rose to become a dubious supporter of their plan.[162] This shift in perspective was already evident in the pages of the slender pamphlet that the small group published. The first two issues' covers were a drawing of an international group of armed fighters, led by a man with a machine gun. The young Israelis wanted to adopt the visual language of guerrilla warfare for their own context. Later, at trial, Udi Adiv personally described his path towards self-sacrifice and identification with the struggle of the Palestinians. He only considered a joint Jewish–Arab organisation possible in the context of an allied armed struggle:

> This can only be done if the Jews will prove to the Arabs, who have been fighting Zionism for dozens of years, that they [the Jews] are on their side, that they are prepared to sacrifice everything they have, to be subjected to the same 'treatment' and to share everything with them.[163]

Ultimately, the meeting with the Haifa-based bookseller Daud Turki prepared Adiv's circle for their departure from the political reality and their descent into the underground, where the young Israelis hoped to squeeze their way into the cockpit of world history. Turki, a Christian Palestinian who was born in 1927 in the Arab village of El-Maghar and raised in Haifa, had a long political saga before that fateful meeting. During the British Mandate, he belonged to the Arab Communist National Liberation League before he joined Maki and later associated with the Al-Ard group. Eventually, in 1963, Turki joined Matzpen, only to leave it after just two years. In his view, Matzpen's alliance with Uri Avnery's *Haolam Hazeh* was an unforgivable compromise with Hebrew nationalism.[164] When he found out about the establishment of Hazit Aduma (Red Front) six years later, he reached out to Udi Adiv and proposed the possibility of a joint Judeo–Arab struggle. The first step of this entailed meeting directly with a PLO member for a discussion in Athens – an offer the young Adiv accepted with enthusiasm. But when he flew to the Greek capital on 28 September 1971, it was not only his first international trip, it was a border-crossing that made him a turncoat. From that point onward, Adiv identified wholeheartedly with the Palestinian cause and set out to join the nationalist movement in the hopes of 'pav[ing] the way for true coexistence in a Palestine freed of Zionism'.[165] His political activities underwent a sea change. When he met with his contact, who went by the name Abu Kamal and introduced himself to the young Israeli as a member of an independent Palestinian organisation with Marxist–Maoist leanings, the main item on the agenda was passing on information about the Israeli military. But it did not stop there.[166] In August 1972, Dan Vered also travelled to Athens. From the Syrian Embassy, the Palestinian intermediary escorted him – under a fake passport – to Beirut and then Damascus. His border-crossing was symbolic at first, but socially and morally, he transgressed a real boundary. In Damascus, Vered was familiarised with military codes. He was then drilled in the use of firearms at a Palestinian training camp near the capital. The proximity to Syrian institutions made Vered realise that he was not exclusively serving the Palestinian cause, but had become a tool of the Syrian government. Udi Adiv had no such misgivings. Vered decided to end his involvement in the meetings with the Palestinians.[167] Soon after, in September 1972, Adiv boarded another plane to Athens and travelled by the same route to the training camp near Damascus. He readily shared all the information he had gained about the Israeli military, his military education and weapons technology. The only request he denied was to bring along photographs of military installations in Israel.[168] He maintained the steady conviction that he was a trailblazer for a just cause. 'I understood that I had gone too far in my actions and that I was sinking into a dangerous underground operation with no way back', he later reflected. 'This feeling only strengthened my appreciation of the significance of my action, which I for my part understood as an advancement of revolutionary solidarity with the Palestinians. This act illustrated my own commitment to their revolutionary strategy but also a gesture of trust on their part.'[169]

Although all of Udi Adiv and Dan Vered's trips were planned and carried out in secret, they did not escape the notice of Israeli intelligence. In the early morning of 6 December 1972, several weeks after Adiv returned from his second trip, roughly twenty police officers forcibly entered his flat and arrested him. The Israeli authorities had concluded that he was planning terrorist attacks and intervened. The intelligence officers confronted Adiv and Vered with numerous photographs of their meetings in Athens, along with documents attesting to their cooperation with Syrian intelligence. This was soon explained by the invisible role of Habib Kahwaji, who had introduced himself in Athens by the code name of Abu Kamal. After his release from Israeli prison in 1968, the former Al-Ard member had agreed to leave the country and was soon approached by Syrian intelligence with an assignment to build a Jewish–Arab network for espionage and sabotage.[170] The core of the network was comprised of the Arab group members, including Daud Turki, Subhi Na'arani, Anis Kar'awi and Simon Haddad. By way of Turkey, they all kept in regular touch with both Kahwaji and contacts in Beirut and Damascus. Turki was also tasked with identifying sites in northern Galilee that could be used as 'drop-off points for weapons and explosives'.[171] Under these circumstances, Turki and Adiv's claims that they did not know about Kahwaji's connections with Syrian intelligence were not very credible. They could do nothing to stave off a sensational trial and sentencing hearing (Figure 4.3). Adiv's perception that Kahwaji had betrayed him did not help his case. 'All I planned was a Jewish-Arab revolution in Israel', he said on the record during a hearing. 'They wanted to destroy the state; I only wanted a more just regime.'[172] By then, the trial had become a public occasion. Partly for that reason, when the verdict was pronounced on 26 March 1973, the prison sentences handed down to the members of the network were unusually long. For their involvement in an illegal organisation, their connections to foreign agents, their establishment of an espionage organisation, their provision of information to the enemy and their illegal entries into Lebanon and Syria, Daud Turki and Udi Adiv were each sentenced to seventeen years in prison. On similar charges, Subhi Na'arani and Anis Kar'awi were sentenced to fifteen years, Dan Vered to ten and Simon Haddad to two.[173]

Throughout the trial, there were numerous demonstrations in Haifa, where members of Ma'avak and Matzpen agitated for the release of the accused – even while both groups were vocally distancing themselves from the activities of their former comrades. 'We rely on the strength and conscious[ness] of the

Figure 4.3 The defendants in the courtroom, left to right: Dan Vered, Subhi Na'arani, Udi Adiv and Daud Turki, Haifa, 1973.

masses, not on the personal bravery of individuals or a vanguard without roots in the concrete struggle of any class', pledged the members of the Ma'avak group; they wrote off the spy ring as a 'revolutionary excitement for political adventure without value'. Equally, they feared the trial would provide the authorities with an 'excellent pretext' for launching a 'witch hunt' and 'for the oppression and silencing' of opposition voices in general.[174] During the police investigation that followed the discovery of the spy ring, there was a second wave of arrests on 26 December 1972. The police rounded up about twenty Israeli Arabs and two members of Ma'avak: Rami Livneh and Meli Lerman. The pair were not accused of directly collaborating with Udi Adiv's ring, though the police did charge them with possessing information that could have been useful to the investigation. The main charge against them was of meeting with the Fatah member Ahmed Khaladi. Livneh had first met the Palestinian student from the occupied territories in the summer of 1970 in a forest outside Nazareth. In 1972, Khaladi had also visited Lerman in the latter's house in Kiron.[175] But even though Livneh repeatedly emphasised that the meeting was solely for the sake of dialogue and that he had staunchly opposed any form of violence, suspicions that he had committed 'offenses

[. . .] aimed against the sovereignty of the state' and had 'provid[ed] cover' for the enemy hung in the air. In a separate trial, he was eventually sentenced to ten years in prison for having had 'contact with a foreign agent'. Lerman was sentenced to seven.[176]

But the greater significance of this trial was not about the charges; it had to do with the public scandal over the interrogation methods used. Soon after Livneh and Lerman's apprehensions, their lawyers Felicitas Langer and Lea Tsemel lodged preliminary complaints about the use of force during the authorities' interrogation of their clients. It was Rami Livneh's father Avraham Levenbraun, a Member of the Knesset from the communist Rakah party, who raised allegations of torture before the Israeli public. On 8 January 1973, the day after he visited his son at Jalameh Prison, Levenbraun held a press conference in the Knesset building to report on the interrogation techniques. He said that interrogators used punches, kicks and electric shocks to extract information and confessions.[177] At first, Levenbraun accused the authorities of using violence against his son. However, the subsequent public debate centred on the use of violence against Arab prisoners as a way to coerce confessions from their Jewish friends.[178] The discussion of the treatment of prisoners drew attention throughout the left-wing political spectrum in Israel. The human rights activists Israel Shahak and Uri Davis drafted various communiqués protesting the prisoners' conditions. The dramatist Hanoch Levin even considered writing a play based on Livneh's trial.[179] Significantly, Matzpen and Ma'avak felt duty-bound to act. They published letters of protest in Israel, while mobilising their international contacts. A statement against the interrogation methods was signed by the likes of Maxime Rodinson, Charles Bettelheim, Pierre Vidal-Naquet and Jean-Paul Sartre, and Amnesty International also investigated the case.[180] Yet the public engagement in the trial had no effect on the outcome. Matzpen and Ma'avak tried to protect Rami Livneh from imprisonment by appointing him as the top candidate of a new Jewish–Arab list in the upcoming election, but this attempt also failed.[181] In the end, Livneh's early release was a result of an official decision, after one year, to reduce his sentence from ten years to four and Lerman's from seven to two.[182]

These events would not be the final instalment of the dialogue between Matzpen members and representatives of Palestinian organisations. But whereas the first overtures were sparked by the military and territorial changes in the aftermath of the Six-Day War, and by the Palestinian political awakening, later contacts grew out of the fourth round of Israeli–Arab fighting: the October 1973 War and the subsequent shift from violence to diplomacy. The war was waged by the Egyptian President Anwar as-Sadat, together with Syria, as a limited engagement aimed at breaking the gridlock that had set in since the Six-Day War and initiating a political process in the Middle Eastern conflict.[183] For the Palestinians, it also opened the door to diplomacy and political compromise. A national and territorial settlement finally seemed possible for the first time in the history of the Israel–Palestine conflict, which had been irresolvable as a result of its colonial structure. For an Israeli Left that articulated its agenda based on the distant horizon of a socialist revolution, the prospect of a geopolitical solution threw a spanner in the works. The Left was now forced to choose between the state and revolution. This question deepened a second rift in Matzpen, which had already come to light during 1971–2. This time, the rift was not situated at the group's margins: it ran straight down the middle.

State or Revolution

The Israeli Socialist Organization had not called many press conferences. After all, Matzpen was a revolutionary organisation with the objective of a long-term socialist transformation of society as a whole. The revolution could hardly be announced at a press conference. The dull procedures of short-term, day-to-day politics were as foreign to the group as the associated public appearances. Yet in mid-December 1975, when the group sent invitations to the country's newsrooms – almost in the fashion of a political party – Matzpen had an extraordinary event to report, virtually a political affair of state. A month prior, on 10 November, Moshé Machover had met in London with Said Hammami (1941–78), the local representative of the Palestinian Liberation Organisation (PLO), which had just attained international recognition a year earlier.[184] The two of them had met before in the secrecy of Hammami's apartment, but this was their first semi-official conversation. In anticipation of peace talks, they spent a long time discussing the Israel–Palestine conflict in detail: the history, its present status and prospects for a solution. The conversation's unusual nature was underscored by the fact that it was recorded and later distributed as a special edition of *Matzpen*.[185] Probably for the first time ever, a leading representative of the PLO had consented to a face-to-face interview by an Israeli – for the purposes of publication, no less. This resulted in a kind of role reversal, with Moshé Machover essentially serving as an unappointed emissary. Despite being a proponent of revolution, he served a pioneering 'diplomatic' role. By holding the press conference and publishing the transcript of the meeting, the Matzpen members wanted to emphasise the meeting's significance even further. The theatrics hit the mark. The Israeli newspapers immediately ascribed political relevance to the meeting. *Yediot Aharonot* treated the encounter as a formal political meeting, running the headline: '"Matzpen" Member Meets PLO Reps in the UK; Transcript Published' – as though Moshé Machover were a recognised envoy of Israeli interests, or even conducting government-like policy.[186]

The conversation between Machover and Hammami comprised just such a blend of revolutionary utopianism and political pragmatism, as it moved back and forth between long-term scenarios for the future and short-term steps to reconcile the longstanding conflict. The dialogue began by explicating the perspective Matzpen favoured: that the Israel–Palestine conflict could be permanently transformed by transcending the Jewish–Arab antagonism in a binational society within a region turned socialist. This society would not feature any 'national discrimination', and all people would 'have the right to form their own political and *national* organisations'.[187] Both Palestinian Arabs and Israeli Jews would be able to maintain their language, beliefs, culture and traditions without restricting the rights of the other national group.

The need to postpone a solution to a utopian era's distant horizon had grown out of the politically hopeless set-up of a conflict over national settlement that seemed nearly intractable in territorial terms. The very life of Said Hammami, born in 1941 in Jaffa, had been imprinted with this founding conflict of the Jewish state. In 1948, his family was forced to leave that coastal city bordering Tel Aviv; after the war, they found refuge in Lebanon and finally resettled in Amman, Jordan. Hammami later moved to Damascus to study, where he joined Syria's Baath party, before joining Fatah for its Palestinian nationalism and its resistance against the Jewish state.[188]

His interviewer, Moshé Machover, was willing to confront Palestinians' suffering head-on and shared their demands for individual equality and collective recognition. Hammami, for his part, had promised Machover that he would recognise the collective existence of Israeli Jews, the same recognition Matzpen had been pushing for from the Palestinian organisations. Less than thirty years after the Palestinian catastrophe, Hammami said he no longer blamed 'the present Israeli generation for what their fathers did to me personally, expelling me from my country. But they should also know that we exist as a people and have a just claim to that country.' Hence, his opinion about the country's future was guided by the indisputable existence of both peoples:

> Not a single progressive Palestinian can say to an Israeli Jew, 'You don't have a right to this country'. But not a single Israeli Jew can say to a Palestinian Arab, 'I have more right to this country than you'. We probably have a bit more right to Palestine than the Israeli Jews. The fact is that we both exist as peoples. The question is: Is conflict the only relation possible between these two peoples? My reply is: Definitely not.[189]

In London, far from the site of the virtually irresolvable conflict, Machover and Hammami felt ready to leave history behind them and together look to the future.

The dialogue partners did not content themselves with the utopian appeal for a binational polity. Their conversation led them to a pragmatic realism and possibilities for short-term measures that would blaze a passable trail to political reconciliation beyond the origins of the conflict. Alongside their shared hopes for the future, they had taken pragmatic diplomatic strides. 'Probably as a first step – and I believe that it is a necessary step, an inevitable step, whether we or they like it or not – Palestine should be partitioned between the two peoples', Hammami therefore argued. '[F]or the sake of peace between the two peoples, there must be two states as a first step.'[190] However, in his view, the idea of partitioning the country and establishing a Palestinian state was not at all synonymous with solving the Israel–Palestine conflict. Still, Hammami saw this as a 'realistic step', in order to give Palestinians their first direct sovereignty and to allow refugees from previous wars to return to their own state. Machover got on board with this first preparatory step towards a new long-term prospect for Israelis and Palestinians. He pinned the transitional compromise of a two-state solution to his hopes that Israelis would start 'to acknowledge that another people exists in Palestine who can legitimately lay claim to this country'.[191] A few days after their conversation, he asked Hammami to quickly review the transcript so that he could send it to Israeli Matzpen members as part of a campaign seeking Israeli recognition of the PLO as a political negotiation partner.[192] At the subsequent press conference in Tel Aviv, Matzpen announced, Hammami's stance amounted to no less than a general shift in the PLO's position.[193] The Israeli press likewise welcomed this development: 'Said Hammami spoke of a Palestinian state in the West Bank and Gaza', reported *Yediot Aharonot*.[194] For the first time, there were real prospects of a compromise and a political solution.

The PLO's new position did not, in fact, derive from the talk between Machover and Hammami. Neither did it come as a complete surprise. It was simply the expression of political shifts within the Palestinian organisation that had been underway for some time, but had only crystallised once the war of October 1973 rearranged the international puzzle pieces of the Middle Eastern conflict.[195] The fourth round of military escalations was unique among the Israeli–Arab clashes. By accepting UN Resolution 242, which stipulated that Israel withdraw to the pre-5 June 1967 borders, Egypt, Jordan and later Syria had already shown that they had, theoretically, resigned themselves to the Jewish state and given up on the triple 'no' of the Khartoum Summit.[196] Instead, Egypt's President Sadat had started taking Israel's offer to swap land for peace very seriously – in fact, insisting on it, violently at times. A limited war against Israel was intended to set things back in motion. The state of play had been at a standstill since 11 June 1967, and Sadat hoped to extract the occupied territories from the Jewish state through military force. In retrospect, the war that October proved to be nearly 'preparatory for peace'.[197] For Israel, it was the obverse of the Six-Day War: its element of surprise destroyed the state's sense of military invincibility. The takeaway for the Arab states, meanwhile, was that it would be impossible to vanquish Israel through military force. Most of all, it created a new basis for political negotiations. Under political pressure from the international community, especially the US Secretary of State Henry Kissinger, the war became the starting point for the 1973–5 peace talks in Geneva. Those talks laid the groundwork for the negotiations at Camp David in 1978, which eventually led to the Israeli–Egyptian Peace Treaty in March 1979 and Israel's subsequent withdrawal from the Sinai Peninsula.

The Palestinians could not rule out such a shift from force to diplomacy either. Even before the war, scattered voices in Nayef Hawatmeh's PDFLP had already abandoned the 'liberation of the whole of Palestine' and urged a provisional diplomatic solution; after the war, these voices were magnified. A process was set in motion, and after the 1973 War, the Palestinian leadership wanted a seat at the table, expecting recognition of their independent position on the international stage. Meanwhile, they signalled their willingness to make political compromises.[198] Said Hammami embodied the clearest manifestation of this, and he became the voice of this transformation. At the peak of Palestinian guerrilla activities, he had already foresworn an armed struggle in favour of navigating political terrain. The death of Israeli children at the hands of his unit had given him significant doubts about the legitimacy of military action.[199] As the PLO's London representative, he first personally advanced the internal shift in his organisation, before communicating it to the international public. In two highly regarded articles for the London *Times*, he appealed for the Palestinians to be given diplomatic recognition and to be included as participants and negotiation partners in future peace talks in Geneva.[200] This introduced a new perspective on the conflict with Israel. The adoption of the idea, propagated by the United Nations, of establishing a Palestinian state in the territories that Israel had occupied six years earlier testified to the Palestinians' growing pragmatic self-restraint and their previously withheld acknowledgment of the existence of two peoples in Palestine as a basis for future developments. 'Many Palestinians believe that a Palestinian state on the Gaza Strip and the West Bank [. . .] is a necessary part of any peace package', read Hammami's public statement, in which he turned towards a two-state solution.[201] 'The Israeli Jews and the Palestinian Arabs should recognise one another as peoples, with all the rights to which a people is entitled.'[202] This interpretation of the political circumstances from a PLO representative was unprecedented. Yet his article heralded a much broader transformation. For all its insistence on the rhetoric of the 'whole of the soil of their homeland', the entire PLO had signed off on its first transitional programme at the organisation's assembly of June 1974:[203] on principle, the agenda opposed the United Nations' two-state approach, but it made concessions by invoking the establishment of an 'independent combatant national authority for the people over every part of Palestinian territory that is liberated'.²⁰⁴ Before long, the idea of a new Palestinian mini-state was the talk of the town.²⁰⁵

However, this pragmatism was mostly championed by Fatah, and it did have detractors within the PLO, most of all the fiercely dissenting Popular Front for the Liberation of Palestine (PFLP), led by George Habash, and its breakaway group, the PFLP-General Command (GC), headed by Ahmed Jibril. Committed to 'territorial maximalism', the PFLP preferred to skip short-term political steps such as international peace talks in Geneva. Under no conditions would they accept a Palestinian mini-state and the 'renunciation of the liberation of all Palestine'.²⁰⁶ On 26 September 1974, the group withdrew its membership from the Palestinian umbrella organisation on those grounds and soon afterwards formed the Rejectionist Front together with the PFLP-GC and the Iraqi Baathists of the Arab Liberation Front.²⁰⁷ This opposition to the Palestinian leadership's pragmatic realism had already erupted with dramatic results earlier that year. On 11 April, armed PFLP-GC units broke into an Israeli block of flats in the far-northern town of Kiryat Shmona and murdered eighteen Israeli civilians. In a communiqué, the group quickly claimed responsibility for the massacre, explaining its rejection of the PLO's new diplomatic, compromising approach. '[We] will continue the revolutionary struggle until the total liberation of Palestine', reads the statement, an intent underscored by the attack's chosen target. 'We have launched an operation against Kiryat [Shmona] [. . .] situated within the 1948 borders, to underline that our liberation struggle is not limited to the West Bank and Gaza.'²⁰⁸ Israeli civilians would eventually pay a bitter price for this internal conflict among Palestinians over diplomacy versus violence and a Palestinian mini-state versus territorial maximalism.

Yet the diplomatic turn among Palestinians was unstoppable. The PLO's willingness to make territorial compromises and their efforts to secure a seat at the table for future peace talks had vastly improved their international standing. Under Yasser Arafat's leadership, the PLO was confirmed in October 1974 as the 'sole legitimate representative of the Palestinian people' by the League of Arab States.²⁰⁹ The Palestinian organisation primarily attained international legitimacy thanks to the United Nations, however. Arafat was invited to give a speech on the Israel–Palestine conflict. Only nine days after his historic address to the General Assembly in New York, on 13 November 1974, the

Palestinian umbrella organisation was granted international observer status.[210] In the spirit of this diplomatic breakthrough, and in anticipation of further political negotiations, Said Hammami tirelessly tried to keep advancing the process of collective recognition by appealing for a transitional two-state compromise. In March 1975, he presented a new position paper. It would become more than just the next milestone in the PLO's internal clash; indeed, it called for a 'dialogue with any elements within Israel who were prepared to meet and talk with Palestinians regarding the form of a mutually acceptable coexistence which might in time be developed between the two peoples living in the country to which they both lay claim'.[211]

This development, and his appeal for mutual understanding, did not go unanswered. Hammami's advocacy had aroused interest both in Israel and among the broader Jewish public, not only Matzpen members. This interest grew out of a very diverse range of political players' expansive yearnings for dialogue. Shortly after the publication of his *Times* article, Hammami agreed to an exclusive interview with Britain's *Jewish Chronicle*. 'Arafat Ready to Make Peace with Israel', ran the headline, which certainly left its mark.[212] In Israel, Uri Avnery had been the central figure seeking political dialogue and contact with Hammami.[213] Avnery had repeatedly promoted a two-state solution in *Haolam Hazeh* and published open letters to the Palestinian leadership with that in mind. Perceiving an opportunity for dialogue in Hammami's initiative, he contacted the PLO's representatives and tried to arrange direct talks with the Israeli government under Yitzhak Rabin, who declined the proposal. However, Rabin did not stand in the way of further meetings between Avnery and Hammami. To that end, in June 1975, Avnery joined forces with Amos Kenan and Yossi Amitai to form the Israeli Council for Israeli–Palestinian Peace (ICIPP). But despite various meetings between the two of them, Hammami did not agree to Avnery's wish to publish their exchange.[214] He reserved this privilege for Moshé Machover and *Matzpen*.

Still, the Israeli socialists in and around Matzpen had a difficult path, full of rifts and organisational quarrels, before the self-declared revolutionaries were willing to engage in dialogue with the PLO and to update their own agenda for the shifting order of the Middle East. Since 1967, the group had pronounced its opposition to a two-state solution before both Israeli and international audiences under the conviction that only a social and political transformation of the whole region could bring about a genuine solution. At any rate, there had been no talk of externally mediated great-power diplomacy. But just as the October 1973 War shattered the myth of an invincible Israel, the Arabs' subsequent diplomatic turn made some of the Israeli leftists question the utopia of a socialist revolution throughout the Middle East. Ilan Halevi's political circle was the first to revise its former positions in view of this historically novel situation. 'Because of the [October 1973] War', Halevi later reflected, 'I began to understand that the world had no intention of aligning itself to my dreams and that my friends and I would not be successful at forcing our wills on the world'.[215] This analysis of the times was evident in a self-critique by HaBrit HaKomunistit HaMahapachnit, written later that year.[216] The previous assumption that the Arab governments in Egypt, Syria and Jordan would make no efforts to solve the Palestine question or to influence Israel was reconsidered, as was the insistence on a regional revolution as the only prospect for peace. The group adopted a stance of realpolitik, a 'transitional programme', and began considering a partition of historical Palestine for the sake of a temporary two-state solution.[217] However, this would not bury the claim of a Palestinian right of return and a de-Zionisation of Israel; neither would it occlude the long-term prospect of a socialist solution to the Palestine problem. Meanwhile, the Ma'avak group responded to the Palestinian leaders' political shift by demanding that the Jewish state immediately retreat to the 1967 borders, with the aim of giving the Palestinians an immediate, preliminary entitlement to national sovereignty. With this turn to realpolitik, Ilan Halevi himself blazed a new trail that went far beyond adapting his political positions to the changed circumstances and laid the foundation for his departure from Israel and his self-reinvention as a Palestinian. In the summer of 1976, he left Israel for Paris, where he joined the PLO as its first Israeli Jewish member. Beginning in 1978, he made regular visits to Beirut, where his talks at the Palestine Research Centre made his name among the networks of Palestinians moving between Paris and Lebanon. His book *Sous Israël, la Palestine* reinforced this reputation. He obtained his first official position within the PLO in 1982, after the PLO envoy Fadel El-Dani was assassinated on his way to a speaking tour. Ibrahim Souss, the PLO representative in Paris, had encouraged Yasser Arafat to assign El-Dani's former duties to Halevi.[218] From September 1982 onward, he was the PLO's liaison to the media in Paris and edited the PLO bulletin *Revue d'études palestiniennes*. The same year, he became the PLO spokesperson at the UN Human Rights Committee in Geneva. Finally, in the spring of 1983, Halevi took over Issam Sartawi's former post as the Palestinian delegate to the Socialist Internationale after Sartawi, too, was assassinated.[219] 'I know that the vast majority of Israelis consider me a traitor [. . .] given that Israel is technically in a state of war with the PLO', acknowledged Halevi in an interview for French television. In contrast, he described his personal case as an outstanding example 'of democracy and tolerance on the part of the Palestinians, who consider a Jew and Israeli as equal among equals and completely trustworthy'.[220]

His transformation from an Israeli Jew to a Jewish Palestinian, not to mention his decision to join the PLO, made Ilan Halevi an outlier. Yet he was not alone in turning from revolution to diplomacy, or from a radical vision for a resolution to the Israel–Palestine conflict towards a politics of interim solutions. The core group of Matzpen could not ignore that the 1973 War had drawn the major powers back into the Palestine question, which now became the subject of international diplomatic negotiations that linked the existence of a Jewish state to the prospects of Palestinian sovereignty in the West Bank and Gaza. 'This time – as a result of the [October 1973] War and the ensuing conversations – the Palestine question is now presented "realistically", practically, even pragmatically', they wrote, describing the new modus of diplomacy 'as a kind of give and take'.[221] Given the international debates over a sovereign Palestinian territory alongside the Jewish state, the Israeli socialists had no illusions that a Middle Eastern peace negotiated by Israelis, Americans and the Arab states could bring a true solution to the Palestine question. Yet they did not wish to oppose the realisation of the Palestinian demand for sovereignty in all territories that would be wrested from the Jewish state. 'Contrary to the current situation', they explained, 'no direct Israeli suppression would occur there', and, at the very least, the colonial situation between Israeli Jews and Palestinian Arabs would be over there. 'And even if prisons within [that sovereign territory] will still be full of Palestinian detainees and prisoners', they went on, 'the prison guards will be Palestinian Arabs, who will serve under a Palestinian flag'.[222] Alongside all their customary words of support for the Palestinian efforts towards national self-determination and a revolutionary solution to the Palestine question, the group's revised platform added their support for the Palestinians' struggle: 'Including their struggle for the full and unconditional Israeli withdrawal from the territories occupied in 1967 in order to establish an independent political framework there'.[223] This was a conscious compromise in the direction of an interim political solution, a compromise that demonstrated the intrusion of realpolitik into socialist utopia.

Yet just as the transition to diplomacy had revealed differences and awakened antagonisms among the Palestinians, the tension between state and revolution exposed discrepancies among the Israeli leftists' principles. In Machover's conversation with Hammami, he reported that: 'Also in Israel, there is a Trotskyist group, which split off from Matzpen [in 1972] [. . .] These Trotskyists, although they accept the principle of self-determination in general, oppose this immediate demand for a Palestinian state.'[224] Although these differences of opinion were not the trigger for Matzpen's early 1972 split, the rival camps would increasingly coalesce around different proposed solutions to the Palestine question. At first, though, the conflict primarily related to habitual and ideological differences with opposite poles in Jerusalem and Tel Aviv. First, Matzpen's Jerusalem-based core – grouped around Michel Warschawski, Arie Bober, Eli Aminov, Nabil Saad and Yossi Ben-Akiva – accused the Tel Aviv group, who gathered around Haim Hanegbi and Oded Pilavsky, of lacking political seriousness.[225] Instead of Marxist theory and revolutionary commitment, the Jerusalemites claimed, they had fallen prey to anarchistic machinations and an anti-Marxist, bohemian lifestyle.[226] They therefore set out to turn Matzpen into a 'revolutionary Marxist' organisation, where a commitment to Marxism–Leninism and Trotsky's idea of a 'permanent revolution' was a tacit membership requirement.[227] This ideological programme may be the reason Sylvia Klingberg, the daughter of the scientist and former Soviet spy Marcus Klingberg, was the only member from Tel Aviv to join the Jerusalem-based group. Michel Warschawski was one of the driving forces in this new direction. Having joined Matzpen not long after the Six-Day War, together with his comrades, he now wanted to commit Matzpen to a more distinct revolutionary programme and political outlook, which meant both a unity of revolutionary theory and lifestyle and a convergence with a worldwide revolutionary organisation – that of international Trotskyism.[228]

'Mikado [Michel Warschawski] was apparently convinced not only that the world revolution was at hand', Moshé Machover wrote later, still somewhat angry, 'but also that it was going to be orchestrated by [. . .] Brussels HQ [of the Trotskyist Fourth Internationale].'[229] Due to this evidently institutional geography of revolution, the divisive conflict within Matzpen was set off, at least formally, by the question of whether to join the international Trotskyist organisation. In the end, both groups claimed to be carrying on the original legacy of the Israeli Socialist Organization and called the other group the spin-off. It was not long before the Trotskyist group, which also became the new home of veteran Jakob Taut and some other Matzpen members from Haifa, published its newspaper with the standalone title *Matzpen–Marxisti* and the symbol of the Fourth International on its cover.

In its magazine *Matzpen–Marxisti*, the new group proclaimed revolutionary ambitions that also ran counter to the diplomatic developments after the October War of 1973. 'No to the Accord' was one of their main slogans; they decried the great powers' Geneva peace talks as cementing imperialist interests and also vilified Palestinians' political pragmatism.[230] Ever since the first diplomatic proposals by Nayef Hawatmeh, Said Hammami and the greater PLO, the Jerusalem group had spoken out volubly against the turn toward a 'Palestinian mini-state'. They saw any willingness to postpone a thorough and complete solution to the Israel–Palestine conflict for the sake of a feasible temporary compromise as nothing less than capitulation – 'de facto recognition of Zionism and the legitimisation of some of its conquests' – and as surrender by the international revolution to the major power's interests.[231] Their accusation that the PLO was 'liquidating the Palestine question' and their attachment to the idea of an 'Arab revolution' were indications that this disagreement had deeper origins.[232] When they insisted that the Israel–Palestine conflict could only ever be solved through a revolution that both rectified its historical origins and upended the entire region, they were also deflecting issues of negotiations and reconciliations in the political present.

By choosing to let the utopian temporality of revolution overshadow the political present, the Jerusalem-based group placed itself in direct contrast to parallel developments in Matzpen and Ma'avak. In his 'Open Letter to Our Former Anti-Zionist Comrades (?)', Michel Warschawski attacked the turn towards realpolitik that had started with Ilan Halevi and Ma'avak, spreading to Matzpen–Tel Aviv. First, he lashed out against Halevi's circle:

> The same comrades who once criticised Matzpen for its recognition of the principle that Israeli Jews have a right to self-determination, and for failing to emphasise the colonial nature of the Israeli-Arab conflict, today support the principle of partition as the culmination of both people's rights to self-determination. Today, 'realism' leads them – just like the Democratic Front – to reconcile with the existence of the Israeli state [. . .].[233]

He further complained that when Matzpen's Tel Aviv members looked for broader allies against the occupation, they were increasingly approaching members of Rakah or Siach, giving Warschawski the impression that Israel's political map had been rearranged:

> Suddenly the political boundary no longer runs, as in the past, between the 'united Matzpen' on one side and Siach or Rakah on the other. Instead it runs between Matzpen-Marxisti and Brit HaPoalim on one side and Rakah, Siach, Matzpen-Tel-Aviv and Ma'avak on the other. [. . .] We truly regret seeing our former comrades, who used to share our principled anti-Zionist position, join the reformist camp of non-Zionists.[234]

Hence, the conflict between political pragmatism and a revolutionary solution to the Palestine question had evolved into a dispute, even within Matzpen. The Jerusalem splinter group's unconditional insistence on revolution, and on a solution to the Israel–Palestine conflict beyond territorial compromise, would lead it to take the new name of HaLiga HaKomunistit HaMahapachnit (Revolutionary Communist League) and to seek new political alliances. The Jerusalemites found a new ally in Lebanon's Revolutionary Communist Group, which was one of the Israeli Trotskyists' sibling organisations in the Fourth International. Shortly after the 1973 War, Warschawski and Gilbert Achcar, the group's Senegalese-born theorist, co-drafted a new joint programme for the next steps of the Arab revolution in the region.[235] Contrary to all current diplomatic negotiations, they pinned their hopes on 'a revolutionary overturn in the entire Near East', with the 'destruction of the Zionist state' as a central mission, in order to restore the rights of the Palestinian Arabs. This alone would make it possible 'to deal concretely and correctly with the question of the rights of the Jewish national minority in

Palestine' and to guarantee 'complete equality between Jew and Arab'. Meanwhile, they asserted that the only 'revolutionary attitude' regarding the Israel–Palestine conflict was 'to recognise the complete and unconditional right of the Palestinian Arabs to self-determination, that is their right to return to all the territories from which they have been expelled'.[236]

Even if this uncompromising stance in their alliance with the Lebanese communists was rooted in their shared socialist vision for the future of the whole Arab region, the local conflict over Palestine and the fragmentation of Palestinian organisations politically situated the Jerusalemite opponents of pragmatism and realpolitik in a distant closeness to the Rejectionist Front.[237] To be sure, immediately after the events of Kiryat Shmona, Matzpen–Marxisti published an unambiguous statement condemning it as a massacre by the Palestinian group and accused them of failing to distinguish between the 'operations of Zionist policies and the Jewish-Israeli masses exploited by those policies'.[238] Soon after, in another article written a year before his own involvement with Israeli intelligence became known, Yossi Ben-Akiva summarised his group's doubts and criticism:

> Their petty bourgeois nature prevents them from taking a revolutionary socialist path – the only path on which the Palestinian struggle can defeat Zionism. Their narrow Palestinocentric and militaristic outlook, which separates the struggle of the Palestinians from the social struggles of the entire region, but also their nationalistic approach towards the Israeli Jews, which offers them no alternative to Zionism, were the reason for their defeats in the past and will be the reason for their failures in the future.[239]

However, in the same article, in which he distanced himself from the militancy of the Rejectionist Front and rejected its narrow nationalism for offering Israeli Jews no alternative to Zionism, he took on a different tone:

> Still [. . .] we are by no means neutral in the conflict, which currently pits Fatah and the PDFLP against the Popular Front and the organisations of [Ahmed] Jibril. While the first group is playing a significant role in putting an end to the Palestine question, the others oppose that plan and continue the struggle against the Zionist state. And in the conflict between the liquidators, devotees of an accord and those who oppose it – though on a nationalistic foundation – we stand with the latter group.[240]

Meanwhile, the escalating violence that emanated from the Rejectionist Front and set off a new wave of Palestinian guerrilla activities kept pushing the Israeli 'realists' farther down the moderate path favoured by Said Hammami, especially when faced with a new form of terrorism, inaugurated by the PFLP's attack in Kiryat Shmona, that made Israeli civilians into the targets of 'indiscriminate terror', undermining any hopes for a future common ground between Israeli Jews and Palestinian Arabs.[241] Yet no event had a greater impact on the Israeli Left than the terrorist attack on 15 May 1974, for which Nayef Hawatmeh's PDFLP claimed responsibility.[242] In the northern town of Ma'alot, a three-person terrorist unit had attempted to secure the release of political prisoners by taking teachers and students hostage at a primary school. When the Israeli armed forces tried to free the hostages, thirty-one of them were killed by explosives installed by the unit, whose members also died during the operation to free the hostages. For Matzpen and Ma'avak, this terror attack destroyed any hope of finding an ally in the Palestinian group, which belonged to the camp of 'revolutionary realists' and was willing to strike political compromises, but held firm to the idea of transforming the entire region through revolution in the longer term.[243] In fact, Hawatmeh's group was the first Palestinian organisation with which Matzpen ever engaged in dialogue – because they were willing to consider recognising the Israeli Jews as a national group and to discuss the Palestine question in the context of a regional transformation of the Arab world. Even before Fatah announced its official support for a Palestinian mini-state as a transitional measure, the PDFLP advocated for establishing an 'independent [Palestinian] national authority' in the occupied territories – a step in the same direction proposed by Hammami in London.[244] Only a few weeks before the events of Ma'alot, Hawatmeh had doubled down on this stance in a widely read interview for the *Washington Post*, reprinted in Israel's *Yediot Aharonot*, in which he stressed his willingness to discuss the issues with representatives of the Israeli – even Zionist – Left.[245] The group's terrorist attack exposed the hypocrisy of this statement and demonstrated the effects of splintering among Palestinian organisations. As the realists of Fatah, adopting an approach of territorial compromise, drifted away from the maximalists of the Rejectionist Front, who violently opposed a political solution, the PDFLP's 'revolutionary realism' became more and more meaningless. Thus, by carrying out the attack, the PDFLP was to trying to 'shake off [its] stigma of being an opportunistic party of restraint' and prove itself in the competitive field of Palestinian organisations with an act of violence.[246]

The bloody events of Ma'alot left Israeli society in shock, and also struck members of Matzpen and Ma'avak deeply. Ilan Halevi's group was the first to put this into words. Their analysis of the escalating violence as an integral part of colonial conflicts certainly did not prevent them from raising some 'tough questions' about the Democratic Front. In this indiscriminate violence, Ma'avak saw the erstwhile difference between the Democratic Front and the 'Rejectionist Front' eliminated in the 'most cruel way' and replaced with a turn towards reactionary Arab nationalism.[247] It was not long before *Matzpen* published an open letter in Hebrew and Arabic, also printed by international left-wing media, in which the group categorically dissociated itself from both Ma'alot and the PDFLP.[248] 'We will not conceal this', they declared to their former contacts: 'Your action strengthened and deepened the hostility between the masses of both nations.' The indiscriminate violence against Israeli civilians 'ignored elementary moral principles'. In addition to this layer of immorality, Matzpen pointed out another aspect, one that was related to the social stratification of Ma'alot. As a town 'mainly populated by poor workers, who belong to the most exploited and oppressed within Israeli society', its residents were basically the 'cannon fodder of Israeli policy, neither responsible for it nor enjoying it'.

> For these inhabitants of Ma'alot, your action made Zionism their last resort. If the Palestinian movement offers them no alternative to Zionism, they will prefer Zionism, despite the dangers and the high price they will continue to pay for it.

For Matzpen, the events of Ma'alot had 'turned every piece of fertile soil into a desert'. In their eyes, this act of violence quashed both their dialogue and the Palestinian organisation's credibility.[249]

Yet the criticism found an ally: Said Hammami. Although he did not reject the Palestinian armed struggle on principle, he distanced himself from this new form of terrorism soon after the attack in Kiryat Shmona. Certainly, his statement also condemned the cyclical, indiscriminate violence by the Israeli military against the Palestinian population. However, his central rejection of any justification for 'the killing of women and children whatever the circumstances' drew a line between himself and the Palestinian guerrilla group's terrorist methods against Israeli Jews.[250] Emblematic of that rejection was his meeting in London with Machover in the autumn of 1975. 'I cannot accept terrorism, not only for moral but also for political reasons', replied Hammami during the meeting, when Machover pressed him on his views of the massacre in Ma'alot. 'Because I am a progressive Palestinian, and I believe that if you kill Israelis indiscriminately, you are playing into the hands of the Zionist establishment. Our enemy is Zionism, not all the Israelis.'[251]

His own plan, which he promoted among the Palestinians, was to establish Palestinian sovereignty that would pave the way to a long-term solution to the Palestine question. The plan was not just another attempt to defy the Jewish–Israeli claim on the territory of historical Palestine and to attain recognition for the 'existence of the Palestinian people, and our right to have our own state in Palestine'.[252] Moving away from the endless violence of the conflict's history to date, he believed that accomplishing Palestinian sovereignty would help de-escalate the violence and ease tensions on both sides. 'So I say, let us have a state', Hammami concluded. 'This would relax the exaggerated alarm of the Israeli Jews; this would reduce the tension among the Palestinians.'[253] As long as this aspiration remained unconsummated, the dialogue that had begun between Machover and Hammami brought a further convergence of ideas. 'If it was not a crime under Israeli law, we would invite progressive anti-Zionist Israelis to come and participate with us in the [Palestinian National Council] [. . .] and to come and participate in planning our policy', Hammami said, concluding his conversation with Machover. 'We need a continuous dialogue.'[254]

Yet this joint effort between two individuals would remain symbolic. Although representatives of the different political wings of Matzpen participated in several meetings with the PLO in Febuary 1976, the intended objective – a joint statement by Israelis and Palestinians – did not materialise.[255] After all, these meetings had occurred outside the auspices of Israel's state institutions, and before the era of political negotiation. Hammami and Machover had subsequent meetings, and in 1977, shortly before Sadat visited Jerusalem, Haim Hanegbi was invited to London as a guest at a conference organised by Hammami, where Hanegbi served as the lone Israeli speaker among representatives of many

Arab states. However, Hammami's introduction of the Israeli dissident quickly revealed the narrow scope of the encounter: 'We have no need of making peace with our friends from Matzpen and Rakah. They are not enemies. They are friends', he declared, alluding to the sobering fact that their political proximity to Matzpen had no bearing on the real prospects for peace and recognition.[256] Indeed, genuine peace could only be made with the official Israel. Menachem Begin, now the Israeli Prime Minister, had signed a peace treaty with Egypt six years after the October 1973 War. Yet a peace process with the Palestinians would not begin until 1993 with the Oslo Accords. Before then, the PLO was treated as a political enemy and meeting its representatives was a punishable crime.[257]

Hammami's position was by no means as stable among his fellow Palestinians as it might have seemed in the aftermath of the October 1973 War. For Palestinians, the question of whether to recognise the Israeli Jews remained contested. All attempts at negotiations were jeopardised by the same organisations who had rejected the prospect of mutual recognition from the outset. No one would pay a greater price for this opposition to diplomacy than Said Hammami himself. His assassination on 4 January 1978 is universally attributed to the Abu Nidal Organisation, founded by Sabri Khalil al-Banna. Al-Banna, whose *nom de guerre* gave the group its name, came from Jaffa like Hammami. Yet whereas Hammami advocated the prospect of a common future with the Israeli Jews in the country, al-Banna found the Israelis' very presence abhorrent. Politically at home in Arab nationalism, Al Banna found his first institutional domicile in the Baath party, before he joined Fatah in the 1960s and finally turned towards the Arab Rejectionist Front after the organisational fractures of the 1970s. Terrorism became his 'political' weapon.[258]

But secular Arab nationalism was not the only ongoing threat to any attempts at a negotiated compromise. The prospects of an Israeli–Palestinian reconciliation were no less jeopardised by other developments that had also begun with the Six-Day War and shifted the long-term likelihood of a compromise. Whereas the war of June 1967 had revealed the sacred foundation of secular Zionism, the Arab states' defeat caused a gradual erosion of nationalism in the Arab world. This ushered in the rise of political Islam, affecting various states and societies in the Middle East. It was in the context of this shift, which threatened to turn the conflict over Palestine into a rivalry between Jews and Muslims, that a new dialogue was unfolding between the Israeli dissidents of Matzpen and members of the Arab Left.

Notes

1. 'Hostilities and Clashes at the Maki-Demonstration in Tel-Aviv', *Ma'ariv* (2 May 1969), p. 3 [Hebrew].
2. Rubenstein, *The Communist Movement in Palestine and Israel, 1919–1984*, p. 353; 'Israeli Communist Party Backs Israel's Aggression', *World Outlook* 25 (30 June 1967), p. 644.
3. 'May 1st 1969', *Matzpen* 49 (1969), pp. 8–9, at p. 9 [Hebrew].
4. Ibid; 'Clashes During Maki-Demonstration', *Al Hamishmar* (2 May 1969), p. 1.
5. 'Joint Israeli-Arab Statement on the Middle East Crisis'.
6. A. Orr, Interview with the Author, Tel Aviv (1 November 2012) [English].
7. 'Joint Israeli-Arab Statement on the Middle East Crisis'.
8. Amos Elon, *The Israelis: Founders and Sons*, 1st edn (New York: Holt, Rinehart and Winston, 1971), p. 6.
9. Government of Israel, 'The Land-for-Peace Principle, 19. Juni 1967', pp. 238–9; Segev, *1967: Israel, the War, and the Year that Transformed the Middle East*, pp. 500–6.
10. Israeli Socialist Organization (Matzpen), 'The Third Round', in Arie Bober (ed.), *The Other Israel: The Radical Case Against Zionism* (Garden City: Doubleday, 1972), pp. 214–25, at p. 222 [first: *Matzpen* 36 (1967)].
11. Quoted in Segev, *1967*, p. 500.
12. Israeli Socialist Organization (Matzpen), 'General Declaration by the ISO, 22 March 1968', p. 226.
13. Morris, *Righteous Victims*, p. 336.
14. Cover page, *Matzpen* 37 (1967).
15. Moshé Machover (Pe'er, Z.), 'An Old Story', *Matzpen* 37 (1967), pp. 2–3, at p. 2 [Hebrew].
16. Segev, *1967*, pp. 455–81.
17. Oded Pilavsky, 'National Ethics', *Matzpen* 39 (1967), p. 8 [Hebrew].
18. Israeli Socialist Organization (Matzpen), 'General Declaration by the ISO, 22 March 1968', p. 228.
19. Tikva Honig-Parnass, 'On the Apartheid Nature of Israel, Matzpen and the Contradictions of the Zionist Left. The Flying Carpet Institute Interviews Israeli Socialist Tikva Honig-Parnass', https://theflyingcarpetinstitute.wordpress.com/2010/04/30/on-the-apartheid-nature-of-israel-matzpen-and-the-contradictions-of-the-zionist-left-the-flying-carpet-institute-interviews-israeli-socialist-tikva-honig-parnass/ (accessed 7 October 2019).

20. Ibid.
21. Erel, *Matzpen: Conscience and Fantasy*, pp. 47–75.
22. Ibid., p. 47; Rachel Jones, *Advocate. Lea Tsemel*, 2019, Israel, 108 min, documentary.
23. Warschawski, *On the Border*, p. 18.
24. Rachel Fish, 'Configurations of Bi-Nationalism. The Transformation of Bi-Nationalism in Palestine/Israel 1920's-Present' (PhD thesis, Brandeis University, 2013), p. 129.
25. Warschawski, *On the Border*, p. 18.
26. Quoted in Isaac, *Israel Divided*, p. 74.
27. Amos Oz, 'Minister for Defence/Lebensraum', *Davar* (22 August 1967), p. 4 [Hebrew]. An English translation was published in *Jewish Currents* ([February] 1968), pp. 18–21, 35.
28. Adi Portugez, 'Siah. The Case of a New Left Movement in Israel', *Israel. Studies in Zionism and the State of Israel* 21 (2013), pp. 225–51 [Hebrew].
29. Israeli Socialist Organization (Matzpen), 'They All Promise Peace. October ISO Statement on 1969 General Elections', in Arie Bober (ed.), *The Other Israel: The Radical Case Against Zionism* (Garden City: Doubleday, 1972), pp. 243–5.
30. 'Today peace is possible only if three elements exist: total Israeli withdrawal from the areas she has been occupying since 1967; Israeli acceptance of the right of self-determination of the Palestine Arab Nation, including a state of its own; Arab acceptance of the right of the Jews to live in a state of their own.' Quoted in Schnall, *Radical Dissent in Contemporary Israeli Politics*, p. 79.
31. Israeli Socialist Organization (Matzpen), 'They All Promise Peace', p. 244.
32. Machover, 'Resurrection of the Dead (October 1967)', p. 148.
33. Ariel Renan, 'The "Hallucinating a Myth" Has a Meaning', *Davar* (14 September 1967), p. 3 [Hebrew]; quoted in Machover, 'Resurrection of the Dead (October 1967)', p. 148.
34. Baruch Kimmerling and Joel S. Migdal, *Palestinians: The Making of a People* (New York, Toronto, New York: Free Press; Maxwell Macmillan Canada; Maxwell Macmillan International, 1993), pp. 209–39; Helga Baumgarten, *Palästina: Befreiung in den Staat: die palästinensische Nationalbewegung seit 1948* (Frankfurt am Main: Suhrkamp, 1991), pp. 216–19.
35. Palestine Liberation Organization, 'The Palestinian National Charter. Resolution of the Palestine National Council July 1-17, 1968', in Leila S. Kadi (ed.), *Basic Political Documents of the Armed Palestinian Resistance Movement* (Beirut: Palestine Liberation Organization, Research Center, 1969 [1970]), pp. 137–42, at p. 140 (Article 21).
36. Morris, *Righteous Victims*, p. 365.

37. Alain Gresh, *The PLO: The Struggle Within: Towards an Independent Palestinian State*, rev. and updated edn (London: Zed Books, 1988), p. 14 [Translation of: *OLP*].
38. Rubenstein, *The Communist Movement in Palestine and Israel, 1919–1984*, p. 354.
39. Israeli Socialist Organization (Matzpen), 'General Declaration by the ISO, 22 March 1968', p. 228.
40. Ibid.
41. Wolfensohn, 'The Conscience of Matzpen: Part III'.
42. Israeli Socialist Organization (Matzpen), 'General Declaration by the ISO, 22 March 1968', p. 228.
43. A comprehensive overview of the different groups and their programmes can be found in Leila S. Kadi (ed.), *Basic Political Documents of the Armed Palestinian Resistance Movement* (Beirut: Palestine Liberation Organization, Research Center, 1969 [1970]).
44. Akiva Orr and Moshé Machover, 'The Zionist Left and the Palestinian Resistance', in Arie Bober (ed.), *The Other Israel: The Radical Case Against Zionism* (Garden City: Doubleday, 1972), pp. 182–90, at p. 186.
45. 'Signs for 1968', *Matzpen* 40 (1968), p. 1 [Hebrew]; see also Moshe Shemesh, 'Did Shuqayri Call For "Throwing the Jews into the Sea"?', *Israel Studies* 8: 2 (2003), pp. 70–81.
46. Palestine Liberation Organization, 'The Palestinian National Charter', p. 137 (Article 6). 'Jews who were living in Palestine until the beginning of the Zionist invasion will be considered Palestinians.'
47. Pilavsky, 'National Ethics'; see also Erel, *Without Fear and Prejudice*, p. 128.
48. Baumgarten, *Palästina*, p. 238.
49. Address by the Al-Fateh Delegation to the Second International Conference in Support of the Arab Peoples (Cairo, [January] 1969), p. 7; see also Gresh, *The PLO*, pp. 30–3.
50. Moshé Machover and Jabra Nicola, 'The Middle East at the Crossroads (September 1969). A Position Paper on the Palestinian Movement by the ISO', in Arie Bober (ed.), *The Other Israel: The Radical Case Against Zionism* (Garden City: Doubleday, 1972), pp. 237–42, at p. 241 [first: *Matzpen* 50 (1969)].
51. Ibid., pp. 240–1.
52. Ibid., pp. 238 and 240.
53. Ibid., p. 241.
54. Popular Democratic Front for the Liberation of Palestine, 'A Democratic Solution to the Palestine Question', in Leila S. Kadi (ed.), *Basic Political Documents of the Armed Palestinian Resistance Movement* (Beirut: Palestine Liberation Organization, Research Center, 1969 [1970]), pp. 173–4, at p. 173.

55. Ibid.
56. See Torbiner, *Matzpen. Anti-Zionist Israelis*, 54 min.
57. 'Head of the "Popular Democratic Front for the Liberation of Palestine" Claims: We Have a Dialogue with "Matzpen"', *Haolam Hazeh* 1681 (19 November 1969), p. 14 [Hebrew].
58. Nayef Hawatmeh, 'A Democratic Solution for the Palestine Problem', *Al-Hurriya* (12 January 1970) [Arabic] (a French translation was published in *Le Monde*, 27 January 1970); quoted from the English translation Nayef Hawatmeh, 'A Democratic Solution for the Palestine Problem', in Leila S. Kadi (ed.), *Basic Political Documents of the Armed Palestinian Resistance Movement* (Beirut: Palestine Liberation Organization, Research Center, 1969 [1970]), pp. 175–8, at p. 177 [first: *Al-Hurriya*, 12 January 1970].
59. Nayef Hawatmeh, 'For a Democratic Solution to the Palestinian Problem and the Israeli Problem', M*atzpen* 52 (1970), p. 5 [Hebrew].
60. Oded Pilavsky, 'Palestinian–Israeli Dialogue. Controversy and Debate', *Matzpen* 53 (1970), pp. 3–4, at p. 3 [Hebrew].
61. Ibid.
62. See also Erel, *Matzpen*, p. 131.
63. Pilavsky, 'Palestinian–Israeli Dialogue', pp. 3–4.
64. Ibid., p. 4.
65. Erel, *Matzpen*, pp. 58–9; Emanuel Bar-Kedma, 'Who Remembers Rami Livneh?', *Yediot Aharonot. Weekend Supplement* (23 April 1992), pp. 29–30 [Hebrew].
66. The Hebrew translation of the interview with Hawatmeh slightly differs from the English translation; whereas the English version reads: 'This proposed democratic solution, in fact, calls on all progressive Israelis and Jews to organize themselves into an armed popular Palestinian front to ensure the day by day objective implementation of this solution', the Hebrew translation in Matzpen reads: '[W]e called on all progressive Israelis to enter the struggle – separately or within the armed Palestinian movement – to enable the realization of this democratic solution.' See Hawatmeh, 'For a Democratic Solution to the Palestinian Problem and the Israeli Problem'.
67. Rami Livneh, 'For a Joint Programme in a Joint Struggle', *Matzpen* 53 (1970), pp. 4 and 15, at p. 15 [Hebrew]; see also Erel, *Matzpen*, p. 131.
68. Michel Warschawski, Letter to Jabra Nicola and Moshé Machover (1 October 1970), Private Archive of Moshé Machover, London, p. 1 [Hebrew].
69. See Greenstein, *Zionism and its Discontents*, pp. 172–82; Erel, *Matzpen*, pp. 160–80.
70. See Ghilan, *How Israel Lost its Soul*, pp. 158–9; Yuval-Davis, 'Matzpen. The Israeli Socialist Organisation', p. 92.

71. Lutz Fiedler, Phone Call with Menachem Carmi (12 July 2013) [Hebrew].
72. Menachem Carmi, 'Towards a Critique of the Traditional Israeli Left', *Matzpen* 44 (1968), pp. 6–8 [Hebrew].
73. Eli Lobel, Letter to Moshé Machover (4 February 1969), Private Archive of Moshé Machover, London.
74. Lutz Fiedler, Email Communication with Sylvain Cypel (15 July 2013) [English].
75. Ibid.
76. Ibid.
77. Lobel, Letter to Moshé Machover (4 February 1969).
78. Quoted in Erel, *Matzpen*, p. 131.
79. For my brief remarks on the history of Brit Hapoalim following its foundation, I rely on Greenstein, *Zionism and its Discontents*, pp. 178–82; see also the documentary of T. Carmi, *Away from the Tribe's Center*, 2009, Israel, 58 min, documentary.
80. 'From Petty-Bourgeois Radicalism to the Building a Revolutionary Party of the Working Class', *Matzpen* 57 (1971), p. 13 [Hebrew].
81. Moshé Machover and Akiva Orr, 'The Class Nature of Israeli Society', *Matzpen* 55 (1970), pp. 3–4 [Hebrew].
82. Yehuda K[upperman], 'Criticism of the ISO (Matzpen)', *Avangard* 1 (November 1970), quoted from Greenstein, *Zionism and its Discontents*, p. 178.
83. Ibid; Erel, *Matzpen*, p. 171.
84. Warschawski, 'Letter to Jabra Nicola and Moshé Machover', p. 5.
85. Greenstein, *Zionism and its Discontents*, p. 179.
86. Ibid., p. 180.
87. 'Toward A New Perspective', *Ma'avak* 1 (1970), pp. 2–6; quoted from the English translation 'Toward a New Perspective', The Israeli Left Archives, https://hdl.handle.net/10622/5D4051EE-BF1A-11E7-A02F-E355B54FC576?locatt=view:master (accessed 14 April 2020).
88. 'Toward a New Perspective'.
89. Ibid.
90. Christoph Kalter, *Discovery of the Third World: Decolonization and the Rise of the New Left in France, c.1950–1976* (Cambridge: Cambridge University Press, 2016).
91. 'Toward a New Perspective'.
92. Quoted in Lilian Smith, 'From Nowhere to the End of Night', *The Saturday Review* (4 April 1964), pp. 39–40, at p. 40.
93. Ibid.
94. Marc Albert-Levin, 'Ah, les vies d'Halévi! Une autre face de la vie d'Ilan Halevi', *La Gazette de la Lucarne* 63 (15 October 2013), pp. 2–3.

95. Aryeh Dayan, 'Some Comrades Started to Complain about Strange Things that Happened around Ilan', *Haaretz* (27 May 2001), pp. 8ב–9ב [Hebrew].
96. For Halevi's biography, see Nicole Lapierre, *Causes communes: Des Juifs et des Noirs, Un ordre d'idées* (Paris: Stock, 2011), pp. 123–42.
97. Smith, 'From Nowhere to the End of Night'.
98. Farouk Mardam-Bey, 'Ilan Halevi. Palestinian Jew and Citizen of the World, 1943-2013', *Journal of Palestine Studies* 43: 4 (2014), pp. 67–70, at p. 67.
99. Ilan Halevi, *Allers-retours* (Paris: Flammarion, 2005), p. 106.
100. Lapierre, *Causes communes*, p. 133; Mardam-Bey, 'Ilan Halevi', p. 67.
101. Allyson Tadjer, 'Triangulating Racism. French and Francophone African Reactions to the African American Freedom Movement (1954-1968)' (Dissertation, Georgia State University, 2015), pp. 39–46.
102. Alain Albert, *The Crossing* (New York: G. Braziller, 1964).
103. Dayan, 'Some Comrades Started to Complain about Strange Things that Happened around Ilan'.
104. Smith, 'From Nowhere to the End of Night'; Mardam-Bey, 'Ilan Halevi'.
105. Dayan, 'Some Comrades Started to Complain about Strange Things that Happened around Ilan'.
106. Lapierre, *Causes communes*, p. 138.
107. Mardam-Bey, 'Ilan Halevi', p. 68.
108. Lapierre, *Causes communes*, p. 138.
109. Quoted in Dayan, 'Some Comrades Started to Complain about Strange Things that Happened around Ilan'.
110. Ibid.
111. The letter itself could not be located, but Haim Hanegbi reports on it. See Haim Hanegbi, 'Ilan Halevi. From Udi Adiv until Sartawi', *Koteret Rashit* (14 April 1983), pp. 18 and 39.
112. Ibid., p. 39.
113. Erel, *Matzpen*, pp. 162–3.
114. Machover, 'Matzpen. The Israeli Socialist Organisation', p. 322.
115. Erel, *Matzpen*, p. 120.
116. Warschawski, 'Letter to Jabra Nicola and Moshé Machover', p. 2.
117. Machover, 'Matzpen. The Israeli Socialist Organisation', p. 322.
118. Warschawski, 'Letter to Jabra Nicola and Moshé Machover', p. 3.
119. 'Toward a New Perspective'.
120. Letter to Moshé Machover (12 October 1970), Private Archive of Moshé Machover, London.
121. 'Toward a New Perspective'.

122. Roi Bet-Levi, 'A Bad Tropical Country', *Haaretz* (18 September 2007).
123. Erel, *Without Fear and Prejudice*, p. 161.
124. Machover, Moshé (Avital, M.), 'Go in Peace', *Matzpen* 56 (1970), pp. 6–8 and 15, at p. 8 [Hebrew].
125. Oded Pilavsky, 'Left-Wing Slogans with a Right-Wing Meaning', *Matzpen* 56 (1970), pp. 5–6, at p. 6.
126. Ibid., p. 5.
127. Machover, 'Matzpen. The Israeli Socialist Organisation', p. 323.
128. Hanegbi, 'Ilan Halevi', p. 39; Erel, *Matzpen*, pp. 163–4.
129. Warschawski, 'Letter to Jabra Nicola and Moshé Machover', p. 6.
130. 'Dare to Struggle!', in 'Toward a New Perspective'.
131. *Haaretz* (8 December 1972), p. 1, quoted in 'The Spy Ring Story', *Israleft. News Service* 8 (15 December 1972), pp. 1–7, at p. 1.
132. Gerald Cromer, 'Udi Adiv', in Gerald Cromer, *The Writing Was On the Wall: Constructing Political Deviance in Israel* (Ramat-Gan: Bar-Ilan University Press, 1998), pp. 110–33.
133. *Yediot Aharonot* (8 December 1972), p. 1. For an overview of Israels' media coverage, see 'The Spy Ring Story'.
134. *Ma'ariv* (11 December 1972), quoted from Ibid., p. 5.
135. Ibid.
136. Yossi Klein Halevi, *Like Dreamers: The Story of the Israeli Paratroopers who Reunited Jerusalem and Divided a Nation* (New York, London: Harper Perennial, 2013), p. 214; Eitan Haber and Yossi Melman, *The Spies: Israel's Counter-Espionage Wars* (Tel Aviv: Yediot Ahronot, 2002), pp. 166–90 [Hebrew].
137. *Jerusalem Post* (12 December 1972), quoted from Cromer, 'Udi Adiv', p. 111.
138. *Haaretz* (8 December 1972), p. 1, quoted in 'The Spy Ring Story', pp. 1–2.
139. Aharon Bachar, 'Gan Shmuel. Udi versus Uri', *Yediot Aharonot. Weekend Supplement* (15 December 1972), pp. 1–2 [Hebrew].
140. Ibid.
141. Quoted in Cromer, 'Udi Adiv', p. 129.
142. 'The Spy Ring Story'; Sprinzak, *Brother Against Brother*, p. 121.
143. Sprinzak, 'The Emergence of the Politics of Delegitimization in Israel, 1967–72', pp. 50–1.
144. Aharon Bachar, as quoted in 'The Spy Ring Story', p. 4.
145. Haim Hanegbi, 'Udi, Ran and Uri. All From the Same Village', *Koteret Rashit* 129 (22 May 1985), pp. 16–17, at p. 17 [Hebrew]; see also Morris, *The Birth of the Palestinian Refugee Problem Revisited*, p. 245; Vidal, 'If I Forget Thee, O Zion'; Klein Halevi, *Like Dreamers*, p. 131.

146. Hanegbi, 'Udi, Ran and Uri'; Klein Halevi, *Like Dreamers*, pp. 162–3 and 218.
147. Haber and Melman, *The Spies*, p. 168.
148. Quoted from Erel, *Matzpen*, p. 165.
149. Ibid.
150. Warschawski, *On the Border*, p. 51.
151. Aharon Bachar, 'The Suspects of Belonging to a Joint Network', *Yediot Aharonot* (10 December 1972), p. 11 [Hebrew].
152. Jon Broder, '"Mideast War Now International". Conflict's Shadow Follows Expatriates', *Daytona Beach Sunday News-Journal* (22 July 1973), p. 8B.
153. Harvey Klehr, *Far Left of Center: The American Radical Left Today* (New Brunswick: Transaction, 1988), p. 92.
154. Haber and Melman, *The Spies*, p. 169.
155. Bachar, 'The Suspects of Belonging to a Joint Network'.
156. For a more detailed analysis of the group's ideological position, see Greenstein, *Zionism and its Discontents*, pp. 175–7.
157. Ibid., pp. 176–7.
158. Ibid., p. 177.
159. Yehuda Palestinai (Adiv, Udi), 'Matzpen and the Palestinian Resistance Organizations', *Hazit Adumah* 3 ([April–May] 1972), pp. 15–17 [Hebrew]; quoted from the English translation in Greenstein, *Zionism and its Discontents*, p. 177.
160. Warschawski, *On the Border*, p. 51.
161. Lutz Fiedler, Email Communication with Udi Adiv (6 May 2015) [English].
162. Habib Kahwaji, '"El Ard" Movement on the "Red Front"', https://hdl.handle.net/10622/90A6C004-BF1A-11E7-ADF-6FB495D231EF?locatt=view:master (accessed 20 April 2020).
163. 'The Red Front Trial. The Depositions of Turki and Adiv', *Journal of Palestine Studies* 2: 4 (1973), pp. 144–50, at p. 150.
164. Orr, 'A Brutal Revolution'.
165. Warschawski, *On the Border*, p. 50; on the concept of turncoat, see Memmi, *The Colonizer and the Colonized*, pp. 66 and 81.
166. Haber and Melman, *The Spies*, pp. 171–3.
167. Ibid., pp. 175–6.
168. Ibid., pp. 178–9; Klein Halevi, *Like Dreamers*, p. 213.
169. Quoted from Haber and Melman, *The Spies*, p. 177.
170. Ibid., pp. 182–3.
171. Mandred Schröder, 'Spionage-Prozess in Israel', *Süddeutsche Zeitung* (10 March 1973).
172. Quoted from *Israleft. News Service* 13 (20 March 1973), at p. 3.

173. See *Israleft. News Service* 14 (3 April 1973), at pp. 6–7.
174. 'Declaration of the Revolutionary Communist Alliance (16.12.1972)', *Israleft. News Service* 9 (15 January 1973), pp. 8–9; see also Erel, *Matzpen*, p. 167.
175. *Israleft. News Service* 12 (4 March 1973), pp. 8–10; see also Bar-Kedma, 'Who Remembers Rami Livneh?'.
176. *Haaretz* (15 February 1973), as quoted in *Israleft News Service* 12 (4 March 1973), at p. 8. See also Zachary Lockman, 'The Left in Israel. Zionism vs. Socialism', *Merip Reports* 49: July (1976), pp. 3–18, at p. 15.
177. Avraham Levenbraun, Letter to the Minister of Justice, the Minster of Police and the Speaker of the Knesset (8 January 1973), The Israeli Left Archives [Hebrew].
178. 'Les Procès du Réseau Judéo-Arabe', *Le Monde* (14 July 1973); Glass, 'Jews Against Zion', p. 72; Lea Tsemel, 'Notes on the History of Torture in Israel', in Adalah – The Legal Center for Arab Minority Rights in Israel (ed.), *On Torture* (Haifa: Adalah, 2012), pp. 7–11, at p. 7.
179. Yaacov Haelion, 'Rami Livneh's Trial as "Inspiration" For a Play', *Ma'ariv* (23 July 1973), p. 2 [Hebrew].
180. Amnesty International, *Annual Report* (London: Amnesty International, 1973–4), p. 72.
181. 'Representatives of Matzpen and the Revolutionary Communist Alliance Prepare a List Headed by Ramil Livneh', *Ma'ariv* (3 July 1973), p. 9 [Hebrew].
182. 'Sentences Reduced for Two Jewish Security Prisoners', *Jewish Telegraphic Agency* 138 (19 July 1974), p. 2.
183. Fred J. Khouri, *The Arab-Israeli Dilemma*, Contemporary Issues in the Middle East, 3rd edn (Syracuse: Syracuse University Press, 1985), p. 370.
184. Shlomo Nakdimon, 'A "Matzpen" Member Met with a PLO Representative in the UK. Transcript to Be Released', *Yediot Aharonot* (16 December 1975), pp. 1 and 7 [Hebrew].
185. 'Full Report of the Conversation between a Matzpen Member and a PLO Representative in London' (Tel Aviv: Matzpen Publications, 1975) [Hebrew]; quoted below from the English translations, Moshé Machover and Said Hammami, 'To Live Together', in Jon Rothschild (ed.), *Forbidden Agendas: Intolerance and Defiance in the Middle East* (London: Saqi Books, 1984), pp. 382–400.
186. Nakdimon, 'A "Matzpen" Member Met with a PLO Representative in the UK', p. 1.
187. Machover and Hammami, 'To Live Together', pp. 385–6 (emphasis in original).
188. See Avnery, *My Friend, the Enemy*; Part II: Hammami.
189. Machover and Hammami, 'To Live Together', p. 384.
190. Ibid., p. 385.

191. Ibid., p. 392.
192. Moshé Machover, Letter to Said Hammami (4 December 1975), Private Archive of Moshé Machover, London.
193. Adi Ophir (ed.), *50 to 48: Critical Moments in the History of the State of Israel* (Jerusalem: Hakibbutz Hameuchad, 1999), p. 294 [Hebrew].
194. Nakdimon, 'A "Matzpen" Member Met with a PLO Representative in the UK', p. 1.
195. Khouri, *The Arab-Israeli Dilemma*, pp. 370–86.
196. Baumgarten, *Palästina*, pp. 240–1.
197. Dan Diner, 'Die Palästina-Frage im Vorderen Orient. Entwicklungen und Perspektiven', in John Bunzl (ed.), *Israel/Palästina: Klasse, Nation und Befreiung im Nahost-Konflikt* (Hamburg: Junius Verlag, 1980), pp. 169–82, at pp. 169–73; Morris, *Righteous Victims*, pp. 387–98.
198. Gresh, *The PLO*, pp. 122–6; Baumgarten, *Palästina*, pp. 240–5.
199. Omar Kamil, *Die Araber und der Holocaust: Eine Diskursgeschichte* (Göttingen: Vandenhoeck & Ruprecht, 2012), pp. 149–50.
200. See Gresh, *The PLO*, pp. 143–6.
201. Said Hammami, 'The Palestinian Way to Middle East Peace', *The Times* (16 November 1973), p. 20.
202. Said Hammami, 'Making the First Move Towards Peace in Palestine', *The Times* (17 December 1973), p. 14.
203. Palestine Liberation Organization, 'Political Program (June 9, 1974)', in Itamar Rabinovich and Jehudah Reinharz (eds), *Israel in the Middle East: Documents and Readings on Society, Politics, and Foreign Relations, Pre-1948 to the Present*, 2nd edn (Waltham: Brandeis University Press, 2008), pp. 344–6, at p. 345.
204. Ibid.
205. Baumgarten, *Palästina*, pp. 243–6.
206. Quoted in Ibid., pp. 246–7; Gresh, *The PLO*, pp. 146–9.
207. Gresh, *The PLO*, pp. 185–7.
208. Quoted from Ibid., p. 164.
209. The League of Arab States, 'Seventh Arab Summit Conference (October 1974)', in Itamar Rabinovich and Jehudah Reinharz (eds), *Israel in the Middle East: Documents and Readings on Society, Politics, and Foreign Relations, Pre-1948 to the Present*, 2nd edn (Waltham: Brandeis University Press, 2008), pp. 342–4, at p. 344.
210. Baumgarten, *Palästina*, p. 247.
211. Said Hammami, 'A Palestinian Strategy', *Intercontinental Press* 13: 34 (1975), pp. 1308–10, at p. 1309.

212. Joseph Finkelstone, 'Arafat Ready to Make Peace. Exclusive Interview with PLO-Leader', *Jewish Chronicle* (5 April 1974), p. 2.
213. Avnery, *My Friend, the Enemy*, Part II: Hammami.
214. Ibid., p. 71–5; Silke N. Minning, *Der Dialog zwischen der israelischen Friedensbewegung und den palästinensischen Friedenskräften: Divergenzen und Konvergenzen 1973–1993* (Münster: Lit-Verl., 2005), pp. 27–35; Beinin, *The Dispersion of Egyptian Jewry*, pp. 175–6.
215. Dayan, 'Some Comrades Started to Complain about Strange Things That Happened around Ilan'.
216. Revolutionary Communist Alliance, *The Palestinian Question and the Right to Self-Determination* (Jerusalem: Ma'avak Publishing, 1974) [Hebrew]; an abridged French translation of the text can be found as 'La tâche des révolutionnaires israéliens et palestiniens', *Khamsin. Revue des Socialistes Revolutionnaires du Proche-Orient* 1 (1975), pp. 50–69.
217. See also Erel, *Matzpen*, pp. 167–8.
218. Dayan, 'Some Comrades Started to Complain about Strange Things That Happened around Ilan'.
219. Zvi Singer, 'An Israeli in the PLO', *Yediot Aharonot* (18 April 1983), pp. 1 and 7 [Hebrew].
220. David Zohar and Gil Keisari, 'Who Are You, Ilan Halevi?', *Ma'ariv* (15 April 1983), p. 26 [Hebrew]; Mardam-Bey, 'Ilan Halevi'.
221. 'Editorial: And Again – The Palestinian Question', *Matzpen* 71 (1974), p. 3 [Hebrew].
222. Ibid.
223. 'On the Palestinian Question – Here and Now', *Matzpen* 72 (1974), pp. 8–9, at p. 9 [Hebrew].
224. Machover and Hammami, 'To Live Together', p. 390.
225. See Erel, *Matzpen*, pp. 173–4.
226. 'On the Split', *Matzpen* 62 (1972), p. 2 [Hebrew].
227. 'Go in Peace!', *Matzpen-Marxisti* 62 (1972), p. 3 [Hebrew].
228. Lea Tsemel and Michel Warschawski (Mikado), 'Democratic Centralism is Not the Problem', *Israeli Socialist Organisation: Discussions on the Question of the Organisation* (1971), pp. 9–15 [Hebrew].
229. Moshé Machover, 'A Peace Activist on the Border', in Moshé Machover, *Israelis and Palestinians: Conflict and Resolutions* (Chicago: Haymarket Books, 2012), pp. 249–56, at pp. 254–5.
230. See *Matzpen-Marxisti* 73 (June 1974), cover page and the statement on p. 3.

231. Michel Warschawski, 'Arafat Wants to be President', *Matzpen-Marxisti* 71 (1973), p. 17 [Hebrew]; all the quotes come from Michel Warschawski, 'Who Will Benefit From a Palestinian Ministate?', *Intercontinental Press* 12: 22 (1974), pp. 736–7.
232. Warschawski, 'Who Will Benefit From a Palestinian Ministate?'.
233. Warschawski, Michel (Mikado), 'Open Letter to Our Former Anti-Zionist Comrades (?)', *Matzpen-Marxisti* 74 (1974), pp. 4 and 15, at p. 4 [Hebrew].
234. Ibid., p. 15.
235. See Greenstein, *Zionism and its Discontents*, pp. 182–6.
236. Quoted from Ibid., p. 185.
237. See Erel, *Without Fear and Prejudice*, p. 178.
238. 'Public Statement', *Matzpen-Marxisti* 73 (1973), p. 3 [Hebrew].
239. Yossi Ben-Akiva, 'The Palestinian Resistance – Where To?', *Matzpen-Marxisti* 75 (1974), pp. 6–7, at p. 7 [Hebrew].
240. Ibid.
241. 'To the Reader', *Matzpen* 72 (1974), p. 2 [Hebrew]; Revolutionary Communist Alliance, 'On Kiryat Shmona, Ma'alot and All Similar Upcoming Operations' (May 1974), The Israeli Left Archives [Hebrew].
242. See Gresh, *The PLO*, p. 165.
243. Revolutionary Communist Alliance, 'On Kiryat Shmona, Ma'alot and All Similar Upcoming Operations'.
244. Gresh, *The PLO*, pp. 138–41.
245. ISRACA, *Der Palästinastaat* (Frankfurt am Main: Israca, 1974), pp. 25–30.
246. Baumgarten, *Palästina*, p. 249.
247. Revolutionary Communist Alliance, 'On Kiryat Shmona, Ma'alot and All Similar Upcoming Operations'.
248. 'Open Letter to the Democratic Front for the Liberation of Palestine (June 1974)', *Matzpen* 72 (1974), p. 18 [Hebrew].
249. Ibid.
250. Said Hammami, 'Middle East Terrorism (Letter to the Editor)', *The Times* (17 April 1974), p. 15.
251. Machover and Hammami, 'To Live Together', p. 399.
252. Ibid., p. 396.
253. Ibid., p. 394.
254. Ibid., p. 400.
255. 'On the Meeting Between Matzpen Members and PLO-Representatives', *Matzpen* 80 (1977), p. 4 [Hebrew]; see Erel, *Matzpen*, pp. 138–9.

256. Quoted from Erel, *Matzpen*, p. 139.
257. Alexander Flores, *Der Palästinakonflikt* (Freiburg im Breisgau: Herder, 2009), p. 87.
258. Adam LeBor, *City of Oranges: Arabs and Jews in Jaffa* (London: Bloomsbury, 2006), pp. 231–4.

5

Khamsin: A New Vision for the Middle East

London–Paris–Beirut

Not even a full year after the October 1973 War, Moshé Machover received a letter in London from Eli Lobel in Paris. The two of them had shared the same political trajectory for more than twenty years. Machover and Lobel had both been part of Israel's communist movement in the early 1950s, and since the Six-Day War, when Lobel rose to become Matzpen's main representative in France, their friendship had flourished. Lobel's letter from the summer of 1974 was part of a years-long correspondence that centred mainly on Matzpen's activities and the Israel–Palestine conflict. But this time, the letter contained a handwritten draft by Lobel that stretched beyond this narrow regional context and revived former ideas for a collaboration of revolutionaries across the whole Middle East. Now, with the political order of the Middle East back on the negotiating tables of Geneva and Washington, Lobel asserted that it was time to consolidate the region's freedom fighters in preparation for social progress and a prospective revolution.[1] His ideas, such as publishing a journal or arranging conferences, found a receptive audience in Machover. Shortly afterwards, on the first weekend of October 1974, they laid the cornerstone. At the London home of Ilana and Moshé Machover, Eli Lobel from Paris and Emmanuel Farjoun from Jerusalem participated in the founding meeting of a new journal. The political writer Leila S. Kadi (b. 1939) and the Syrian philosopher Sadik J. Al-Azm (1934–2016) had both travelled from Beirut for the meeting.

Before another year was out, the first edition of *Khamsin. Revue des socialistes revolutionnaires du Proche-Orient* (Khamsin: A Journal of Revolutionary Socialists of the Near East) was released (Figure 5.1). Although the journal struck a scholarly tone with its blend of political, economic and social analysis, alongside book reviews, there was no doubt as to its true intentions: revolutionary change.

The journal's title, *Khamsin*, was a symbol of the proposed change. This word for the dry and hot desert wind that crosses the Middle East several times a year was a metaphor for the tempestuous changes and upheavals that had roiled the entire region over the preceding century. Meanwhile, the subtitle *Revue des socialistes revolutionnaires du Proche-Orient* signposted the group's eagerness for a revolution that would reunite the region. Thus, the journal represented a disparate network, beyond any national or religious loyalty, that sought to develop a common perspective for the various collectivities in the Middle East. It testified to an unprecedented coalition: an organisational alliance of both Israeli and Arab intellectuals who had transcended national and religious boundaries with their common leftist worldview. Although *Khamsin* was edited and published outside the Middle East, in the European metropolises of Paris and London, the journal would become a vibrant symbol of the region – in a way, a new vision of the Middle East on paper.

Khamsin's emergence had its own prehistories. One of these strands began in August 1969, several months before *Matzpen* printed its first articles on the dialogue with Nayef Hawatmeh's Democratic Front. This was when Moshé Machover, then living in London, received a letter from Leila S. Kadi in Beirut, the Lebanese capital, proposing a collaboration.[2] Kadi, a Druze from Lebanon, introduced herself as a sympathiser of Hawatmeh's revolutionary leftist PDFLP. Most importantly, as an employee of Beirut's Palestine Research Centre, a PLO think tank, she had access to an impressive quantity of publications and collections of documents dealing with the history of the Israel–Palestine conflict and its international dimension. She had also authored a monograph on the history of the Histadrut, the Israeli labour organisation.[3] Her letter, she informed Machover, conveyed a matter of primary importance to the Israeli Socialist Organization. She planned to publish the first Arabic monograph about Matzpen and the group's political outlook. In so doing, she aimed to show her own solidarity, while satisfying the Arab

Khamsin

REVUE DES SOCIALISTES REVOLUTIONNAIRES DU PROCHE-ORIENT.

La stratégie révolutionnaire
au Proche-Orient

ETAT PALESTINIEN ?
PAX AMERICANA ?

Le débat
à l'intérieur du camp arabe
à l'intérieur du camp israélien

n° 1. 1975

Figure 5.1 The prospect of a socialist Middle East: cover image of the first issue of *Khamsin. Revue des socialistes revolutionnaires du Proche-Orient*, 1975.

Left's avid interest in the Israeli socialists, which had grown since the Six-Day War: 'I hope, by writing this book, to serve in my humble way the cause of mutual understanding, cooperation and eventual solidarity between the revolutionary left "on both sides of the fence."' Issuing such a publication under the umbrella of the Palestine Research Centre would play a part in achieving this aim. 'To get the PLO to publish a book favourable to an Israeli party is a step forward as well as a good cover, (it makes the book more kosher).'[4]

Given these opportunities, she did not have to ask Machover twice. Without hesitation, he offered her material for her research. The book project fostered an intensive, trusting exchange that continued after the book's release, two years later in Beirut, by the Palestine Research Centre's publishing arm. Yet the book unsettled Machover at first. Ghassan Kanafani's foreword included some defamatory statements, alleging that Matzpen's London group, specifically, had been infiltrated by Israeli intelligence.[5] By explaining that Kanafani's text had been a proviso of the book's publication, Kadi tried to curtail the damage to the rest of her book. At the same time, she gave Machover a glimpse of a small circle of Arab leftists who were involved or loosely associated with the Beirut research centre and supported Kadi's project against institutional pressure from the centre's director, Fayez Abdullah Sayegh. She had originally proposed that the foreword be written by her closest confidant, the Beirut philosophy professor Sadik J. Al-Azm (1934–2016), but the editorial board of the Research Centre ruled him out as overly friendly towards the Israeli socialists. When it became clear that the disparaging foreword would be retained against her wishes, the Tunisian-born Lafif Lakhdar (1934–2013) offered to review the book positively in a left-wing Arab paper. To solve the problem once and for all, Kadi finally offered her London based penfriend the opportunity to write a rebuttal of the foreword, which she and Sadik J. Al-Azm would co-translate into Arabic for publication in either *Palestine Affairs*, *Al-Hurriye* or *Al-Hadaf*. The controversy within the editorial board over the foreword had also led her to an inevitable decision. As she wrote to Machover: 'Following that I resigned from my post with them.'[6]

Their correspondence, so euphoric at first, was quickly dampened by a sense of defeat and disillusionment and soon devolved into a litany of the ejections from both the Palestinian and Israeli Left. To this laundry list, Machover added the split within Matzpen, which had been announced in early 1972.

'This time it is going to be a really serious and damaging split', he wrote to Kadi, diagnosing the processes that, for him, symbolised the 'self-destructive' trend among the 'revolutionary left in our region and throughout the world'.[7] For her part, Kadi had even more dramatic disappointments to report on. By early 1972, she was already complaining to Machover about the PDFLP. She wrote to him about her worries that the revolutionary leftist Palestinian organisation had set aside its earlier ethical and political standards and was no longer distancing itself from aeroplane hijackings as a means for Palestinian resistance.[8] But nothing shook the two of them more than the terror attack in Ma'alot, perpetrated by the same organisation on which they had once pinned their hopes. 'They claim to believe in something and do the opposite', wrote the enraged Kadi to Machover, airing her growing mistrust of the leftist Palestinian organisation without even mentioning the incident itself.[9] In detail, she pointed out that the group financed itself through drugs and arms trafficking. By selling its weapons to nationalist organisations, among other customers, it had already compromised its own political principles. The attack in Ma'alot put her at a loss:

> Moshé, I am disgusted. [. . .] A human being for me has a value, a right to live. Revolution does not mean butchering. [. . .] What we need is a conference where revolutionary Arabs and Israelis sit and talk, discuss the problem, propose solutions, work together, etc.[10]

In his response to Kadi, Machover made no secret of his rage and disenchantment at recent events. He called the Palestinian group's tactic a moral catastrophe and an 'act of sheer political madness and crime', in part because it also dealt a blow to all efforts at cooperation between the Israeli and Palestinian Left. Almost fatalistically, he wrote: 'God knows how long it will take us to recover the ground lost in this way'.[11] Nevertheless, despite the escalating violence and his nearly drained reserves of once abundant optimism, he concluded with new prospects for cooperation:

> The only bit of hopeful news comes from Paris. My close friend Eli Lobel tells me that he and a few comrades from the Arab world are planning a common journal. It seems that after years and years of unsuccessful efforts to bring about such a common publication, it is finally going to happen.[12]

Things proceeded very quickly. Only a few days prior, Machover had received Lobel's proposal outlining a plan for a new association of Arabs and Israeli Jews. By the first editorial meeting at Machover's home in London, four months later, Lobel had already persuaded François Maspero, a publisher from the French Left, to co-publish the first four issues with Leila Kadi. Although the first issue was fully devoted to the Palestine conflict and the internal discussions among Israeli and Palestinian leftists over the future of a Palestinian state, the journal had a much broader thematic profile from the beginning. It spoke of working together to transform the entire Middle East, an ambition that was fissured by national and colonial battle lines and stunted by the potent and menacing rise of religion. Instead of pledging national or religious allegiances, the journal held up the shared utopia of a socialist society that promised to neutralise national, ethnic and religious conflicts in the region.

The commitment to such a thoroughgoing internationalism traced its roots further than the evolution of the Israel–Palestine conflict and the political advocacy of Matzpen. It was most directly and personally connected to Eli Lobel (1926–79), the founding father of *Khamsin*. Although the quest for a shared Jewish–Arab future had led him to Matzpen, Lobel embodied the archetype of the travelling 'salesman of revolution', who, in the age of anticolonialism, was agitating worldwide for the causes of internationalism, social emancipation and national equality. The founding of *Khamsin* was the journalistic apex of that advocacy. This universalist perspective had equal support from the Arab members of the *Khamsin* group, which at first centred on Sadik J. Al-Azm and Lafif Lakhdar, as well as Leila Kadi. Besides their ongoing analysis of the Palestine question, they chiefly represented the project of a new Arab Left, which, after the Arab states' defeat in the Six-Day War, began with the demand for a socialist revolution and spoke out for the project of secularising and modernising the entire Arab world. Around the time of the journal's founding, the civil war in Lebanon was breaking out, a war that would transfix the region for four years and expose its fractures along national and religious battle lines. This, too, contributed to *Khamsin*'s adoption of a perspective that enveloped the region. Given the ongoing Israel–Palestine conflict and the steady erosion of the Middle East – stretching from Lebanon to Iran to Turkey – the journal would take on a plurality of political meanings.

If *Khamsin* was in one sense an extended mouthpiece of Matzpen, it also became a platform and gathering place for dissidents of many stripes from the Arab and Muslim world.

Eli Lobel: 'A Foreign Minister without a State'

After Eli Lobel died by his own hand, his funeral was in keeping with the spirit of his life. Guests from around the world travelled to see him off at the Jewish section of Paris's Bagneux Cemetery on 8 October 1979; guests whose varied origins mirrored the border-crossing of his political advocacy. The mourners included members of the European, Arab and Israeli Left. Moshé Machover travelled from London to pay his respects as friend and as a representative of Matzpen. Lobel's brother came from Tel Aviv to say Kaddish, the Jewish prayer for the dead, and to bid his brother farewell. The next to speak was Ibrahim Souss (b. 1945), the official representative of the Palestinian Liberation Organisation in Paris. He had met Lobel ten years prior, 'at a time when there were still only few of his kind fighting around the world for the respect and the rights of the Palestinian people'. As he saw it, the significance of their relationship extended beyond personal friendship: 'Despite some points of disagreement, the entire Palestinian people sees Eli Lobel as a comrade and friend.'[13] A few days later, the Israeli press also reported on the PLO representative who had mourned the Israeli leftist and Matzpen member.[14] So it was that Lobel's burial became an allegory: a symbol for his lasting efforts to solve the Israeli–Palestinian conflict on the basis of equality and mutual recognition.

From the start, Lobel's life story was at odds with the Israeli–Zionist perspective of the Jewish people's return to Eretz Israel. His family, who came from Poland's practising Jewish community, had been driven to Palestine by utter desperation, not Zionist fervour. After the First World War, his parents had fled Brzostek, in Polish Subcarpathia, and settled in Berlin, where Eli was born in 1926.[15] German was one of his first languages. His father, Solomon Lobel, was imprisoned by the authorities in Nazi Germany, then released in 1938, whereupon his entire family hurried back to Brzostek. Even Shabbat did not delay Eli's strictly observant father on a journey that passed through Poland and Romania and eventually led to Palestine. Thus, this land was not their first choice, but their only option and last resort.[16]

They arrived in Tel Aviv during the final months of the Arab Revolt of 1936–9, which experience quickly gave the young Lobel a sense of the inherent conflict of Jewish settlement in Palestine.[17] He soon joined the youth movement of Hashomer Hatzair, which sought to reconcile its socialist internationalism with the Zionist *raison d'État* by advocating the idea of a binational Jewish–Arab state.[18] In the evenings, when Lobel's father was at synagogue, Eli would go with Amos Kenan, his classmate at Tel Aviv's Tikhon Hadash High School, to meetings of the Zionist socialists.[19] In retrospect, at that time, Hashomer Hatzair evidently represented the still-united nucleus of an Israeli Left that would later fracture along various fault lines. For example, when Amos Kenan later recalled an excursion with Hashomer Hatzair in May 1945, it turned out that besides him and Lobel, three of the future military governors of the post-1967 occupied territories in the West Bank had also been on the trip.[20] In 1946, one of them, Shaul Givoli, would become a co-founder with Eli Lobel of Kibbutz Nirim in the Negev Desert to the south, where their shared utopia of Zionist-style universalistic socialism was to be realised.

These hopes collapsed with the first Israeli–Arab war that followed the United Nations Partition Plan. Even before that, the former comrades from Hashomer Hatzair had parted ways when Amos Kenan joined Lehi, while Lobel devoted himself to establishing his kibbutz. But even within that utopian lifestyle, the aftermath of the war soon exposed differences in how they each perceived what was necessary for existence. While Israeli frontier outposts such as Nirim keenly experienced the Israeli necessity of defending the community by military force, Eli Lobel's intellectual viewpoint evolved at a spatial distance from events – from the outside, looking in. Because of health troubles, he followed Israel's founding war from distant Prague – by radio. This may have been one of the reasons why he continued to hope for a binational Palestine, even after such aspirations had gradually faded away within Hashomer Hatzair.[21]

With even more significant implications for Lobel, the kibbutz decided to send him onward from Prague to study economics at the Sorbonne in Paris, where he also wrote regular articles for *Al HaMishmar* as a correspondent for the Kibbutz HaArtsi umbrella organisation. These included many reports on current affairs in the French Fifth Republic, such as the labour strikes and colonial conflicts. In the spring of 1952, his work also enabled him to travel to Egypt as part of a delegation for the weekly *Observateur*, and ultimately to visit Palestinian refugee camps in the Gaza Strip. This led to a whole series of articles for *Al HaMishmar* titled 'Among the Refugees in Gaza', which Lobel wrote under the pseudonym P. Weiss.[22] In early 1950s Israel, when the country was a sworn enemy of neighbouring Egypt, the reports drew significant attention. Both their authenticity and the reporter's existence were cast into doubt.[23] For Eli Lobel, his time in the camps amounted to an unsettling confrontation with the situation of the Palestinians, most of whom had lived on what was now Israeli territory before they became refugees. He began seeing both the Israeli state and his own kibbutz with different eyes: those of the Palestinian Arabs. 'And so I find myself here [in Gaza] among "our" Arabs', he wrote in the final instalment of the series, reflecting on his own conflicted feelings:

> North of me is Yad Mordechai; a chain of kibbutzim surrounds the entire Gaza Strip: Be'eri, Magen, Nirim. In the kibbutz, some guards stay up every night watching the fields for infiltrators, whom I might run into here as I walk down the street. [. . .] These people are suffering.[24]

Before long, he left Paris and returned to his kibbutz in Israel, but this experience did not leave him. In a letter to his friend Lilia Peter, he wrote once again about the contradictions that seized him while riding a tractor to plough fields he had previously seen from the other side:

> When the tractor reaches the border, and I see the Arabs watching me plough the earth that once belonged to them, I turn around with the tractor and reach the graves of my comrades who died defending the kibbutz and the Negev.[25]

But although the visit to the Gaza Strip marked a major turning point in Eli Lobel's life, leaving early cracks in his notion that socialism, Zionism and internationalism were mutually compatible, neither his trip nor the resulting articles brought about an immediate rift with the rest of the kibbutz. 'It was not seen as betrayal or anything like that', recalled Vivi Katzir, who lived in Nirim at the same time, many years later. 'It seemed more like a kind of personal adventure; he was one of us, after all.'[26] The rupture would finally come in the wake of the Slansky trials in Prague, when one of those accused of being 'cosmopolitans' and 'Zionist agents' was Mordechai Oren, a Mapam member and representative of the kibbutz movement. His charge: collaborating with British intelligence. According to the prevailing explanation by Yaakov Hazan, Meir Ya'ari and the rest of the party leadership, this was an outbreak of antisemitism in a socialist guise and with Soviet support. Eli Lobel begged to differ. He felt much more drawn to the Left Socialist Party that was gathering around Moshe Sneh, which declared its unconditional solidarity with the USSR and believed the allegations of Oren's espionage activities against the Czechoslovak People's Republic. Lobel's fellow kibbutzniks were unconvinced, and gradually distanced themselves from him, despite all their personal connections. When information about his contacts with the Communist Party became public, this internal disagreement led to an open conflict with the entire league of kibbutzim. The leadership of Kibbutz Arzi ordered a search of Lobel's quarters, and he publicly called their disciplinary measures 'intellectual censorship' until the situation finally came to a head.[27] In the spring of 1953, before the death of Stalin, Lobel was ejected from his party by a resolution of Mapam and finally had to leave his own kibbutz, Nirim. Without much delay, he found a new political home in Tel Aviv with Moshe Sneh's Left Socialist Party, embarking on a remarkable political career at Sneh's side. He also struck up lasting friendships with Oded Pilavsky and Akiva Orr.[28] Still, his ejection from the erstwhile socialist utopia of Nirim cast a long shadow on him. More than marking the end of his old hopes, the controversy and his general political activities made it difficult for him, personally, to find work in Israel. When Lobel lost his job as a factory bookkeeper, he decided to leave the country and return to Paris. It was a final farewell. From then on, he would align his internationalist outlook with an international existence.

Lobel continued to take part in the conflicts of his country and region, even from Paris. Soon after his arrival, still shaken by his visit to the Gaza Strip, Lobel joined a group headed by Maxime Rodinson, the Jewish communist and professor of classical Ethiopian studies, to discuss the Palestine question. Other Israeli exiles, such as Gila Ballas and Chaya Harari, were responsible for founding the group and established direct contact with both Palestinian and Arab leftists. Over time, the regular gatherings took the name

'Arab–Israeli Committee for Peace'.[29] Later, Amos Kenan would even claim that Lobel was the first of their generation to engage in dialogue directly with the Palestinians for peace and mutual recognition.[30] Lobel's political and economic activities went far beyond the Palestine question and the situation in the Middle East. In the context of contemporary decolonialisation processes, his perspective on the Israeli–Palestinian conflict had radicalised, while the range of his internationalist activities expanded. In 1950s Paris, where important representatives from the 'Third World' were assembling to plan 'the future revolution' that would bring their national independence, Lobel quickly integrated into the networks of socialist anticolonialism.[31] 'Years later, when all the African states had achieved independence', Akiva Orr later recalled, 'he had friends everywhere. People who had studied with him back then and had since become prime ministers or finance ministers'.[32] Kenan, impressed by his friend's enterprise and internationalist activism, dubbed him a 'foreign minister without a state' (Figure 5.2).[33] Yet Lobel's political solidarity was not merely symbolic; it was based on his practical support and his skills as an economist. As early as the mid-1950s, he travelled to India

Figure 5.2 'Foreign minister without a state': Eli Lobel in the 1960s.

with a group of Marxist experts in economics, including Charles Bettelheim and Joan Robinson, to help with the development of an independent five-year plan under Jawaharlal Nehru. He continued this consulting work as a United Nations employee after his return to the French capital. But his work at the international organisation, which his teachers had recommended he pursue partly for the sake of his career, quickly grew monotonous for Lobel. More importantly, he felt it did not make an adequate impact.[34] Besides his work as an economist, he devoted himself to supporting the fight for Algerian independence and joined the movement in solidarity with the FLN, which was clandestinely organising in Paris.[35] Lobel had befriended Lakhdar Brahimi, the future Algerian Ambassador to Sudan, Egypt and the UK, and also joined the French FLN solidarity network which first evolved around Francis Jeanson and was later led by Henri Curiel. Lobel also got Amos Kenan and Uri Avnery to support the anti-colonial movement in Algeria. After a meeting between Avnery and Henri Curiel, this resulted subsequently in the founding of the Israeli Committee for a Free Algeria.[36] It was not long after the dismantling of the so-called 'Jeanson network' network in early 1960 that Lobel also relocated his political activities. Thanks to his contacts from his Parisian student days, he was invited to Mali as an economic advisor to the new government.[37]

Lobel's six-year stay in the former French colony was his longest in Africa, and it became almost legendary. The main subject of sensationalism and anecdotes was the Israeli's quasi-diplomatic advocacy for political and economic matters in sub-Saharan Africa: primarily, his work there as a 'consultant and de-facto finance minister' for Modibo Keita's socialist government, representing the country to the World Bank and working on its development with a group of Marxist economists led by the Egyptian-born Samir Amin.[38] But Lobel was not the only Israeli whose studies in Paris led him to solidarity with the anticolonial independence movements and who was now serving as a consultant for the post-colonial states. Uri Avnery reported several times on Lobel's meeting with Joe Golan, a former employee of the World Jewish Congress (WJC): the two Israelis sat at opposite sides of the table during a bilateral meeting between Mali and Senegal a while after the federation of the two neighbouring states broke down in the autumn of 1960.[39] In his WJC days, during the 1950s, Golan had been a close confidant of Nahum Goldmann and had initiated some early peace discussions between Israel and the Arabs, as well as the idea of a Mediterranean Union. As a unique connoisseur of the Arab world, Golan was also involved in the WJC's efforts to safeguard North African Jewry in the age of decolonisation.[40] Yet his independent meetings with the Algerian FLN leadership had made him an *enfant terrible* of the Israeli state, resulting in the 'Golan affair' over Golda Meir's refusal to renew his Israeli passport. Golan went on to accept Leopold Senghor's invitation to serve as a political consultant in his administration in Senegal.[41] So it was that Lobel and Golan, two Israeli dissidents who became economic advisers for sub-Saharan states, helped to mediate the dispute between Mali and Senegal.[42]

This legend-in-the-making had a sequel at the World Bank headquarters in Washington, D. C., Lobel would later tell his friends that he was once standing in the lift at the headquarters of the World Bank across from the Israeli representatives Levi Eshkol and David Horovitz when they saw that his name tag identified him as a representative of Mali. They asked him about his background, perplexed. When Lobel identified himself as an Israeli, in fluent Hebrew, they turned their backs to him.[43] Lobel's consultancy failed to prevent Mali's economic upheavals, but this did not harm his reputation as an economist fully devoted to establishing post-colonial economic systems. In 1966–7, at Charles Bettelheim's recommendation, he travelled twice to Cuba to assist with the country's economic planning.[44] His ensuing report sharply criticised Fidel Castro and Che Guevara's monocultural planned economy and recommended that the country open up economically to end its dependence on sugar, its main export crop. This led to a rift with the government of a country he had previously gushed about. Looking back, he later confided in some close friends: 'The indignant reactions of my hosts made clear to me that I had no place in Cuba anymore.'[45]

Lobel's return from the Caribbean would lead him and his internationalism all the way back to the Israel–Palestine conflict, and not only because the events of 1967 had made the Palestine question the focus of international attention. In May 1968, when the political utopia of a future socialist revolution was gathering steam, the same momentum fuelled hopes of a common future for Israeli Jews and Palestinian Arabs. More than anyone else, Lobel – now swept up in that euphoria – represented Matzpen's international voice in Paris, just as Moshé Machover, Akiva Orr and Shimon Tzabar did in London.

There in Paris, together with Nissan Rilov (1922–2007), he co-edited the French edition of *Israca/ISRAC*, which rapidly became the centre of gravity among Jewish and Israeli leftists in France and also had readers at universities.[46] Rilov had immigrated to Palestine from the Soviet Union and grew up in the Zionist moshav of Nahalal with childhood friend Moshe Dayan of later fame. As part of the first generation of Israeli artists, Rilov would become part of the same cultural scene as Shimon Tzabar. Yet in the early 1950s, he left Israel due to cultural and political disillusionment and resettled in France.

As part of a group of Israeli artists in the French capital, Rilov was also one of Lobel's main public companions after the Six-Day War,[47] but Lobel gathered support far beyond the immediate circle of leftist Israelis. He even got Jean-Paul Sartre to support the cause of Giora Neumann, Israel's first counscientious objector after the Six-Day war. Lobel was friends with Maxime Rodinson, Pierre Vidal-Naquet and also Eric Rouleau, who wrote for *Le Monde* as their reporter on the Arab world and the conflict in the Middle East. Like Henri Curiel, Rouleau came from a family of Egyptian–Jewish communists and was forced into French exile in 1951 under the reign of Farouk I.[48] As an aficionado of Arab politics and a section editor at *Le Monde*, Rouleau reported, in turn, on Matzpen, travelled personally to Tel Aviv in 1969 to meet Haim Hanegbi and Rami Livneh and occasionally gave voice to the Israeli socialists' stance in *Le Monde* when describing the public debate over the Palestine question.[49] But Lobel's greatest media impact was neither in *Le Monde*, nor in the radical-left *Partisan*, where he was responsible for covering Middle Eastern issues. He reached his largest audience by editing and writing the introduction to Sabri Geries's book *The Arabs in Israel*, whose publication by Maspero Press he oversaw in 1969.[50] The book was translated into several languages and quickly became one of the New Left's standard texts on the Israeli–Palestinian conflict, while representing Lobel's own hopes for its resolution.[51]

Lobel's political activities related to Matzpen had drawn ample attention to him, but also made him a target of his political opponents – especially when he used his public appearances not only to invoke his allies, but to express his clear opposition to representatives of the Israeli government. In the summer of 1969, when Israel's Ambassador to West Germany, Asher Ben-Nathan, tried to deliver a speech at the University of Frankfurt, but was shouted down by German students, the Israeli Ambassador drew certain parallels with the menacing mood of the 1930s.[52] But the students appealed for a follow-up speech by Eli Lobel, as an Israeli and a spokesperson for Matzpen. This prompted *Haolam Hazeh* to ask: 'Who is the Israeli waging war against the Israeli ambassador to Germany?'[53] Ben-Nathan himself considered the Israeli Left to be merely 'a pathological symptom', a 'symptom of self-hatred' and certainly not a political group to be taken seriously.[54] Just three days after the ambassador's event, the rhetorical accusations against Matzpen were overshadowed by outright violence. The Socialist German Student Union (SDS) planned a side event in protest of the ambassador's talk. When both Eli Lobel and Abdallah Frangi from the General Union of Palestinian Students took their seats on the podium, a dramatic situation commenced, loaded with history and memory. The mood soured before the event had even started. First, an elderly man addressed the audience, identified himself as a Holocaust survivor and announced his categorical opposition to any criticism of the Jewish state in view of his experience. When the microphone was taken from him, another similarly minded group stormed the podium, struck the speakers with planks of wood and tried to throw the film projector at the head of Eli Lobel, who had already fallen to the floor. Lobel made it out of the mêlée with light injuries, but Frangi suffered a basal skull fracture and was confined to hospital for an extended stay.[55] The scenario repeated itself not long after, in December 1969, in Paris. At an event, Lobel and his political friends were attacked by a group of people whom he later identified as members of Betar, a right-wing Zionist youth movement. The confrontation occurred when Lobel and his friends were approaching the venue, and afterwards Lobel and a badly injured Klaus Rürup had to be taken to hospital. 'The attack was targeted against our little group and especially against me', Lobel wrote to Haim Hanegbi soon afterward. 'Ruth's husband was violently attacked. I have a concussion and I got some stiches. I only spent two days in hospital.'[56] These incidents would not be the last.

However, the conflicts over Lobel's political advocacy for a common Jewish–Arab perspective in the Middle East were not limited to quarrels with Jewish and Israeli opponents. He was also moved to voice open criticism of Palestinian and Arab groups that rejected him on the basis of his Jewish–Israeli background. His childhood friend Yaakov Malkin later remembered that this was why, when he visited PLO members in Beirut, he was unwilling to discard his Israeli passport: a symbol of collective belonging.[57] For the same reason, he found it intolerable that members of the Israeli Left were not allowed to speak at political events with Palestinian groups, solely because of their nationality. 'He supported the Palestinians' struggle against oppression', recalled Marius Schattner, who became acquainted with Lobel in Paris in the 1970s. 'But he did not accept their nationalism, just as he didn't accept the Israeli kind.'[58] His insistence on collective recognition and equality eventually led to a falling out with his one-time friend Samir Amin, whom he had met back in Mali. When Amin edited Lobel's essay 'Palestine and the Jews' to include in a collection reprinting writing by both of them, Amin's tacit changes to Lobel's text prompted ruptures in their former friendship. Amin also intervened in places where Lobel had rebuked Arab nationalism and 'voiced solidarity-based critique of Palestinian resistance'.[59]

Eli Lobel's friendship with the Jerusalem-born Ibrahim Souss was a different story, and a much more uplifting one. The future Paris representative of the PLO had befriended Lobel in the late 1960s and respected his political activism, specifically as a Jewish Israeli – long before the Palestinians publicly approved such a stance. In the heydays of internationlism, when Lobel opened his house for many politically like-minded people, the talented pianist Souss was soon counted among Lobel's many guests, who included European and Israeli socialists as well as Paris-based exiles from the Arab Left.[60] Another of Lobel's close confidants was the Tunisian-born Lafif Lakhdar, who had also settled in Paris in the early 1970s. Lakhdar had already distributed Matzpen leaflets with Leila S. Kadi in Beirut, where he spoke out in support of collaborating with the socialist Israelis.[61] Now in Paris, he wanted to join forces with Lobel. In retrospect, Lakhdar recalled their shared enchantment with King Hassan II's dream of 'recreating al-Andalus'. Far from the region to which both felt wedded, the Moroccan King's Middle Eastern mediation efforts gave them new hope for Jewish–Arab reconciliation after the war of October 1973.[62] But their own dream of Judeo–Arab coexistence in the contemporary Middle East was not as much about a return to the premodern past – to the 'Golden Age of a Muslim-Jewish synthesis' – as it was in the spirit of a shared socialist future. Many years later, the writer Shimon Ballas ironically described this shared ambition, which put them both at odds with their communities of origin, as a 'fraternity of traitors' (*ahvat bogdim*) and a kind of anti-nationalist fraternity of peoples (*ahvat amim*).[63] In the journal *Khamsin*, which Lobel co-established in 1974–5 and to which Lakhdar would soon regularly contribute, the two men found a joint forum for their shared vision of a new Middle East.

Arab Self-Criticism and Palestinian Revolution

The first order of business for *Khamsin*, the journal for the revolutionary transformation of the Middle East, was to come up with a vision of a shared future. But even though the New Left of Israel and the Arab world had a common vocabulary – the language of socialism – they were motivated by different political and historical experiences. In the case of Leila S. Kadi, Sadik J. Al-Azm, Lafif Lakhdar and their circle, these experiences placed them at the margins of their Arab environments, sidelined in much the same way as Matzpen was in Israel. Granted, they, too, had taken on both the Palestinian cause and the integration of Israeli Jews within the Levant as their own political concerns. First and foremost, however, their socialist affinities sprang out of the failure of a universalistic anticolonialism in the Arab world. As their critique of post-colonial lived realities spread to criticising religion's dominance in public space, their talk of a socialist revolution came to represent the demand for a secular road to modernity.

The life of Lafif Lakhdar, whose writing appeared in *Khamsin* from the third issue onwards, exemplified some of these historical experiences. Lakhdar was born in 1934 in rural Tunisia to a family of *fellahin*, and his village-based schooling consisted almost exclusively of Qur'an studies.[64] A six-month stint at a French school ended abruptly when German troops destroyed the schoolhouse during the Second World War. To continue his education without tuition fees, Lakhdar first enrolled at Al-Zaytuna University in Tunis, a religious institution – but the young man was already reading Charles Darwin surreptitiously under his desk.[65] His father's early demise had sent him on a search for new role models that led him from Sheikh Muhammad al-Tahir Ibn Ashour to Taha Hussein, the former Egyptian Education Minister and a lodestar of Arab modernity. Lakhdar even wore an eyepatch to emulate his idol, who was blind.[66] It was his subsequent law studies, however, that first familiarised him with modern Western disciplines and inspired him to become a follower and defender of Habib Bourguiba,

Tunisia's first president, who, shortly after the country's independence in 1956, announced a Code of Personal Status emancipating Tunisian women. By then, Lakhdar was working as a lawyer. When he spoke out against Al-Zaytuna University's unchanged religious educational system, advocating a switch to a modern French curriculum, it was Bourguiba who initiated educational reform along those lines and separated Al-Zaytuna University from the mosque out of which it originally sprung.[67]

Yet Lafif Lakhdar's activism as a political lawyer brought him head to head with his country's political authorities. His defence of a political dissident was a tragic failure: the defendant was executed, and Lakhdar was forced to flee political persecution.[68] His escape from Tunisia to France, assisted by the FLN in Algeria, was followed by an odyssey through numerous countries on several continents, starting in 1961 in Paris, where he was clandestinely backing the Algerian War of Independence. A year before the FLN's historic victory, Lakhdar was already part of the inner circle of Ahmed Ben Bella, who would soon be elected president of an independent socialist Algeria.[69] It was here that Lakhdar also became more involved with the Palestine question. He worked for three years as a translator at the Fatah office in Algiers, which opened in 1962 under the leadership of Khalil Al-Wazir, also known by his *nom de guerre* Abu Jihad. In 1965, when Che Guevara came to discuss the Israel–Palestine conflict with Al-Wazir at Algiers's Hotel Elité, Lafif Lakhdar was also involved in the discussions.[70]

Yet the 1965 putsch against Ben Bella and the new authoritarian regime in Algeria snuffed out all dreams of a universalist anticolonialism that still seemed possible in 1961, when Frantz Fanon published his seminal book *The Wretched of the Earth* in support of the Algerian independence struggle and against colonialism.[71] The forces of General Houari Boumédiène, who seized power on 19 June 1965, aimed their weapons at Ben Bella, but also – and especially – against socialist anticolonialists. Since Algerian independence, Lakhdar had had close relations with the Algerian Left, specifically a group around Mohammed Harbi and the leftist journal *Revolution Africaine* that protested the political leadership's increasing bureaucratisation and championed a full democratic transformation of Algerian society.[72] While Ben Bella was in power, Boumédiène had asked him to exclude Harbi's group from the editorial team of *Revolution Africaine*; this led the group to establish the

Socialist Vanguard opposition party.⁷³ Their outright persecution began after the coup and Ben Bella's imprisonment. Harbi and his allies, who had been among the pioneering fighters for Algerian independence, now found themselves in the hands of an authoritarian regime; many were detained and brutally tortured.⁷⁴ If Lafif Lakhdar wanted to escape the government's minions, his only choice was to flee once more.⁷⁵

Lakhdar found refuge in Czechoslovakia and East Germany, where he also learned German. However, his encounters with the local population quickly sensitised him to the restrictive political structures of 'real existing socialism' and converted him into a staunch anti-Stalinist.⁷⁶ His exile led him next to the freshly independent state of South Yemen. By 1969, when he took part in a conference of ministers, his recommendations were not coming from a Marxist–Leninist playbook. Instead, he was pushing the same reforms and modernisation measures that Bourguiba had already introduced in Tunisia with his Code of Personal Status. After discussing the future of a secular South Yemen with President Salem Rubaya Ali, his travels took him to Jordan and later to Beirut, where he joined the Palestinian cause, once and for all.⁷⁷

The experience of the violent shift of power in post-colonial Algeria was formative for Lakhdar, shaping his future ideas and actions. He was not just reacting to Boumédiène's statist and authoritarian leanings, but was, more importantly, engaging with an emergent post-colonial Algerian identity that, for all its socialist justifications, invoked nationalistic and religious myths. This was typified by Boumédiène's reference to 'Islamic socialism' as the one true socialism, a rejection of Western universalistic traditions in favour of Arab–Islamic values: a nationalistic and religious clampdown that resulted in an abrogation of universalist values, such as women's equality and the freedom of culture, expression and academic enquiry.⁷⁸ During the 'Arabisation of the cadres' and the FLN's Islamic turn, the new regime even declared Frantz Fanon himself (who had died in 1961) to be a 'non-Arab foreigner'.⁷⁹

After he fled Algeria, Lakhdar gradually made this politicisation of Islam into the main target of his political criticism. A few years later, he was the first to translate the entirety of Lenin's essays on the critique of religion as part of a larger collection of Lenin's writings.⁸⁰ At a time when even nominally secular Arab movements were defining themselves in reference to a religious paradigm of history and the Golden Age of Islam, Lakhdar's manifesto-like introduction to *From the Critique of Heaven to the Critique of Earth* rejected 'those Middle Ages we are still living in' and called for the total separation of politics and religion.[81] This was followed, in short order, by a translation of the *Communist Manifesto* from German to Arabic – the first unfalsified edition, as he put it. But he could only find a publisher for it among Israeli leftists. Years later, Lakhdar would be dubbed the 'Arab Spinoza' for his defence of enlightened rationalism.[82] In the politically charged 1970s, this critique of religion was linked to a call for an Arab revolution.

Actually, the pervasiveness of religion in everyday life in the Arab world had already sparked a debate there immediately after the Six-Day War of 1967. The attempted explanations by Gamal Abdel Nasser, the President of Egypt, that 'the enemy we expected from the east and north came from the west' seemed flimsy, and the Arab defeat looked avoidable in hindsight.[83] While large parts of the Arab world were turning to Islam in greater numbers, the year 1967 saw the emergence of a new secular Arab Left, in which Lafif Lakhdar also played a seminal role.[84] In the spirit of 'self-criticism', the loss of the war prompted an unsparing reflection on all models of Arab socialism to date – whether Nasserite or Baathist – culminating in a fundamental critique of Arab society.[85]

This New Leftist movement represented no less than an appeal for a reform encompassing both political and cultural dimensions that would propel the region into enlightened modernity. Alongside institutional democratisation, the reformers demanded a radical transformation of Arabic that would eliminate the distinction between the written, sacred language and the spoken, profane language – in order to drive religion out of public space.[86] The most influential book related to these New Left demands for modernisation and secularisation was an essay collection by Lakhdar's political ally Sadik J. Al-Azm, published in 1968 under the title *Self-Criticism After the Defeat*.[87] The author came from a famous Damascene family, defended his doctorate at Yale in 1961 and had taught at the American University of Beirut and the University of Jordan in Amman. Soon after the book's release, one commentator reported that Al-Azm had succeeded in 'slaughter[ing] a surprisingly large number of sacred cows – and has taken in his stride not only so-called reactionary Arab thinkers and regimes, but has included nearly everyone, not even sparing President Nasser and his Arab Socialist regime'.[88]

Al-Azm's book began by taking stock of Arab explanations for the loss of the war, before expanding into a work of fundamental ideological and social criticism. After concluding that it was difficult 'to find a shortcoming, weakness or error in Arab organisation, preparation and planning revealed by the June [1967] War that some Arabs have not ascribed to colonialism and international imperialism', the author appealed for Arabs to engage in self-criticism and take responsibility for the outcome of the war.[89] Taking aim at would-be conspiracy theories, he railed against the Arab states' failure to modernise, to encourage civic consciousness and, on that basis, to build capable armies.[90] Even for Gamal Abdel Nasser and the other self-appointed spokespeople of Arab revolution and Arab socialism, Al-Azm attested, 'the defeat in June had revealed that the Arab socialist revolution [. . .] was neither revolutionary enough nor socialist enough'.[91] Partly for that reason, Al-Azm held that the military defeats of 1956 and 1967 could be attributed to the Egyptian revolution of 1952.[92]

The farther Al-Azm's criticism strayed from the events of those wars, the more bitingly he disparaged the self-proclaimed Arab revolution of Nasserism. Perhaps it styled itself as socialist, but 'in contrast to the other socialist revolutions', he argued, 'the Arab revolution has yet to proclaim, in a frank, clear, and official way, the scientific character of its socialism and its secularism'.[93] Al-Azm criticised the talk of an 'Arab adaptation of socialism', which he argued got in the way of resolving the relationship between politics and Islamic tradition. With equal vehemence, he repudiated the insistence on a 'middle-roadism' in Arab socialism as a supposed compromise between progress and tradition.[94] For Al-Azm, all these self-assertions by Arab socialists mostly showed that even the progressive elements in society were still deeply dictated by religious tradition. Those who claimed to be socialist, revolutionary and secular were, in fact, beholden to religious values; Al-Azm considered such people a 'concealed reactionary resistance to the scientific progress, scientific socialist practice, and the cultural revolution that societies walking these paths seek'.[95] In 1969, he published another essay collection, this time investigating the role of religion in Arab public spaces. Thus, *Self-Criticism After the Defeat* was supplemented by *Critique of Religious Thought*.[96]

Although his next book did not delve into the tempestuous events occurring in the region to the same depth, it was no less political. *Critique of*

Religious Thought's academic and critical reasoning did not stop at attacking Arab scholarly thought for clinging to the authority of sacred sources, a habit the book blamed for hindering development and knowledge in the Arab world.[97] The call for a separation of faith and knowledge gave way to a demand for a historical–critical textual analysis of the Qur'an, a scholarly process that had so far been avoided out of deference to the sacredness of the texts. Similar to modern biblical scholarship and Jewish studies, the volume invoked a kind of 'Islamic studies' that would pave the way to secularising and modernising Arab society.[98]

The responses to this unsparing criticism went beyond public attacks on Al-Azm 'in a few newspapers and by the pulpits of the mosques'.[99] Under the accusation of 'inciting sectarianism', the (Sunni) Grand Mufti of Lebanon ordered the confiscation of the book on 16 December 1969. On 8 January 1970, he was finally accused of violating the law governing publications, as well as section 317 of the Lebanese Penal Code for publishing a book that 'intended to or result[ed] in instigating confessional or racial bigotry, or that provoke[d] conflict between the sects'.[100] Although the highly visible trial and the accompanying heated public debate ended in the defendant's acquittal that July, the affair had marked the boundaries of criticism and highlighted the precarious status of secular critics in the Arab world.

However, not only had the Six-Day War exposed the delayed modernisation of the Arab world, but in the eyes of the Arab Left, it also seemed to establish the prerequisites for a new revolutionary situation.[101] Just as the 1967 defeat led to the abandonment of the outdated political models of Nasserism and Baathism, an entire generation of Arab leftists associated the return of the Palestine question with their hopes for the awakening of a new revolutionary subject in the region. Contrary to the former claim by certain Arab states, especially Egypt, to represent the Palestinian cause, the Palestinians themselves were to become the embodiment of a contemporary revolution that would embrace the entire Arab world.[102] Sadik J. Al-Azm was affected by these expectations. To protect himself from political censorship, he had even placed himself briefly under the care of the small, radical-left PDFLP, which more than any other group had linked the project of Palestinian self-determination to the political emancipation and social progress of the entire

Arab world at large.[103] After relocating to Beirut, Lafif Lakhdar had risen to become one of this Palestinian group's prominent theorists and viewed it as the 'revolutionary vanguard of the Arab revolution'.[104]

The expectation that Palestinians would essentially become the hotbed of the entire Arab world's emancipation also influenced the perception of the Palestine question and emboldened outspoken advocacy for a solution based on the equal rights to existence of Palestinian Arabs and Israeli Jews. In his earlier book *Self-Criticism After the Defeat*, Al-Azm had reasoned against conspiracy theory style portrayals of the Israeli–Palestinian conflict, which were notorious for taking cues from the *Protocols of the Elders of Zion*.[105] Now, in *Leftist Studies on the Palestine Question*, which was influenced by Maxime Rodinson, Al-Azm also turned to Judeo–European historical experiences and non-Zionist Jewish approaches to solving the Middle Eastern conflict.[106] Lafif Lakhdar, likewise, stridently spoke out for separating 'the liberation of Palestine from demagogic, chauvinistic and religious slogans'. His appeal for a 'human, revolutionary and internationalist solution to the question of Palestine and Israel' was guided in no small part by his experience of the nationalist and religious constriction of the post-colonial Arab states.[107] In an open letter to the Algerian communist Larbi Buhali dated 12 December 1968, Lakhdar emphasised that Arab states' discrimination against their own Jewish populations had reinforced the Zionist narrative of a Jewish nation that could only find a safe home in a Jewish state.

> Did not the Egyptian government force Egyptian communists of Jewish origin to emigrate? [. . .] Did not the [Algerian] government of Bu Medien [sic] expel, in 1966–67, a number of Marxists of Jewish origin [. . .] [and] tell them, at the airport, that 'your country is Israel and not Algeria'?[108]

Thus, Lakhdar's portrayal of the post-colonial Arab–Islamic world was paired with fierce criticism of antisemitism, the Arab strain of which had contributed, in his view, to the Israeli insistence on a sovereign Jewish state. In contrast to the widespread call, disseminated by the likes of Gamal Abdel Nasser and the PLO's first Chairman Ahmad Shukeiri, to throw the Jews into the sea, Lakhdar stressed that the 'liberation of Palestine does not mean at all its liberation from its Jewish inhabitants [. . .] It does not mean, at least as far as I am concerned, the prevention of the Jews of Israel from sharing power in a future Palestinian Jewish-Arab state'. In that vein, he declared that 'it would be natural for the head of a future democratic Palestinian state to be an elected Jew, and for the Jewish majority to be represented democratically [. . .] at all levels of power'.[109] Hence, Arab self-criticism after the defeat had spawned a vision on the Palestine question of a united socialist federation within the Arab world, where all national groups in the region would be guaranteed equal recognition.

The faith in the Palestinians as the new protagonists of the Arab revolution would not even last three years. It was abruptly smothered by the 'Black September' of 1970, when the Jordanian Army massacred local Palestinian groups, setting off the Jordanian Civil War.[110] In the run-up to these events, Lafif Lakhdar had warned 'that revolutionary leadership should not under any circumstances be confused with a leadership that glorifies military action'. The violent efforts by Palestinian organisations to seize political power in Jordan now seemed to confirm their 'mystical relationship with guns'.[111] What began with a failed assassination attempt on the King of Jordan and proceeded with multiple hijackings, prompting a military escalation and Syrian intervention, was certainly not the liberating revolution of the Arab Left's hopes and dreams. Instead, the bloody murder of hundreds or thousands of Palestinian guerrillas and civilians led to the PLO's retreat from Jordan.[112] Soon after these dramatic events, Lafif Lakhdar and Mustapha Khayati published a critique of the Palestinians' political practice, which they had begun writing earlier, under the provocative title *Waiting for the Massacre*. The pamphlet paired accusations of 'fetishism of purely military activity' with a conclusion that the Palestinians were clearly unfamiliar with the social contexts of their actions.[113] Military hubris had won out over political rationality. Given the dearth of long-term social and political prospects, Lakhdar and Khayati argued that the top priorities were a substantive discussion and a shake-up of roles within the Palestinian movement. If the hopes of a revolution had so recently been pinned on the Palestinians, the same Palestinians were now in need of an inner revolution of their own: 'The bases of the Resistance must know, from now on, that the most perilous enemy is within our borders and within our ranks.' They therefore called on the 'rank and file of the Resistance' to go so far as to 'liberate itself from its leaders'.[114] For Lakhdar personally, this treatise was his first step away from the existing political movements, before he finally created a political alternative in 1972, the revolutionary 'popular councils'.[115] However, this small-scale political experiment would not last long either. In the mid-1970s, following the outbreak of the Lebanese Civil War, Lakhdar eventually relocated to Paris.

Sadik J. Al-Azm made the most conspicuous switch, from hailing Palestinian organisations as pioneers to railing against them in public.[116] His *Critical Study of the Thought of the Palestinian Resistance*, released after the Jordanian Civil War, was essentially a modified sequel to his *Self-Criticism After the Defeat*, this time using the Palestinians as his case study.[117] Yet his assertion that 'September 1970 signifies to the Palestinian struggle what June 1967 signified to the limping Arab liberation movement in general' went beyond a reprise of earlier critiques.[118] His characterisation of the movement, particularly Yassir Arafat's leading Fatah group, as having a 'vaguely progressive, strongly anti-imperialist and basically militaristic orientation' likewise accused them of more than just the same military hubris that had supressed any social and political analysis of the region's social circumstances.[119] Al-Azm perceived a Palestinian tendency to be 'more often driven by their wish to die for their cause instead of fighting well and live – if possible – to see their cause win'.[120] Thus, according to Al-Azm, prospects for the future were sacrificed on the altar of willing martyrdom. He did not even exempt organisations that self-identified as socialist, such as the Democratic Front for the Liberation of Palestine, which Al-Azm had previously supported, from this line of criticism. They, too, had succumbed to that impulse of fetishising violence, an impulse that went hand in hand with a lack of socio-political ideas for the future. He extended his critique:

> These organisations [. . .] often expressed quite accurately and correctly the dilemmas of the Resistance and articulated very well the type of organisation, political orientation and relationships with the masses that are needed in order to overcome these dilemmas. However, these same organisations remained unable to live up to what they mentally saw and preached. [. . .] In the end the prevailing petit bourgeois current swept them along like everyone else, for within their own ranks the struggle against its outlook, values, loyalties and modes of individual and collective behavior was never that strong in the first place.[121]

However, his fierce criticism of the events of 'Black September' and the new direction of Palestinian violence left him isolated and without political alternatives. After *Critical Study of the Thought of the Palestinian Resistance* was published, Arafat personally ordered his dismissal from the Palestine Research Centre in Beirut. From then on, Al-Azm was forced to use a pseudonym if he wished to publish in Palestinian publications in Lebanon.[122]

Al-Azm was no loner in developing his theses, however, and neither was his gradual dissociation from Palestinian organisations any exception. As a symptom of a collective development under the new Arab Left, his case also reflected his exchange of ideas with Leila S. Kadi, one of his political and personal confidants. Some of Al-Azm's published phrases reproduced verbatim the phrasing of Leila S. Kadi's concurrent letters to Moshé Machover in London. While both thinkers' writings reflected their disassociation from the Palestinian movements, they were also signs of new common ground with the Israeli socialists of Matzpen. Kadi and Al-Azm both travelled to London for their first visit in the summer of 1972 and returned two years later to co-found *Khamsin*. Thus, although the journal's founders had begun with revolutionary aspirations, their formation also represented a move in the opposite direction. The political revolutionaries were becoming passionate intellectuals, whose task was no longer to change the world, but to interpret historical events for academic purposes.

Journal of Revolutionary Socialists of the Middle East

There were six attendees at the autumn 1974 meetings in London, where the first four issues of *Khamsin* were outlined (to be released in Paris by Maspero over the years to come): Moshé and Ilana Machover, Emmanuel Farjoun, Eli Lobel, Sadik J. Al-Azm and Leila S. Kadi. The journal would, however, find readers far beyond major European cities; it was even for sale in some bookshops in the Middle East. By the time the thirteenth and final edition was published in 1987, the language had changed from French to English and the publisher had changed too: first, to London's Pluto Press and later to Ithaca Press. The cumulative forty-plus contributors represented many countries of origin in the Middle East, which was also a reflection of the periodical's broad thematic orientation. From the Israel–Palestine conflict and the Lebanese Civil War to the Iranian Revolution and Turkey's 1980 military coup, virtually all major incidents and conflicts in the region underwent universalistic critiques.

Khamsin attracted recruits from among Matzpen's close friends and allies from the outset, and soon became a magnet for Jewish and Israeli leftists who had links to the Middle East, but were now living in Europe. This development was largely thanks to Eli Lobel, who had already successfully recruited more collaborators and contributors in Paris, like Mikhal Marouan. The first couple of issues included a conversation on 'Judaism and Zionism' between Lobel, the Israeli human rights advocate Israel Shahak and – even more impressive – his friend, the distinguished leftist intellectual Maxime Rodinson.[123] Excited by the journal's perspective, the Londoners Avishai Ehrlich and Nira Yuval-Davis joined *Khamsin*. The two of them met in the mid-1960s during their studies at the Hebrew University of Jerusalem, by which point they were both involved in the struggle against the military administration. Ehrlich, a Tel Aviv-born sociologist, had been a member of the Communist Party's student organisation until the party's split in 1965. Three years later he left the country to visit some of the hotspots of the year's student revolt and eventually settled in London. Shortly after *Khamsin* was founded, he joined the journal's editorial collective along with Nira Yuval-Davis, who had already written her master's thesis on Matzpen. Both of their work for *Khamsin* was also crucial for their parallel scholarship on conflicts in the Middle East, the unsettling of settler societies, the politics of belonging and the intersection between nationalism and gender.[124] Later, the *Khamsin* collective was joined by Dina Hecht and Haim Bresheeth, two further Israeli leftists, who were likewise living in London. Meanwhile, in Tel Aviv, Ehud Ein-Gil decided to work with the journal. Born in 1950 in Petah Tikva, he joined Matzpen after a long political journey that led him from Aharon Amir's Action Staff for the Retention of the Territories to the radical left. His disillusioning experience of Israeli military service during the war of attrition and his arrest at a demonstration in support of the Israeli Black Panthers in 1972 were further steps on this path. After two more years during which he collaborated on a small journal called *Alternative* with Avi Glezerman, Ali Al'Azaari and Herzl Schubert, he finally joined Matzpen in 1974.[125] Having found a political home in the group's internationalism, he expanded his own efforts to an international level in *Khamsin*. For Ein-Gil, becoming acquainted with representatives of the Arab Left had been a formative experience, and he later frequently praised Lafif Lakhdar and Sadik J. Al-Azm in the Israeli press.[126] In 1981, when *Khamsin* ran an issue on the theme of 'politics of religion in the Middle East', his essay 'Religion, Zionism and Secularism' was printed alongside contributions by the two Arab critics of religion.[127]

Dan Diner came to the journal from Frankfurt, a stone's throw from Khalil Toama in Offenbach, who also sat on the editorial board of *Khamsin*. Diner had been the chair of both the West German and European associations of Jewish students and also co-founded the left-wing Zionist Borochov Press. The attacks on Eli Lobel during Lobel's visit to Frankfurt marked a crossroads in his life: 'For me, my experience of violence back then signified an emotional break and the start of my separation from left-wing Zionism', Diner later recalled.[128] Only a few years after his political conversion, he published in *Khamsin* the early musings that would lead to his monograph, *Israel in Palästina: Über Tausch und Gewalt im Vorderen Orient* (Israel in Palestine: On Trade and Violence in the Middle East).[129] From Vienna, John Bunzl joined the journal's editorial collective. Born in London, his socialist parents' place of exile, he was raised in Austria (his father's country of origin). The younger Bunzl's encounters with the antisemitism of post-war Austrian society led him to find a home in the New Left, particularly in Trotskyist circles. Troubled ever since his first visit to Israel by questions about the Israel–Palestine and the Middle Eastern conflict, he found answers in Matzpen's universalist outlook.[130] Unlike the leftist Israelis, Bunzl also identified politically with older traditions of a Jewish Diaspora class struggle, exemplified by General Jewish Labour Bund (often known simply as The Bund).[131]

The Tel Aviv-born, Berlin-based Mario Offenberg was also guided by a desire to resurrect Jewish historical experiences. Like the Middle East scholar Alexander Flores, Offenberg defended a dissertation on the Communist Party of Palestine; they both wrote about the party's political legacy in *Khamsin*.[132] Together with Eike Geisel, Offenberg had also published writing on the 'Jewish question' by Isaac Deutscher (1907–67), as well as a German translation of Nathan Weinstock's *Le sionisme contre Israël* (published as *Das Ende Israels*, 1975).[133] At the autumn 1977 DOK Leipzig film festival, he was awarded a PLO-sponsored prize for his documentary about the Palestinian 'Day of the Land'.[134] At *Khamsin*, Offenberg and Flores were now members of the journal's editorial collective. They found a home in the political utopia of a harmonious coexistence, the likes of which scarcely existed in the journal's region of focus.

The expanded involvement of leftists from Europe and Israel in *Khamsin* was only part of the story. In parallel, the journal had become a gathering place for internationalist leftists from all over the Arab–Islamic world; it thus covered the various other crises in the Middle East. More and more, its contributors' articles and essays were reacting to the social shift of the 1970s, marked by the increasing politicisation of religion and a fissure of the region along ethnic and religious lines. It was against this political backdrop, soon after the *journal's founding*, that Kanan Makiya (b. 1949) joined the editorial team and began publishing under the pen name Mohammad Ja'far. Growing up in Iraq to a British mother had made Makiya feel like an 'insider with an outsider's perspective'; at a young age, he came to doubt the rhetoric peddled there about a soon-to-come Arab victory against Israel during the Six-Day War, for he had information to the contrary as a BBC listener.[135] When he left to study at the Massachusetts Institute of Technology, he quickly found his place among American leftists and dedicated himself to solidarity with Palestine. This was how he met Emmanuel Farjoun of Matzpen, who impressed him with his critique of his own society, as well as his wealth of socialist knowledge. They soon became close personal and political friends, a friendship that also became decisive for Makiya's road to *Khamsin*.[136] The journal offered him a platform for his support for, and recognition of, Palestinian nationhood and self-determination. At the same time, it provided a forum for his growing criticisms of Palestinian organisations. Beyond all their internal rifts, his dissociation was primarily due to the role of the PLO, under Arafat, in the first phase of the Lebanese Civil War, in 1975–6. 'I hope that we can have a discussion', wrote Makiya in *Khamsin*, '[on] the mafia-like behaviour of the PLO during the Lebanese civil war and the fact that it stands today as probably the most loathed organisation amongst the Lebanese masses (Christian and Moslem alike) [. . .]'.[137]

Apart from that, the Lebanese Civil War became the subject of an independent conflict for *Khamsin*, because it violently unleashed the political tensions over religious affiliation in the clash between the country's Muslims and Maronite Christians, and because the Palestinians' involvement and the

Syrian intervention transformed it into a proxy war for other fundamental sources of strife throughout the region.[138] For these reasons, the journal's contributors resisted a 'heroic interpretation' of the conflict that separated the warring parties into the progressive left of Kamal Jumblatt's Lebanese National Movement and the reactionary forces of the Maronite Phalange.[139] While both main adversaries were waging the war as a religious, political and economic conflict, *Khamsin* interpreted the escalation basically as a failure of confessionalism and of Lebanon's National Pact of 1943. Its approach of dividing parliamentary seats and government posts according to religious affiliation had intensified the country's religious antagonisms, instead of neutralising them.[140] The competing religious claims to the truth merged into a fight for political supremacy and exploded violently in the war. The conflict took on a growing territorial dimension and caused displacements motivated by ethnicity and religion. In the face of these trends, the Lebanese activist Nada Kadir – and, years later, the London-based émigrée Mai Ghoussoup – found an opportunity in *Khamsin* to defend the idea of a Lebanon that transcended religions and factions.[141] Partly, this meant demanding the restoration of state sovereignty over the full territory of Lebanon on the basis of a shared Arab culture beyond Christian or Muslim affiliation. On the other hand, this perspective was linked to the secularity of the state. 'This, perhaps', Nada Kadir concluded, 'may ultimately be Lebanon's contribution to severing the bond between Arabism and Islam'.[142] The discussion of the Lebanon War in *Khamsin* therefore extended the question of the relationship between political Islam and the political culture of the Arab world.

Soon enough, the 1979 Islamic Revolution in Iran became the focus of this debate. After the authoritarian regime of the Shah (Muhammed Reza Pahlavi) was overthrown, Ayatollah Ruhollah Khomeini seized political control in February 1979. The subsequent declaration of the Islamic Republic of Iran marked a major shift: before, political theology had exerted power under the surface; now, religion would be the explicit foundation of politics and the state. In contrast to some on the left, who had initially supported the anti-Shah movement as a mass protest and even greeted the nouveau regime with euphoria, the establishment of the Islamic Republic prompted political fears and principled opposition in *Khamsin*. Writing under the pseudonym of Mohammed Ja'far, Kanan Makiya and his wife Afsaneh Najmabadi (Azar

Tabari) stressed that the Iranian Revolution was proof that a mass uprising could be reactionary. After the revolt, the Iranian-born Najmabadi had travelled to Tehran in support of women's liberation struggles, but soon witnessed the nouveau régime's 'August 1979 attacks against the press, the left and Kurdistan'.[143] Meanwhile, on the front pages of *Le Monde*, Maxime Rodinson was arguing against the ecstatic Michel Foucault and sounding a note of caution, in reference to the anti-Shah movement, about 'a provisional alliance against one form of despotism which usually numbered among its members people dreaming of another form of despotism'.[144] This new face of political Islam in Iran meant reviving older forms of law with religious justifications; accordingly, he responded to Foucault's hopes for a new 'political spirituality' with his own fears of an 'archaic fascism' – 'an authoritarian and totalitarian state whose political police would brutally enforce the moral and social order'.[145] Similarly, Makiya and Najmabadi emphasised in *Khamsin* that the Iranian masses' turn towards Islam was not a sign of increased religious devotion, but a political act: a 'revolt against the present and the future, to reconquer a mythical past that had never really existed'.[146] It was Lafif Lakhdar who, in a far-ranging essay, asked why Islam retained that political aspect in the Middle East. Why, indeed, was there such a conspicuous, proliferating craving for its archaic forms?[147] The events of 1979 thus revived questions from 1967, with fresh urgency. In view of the visible rise of the Muslim Brotherhood in Egypt and other Arab countries, around the same time as the Iranian coup, Lakhdar turned his attention to the failed modernisation movements of the nineteenth and early twentieth centuries. For lack of a revolution in civil society, a 'self-sufficient modern state which does not need to lean on the crutches of Islam' had never been established. In the Arab and Islamic worlds, Lakhdar concluded, the state had remained a 'confessional state'.[148]

What began with the a gradual rise of political Islam after the Six-Day War and culminated in the Iranian Revolution and the creation of a political theocracy became a tragic symbol of the failure of a socialist dream of a progressive, emancipatory revolution. When even some on the European Left began supporting the Arab–Islamic recourse to premodern religious traditions, seeing this as a rejection of the colonialist and imperialist West, *Khamsin* viewed this turn as an abandonment of traditional leftist positions. If both Foucault and the Trotskyists of the Fourth International considered the

Iranian Revolution a step in the right direction, Kanan Makiya and Afsaneh Najmabadi saw it as final proof that the existing descriptive categories were no longer adequate.[149] In their article, they explained that apart from the now-secondary economic demands, 'hostility to this theocratic Islamic regime and the very idea of an Islamic republic' must therefore 'form the central axis of a revolutionary socialist programme'.[150] However, the growing emphasis on the independent importance of political systems over societies' economic structures brought a radical transformation of the Arab leftists in *Khamsin*'s orbit. Gradually, they came to base their defence of individual freedoms and rights, including the rights of women and national minorities in the region, on the European Enlightenment's emancipatory principles and universalist tradition – despite the stain of the West's colonising history.[151]

This shift also applied in part to Lafif Lakhdar, whose political hopes for an emancipation of the Arab world had grown out of confidence in universalist anticolonialism and the prospects of an Arab revolution. Yet by the late 1970s, his political analyses about the failure of secularism in the Arab world were also pointing to the experiences of the European Reformation and the neutralisation of religion in the modern nation-state.[152] Many years later, beyond his critique of political Islam and his demand for the secularisation of the Arab world, he tried to apply the Jewish tradition of *dina demalchuta dina* (the law of the ruler is the law) to the integration of Muslims in Europe.[153] Likewise, Sadik J. Al-Azm's critique of Edward Said's book *Orientalism* (1978), which was first printed in *Khamsin*, was concerned about a negative essentialisation of the West, as presented in Said's bestselling book.[154] Although Al-Azm positioned himself as a critic of colonialism and imperialism, he cautioned against Said's general distrust of the West. Such a sweeping dismissal, especially if it rejected the universalist traditions of secularisation and the Enlightenment, was tantamount to 'Orientalism in reverse'. He later extended his project of Arab self-criticism with a critique of Occidentalism and a quest for possibilities for secularisation within Islam.[155]

No one embodied the shift towards Western political and theoretical traditions more than Kanan Makiya. In 1989, when he published his most important book, *The Republic of Fear*, under the pseudonym Samir Al-Khalil, his fundamental analysis of the totalitarian nature of Saddam Hussein's rule in Iraq was rooted in the political theories of John Stuart Mill, Thomas Hobbes, Isaiah Berlin and, especially, Hannah Arendt's *Origins of Totalitarianism*.[156]

Verso Books, a leftist publisher, lost interest in publishing Makiya when it came to this sort of political analysis. After more than seventy rejections, the editors at California University Press agreed to take the book. Makiya's turn towards the West became more than theoretical. Years later, after 11 September 2001, when the United States was planning to intervene in Iraq and overthrow Saddam Hussein, Makiya (as an exiled Iraqi) had become one of the resolute advocates of the US Army deposing the Iraqi dictator. 'If I can reduce the amount of human suffering in the world by even a jot, if it is possible to demonstrate that overall suffering has been reduced, then the right position in politics is always to be for that reduction', he later explained in response to leftist criticisms of his turn towards realpolitik.[157]

Witnessing the collapse of their former utopia and the failure of emancipation and progress, few *Khamsin* contributors took a path as rigorous as Makiya's. His position in favour of the Iraq War caused a huge rift in his longstanding friendship with Emmanuel Farjoun. Back in 1980, in his book on the Israel–Palestine conflict, Dan Diner had already considered the possibility of returning to previous historical spaces and imperial orders. He linked the future of a binational Palestine with a 'transition period of international guarantees, including multinational troops in Greater Palestine'. Hence, the idea of a 'de-facto re-Mandatisation' came to replace his former revolutionary hopes for the region.[158] Hardly anyone from the *Khamsin* collective remained untouched by the decline of former hopes in a revolutionary transformation of the region. For some of them – Alexander Flores, Sadik J. Al-Azm, John Bunzl and Dan Diner – it prompted a retreat from politics and the beginning of academic careers. Others, such as Mario Offenberg, rediscovered their Jewish roots and turned to religion. In the early 1990s, Offenberg became the executive director of Berlin's Orthodox Adass Yisroel congregation.[159]

Eli Lobel was the only one existentially wounded by the collapse of the political utopia. After the Paris uprising of May 1968, his political euphoria was largely fuelled by dreams of overcoming the battle lines of the Middle East; dreams of this historic chance to shape history in the spirit of an undivided humanity. He was especially shattered to see the outbreak of Lebanon's civil war and the country's subsequent internal collapse, which buried those dreams in the rubble. 'He became so negative', Akiva Orr later recalled of their meeting at the time. 'Whatever people suggested to him, he would answer: That won't help anything. Nothing is going to change.'[160] That

Palestinian organisations were fighting on Jumblatt's side played a significant role in his lingering disillusionment. Unlike some in Matzpen, who sided with the Palestinians in Lebanon, he argued that their organisations there had turned into oppressors of the Lebanese masses and were among the first 'to drop indiscriminatory bombs on neighbourhoods [of Beirut] and entire villages'. Lobel therefore warned against taking sides in a conflict that no longer accommodated a universalist perspective. 'This war is not our war', he wrote to his Matzpen friends in Israel in October 1976.[161]

Devastating present-day experiences from the period before his death were accompanied by the re-emergence of a long-concealed chapter of the past: the period of Nazi rule and the Holocaust.[162] Not long after the Second World War, when he reported for *Al HaMishmar* from Berlin, he wrote with sensitivity about both: the new beginnings of Jewish life there and migration to Israel in the shadow of catastrophe.[163] As the Israel–Palestine conflict took centre stage, past experiences were increasingly sidelined by the urgency of resolving the conflict between Israeli Jews and Palestinian Arabs. The genocide never lost its hold on him, however. 'Painful memories of the Holocaust [had] traumatised Eli', Lafif Lakhdar later wrote of his friend.[164] In the late 1970s, the costs of providing for his family raised the long-neglected question of whether Lobel should apply for the compensation to which he was entitled as a result of his parents' forced departure from Nazi Germany.[165] At the same time, that question awakened much deeper memories of his family's fate during the Second World War. Lakhdar recalled how Eli 'kept telling me about the persecution of his cousin, who was the same age as him'.[166] Most of their relatives had not escaped the Nazis' collective death sentence. Lobel faced a nearly intolerable impasse: an aporia between the drive for a universalistic resolution that would transcend all conflicts between ethnic and religious groups – and the experience of annihilation on the sole basis of Jewish descent. It was that aporia that crushed all hopes of historical progress.

Notes

1. Eli Lobel, Letter to Moshé Machover (8 June 1974), Private Archive of Moshé Machover, London. Lobel enclosed the Hebrew-language document *Khamsin Programme*, dated May 1974, which was later reprinted in French in a similar form under the title 'La stratégie révolutionnaire au Proche-Orient', in Khamsin. *Revue des socialistes révolutionnaires du Proche-Orient* 1 (1975).

2. Leila S. Kadi, Letter to Moshé Machover (27 August 1969), Private Archive of Moshé Machover, London.
3. Leila S. Kadi (ed.), *Arab Summit Conferences and the Palestine Problem: 1936–1950* (Beirut: Research Center, 1966); Leila S. Kadi, *Histadrut* (Beirut: Palestine Liberation Organization, Research Center, 1967) [Arabic]; Leila S. Kadi, *A Survey of American-Israeli Relations* (Beirut: Palestine Liberation Organization, Research Center, 1969).
4. Kadi, Letter to Moshé Machover (27 August 1969).
5. Moshé Machover, Letter to Leila S. Kadi (22 July 1971), Private Archive of Moshé Machover, London: 'I am referring to the remark made by Gh. Kanafani in his introduction to your book, alleging that "the Matzpen people in London have been infiltrated by the Shin Beth". Now, you & I know very well (but the reader of your book would not know) that Mr. Kanafani has absolutely no direct knowledge of Matzpen in London or anywhere else. His remark can therefore base either on shady sources or a figment of his own imagination.' See also the Preface by Ghassan Kanafani to Leila S. Kadi, *The Israeli Socialist Organization (Matzpen)* (Beirut: Palestine Liberation Organization, Research Center, 1971), p. 9 [Arabic]. I am grateful to Walid Abd el Gawad for his help with the translation.
6. Leila S. Kadi, Letter to Moshé Machover (1 August 1971), Private Archive of Moshé Machover, London.
7. Moshé Machover, Letter to Leila S. Kadi (6 February 1972), Private Archive of Moshé Machover, London.
8. Leila S. Kadi, Letter to Moshé Machover (23 February 1972), Private Archive of Moshé Machover, London. Kadi was referring here to the attempted hijacking of a Jordanian airliner. The Iraqi Saleh Mahdi Mustaufi, who was stopped by security guards, first claimed he was a member of Fatah, which the Palestinian organisation denied. A short time later, he declared himself a member of the Democratic Front for the Liberation of Palestine and stated that his act was intended to 'make trouble for Al-Fatah'. In the end, the Jordanian Movement for National Liberation claimed responsibility for the attempted hijacking. See 'Attempted Hijack of Jordanian Airliner', *Arab Report & Record* 4 ([16–29 February] 1972), p. 102.
9. Leila S. Kadi, Letter to Moshé Machover (22 May 1974), Private Archive of Moshé Machover, London.
10. Ibid.
11. Moshé Machover, Letter to Leila S. Kadi (12 June 1974), Private Archive of Moshé Machover, London.
12. Ibid.

13. The Israeli Socialist Organisation, 'The Parisian PLO Representative at a Matzpen Member's Funeral in Paris. "Eli Lobel Was a Friend of the Palestinian People"', https://matzpen.org/1979-10-13/נציג-אשף-בפאריס-בהלוויית-איש-מצפן-אל/ (accessed 21 April 2020) [Hebrew].
14. 'The Parisian PLO Representative at a Matzpen Member's Funeral in Paris', *Haaretz* (14 October 1979) [Hebrew]; Arnon Yaffe, 'A PLO Representative Grieves for Eli Lobel', *Al Hamishmar* (9 October 1979) [Hebrew]; shortly thereafter, an appreciative obituary was published in the Arabic newspaper *Al-Hurriya*: 'A Salute to the Militant Eli Lobel', *Al-Hurriya* 937 (22 October 1979) [Arabic].
15. See the autobiography of Eli Lobel's cousin, Ruth W. Pagirsky, *Memoirs* (New York: Pagirsky Family Press, 2013).
16. Hannu Reime, *Century as a Fate. The Life and Times of Eli Lobel*, 31 December 2002, Finnish Broadcasting Company (Channel 1), radio documentary. I am grateful to Hannu Reime for providing a transcription of the radio recording.
17. C. D. Edwards, 'Interview with Eli Lobel. Matzpen's Voice Abroad', 1972, Berkeley, audio recording.
18. Beinin, *Was the Red Flag Flying There?*, pp. 25–31; Hattis, *The Bi-National Idea in Palestine During Mandatory Times*, pp. 293–8.
19. Amos Kenan, 'Meeting Palestinians', *Yediot Aharonot* (13 September 1985), pp. 16–17 [Hebrew].
20. Amos Kenan, 'A Short Trip to the Hermon', in Amos Kenan, *Israel: A Wasted Victory* (Tel Aviv: Amikam, 1970), pp. 152–4 [first: *Yediot Aharonot* (19 June 1969)].
21. Sarit Fuks, 'Yaakov is Emanuel is Eli', *Ma'ariv. Weekend Supplement* (16 July 1993), pp. 20–4, at p. 21 [Hebrew]; Lockman, 'The Left in Israel. Zionism vs. Socialism', p. 6.
22. P. Weiss, 'Among the Refugees in Gaza (Series of Four Parts)', *Al Hamishmar* (4 April 1952); (7 April 1952); (11 April 1952); (13 April 1952) [Hebrew].
23. After the publication of Lobel's first articles from Egypt, but before his series of articles about the refugees in the Gaza Strip, the editorial board of Al HaMishmar already felt compelled to print a letter by the publisher of *L'Observateur* corroborating the existence of P. Weiss, though acknowledging it was a pseudonym. See 'The Publisher's Witnesses', Al HaMishmar (24 March 1952), at p. 2 [Hebrew].
24. P. Weiss, 'Among the Refugees in Gaza. Part 4: The City Cut Off from its Homefront', *Al Hamishmar* (13 April 1952), p. 2 [Hebrew].
25. Quoted from Fuks, 'Yaakov is Emanuel is Eli', pp. 21 and 24.
26. Quoted in Roli Rosen, 'Eli Lobel Committed Suicide in Fall of '79', *Kol Ha'Ir* (11 June 1993), pp. 65–70, at p. 66 [Hebrew].

27. 'A Mapam Official in the West was Expelled from the Party', *Ma'ariv* (14 January 1953), p. 4 [Hebrew].
28. Ghilan, *How Israel Lost its Soul*, p. 153.
29. Beinin, *Was the Red Flag Flying There?*, p. 150.
30. Kenan, 'Meeting Palestinians'; see also Beinin, *Was the Red Flag Flying There?*, p. 150.
31. Rosen, 'Eli Lobel Committed Suicide in Fall of '79', p. 67.
32. Ibid.
33. Reime, *Century as a Fate*, p. 1.
34. 'An Israeli Life. Obituary for Eli Lobel', *Haolam Hazeh* 2197 (10 October 1979), pp. 35 and 38, at p. 35 [Hebrew].
35. Reime, *Century as a Fate*.
36. Avnery, 'The Silent Idealist'; Amos Kenan, 'Hubris', *Yediot Aharonot* (4 June 1982), p. 9 [Hebrew]; see also Beinin, *The Dispersion of Egyptian Jewry*, pp. 165–6.
37. Kenan, 'Hubris'; Dan Diner, 'Für ein Israel der Gegenwart. Eli Löbel oder Eine politische Gegenbiographie', *Blätter für deutsche und internationale Politik* 43: 5 (1998), pp. 613–17, at p. 614.
38. Dan Diner, 'Zum Tod von Genossen', *Links* 116 (1979), p. 4; Samir Amin, *A Life Looking Forward: Memoirs of an Independent Marxist* (London, New York: Zed Books, 2006), pp. 109–51.
39. Avnery, *Optimistic*, p. 560.
40. Bar-On, *In Pursuit of Peace*, pp. 19–22.
41. Amos Kenan, 'Who Is Afraid of Joe Golan?', *Yediot Aharonot* (8 September 1978), pp. 12–14 [Hebrew].
42. 'An Israeli Life'; Avnery, *Optimistic*, p. 560.
43. 'An Israeli Life', p. 38.
44. Ibid., p. 35.
45. Ibid; see also Rosen, 'Eli Lobel Committed Suicide in Fall of '79', p. 67.
46. *ISRAC*, published by C.A.R.I.S.E. (Comité d'action revolutionnaire Israélien à l'étranger, lit. Committee of Revolutionary Israeli Action Abroad), at first consisted of translations from the English-language publication *Israca*. By the time the fifth issue appeared under the title *Sur la conception matérialiste de la question Juive* (On the Materialist Conception of the Jewish Question), Lobel himself took charge of shaping the magazine.
47. Ygal Sarneh, 'In Nahalal They Think He is a Traitor', *Yediot Aharonot* (7 February 1992), pp. 22–3 and 54 [Hebrew].
48. Eric Rouleau, *Truths and Lies in the Middle East: Memoirs of a Veteran Journalist, 1952-2012* (Cairo, New York: The American University in Cairo Press, 2019).

49. See, for example, Moshé Machover's article 'Pour un état Judéo-Arabe', *Le Monde* (9 January 1969). For more on Rouleau's trip to Israel, see Halevi, Allers-retours, p. 61. The first report by Rouleau about Matzpen dates back to 20 May 1967, when he wrote an article for *Le Monde* about the Paris gathering of Arab students for Nakba Day, at which Nathan Weinstock read Matzpen's statement as one of the speakers. See the section on 'Foreign Natives' in Chapter 2.
50. Sabri Geries, *Les Arabes en Israël: Précédé de Les juifs et la Palestine par Eli Lobel* (Paris: François Maspero, 1969).
51. In addition to the French original, there is an Italian and German edition: Sabri Geries, *Gli Arabi in Israele: Con un Saggio di Eli Lobel* (Roma: Editori Riuniti, 1970); Geries and Lobel, *Die Araber in Israel*; however, the English translation – Ahmad E. Kodsy and Eli Lobel, *The Arab World and Israel* (New York: Monthly Review, 1970) – only contains the introductory essay by Lobel, 'Palestine and the Jews', pp. 63–137, and another essay by Ahmed El-Kodsy (Samir Amin).
52. Wolfgang Kraushaar, *Fischer in Frankfurt: Karriere eines Aussenseiters* (Hamburg: Hamburger Edition, 2001), pp. 202–15.
53. *Haolam Hazeh* 1659 (18 June 1969), at p. 19 [Hebrew].
54. Quoted in Kraushaar, *Fischer in Frankfurt*, p. 205.
55. Ibid., pp. 205–7; Abdallah Frangi, *Der Gesandte: Mein Leben für Palästina; Hinter den Kulissen der Nahost-Politik* (München: Heyne HC, 2011), pp. 140–3.
56. Rosen, 'Eli Lobel Committed Suicide in Fall of '79', p. 69. The badly injured victim was Klaus Rürup, who lived in Karlsruhe, Germany, and was married to Ruth Rürup-Braun. They were both close friends of Lobel and represented Matzpen's positions in Germany.
57. Fuks, 'Yaakov is Emanuel is Eli', p. 21.
58. Quoted in Rosen, 'Eli Lobel Committed Suicide in Fall of '79', p. 69.
59. Diner, 'Zum Tod von Genossen', p. 4.
60. 'An Israeli Life', p. 38.
61. Rosen, 'Eli Lobel Committed Suicide in Fall of '79', p. 70.
62. L. Lakhdar, Email from Lafif Lakhdar, via Kristin Couper, to the Author (2 April 2009): 'Les discussions se faisaient entre moi et Eli sur l'avenir de la paix au Proche Orient – une réconciliation judéo-arabe. Le slogan de Hassan II, roi de Maroc, "Refaire l'Andalousie" nous enchantait tous les deux.'; for more on King Hassan's reference to multinational and multireligious Andalusia, see Samir Ben-Layashi and Bruce Maddy-Weitzman, 'Myth, History and "Realpolitik". Morocco and its Jewish Community', *Journal of Modern Jewish Studies* 9: 1 (2010), pp. 89–106.
63. Shimon Ballas, *Last Winter* (Jerusalem: Keter, 1984), p. 34 [Hebrew].
64. Ein-Gil, 'The Roots of Jihad'.

65. Ibid.
66. Abdulkhaliq Hussein, 'Farewell to Lafif', http://almuslih.com/index.php?option=com_content&view=article&id=253:farewell-to-lafif&catid=38:obstacles-to-reform&Itemid=207 (accessed 7 October 2019).
67. Ibid; see also Pessah Shinar, 'Ulama, Marabouts and Government. An Overview of their Relationships in the French Colonial Maghrib', *Israel Oriental Studies* 10 (1980), pp. 211–29, at p. 221.
68. Ein-Gil, 'The Roots of Jihad'.
69. Menahem Milson, 'Lafif Lakhdar. A European Muslim Reformist', *Memri. Inquiry and Analysis Series* 314 (5 January 2007).
70. Fadi A. Bardawil, *Revolution and Disenchantment. Arab Marxism and the Binds of Emancipation* (Durham and London: Duke University Press, 2020), pp. 173 and 235, note 17; Ein-Gil, 'The Roots of Jihad'.
71. 'Conclusion', in Frantz Fanon, *The Wretched of the Earth* (London: Penguin Books, [1961] 2001), pp. 251–5.
72. See Mohammed Harbi, 'Bauern und Revolution', in Bassam Tibi (ed.), *Die arabische Linke: Hrsg. u. eingel. von Bassam Tibi. (Aus d. Arab. von Bassam Tibi)*, (Dritte Welt) (Frankfurt a.M.: Europäische Verlags-Anstalt, 1969), pp. 123–37.
73. Bassam Tibi, 'Einführung. Skizze einer Geschichte des Sozialismus in den arabischen Ländern', in Bassam Tibi (ed.), *Die arabische Linke: Hrsg. u. eingel. von Bassam Tibi. (Aus d. Arab. von Bassam Tibi)*, (Dritte Welt) (Frankfurt a.M.: Europäische Verlags-Anstalt, 1969), pp. 7–41, at pp. 38–9; Bassam Tibi, 'Vorbemerkung des Herausgebers', in Bassam Tibi (ed.), *Die arabische Linke: Hrsg. u. eingel. von Bassam Tibi. (Aus d. Arab. von Bassam Tibi)*, (Dritte Welt) (Frankfurt a.M.: Europäische Verlags-Anstalt, 1969), pp. 119–22.
74. Tibi, 'Einführung', pp. 38–9.
75. Milson, 'Lafif Lakhdar'.
76. Hussein, 'Farewell to Lafif'.
77. Ibid.
78. Tibi, 'Einführung', p. 38.
79. Udo Wolter, 'Die Arbeit des Global Theorist', *Jungle World* 51 (12 December 2001).
80. Lafif Lakhdar (ed.), *Lenin: Texts on the Attitude towards Religion (New Anthology)* (Beirut: Dar al-Talia, 1972) [Arabic].
81. Lafif Lakhdar, 'From the Critique of Heaven to the Critique of Earth', in Lafif Lakhdar (ed.), *Lenin: Texts on the Attitude towards Religion (New Anthology)* (Beirut: Dar al-Talia, 1972); quoted from Emmanuel Sivan, 'Arab Revisionist Historians', in Emmanuel Sivan, *Interpretations of Islam: Past and Present* (Princeton: Darwin Press, 1985), pp. 45–72, at pp. 54–5.

82. Ein-Gil, 'The Roots of Jihad'.
83. Quoted in Ajami, *The Arab Predicament*, p. 32.
84. Ibid., pp. 30–48; Tareq Y. Ismael, *The Arab Left* (Syracuse: Syracuse University, 1976), pp. 101–17.
85. Ajami, *The Arab Predicament*, pp. 30–48.
86. Ibid., pp. 32–3; see also Dan Diner, *Lost in the Sacred: Why the Muslim World Stood Still* (Princeton: Princeton University Press, 2009).
87. Al-Azm, *Self-Criticism After the Defeat*.
88. Nissim Rejwan, 'A Dissenting Voice in the Arab World', *Midstream* ([April] 1971), pp. 71–80, at p. 72.
89. Al-Azm, *Self-Criticism After the Defeat*, pp. 51–2.
90. Ibid., pp. 39–40.
91. Quoted from Rejwan, 'A Dissenting Voice in the Arab World', p. 73.
92. Ibid.
93. Al-Azm, *Self-Criticism After the Defeat*, p. 114.
94. Ibid., pp. 114–26.
95. Ibid., p. 118.
96. Sadik J. Al-Azm, *Critique of Religious Thought* (Berlin: Gerlach Press, 2015).
97. Ibid.
98. See also Sadik J. Al-Azm, 'A Criticism of Religious Thought', in John J. Donohue and John L. Esposito (eds), *Islam in Transition: Muslim Perspectives* (New York: Oxford University Press, 2007), pp. 113–19; Sadik J. Al-Azm, 'Islamisches Denken in der heutigen Welt', in Evangelischen Gemeinde Beirut (ed.), *Libanon. Kleine Orientierung* (Beirut: Evangelisch Gemeinde, 1969), pp. 70–5.
99. Stefan Wild, 'Gott und Mensch im Libanon', *Der Islam: Journal of the History and Culture of the Middle East* 48: 2 (1971), pp. 206–53, at p. 229.
100. 'Documents from the Trial of the Author and Publisher', in Sadik J Al-Azm, *Critique of Religious Thought* (Berlin, Germany: Gerlach Press, 2015), pp. 207–26; Wild, 'Gott und Mensch im Libanon', pp. 229–32.
101. Ajami, *The Arab Predicament*, pp. 174–6.
102. Ibid., pp. 174–6.
103. Wild, 'Gott und Mensch im Libanon', p. 231.
104. Lafif Lakhdar, 'Zur Situation in der palästinensischen Widerstandsbewegung', *Al-Djabha. Die Front* 3/4 (1969), pp. 11–15, at p. 14.
105. Al-Azm, *Self-Criticism After the Defeat*, pp. 61–72.
106. See Kamil, *Die Araber und der Holocaust*, p. 152.

107. Lakhdar, 'Zur Situation in der palästinensischen Widerstandsbewegung', pp. 11–12.
108. Lafif Lakhdar, 'A Letter from 'Afif al-Akhdar to Al-'arabi Bu-Hali (12.12.1968)', in Al-Sherrara (Spark) (ed.), *The Arab Left and the Palestinian Revolution* (Durham: The Committee for the Support of the Popular Democratic Front for the Liberation of Palestine, 1969), pp. 1–11, at pp. 8–9 [first: *Al-Hurria* 463 (12 Mai 1969)].
109. Ibid., pp. 2–3.
110. Ajami, *The Arab Predicament*, p. 177.
111. Lakhdar, 'Zur Situation in der palästinensischen Widerstandsbewegung', pp. 11–12.
112. See Morris, *Righteous Victims*, p. 372.
113. Lafif Lakhdar and Mustapha Khayati, 'Waiting for the Massacre', *On Target. Socialist Journal Concerned with the Middle East* 1: Winter (1975/6), pp. 39–53, at p. 45.
114. Ibid., pp. 42 and 46.
115. Yezid Sayigh, *Armed Struggle and the Search for State: The Palestinian National Movement 1949–1993* (Oxford, New York: Oxford University Press, 2011), p. 303.
116. Ajami, *The Arab Predicament*, pp. 180–1.
117. Sadik J. Al-Azm, *A Critical Study of the Thought of the Palestinian Resistance* (Beirut: Dar al-'Awda, 1973); an English summary is available in Sadik J. Al-Azm, 'The Palestine Resistance Movement Reconsidered', in Edward Said (ed.), *The Arabs Today: Alternatives for Tomorrow* (Columbus: Forum Associates, 1973), pp. 121–35.
118. Al-Azm, 'The Palestine Resistance Movement Reconsidered', pp. 122–3.
119. Ibid., p. 122.
120. Quoted from Manfred Sing, 'Brothers in Arms. How Palestinian Maoists Turned Jihadists', *Die Welt des Islams* 51: 1 (2011), pp. 1–44, at p. 28.
121. Al-Azm, 'The Palestine Resistance Movement Reconsidered', p. 134.
122. Ghada Talhami, 'An Interview with Sadik Al-Azm', *Arab Studies Quarterly* 19: 3 (1997), pp. 113–26, at p. 122.
123. Eli Lobel, Maxime Rodinson and Israël Shahak, 'Judaïsme et sionisme', *Khamsin. Revue des Socialistes Revolutionnaires du Proche-Orient* 1 (1975), pp. 67–81.
124. Avishai Ehrlich, 'Settler Societies', in Paola Cardullo, Rahila Gupta and Jamie Hakim (eds), *Sociology, Politics, Thinking and Acting: A Festschrift for Nira Yuval-Davies* (London: Centre for Research on Migration, Refugees and Belonging, University of East London, 2014), pp. 48–52; Nira Yuval-Davis, 'Avishai Ehrlich',

in Nea Ehrlich, Lesley Marks and Nira Yuval-Davis (eds), *The Work of Avishai Ehrlich: Political Sociologist, Activist and Public Intellectual* (Newcastle upon Tyne: Cambridge Scholars, 2013), pp. 171–7.
125. Erel, *Matzpen*, p. 68–9.
126. Ehud Ein-Gil, 'In One Point We Will Remain the Same. In the Love for this Middle East. Ehud Ein-Gil Talks About Meetings with Arab Revolutionary Intellectuals', *Haaretz* (1 March 2017) [Hebrew]; Ein-Gil, 'The Roots of Jihad'.
127. Ehud Ein-Gil, 'Religion, Zionism, and Secularism', *Khamsin. Journal of Revolutionary Socialists of the Middle East* 8 (1981), pp. 105–20.
128. Diner, 'Zum Tod von Genossen'.
129. Dan Diner, 'Marché mondial, sionisme et violence. Thèses sur l'integration capitaliste du Mashreq et ses consequences politiques', *Khamsin. Revue des Socialistes Revolutionnaires du Proche-Orient* 4 (1977), pp. 66–87.
130. John Bunzl, 'Left Memories', in Raimund Löw (ed.), *Die Fantasie und die Macht: 1968 und danach* (Wien: Czernin, 2006), pp. 261–73.
131. John Bunzl, *Klassenkampf in der Diaspora: Zur Geschichte der judischen Arbeiterbewegung, Schriftenreihe des Ludwig Boltzmann Instituts fur Geschichte der Arbeiterbewegung* (Wien: Europaverlag, 1975), vol. 5.
132. Alexander Flores, *Nationalismus und Sozialismus im arabischen Osten: Kommunistische Partei und arabische Nationalbewegung in Palästina, 1919–1948, Reihe Dissertationen zur Politik und Ökonomie in der Dritten Welt* (Münster: Periferia Verlag, 1980). See also Flores' contributions in *Khamsin* 7 (1979): 'Communist Parties in the Middle East'.
133. Weinstock, *Das Ende Israels?*; Isaac Deutscher, *Die ungelöste Judenfrage*, ed. by Eike Geisel and Mario Offenberg (Berlin: Rotbuch-Verlag, 1977).
134. Horst Richter and Horst Schiefelbein, 'Manifestation brüderlicher Solidarität', *Neues Deutschland* (26 November 1977), p. 12.
135. Alan Johnson, 'Putting Cruelty First. An Interview with Kanan Makiya', in Alan Johnson (ed.), *Global Politics after 9/11: The Democratiya Interviews* (London: Foreign Policy Centre, 2007), pp. 93–137, at p. 94.
136. Ibid., p. 95.
137. Ibid., p. 96.
138. Lafif Lakhdar, 'De la guerre à la réconciliation arabo-palestinienne. Entretien avec Lafif Lakhdar', *Khamsin. Revue des Socialistes Revolutionnaires du Proche-Orient* 4 (1977), pp. 6–24.
139. Jon Rothschild, 'Civil War in Lebanon', in Jon Rothschild (ed.), *Forbidden Agendas: Intolerance and Defiance in the Middle East* (London: Saqi Books, 1984), pp. 233–5, at p. 234.

140. See Alexander Flores, *Die arabische Welt: Ein kleines Sachlexikon* (Stuttgart: Philipp Reclam, 2008), pp. 139–41 and 150.
141. Nada Kadir, 'In the Maelstrom of Confessionalism', in Jon Rothschild (ed.), *Forbidden Agendas: Intolerance and Defiance in the Middle East* (London: Saqi Books, 1984), pp. 237–59 [first: *Khamsin* 3 (1976), pp. 101–23]; Magida Salman, 'The Lebanese Communities and their Little Wars', in Jon Rothschild (ed.), *Forbidden Agendas: Intolerance and Defiance in the Middle East* (London: Saqi Books, 1984), pp. 260–8 [first: *Khamsin* 10 (1983), pp. 13–20]; Mai Ghoussup, who wrote for *Khamsin* under the name Magida Salman, grew up in Lebanon and only moved to London in 1977 after an incident in which she tried to transport a wounded Palestinian to a hospital and sustained a serious eye injury. In London, the artist and writer wrote for *Khamsin* while co-running the Al Saqi bookshop and press with André Gaspar. See also Mai Ghoussoub, *Leaving Beirut: Women and the Wars Within* (London: SAQI, 2007).
142. Kadir, 'In the Maelstrom of Confessionalism', p. 259.
143. Mohammed Ja'far (Makiya, Kanan) and Afsaneh Najmabadi (Tabari, Azar), 'Iran. Islam and the Struggle for Socialism', in Jon Rothschild (ed.), *Forbidden Agendas: Intolerance and Defiance in the Middle East* (London: Saqi Books, 1984), pp. 322–48, at p. 333 [first: *Khamsin* 8 (1981), pp. 83–104]; Johnson, 'Putting Cruelty First', p. 94.
144. Maxime Rodinson, 'Islam Resurgent?', in Janet Afary and Kevin Anderson (eds), *Foucault and the Iranian Revolution: Gender and the Seductions of Islamism* (Chicago: University of Chicago Press, 2005), pp. 223–38, at p. 235 [first: *Le Monde* (6.–8. December 1978)].
145. Ibid., p. 233.
146. Mohammed Ja'far (Makiya, Kanan) and Afsaneh Najmabadi (Tabari, Azar), 'Iran', p. 325.
147. Lafif Lakhdar, 'Why the Reversion of Islamic Archaism?', in Jon Rothschild (ed.), *Forbidden Agendas: Intolerance and Defiance in the Middle East* (London: Saqi Books, 1984), pp. 275–301 [first: *Khamsin* 8 (1981), pp. 62–82].
148. Ibid., p. 279.
149. Johnson, 'Putting Cruelty First', pp. 96–100.
150. Janet Afary and Kevin Anderson (eds), *Foucault and the Iranian Revolution: Gender and the Seductions of Islamism* (Chicago: University of Chicago Press, 2005), pp. 343 and 347.
151. 'Editorial', *Khamsin* 8 (1981), pp. 2–4.
152. Lakhdar, 'Why the Reversion of Islamic Archaism?'.
153. Milson, 'Lafif Lakhdar'.

154. Sadik J. Al-Azm, 'Orientalism and Orientalism in Reverse', in Jon Rothschild (ed.), *Forbidden Agendas: Intolerance and Defiance in the Middle East* (London: Saqi Books, 1984), pp. 349–76 [first: *Khamsin* 8 (1981), pp. 5–26].
155. Sadik J. Al-Azm, 'Orientalism, Occidentalism, and Islamism', *Orientalism, Occidentalism, and Islamism* 30 (2010), pp. 6–13.
156. Samir Al-Khalili (Makiya, Kanan), *The Republic of Fear: The Politics of Modern Iraq* (Berkeley: University of California Press, 1989); Johnson, 'Putting Cruelty First', p. 98.
157. Johnson, 'Putting Cruelty First', p. 131.
158. 'Politisches Nachwort', in Dan Diner, *Israel in Palästina: Über Tausch und Gewalt im Vorderen Orient* (Königstein/Ts.: Athenäum, 1980), p. 272.
159. Henryk M. Broder, 'Tote Seelen in Berlin', *Die Zeit* (27 September 1991).
160. Quoted in Rosen, 'Eli Lobel Committed Suicide in Fall of '79', p. 70.
161. Eli Lobel, 'Maintain the Outcry. Letter to the Members of Matzpen (October 1976)', *Matzpen* 88 (1980), p. 7 [Hebrew]; see also Erel, *Matzpen: Conscience and Fantasy*, p. 157.
162. Diner, 'Für ein Israel der Gegenwart', p. 614.
163. Eli Lobel, 'Amidst the Jews of Berlin', *Al Hamishmar* (13 January 1950), p. 4 [Hebrew].
164. Lakhdar, Email from Lafif Lakhdar, via Kristin Couper, to the Author.
165. Fuks, 'Yaakov is Emanuel is Eli', p. 24.
166. Lakhdar, Email from Lafif Lakhdar, via Kristin Couper, to the Author.

6

Beyond the Holocaust: Jewish Past, Hebrew Present, Socialist Future

Cohn-Bendit's Departure: Israel and the Holocaust

'It was just too much for me. Originally I was supposed to stay longer', Daniel Cohn-Bendit wrote, with a few years of hindsight, of his whirlwind stay in Israel in the spring of 1970. But he 'left after fourteen days, completely exhausted.'[1] 'Red Danny' had arrived in Israel brimming with enthusiasm and excitement for the future. With his friends and political allies from Matzpen, he had travelled the length and breadth of the country to spread the revolutionary spirit and the dream of a common Jewish and Arab perspective in the region, despite the entrenched positions on the ground. But whenever his comments about the Israel–Palestine conflict became critical, particularly when he spoke out against maintaining Israel as a Jewish nation-state, the recent European–Jewish past entered the discussion and, frankly, flew in his face. There was a confrontation at the very start of his trip during an appearance at Hebrew University's Colloquium of Jerusalem Students. Cohn-Bendit's morning talk was followed in the afternoon by a speech from an Israeli pacifist, who wasted no time in voicing his condemnation of the Israeli Army, calling it, like all other military forces, an 'army of murderers'. He was loudly interrupted by a right-wing Member of Knesset from the audience (Figure 6.1):

> This man here and the one you have heard this morning are trying to put us in the same situation our parents experienced in Auschwitz. There are only two options: either we wipe them out, or they wipe us out. And we can't just stick with words, we must follow up with action.

Figure 6.1   Daniel Cohn-Bendit and Dan Ben-Amotz at the Hebrew University of Jerusalem, 1970.

Of the ensuing clash, Cohn-Bendit later recalled 'hysterical shouting and applause'.[2] The episode left him shocked and publicly demonstrated how strongly the Jewish past was still influencing the Israeli present. But none of that visit's many stops would shake the young man more enduringly, or stir him more profoundly, than a gathering in Kibbutz Gan Shmuel. This was not the evening discussion at which he quarrelled with Benjamin Gruenbaum on stage, then spent the whole night on the roof of the venue arguing at length about socialism, internationalism and how to resolve the Israel–Palestine conflict. This occurred the following day, when he met a group of older German Jews. They had survived the Holocaust back in Europe and found a new home in Gan Shmuel after the war. They showed their young guest the numbers tattooed on their arms, which remained there as physical reminders of the crimes committed against them. 'So what would you have done in '45?' they challenged the optimistic 1968 radical.[3] Could he have gone on living in Germany after suffering under the atrocities committed by that country? Their life situations left the ever-glib figurehead of the student rebellion tongue-tied. 'In their eyes, the existence of an Israeli state meant that they would never again be forced into a concentration camp simply for being Jews', he wrote later, empathetically recalling his meeting with people who felt that their survival was tied to the obligation to tell the world about the Holocaust. 'They couldn't accept that the logical consequences of founding an Israeli state were the suppression and enslavement of Arabs and Palestinians.'[4] Hence, Daniel Cohn-Bendit saw a chasm opening up before his eyes. On one side was the experience of the Holocaust, which lent an existential justification for the Jewish state. On the other was the inevitable link between the founding of the Jewish state and the Israel–Palestine conflict. 'Current, historical and future claims to legitimacy were in harsh conflict', he reasoned, summing up the discussions during his time in Israel, which he remembered as both 'passionate and desperate'. In the end, he returned home to Europe sooner than planned.[5]

Another reason for the visit's 'traumatic impression' on Cohn-Bendit must have been that the integral link between the experience of the Holocaust and the existential necessity of the Jewish state was connected, in turn, to his own life story, within a broader transformation of Jewish identity after Auschwitz. Hannah Arendt, the famous philosopher and a Cohn-Bendit family friend, was one of the first, straight after the war, to notice the sense of urgency with which the 'surviving remnant' (*she'erit hapletah*) of European Jews regarded Palestine and to perceive the bitter timeliness that the Nazis' genocide had given the idea of the Jewish state. Because '[a]mong all those who were persecuted, only Jews were singled out for certain death', and because this experience had drawn a dividing line beyond which 'all Gentiles became alike', this new, unprecedented mode of persecution and murder, unlike all previous versions, had instilled a 'strong desire to go to Palestine. It is not that they imagine they will be safe there – it is only that they want to live among Jews alone, come what may.'[6] Soon afterwards, Arendt stressed that it would also be 'frivolous to deny the intimate connection between this mood on the part of Jews everywhere and the recent European catastrophe'.[7] Rather, she had observed the formation of a proto-Zionist Jewish consciousness borne by the conviction that a Jewish state was necessary. Responding to the question of what made someone a Jew, Isaac Deutscher wrote that: 'Auschwitz was the terrible cradle of the new Jewish consciousness and of the new Jewish nation.'[8] After the annihilation and destruction of a multitude of Jewish environments and identities, the Jews had now delegated their share of their collective self mostly to the Jewish state, to Israel.⁹ Cohn-Bendit offered a parallel explanation of his own, reconstructing his earliest thoughts about a Jewish country.

> Coming from a Jewish family, I never questioned the *raison d'être* for the state of Israel. For Jews, and especially German Jews, the State of Israel is the logical and necessary consequence of antisemitic barbarism. Not that I felt the need to live in Israel myself – but it made perfect sense to me that people would want to live there after all that had happened.¹⁰

For all those earlier questions, it was his encounters during his visit in the spring of 1970 that eventually eroded his unconditional solidarity with the Jewish state:

> Before that, I had never quite managed to define my relationship to Israelis. For me, they had always been poor, beaten-down people, oppressed and threatened with destruction by antisemitism all around the world.¹¹

When he met Matzpen, that perspective changed. The 1967 War had forced the Palestine question to the surface; now Cohn-Bendit turned his attention to Israel's founding conflict of 1948, which brought him face to face with the blatant link between the Jewish state's establishment and the Palestinian catastrophe.

Cohn-Bendit's ambivalence during his visit to Israel resulted from an entanglement of histories: the Six-Day War had forced a collision between the disparate times and spaces of Jewish historical experience; a collision that also permanently alienated the New Left of Matzpen from mainstream Israeli society. Indeed the post-war occupation had unearthed even more than the Palestine problem and the Jewish state's unresolved founding conflict. In the weeks leading up to the war, both the Egyptian President Gamal Abdel Nasser and the PLO Chair Ahmad Shukeiri had threatened to 'throw the Jews into the sea': warnings of total annihilation that evoked memories of the Nazis and the Holocaust.¹² In response, *Haaretz* commentators dubbed Nasser the 'new Hitler' or the 'Egyptian Hitler', and new fears of obliteration emerged. In the same newspaper, former Mapai Member of Knesset Eliezer Livneh declared that the very 'existence or nonexistence of the Jewish people' hung in the balance.[13] In that light, Israeli Jews' existential endangerment in the Israel–Palestine conflict seemed like a sequel to the Nazis' collective death sentence for the Jews. Shortly after the war, when the Israeli Foreign Minister Abba Eban refused to retreat to the borders of 4 June 1967, he argued that defending Israel's borders always meant defending the 'Auschwitz lines'.[14]

That historical situation only compounded the Israeli public outcry and vilification of the Israeli leftists of Matzpen as the group expressed solidarity with Palestinian organisations, spoke out against the occupation and thereby distanced itself from Israel's status as a Jewish state. Throughout the Hebrew press, they were accused of greeting 'national suicide' with open arms and condemned as 'self-hating Jews'.[15] Avraham Wolfensohn, a writer for the newspaper *Davar*, went so far as to conflate Matzpen, in its support for the Palestinians, with the fascist sympathisers in England and France who had sided with the totalitarians of Germany and Italy against their own countries' democracies. 'The Objective: The Extermination of Israel', ran the headline of one his articles about the Israeli leftists.[16] In another part of this series, he went on to say: 'In the Middle Eastern conflict, their mercy is only with the Arabs' side. The Jews persecuted worldwide do not deserve concern or mercy in their eyes [. . .] Rescuing the Jews from annihilation is not a general or primary problem for the Matzpen people.'[17] The journalist Shlomo Grodzenski accused the Israeli leftists of depriving the Jewish people, and only them, of the right to a nation-state, charging them as 'traitors of the Jewish-Israeli homeland' on those grounds. His polemic did not end there: 'Actually, in this regard the Matzpen people are the disciples of Hitler (and somewhat those of Stalin too, who from time to time also decided whether this or that nation had a right to exist).'[18]

In light of the New Left's rise and the Jewish and Israeli radicals' departure from the idea of the Jewish state, the Communist Party (Maki) levelled an equally strong allegation of Matzpen's failure to learn the lessons of history. 'If it comes down to it, we'll even give you a visa', shouted an enraged Moshe Sneh, Maki's chief theorist, during a session of the World Union of Jewish Students' annual congress in France in February 1969. The 'you' was a participant who had just spoken approvingly of the Israeli leftists in Matzpen and their positions.[19] The event at the Foyer de Neuilley in Paris had been initiated with the express purpose of arming visitors from the Jewish student organisation with talking points against Matzpen and the New Left.[20] After repeated complaints that Matzpen themselves had not been invited, Sneh called the Israeli leftists 'psychopaths' for their positions on the Israel–Palestine conflict. Next, his furious tirade dug deeper, and the Polish Jew turned to his own survival in the Palestinian Yishuv. He argued that criticising Israel was off-limits for the simple reason that only a Jewish state would guarantee open immigration for Diaspora Jews. If that option had existed during the Nazi period, many more Jews could have been saved. The socialist Alfred Moos published an indignant article, full of similar arguments, in the pages of the communists' *Kol Ha'am*: 'Young Israelis, who are calling upon people to participate in the struggle against Zionism, shouldn't forget that their parents or grandparents in most cases were persecuted people for whom Palestine/Israel was the only refuge.'[21] Moos himself had found refuge from the Nazis in Palestine. Based on that experience, he now suggested that criticising Israel was off limits for the simple reason that only a Jewish state would guarantee open immigration for Diaspora Jews. If that option had existed during the Nazi period, many more Jews could have been saved. Opposing Matzpen and Jewish involvement in the New Left, he now insisted that 'they would hardly have the right today to close Israel's borders if sometime in the future Jews should be forced to flee to Israel in the face of anti-Semitic persecution. The old Jewish self-hatred sometimes gives rise to queer practices.'[22]

The existential retreat to Zionism and the Jewish state that emerged from the Holocaust seemed to deprive Matzpen of any legitimacy. Meanwhile, Zionists felt historically vindicated in their interpretation of the world. After all, the Zionist movement had been foretelling an imminent Jewish catastrophe since the late nineteenth century.[23] The conflation of centuries of remembered oppression with the experiences of violence and pogroms in the era of the nation-state and modern antisemitism had invited the conclusion that Jewish life was incompatible with a non-Jewish environment. The only escape from the predicted collapse of Diaspora Jewish existence was an exodus from the Gentile world.[24] Hence, the Israeli leftists' criticisms could not confine themselves for long to the reality of the Israel–Palestine conflict. Matzpen also dissented from the Zionist interpretation of history that drew a direct link from Jews' oppression and annihilation to their collective survival, thanks to the Jewish national project in Palestine. This recourse to Zionism's historical confirmation in the Jewish consciousness would, almost automatically, block any development as regards the Israel–Palestine conflict, let alone an end to Israel's character as a Jewish state. 'Many good people claim that our proposals amount to exposing Diaspora Jews to pogroms and physical annihilation – and those people point to the experience of the Second World War and the Holocaust', Oded Pilavsky observed as early as 1964.[25] He therefore urged that the Zionist movement's role and significance be re-examined against the background of Nazism and the mass murder of Jews. Indeed, Zionists were far from the only ones to claim that history confirmed their theories of an impending catastrophe. Zionism's negative teleology, as an apparently unscathed interpretation of the world, granted psychological relief and constructed political meaning out of what Hannah Arendt called 'complete senselessness'.[26] Eventually, this narrative swayed even the Zionist movement's former adversaries. Nine years after the war, the Jewish communist Isaac Deutscher wrote: 'If, instead of arguing against Zionism in the 1920s and 1930s I had urged European Jews to go to Palestine, I might have helped to save some of the lives that were later extinguished in Hitler's gas chambers.'[27] There was no getting around an historical experience of this magnitude. It was not enough to assert the legitimacy of socialist Jewish perspectives or to point out that varied groups of *fin-de-siècle* European Jews had believed in a universalist dream of integration into their non-Jewish environment, rather than in an ethnic division of the world.[28] Neither was it enough to deny the Zionist monopoly on responses to modern antisemitism. The Israeli leftists of Matzpen picked up on this historical impasse. Their critique aimed, instead, to confront the Zionist movement with its own historical position, in order to document that position's failure: did the Jews in the Palestinian Yishuv truly survive thanks to Zionism? And had the local political leadership truly prioritised rescuing the European Jews on the eve of the catastrophe?

As to the latter question, Matzpen's historical judgement was unanimous. 'The situation of Jews living outside Palestine interests Zionism only in so far as they are moved by their situation to emigrate to "the Promised Land" or at least to support Zionism', concluded Moshé Machover in a polemic appraisal of the Yishuv's Zionist leadership that borrowed liberally from the critical writings of the historian Yigal Elam.[29] In fact, he argued, their 'Palestino-centrism' – i.e. their political prioritisation of Zionism and the Yishuv – had limited the efforts to help European Jews even after the rise of the Nazis. The two faces of the Zionist movement, whose retreat from the Gentile world had been guided from the start by the telos of the Jewish people's rebirth in Eretz Israel, had ultimately extended to their concept and practice of rescuing fellow Jews. Just as the future Prime Minister David Ben-Gurion was inspired, in the 1930s, to transform the disaster of German Jewry 'into a productive force' for Zionism and 'to use Hitler [. . .] for the building of our country',[30] the political existence of various groups of Diaspora Jews and the defence of their individual and collective rights outside Palestine receded into the background.[31]

To be sure, a committee to rescue Germany's Jews was quickly established in the Yishuv.[32] However, at a board meeting of the Jewish Agency on 31 December 1935, Ben-Gurion sought to clarify the commission's scope: to discuss 'the question of the Jews in Germany only from the aspect of their immigration to Palestine' and to prioritise the 'Zionist aspect' over 'measures to be taken in support of the rights of the Jews in the Diaspora'.[33] Moshe Sharett's defence of the *Ha'avara* (Transfer) Agreement, even if it contradicted the Jewish call to boycott Nazi Germany, was even more explicit: 'It is Zionism's lot to have to be cruel to the Diaspora at times, when the development of the country demands it'.[34]

In the summer of 1938, after Nazi Germany annexed Austria, the Évian Conference convened to rally international assistance for the Jewish refugees and became a focal point for Jewish non-state diplomacy.[35] The conference's failure rested on the refusal of the major powers, almost without exception, to open their doors to Jewish refugees. Notwithstanding, the Yishuv leadership's lack of efforts to advance mass Jewish migration to countries besides Palestine was an additional source of hand-wringing in hindsight.[36] 'We are risking Zionism's very existence if we allow the refugee problem to be separated from the Palestine problem', declared Ben-Gurion before the Palestine Zionist Executive in December 1938, further cementing the image of 'cruel Zionism' for his future critics.[37] Reconstructing that very same historical development, the political rhetoric of *Matzpen* climaxed in an accusation:

> It is not just that Zionism and saving Jews in danger of extermination are not one and the same thing; at a critical historical moment, Zionism took a stand *against* saving the Jews.[38]

Yet such criticism was not altogether free of bluster, nor of the hubris of historical hindsight. In their reckoning with the Zionist movement, Matzpen did not acknowledge that even the Zionist leadership – for all its catastrophic rhetoric – could by no means have foreseen the scale of the mass murder of Jews to come, which went beyond anyone's wildest nightmares whilst leaving the Yishuv helpless and powerless.

Their exploration of Zionism's Palestino-centrism gave the young leftists further insight in other areas. For example, these ideas illuminated Zionists' belief of having survived in Palestine thanks to Zionism alone, almost as though Jews could '"get out of" world history through Zionism' – as though the Jews in Palestine had been exempted from the Nazis' death sentence.[39] Chaim Weizmann's claim that 'Zionism is eternal life and, compared with that, saving thousands of Jews is merely extending their lives on borrowed time', which was quoted by Matzpen as another example of so-called 'cruel Zionism', was in fact an expression of concern about mass immigration to the land of Israel: 'This land is not only the land of rescue [*hatsala*], but also the land of redemption [*ge'ula*]', he stressed. Based on the sacredly imbued idea of an eternal connection of the Jewish people and the land of Israel, his views demonstrated the depths of a political theology that intertwined catastrophe, rescue and redemption; a perspective that had taken shape long before the Nazi extermination of Jews.[40] In late 1942, Ben-Gurion was the one who again proclaimed the link between catastrophe and redemption: 'The essence of Zionist strategy is that it knows how to transform our catastrophe not into a source of despair and paralysis, as did the Diaspora, but into a spring of creativity and spiritedness'. Only one year later, Ben-Gurion's political companion Moshe Sharett saw the reports on the systematic annihilation of European Jews as ultimate proof of the Zionist movement's narrative of history. He wrote in the daily *Davar*:

> The Zionists do not mean to exploit the horrible tragedy of the Jews of Europe [but still] they cannot refrain from emphasising the fact that events have totally proven the Zionist position on the solution of the Jewish problem. Zionism predicted the Holocaust decades ago.[41]

After the war, this perception was further integrated into the Zionist narrative of destruction and rebirth (*Shoah ve-tekuma*), although that worldview had long been rendered obsolete by the shift from a modern antisemitism of oppression to the Nazi antisemitism of annihilation.[42]

'There in Palestine, they would be safe from their enemies', Hannah Arendt wrote as early as 1944, pointing out the oddity that 'by their interpretation of Palestine in the future life of the Jewish people, the Zionists shut themselves off from the destiny of the Jews all over the world'.[43] Zionists acted as if there were 'special conditions for Palestine, unrelated to Jewish destinies elsewhere, while at the same time generalising adverse conditions for Jews everywhere else in the world'.[44] However, the horrific dimension of the Nazi genocide had, in fact, created a different truth at this point, 'when Rommel's army threatened Palestine Jewry with exactly the same fate as in European countries'.[45] After all, the Nazis had not planned to spare the Jews of Palestine from the fate of European Jewry, and the Yishuv owed its survival not to Zionism, but to the victory of the British troops over the Germans at El-Alamein in 1942.[46] Notwithstanding, the Zionist utopian idea of Eretz Israel as a secure refuge during the Holocaust was preserved in the young state's structure and was considered a political instance of salvation that had proven correct and historically proactive in comparison to European Jewry.[47]

Now, more than two decades later, concerned that the alleged vindication of the Zionist worldview by the Holocaust would obstruct any solution to the Israel–Palestine conflict, Matzpen took aim at the political theology of Zionism. They insisted that no '"magical mystical" power of Zionism's' had protected the Jews of Palestine from the Nazis, while only the Jews of Europe were condemned to annihilation.[48] The Jews who came to Palestine in the 1920s and 1930s had, indeed, outlasted the ultimate genocide by virtue of living there. Yet their survival was no different from that of Jews who had escaped the Nazis' grasp 'without Zionism, indeed contrary to Zionism' – by emigrating to the United States or relocating to the Soviet interior, either by choice or by force.[49] In 1942, with the German Army in spitting distance of Palestine, parts of the Yishuv had prepared for their own end with the Massada Plan. Like the rebels of the Warsaw Ghetto, many in the Yishuv found themselves choosing what sort of imminent death they would face. When the Jews of Palestine escaped the horrible end of the European Jews, their salvation came not from Zionism and their own political efforts, but rather from British military protection.[50] As *Matzpen* later had it: 'If Rommel's army had conquered Palestine and had got as far as Syria, the fate of the Jews in Palestine would undoubtedly have been the same as their brothers' in Poland.'[51] For Zionism, Moshé Machover concluded, the Holocaust basically proved nothing.[52]

Even before the war's end, quiet doubts as to Zionism's historical teleology were even registered in the centre of the Zionist movement. At a January

1945 gathering of the Poale Zion World Congress in Jerusalem, the Polish-born Yaakov Zerubavel cautioned against expressing undue hubris towards Diaspora Jews, and said the Zionists should not pretend to have truly possessed the foresight to avoid the imminent catastrophe in good time by casting their political lot with Zionism. In response to a speech by David Ben-Gurion, he asked:

> Is it admissible to build everything on this catastrophe? [. . .] Wasn't Hitler at the gates of the country? What would have been our situation and fate here then? [. . .] Hitler didn't only plan to annihilate the Diaspora but *Jewry*, all Jews everywhere. We have saved ourselves by *pure chance*.[53]

Zerubavel's voice might have been soft in 1945, but many years later it provided historical support for Matzpen's theories. The young leftists claimed that the theoretical and political premises underlying the insistence on Zionist policies had been all but disproved by history.[54] But this same argument could be turned right back against them when it came to their own worldview. In the present era of the Israel–Palestine conflict, the only way to sustain their sense of self, their political utopias, their self-perceptions and their dreams of securing a safe existence for both Israeli and Diaspora Jews was by circumventing the history and meaning of the Holocaust. Despite all substantial differences, the 'post-Zionist children of Zionism' had been raised in the political culture of a country in which – away from events in Europe – the political and ideological discourses had been preserved from a time before the Holocaust.[55] For many years, the political and cultural outlook of Matzpen would impede its members from acknowledging the impact of the Nazi mass annihilation of Jews on the Jewish collective consciousness. Their sense of belonging to a new Hebrew nation seemed, instead, to somehow extract Israeli life from Jewish history entirely. But being part of a new Hebrew milieu – which had emerged and culturally reinvented itself in distinction to the Jewish Diaspora, and had, by good fortune, been spared the tragic fate of European Jewry,– entailed a collective sense of distance from the history and memory of mass extermination. By adhering to their faith in progress rooted in the socialist teleology of history, the Hebrew leftists of Matzpen further accentuated this disregard of the consequences of the Holocaust – despite the connections linking these Israeli Leftists and their socialist internationalism to the revolutionary hopes of Eastern European Jewish communists of the interwar period. Back then, the Zionist proposal of 'a modern solution to the Jewish question' (Theodor Herzl's phrase) had been contrasted with the emancipatory hope for a kind of 'Red assimilation', which promised the emancipation and integration of Jews into their non-Jewish surroundings as part of a communist future. Now those old dreams of progress were being updated – as a voluntary renunciation of a Jewish state in favour of an aspired Israeli–Palestinian society. However, this social and national utopia played a reinforcing role in the Israeli New Left's habit of side-lining Jews' post-Auschwitz collective consciousness.

Jewish and Hebrew Memories Juxtaposed

Akiva Orr was living in far-off London, but still representing Matzpen, when the war of June 1967 drew him back with a vengeance into the conflicts between Israelis and Arabs. He had been born Karl Sebastian Sonnenberg to a family of Polish and German Jews, only to transform into the Hebrew–Israeli Akiva Orr. Now, the war confronted him with the depths of a Jewish collective memory whose effects had, until then, mostly eluded him. Just a few months earlier, Orr had moved into the small London neighbourhood of Golders Green, which had a large middle-class Jewish population. That demographic included his landlord, an eighty-year-old German Jew who had managed to escape to Britain after the Nazis took power and had lived there ever since as a secular Jew, far from the Jewish state and the Jewish religion. But on the eve of the war, with Israel cornered by three enemies – Egypt's troops stationed in the Sinai, and their allies Syria and Jordan to the north and west – the man was overwrought by a nearly existential fear for that state. His exchanges with his Israeli lodger had so far been limited to pleasantries, but now the old man greeted Orr with questions when he arrived home: 'What do you think, Mr Orr, will they destroy us?'[56] He clearly saw the Jewish state's peril as his own.

'This stopped me in my tracks', Akiva Orr recalled. 'What the hell did he mean by "us"? He lived in England, never visited Israel, had no relatives there, yet spoke like someone about to be attacked personally.'[57] Aware of his landlord's sense of existential danger, Orr stifled his impulse to quip that Nasser's troops were not exactly amassing in Calais for an attack on Britain, let alone on Golders Green. What stuck in his mind was that collectivising 'us' by which the worried man tried to link the two of them. The question of what had led a German Jew living in the UK to have so strongly 'embedded Israel in his identity'[58] inspired Orr to write several books about Jewishness and the Jews' self-conception in the modern age.[59] Astutely, he proceeded to explore secular Jews' difficulties at characterising their Jewish identities, addressing how challenging it was to build a secular Jewish life that was fully distinct from the religion. He concluded that for non-religious Jews, 'the state of Israel serves as a psychological prop for their sense of identity. It enables them to overcome the lack of clarity – caused by their loss of belief – of their Jewishness'.[60] However, Orr may have been oversimplifying when he interpreted their defence of, and identification with, the Jewish state as merely an 'externalised' insecurity and therefore a personal problem.[61] In fact, after the real persecution as a Jew that had forced his landlord to leave Germany, he had folded that externally imposed label into his own Jewish identity. The experience of oppression and annihilation solely on the basis of descent must have been singed into the man's psyche, for that same experience justified his sense of connection to the Jewish state as a guarantor of even his own life. In light of the Arab threats of annihilation on the eve of the Six-Day War, this Holocaust-derived memory tightened the already-close bond between Israel and the Diaspora and united dispersed groups of worldwide Jewry in a fear of a potential 'second Holocaust'.[62] Orr had similarly witnessed this resurgence of fear in his own parents, who had also left Germany for Palestine shortly after Hitler's rise to power. A few days after the June war, they informed their incredulous son that they had organised pills so that, if worst came to worst, they could escape a new doom with a death of their own choosing.[63]

Their son did not share their fear of annihilation, which arose from their experience. Reflecting years later on both reactions, Orr remained mystified by the panic of his usually calm parents, just as he had been perplexed by his London landlord's identification with Israel. Around the period of the 1967 War, when London Jews repeatedly denigrated Orr for his public criticism of Israel, he wondered:

> [W]hy did so many British Jews react so emotionally whenever I criticised Israel? After all, I was an Israeli citizen, they were not; I served in the Israeli army in 1948, they did not [. . .] what right did they have to react so hysterically to my criticism of my government?[64]

The political disagreements over the legitimacy of Israeli policy ran deep, but there was an even deeper chasm between the contradictory meanings people assigned to the Jewish collective experience of the Holocaust and the consequential importance of the Jewish state. The experience of annihilation served as a collective memory, one that Jewish populations in the Diaspora shared with the generation of survivors who had found a safe haven in Israel. By contrast, young, critical Israelis were a step removed from that collective feeling – almost as if it had nothing to do with them. Akiva Orr's exploration of the forms of Jewish belonging in the modern age asked why the Jewish state had also become the existential reference point for Diaspora Jews. But more than that, it justified and legitimated his own cultural sense of self: his belonging to a new Hebrew nation that materialised in Israel as a result of the Zionist settlement in Palestine, but had gradually decoupled itself from its origins. In his view, this culture could no longer be considered truly Jewish; for one thing, it 'lack[ed] minority complexes' that he ascribed to Diaspora Jews.[65] His friend Shimon Tzabar made a similar observation in his autobiography:

> The feeling of being a member of a minority group, whether persecuted or not, that Jews feel anywhere else, escaped me. I was one of the first generation of Hebrew-speaking natives in a town of Hebrew speakers. I belonged to the majority indigenous population from the outset. As it happened, the culture of my generation shaped the culture of Israel today. To understand the chutzpah, the cruelty and the cynicism of the Israeli society today, one must be familiar with the culture of my generation.[66]

This idea of culturally belonging to a new (and, indeed, newly invented) Hebrew–Israeli nation had estranged Akiva Orr, Shimon Tzabar and Matzpen from the Jewish experience of the Holocaust – and seemingly shielded them from it. That became one premise of their radical critique of the Jewish state.

Matzpen sharply opposed the Jewish state's self-definition, but their distance from the experience of the ultimate genocide equally exemplified the outlook of an Israeli culture that had, itself, arisen from the Zionist movement. 'We did not occupy ourselves much with the Holocaust or the Jews' history of oppression because that was not generally a topic in Israeli society until the early '60s', Khalil Toama elaborated later, regarding the cultural environment that gave rise to Matzpen.[67] That societal fork in the road had come long before the Holocaust and related to the way a new political culture was invented in the course of territorialising disparate European Jews, an invention accompanied by Zionism's 'negation of exile'. For the Jews of Palestine in the first half of the twentieth century, regaining sovereignty and resuming history signified more than just turning their backs on the torments of marginalisation, oppression and pogroms. In everything from language to professions to everyday habitus, that meant rejecting the old 'exilic Jewish way of life'.[68] Akiva Orr, who went to school in Tel Aviv in the 1940s, noticed this too:

> Because the Zionist upbringing we received described 'exile Jews' as 'subordinate to Gentiles' and made us, instead, into 'proud independent sabras', my generation developed a sense of superiority over all Jews who had not grown up in the country. We even looked at Chaim Weizmann, David Ben-Gurion and Menachem Begin with some disdain.[69]

The country's native children thus distinguished themselves culturally from the Jews of the Diaspora. And it was that difference that fundamentally shaped their reaction to early news of the annihilation. As the sabra generation was confronted by the scale of the Nazis' crimes, a scale beyond anyone's imagining, the fate of European Jews somehow ricocheted off their new patriotic self-image. The accusation that the Diaspora had missed its chance to immigrate to Palestine was compounded by the charge 'that they prefer the life of a beaten dog to death with honour'.[70] Orr later recalled, by then with more critical distance:

> Around 1944 [sic – actually 1942], when the first news of the annihilation of European Jews reached the country, it fit into the image of the exilic Jew we were already instilled with by our Zionist upbringing: a submissive population that did not dare fight the Nazis. We were proud of the Jewish partisans and the insurgents of the Warsaw Ghetto, but we knew that they represented a very tiny fraction of the entire population.[71]

This self-distancing from the fate of Diaspora Jews reached its utmost in the Young Hebrews movement's enigmatic *Opening Speech at the Meeting of the Committee with Representatives of the Cells* (1944). Yonathan Ratosh's document intensified Zionism's 'negation of exile' into a radical heresy of an indigenous Hebrew nation fully decoupled from Jewish life. This went hand in hand with an utter disregard for the fate of European Jews under the swastika, as evidenced by the text's publication date and the fact that the Young Hebrews formed their ideology at the precise moment in time when the Jews were being annihilated. This historical pattern comes into even sharper relief in light of that founding document's actual content. The publication could also be seen as a defensive response to the news from Europe, which Ratosh saw primarily as a threat to his own nationalist project – of building a Hebrew nation.[72] '[T]he Nazi slaughter increased and intensified the power of the *shtetl* in the hearts of the immigrants', he argued with a mixture of worry and cynicism, as the atrocities brutally begged the question of Jewish belonging in the country. The events in Europe 'shook all of the Jewish immigrants down to the very depths of their personal and Jewish being' and threatened to undermine the establishment of a distinct Hebrew nation.[73] Yet the writer went on to argue that 'the Hebrew youth' were immune to the Jewish experience emanating from the Diaspora; the horrors in Europe 'only touched the human element in [their] soul'. But 'in the heart of Hebrew youth not a thing remains of all this'.[74] In some respects, this averting of eyes was itself a divisive act.[75] In the face of the annihilation that was being physically perpetrated at the time, the absolute dividing line he drew between the fate of Jews in Europe and the Hebrew existence in Palestine provided a kind of ideological inoculation – as though 'by defining themselves as Gentile Hebrews [. . .] they had escaped the Nazis' collective death sentence'.[76]

The Young Hebrews' disquieting dissociation from the fate of the Jews in Europe overlooked the new nature of the Nazis' ultimate genocidal intentions, which went undeterred by a self-declared secession from Judaism. However, as symbols of divergent historical experiences, and as products of the polarity between European–Jewish destiny and a Hebrew self-confidence that arose from the Yishuv's realities, they were an extreme example of a more general trend. This was one reason why, in the first decade of the Jewish state, Holocaust survivors' tales of their experiences found little reception.[77] 'For the truth was that, notwithstanding the Yishuv's and then Israel's eager acceptance of so many victims of the Holocaust during the postwar period and the

War of Independence, survivors had not in general had an easy time in the new Jewish state', explained the historian Michael R. Marrus. 'The new country found it difficult to fit them into the new national narrative.'⁷⁸ For many years of Israel's history, this discrepancy would live on in a younger generation of Israeli sabras whose culture and habits primed their incomprehension of survivors' horrific experiences. Perhaps its most disturbing symptom manifested in one area where the new environment was fully fledged, blocking out survivors all the more: the slang of the Hebrew youth. For example, Shimon Tzabar recollected his generation's stereotypes about survivors: 'Who were we? We were the young Israelis. On top of being rude and nasty, we were also capable of jokes in very bad taste indeed like, for example, we nicknamed the Jews who managed to survive the Holocaust "the Soaps".'⁷⁹ This insulting and unsettling slur was a reference to the rumour that soap had been produced using fat from the bodies of murdered Jews, and for years it featured in the slang of Hebrew teenagers. It then entered the vernacular as a synonym for weakling and a description for anyone 'lacking in character'.⁸⁰ In the 1970s, 'soap' was a headword in *The World Dictionary of Hebrew Slang*, compiled by Netiva Ben-Yehuda and Dan Ben-Amotz, a man who was personally shaped by Hebrew slang and shaped it in turn. As a final, toned-down artefact of the painful collision between Hebrew and Jewish experiences, the word was defined there as weakness or an unathletic person.⁸¹

The level to which the sabra generation's mental dissociation shaped Israel's public political discourse was apparent at 'the first great Holocaust trial held in Israel', the Kasztner trial of 1954.⁸² The year before, the Hungarian-born Holocaust survivor Malchiel Gruenwald had announced that the Jerusalem Mapai member Israel Rudolf (Reszö) Kasztner was the same man who had led the Jewish rescue committee in Hungary during the war. Kasztner had personally negotiated with Adolf Eichmann to save the lives of 1,685 Jews via a special chartered train. Gruenwald now accused Kasztner of collaborating with the Nazis, of exploiting his role for personal advantage and of sacrificing the lives of most Hungarian Jews.⁸³ Gruenwald's claims touched on existential questions that had plagued the Jewish community for years. Nevertheless, the ensuing trial became a venue for negotiating the young state's political and cultural identity instead, and the trial therefore failed to address the hopeless plight European Jews had faced during the Holocaust.

First, the Mapai leadership, as represented by Attorney General Haim Cohn, charged Gruenwald with defaming Kasztner, who was now a member of their party. In the years after the court proceedings began at the Jerusalem District Court, on 1 January 1954, the accusations kept shifting direction. First, the trial of Malchiel Gruenwald morphed into the Kasztner Affair. Then Mapai itself stood accused, before the trial finally implicated 'the victims and survivors of the Holocaust'.[84] This progression was largely shepherded by Gruenwald's lawyer, Shmuel Tamir, and enabled by news coverage from his ally Uri Avnery, the editor of the weekly *Haolam Hazeh*.

In defending Malchiel Gruenwald, Tamir, 'the foremost political lawyer in the country', was only nominally acting in his client's interests.[85] His deeper motive dated back to his former membership in the right-wing Zionist Irgun Tzva'i Le'umi (Etzel) paramilitary organisation: his belief in 'the contemptible wretchedness of the Jews of the Exile as compared to the "stalwart" character of the Israelis'.[86] Tamir made clear that he, too, faulted Ben-Gurion's government for the same exile mentality and blamed the founding prime minister for collaborating with the British on the eve of statehood, instead of supporting the Hebrew underground's Lehi and Etzel brigades as they fought for national sovereignty. Kasztner's decisions in Budapest seemed to represent just another facet of the same mentality. 'There were collaborators there, and here as well', as the historian Tom Segev later paraphrased Tamir's interpretation. 'Mapai in Budapest, Mapai in Tel Aviv – a single party with a single mentality.'[87] Outside the courtroom, Avnery helped to popularise this equation in *Haolam Hazeh*. It was his journalism that first reframed the trial as the Kasztner Affair. He had offered Tamir space in the magazine, and he cast the trial in sensational terms as a face-off between the young Hebrew–Israeli attorney and the 'exile–Jewish' official from Budapest.[88] Ultimately, *Haolam Hazeh* crowned Tamir 'Man of the Year'.[89] Most importantly, Avnery wanted to extend the journalistic debate over the country's political, cultural and generational future to questions about Israel's relationship to the past. Besides accusing both Rudolf Kasztner and Moshe Sharett of being collaborators – Kasztner with the Nazis and Sharett with the British – Avnery painted an ugly picture of a small number of 'Jewish Ghetto leaders', functionaries who had, in his telling, prevented insurrection and rebellion.[90] In the case of the War of Independence, he had glorified a young generation of Hebrew fighters for wresting national sovereignty from the

British Crown; now he connected that experience to the Jews' plight before and during the Holocaust. In reference to the European Jews, he made a grandiose assertion:

> There is no doubt that it was possible to save a great many of them [...] In Palestine there was a centre of Hebrew power, organised Hebrew power, national authority that could decide and act. Had such a centre declared a holy war to save Jews, it might well have changed the situation. But nothing of the sort happened. [...] Thus, a great guilt hovers over the politicians who set the course of the Yishuv.[91]

Finally, Avnery held up the supposed morality of the Hebrew rebellion as a yardstick for the behaviour of European Jews in the lead-up to their annihilation. Unlike their hopeless European cousins, who could only make a grim choice between deaths, Avnery mythologised the Hebrew fighters with the haughty claim that his generation had not gone 'like lambs to the slaughter'.[92] The Kasztner trial stretched out an impossibly wide gap between the Hebrew youth's self-confidence and the Jewish experience of annihilation.

In the end, Malchiel Gruenwald was acquitted of almost all charges. The ultimate victim of the proceedings was, instead, Rudolf Kasztner. For years to come, his name would be stained by the verdict of the Jerusalem judge Benjamin Halevi, who wrote that in the negotiations with Eichmann, Kasztner had 'sold his soul to the devil'.[93] This stoked the rage of some former members of the pre-state terrorist underground and culminated in Kasztner's murder in March 1957. Only a year later, Kasztner's criminal record was cleared, but this could not undo the lasting impact of the press's public condemnation. As late as 1961, the New York-based dramatist Ben Hecht wrote a polemical play called *Perfidy*, rebuking Kasztner's rescue of 1,685 Jews by implying that Kasztner had kept the rest of Hungary's Jewry in the dark about their grim future. (Hecht had previously been part of a group of Hebrew heretics in New York, along with Hillel Kook and Shmuel Merlin.) In Israel, meanwhile, discussion of the Kasztner trial quickly spread to the Israeli Left, including *Matzpen*. Even before founding the organisation, Akiva Orr had attended several sessions of the trial at Jerusalem's Russian Compound and obtained information from *Haolam Hazeh* and from a lawyer friend who was assisting Tamir during the trial. 'What emerged was beyond anything I – and most Israelis – could have imagined [...] New, alarming and unexpected questions emerged that have never been answered.'[94] At the time, Orr was still a member of the Communist Party, which tried to square Kasztner's verdict with its own anti-imperialist assumption that the Zionist leadership was continuously cooperating with the major Western powers.[95] The Party Chair Shmuel Mikunis told his comrades:

> The verdict about Kasztner is a verdict on the Jewish Agency, the heads of State in Israel and all their accomplices who share the *Judenrat*'s responsibility of the Holocaust. This is a verdict on those, whom our party has rejected throughout the years as collaborators and those who carried out the policy of the enemies of peace and the nation, of the black forces of imperialism.[96]

The communists thus fit Kasztner's desperate efforts to rescue Hungarian Jews from certain death into an old, pre-war interpretation of Zionist diplomacy – even though Nazi rule and the Holocaust had upended that interpretation. Matzpen publications later adopted a similar tone – integrating Kasztner's story into a history

> in which the antisemite appears to the Zionist not as an enemy against whom an implacable struggle must be waged, but as a potential bargaining partner with whom arrangements can be negotiated to achieve a common goal; e.g., the removal of Jews from non-Jewish society and their concentration in a society of their own.

'Most infamous of all such negotiations', this account summarised, 'were probably those carried out in Budapest between Rudolph Kasztner, secretary of the Zionist committee in that city, and Adolph Eichmann in 1944'[97] – as if to suggest that Kasztner had been in a similar position as that of Theodor Herzl many years earlier, when Herzl tried to win over the antisemitic Russian Interior Minister Vyacheslav Konstantinovich von Plehve in support of his Zionist programme. The Israeli Radical Left was perpetuating a political discourse that originated among the Hebrew nationalist milieu, but had its cultural basis in the spatial/temporal distance between Palestine and the fates and experiences of European Jews. And yet, maybe the most prominent denunciation of Kasztner came from Hannah Arendt, whose own portrayal strikingly resembled the Hebrew scene's take on Kasztner during the trial.[98] Arendt's own portrait of the 'strange Mr Kasztner', whom she read as a symbol of the 'extent to which even the Jewish victims had accepted the standards of the Final Solution', would not be published until 1963, two years after the Eichmann trial, an event that fundamentally changed the public memory of the Holocaust.[99]

The Eichmann trial represented one more phase, presumably the last, of the split between the native Hebrew consciousness and the Jewish experience of the Holocaust. At the same time, the trial in Jerusalem – broadcast from Israel – lent public validity and recognition to the victims and survivors of the annihilation for the first time.[100] However, even as the collective Jewish memory of the Holocaust was gaining ground, the cultural policy conflict between the Ben-Gurion government and the Hebrew subculture persisted. After all, the Israeli Prime Minister had his own political agenda: '[A] great number of purposes the trial was supposed to achieve, all of which were ulterior purposes'.[101] These aims were not all related to the repeatedly emphasised parallels between Nazi crimes and Arab propaganda about the Israel–Palestine conflict.[102] Israel's founding father strongly preferred for Zionism to integrate Auschwitz into the Jewish state's own teleological history, which would lend the state fresh legitimacy as a refuge from an endless chronicle of persecution.[103] Thus, Ben-Gurion presented the Jewish state to his international audience as 'the only inheritor of these [murdered] Jews'.[104] He also appealed to the Israeli youth, whose apathy towards Holocaust victims he found disturbing.[105] Before the trial began, Ben-Gurion declared: 'One of our motives in bringing Eichmann to trial is to make the details of his case known to the generation of Israelis who have grown up since the Holocaust. We want them to know the most tragic facts in our history, the most tragic facts in world history.'[106]

This linkage between Israeli society and Jewish tragedy seemed to damage the notion of a separate Hebrew present, and it was resisted by the native Hebrew–Israeli subculture.[107] Their wording was not always as harsh as that of Yonatan Ratosh, who asserted that the 'Holocaust dealt cruelly with the Jewish religious community. But the Hebrew nation that rose in the land of Israel has no connection with the Jewish religious community'.[108] Still, Ratosh was not alone in his determination to defy Zionism's historical teleology by universalising the experiences of antisemitism and the Holocaust so as to safeguard the separate legitimacy of the Hebrew state. In fact, his peers unanimously shared this view. When Uri Avnery, Amos Kenan and Boaz Evron reacted to the Eichmann controversy in *Etgar* and *Haolam Hazeh*, they, too, tried instinctively to detach the annihilation of European Jews from both Jewish victims' experiences and Zionist interpretations of them. Instead, the three men focused on the implications of Nazi crimes for all humanity. In the summer of 1960, two months after Eichmann's imprisonment, Boaz Evron insisted that the annihilation of Jews 'is not to be separated from the general framework of Nazism and modern totalitarianism. Not only Germans were capable of killing, and not only Jews were victims.'[109] In that context, Evron pointed at Nazi plans to murder Slavic ethnic groups. Evron and Avnery reacted euphorically in *Etgar*, Semitic Action's magazine, to the publication of Hannah Arendt's serialised report from the Eichmann trial in the *New Yorker*. In one of his columns, Avnery mentioned the sensational articles, then immediately highlighted the striking similarities between Arendt's attitude and those of the Hebrew journalists – 'even though she has not read our texts at all'. In particular, Avnery emphasised her criticism that the trial in Jerusalem had treated the Nazi annihilation of Jews as the latest chapter in a litany of anti-Jewish persecution, reducing it to a reprise of 'yesterday's pogrom', instead of recognising what made the Holocaust fundamentally new.[110] 'The trial missed its chance to ask the most important questions.' Building on Arendt, Avnery subordinated the Jewish particularist question of *why* Jews were victimised to the universal question of *how*, which is largely directed towards the collective of perpetrators: 'How can such a great, cultivated nation be yoked to such a criminal regime and support it so zealously until the very end?'[111] In that vein, after reading Arendt's series of articles, Boaz Evron asked a no less universalist question about the nature of genocidal crimes in the modern age – a question that likewise veered away from the Jewish experience.[112]

The public questioning of Zionist accounts on Jewish history and the Holocaust was only one side of the reaction from the younger Hebrew–Israeli milieu. In the long run, their generation could not extract itself from the effects of the Jewish experience of the ultimate genocide. After the Eichmann trial, this accelerated the erosion of a distinct Hebrew consciousness, both visibly and irreversibly.[113] Parallel to the political aim of universalising the memory of the Holocaust, Avnery predicted this shift at the beginning of the trial. In the very first week of hearings, he wrote in *Etgar* that the trial would 'have the greatest impact on the Hebrew nation in Israel. A profound transformation is under way, the earliest manifestations of which are already catching our eyes.'[114] For sixteen years, the Hebrew youth had overlooked the Holocaust, had refused to listen to anything about it, and had resisted 'identifying with the degraded Jews who went into the gas chambers'. He now discerned the beginnings of a contrary trend. As Israelis faced the survivors' appalling testimony, he saw the 'implosion' of all the sentiments that had prevented Israeli society from grappling with this history. Despite Avnery's emphatic distinctions between the Jewish past and the Hebrew present, he, too, saw Eichmann's trial as the start of a change 'that is helping to form a normal relationship to yesterday, a dismantlement of the complexes that previously impeded the new Hebrew from a healthy relationship with the Jewish past and present'.[115] He viewed the lack of Hebrew literature about the Holocaust in the post-war period as characteristic of that era and surmised 'that it is quite possible that the [trial's] significant influence will show itself in the realm of literature'.[116]

Indeed, literature was where Hebrew identity first opened up. The poet Haim Gouri, formerly associated with the Canaanites, famously remarked that nobody walked out of the Eichmann trial the same person as when they walked in.[117] A group of writers from the Palmach generation, including Hanoch Bartov, Yehuda Amichai and Yoram Kaniuk, finally began addressing the horrors of the Holocaust and the fate of Diaspora Jews.[118] This shift was most noticeable in the case of Dan Ben-Amotz, who in 1966 began working on his first Hebrew novel *Lizkor ve-Lishkoah* (To Remember, To Forget), which was published two years later.[119] Ben-Amotz had been considered the quintessential Israeli sabra since his youth, and had helped to shape Israeli Hebrew and Israeli vernacular culture together with Shimon Tzabar and Amos Kenan. However, as he turned his gaze towards the Holocaust, his novel marked a twofold transformation.

The first transformation was written into the novel's plot. The Israeli protagonist Uri Lam travels to Frankfurt am Main to resolve his reparation claims.[120] In the course of this encounter with the Old World and a successor state of the Third Reich, the life of the German Jew Zvi Hirsch Lambert emerges from behind that of the Israeli Uri Lam. 'So many years of silent data, yellow with age, clouded with dust, but all forgotten', Lam pronounces. The character arrived in Palestine before the Holocaust as a child, leaving his own backstory behind.[121] 'I changed Hirsch to Zvi. In Hebrew, Zvi is Hirsch. To get a little more distance I changed Zvi to Uri.'[122] Having papered over his diasporic roots, Uri Lam begins telling people he is from Tel Aviv, not Frankfurt.[123] This biographical reinvention will not last. When he travels back to Europe, his transformation from a German Jew to a Hebrew Israeli is disrupted: 'Suddenly, on the heels of my rash decision [to go to Germany], what was long dormant begins to stir. Scenes I had managed to forget I was now required to dredge up.'[124] From the beginning of the trip, even before Lam/Lambert arrives in Germany, his confrontation with Europe becomes both a biographical self-discovery and an encounter with the history of his own family, who did not escape to Palestine and instead fell victim to the annihilation in Europe. On a visit to a cemetery in Florence, he has a repressed revelation: his individual choice to forget was bound up with the fact that all Europe had become a Jewish cemetery, and he himself – Uri Lam, or Zvi Hirsch Lambert – served as the final heir and witness: 'I have no message for my dead, dead who lie unknown in foreign fields, with no monument', declares Ben-Amotz's protagonist. 'No trace of them remains but me.'[125]

The second transformation revealed by Ben-Amotz's book, besides the fictional narrative, was the author's 'coming out' about his own Jewish past, which had been a closely guarded secret. 'Who Are You, Dan Ben-Amotz?', ran the headline in *Haolam Hazeh* upon the novel's release.[126] Behind the life of Dan Ben-Amotz, the story of Moshe Tehilimzeiger emerged. The writer was born with this name in 1923 in the Polish–Ukrainian town of Rowno/Rivne and did not resettle in Palestine – in the Zionist youth village of Ben Shemen – until after the Nazis invaded Poland. He was the only member of his family to choose emigration to Palestine, and therefore the only one to survive the Holocaust. But after arriving in Ben Shemen, he had already changed his name – initially to Moshe Shaoni – and before long had also invented a new life story for himself in Palestine that omitted Europe.[127] 'It was a very clear process of assimilation to the sabra environment', Ben-Amotz admitted, recalling his first years in Palestine, when he devised a local origin story for himself, including a new family complete with uncles and aunts. 'Like any kid, I didn't want to be different. And it was impossible to be like everyone else if you came from another place and your parents lived somewhere else.'[128] Perhaps it was his difference from his locally born peers that led him to adopt so keenly the mannerisms and speech patterns of the new culture, ultimately becoming its personification as Dan Ben-Amotz. Just as Uri Lam's trip led to the emergence of Zvi Hirsch, the novel was Ben-Amotz's way of coming to grips with the story of Moshe Tehilimzeiger: 'I came to the conclusion that you can only forget events that you don't refuse to remember', he wrote, shortly after the novel's release, in a summation of his inner struggle. 'The first step must be remembering – not commemorating – but being aware, and only then is it possible to forget.'[129] However, despite the similarities between Ben-Amotz and Uri Lam, *To Remember, To Forget* was no autobiographical novel. Rather, it was the fictional herald of a paradigm shift: the re-entry of the Jewish Holocaust experience into Israeli society's public memory, which gradually eroded the myth of a disconnected Hebrew culture, even for those who actually *were* born there.

Six years after the Eichmann trial, the Six-Day War of June 1967 and the preceding Arab threats of annihilation once again evoked the integration of a Jewish Holocaust experience into Israel's self-definition. When the war was over, even the Hebrew dissidents in the circle of Uri Avnery, Nathan Yellin-Mor and Amos Kenan described it as a 'defensive war against a clear attempt at genocide on the part of Egypt'.[130] The most striking evidence of the advent of memories of the Holocaust – and of their links to the current threats in the conflicts of Israel–Palestine and the greater Middle East – was Amos Kenan's 'A Letter to All Good People'.[131] This essay is symptomatic of Kenan's personal and political incorporation of Holocaust memory and a sign of his quarrel with representatives of the European Left, who had previously been at his side in the struggle against European colonialism. After the Six-Day War, the New Left had officially shifted allegiances from the Jewish state to the Palestinian cause; Kenan reminded them of the menacing pre-war scenarios: 'Today, no less than in June 1967, Israel is in danger of annihilation'.[132] Still, far from recounting the genuine history of the Israel–Palestine conflict, he, too, cloaked these threats in the imagery of the Nazis and the Holocaust: 'If the Allies had defeated Germany in 1940, there would have been no Auschwitz death camps. At that time, if anyone had claimed that the Germans intended to murder 6 million Jews, people would have said:

"This is merely propaganda."'¹³³ In the same breath, defying the New Left and their 'optical illusion of 1968', he rationalised Israel's preventive attack on its Arab neighbours.¹³⁴ 'After the death camps, we are left with only one supreme value: existence.'¹³⁵ Thus, Kenan had slowly formed a worldview that interwove Arab hostilities and antisemitic incidents in 1950s Prague and late 1960s Poland with the New Left's pro-Palestinian stance. The world was increasingly divided into Jews and non-Jews in his eyes. A few months after writing his 'Letter', Kenan travelled to Paris with Moshe Sneh, Shlomo Avineri and others to attend a conference on 'Israel and the New Left', to which the World Union of Jewish Students had been invited in late February 1969.¹³⁶ There, he came to the Jewish state's defence and railed against the New Left, which since the Six-Day War had been increasingly withdrawing its recognition of Israel. Soon afterward, he wrote an article for *Yediot Aharonot* with the headline 'New Left, Go Home!'¹³⁷

At the same time, Kenan's trip was intended as a challenge to Matzpen and its public fraternisation with the European New Left. They had all spent so much time together in the same cultural dissident scene, in which Kenan and Avnery had first met Shimon Tzabar, Haim Hanegbi and others, and that personal connection might have lent fuel to the fire. Yet, for Kenan and Avnery, the public performance of hostility was, at its core, less about positioning within Israel and more directly about Matzpen's involvement with the European New Left. '"Matzpen" Seeks Admission Cheaply', wrote Kenan in *Yediot Aharonot* of the strengthening ties between the Israeli leftists and the New Left in Europe, contentiously claiming that 'even the slogan of brotherhood of the workers of the Middle East [. . .] does not work well, on account of the fact that astute scoundrels long ago used it as an alibi for genocide'.¹³⁸

Kenan's hostility did not go unanswered. While 'A Letter to All Good People' was circulating abroad, Haim Hanegbi and Moshé Machover responded with a 'Letter to All Those "Once-Good" Israelis', which targeted Avnery, Kenan and Yellin-Mor with equal ferociousness:

> It took a situation as radical as the June War to expose the fact that all of you and Dayan share the same basic assumptions about the Jewish state on this land [. . .] You've suddenly also realised that if you don't set aside Israeli [Hebrew] nationalism, you will be driven into the arms of Dayan et al. – into the arms of Zionism.¹³⁹

In addition to the former allies' disagreements over present-day politics and justifications for the most recent war, their attitudes towards the collective Jewish memory of the Holocaust deepened the rift. Matzpen had remained resistant to its pull, which by then was even entering the Hebrew consciousness. When people called the Six-Day War 'a battle for Israel's existence' – a frequent claim – Matzpen did not realise that this was also tied to the emergence of Holocaust memories; they simply saw one more instance of Zionists spouting catastrophic rhetoric. After all, Zionists had been talking about the never-ending persecution of the Jews 'from generation to generation' since long before the Holocaust. Hanegbi and Machover took issue with this dominant national narrative of history:

> This self-justifying and self-righteous philosophy of history customarily seeks to comprehend the Jewish fate in separation from – and even in opposition to – the fate of the Gentiles. [. . .] Whoever accepts the assumption that discrimination against national minorities is inherent in human nature must also accept the Zionist solution to the Jewish problem.[140]

Such a rejection of a Zionist narrative of history, which also integrated the reality of the Israel–Palestine conflict into a centuries-long Jewish history of persecution, might be at the core of Matzpen's critique. At the same time, though, this rejection concealed the reality of an historical experience that had, indeed, separated Jews from the rest of the world in the wake of the ultimate genocide: an experience reflected in the gradual emergence of a collective memory of the Holocaust.

When Matzpen adopted the concept of a new Hebrew nation for their own cause, they deployed it in opposition to a religious justification for the Jewish state. It also served as a helpful tool for demanding that Palestinians recognise Israeli Jewry as a post-Zionist nation inherent to the region. However, in light of the catastrophe of European Jewry, which united most Jews in a shared experience or memory, the concept of a distinct Hebrew nation had already gone obsolete. By this point, the land of the new Hebrew nation had already become also the state of the Jewish survivors.

Matzpen's immunity to the Holocaust's increasing impact was, however, only partly due to the Hebrew cultural milieu from which the group had sprung, and whose ideas they had continued to develop in their own way, even if they were at odds with the chronology of memory. The group's circumvention of the Jewish catastrophe was facilitated far more by their revival of a Jewish political tradition that, long before the genocide, had offered an alternative to founding a Jewish state. They may have arisen generationally from the milieu of Hebrew culture, but politically they were building on the tradition of the Jewish labour movement in East–Central Europe that extended to Palestine and Israel. The movement's longstanding faith in the future and in historical progress, with the aim of ending the Jewish people's suffering as a community and a nation, had also made a Jewish state superfluous. After Auschwitz, when Matzpen restabilised its own outlook by adopting a universalistic utopia, the young Israeli leftists were building on a tradition that had already been most dreadfully disproven in the eyes of its former advocates.

Socialism or Barbarism

In late July 1969, not even half a year after Kenan's appearance in Paris at the convention of the World Union of Jewish Students, Haim Hanegbi of Matzpen embarked on a trip to Europe of his own. For many years, Hanegbi and Kenan had been acquaintances who moved in the same circles. But the political upsets that followed the Six-Day War had turned them into political adversaries. This much was evident from the nature of Hanegbi's trip. He had been invited to give talks about the conflict in the Middle East in Stuttgart, Tübingen and Frankfurt – but the invitation came from the New Left organisations in Germany, not from the World Union of Jewish Students. His role was to represent the Israeli Radical Left. Flyers in Frankfurt announced: 'Haim Hanegbi from the Israel[i] anti-Zionist soc[ialist] group Matzpen. Come out in droves'.[141] Separately, the Socialist German Student Union (SDS) extended a spontaneous invitation to a conference in Berlin. 'People here know Matzpen', Eli Lobel had already written to Hanegbi from Paris. 'We're invited everywhere and the people want to know our opinions.'[142] A few weeks earlier, he, too, had travelled to Germany and presented the group's positions in Frankfurt and Hamburg. Back in Israel, Matzpen was seen as heretical for its utopia of a Middle East united in socialism, but the group's political visions for the future resonated in Europe with the New Left.

However, although Diaspora Jews were well-represented in the protest movements after 1968, their opinions on Israel–Palestine generally diverged from those of their non-Jewish comrades.[143] The war of June 1967 had caused a fracture along ethnic lines there too. While the European Left had sided with the Palestinians and against Israel, groups of Diaspora Jews demonstrated their solidarity and existential links to the Jewish state – setting aside such basic criticisms. For example, Eli Lobel pointed out:

> The Palestine-Zionism complex is undeniably a far from negligible divisive factor within the revolutionary movements in the West. The May movement in France, for instance, in its active phase a magnificent example of internationalism [. . .] nevertheless came up against the troublesome problem of Palestine. At the only demonstration with an ethnic character, whether provoked or not, Arabs and Jews in Paris came to blows on the occasion of the anniversary of the June 1967 war.[144]

Given this bond between diasporic Jewry and the Jewish state, Lobel scarcely wished to limit Matzpen's activities and those of its sympathisers to criticising Zionism in connection with the Israel and Palestine question. 'We believe that Jewish revolutionaries have a particular, but not exclusive, role to play in this international struggle', he wrote, going on to describe Diaspora Jews' feelings about Zionism and the Jewish state as 'fallacious answers to the problem of Jews anywhere in the world'.[145] Hence, the quest for a common future for Israeli Jews and Palestinian Arabs also led Matzpen back to the circumstances of world Jewry – in the aim of breaking their political affinity for the Jewish state. Aside from persistent antisemitism, the mutual political affiliation between Israel and the Diaspora was at risk of drawing Jews from outside Israel into the maelstrom of the Israel–Palestine conflict, which 'poses a serious threat to Jews everywhere'.[146] Outside the Middle East, among both Jewish and non-Jewish leftists, Matzpen strove to sever the 'equation of support for Zionism with struggle against anti-Semitism' and to discredit the recourse to the Jewish state as an 'internationalism of fools'.[147] Still, the premise that a 'worldwide struggle against fascism' was the only 'effective answer to antisemitism' renewed a universalist tradition and a political utopia that had long ago fizzled out for its one-time champions during the upheavals of the twentieth century.[148] Matzpen could scarcely pretend otherwise.

With its rhetoric of socialist internationalism and voluntarily relinquishing a Jewish nation-state, Matzpen had inherited a political worldview from the

Eastern European Jewish communists of the early twentieth century and the interwar period. Michel Warschawski later wrote:

> More or less consciously, the wandering Jew, and later the revolutionary Jew of 'Yiddishland' were the archetypes with which they identified – activists such as Hersh Mendel or Israel Feld, known as Sroulik-the-Red, who, from the Russian Revolution to the French resistance, through the MOI [a trade unionist organisation for immigrant workers in France] and Republican Spain, never had any fatherland other than world revolution.[149]

Long before statehood, the conflict among Jews over the Jewish question had pitted the universalist perspective, which looked towards the larger communist movement, against a Zionist retreat from the Gentile world that emphasised Jewish particularism. Instead of seeking to establish a separate nation-state, the Jewish communists put their faith 'in the aspect of the revolution that changes society and by extension people, in order to escape the antisemitism that goes hand in hand with ethnic nationalism'.[150] Thus, the social revolution, in their eyes, would also become an engine of the Jews' national liberation. The rivalry came to a head in 1917, when the British pledge to create a 'national home for the Jewish people' in Palestine was juxtaposed against the October Revolution's guarantee of equal rights for Russian Jews. Lenin's decisive action against antisemitism may have been one reason that Jews were disproportionately represented in communist movements throughout Europe.[151] As Isaac Deutscher wrote years later in 'The Russian Revolution and the Jewish Problem': 'It should be realised that the great majority of Eastern European Jews were, up to the outbreak of the second World War, opposed to Zionism.'[152] Accordingly, Leopold Trepper reflected, 'I became a communist because I am a Jew', years before emigrating to Palestine.[153]

The origins and platform of Palestinian communism were fuelled by this universalist historical perspective. The party's founders, such as Joseph Berger-Barzilai, Wolf Averbuch and later Leopold Trepper, had biographical links to both the Zionist movement and socialist horizons of the future. However, against the backdrop of the radicalising 'Arab question' and the awareness that the project of Zionist settlement was explicitly trying to establish a homogeneous Jewish society, the arrival of communism in Palestine marked a departure from Zionism's particularist perspective. In the spirit of a common vision, it brought with it a conversion to communist internationalism.[154] Trepper later wrote about this final divorce from the Zionist movement:

> Since 1917, I had been living with my eyes turned toward that vast and dazzling light in the east. [. . .] Convinced henceforth that only socialism could free the Jews from their centuries-old oppression, I threw myself into the fray. [. . .] As for me, in those days I did not believe that it was either possible or desirable to create a Jewish state. I could not see why the five million American Jews, the three million Jews in the Soviet Union, and the millions of Jews scattered throughout the world should leave their homes and emigrate to Palestine in search of a hypothetical native land. [. . .] Those who were conscious of belonging to the Jewish race should be able to enjoy in each country the rights of a national minority.[155]

The birth of Palestinian communism was also inextricably linked to the perspective of the Jews' socialist emancipation and their integration into non-Jewish majority societies.

The last person to tout this yet unbroken tradition of Jewish internationalism was the Belgian–Jewish Trotskyite Abraham Léon (1918–44). In December 1942, already living underground at the tender age of twenty-four, he completed his treatise *The Jewish Question: A Marxist Interpretation*, which was to be published only posthumously. Léon, born Abraham Wajnsztock in 1918 in hotly contested Warsaw, had personally passed through various stages of Eastern European Jewry's winding path into modernity. Raised by a Zionist family, he first emigrated with them to Palestine in 1925, only to return to Poland the following year, before moving once again to Belgium, where the young Léon joined the left-wing Zionist Hashomer Hatzair. Yet as he contemplated the rivalling visions of territorialisation versus universal liberation, he began to distance himself more and more from Zionist utopia and ultimately signed on to the communist vision for the future.[156]

This shift culminated in Léon's completion of his famous manuscript *The Jewish Question: A Marxist Interpretation*, in which Léon, who had studied Marx and the Marxist debates about modern Jewish existence, proposed the concept of the 'people-class'.[157] Premised on the intersection between Jews' ethnicity and their unique roles in premodern society, the concept proposed a socio-economic explanation for Jews' persistence as a collectivity. Léon went on to describe antisemitism as the incapacity of a bourgeois capitalist mode of production to incorporate the particularities of Jewish life into its model of modern society, a discrepancy which he resolved by positing a revolutionary utopia that would rise above both antisemitism and bourgeois society in one fell swoop. Challenging the 'illusion of Zionism', which 'consists in believing that the insurmountable difficulties which decaying capitalism puts in the way of these tasks will disappear as if by magic in Palestine', Léon insisted socialism and a complete revolution of society constituted the only viable prospect of Jews being emancipated and integrated into the global economy.[158] 'We still cannot foresee exactly what the "offspring" of present Judaism will be', Léon concluded his treatise, in December 1942, maintaining his optimism even then, but 'socialism will take care that the "birth" will take place under the best possible conditions'.[159]

Until early 1944, Léon supported numerous mass protests in Belgium and sought to 'direct them toward the revolutionary proletarian movement'.[160] Despite the pressures of living underground during the Nazi occupation, he undertook the journey to the convention of the Trotskyist Fourth International in February 1944. But even in the Belgian underground, Léon could not escape the Nazis. In Charleroi, where he hoped to hide out with his wife, he fell into the hands of the Gestapo a year before the war ended. After weeks of detainment and torture, he was deported to Auschwitz and murdered at the age of twenty-six. The extermination of Eastern European Jewry eventually stripped his utopia of its human foundation; this testified in brutal fashion to the failure of his universalist hopes for the future.

Nevertheless, Léon's magnum opus became a primary source for the New Left, untainted by the circumstances of its author's demise.[161] *The Jewish Question: A Marxist Interpretation* was published in France in 1946 and as an English translation in Mexico in 1950, leaving barely a ripple.[162] In 1968, a Parisian press reprinted it, adding an extensive foreword by Maxime Rodinson. Soon enough, it became a veritable textbook on the Jewish question and was passed around in Jewish leftist circles. Reprints and translations into Italian, Swedish and German followed.[163] In Paris, Eli Lobel organised a symposium on the enduring significance of Léon's work;[164] in Beirut, Maxime Rodinson organised an Arabic translation. His theses were soon discussed by such Arab intellectuals as Sadik J. Al-Azm and Elias Murqus.[165] Wherever it was read, the book's reception was propelled by the dream of a universalist utopia that would eliminate antisemitism while transcending Zionism – as though nothing had changed since the 1930s. Eliding Auschwitz, the very real 'de-universalisation of humanity', and its collective effect on Jewish consciousness, the catastrophe was integrated into socialists' teleology of progress and interpreted as a confirmation of their historical philosophy.[166] 'In our epoch humanity is faced with the alternative of socialism or barbarism', asserted Nathan Weinstock in his interpretation of Léon's text, arguing that the Holocaust was the 'the terrible price mankind must pay for delay in carrying out the socialist revolution or for failure to arrest its degeneration'.[167]

In the context of the Israel–Palestine conflict and persistent antisemitic attitudes in European society, the new edition of Léon's book reframed and updated his position, but in a sense ignored the tragic ending of the author's biography. Weinstock concludes his introduction to Léon's book: '[A]ssuming that one could spell out a "Jewish" stand in the political struggle, it could only be the admission of the fact that the Jewish people have a vested interest in the emancipation of humanity [. . .] Socialism is the only road to Jewish survival.'[168] Hence, the efforts by the New Left to build on Léon's theories simultaneously testified to their evasion of both Léon's personal fate and the implications of the Holocaust for their own ideology.[169]

Of all the reviews and articles that were released in parallel to the publication of Léon's book, only Isaac Deutscher's was less optimistic. Deutscher's essay 'The Russian Revolution and the Jewish Problem', written in 1964, before the New Left's emergence, was included in the French reprinting of Léon's book. The 'Jewish opposition to Zionism was a tragic opposition – it failed and ended in the perdition of the Jews', Deutscher concluded gloomily, considering it impossible to extend a past generation of communist anti-Zionism to the present day.[170] The Jewish communists' old dream, which now served as a reference point for the New Left, could not stand up to Auschwitz. In 1954, Deutscher explained:

> I have, of course, long since abandoned my anti-Zionism, which was based on a confidence in the European labour movement, or, more broadly, in European society and civilisation, which that society and civilisation have not justified. [. . .] For the remnants of European Jewry – is it only for them? – the Jewish State has become an historic necessity.[171]

Thus, the New and the Old Left held diametrically opposed views about the lessons of the Holocaust. The New Left wanted to continue the same utopian programme, but the Old Left felt it had been destroyed by historical experience. The optimism of the few survivors from the Jewish labour movement had likewise been crushed. Confronting their historic defeat, they made their peace, one way or another, with the Jewish state.[172]

Still, the members of the New Left were not the first ones after the Holocaust who wished to revive the shattered political utopias from before the war. They had been preceded by Jakob Moneta and Rudolf Segall's circle of Trotskyist returnees, who had waited out the Nazi era in Palestine and, together with Jakob Taut and Jabra Nicola, preserved a political tradition that Matzpen would soon join. Their focus on the Palestine question and their political advocacy for a joint Jewish–Arab society were more than just extensions of their earlier internationalist worldviews and activism from Europe. In Palestine – far removed from the events in Europe and their effects – their universalistic expectations were preserved nearly unscathed. Besides, most of them had moved to Palestine planning to stay only as long as necessary, to maintain their ties to Europe and to return after the war. 'We are in exile here in Palestine', Rudolf Segall later wrote, exemplifying the group's attitude. 'It is our duty to return to our home countries as soon as possible to work in the service of revolution.'[173] Even before Israeli statehood, Jakob Moneta had returned to Germany with an untainted dream of progress and a belief – very belatedly revised – 'that history there would pick up where it had left off after the 1918 Revolution'.[174] Like Rudolf Segall, he jumped into the thick of the labour movement, where he resumed the struggle from the old days in German unions and paved the way for an international New Left. 'In that regard, the Palestinian periphery was the bridge that led over Nazism and Auschwitz, which seemed like a kind of no-man's-land' and enabled the Trotskyists from Palestine 'to build on [. . .] the traditions of the 1920s'.[175]

Many years later, the dichotomy between a renewed dream of the future and the Jewish experience of annihilation was expressed in the memoirs of the Polish–Jewish Trotskyist Hersch Mendel (1900–68), translated into German and published by Jakob Moneta.[176] Moneta loudly hailed the significance of his kindred spirit's life's work. With his epilogue to Mendel's memoir, he hoped to immortalise both Mendel and Poland's Jewish labour moment, which the Nazis had eradicated. Mendel, born Hersch Stockfisch at the turn of the century, represented more than anyone the many facets of that history, of which his autobiography became the most important chronicle. A native of Warsaw's Yiddish-speaking proletariat, he joined the struggle for the Jews' social and national liberation by way of the Jewish Labour Bund and the Communist Party of Poland, then became a Trotskyist dissident outside the party during the Stalin era. Different existential experiences during the Second World War – Moneta was living in the Palestinian Yishuv, while Mendel survived the war in Nazi-occupied France – pushed the two men's lives in opposing directions. In his epilogue to Mendel's memoir, Moneta wrote:

> I crossed political paths with Hersch Mendel [. . .] Whereas the extermination of the Jewish people in Poland and in the countries under Nazi occupation turned him from an internationalist into a Zionist, my fifteen years living in Palestine and the terrible fate of the Palestinian people led me from proletarian Zionism to internationalism.[177]

As early as 1939, one year after Stalin liquidated the Polish Communist Party and struck a pact with Nazi Germany, Mendel's progressive socialist optimism started to crack. 'The thirty odd years which I had devoted to the struggle for socialism were lost', he reflected bleakly in his memoir. 'In the name of that struggle I had given everything of which a man is capable. I had never given a moment's thought to anything else. And now I was witness to a frightful storm which would destroy everything.'[178] But the Holocaust was the trigger of his 'deepest moral crisis'.[179] An episode in which the Nazis shot a Jewish child in front of the child's mother became symbolic to him. 'She was afraid to cry, for she was terrified that the Nazis might single her out [. . .] I literally felt her unshed tears.' At the end of his memoir, he declared:

> He who has been witness to such a scene will never forget it. And he will never rest until the conditions have been created in which its recurrence is no longer possible. He will ever and always be ready to devote his body and soul in order to guarantee the existence of the Jewish people in a Jewish land.[180]

On those grounds, Mendel had no desire to remain in Europe after the war. Devastated by Stalinism and Nazism, he turned to proletarian Zionism as a 'twice-broken revolutionary' and emigrated to Israel in the early 1950s.[181] In a conversation with Jakob Moneta and Eike Geisel regarding the memoir, Jakob Taut later recalled meeting Mendel in Israel:

> In the moment when the Jewish population, including the Jewish workers, were exterminated, he too was a broken man. Not only did his family perish, but so did the entire environment of his upbringing that had once given him the strength to work for the international labour movement. That was why he lost all faith in socialist internationalism; that was why he went to Israel.[182]

Around the same time, Eike Geisel asserted elsewhere: 'His memories deal with [...] the ultimate annihilation of an historical possibility. What he recorded is unrecoverable. He wrote about the transience of the historical conditions that underlay the choice between socialism or barbarism. That question has been decided.'[183] But although Taut and Moneta were deeply affected by Mendel's personal and political breakdown, they did not agree about the personal ramifications. '"Labor Zionism" Narrowed Hersch Mendel's Perspective', ran Moneta's headline, showing that, at least for him, the socialist history of progress was not over, and neither had a fate been definitively chosen at the crossroads of socialism and barbarism.[184] Mendel's memoir ends with the statement that 'the sole hope for the Jewish proletariat in leading the Jewish people along the path to socialism is the construction and defense of this [its own] country'.[185] Moneta and Taut, meanwhile, could scarcely reconcile themselves with the Jewish state, and not only because of the Palestine question. To their mind, the forgotten Jewish proletariat still played a part in a history of progress – as if there were one straight throughline connecting the old battles against the Nazis with the anticolonial movements of the 1950s and 1960s:

> In that sense, the victory of the colonial revolution is also a posthumous victory for the Jewish proletariat in Poland. In the history of liberation movements, the Warsaw Ghetto Uprising occupies a valuable place alongside the Paris Commune, the uprising of the Spanish people [and] the Algerian people's liberation struggle.[186]

The contradictory expectations of history that divided Moneta and Taut from Mendel, which grew out of divergent existential experiences, could not have been phrased in starker terms.

In the last decade of his life, Mendel found an ally in Joseph Berger-Barzilai. Shortly after Mendel's death on 22 July 1968, Berger voiced his public support for his late friend's decision to make the Jewish state and the 'struggle for the existence of the Jewish people' into the focal point of his sunset years.[187] Berger's attitude, likewise, was the outcome not so much of an ideological choice as of the common experience of the 'shipwreck of a generation', to which his memoirs sadly testify.[188] His memoirs became a gravestone for the dreams of socialist revolution, which had been buried under the ruins of the twentieth century. The world–historical experience of the defeated past visions of the future had sent him back into the arms of the Jewish state, even though, after arriving in Palestine in 1920, he had become a committed communist and political opponent of the Zionist movement against the backdrop of the conflict over Palestine. The twenty-one years he spent in Soviet prison camps from 1935 onwards, in the meantime, confronted him with the total arbitrariness of Stalinist rule and destroyed his faith in the socialist project of a universalistic future. And so, during his interment in Siberia, he converted back to his ancestral Jewish faith. 'What helped Berger survive was his turn toward Jewish religion', wrote his biographer Mario Kessler. 'There was no abrupt change of his conviction, but the longer he stayed in the camps, the more he found comfort in the faith.'[189] After Berger was fully rehabilitated and released in 1956, several weeks after the Twentieth Congress of the Soviet Communist Party, he eventually moved to Israel.

Berger wanted to be more than just a witness to his 'lost generation of revolutionaries', despite his many biographical and autobiographical publications.[190] After his arrival in Israel, besides teaching at Bar-Ilan University and reporting for the newspaper *Davar* and the magazine *Molad*, he adopted the cause of Soviet Jews. He wrote numerous columns advocating for their 'inalienable right for "repatriation", i.e. their return to their homeland, and this, they say, is only one country in the world – the State of Israel'.[191] As early as September 1960, he participated in an international convention of the World Jewish Congress, directed by Nahum Goldmann.[192] Aside from his own background and experience of Stalinist purges, the plight of the Soviet Union's Jewish population gave further strong evidence that a communist utopia to resolve the Jewish question had tragically failed: '[T]he events of the thirties destroyed completely the doctrine of assimilation. It was drowned in the blood of the six million Jews who became the victims of German Nazism, and in the rising tide of Great Russian chauvinism.'[193] The divergent memories of the Second World War and the Holocaust cracked apart the Jewish–Communist symbiosis.[194] The experience of collective persecution and annihilation – as Jews – was excluded from the Soviet commemoration of the Great Patriotic War. After the Holocaust, the collective memory of Soviet Jewry was increasingly attacked as particularist and became a conduit for redirected traditional antisemitism.[195] Finally, the destruction of Jewish culture under Stalin and the murder of the Jewish Antifascist Committee's representatives on the Night of the Murdered Poets (12–13 August 1952) was another reminder to Soviet Jews of their precarious Jewishness. As Berger wrote almost twenty years later: 'This great traumatic experience of naked anti-Semitism sparked off the search for a final remedy to the disease. It revived old memories and was the start of the Neo-Zionism in the Soviet Union we are witnessing today.'[196]

The New Left of Matzpen did not turn a blind eye to the fate of Soviet Jews, nor to Jews' failed communist dreams. In his writings on the plight of Soviet Jews, Oded Pilavsky empathised with those communists who 'have been fed up with the Soviet regime, which has distorted socialism beyond all recognition. Broken by the camps [. . .] they have decided to emigrate.' Still, it was clear that the founder of Palestine's Communist Party in the 1920s had long diverged from his former viewpoints, which his Israeli disciples on the New Left wished to continue nevertheless. For Berger, the path to the Jewish state had symbolised a territorialised retreat into his Jewish identity. By contrast, the members of Matzpen universalised the conflict over the situation of Soviet Jews and tried to attach it to their revived hopes for a revolutionary transformation. In an article titled 'Judaism versus Humanism', Pilavsky asserted that he could not 'approach the problem [of the situation facing Soviet Jews] from a Jewish point of view, because a Jewish perspective, by its very nature, also distorts the humanistic-socialistic view of the problem'.[197] Hence, Pilavsky expanded the Jewish aspirations for free emigration to Israel into a much broader demand for the right to emigrate and for the freedom to choose one's place of residence, regardless of ancestry or affiliation. Most of all, building on a socialist stance towards the Jewish question, he insisted on future prospects within the USSR, on 'a struggle for a revolutionary transformation of the regime and of the structure of Soviet society, to realise a socialist society and not only a caricature of one'. He also expressed the same demand to the old Jewish communists who were now living in Israel. 'We call upon them to join the ranks in the struggle for a socialism according to your vision here [. . .] and to fight against the Jewish chauvinism that rules in Israel.'[198] Yet such a call could hardly bridge the existential gap between the past Jewish hope in the universal promise of communism and the resigned, disillusioned choice to immigrate to the Jewish state.

The drama of Berger and Mendel's shipwrecked generation was still not over yet. Even as the New Left in Israel and Europe sought to pick up the old socialist perspectives on Jewish life right where they left off, the fate of Berger's former comrade Leopold Trepper was already demonstrating the latest stage in this universalistic project's collapse. Trepper had co-founded the Communist Party in Palestine, then witnessed its liquidation from afar. After working underground for the anti-Nazi resistance group Red Orchestra, he had been incarcerated in Stalin's prisons, after which he deliberately chose to return to his birth country, Poland, instead of Israel. 'In my country, three million Jews were exterminated during the last war', he explained to the communist officials, who offered him a dignified retirement in the Soviet Union after his release and rehabilitation. 'My place is with the little community that survived the Holocaust.'[199] Also, after the liberalisation efforts during the Polish October, he harboured hopes for the country's post-war socialism and worked to cultivate the Jewish community there, where he played an active role as the president of the Yiddish Buch publishing house and the director of the Sociocultural Association of Polish Jews (T.S.K.Z.P.). His hopes would be shredded by bitter disappointment. The news of the destruction of Jewish institutions and the murder of Jewish artists and writers in the Soviet Union had already demonstrated the return of antisemitism in a socialist guise. But the initial pledge of equality collapsed outright with the events of 1967–8 in Poland. The Communist Party, in which the Polish nationalists and antisemites of the pre-war period had also been gathering around General Moczar since the end of the Second World War, itself fuelled anti-Jewish sentiment for years.[200] The Six-Day War merely provided a pretext for the Polish government's antisemitic campaign, now posing as anti-Zionism. 'It was not long before hostility toward Israel and Zionism turned into open hostility toward Polish Jews', Trepper wrote in his memoir, exasperated. His 'last battle' was now to leave Poland.[201]

'We wanted to change man, and we have failed', he concluded, as he completed his memoir in Denmark. He only managed to relocate there in 1973, after a fierce struggle and with the help of an international campaign of support. 'This century has brought forth two monsters, fascism and Stalinism, and our ideal has been engulfed in this apocalypse.'[202] He did not want to give up his dream of a reformed socialism, but he could only find a new, safe home in the Jewish state. He had not chosen Israel, but for him, as for Mendel and Berger and indeed for an entire 'lost generation', the country became his last resort. 'How does one approach such people [. . .] people who came to Israel as a "shipwreck of a generation"?' Eike Geisel later asked, perturbed, in a long interview with Taut and Moneta about the lives of Mendel, Berger and Trepper: 'Aren't such broken people living proof of the correctness of the Zionist ideology?'[203] Perhaps this was one reason Trepper's move to Israel and the tortuous life of Berger-Barzilai were scarcely addressed in *Matzpen*. That would have meant coming to terms with a generation whose personal 'testimony of recent history put a thumb on the scales of Zionism'.[204] As founders of Palestinian communism, Trepper and Berger's legacy could be advanced and their political vision revived. As members of a failed generation who had abandoned their historical optimism, they did not set useful examples of how to shape a political future, certainly when it came to the ever-pressing Palestine question. What divided the Old and New Jewish Left was not their politics or agendas so much as a near-unbridgeable gulf between an optimistic faith in progress and lived experiences of a miserable century.

This form of failure had its own irritating repercussions for the New Leftists of Matzpen, even if their acknowledgment of this lived history carried over to their encounters with leftists in West Germany. When Haim Hanegbi travelled to Germany in the summer of 1969, he made his last stop in West Berlin for an appearance at an event held by the Socialist German Student Union (SDS). Out of solidarity, since he was short on funds, SDS offered its Israeli guest a place to stay at the home of an old communist who had since joined the New Left. Hanegbi forgot his host's name soon after returning home from Germany. But the man's stories left a lasting impression on the much younger Israeli. Still wearing the garb of his Weimar Republic days, with a beret on his head and a briefcase under his arm, the German host told Hanegbi about his pre-war experiences and the years of Nazi rule, which he survived in a concentration camp. Dashed hopes of a new socialist beginning in the German Democratic Republic had ultimately led the committed communist to move to West Berlin. But it was the knowledge of Auschwitz and its meaning as a 'rupture in civilisation' (Dan Diner) that seared the man's mind and maimed his own universalism. This was all palpable to the young Hanegbi. When he made critical comments about Israel's nationalism and its constant 'policy of conquest', the German communist interrupted him and insisted: 'I don't want to hear a single word discrediting the Jewish state'. Hanegbi pointed out his own Jewishness, as a kind of licence, but his host would not budge from this strict stance. He himself had been detained in a concentration camp, and after everything the Nazis had done to the Jews, 'whatever the Jews are doing is completely fine'.[205] Though a debatable position, this was an ethical decision – in light of past horrors – to reject any criticisms of the Jewish state as a home for the survivors. The young Hanegbi, as he himself later recalled, walked away from this encounter in a pensive mood. It had taught him an important lesson about the long shadow of the past.[206]

That meeting took place in August 1969. Three months later, on 9 November, thirty-one years after the pogroms known by the euphemism *Kristallnacht*, a group of German leftists kissed this moral imperative goodbye. Members of the group planted a bomb in the Jewish Community House on Berlin's Fasanenstrasse, which was scheduled to host a 250-guest event commemorating the anniversary. For unknown reasons, the bomb never went off. If it had exploded, it would have 'shredded the building' and claimed many lives.[207] The next day, in a statement headlined 'Shalom and Napalm', the would-be bombers identified themselves as members of the Black Rats TW (Tupamaros Westberlin), and verbally affirmed their ideological lineage.[208] At any rate, their arguments had little to do with the realities of the Israel–Palestine conflict. Instead, they spoke of the necessity of the German Left setting aside the 'guilt-laden pretext of coming to terms with the fascist atrocities against the Jews', then cavalierly invoked 'fascist atrocities against Palestinian Arabs'.[209] At a far remove from the actual antagonism between Israeli Jews and Palestinian Arabs, the German leftists used the Palestine question as a way to move on from a past they preferred not to face, a past in which the Nazis and the Holocaust loomed large. They projected attributes of the Nazi annihilation programme onto the policies of Israeli Jews, distorting those policies to fit. Portions of the New Left in Germany were resuming an old tradition of antisemitism and starting to enact it, often with lethal violence. 'All political power comes from the barrel of a gun', concluded the would-be bomber's statement with a menacing quotation by Mao Tse-tung.[210]

The events did not go unchallenged, however. Just three weeks later, on 1 December, the Frankfurt Palestine Committee released a 'Statement on the Attempted Bombing of the Jewish Community House in Berlin', fiercely condemning the attack: 'The Jews in the Diaspora can only interpret acts of terror such as the one against the Community House in Berlin within the context of their persecution and annihilation as Jews.' In contrast to the left-wing trend of using the Israel–Palestine conflict as an arena for renewed anti-Jewish sentiment, this was a show of solidarity with Holocaust victims that was otherwise conspicuously absent from that scene.

> The attempted bombing, the slogans at memorials to the victims of fascism, and their justifications represent a provocation *objectively*. Within the movement, we need to fight against such actions if we do not want our internationalism to culminate in ahistorical moralism.[211]

The statement was written by Daniel Cohn-Bendit, Detlev Claussen, Burkhard Bluem, Heiner Roetz and Ronny Loewy. Surely by no coincidence, some of the signatories themselves were Jewish or of Jewish descent. Far beyond its immediate purpose, the statement symbolised the need for the left to engage in a public debate over how to combine criticism of Israel's policy around Palestine with solidarity towards the victims of the Holocaust. This was the beginning of a gradual split that would tear apart the left, particularly in Germany. A parallel process, originating at the same time in the periphery of the Diaspora, would lead some Matzpen members to begin debating questions of the Holocaust as well.

Lebanon 1982: 'The Real War and the Imaginary War'[212]

In the early morning hours of 13 June 1982, a small cohort of Frankfurt-based Jews set off in a convoy to Bonn. Their precise destination was the Israeli Embassy in the district of Bad Godesberg, where they planned to demonstrate against the war in Lebanon that had begun a few days earlier. Moishe Postone, a Canadian-born lecturer at Goethe University Frankfurt, explained the protest to a correspondent from Berlin's left-wing *Tageszeitung*, who had travelled along with them to cover it:

> We are a group of Jews from Frankfurt. [. . .] We are outraged at the Israeli forces' attempt to wipe out Palestinian organisations. But our reasons for rejecting the actions of the Tel Aviv government are not only humanitarian: we also know that there will be no peace in the Middle East without a right of self-determination for the Palestinian people.[213]

The initiative was spearheaded by Dan Diner, who at the time was serving as a guest professor at the University of Kassel. Three years earlier, he had completed a postdoctoral thesis in Frankfurt on *Tausch und Gewalt im Vorderen Orient* (Exchange and Violence in the Middle East), which was published under the title *Israel in Palästina* (Israel in Palestine) and caused quite a stir.[214] It was Diner's suggestion to protest directly in front of the embassy. He was joined by a whole group of left-wing Jews from Frankfurt, including Micha Brumlik, who had recently been appointed as a professor of education at the University of Heidelberg; Daniel Cohn-Bendit, who by then was publishing the Frankfurt local magazine *Pflasterstrand*; Cilly Kugelmann, who years later would direct the educational programme and curate exhibitions at the city's Jewish Museum; and the future psychoanalysts Dina Stein and Susann Heenen. Yet the mere twenty-five participants were prevented from delivering a statement right outside the embassy grounds. 'An embassy is always in danger', argued the police officers on the ground, 'especially the embassy of a country at war'.[215] At some distance from the desired location, Diner finally addressed a few words to the group that had travelled with him, who held up signs and banners bearing captions in German, English, Hebrew and Arabic.[216] 'Stop the Israeli Liquidation of the Palestinians in Lebanon', demanded one placard.[217] Cohn-Bendit posed behind it, while holding up a solidarity slogan in Arabic. Dan Diner's poster read *Hal'a HaKibush*; Cilly Kugelmann appeared in a photograph alongside a German slogan that translated as 'Jews For the Rights and Lives of Palestinians'. Almost all the invited members of the press had stayed away. 'To them, we don't matter', Cohn-Bendit told the lone correspondent, disillusioned.[218] Still, it was the very first demonstration in West Germany in opposition to the current war and in favour of Jewish–Palestinian coexistence. 'For a Joint Perspective', read another poster; that was the refrain that stuck.[219]

One week had passed since 6 June, when the Israeli government had decided to send troops into Lebanon in response to the attempted assassination of their Ambassador to the UK, Shlomo Argov, who had sustained serious injuries. Moreover, there had been Palestinian rocket fire from Lebanon on northern Israel some weeks before. Within 48 hours, such incursions were held back by a 40km 'safety corridor', or buffer zone. The offensive was the beginning of 'Operation Peace for Galilee'. In the middle of the Falklands Crisis between the UK and Argentina, a period of Syrian isolation and military weakness, and a tense moment between the major powers of the Cold War, the Israeli military considered this excellent timing for their operation. Yet the plans for the military operation were older and connected with efforts to bring an end to the PLO's political existence in Lebanon and, by extension, to strike a blow to Palestinian institutions on the West Bank and in the Gaza Strip. Ariel Sharon, who was coordinating the military campaigns for Begin's government, had for some time been openly advocating an Israeli 'war against the PLO' that would contribute to restructuring Lebanon.[220] The 'objective was the restoration of Christian dominance' under the leadership of Bashir Gemayel, who 'would then sign a peace treaty with Israel', while the Palestinians would be driven out into Syria.[221] But the Israeli Army soon broached the boundary of the planned 'security zone', and before long its soldiers were approaching West Beirut, gearing up to fight the Palestinian troops who were entrenched there. It was the first war that Israel fought solely against Palestinians and not against an Arab state. The war would be Israel's most protracted.

Public reactions to the military conflict were not slow in coming. In Israel, Matzpen had already sounded the alarm about an imminent war in Lebanon, both in their own publication and in *Haaretz*. To reach a larger audience, individual members of the group participated in the inter-party 'Liberated Territory' initiative – a group whose very name 'inverted the meaning of the right-wing term for the Occupied Territories'.[222] From December 1981, the group published a weekly paid-for column in *Haaretz* that declared itself a 'liberated territory' for information and expressed the 'fiercest and most continuous criticism of the government's policy'.[223] Their twentieth column, dated

9 June 1982, was headlined 'No to the War' and read: 'With immediacy and urgency, as an imperative in a state of emergency, we propose a nationwide assembly of the peace camp to deliberate paths of action and guiding principles, faced with the opening of a new chapter drenched in blood and tears.'[224] A few days earlier, the similarly marginal ad hoc 'Committee for Solidarity with Bir-Zeit University' had assembled in opposition to the war in Lebanon. It consisted of a circle of the Palestinian educational institution's supporters, with Matzpen's Michel Warschawski among its founders the previous year. The first public demonstration in Tel Aviv calling for an immediate stop to the war had only fifty attendees.[225] Notwithstanding, the protest quickly spread to Jews outside Israel. First, in Paris, Maxime Rodinson came out with a letter of protest in *Le Monde*, which then printed a much higher-profile joint statement by Nahum Goldmann, the former president of the World Jewish Congress, his successor Philip Klutznik and Pierre Mendes-France three weeks later. 'The war in Lebanon must stop', it declared. 'And there should be negotiations with the aim of achieving co-existence between the Israeli and Palestinian peoples based on self-determination.'[226] By then, similarly worded declarations with hundreds of signatories had been published in British, Belgian, French and American dailies. In Germany, the first statement by Berlin Jews would soon be released. Individual members of the Jewish communities in Hamburg and Munich had also met to co-draft letters of protest.[227]

Thus, the demonstrators near the Israeli Embassy in Bonn on 13 June 1982 were far from alone. Nevertheless, their public stand against the policies of the Jewish state represented a fundamental challenge, specifically to the outlook of Jews living in Germany. Merely by choosing to live in the ostracised successor state to Nazi Germany, the Jews there found themselves in the situation of a 'pervasive, omnipresent ban'; 'a Jewish ban hovering over Germany that came alive through the liturgical resonating board of memory' and that became a 'source of the overall Jewish rejection of Jewish life on German soil, [. . .] in the "land of the murderers".'[228] From the outset, the new start of Jewish life in post-war Germany rested therefore on a deep feeling of guilt and transformed their lives into an existence 'on the go'.[229] Their gaze was primarily directed inwards, at Jewish community life. 'For my parents, the divide was clear-cut', wrote Cilly Kugelmann, recalling this era. 'My parents didn't have any German friends at all. It was a problem for me to invite German friends from school to our house.'²³⁰ Consistent with this communal retreat to their own collectivity, Jews in Germany maintained a political stance of unconditional solidarity with the Jewish state and 'attempt[ed] to be utterly loyal to Israel'.²³¹ Meanwhile, in their country of residence, they muddled through for many years in a 'Jewish habitus of withdrawal, of absent presences'.²³²

This only changed with the first post-war generation, some of whom had been born in Germany's DP camps immediately after the war and knew each other, sometimes since childhood, from the local Jewish communities' educational programmes for children.²³³ Others had grown up in Israel before their families' return to Germany in the late 1950s. For Dina Stein or for Sammy and Moshe Speier, for example, relocating to Germany had been a traumatic turning point. Although, as socialist Zionists, they believed their roads would eventually lead back to Israel, realistically, they were more and more focused on their ongoing lives in Germany and on political activism there. Because of its public departure from the parental cohort, the New Left became one of the first havens and gathering places for this new generation.²³⁴ Many years later, Dan Diner recalled the political path that had led him to the West German Social Democrats and from there to the New Left:

> Another important aspect is that we intuitively understand whatever people in Germany perceived as left-wing to be a concession to our own history. [...] The left felt like neutral ground. As left-wingers, Jews and Germans alike left the past behind.²³⁵

Club Voltaire, in Frankfurt's Kleine Hochstrasse, became an important 'conversion site', where young Jews experienced a sort of 'acculturation' and moved 'from the Jewish world into the general public'.²³⁶ The practical and political manifestation of this was their direct involvement in the New Left and its alternative political structures. For example, Dina Stein started off in the left-wing German–Israeli Study Group, but joined SDS in 1967 after her second departure from Israel.²³⁷ Meanwhile, from the mid-1970s onward, Dan Diner played an active role in the Sozialistisches Büro (Socialist Bureau) of Offenbach, where he co-published the magazine *Links* (Left). He was later joined there by Micha Brumlik. According to Cilly Kugelmann, most of the young left-wing Jews who had been politicised in Frankfurt led their lives as a 'balancing act [...] with one foot in the Jewish community and the other in the leftist scene'.²³⁸ In the late 1970s, this shared frame of reference finally coalesced into the Frankfurt Jewish Group, which combined both sides of that existence.²³⁹

It was just a matter of time before the group came into conflict with the Jewish community, especially as left-wing Jews increasingly distanced themselves from Israel and viewed 'the Zionist experiment [as having] already failed from a political and moral standpoint'.²⁴⁰ But there was no actual dispute until the group made its first public comments against the Jewish state's policies. When 4,000 Palestinians demonstrated in Bonn against the closure of Bir-Zeit University in the West Bank, the group published a statement in the *Frankfurter Rundschau* expressing their solidarity with the Palestinians in opposition to the 'land grab in Palestine'. This prompted turbulent protests from the Jewish community.²⁴¹ 'A cut-out from the newspaper was pinned up in a display case in the Westend synagogue', Micha Brumlik later recalled. 'That turned our self-stigmatisation into public stigmatisation and, logically, we were pilloried for it.'²⁴² The tensions only truly escalated during the Lebanon War, when a few members were almost expelled from the community. As late as 1994, Arno Lustiger – who was perhaps the most upset by the leftist Jews – published a furious article railing against 'the disgraceful role played by anti-Zionist Jewish leftists, especially in Germany, in the '70s and '80s': 'Dina Stein and Dan Diner were Matzpen's exponents in Germany.'²⁴³

The Frankfurt Jewish Group was certainly not Matzpen's mouthpiece in Germany. But encountering Matzpen did catalyse many of these left-wing Jews' dissociations from a long-shared Zionism that had provided theoretical explanations for, and political answers to, the Nazis' unfathomable mass murder. This was true of Daniel Cohn-Bendit, whose biographical transition peaked during his spring 1970 visit to Israel, but was just as evident in Dina Stein's path to the Israeli Radical Left. In the summer of 1968, her romance with Khalil Toama exposed her to the status of Israel Arabs in the Jewish state, as well as to the reality of the occupation. Both situations disturbed her egalitarian sensibilities.²⁴⁴ It was she who brought Matzpen to Germany. An encounter with Israeli leftists also rerouted the political trajectory of Micha Brumlik. In the autumn of 1967, when he first travelled to Kibbutz Matzuva for a nearly two-year stay in Israel, he found many things disturbing, beginning with the situation in the wake of the Six-Day War. Instead of devoting himself to his social science studies in Jerusalem, he spent his time engaged in the city's leftist scene. Brumlik was especially captivated by Ilan Halevi, who was then still spouting anticolonial rhetoric at Café Ta'amon, long before he became a Jewish PLO member.[245] If Brumlik had arrived in Israel a 'youthful, fiery Zionist', he returned to Germany a 'young, leftist, binational-minded Jewish anti-Zionist'.[246] Yet the most ardent representative of Israeli Left's ideas in Germany was Dan Diner. With his Eastern European, Polish–Lithuanian Jewish family, Diner differed from most of the other members of the Frankfurt Jewish Group, who shared a German–Jewish background. He was born on 20 May 1946 in a DP camp near Munich, and his family immigrated to Israel in 1949, before they finally settled in Frankfurt am Main in 1954. With his 'Jewish-Israeli experience against a German foreground',[247] he played a formative role in the German Left's conflict over the Lebanon War as a spokesperson for the Israeli opposition movement. By then, he had proclaimed himself 'long-married to the conflict', which he now sought to help with solving.[248]

Diner had been a relative latecomer to Matzpen. When Brumlik returned to Frankfurt in the summer of 1969, Diner was still serving as a political activist and theorist, having signed on to the philosophy of the left-wing Zionist Ber Borochov and named a new small press after him.[249] The first of the press's two publications was a reprint of Borochov's *Foundations of Socialist Zionism*, for which Diner wrote a foreword combing Borochov's Jewish national ideas of socialism and emancipation with the theories of Jean-Paul Sartre and Frantz Fanon.[250] 'Be a Revolutionary in Zion and a Zionist in the Revolution': this was the era's basic formula for a left-wing interpretation of the Zionist movement as a movement to emancipate the Jewish people.[251] Diner also embodied this interpretation institutionally, first as chairman of the Federal Union of Jewish Students in Germany and then as the European chairman of the World Union of Jewish Students.[252] At the World Union's 1969–70 conference in Helsinki, he concluded his talk with the statement: 'Aliyah and socialism are the only path to Zionism', foreshadowing his own next move.[253] He completed his dissertation in law at Goethe University in Frankfurt, then went to Israel in 1973. However, although he had long considered 'Zionism itself [. . .] merely an ideological form of justification of the Jewish state' but not 'a material form of domination', Diner had already stretched his left-wing Zionist position on the Palestine question as far as possible towards universalism.²⁵⁴ As chairman of the German Union of Jewish Students, he co-introduced (with Ella Weinstein) a resolution on the situation in the Middle East that advocated the 'Palestinian people's legitimate rights to national self-determination and self-actualisation'.²⁵⁵ In June 1970, when the World Union of Jewish Students passed a resolution linking the enactment of the Zionist project to Palestinians' recognition of it, Diner concluded: 'Thus the Palestinians have become an element of Jewish emancipation. Both have to realise that only common action will lead to socialist liberation [. . .]'.²⁵⁶

It was not long before Dan Diner reconsidered his political analysis. Like some of his peers, he came to believe that a common Jewish–Arab perspective was incompatible with the Zionist idea of preserving an exclusively Jewish state, and that the Israel–Palestine conflict was for one thing a confrontation between national collectivities, but for another colonial in nature. Various elements contributed to this reconsideration. One was an altercation during the summer of 1969, at the Week for Freedom and Understanding in the Middle East, which left Abdallah Frangi severely injured and Eli Lobel somewhat battered. Beyond his friendship with Lobel, Diner's life had exposed him to a mix of experiential influences that ultimately, in a 'long-lasting and bitter process', shaped his divorce from Zionism.²⁵⁷ Diner's 'Israeli-Oriental childhood'²⁵⁸ may have been a background factor, along with the role of his uncle David Tilman, whose former membership in Lehi, the anti-imperialist underground organisation, had encouraged the nephew into Hebrew nativism and prompted him to 'identify with anything that had a direct connection to the country'. The result was, 'paradoxically, an identification with its direct inhabitants, the Arabs of Palestine'.²⁵⁹ A childhood experience, walking with his father on the family land in the north of Israel, had a lasting impact on him as well. When they suddenly spotted an elderly Arab in the distance, Diner's father paused and rested on his rifle as the traditionally dressed man approached him. Much later, the son came to decode this perhaps harmless situation as a 'covertly colonial gesture of superiority';²⁶⁰ this realisation might have been prompted by members of the Jewish youth organisation in Frankfurt am Main, where Diner's family had settled after five years of living in Israel. Now in Germany, Harry Maor and Berthold Scheller, in the more immediate vicinity of the official Jewish community, and Jakob Moneta, at its periphery, carried on the legacy of international dissent, as reflected in their attitude towards the Palestine question.[261] In addition, Diner was deeply affected by the Algerian War – not only the event itself, but also its portrayal in Gillo Pontecorvo's masterpiece film *La Battaglia di Algeri* (The Battle of Algiers, 1966). For Diner, the role of the French paratrooper commander Colonel Mathieu shed valuable light on the context of the Israeli–Palestinian conflict. In the film, Mathieu angrily denies applying fascist torture methods, pointing out that the French soldiers, as former members of the Resistance, lived through Buchenwald and Dachau themselves. For Diner, this line of argument implied the sad insight that '[t]he biographical self-perception of the victim – displaced in space and time – can become a noose for new victims'.[262] He went on: 'Only later did I begin to understand that the establishment and maintenance of an exclusively Jewish state in Palestine was only possible through the employment of discriminatory measures and the continued use of colonial force.' Back in Israel, when Diner was a soldier patrolling the occupied West Bank, he 'experienced directly what had originally been an intellectual insight'.[263]

Diner's shift in perspective on the Israel–Palestine conflict, past and present, was accompanied by a transformation of the framework in which he expressed his positions. An article he wrote, 'Social Democracy and the Colonial Question', was published in April 1973, alongside contributions by Maxime Rodinson and Sadik J. Al-Azm.[264] In Israel, he moved closer to Matzpen and befriended Haim Hanegbi and other members. Over the course of his dynamic life – which straddled Israel and Europe, politics and academia – he found his firmest footing in the journal *Khamsin* and its associated personal network. From then on, Diner's engagement with the Palestine question was linked to his activism directed at the whole Middle East.[265] In the early days of the Lebanon War, Diner reiterated a finding drawn from *Khamsin* about a trend in the Middle East that for a decade had been jeopardising any reconciliation on the Palestine question:

> For the further future: The tide of Islam will keep rising. [. . .] The problem that Arab nation-states are pitted against a Jewish nation-state, as was the case in the Fifties and Sixties, has been increasingly forgotten. [. . .] That is the future of the Orient – and then it will only be Muslims versus nonbelievers. No chance left of a compromise.[266]

Diner would have his greatest impact in Germany through the debates sparked by his politically motivated academic writings, which centred on the historic project of depoliticising national identity – in analogy to religion in early modern Europe. He first presented his political programme for a binational Israeli-Jewish and Palestinian-Arab polity, with which he concluded his contribution to Fischer Verlag's series of books on world history, at a meeting of Matzpen members. The text was later distributed in Vienna as a special edition.[267] Billed as 'aspects of a theory of binationality' and theses on 'Jewish-Israeli nationality', these same ideas were also the subject of two seminars given at the Protestant Student Union in June 1980 and October 1981.[268] They also laid the foundation for a new forum for Germany-based Arabs, Jews and non-Jewish Germans. The discussion group was called the 'Halterner Kreis' (Haltern Circle). Its composition overlapped with that of the Frankfurt Jewish Group, and it took its name from the town of Haltern am See, where the group met sporadically at the home of Nicola Abu-Khalil.[269] In addition to the Jerusalem-born Palestinian Abu-Khalil, the group also included Khalil Toama and attracted another circle of Arab intellectuals in Germany, including the Syrian-born writer Rafik Schami and the Egyptian-born translator Cherifa Magdi.[270] Under the heading 'For a Joint Perspective', one of the group's first signed statements, in March 1982, expressed solidarity with the Israeli 'Liberated Territory' initiative and appealed for a common future for Israeli Jews and Palestinian Arabs on the land of historical Palestine.[271] With the involvement of Alexander Flores and Eike Geisel, a 'joint perspective' also meant enabling the inclusion of non-Jewish German allies during the Lebanon War – a perspective beyond ethnic belonging, countered by trends that saw the left in Germany increasingly adapting to its German national identity. The real war Israel was waging in Lebanon became, simultaneously, a war over the past. By blurring the contemporary conflict with imagery from the Nazi past, left-wing ethnic Germans were removing the basis for their cooperation with the Jewish Left in Germany – ignoring their connected but contradictory histories and, in a way, withdrawing their recognition as equals. With their resolute stand against the intrusion of images from the Holocaust into the discussions about the Israeli–Palestinian conflict, the Jewish leftists were not only bucking the political trend in Germany, however, but also parallel tendencies within the Jewish state. In the 1982 War, the Israeli Prime Minister Menachem Begin had declared war on more than the Palestinians in Beirut: 'I feel as though I have sent an army to Berlin to wipe out Hitler in the bunker', he wrote to US President Ronald Reagan in the middle of the fighting.[272]

Menachem Begin's election as prime minister, in 1977, represented a transformation of Israel's political landscape. Most visibly, it marked the end of Labour Zionism's many years of political domination. Begin was also the first survivor from Europe to take the helm of the Jewish state, and his realms of experience and perception were partly rooted in that previous catastrophe. One year after the outbreak of the Second World War, he had been imprisoned by the Soviet secret police and deported to a labour camp in north-western Russia, before he was released under the Sikorski–Mayski Agreement following the German attack on the Soviet Union. As part of the Polish Armed Forces in the East under the command of Władysław Anders, he eventually made his way to Palestine in 1942. 'There were many indications that he had brought with him what was later described as "survivor syndrome"', Tom Segev wrote: 'a sense of guilt for having remained alive'.[273] His views on the Holocaust also differed decisively from those of David Ben-Gurion, the architect of the Jewish state. According to Avi Shilon, 'Ben-Gurion emphasised that after the State of Israel had gained its independence, the Holocaust became a distant memory';[274] by contrast, the Holocaust was the 'dominant force' motivating Menachem Begin's politics.[275] Most likely, he 'did more than anyone else to politicise' the Holocaust.[276] The experience of annihilation was virtually the engine of his later policy. First, this became evident in his resolute campaign against Ben-Gurion's politic of reparations, when his party claimed that 'the reparations money is dipped in Jewish blood'.[277] His 'lifelong suspicion of Gentiles' also determined his understanding of Israel's conflict with the Palestinians, integrating it into the long history of Jew-hatred.[278] Vitally, Begin situated Israel's position in the Israel–Palestine conflict and in the greater Middle East within a mental framework shaped by the experience of annihilation, whose horrors he kept seeking to fend off afresh.

Beyond all strategic military concerns, the bombardment of Iraq's Tammuz nuclear reactor in 1981, a year before the Lebanon War, furnished an earlier example of this transferral of Nazi imagery. Even if the main purpose of destroying the reactor outside Baghdad was to uphold Israel's regional monopoly on nuclear arms, the decision was informed by a much deeper feeling concerning the need to prevent a possible reprise of Nazi annihilation. 'We must protect our nation, a million and a half of whose children were murdered by the Nazis in the gas chambers', declared Begin, justifying the air strike to the Israeli public.²⁷⁹ For Dan Diner, there was a clear psychological logic behind Israel's actions. He commented on the latest developments in the magazine *Links* (Left):

> The imagery is unambiguous. [. . .] The bombardment of the reactor stands for the failure of the Western allies in the Second World War to destroy the death factory of Auschwitz and the railway lines leading there from the air. But that is not all. Israel's publicly declared nuclear option is also directed at Europe, which spat out the Jews and drove them to Palestine into a life-or-death colonial conflict.²⁸⁰

In regard to the Palestinians, the conflation of memories from the European past and the Holocaust with Israel's present Middle Eastern conflicts soon took on new meaning in the 1982 War in Lebanon. Begin publicly belaboured the comparison between Hitler and Arafat, demonstrating that the only pattern he discerned in the Israel–Palestine conflict was the endless loop of Jews being attacked by their enemies. When he laid out his case for a military invasion, he resurrected the past for his cabinet and declared that this time, the Jews would not be victims. 'There is no way other than to fight selflessly', he argued, defending the decision to invade Lebanon. 'Believe me, the alternative is Treblinka, and we have decided that there will be no more Treblinkas.'²⁸¹

Begin's political practice sparked criticism and debate among the Jewish Left in Germany on many grounds. It was not only that the horizon of the prime minister's perceptions essentially obscured the historical origins of the Israel–Palestine conflict or that the Palestinians were today paying the price for yesterday's Jewish traumas. After the destruction of the Iraqi reactor, members and associates of the Frankfurt Jewish Group formed a new discussion circle, partly out of fear that displaced trauma from the Holocaust was now shaping the Middle Eastern conflict and could lay a terrible trap for Israeli Jews.²⁸² 'The colonial and thus absolute nature of the conflict over Palestine is the *actual gateway* through which images and metaphors from the extermination of the Jews in Europe flow', Dan Diner observed at the time. Given this, he warned that 'an outlook formed by the experience of the Holocaust is oriented around guaranteed doom in the concrete conflict over Palestine. [. . .] The constant efforts to prevent [that doom] increase its likelihood.' Given the urgent escalation in Lebanon, Diner expressed the provocative wish that the opposing fronts of the Cold War would smother the fire of the hot war in Lebanon. In the short term, he was essentially asking for a political confrontation between the superpowers that would, as a side effect, help to de-escalate the real war.[283] However, there was no hope that this power play could pacify the Israel–Palestine conflict once and for all. In the long run, he believed that it was crucial to detach the interpretation of that conflict, past and present, from the memories of the catastrophe in Europe. 'As long as the [. . .] Zionist Israelis perceive themselves as transhistorical victims, then every possibility of overcoming the real controversy is bound to remain blocked', Diner concluded:

> The political consciousness remains blinded by the European experience. The confusion of the constitutive Holocaust in Europe with the real conflict in Palestine can never heal the wound caused by having missed the decisive battle at the right time. For the life and survival of Israelis and Palestinians such a consciousness represents a collective danger.[284]

This plea against conflating the European past with the Israeli–Palestinian present was levelled not only at Israeli society. From the very beginning of the war, when Diner gave his first interview on the situation, he tried to extend the same obligation to German society: 'What is happening there is the extension of German, European history. The suffering of Jews, which blinds them [. . .] Germans have a very special obligation there: to stand up for the Palestinians – and at the same time for the Israeli population's right to live in that land', he pronounced, in an appeal for, specifically, the German Left to 'reflect on their own history which forced Jews to Palestine' and became fundamental to the conflict there.[285] Those hopes did not materialise. The non-Jewish Left had, indeed, participated in the public debate over the Lebanon War, and in large numbers. However, instead of taking historical responsibility, these leftists soon revealed that they were repressing both the Jews' historical experiences and their own role as the post-war generation in Germany – and therefore also the implications for the Israel–Palestine conflict. For the Jewish leftists in Germany, the Lebanon War became the 'first lesson on the reality of antisemitic anti-Zionism'.[286]

The relationship on the left between Jews and Germans had been fraught from the beginning. Even if forgetting differences in historical affiliations may have energised the New Left, the contradictory experiences of history could not be entirely papered over. In the wake of the Six-Day War, there had already been a 'decline in the apparent consensus between the New German Left and their Jewish Zionist comrades, but also in left-wing Jews' relationship to Israel'.[287] When the New Left suddenly abandoned its kibbutz-happy philosemitism and took the Palestinians' side against the Jewish state on an anticolonial basis, left-wing Jews were offended: '[T]he Left in West Germany did not perceive the link between their history and that of those people who, as victims of Nazism, had been catapulted to Palestine', Diner recalled.[288] Among the Germans, amnesiac blindness towards the ongoing traumatic effects of the Holocaust accompanied an uncritical position towards Palestinian movements, even on issues about which Jewish and Israeli leftists made nuanced distinctions for the sake of establishing a common perspective for Jews and Arabs in Israel and Palestine.[289] The 'Al-Fatah summer camp', attended by an SDS delegation in the summer of 1969, inaugurated a dangerous, if not fatal, path that Dieter Kunzelmann was the first to tread.[290] In November 1969, he sent the German Left a 'Letter from Amman' that railed against their 'Jewish complex' (*Judenknax*) and called for an armed struggle against the 'fascist ideology of "Zionism"'.[291] The low point of this development was the hijacking of a plane to Entebbe, Uganda, in the summer of 1976. In addition to the Palestinian terrorists of the PFLP, German leftists from the Revolutionary Cells were involved in the 'selection' of Jewish and non-Jewish passengers. This marked a dramatic turn of events that saw historically forgetful leftist Germans re-enacting their own history.[292]

During the Lebanon War, this development was continued in the press as the left sought to normalise the German past by finding an analogy for Auschwitz. First, the journalist Reinhard Hesse called the invasion of Lebanon a 'reverse Holocaust' in the pages of Berlin's *Tageszeitung* newspaper, indicating that the German Left had washed its hands of the genocide and was now prepared to deploy it as a talking point against the Jewish state's policies. In an interview soon afterwards, the former Social Democratic Member of Parliament Lenelotte von Bothmer invoked the 'dreadful parallels' between the persecution and murder of European Jews and the Israelis' military operation against the Palestinians. When an excerpt from an interview Dan Diner had given for *Pflasterstrand* was reprinted in the *Tageszeitung* with the added subtitle 'On the Israeli Final Solution', Diner felt compelled to intervene in the debate.

Diner's written intervention against overreaching journalism and the recycling of Nazi era terms for the conflict that was escalating in the Middle East sought primarily to bring back a sense of historical judgement to the current debate.[293] In differentiating between different kinds of deaths, between the colonial violence of the Israel–Palestine conflict and the Nazis' historically singular practice of annihilation, he stressed that he had no intention of unequally valuing human lives that ended violently in different historical situations. Yet, Diner demanded that left-wing Germans consider 'the type of death [. . .] that has different respective characteristics for the outlook and the life and survival of those who go on living'. Specifically, he called for distinguishing between the collective death of the Jews in Auschwitz and the deadly violence against the Palestinians in the Israel–Palestine conflict, which had much closer historical parallels with the Algerian War. Although the victims in the Israel–Palestine conflict were also subjected to a form of indiscriminate violence that targeted combatants and civilians alike, said violence arose from a 'conflict that was antagonistic from the outset [. . .] over interests that are irreconcilable, i.e. incapable of compromise'. Unlike that 'real existing conflict', the Nazis' antisemitism had been based on the constructs of modern-day conspiracy theories and racial ideology in the complete absence of any underlying political conflict. Most of all, Diner stressed the unprecedented nature of the Nazi genocide: a 'death sentence against all Jews' everywhere, 'only because they were Jews', which had been 'proclaimed by the Nazis and almost executed to completion. This type of death lives on in the survivors.'[294]

Given this historic specificity, he found it unsettling and disturbing 'that in Germany of all places, the term "Final Solution" should be applied so carelessly' to Israel's military operation in Lebanon. This led Diner to the 'scarcely deceivable feeling [. . .] that people in this country are practically wishing' for the Israeli operation against the Palestinians 'to be a truly planned genocide, a true murder of a people [*Völkermord*]'. Instead of showing solidarity with the situation of Palestinians in this specific conflict, he argued, the comparison mostly attested to the degree to which 'such a qualitative distortion serves a significant implicit function of easing a burden on the collective-German aspects of the local mindset, even on the left' and was a product of German leftists' repression of the Nazis' annihilation of Jews.[295] For the surviving victims of Nazism, Diner emphasised elsewhere, the reuse of terminology from the Holocaust in reference to the Jewish state 'can only serve the purpose of robbing the Nazis' victims of their history and thus excusing the collectivity of the perpetrators'.[296] On either side of the Nazi annihilation programme's traumatic shadow, a trench widened between Jewish and non-Jewish leftists, a trench that could not be bridged by the abstract notion of equality, which disregarded the opposing collective experiences and memories of Germans and Jews. The Jewish leftists were, indeed, denied recognition as equals when German leftists ignored the difference between former perpetrators and victims in conflating the Israel–Palestine conflict with the Holocaust. This comparison partially exculpated their own parents, while it dismissed the memories of surviving Jewish communities. Hence, the legitimacy of Germans critiquing the Jewish state was dubious to say the least, even based upon optimistic and universalist stances on the Israel–Palestine conflict, as such criticisms helped to conceal the conflict's European origin story and negated the fact that Israel itself had become a very real refuge and a retreat of failed Jewish hopes. At the end of his intervention, Diner sounded a note of warning:

> Again, what happens there is also a continuation of German and European history. And anyone who wishes to understand that misery, to change it for the sake of Arab Palestinians and Israeli Jews, must learn to grasp history in its wholeness and, importantly, must feel a sense of responsibility – now more than ever, and particularly for the Palestinians.[297]

That was not the last word on the subject. Rather than in the pages of the *Tageszeitung*, the next chapter came during the planning stages of a joint West German demonstration that was co-initiated both by the Frankfurt Jewish Group and sympathetic Arab members of the Haltern Circle, among other groups. The initiative for a Palestine–Lebanon demonstration on 21 August 1982 in Frankfurt am Main sought to build the greatest possible consensus, but it also fit a pattern: it was 'often easier for leftist Jews in [West Germany] to enter a dialogue with the Palestinians over the future of both peoples in the Middle East', whereas comparable efforts to engage with non-Jewish German leftists were usually marred by examples of 'historical blending' of the Palestine question with the Nazi era.[298] The public panel discussions that featured Abdalla Frangi, the PLO representative in Bonn, alongside

Dan Diner, representing the Israeli opposition movement, were marked by mutual recognition and even harmony on the issues. By contrast, the group discussion held to come to some form of agreement on the content of the demonstration announcement took a different route.[299] The latter event brought together numerous groups from the radical left-wing scene, which not only demonstrated their usual sectarianism, but exposed naked hostility towards the members of the Frankfurt Jewish Group. For example, one splinter group derided the announcement as 'pro-Zionist', because it neither called the Israeli operation an act of 'genocide' (*Völkermord*), nor denounced Zionism as a form of racism. The leftist Jews were accused of 'betrayal' when they voiced positive views of the Israeli opposition movement. 'One Jew is enough', blurted out a participant during the discussion, rejecting out of hand the suggestion to invite Erich Fried to speak at the concluding event alongside Abdallah Frangi, Dan Diner and Jakob Moneta. The protest by Hamburg's 'Große Freiheit' (Great Freedom) group was one distressing climax of the hours-long debate: 'We won't allow ourselves to be catapulted out of the worldwide fight against imperialism and racism over a few so-called progressive Jews.'[300] The meeting finally resulted in two different demonstration announcements. The Frankfurt Group, which consisted of Jews and Arabs, felt compelled to supplement the announcement by their rival leftists with a statement of their own, which emphasised the Israeli opposition movement along with the objective of a joint perspective for Jews and Arabs. The day before the demonstration, the Frankfurt Jewish Group felt forced to publish another declaration titled 'The War Over the Past', which cautioned against a 'gigantic exculpation' that aired antisemitic resentments under the guise of supposedly universal morality:

> If people in this country don't learn to distinguish between the War in Lebanon and Germans' war over their past, then the effort to express solidarity with the Palestinians will fail and the floodgates of antisemitism will swing open.[301]

This trend on the left continued to prompt critical responses, and not only from left-wing Jews. They were joined by non-Jewish detractors, such as Dietrich Wetzel, Eike Geisel, Detlev Claussen and others, who took pains to integrate what Diner called the 'rupture in civilisation' into their own frame of reference and called upon the post-war generation to take historical responsibility. Adorno's student Detlev Claussen had himself been part of the delegation from the Frankfurt SDS that travelled to Jordan in August 1969.[302] After his return, however, he shared his deep dismay with friends, despairing over the political shape of the Palestinian guerrilla groups, which were at odds with his own socialist utopias and sought, above all, to destroy Israel.[303] A few months later, when the bomb was discovered at the Jewish Community Centre in West Berlin, Claussen was among the pioneering critics of the nascent left-wing antisemitism, together with Daniel Cohn-Bendit, Ronny Loewy and Bernhard Blum. Claussen also reacted immediately to the Entebbe aeroplane hijacking and to the involvement of two members of the 2 June Movement in 'selecting' Jewish passengers. As in November 1969, this was no longer a case of distinguishing between forms of left-wing criticism of the Israel–Palestine conflict; it was about clearly repudiating left-wing antisemitism. 'To criticise this ahistorical anti-Zionism, one that places any use of violence [by] Germans against Jewish civilians into the continuity of German antisemitism' was not the same thing as defending Zionism, Claussen wrote in his trenchant intervention against the German Left, before turning to the Palestinian groups:[304] 'Palestinian organisations that fail to exclude Germans from armed actions against Israel inflict great damage on the anti-racist character of the Palestinian revolution.'[305] A year after the Lebanon War, Dietrich Wetzel, a future member of parliament for the Greens, released an edited volume of essays, based on a Frankfurt Jewish Group discussion series and titled *Die Verlängerung von Geschichte. Deutsche, Juden und der Palästinakonflikt* (The Prolongation of History: Germans, Jews and the Palestine Conflict). Claussen contributed a chapter about the Nazi past's ongoing impact, including on the German Left; he titled it 'In the House of the Hangman'.[306]

The fiercest critic of the left in Germany and its endeavour 'to be unscrupulously German' was Eike Geisel, who was one of very few people to advance the spread of Matzpen's writings and ideas in the German language.[307] A few months before the war in Lebanon, Geisel (himself born in 1945) wrote furiously 'about the disgrace of the German left' for having 'forgotten where it lives: in the house of the hangman'. At the time, left-wing publications in Germany had either kept mum or joined the country's indignant chorus after Menachem Begin reminded the German Chancellor Helmut Schmidt of his past as a soldier in the Wehrmacht and the oath of allegiance that he had sworn to Hitler. Deviating from the others, Geisel took Begin's statement as an urgent reminder for the German Left to take a critical look in the mirror:

> Writing off Begin's fit of anger as the idiotic gesture of a Zionist Zorro or a senile Middle Eastern sheriff – in Germany, that remains the sole privilege of Jews. If the left had called out this latest show of growing national unanimity, it would not have been making common cause with Israel's occupation policy, but on the contrary would have earned the moral standing to criticise it.[308]

However, this reaction was only partly responding to the rampant nationalism on the left and its historically forgetful hostility towards the Israeli state. In the period between the publication of Nathan Weinstock's monograph *Das Ende Israels* (released in English as *Zionism: False Messiah*), within which Geisel co-wrote an introduction with Mario Offenberg, and Geisel's increasing focus on critiquing the German Left, he became more and more concerned with the effects of the Holocaust on the lives of former communist Jews. Geisel and Offenberg had already co-edited an edition of Isaac Deutscher's essays that centred on the rupture Auschwitz tore into Deutscher's former optimistic universalism. The publication of Hanna Levy-Hass's *Diary of Bergen-Belsen* similarly reflected this impulse. On Geisel's many trips to Israel, he kept crossing paths with Levy-Hass, a Yugoslav communist. In a series of long interviews in 1978, she offered insights into her life, showing how it was Nazism that first made her care about her Jewishness and revealing that the destruction of her childhood world was ultimately what compelled her move to Israel.[309] Finally, Geisel's encounter with the shattered life of Hersch Mendel and his own road to Israel moved him to accuse the left of an exceedingly short memory. What hung over Israel, Geisel asserted, 'was not the glory of Herzl [. . .] but the traumatising shadow of Hitler'.[310]

'He wasn't stuck on Auschwitz', Geisel's friend Wolfgang Pohrt later wrote. 'That distinguished him from the adherents to the singularity [premise]. But he stuck with people in whose lives Auschwitz played the central role.'[311] That was partly why the intensifying debate over antisemitism in various aspects of German society did not diminish Geisel's solidarity with the Israeli Left on the question of Palestine. Unlike his future comrades in Germany, whose critique of German society involved a – likely unintended – withdrawal to their own German identity, Geisel served as a connecting link to the Israeli Left's efforts to establish a Jewish–Arab common ground in the Middle East.[312] Eventually, the Lebanon War of 1982 was more than the latest escalation of the conflict between Israelis and Palestinians. It had also 'changed the face of Israeli society and politically unearthed many of its buried contradictions'.[313]

The observation that Israel had 'no opposition and no antiwar movement', which the 'Liberated Territory' group used to rally people to its cause at the beginning of the war, quickly became outdated as a new reality emerged. Three weeks after the outbreak of the war, when the Committee against the War in Lebanon appealed for an immediate withdrawal from Lebanon and the initiation of political negotiations with the Palestinians' representatives, more than 20,000 people heeded the call. Unlike previous wars, which invariably brought Israeli society together in a united front, there was audible protest, even during the military operations. These voices grew louder, partly because they also had some support from within the Israeli Army. Shortly after the outbreak of the war, the organisation Yesh Gvul (There Is a Border/Limit) was launched by a small group of combat veterans who refused to serve in the war and mobilised against any military solution to the Israel-Palestine conflict. They felt bolstered by reports from individual active duty soldiers, who, when returning from battle, explained their horror upon realising that the war's targets included Palestinian civilians.[314] Another group, 'Chayalim Neged Shtika' (Soldiers Against Silence), channelled the gathering dissent of Israeli soldiers. Their spokesperson was Avraham Burg, a former member of the Israeli Paratrooper Brigade, who gained particular popularity as the son of Yosef Burg, the Israeli Interior Minister and chair of the National Religious Party.[315] The younger Burg personified the disagreement of many soldiers and voiced the widespread doubts as to the latest war's legitimacy and military benefit.[316] Thus, the Lebanon War marked a rupture within Israeli society, which for the first time publicly questioned the justification of all Israel's wars to date as 'no choice wars'.[317]

Uri Avnery pulled a sensational stunt during the military offensive that embodied a political alternative and the call for an immediate end to the fighting. As a reporter for *Haolam Hazeh*, he crossed the Lebanese border and conducted an interview with Yasser Arafat on 3 July in embattled Beirut. This mid-war act came to symbolise coexistence and mutual recognition. 'Yasser Arafat said important things', Avnery wrote in *Haolam Hazeh*, which printed the interview in full, 'but more than anything he said, what matters most is that the meeting took place'.³¹⁸ When the group 'Shalom Akhshav' (Peace Now) mobilised for a demonstration against the war, a few days later, one of its demands was that the government refrain from charging Avnery with treason, a step already being considered. Shalom Achshav had been founded in March 1978, following Sadat's visit to Israel, to demand the continuance of the endangered peace talks between Israel and Egypt and to seek peace and reconciliation with Israel's Arab neighbours and the Palestinians. During the Lebanon War, their mobilisation of the mass protest symbolised the shifting public opinion. On 5 July, 100,000 Israelis protested the war, demanding 'Begin must go'. Before long, there was talk of an 'implosion of the national consensus'.

This rapid change within Israeli society also entailed extracting the memory of the Holocaust from the Israel–Palestine conflict. The public protest increasingly rejected Begin's Holocaust references as a rationale for the massive military operation against Palestinian fighters and civilians alike. 'Hitler is already dead, Mr Prime Minister', wrote the author Amos Oz in *Yediot Aharonot*, rebuffing Begin's metaphor of fighting Hitler in his Berlin bunker. 'Hitler is not in hiding in Nabatea, in Sidon, or in Beirut. He is dead and gone.'³¹⁹ The public protest by the molecular biologist Shlomo Schmelzman also drew attention. Schmelzman was the first Holocaust survivor ever to embark on a hunger strike on the grounds of Yad Vashem. In his statement of protest, he raised fierce accusations against his state's military campaign and against Menachem Begin's rhetoric:

> In my childhood I have suffered fear, hunger and humiliation when I passed from the Warsaw Ghetto, through labour camps, to Buchenwald. [. . .] I hear too many familiar sounds today [. . .] I hear 'dirty Arabs' and I remember 'dirty Jews'. I hear about 'closed areas' and I remember ghettos and camps. I hear 'two-legged beasts' and I remember 'Untermenschen'. [. . .] Too many things in Israel remind me of too many other things from my childhood.³²⁰

Unlike in Germany, this comparison did not have an ulterior motive. Rather, it expressed his outrage at how his personal history was being appropriated for a political objective that was not his.

The horrific Sabra and Shatila massacre of 16–18 September marked the public protest's mournful climax. The Lebanese Christian Phalangist forces were the direct perpetrators of the lethal violence at the refugee camp. But the Israeli military's enabling role tapped into a particular well of Jewish–Israeli memory. When the entire Israeli opposition – from Matzpen at the leftmost fringes to the critical soldier groups to the Israeli peace movement – mobilised for a demonstration, some 400,000 people answered the call, amounting to 10 per cent of Israel's then population.[321] As well as the demands for an immediate end to the war and a withdrawal from Lebanon, there was now an appeal for a sea change in the Israeli consciousness. 'We have no future on the graves of Palestinians', came the shouts on the streets of Tel Aviv. The slogan did not specify how the conflict with the Palestinians might be resolved, but suggested, at least, that this could only be achieved together.

In the summer of 1983, a year after the end of the war and PLO's departure from Lebanon, the first issue of *Matzpen* was released since the most recent war. It was the ninetieth and final edition of the magazine, which had first been printed in November 1962. Thus, the insidious end of Matzpen also accompanied a shift within Israeli society, a turn towards the Israel–Palestine conflict, which the Lebanon War had brought out into the open. That accomplishment was also to Matzpen's credit. In an interview with Dan Diner and Micha Brumlik conducted by a German magazine during the Lebanon War, Diner also emphasised the historical significance of Matzpen for the emergence of the Israeli opposition movement: 'They never achieved that status as an organisation [. . .] but as a ferment within today's developments, they have attained extraordinary importance.'[322] The shift in Israeli society was not in line with Matzpen's political programme, nor with its socialist utopia. Still, it demonstrated that in the years since the organisation's founding, and at the group's prodding, Matzpen had opened a new window and revealed a path to a common perspective for Israelis and Palestinians. 'That is the decisive factor', Diner concluded. 'Engaging in a process where both sides [Israelis and Palestinians] stand to lose so many of their original demands, but to gain so many things that are new.'[323] Matzpen's lasting legacy is that it opened up a perspective of mutual understanding in the Israeli–Palestinian conflict: it sought to safeguard the endurance of both Israeli Jews and Palestinian Arabs based on equality and mutual recognition, whatever the ultimate structure of their coexistence in the region.

Notes

1. Cohn-Bendit, *Der grosse Basar*, p. 15.
2. Ibid., pp. 13–14; see also Har-Gil, '"Danny the Red" Travelled Israel'.
3. Cohn-Bendit, *Der grosse Basar*, p. 14.
4. Ibid., p. 15.
5. Ibid.
6. Hannah Arendt, 'The Jewish State. Fifty Years After, Where Have Herzl's Politics Led?', in Jerome Kohn (ed.), *The Jewish Writings* (New York: Schocken Books, [1946] 2007), pp. 375–87, at p. 386.
7. Hannah Arendt, 'To Save the Jewish Homeland', in Jerome Kohn (ed.), *The Jewish Writings* (New York: Schocken Books, [1948] 2007), pp. 388–401, at p. 391.
8. Isaac Deutscher, 'Who is a Jew? [1963/1966]', in Isaac Deutscher, *The Non-Jewish Jew and Other Essays* (London: Oxford University Press, 1968), pp. 42–9, at p. 50.
9. Diner, 'Cumulative Contingency', pp. 155–8.
10. Cohn-Bendit, *Der grosse Basar*, pp. 8–9.
11. Ibid., p. 11.
12. 'Everyone Thought About It', in Tom Segev, *The Seventh Million: The Israelis and the Holocaust* (New York: Hill and Wang, 1993), pp. 387–95.
13. Quoted in Ibid., p. 391.
14. Quoted in Ibid., p. 393.
15. Peretz Merhav, 'The "Compass" Astray', *New Outlook* 8 ([October] 1969), pp. 49–52, at p. 51.
16. Wolfensohn, 'The Conscience of Matzpen: Part III'.
17. Wolfensohn, 'The Conscience of Matzpen: Part II'.
18. Shlomo Grodzenski, 'Against Racist Discrimination. For the Forging of the Revolutionary Character', *Davar* (24 July 1970), pp. 13 and 17.
19. This is how Eli Lobel described the scene in his letter to Moshé Machover: Eli Lobel, Letter to Moshé Machover, 2 March 1969, Private Archive of Moshé Machover, London [Hebrew].
20. Yehiel Limor, '"Israeli" Seminar for Students of the "New Left" in Paris. Among the Lecturers: Dr. Moshe Sneh and Amos Kenan', *Ma'ariv* (20 February 1969), p. 7 [Hebrew].
21. Alfred Moos, 'Der Zionismus und sein Popanz', *Links* 33 (1972), quoted from Moshé Machover and Mario Offenberg, 'Zionism and its Scarecrows', *Khamsin. Journal of Revolutionary Socialists of the Middle East* 6 (1978), pp. 33–59, at p. 35, first published in Matzpen 68 (1973), pp. 19–21 [Hebrew].

22. Ibid.
23. Diner, 'Bolschewismus ohne Kommunismus - Ben Gurion und der Holocaust'.
24. Eyal Chowers, *The Political Philosophy of Zionism: Trading Jewish Words for an Hebraic Land* (Cambridge, New York: Cambridge University Press, 2012), pp. 72–114; Thomas Gloy, 'Fritz Bernsteins Soziologie des Judenhasses', in Hans-Joachim Hahn and Olaf Kistenmacher (eds), *Beschreibungsversuche der Judenfeindschaft* (De Gruyter), pp. 286–313.
25. Pilavsky, 'Easternization', p. 6.
26. Hannah Arendt, 'Social Science Techniques and the Study of Concentration Camps', *Jewish Social Studies* 12: 1 (1950), pp. 49–64, at p. 62; Diner, 'Cumulative Contingency', p. 155.
27. Isaac Deutscher, 'Israel's Spiritual Climate [1954]', in Isaac Deutscher, *The Non-Jewish Jew and Other Essays* (London: Oxford University Press, 1968), pp. 91–117, at pp. 111–12.
28. For the whole context, see Moshé Machover (Tzemach), 'An Argument with the Zionist Left. On Zionism and its Scarecrows', *Matzpen* 68 (1973), pp. 19–21 [Hebrew]; Machover and Offenberg, 'Zionism and its Scarecrows', pp. 33–59.
29. Machover (Tzemach), 'An Argument with the Zionist Left. On Zionism and its Scarecrows', p. 20.
30. Quoted from Diner, 'Bolschewismus ohne Kommunismus - Ben Gurion und der Holocaust', p. 128.
31. Yigal Elam, *An Introduction to a Different Zionist History* (Tel Aviv: Levin Epstein, 1972), pp. 115–27 [Hebrew]; Diner, 'Ambiguous Semantics. Reflections on Jewish Political Concepts', pp. 97–9.
32. Segev, *The Seventh Million*, pp. 89–96.
33. Elam, *An Introduction to a Different Zionist History*, p. 123; quoted in Machover and Offenberg, 'Zionism and its Scarecrows', p. 39.
34. Elam, *An Introduction to a Different Zionist History*, p. 122; quoted in Machover and Offenberg, 'Zionism and its Scarecrows', p. 43; see also Boas Evron, 'Zionism without Mercy', in Boas Evron, *Jewish State or Israeli Nation?* (Bloomington: Indiana University Press, 1995), pp. 153–72.
35. Yoav Gelber, 'Zionist Policy and the Fate of European Jewry (1939-1942)', *Yad Vashem Studies* 13 (1979), pp. 169–210.
36. See Diner, 'Bolschewismus ohne Kommunismus – Ben Gurion und der Holocaust', p. 129.
37. Elam, *An Introduction to a Different Zionist History*, pp. 125–6; quoted in Machover and Offenberg, 'Zionism and its Scarecrows', p. 44.
38. Machover and Offenberg, 'Zionism and its Scarecrows', p. 44 (emphasis in original).

39. Ibid.
40. Elam, *An Introduction to a Different Zionist History*, pp. 110–11 [quoted in ibid., pp. 43–4]; see also Diner, 'Ambiguous Semantics. Reflections on Jewish Political Concepts', p. 98.
41. Dina Porat, 'Ben Gurion and the Holocaust', in Ronald W. Zweig (ed.), *David Ben-Gurion: Politics and Leadership in Israel* (London: Cass, 1991), pp. 145–70, at p. 151; Moshe Sharett, quoted in: Segev, *The Seventh Million*, p. 98.
42. Saul Friedländer, 'The Shoah between Memory and History', *Jewish Quarterly* 37: 1 (1990), pp. 5–11.
43. Arendt, 'Zionism Reconsidered', p. 361.
44. Ibid.
45. Ibid., p. 360.
46. Diner, 'Ambiguous Semantics. Reflections on Jewish Political Concepts', pp. 97–9.
47. Friedländer, 'The Shoah between Memory and History'.
48. Machover and Offenberg, 'Zionism and its Scarecrows', p. 44.
49. Ibid.; for the history and historiography on Jewish survival in the Soviet Union, see Laura Jockusch and Tamar Lewinsky, 'Paradise Lost? Postwar Memory of Polish Jewish Survival in the Soviet Union', *Holocaust and Genocide Studies* 24: 3 (2010), pp. 373–99.
50. Yoav Gelber, 'El-Alamein', in Dan Diner (ed.), *Enzyklopädie jüdischer Geschichte und Kultur*, 7 vols (Stuttgart, Weimar: Metzler, 2012–17), vol. 2, pp. 211–15; Michael J. Cohen, *Britain's Moment in Palestine: Retrospect and Perspectives, 1917-1948* (Abingdon: Routledge, 2015), p. 327.
51. Machover and Offenberg, 'Zionism and its Scarecrows', p. 44; Pilavsky, 'Easternization'.
52. Moshé Machover, 'New Premises for a False Conclusion (May 1967)', in Moshé Machover, *Israelis and Palestinians: Conflict and Resolutions* (Chicago: Haymarket Books, 2012), pp. 138–44 [first: *Matzpen* 35 (1967)].
53. *Davar* (5 February 1945), p. 6 [Hebrew], quoted from Machover and Offenberg, 'Zionism and its Scarecrows', p. 45 (emphasis in original).
54. Machover, 'New Premises for a False Conclusion (May 1967)'.
55. Diner, 'Täuschungen', p. 192.
56. Akiva Orr, 'Motives for Writing a Book on Jewish Identity', in Akiva Orr, *Israel: Politics, Myths and Identity Crises*, Pluto Middle Eastern Series (London: Pluto Press, 1994), pp. 4–7, at p. 4.
57. Ibid.
58. Ibid., p. 5.
59. Orr, *The UnJewish State*; Akiva Orr, *Israel: Politics, Myths and Identity Crises*, Pluto Middle Eastern Series (London: Pluto Press, 1994).

60. Orr, 'Motives for Writing a Book on Jewish Identity', p. 4.
61. Ibid., p. 5.
62. Segev, *The Seventh Million*, pp. 387–95.
63. M. Blumenthal and J. Dana, *Author and Activist Akiva Orr on Israel's Wars*, January 2011, 144 min, video interview, https://vimeo.com/19444809 (accessed 15 April 2020), at min. 120–2.
64. Orr, 'Motives for Writing a Book on Jewish Identity', p. 5.
65. Akiva Orr, 'Israeliness', in Akiva Orr, *Israel: Politics, Myths and Identity Crises*, Pluto Middle Eastern Series (London: Pluto Press, 1994), pp. 44–52, at pp. 46–7.
66. Tzabar, *A Prickly Pear Thorn*, p. 6.
67. Toama, 'Zusammenleben in Würde, Gleichheit und Gleichberechtigung', p. 3.
68. Shapira, 'Whatever Became of "Negating Exile"?', p. 72.
69. Akiva Orr, 'How I Came to Politics, to Maki, and to Matzpen', https://matzpen.org/2008-09-01/איך-הגעתי-לפוליטיקה-למקי-ולמצפן-עקי/ (accessed 15 April 2020) [Hebrew].
70. Yitzhak Gruenbaum, quoted in Segev, *The Seventh Million*, p. 71.
71. Orr, 'How I Came to Politics, to Maki, and to Matzpen'.
72. Diamond, *Homeland or Holy Land?*, p. 54.
73. Shavit, *The New Hebrew Nation*, p. 62.
74. Ibid.
75. Ibid.
76. Dan Diner, 'Der hebräische Mythos. Aus Anlass des Buches von Jacob Shavit', *Babylon. Beiträge zur jüdischen Gegenwart* 4 (1988), pp. 119–23, at p. 121; see also Shavit, *The New Hebrew Nation*, p. 177, note 10: 'I was told that during the Nazi occupation of France some members of the group tried to save their lives by claiming that they were not Jews but Hebrews.'.
77. Idith Zertal, *Israel's Holocaust and the Politics of Nationhood*, Cambridge Middle East Studies (Cambridge: Cambridge University Press, 2011), pp. 52–90.
78. Michael R. Marrus, *Lessons of the Holocaust* (Toronto, Buffalo, London: University of Toronto Press, 2016), p. 117.
79. Tzabar, *A Prickly Pear Thorn*, p. 10.
80. Beit-Hallahmi, *Original Sins*, p. 128; Gershon Shaked, 'Watch the Facts!', *Yediot Aharonot* (26 September 1986), p. 20 [Hebrew]; see also Marrus, *Lessons of the Holocaust*, p. 117.
81. Dan Ben-Amotz and Netiva Ben-Yehuda (eds), *The World Dictionary of Hebrew Slang* (Jerusalem: Levin Epstein, 1972), p. 158.
82. Segev, *The Seventh Million*, p. 255; see also Yechiam Weitz, *The Man Who Was Murdered Twice: The Life, Trial and Death of Israel Kasztner* (Jerusalem: Yad Vashem, the International Institute for Holocaust Research, 2011).

83. Segev, *The Seventh Million*, pp. 255–320.
84. Ibid., p. 275.
85. Ibid., p. 268.
86. Ibid., pp. 267–75, at p. 273.
87. Ibid., pp. 271–2.
88. Erel, *Without Fear and Prejudice*, pp. 137–44.
89. 'Man of the Year', *Haolam Hazeh* 884 (30 September 1954), p. 15 [Hebrew].
90. See Erel, *Without Fear and Prejudice*, p. 139; Segev, *The Seventh Million*, p. 279.
91. Quoted from Segev, *The Seventh Million*, pp. 276–7.
92. Quoted in Ibid., p. 279.
93. Quoted in Ibid., p. 283.
94. Akiva Orr, 'The Kastner Case. Jerusalem 1955', in Akiva Orr, *Israel: Politics, Myths and Identity Crises*, Pluto Middle Eastern Series (London: Pluto Press, 1994), pp. 81–116, at p. 82.
95. Eliahu Hazan, 'The Paper as a Mean of Political Taunting. The Mockery of Mapai in the Opposition Press on the Occasion of the Kasztner Trial' (Master's thesis, The Hebrew University of Jerusalem, 2007), pp. 39–47 [Hebrew].
96. Quoted from Yechiam Weitz, 'Political Dimensions of Holocaust Memory', in Robert S. Wistrich and David Ohana (eds), *The Shaping of Israeli Identity: Myth, Memory, and Trauma*, Israel Affairs (London, Portland: F. Cass, 1995), pp. 129–45, at p. 135.
97. N. Israeli, 'Zionism and Anti-Semitism', in Arie Bober (ed.), *The Other Israel: The Radical Case Against Zionism* (Garden City: Doubleday, 1972), pp. 167–75, at p. 172.
98. Dan Diner, 'Hannah Arendt Reconsidered. On the Banal and the Evil in her Holocaust Narrative', *New German Critique* 71 (1997), pp. 177–90, at p. 180.
99. Hannah Arendt, *Eichmann in Jerusalem: A Report on the Banality of Evil* (London: Penguin Books, 2006), pp. 132 and 197.
100. See Annette Wieviorka, *The Era of the Witness* (Ithaca: Cornell University Press, 2006).
101. Arendt, *Eichmann in Jerusalem*, p. 253.
102. Zertal, *Israel's Holocaust and the Politics of Nationhood*, pp. 91–103.
103. Diner, 'Täuschungen', p. 192.
104. David Ben-Gurion, 'The Eichmann-Case as Seen by Ben-Gurion. Interview', *New York Times* (18 December 1960), p. 7 and 62, at p. 7; see also Idith Zertal, *Lords of the Land: The War Over Israel's Settlements in the Occupied Territories: 1967–2007* (New York: Nation Books, 2009).

105. Georges Friedmann, *The End of the Jewish People?* (Garden City: Doubleday, 1967), pp. 213–17.
106. Ben-Gurion, 'The Eichmann-Case as Seen by Ben-Gurion', p. 62.
107. Shapira, 'Whatever Became of "Negating Exile"?', pp. 92–5.
108. Quoted from Ibid., 92.
109. Boas Evron, 'Eichmann. The Monster in Captivity', *Etgar* 2 ([June] 1960), pp. 5–6, at p. 5 [Hebrew]; quoted from Shapira, 'Whatever Became of "Negating Exile"?', p. 92.
110. Uri Avnery, 'Yesterday's Pogrom', *Etgar* 3: 55 ([April] 1963), p. 3 [Hebrew].
111. Ibid.
112. Boas Evron, 'Sin and Punishment', *Etgar* 3: 55 (1963), pp. 2–3 [Hebrew]; on the different meanings of the questions of 'why?' and 'how?', see Dan Diner, 'Epistemics of the Holocaust. Considering the Question of "Why?" and of "How?"', *Naharaim. Zeitschrift für deutsch-jüdische Literatur und Kulturgeschichte/Journal of German-Jewish Literature and Cultural History* 1: 2 (2008), pp. 195–213.
113. Shapira, 'Whatever Became of "Negating Exile"?', pp. 90–103, at p. 94.
114. Uri Avnery, 'The Eichmann-Trial', *Etgar* 1: 5 ([May] 1961), pp. 2–3, at p. 3 [Hebrew]; see also Shapira, 'Whatever Became of "Negating Exile"?', p. 93–4.
115. Ibid.
116. Ibid.
117. Anita Shapira, 'The Eichmann Trial. Changing Perspectives', *Journal of Israeli History* 23: 1 (2004), pp. 18–39, at p. 23.
118. Alan L. Mintz, *Translating Israel: Contemporary Hebrew Literature and its Reception in America* (Syracuse: Syracuse University Press, 2001), p. 194.
119. An English translation was published five years later: Dahn Ben-Amotz, *To Remember, To Forget: A Novel* (Philadelphia: Jewish Publication Society of America, 1973); see also Anat Feinberg, 'Two Different Worlds and a Cemetery Between Them. Dahn Ben-Amotz's Novel "To Remember, To Forget"', *Trumah. Zeitschrift der Hochschule für Jüdische Studien Heidelberg* 21 (2013), pp. 69–80.
120. Ben-Amotz, *To Remember, To Forget*, p. 3.
121. Ibid., p. 102.
122. Ibid., p. 244.
123. Ibid., p. 47: 'I changed my name from Lampel to Lam, and when anybody asked where I was born I would answer defiantly, "Tel Aviv". A simple answer that avoided unpleasant issues.'
124. Ibid., p. 33.

125. Ibid., p. 133.
126. Dan Ben-Amotz, 'Who Are You, Dan Ben-Amotz? Interview with Uri Avnery', *Haolam Hazeh* 1599 (24 April 1968), pp. 12–13.
127. Feinberg, 'Two Different Worlds and a Cemetery Between Them', p. 72; see also Benjamin Harshav, *Language in Time of Revolution* (Berkeley, Los Angeles, London: University of California Press, 1993), p. 167.
128. Ben-Amotz, 'Who Are You, Dan Ben-Amotz?', p. 12.
129. Ibid.
130. Quoted from Moshé Machover and Haim Hanegbi, 'From Generation to Generation They Rise Up to Destroy Us', in Arie Bober (ed.), *The Other Israel: The Radical Case Against Zionism* (Garden City: Doubleday, 1972), pp. 79–86, at p. 79 [first: *Matzpen* 45 (1968)].
131. Amos Kenan, 'A Letter to All Good People. To Fidel Castro, Sartre, Russell and All the Rest', in Amos Kenan, *Israel: A Wasted Victory* (Tel Aviv: Amikam, 1970), pp. 56–69 [first: *Yediot Aharonot* (22 March 1968)].
132. Ibid., p. 62.
133. Ibid., p. 61.
134. Ibid., p. 62.
135. Ibid., p. 64.
136. Yehiel Limor, '"Israeli" Seminar for Students of the "New Left" in Paris. Among the Lecturers: Dr. Moshe Sneh and Amos Kenan', *Ma'ariv* (20 February 1969), p. 7 [Hebrew].
137. Amos Kenan, 'New Left, Go Home!', in Amos Kenan, *Israel: A Wasted Victory* (Tel Aviv: Amikam, 1970), pp. 122–9 [first: *Yediot Aharonot* (21 March 1969)].
138. Amos Kenan, '"Matzpen" Seeks Admission Cheaply', in Amos Kenan, *Israel: A Wasted Victory* (Tel Aviv: Amikam, 1970), pp. 118–21, at p. 120 [first: *Yediot Aharonot* (20 March 1969)].
139. Machover and Hanegbi, 'Letter to All Those "Once-Good" Israelis', p. 8.
140. Machover and Hanegbi, 'From Generation to Generation They Rise Up to Destroy Us', pp. 85–6.
141. Flyer, Private Archive of Moshé Machover.
142. Eli Lobel, Letter to Haim Hanegbi (5 August 1969), provided by Haim Hanegbi [Hebrew].
143. Percy S. Cohen, *Jewish Radicals and Radical Jews* (London: Academic Press, 1980).
144. Lobel, 'Palestine and the Jews', p. 133.
145. Ibid., pp. 132–3.
146. Ibid., p. 135.

147. Ibid., p. 133.
148. Machover and Offenberg, 'Zionism and its Scarecrows', p. 45.
149. Warschawski, *On the Border*, p. 35.
150. Detlev Claussen, 'Entréebillet Kommunismus. Eine Erinnerung an Isaac Deutscher', *Babylon. Beiträge zur jüdischen Gegenwart* 22 (2007), pp. 87–97, at p. 95.
151. Philip Mendes, 'The Rise and Fall of the Jewish/Left Alliance. An Historical and Political Analysis', *Australian Journal of Politics and History* 45: 4 (1999), pp. 483–505.
152. Isaac Deutscher, 'The Russian Revolution and the Jewish Problem [1964]', in Isaac Deutscher, *The Non-Jewish Jew and Other Essays* (London: Oxford University Press, 1968), pp. 60–83, at p. 66.
153. Trepper, *The Great Game*, p. 69.
154. Flores, *Nationalismus und Sozialismus im arabischen Osten*; Mario Offenberg, *Kommunismus in Palästina: Nation und Klasse in der antikolonialen Revolution, Marburger Abhandlungen zur politischen Wissenschaft* (Meisenheim am Glan: Hain, 1975), vol. 29 [German].
155. Trepper, *The Great Game*, pp. 17–18.
156. Ernest Germain (Mandel, Ernest), 'A Biographical Sketch of Abram Leon', in Abraham Léon, *The Jewish Question: A Marxist Interpretation*, 2nd edn (New York: Pathfinder Press, 1970), pp. 15–31.
157. Abraham Léon, *The Jewish Question: A Marxist Interpretation*, 2nd edn (New York: Pathfinder Press, 1970), pp. 79–80.
158. Ibid., p. 251.
159. Ibid., p. 258.
160. Quoted in Germain, 'A Biographical Sketch of Abram Leon', p. 27.
161. See, though with critical intent, Arno Lustiger, 'Wider den Zionismus', in Reinhard Renger (ed.), *Die deutsche "Linke" und der Staat Israel*, 1. Aufl. (Leipzig: Forum Verlag, 1994), pp. 89–100, at p. 91; Henryk Broder, *Der ewige Antisemit: Über Sinn und Funktion eines beständigen Gefühls* (Frankfurt: Fischer, 1986), p. 47.
162. Abraham Léon, *Conception Matérialiste de la Question Juive* (Paris: Édition Pionniers, 1946).
163. Abraham Léon, *Il Marxismo e la Questione Ebraica* (Roma: Samonà e Savelli, 1968); Abraham Léon, *Marxismen och judefrågan* (Mölndal: Coeckelberghs Partisanförlag, 1968); Abraham Léon, *Judenfrage und Kapitalismus* (München: Trikont-Verlag, 1971).

164. The results of the symposium with Maxime Rodinson, Pierre Vidal-Naquet, Many El-Kaïm and Richard Marienstras in May 1970 were later published under the title 'Sur la conception matérialiste de la question juive', *ISRAC* 5 ([January–February] 1971), pp. 17–62.
165. Kamil, *Die Araber und der Holocaust*, pp. 141–57.
166. Diner, 'Täuschungen', p. 193.
167. Nathan Weinstock, 'Introduction', in Abraham Léon, *The Jewish Question: A Marxist Interpretation*, 2nd edn (New York: Pathfinder Press, 1970), pp. 33–70, at p. 34.
168. Ibid., p. 70.
169. Broder, *Der ewige Antisemit*, p. 47.
170. Deutscher, 'The Russian Revolution and the Jewish Problem [1964]', p. 67.
171. Deutscher, 'Israel's Spiritual Climate [1954]', pp. 111–12.
172. See Diner, 'Täuschungen'.
173. Segall, 'Cyrano von Bergerac und die Geduld des Revolutionärs', p. 23.
174. Moneta, 'Mehr Gewalt für die Ohnmächtigen', p. 122.
175. Gerber, *Verborgene Präsenzen*, p. 70.
176. Hersh Mendel, *Memoirs of a Jewish Revolutionary* (London, Winchester, MA: Pluto Press; Distributed in the USA by Unwin Hyman, [1959] 1989); Jakob Moneta, 'Nachwort zur deutschen Ausgabe', in Hersch Mendel, *Erinnerungen eines jüdischen Revolutionärs*, Aus der Reihe, 1.-4. Tausend (Berlin: Rotbuch Verlag, 1979), pp. 265–70.
177. Moneta, 'Nachwort zur deutschen Ausgabe', p. 265.
178. Mendel, *Memoirs of a Jewish Revolutionary*, pp. 320–1.
179. Ibid., p. 327.
180. Ibid., p. 328.
181. Eike Geisel, 'Um wieviel die Welt ärmer geworden ist. "Erinnerungen eines jüdischen Revolutionärs"', in Eike Geisel, *Lastenausgleich, Umschuldung – Die Wiedergutwerdung der Deutschen: Essays, Polemiken, Stichworte* (Berlin: Edition TIAMAT, 1984), pp. 107–15, at p. 115.
182. Eike Geisel, Jakob Moneta and Jakob Taut, 'Die Judenfalle. Hersch Mendel – wie ostjüdische Arbeiter Zionisten wurden', *Forum (Wien)* 27 (1980), pp. 18–24, at p. 22.
183. Geisel, 'Um wieviel die Welt ärmer geworden ist', p. 115.
184. Moneta, 'Nachwort zur deutschen Ausgabe', p. 269.
185. Mendel, *Memoirs of a Jewish Revolutionary*, p. 329.
186. Moneta, 'Nachwort zur deutschen Ausgabe', pp. 269–70.

187. Joseph Berger-Barzilai, 'The Path of a Jewish Worker-Revolutionary. At the Grave of Hersh Mendel', *Davar* (11 August 1968), p. 8 [Hebrew].
188. Joseph Berger, *Shipwreck of a Generation: The Memoirs of Joseph Berger* (London: Harvill Press, 1971).
189. Keßler, 'Joseph Berger', p. 173.
190. Berger, *Shipwreck of a Generation*, p. 272.
191. Joseph Berger-Barzilai, 'The "Neo-Zionist Revolution" in the USSR', *The Jewish Quarterly* 19: 1–2 (1971), pp. 9–10, at p. 9.
192. Yaacov Ro'i, *The Struggle for Soviet Jewish Emigration, 1948-1967* (Cambridge: Cambridge University Press, 1991), pp. 138–41.
193. Berger-Barzilai, 'The "Neo-Zionist Revolution" in the USSR', p. 10.
194. Yuri Slezkine, *The Jewish Century* (Princeton, Woodstock: Princeton University Press, 2006), pp. 290–311.
195. Frank Gruener, 'Jüdisches Antifaschistisches Komitee', in Dan Diner (ed.), *Enzyklopädie jüdischer Geschichte und Kultur*, 7 vols (Stuttgart: Metzler, 2012–17), vol. 3, pp. 268–73.
196. Berger-Barzilai, 'The "Neo-Zionist Revolution" in the USSR', p. 10.
197. Oded Pilavsky, 'Judaism versus Humanism', *Matzpen* 58 (1971), p. 6 [Hebrew].
198. Ibid.
199. Trepper, *The Great Game*, p. 392.
200. Paul Lendvai, *Anti-Semitism without Jews: Communist Eastern Europe* (Garden City: Doubleday, 1971), pp. 89–241.
201. Trepper, *The Great Game*, p. 398.
202. Ibid., p. 409.
203. Geisel, Moneta and Taut, 'Die Judenfalle', p. 22.
204. Dan Diner, *"Keine Zukunft auf den Gräbern der Palästinenser": Eine historisch-politische Bilanz der Palästinafrage* (Hamburg: VSA-Verlag, 1982), p. 128.
205. Hanoch Bartov, 'A Matzpen Envoy Speaks in Washington', *Ma'ariv* (10 July 1970), p. 52 [Hebrew].
206. H. Hanegbi, Interview with the Author, Ramat Aviv (11 December 2008) [Hebrew].
207. Wolfgang Kraushaar, *Die Bombe im Jüdischen Gemeindehaus*, 1. Aufl. (Hamburg: Hamburger Ed, 2005), p. 39 [German].
208. 'Shalom + Napalm', *Agit 883* 40 (13 November 1969), p. 9.
209. Quoted from the English translation in Jeffrey Herf, *Undeclared Wars with Israel: East Germany and the West German Far Left, 1967–1989* (New York: Cambridge University Press, 2016), p. 103.

210. Ibid., p. 104.
211. 'Erklärung zum Bombenattentat auf das jüdische Gemeindehaus in Berlin', *SDS-Info* 25 (1 December 1969), pp. 29–30 (emphasis in original).
212. Dan Diner and Micha Brumlik, 'Libanon. Der reale und der imaginäre Krieg. Interview mit Dan Diner und Micha Brumlik', *Arbeiterkampf* 224 (25 August 1982), pp. 25–7.
213. 'Juden für die Rechte der Palästinenser', *Die Tageszeitung* (14 June 1982), p. 4.
214. Shlomo Shamgar, 'An Israeli Lecturer at Frankfurt University Preaches the Liquidation of the State', *Yediot Aharonot* (16 October 1980), p. 21 [Hebrew].
215. 'Juden für die Rechte der Palästinenser'.
216. See Micha Brumlik, *Kein Weg als Deutscher und Jude: Eine bundesrepublikanische Erfahrung* (München: Luchterhand, 1996), pp. 136–7.
217. Photos of the demonstration are published in Cilly Kugelmann and Hanno Loewy (eds), *So einfach war das: Jüdische Kindheiten und Jugend seit 1945 in Österreich, der Schweiz und Deutschland* (Köln: DuMont, 2002), p. 21; *Links* 181 ([April] 1985), at p. 25.
218. 'Juden für die Rechte der Palästinenser'.
219. Martin W. Kloke, *Israel und die deutsche Linke: Zur Geschichte eines schwierigen Verhältnisses, Schriftenreihe des Deutsch-Israelischen Arbeitskreises für Frieden im Nahen Osten e.V*, 2., erw. und aktualisierte Aufl. (Frankfurt am Main: Haag + Herchen, 1994), Bd. 20, p. 221.
220. Morris, *Righteous Victims*, pp. 508–9.
221. Ibid., p. 509; Uri Avnery, 'Arik's War', *Haolam Hazeh* 2337 (16 June 1982), pp. 15 and 72–3 [Hebrew].
222. Alice Rothchild, *Broken Promises, Broken Dreams: Stories of Jewish and Palestinian Trauma and Resilience* (London: Pluto Press, 2010), p. 28.
223. Avraham Glezerman, '"Der Ring". Über die innerisraelische Opposition gegen den Libanonkrieg', in Dietrich Wetzel (ed.), *Die Verlängerung von Geschichte: Deutsche, Juden und der Palästinakonflikt* (Frankfurt am Main: Neue Kritik, 1983), pp. 126–35, at p. 128.
224. Liberated Territory, 'No to the War!', https://web.nli.org.il/sites/NLI/Hebrew/digitallibrary/pages/viewer.aspx?presentorid=NNL_Ephemera&DocID=NNL_Ephemera700260923 [Hebrew]. The column was printed in *Haaretz* (13 June 1982).
225. Glezerman, '"Der Ring"', p. 126.
226. Quoted in Paul Findley, *They Dare to Speak Out: People and Institutions Confront Israel's Lobby*, 3rd edn (Chicago: Chicago Review Press, 2003), p. 301.
227. See Kloke, *Israel und die deutsche Linke*, Bd. 20, pp. 220–2.

228. Dan Diner, 'Banished. Jews in Germany after the Holocaust. An Interpretation', in Michael Brenner (ed.), *A History of Jews in Germany since 1945: Politics, Culture, and Society* (Bloomington: Indiana University Press, 2018), pp. 7–53, at p. 16.
229. Anthony Kauders, *Unmögliche Heimat: Eine deutsch-jüdische Geschichte der Bundesrepublik*, 1. Aufl. (München: Deutsche Verlags-Anstalt, 2007), pp. 73–89.
230. Cilly Kugelmann, 'Was heißt jüdische Identität? Aufzeichnung eines Gesprächs (Teil 2)', *Alternative* 140/141 (1981), pp. 234–40, at p. 235.
231. Kauders, *Unmögliche Heimat*, p. 10; Anthony Kauders, 'West German Jewry: Guilt, Power and Pluralism', *Quest. Issues in Contemporary Jewish History. Journal of Fondazione CDEC* 1: 1 (2010).
232. Diner, 'Banished', p. 43.
233. Helga Krohn, *"Es war richtig, wieder anzufangen": Juden in Frankfurt am Main seit 1945*, 1. Aufl. (Frankfurt am Main: Brandes & Apsel, 2011), pp. 142–50. Strikingly, a 1956 photo from a group stay at the Wembach holiday retreat portrays Cilly Kugelmann, Dan Diner and Micha Brumlik among others.
234. Dan Diner, 'Fragments of an Uncompleted Journey. On Jewish Socialisation and Political Identity in Germany', *New German Critique* 8: 20 (1980), pp. 57–70, at pp. 64–7.
235. Dan Diner, 'Man hat mit der Sache eigentlich nichts mehr zu tun', in Richard C. Schneider (ed.), *Wir sind da!: Die Geschichte der Juden in Deutschland von 1945 bis heute* (Berlin: Ullstein, 2000), pp. 233–52, at p. 234.
236. Dan Diner, quoted in Tobias Freimüller, 'Mehr als eine Religionsgemeinschaft. Jüdisches Leben in Frankfurt am Main nach 1945', *Zeithistorische Forschungen / Zentrum für Zeithistorische Forschung, Redaktion Zeitgeschichte-online* 7 (2010).
237. Dina Stein, 'Zwischen allen Stühlen', in Cilly Kugelmann and Hanno Loewy (eds), *So einfach war das: Jüdische Kindheiten und Jugend seit 1945 in Österreich, der Schweiz und Deutschland* (Köln: DuMont, 2002), pp. 82–8.
238. Kugelmann, 'Was heißt jüdische Identität?', p. 237.
239. Shila Khasani, 'Minderheit in der Minderheit. Das politische Engagement der linksorientierten Juden in der Frankfurter "Jüdischen Gruppe"', *Trumah. Zeitschrift der Hochschule für Jüdische Studien Heidelberg* 14 (2005), pp. 55–74.
240. Micha Brumlik, in *Cheschbon* ([Spring] 1980), quoted in Kauders, *Unmögliche Heimat*, p. 121.
241. See Krohn, *"Es war richtig, wieder anzufangen"*, p. 171.
242. Brumlik, *Kein Weg als Deutscher und Jude*, p. 134.
243. Lustiger, 'Wider den Zionismus', pp. 89 and 92.
244. Stein, 'Zwischen allen Stühlen', pp. 85–6.
245. Brumlik, *Kein Weg als Deutscher und Jude*, p. 85.

246. Ibid., pp. 100–1.
247. Diner, *"Keine Zukunft auf den Gräbern der Palästinenser"*, p. 2.
248. Dan Diner, quoted in GAL Hamburg, *Krieg im Libanon – Frieden in Europa?: Dokumentation einer Diskussionsveranstaltung der GAL Hamburg* (Hamburg: GAL Hamburg, 1982), p. 30.
249. Inge Deutschkron, 'Jerusalem in All its Colours at the Frankfurt Book Fair', *Ma'ariv* (26 October 1969), p. 19 [Hebrew]; however, the press that Dan Diner co-ran with Heschi Rotmensch only ever published two books: Ber Borochov, *Die Grundlagen des Poalezionismus* (Frankfurt/M.: Borochov-Press, 1969); Simcha Flapan, *5. Juni 1967. Der israelisch-arabische Krieg: Antwort an Isaac Deutscher* (Frankfurt a.M.: Borochov-Press, 1969).
250. Dan Diner, 'Vorwort', in Ber Borochov, *Die Grundlagen des Poalezionismus* (Frankfurt/M.: Borochov-Press, 1969), pp. 7–24; Dan Diner, 'Preface to The Foundations of Socialist Zionism by Ber Borochov' (The World Union of Jewish Students, 1969).
251. See Dan Diner, 'Zionism within the Context of Universalism and Particularism', *Shalom Dialog. Magazine for Jewish European Youth* 20/21 (1972), pp. 70–8, at p. 72; Brumlik, *Kein Weg als Deutscher und Jude*, p. 101.
252. See Krohn, *"Es war richtig, wieder anzufangen"*, p. 160.
253. Dan Diner, 'Der Zionismus und die jüdische Frage heute', *Emuna. Horizonte zur Diskussion über Israel und das Judentum* 5: 3 (1970), pp. 153–9, at p. 159.
254. Diner, 'Fragments of an Uncompleted Journey', p. 69.
255. Bundesverband jüdischer Studenten in Deutschland, *Zur Situation im Nahen Osten: Beiträge von Dan Diner und Ella Weinstein (1968-1969)*, p. 2.
256. Dan Diner, 'Panarabism, Zionism and the Palestinians', *Shalom Dialog. Magazine for Jewish European Youth* 20/21 (1972), pp. 93–9, at p. 99.
257. Diner, 'Fragments of an Uncompleted Journey', p. 70.
258. Ibid., p. 59.
259. 'Gesprächsrunde über jüdisches Leben im Nachkriegsdeutschland', *Münchner Beiträge zur jüdischen Geschichte und Kultur* 6: 1 (2012), pp. 41–60, at p. 47. See also the autobiography of his uncle David Tilman, *From the Cave of Decay to the Anonymous Soldiers. Memories of a Fighter* (Tel Aviv: Yair – Avraham Stern, 1993) [Hebrew].
260. Michael Jeismann, 'Abenteurer. Historiker aus zwei Welten. Dan Diner zum Sechzigsten', *Frankfurter Allgemeine Zeitung* (19 May 2006), p. 41.
261. 'Gesprächsrunde über jüdisches Leben im Nachkriegsdeutschland', p. 47; Diner, 'Man hat mit der Sache eigentlich nichts mehr zu tun', p. 244.

262. Diner, 'Fragments of an Uncompleted Journey', p. 68.
263. Ibid., p. 69.
264. Dan Diner, 'Sozialdemokratie und koloniale Frage, dargestellt am Beispiel des Zionismus', *Die Dritte Welt* 3: 1/2 (1974), pp. 58–87.
265. Diner, *Lost in the Sacred*, pp. 3–4.
266. Dan Diner, 'Ich wäre glücklich wenn die USA und die UdSSR am Rande einer Konfrontation stünden. (Interview)', *Pflasterstrand* 134 (19 June 1982 – 2 July 1982), pp. 24–7, at pp. 24–5.
267. Diner, 'Israel'; Dan Diner, *Zur Kritik der zionistischen Struktur Israels: Für Bi-Nationalität in Palästina* (Wien: Israel-Palästina-Komitee, 1981).
268. Dan Diner, 'Elemente einer Theorie der Bi-Nationalität in Palästina', in Friedhelm Ernst (ed.), *Nahost: Stimmen der Opposition, Palästina zwischen Krieg und Staatsgründung*, Der Schwierige Weg nach Palästina (Stuttgart: ESG-Geschäftsstelle – Bremen, 1981), pp. 67–72; Dan Diner, 'Die jüdisch-israelische Nationalität. Über die Dialektik der Anerkennung', in Friedhelm Ernst (ed.), *Zionismus, Opposition und Bi-Nationalität*, Der Schwierige Weg nach Palästina (Stuttgart: Alektor-Verlag, 1984), pp. 21–6.
269. Nicola Abu-Khalil, 'Mein Al-Quds. Erinnerungen an Ost-Jerusalem', in Yasmeen Hamdan and Hans O. Wiebus (eds), *Palästina: Menschen, Landschaften, mit Fotos von Georg Stein* (Berlin: Elefanten Press, 1989), pp. 111–13. I am greatful to Klaus Rürup and Alexander Flores for information on the Halterner Kreis.
270. Later, the circle found more and more supporters. Among them were: Adel Asi, Munir Kamil, Ahmad Khalid, Ali Murad, Emanuel Bohn, Mandred und Rosel Braun, John Bunzl, Amichai Dreifuß, Susann Heenen, Isidor Kaminer, Tuvia Kwasman, Peter Loew-Beer, Ernst Loewy, Ronny Loewy, Shannee Marks, Jakob Moneta, Alfred Moos, Moishe Postone, Ruth Rürup, Chana Salomon, Moshe Speier, Sammy Speier, Dina Stein, Tanja Weil, Gabi Schoor, Nina Corsten, Friedhelm Ernst, Rosa Kaiser, Klaus Rürup and Alexander Schölch.
271. The text is reprinted in Friedhelm Ernst (ed.), *Palästina* (Kiel: Magazin-Verlag, 1982), pp. 39–40.
272. Quoted in Zeev Schiff and Ehud Ya'ari, *Israel's Lebanon War* (New York: Simon and Schuster, 1984), p. 220.
273. See Segev, *The Seventh Million*, p. 396.
274. Avi Shilon, *Menachem Begin: A Life* (New Haven: Yale University Press, 2012), p. 167.
275. Robert C. Rowland, *The Rhetoric of Menachem Begin: The Myth of Redemption Through Return* (Lanham: University Press of America, 1985), p. 58.

276. Segev, *The Seventh Million*, pp. 397–8.
277. Ibid., pp. 214–15.
278. See Shilon, *Menachem Begin*, p. 65.
279. Quoted in Segev, *The Seventh Million*, p. 399.
280. Dan Diner, 'Israels nukleare Option und das Trauma der Massenvernichtung', *Links* 136 ([July–August] 1981), pp. 8–9, at p. 8.
281. Quoted in Segev, *The Seventh Million*, p. 399.
282. Dietrich Wetzel, '"Die Verlängerung von Geschichte". Anstatt einer Einleitung', in Dietrich Wetzel (ed.), *Die Verlängerung von Geschichte: Deutsche, Juden und der Palästinakonflikt* (Frankfurt am Main: Neue Kritik, 1983), pp. 7–14.
283. Diner, 'Israel and the Trauma of the Mass Extermination', p. 42–3; Diner, 'Ich wäre glücklich wenn die USA und die UdSSR am Rande einer Konfrontation stünden', p. 25.
284. Diner, 'Israel and the Trauma of the Mass Extermination', p. 49.
285. Diner, 'Ich wäre glücklich wenn die USA und die UdSSR am Rande einer Konfrontation stünden', p. 25; Diner, 'Israel and the Trauma of the Mass Extermination', p. 52.
286. Brumlik, *Kein Weg als Deutscher und Jude*, p. 136.
287. Susan Heenen, 'Deutsche Linke, linke Juden und der Zionismus', in Dietrich Wetzel (ed.), *Die Verlängerung von Geschichte: Deutsche, Juden und der Palästinakonflikt* (Frankfurt am Main: Neue Kritik, 1983), pp. 103–12, at p. 108.
288. Diner, 'Fragments of an Uncompleted Journey', p. 69.
289. Heenen, 'Deutsche Linke, linke Juden und der Zionismus'.
290. Hans-Joachim Noack, 'Ferienlager bei El Fatah', *Die Zeit* (15 August 1969), p. 7; see also Kraushaar, *Fischer in Frankfurt*, pp. 202–19.
291. Quoted in Herf, *Undeclared Wars with Israel*, p. 105.
292. Annette Vowinckel, 'Der kurze Weg nach Entebbe oder die Verlängerung der deutschen Geschichte in den Nahen Osten', *Zeithistorische Forschungen/Studies in Contemporary History* 1: 2 (2004), pp. 236–54.
293. Dan Diner, 'Leserbrief [Letter to the Editor]', in Israel-Palästina-Komitee Wien (ed.), *Libanon '82: Der israelisch-palästinensische Krieg. Eine Dokumentation* (Wien: Israel-Palästina-Komitee, 1982), pp. 79–81 [first: *Die Tageszeitung* (30 June 1982)].
294. Ibid., pp. 79–80.
295. Ibid., pp. 80–1.
296. Dan Diner, 'Zionismus und jüdisch-israelische Nation. Zur Begriffsbestimmung in der bundesrepublikanischen Debatte', in Friedhelm Ernst (ed.), *Palästina* (Kiel: Magazin-Verlag, 1982), pp. 22–4, at p. 22.

297. Diner, 'Leserbrief [Letter to the Editor]', p. 81.
298. Heenen, 'Deutsche Linke, linke Juden und der Zionismus', p. 112.
299. GAL Hamburg, *Krieg im Libanon – Frieden in Europa?*
300. All citations as quoted in 'Aktion für eine gemeinsame Perspektive von Juden und Arabern/Vergangenheitsbewältigung', *Arbeiterkampf* (25 August 1982), p. 28.
301. 'Der Krieg mit der Vergangenheit', in Israel-Palästina-Komitee Wien (ed.), *Libanon '82: Der israelisch-palästinensische Krieg. Eine Dokumentation* (Wien: Israel-Palästina Komitee, 1982), pp. 85–6 [first: *Frankfurt Rundschau* (20 August 1982)].
302. Kraushaar, *Fischer in Frankfurt*, p. 209.
303. Moshe Speier, Interview with the Author, Frankfurt am Main (20 February 2008) [German]; consider Kraushaar's view of the delegation's impressions: Kraushaar, *Fischer in Frankfurt*, p. 211: 'Most people's initial enthusiasm for the Palestinians' revolutionary model gave way to an attitude ranging between scepticism and resignation towards the reality in the barren, sunburnt Arab country and the misery in the refugee camps.'
304. Detlev Claussen, 'Terror in der Luft, Konterrevolution auf der Erde', *Links* 9 (1976), pp. 6–8; quoted here in the translation from Herf, *Undeclared Wars with Israel*, p. 336.
305. Quoted from Herf, *Undeclared Wars with Israel*, p. 337.
306. Detlev Claussen, 'Im Hause des Henkers', in Dietrich Wetzel (ed.), *Die Verlängerung von Geschichte: Deutsche, Juden und der Palästinakonflikt* (Frankfurt am Main: Neue Kritik, 1983), pp. 113–25.
307. Eike Geisel, 'Alle sind Sieger', in Eike Geisel, *Lastenausgleich, Umschuldung – Die Wiedergutwerdung der Deutschen: Essays, Polemiken, Stichworte* (Berlin: Edition TIAMAT, 1984), pp. 9–34, at p. 23.
308. Eike Geisel, 'Narziß am Abgrund. Eike Geisel über Alain Finkielkraut: "Der eingebildete Jude"', *Der Spiegel* 17 (26 April 1982), pp. 228–32, at p. 231.
309. Eike Geisel, 'Ein Gespräch mit Hanna Levy-Hass (1978)', in Eike Geisel (ed.), *Vielleicht war das alles erst der Anfang: Tagebuch aus dem KZ Bergen-Belsen; 1944–1945* (Berlin: Rotbuch Verlag, 1979), pp. 61–100.
310. Geisel, 'Alle sind Sieger', p. 25.
311. Wolfgang Pohrt, 'Erinnerung an Eike Geisel', in Wolfgang Pohrt, *Gewalt und Politik: Ausgewählte Reden & Schriften; 1979-1993*, Critica Diabolis (Berlin: Ed. Tiamat, 2010), pp. 378–82, at p. 380.
312. In 1987, Eike Geisel was one of the first signatories – together with Jakob Moneta, Erich Fried, John Bunzl and others – of a petition against the closure of the Alternative Information Centre and the imprisonment of its director Michael Warschawski

by the Israeli authorities. See the statement by the Frankfurt initiative 'Freedom for Michael Warschawski' by the same title. For more on Geisel's significance for the emergence of what became known as the 'anti-German' (*antideutsch*) left in Germany, see Klaus Bittermann, 'Die frühen Jahre. Eike Geisels Weg zum Kritiker des linken Antisemitismus', in Eike Geisel, *Die Gleichschaltung der Erinnerung: Kommentare zur Zeit* (Berlin: Edition TIAMAT, 2019), pp. 457–76.

313. Glezerman, '"Der Ring"', p. 127.
314. Noam Chomsky, *The Fateful Triangle: The United States, Israel and the Palestinians*, updated 2nd edn (Cambridge, MA: South End Press, 1999), pp. 237–41.
315. David Richardson, 'Personal Protest', *The Jerusalem Post* (13 August 1982), p. 7.
316. M. Davis, *40km into Lebanon: Israel's 1982 Invasion*, National Security Affairs Monograph (Washington: National Defense University Press, 1982), p. 103.
317. Inbar, 'The "No Choice War" Debate in Israel', pp. 22–37.
318. Uri Avnery, 'The Topic. The Meeting. Yasser Arafat Said Important Things, But More than Anything He Said, What Matters is that the Meeting Took Place', *Haolam Hazeh* 2341 (11 July 1982), pp. 12–13 [Hebrew].
319. Quoted from Segev, *The Seventh Million*, p. 400.
320. Quoted from Gilbert Achcar, *The Arabs and the Holocaust: The Arab-Israeli War of Narratives* (London: SAQI, 2011), p. 240.
321. Glezerman, '"Der Ring"', pp. 134–5.
322. Diner and Brumlik, 'Libanon. Der reale und der imaginäre Krieg', p. 26.
323. Ibid., p. 27.

Bibliography

In addition to the references already compiled in the bibliography, two books provide the English-speaking reader with direct access to the writings of Matzpen:

Essential writings of the organisation are included in the anthology *The Other Israel: The Radical Case Against Zionism* (Garden City: Doubleday, 1972), edited by Arie Bober. The book is also available online at www.matzpen.org

An English translation of a variety of Moshé Machover's writings – published in *Matzpen* and elsewhere – can be found in his book *Israelis and Palestinians: Conflict and Resolutions* (Chicago: Haymarket Books, 2012).

Furthermore, there are now a number of websites that make the original Hebrew texts of *Matzpen* and other related material accessible:

- Matzpen.org, the website of the Israeli Socialist Organization, offers access to all editions of the journal *Matzpen* and comprises articles on the biographies of individual members of the group.
  - https://matzpen.org/
- The internet archive 'The Israeli Left Archive' provides all scanned editions of *Matzpen* (as pdfs) and provides access to the publications of Matzpen's various spin-offs. Even sources that are difficult to access – such as newspaper articles, letters and leaflets – can be found here.
  - https://search.iisg.amsterdam/Record/COLL00308/ArchiveContentList
- The website 'Aki Orr Books' provides all of the books written by Akiva Orr for download. This includes the Hebrew original and the English translation of the

book *Shalom, Shalom ve-eyn Shalom. Israel and the Arabs 1948–1961* (Jerusalem: Bokhan, 1961), co-authored by him and Moshé Machover.
- http://www.akiorrbooks.com
- On Eran Torbiner's YouTube channel, his documentary on the history of Matzpen, as well as numerous interviews with former Matzpen members and other personalities from the Israeli Left, can be accessed.
    - https://www.youtube.com/channel/UCyIXJSOsrsIG-Z0MqTIFvvg
    'Video Archive of the Left between the River and the Sea' (erantor@gmail.com)

'4 Maki-Activists Ejected From the Party Blamed for "Factional Organization"', *Al Hamishmar*, 2 October 1962, p. 1 [Hebrew].

'A Mapam Official in the West was Expelled from the Party', *Ma'ariv*, 14 January 1953, p. 4 [Hebrew].

'A Salute to the Militant Eli Lobel', *Al-Hurriya* 937, 22 October 1979 [Arabic].

'A "Subversive" Document. Why Four Maki-Members were Expelled?', *Matzpen* 1 (1962), p. 2 [Hebrew].

Abu-Khalil, Nicola, 'Mein Al-Quds. Erinnerungen an Ost-Jerusalem', in Yasmeen Hamdan and Hans O. Wiebus (eds), *Palästina: Menschen, Landschaften, mit Fotos von Georg Stein* (Berlin: Elefanten Press, 1989), pp. 111–13.

Achcar, Gilbert, *The Arabs and the Holocaust: The Arab-Israeli War of Narratives* (London: SAQI, 2011).

Address by the Al-Fateh Delegation to the Second International Conference in Support of the Arab Peoples (Cairo, [January] 1969), https://www.freedomarchives.org/Documents/Finder/DOC12_scans/12.address.by.al-fateh.1969.pdf (accessed 28 July 2020).

Adiv, Udi, Email Communication with Udi Adiv, 6 May 2015 [English].

Afary, J. and K. Anderson (eds), *Foucault and the Iranian Revolution: Gender and the Seductions of Islamism* (Chicago: University of Chicago Press, 2005).

Ajami, Fouad, *The Arab Predicament: Arab Political Thought and Practice since 1967* (Cambridge: Cambridge University Press, [reprint] 1985).

'Aktion für eine gemeinsame Perspektive von Juden und Arabern/Vergangenheitsbewältigung', *Arbeiterkampf*, 25 August 1982, p. 28.

Al-Azm, Sadik, 'Islamisches Denken in der heutigen Welt', in Evangelischen Gemeinde Beirut (ed.), *Libanon. Kleine Orientierung* (Beirut: Evangelisch Gemeinde, 1969), pp. 70–5.

Al-Azm, Sadik, *A Critical Study of the Thought of the Palestinian Resistance* (Beirut: Dar al-'Awda, 1973) [Arabic].

Al-Azm, Sadik, 'The Palestine Resistance Movement Reconsidered', in Edward Said (ed.), *The Arabs Today: Alternatives for Tomorrow* (Columbus: Forum Associates, 1973), pp. 121–35.

Al-Azm, Sadik, 'Orientalism and Orientalism in Reverse', in Jon Rothschild (ed.), *Forbidden Agendas: Intolerance and Defiance in the Middle East* (London: Saqi Books, 1984), pp. 349–76 [first: *Khamsin* 8 (1981), pp. 5–26].

Al-Azm, Sadik, 'A Criticism of Religious Thought', in John J. Donohue and John L. Esposito (eds), *Islam in Transition: Muslim Perspectives* (New York: Oxford University Press, 2007), pp. 113–19.

Al-Azm, Sadik, 'Orientalism, Occidentalism, and Islamism', *Orientalism, Occidentalism, and Islamism* 30 (2010), pp. 6–13.

Al-Azm, Sadik J., *Self-Criticism After the Defeat* (London: Saqi, 2011) [first: Beirut: Dar al-Taliah (Vanguard Press), 1968].

Al-Azm, Sadik, *Critique of Religious Thought* (Berlin: Gerlach Press, 2015).

Albert, Alain, *The Crossing* (New York: G. Braziller, 1964).

Albert-Levin, Marc, 'Ah, les vies d'Halévi! Une autre face de la vie d'Ilan Halevi', *La Gazette de la Lucarne* 63, 15 October 2013, pp. 2–3, https://issuu.com/lalucarnedesecrivains/docs/lucarne_63-15oct-2013-bd (accessed 28 July 2020).

Alexander, Robert, 'Trotskyism in Israel', in Robert Alexander, *International Trotskyism, 1929–1985: A Documented Analysis of the Movement* (Durham: Duke University Press, 1991), pp. 577–85.

Ali, Tariq, *Street Fighting Years: An Autobiography of the Sixties*, 1st Citadel Underground edn (New York: Citadel Press, 1991).

al-Khalili, Samir (Makiya, Kanan), *The Republic of Fear: The Politics of Modern Iraq* (Berkeley: University of California Press, 1989).

Almog, Oz, *Farewell to "Srulik": Changing Values Among the Israeli Elite*, 2 vols (Haifa: Zemorah-Bitan, 2004) [Hebrew].

Almogi, Yosef, *Total Commitment* (New York: Herzl Press, 1982).

Amin, Samir, *A Life Looking Forward: Memoirs of an Independent Marxist* (London, New York: Zed Books, 2006).

Amnesty International, *Annual Report* (London: Amnesty International, 1973–4).

Amnon, K., 'The Group that was Thrown Out of Maki is Preparing to Publish its Own Monthly Magazine', *Al Hamishmar*, 12 November 1962, p. 1 [Hebrew].

'An Israeli Life. Obituary for Eli Lobel', *Haolam Hazeh* 2197, 10 October 1979, pp. 35 and 38 [Hebrew].

'And These are the Demands that One Needs to Struggle For [Program]', *Matzpen* 1 (1962), p. 8 [Hebrew].

'Announcement', *Kol Ha'am*, 28 September 1962, p. 12 [Hebrew].

Ansprenger, Franz, *Juden und Araber in einem Land: Die politischen Beziehungen der beiden Völker im Mandatsgebiet Palästina und im Staat Israel* (München, Mainz: Kaiser; Grünewald, 1978).

'Appeal by the Israeli Committee for a Free Algeria', *Etgar* 22, 22 March 1962, p. 3 [Hebrew].

'Arab States Plan an Offensive Against Israel at the UN', *Herut*, 29 July 1964, p. 1 [Hebrew].

'Arab Student Detained for Sheltering a Leader of the Terror Groups in the West Bank', *Israel Imperial News* 1: 9 (1968), pp. 9–10 and 14.

Arad, Roy C., 'Prophet in Jeans: 25 Years Since Dan Omer's Death', https://chicky00. wordpress.com/2010/02/22/נביא-זעם-בגינס--25שנים-וקצת-למותו-של-דן-ע/ (accessed 13 April 2020) [Hebrew].

Arendt, Hannah, 'Social Science Techniques and the Study of Concentration Camps', *Jewish Social Studies* 12: 1 (1950), pp. 49–64.

Arendt, Hannah, 'The Eichmann Trial. A Missed Opportunity', *Haaretz*, 8 April 1963, p. 9 and 15 [Hebrew].

Arendt, Hannah, *The Human Condition*, 2nd edn (Chicago: University of Chicago Press, [1958] 1998).

Arendt, Hannah, *Eichmann in Jerusalem: A Report on the Banality of Evil* (London: Penguin Books, 2006).

Arendt, Hannah, 'The Jewish State: Fifty Years After, Where Have Herzl's Politics Led?', in Jerome Kohn (ed.), *The Jewish Writings* (New York: Schocken Books, [1946] 2007), pp. 375–87.

Arendt, Hannah, 'To Save the Jewish Homeland', in Jerome Kohn (ed.), *The Jewish Writings* (New York: Schocken Books, [1948] 2007), pp. 388–401.

Arendt, Hannah, 'Zionism Reconsidered', in Jerome Kohn (ed.), *The Jewish Writings* (New York: Schocken Books, [1944] 2007), pp. 343–74.

Ariel, Gideon and Uri Milstein, *The Oasis of Dreams: The Legend of Hadassim* (Ramat Efal: Survival Publishing, 2006).

Ariel, Yaakov, 'From a Jewish Communist to a Jewish Buddhist: Allen Ginsberg as a Forerunner of a New American Jew', *Religions* 10: 2 (2019), pp. 1–16.

Avinoam, Reuven, *The New Left in Israel* (Jerusalem, 1973), https://www.marxists.org/subject/jewish/israel-new-left.pdf (accessed 28 July 2020).

Avnery, U., 'Lover of the Country: Obituary to Amos Kenan', https://www.israeli-occupation.org/2009-08-08/uri-avnery-on-amos-kenan-lover-of-the-country/ (accessed 13 April 2020).

Avnery, Uri, 'The Reactionism of the Fathers', *BaMaavak* ([May] 1947), pp. 6–7 [Hebrew].
Avnery, Uri, *War or Peace in the Semitic World* (Tel Aviv: A. Moses, 1947) [Hebrew].
Avnery, Uri, 'The Eichmann-Trial', *Etgar* 1: 5 ([May] 1961), pp. 2–3 [Hebrew].
Avnery, Uri, 'Yesterday's Pogrom', *Etgar* 3: 55 ([April] 1963), p. 3 [Hebrew].
Avnery, Uri, *Israel Without Zionists: A Plea for Peace in the Middle East* (New York: Macmillan, 1968).
Avnery, Uri, 'Wretched Figures', *Haolam Hazeh* 1627, 6 November 1968, p. 9 [Hebrew].
Avnery, Uri, 'And the Canaanite Was Then in the Land', in Uri Avnery, *The War of the Seventh Day* (Tel Aviv: Daf Hadash, 1969), pp. 145–80 [Hebrew].
Avnery, Uri, 'Caricatures', *Haolam Hazeh* 1657, 4 June 1969, pp. 13–14 [Hebrew].
Avnery, Uri, 'The Topic of Debate: Uri Avnery', *Ma'ariv*, 22 October 1969, p. 34.
Avnery, Uri, 'Arik's War', *Haolam Hazeh* 2337, 16 June 1982, pp. 15 and 72–3 [Hebrew].
Avnery, Uri, 'The Topic. The Meeting. Yasser Arafat Said Important Things, But More than Anything He Said, What Matters is that the Meeting Took Place', *Haolam Hazeh* 2341, 11 July 1982, pp. 12–13 [Hebrew].
Avnery, Uri, *My Friend, the Enemy* (London: Zed Books, 1986).
Avnery, Uri, 'The Man, Who was Ahead of Everyone', *Haolam Hazeh*, 28 January 1990, pp. 18–19 and 41 [Hebrew].
Avnery, Uri, 'I'll Never See Anyone Like Him Again. Obituary about Matti Peled', *Ma'ariv*, 12 March 1995, pp. 4 and 6 [Hebrew].
Avnery, Uri, 'Mein Traum, auch heute noch. . . Uri Avnery: Journalist, Politiker und Friedensaktivist', in Georg Stein and Rudolf Augstein (eds), *Zwei Völker, zwei Staaten: Gespräch über Israel und Palästina* (Heidelberg: Palmyra, 1995), pp. 99–174.
Avnery, Uri, 'Model of a Different Israel. Forty Years to the "Hebrew Manifesto"', *Haaretz Culture and Literature Supplement*, 10 January 1997, p. 17 [Hebrew].
Avnery, Uri, 'The Silent Idealist', *Le Monde Diplomatique* ([April] 1998), https://mondediplo.com/1998/04/14curiel2 (accessed 28 July 2020).
Avnery, Uri, 'Benjamin's Inn', *Haaretz*, 27 December 2007, https://www.haaretz.com/1.4972651 (accessed 28 July 2020).
Avnery, Uri, *Optimistic* (Tel Aviv: Yediot Sfarim, 2014) [Hebrew].
Aytürk, Ilker, 'Attempts at Romanizing the Hebrew Script and their Failure. Nationalism, Religion and Alphabet Reform in the Yishuv', *Middle Eastern Studies* 43: 4 (2007), pp. 625–45.
Bachar, Aharon, 'The Suspects of Belonging to a Joint Network', *Yediot Aharonot*, 10 December 1972, p. 11 [Hebrew].

Bachar, Aharon, 'Gan Shmuel. Udi versus Uri', *Yediot Aharonot. Weekend Supplement*, 15 December 1972, pp. 1–2 [Hebrew].

Bacher, Aaron, 'All the Secrets About Matzpen', *Yediot Aharonot*, 22 May 1970, pp. 5–7 [Hebrew].

Baer, Gabriel (Munier, S.), 'Zionism and the Middle East. The Aftermath of the Jewish-Arab War', *Fourth International* 10: 9 (99) (1949), pp. 277–83.

Bajaja, Nissim (Hanegbi, Haim), 'The Khalil Toama Affair', *Matzpen* (1968), pp. 2–4 [Hebrew].

Bajajo-Hanegbi, Haim, 'Sanctity of Private Property', *Israel Imperial News* 2: 6 ([October] 1968), p. 7.

Ballas, G. (ed.), *Group of Ten, 1951-1960* (Ramat Gan: Museum of Israeli Art, 1992).

Ballas, Shimon, *Last Winter* (Jerusalem: Keter, 1984) [Hebrew].

Bar-Kedma, Emanuel, 'Justice is Money', *Yediot Aharonot. Weekend Supplement*, 14 February 1986, pp. 28–30 [Hebrew].

Bar-Kedma, Emanuel, 'Who Remembers Rami Livneh?', *Yediot Aharonot. Weekend Supplement*, 23 April 1992, pp. 29–30 [Hebrew].

Bardawil, Fadi A., *Revolution and Disenchantment. Arab Marxism and the Binds of Emancipation* (Durham and London: Duke University Press, 2020).

Barnea, Nahum, 'The King of the Jews and His Son', *Koteret Rashit*, 3 December 1986, pp. 24–31 [Hebrew].

Baron, Gabi, 'Attempt to Disrupt Cohn-Bendit's Gathering was a Failure', *Yediot Aharonot*, 1 June 1970 [Hebrew].

Bar-On, Mordechai, *In Pursuit of Peace: A History of the Israeli Peace Movement* (Washington: United States Institute of Peace Press, 1996).

Bartov, Hanoch, 'A Matzpen Envoy Speaks in Washington', *Ma'ariv*, 10 July 1970, p. 52 [Hebrew].

Bartov, Omer, 'Moshe Lewin's Century', *Kritika. Explorations in Russian and Eurasian History* 12: 1 (2011), pp. 115–22.

Baruch, Adam, 'Good To See You, Tzabar', *Yediot Aharonot. Weekend Supplement*, 30 June 1989, p. 21 [Hebrew].

Baruch, Adam, 'Shimon Tzabar. An Adult Hiding Under a Mushroom', *Ma'ariv*, 11 February 1994, p. 19 [Hebrew].

Baruch, Adam, 'Maxim Ghilan Anyway Alone', in Adam Baruch, *How Are Things at Home?* (Kinnereth: Zemorah-Bitan, 2004), pp. 129–55 [Hebrew].

Bar-Yosef, Avinoam, 'On the Left Leg', *Ma'ariv Weekend Supplement*, 6 March 1987, pp. 10–12, 53 [Hebrew].

Barzilai, Gad, *Wars, Internal Conflicts, and Political Order: A Jewish Democracy in the Middle East*, SUNY Series in Israeli Studies (Albany: State University of New York Press, 1996).

Bar-Zohar, Michael, *Ben Gurion*, 3 vols (Tel Aviv: Am Oved, 1975) [Hebrew].

Bar-Zohar, Michael, *Ben-Gurion: A Biography* (Tel Aviv: Magal Books, [1978] 2003).

Batatu, Hanna, *The Old Social Classes and the Revolutionary Movements of Iraq: A Study of Iraq's Old Landed and Commercial Classes and of its Communists, Ba'thists, and Free Officers*, Princeton Studies on the Near East (Princeton: Princeton University Press, 1978).

Baumgarten, Helga, *Palästina: Befreiung in den Staat: die palästinensische Nationalbewegung seit 1948* (Frankfurt am Main: Suhrkamp, 1991).

Beinin, Joel, *Was the Red Flag Flying There?: Marxist Politics and the Arab-Israeli Conflict in Egypt and Israel, 1948–1965* (Berkeley: University of California Press, 1990).

Beinin, Joel, *The Dispersion of Egyptian Jewry: Culture, Politics, and the Formation of a Modern Diaspora* (Berkeley: University of California Press, 1998).

Beit-Hallahmi, Benjamin, *Original Sins: Reflections on the History of Zionism and Israel* (London: Pluto Press, 1992).

Ben-Akiva, Yossi, 'The Palestinian Resistance – Where To?', *Matzpen-Marxisti* 75 (1974), pp. 6–7 [Hebrew].

Ben-Amotz, D. and N. Ben-Yehuda (eds), *The World Dictionary of Hebrew Slang* (Jerusalem: Levin Epstein, 1972) [Hebrew].

Ben-Amotz, Dahn, *To Remember, To Forget: A Novel* (Philadelphia: Jewish Publication Society of America, 1973).

Ben-Amotz, Dan, 'Who Are You, Dan Ben-Amotz? Interview with Uri Avnery', *Haolam Hazeh* 1599, 24 April 1968, pp. 12–13.

Ben-Ari, Nitza, *Suppression of the Erotic in Modern Hebrew Literature* (Ottawa: University of Ottawa Press, 2006).

Ben-Ari, Nitza, 'Popular Literature in Hebrew as Marker of Anti-Sabra Culture', in Rakefet Sela-Sheffy and Gideon Toury (eds), *Culture Contacts and the Making of Cultures: Papers in Homage to Itamar Even Zohar* (Tel Aviv: Tel Aviv University – Unit of Culture Research, 2011), pp. 219–43.

Ben-Chorin, Schalom, 'Pornografie und Zensur', *Jedioth Chadashot*, 2 December 1966.

Ben-Gurion, David, 'The Eichmann-Case as Seen by Ben-Gurion. Interview', *New York Times*, 18 December 1960, pp. 7 and 62.

Benhabib, Seyla, *The Reluctant Modernism of Hannah Arendt*, 2 edn (Lanham: Rowman & Littlefield, 2003).

Ben-Layashi, Samir and Bruce Maddy-Weitzman, 'Myth, History and "Realpolitik". Morocco and its Jewish Community', *Journal of Modern Jewish Studies* 9: 1 (2010), pp. 89–106.

Ben-Tor, Nechemia, *Torch Bearers of Freedom: Short Biographes of the Leaders of the Fighters for Freedom of Israel (Lechi)* (Tel Aviv: Ya'ir, 2008) [Hebrew].
Benziman, Uzi, 'Security is the Quest of Peace (Interview with the Sixth-Formers)', *Haaretz*, 1 May 1970, p. 17 [Hebrew].
Benziman, Uzi, 'Matzpen and the Educational Gap', *Haaretz*, 8 May 1970 [Hebrew].
Berger, Joseph, *Shipwreck of a Generation: The Memoirs of Joseph Berger* (London: Harvill Press, 1971).
Berger-Barzilai, Joseph, 'The Path of a Jewish Worker-Revolutionary. At the Grave of Hersh Mendel', *Davar*, 11 August 1968, p. 8 [Hebrew].
Berger-Barzilai, Joseph, 'The "Neo-Zionist Revolution" in the USSR', *The Jewish Quarterly* 19: 1–2 (1971), pp. 9–10.
Bergmann, Theodor, *"Gegen den Strom": Die Geschichte der KPD (Oppositon)* (Hamburg: VSA-Verlag, 2001).
Bet-Levi, Roi, 'A Bad Tropical Country', *Haaretz*, 18 September 2007, https://www.haaretz.co.il/misc/1.1442943 (accessed 28 July 2020) [Hebrew].
Bichler, S. and J. Nitzan, 'To the New Readers Innocent of the Undeconstructed Past: On the Second Edition of "Peace, Peace, and No Peace"', http://bnarchives.yorku.ca/280/1/20100300_bn_to_the_new_readers.pdf (accessed 30 March 2020).
Bierman, Amnon, 'Where Did Shimon Tzabar Disappear To?', *Yediot Aharonot (7 Days Supplement)*, 29 July 1988, pp. 32–3 [Hebrew].
Bilgin, Pinar, *Regional Security in the Middle East: A Critical Perspective* (London, New York: Routledge, 2005).
Birchall, Ian, *Tony Cliff: A Marxist For His Time* (London: Bookmarks Publications, 2011).
Bittermann, Klaus, 'Die frühen Jahre. Eike Geisels Weg zum Kritiker des linken Antisemitismus', in Eike Geisel, *Die Gleichschaltung der Erinnerung: Kommentare zur Zeit* (Berlin: Edition TIAMAT, 2019), pp. 457–76.
Blumenthal, Max and Joseph Dana, *Author and Activist Akiva Orr on Israel's Wars*, January 2011, 144 min, video interview, https://vimeo.com/19444809 (accessed 15 April 2020).
Bober, A. (ed.), *The Other Israel: The Radical Case Against Zionism* (Garden City: Doubleday, 1972).
Bober, Arie, 'Introduction', in Arie Bober (ed.), *The Other Israel: The Radical Case Against Zionism* (Garden City: Doubleday, 1972), pp. 1–34.
Borochov, Ber, *Die Grundlagen des Poalezionismus* (Frankfurt/M.: Borochov-Press, 1969).
Brecher, Michael, *The Foreign Policy System of Israel: Setting, Images, Process* (London: Oxford University Press, 1972).

Broder, H. M., 'Weinstock wird erwachsen', https://www.achgut.com/artikel/weinstock/ (accessed 28 July 2020).

Broder, Henryk, *Der ewige Antisemit: Über Sinn und Funktion eines beständigen Gefühls* (Frankfurt: Fischer, 1986).

Broder, Henryk, 'Tote Seelen in Berlin', *Die Zeit*, 27 September 1991, https://www.zeit.de/1991/40/tote-seelen-in-berlin (accessed 28 July 2020).

Broder, Jon, '"Mideast War Now International". Conflict's Shadow Follows Expatriates', *Daytona Beach Sunday News-Journal*, 22 July 1973, 8B.

Brossat, Alain and Sylvia Klingberg, *Revolutionary Yiddishland: A History of Jewish Radicalism*, 1st edn (London, New York: Verso, 2016).

Brumlik, Micha, *Kein Weg als Deutscher und Jude: Eine bundesrepublikanische Erfahrung* (Munchen: Luchterhand, 1996).

Buckard, Christian, *Arthur Koestler: Ein extremes Leben 1905–1983* (München: C. H. Beck, 2004).

Budeiri, Musa, *The Palestine Communist Party 1919-1948: Arab and Jew in the Struggle for Internationalism* (Chicago: Haymarket Books, 2010).

Bunzl, John, *Klassenkampf in der Diaspora: Zur Geschichte der judischen Arbeiterbewegung, Schriftenreihe des Ludwig Boltzmann Instituts fur Geschichte der Arbeiterbewegung*, vol. 5 (Wien: Europaverlag, 1975).

Bunzl, John, 'Left Memories', in Raimund Löw (ed.), *Die Fantasie und die Macht: 1968 und danach* (Wien: Czernin, 2006), pp. 261–73.

Bunzl, John, *Israel im Nahen Osten: Eine Einführung* (Wien: UTB/Böhlau, 2008).

Camus, Albert, *The First Man* (Toronto: Alfred A. Knopf Canada, 1995).

Camus, Albert, 'Algeria 1958', in Albert Camus, *Algerian Chronicles*, 1st Harvard University Press edn (Cambridge, MA: Belknap Press of Harvard University Press, 2014), pp. 175–80.

Camus, Albert, 'Letter to an Algerian Militant', in Albert Camus, *Algerian Chronicles*, 1st Harvard University Press edn (Cambridge, MA: Belknap Press of Harvard University Press, 2014), pp. 113–16.

Camus, Albert, 'Preface', in Albert Camus, *Algerian Chronicles*, 1st Harvard University Press edn (Cambridge, MA: Belknap Press of Harvard University Press, 2014), pp. 23–35.

Camus, Albert, 'The New Algeria', in Albert Camus, *Algerian Chronicles*, 1st Harvard University Press edn (Cambridge, MA: Belknap Press of Harvard University Press, 2014), pp. 181–4.

Canaan, Haviv, 'Disgust at the Fossilisation of Communism', *Haaretz*, 15 May 1970, p. 17 [Hebrew].

Canaan, Haviv, 'Matzpen's Aspiration. A State for Everyone', *Haaretz*, 18 May 1970, p. 12 [Hebrew].

Canaan, Haviv, 'The Differences between the Stances of Matzpen and Al-Fatah', *Haaretz*, 19 May 1970, p. 12 [Hebrew].

Canaan, Haviv, 'The Heads of Matzpen and their Careers', *Haaretz*, 20 May 1970, p. 18 [Hebrew].

Carmi, M., Phone Call with Menachem Carmi, 12 July 2013 [Hebrew].

Carmi, Menachem, 'Towards a Critique of the Traditional Israeli Left', *Matzpen* 44 (1968), pp. 6–8 [Hebrew].

Carmi, Tom, *Away from the Tribe's Center*, 2009, Israel, 58 min, documentary.

Carroll, David, 'Camus's Algeria. Birthrights, Colonial Injustice, and the Fiction of a French-Algerian People', *MLN* 112: 4 (1997), pp. 517–49.

Caspi, Mordechai, '"Peace, Peace, When There is No Peace"', *Kol Ha'am*, 8 December 1961, pp. 2 and 7 [Hebrew].

Chazan, Meir, 'Goldmann's Initiative to Meet With Nasser', in Mark A. Raider (ed.), *Nahum Goldmann: Statesman Without a State*, SUNY Series in Israeli Studies (Albany [Tel Aviv]: SUNY Press; Chaim Rosenberg School of Jewish Studies, the Chaim Weizmann Institute for the Study of Zionism and Israel, Tel Aviv University, 2009), pp. 297–324.

Chazan, Meir, 'The Dispute in Mapai Over "Self-Restraint" and "Purity of Arms" During the Arab Revolt', *Jewish Social Studies: History, Culture and Society* 15: 3 (2009), pp. 89–113.

Chetrit, Sami S., *The Mizrahi Struggle in Israel: Between Oppression and Liberation, Identification and Alternative, 1948–2003* (Tel Aviv: Am Oved, 2004).

Chomsky, Noam, *The Fateful Triangle: The United States, Israel and the Palestinians*, updated 2nd edn (Cambridge, MA: South End Press, 1999).

Chowers, Eyal, *The Political Philosophy of Zionism: Trading Jewish Words for an Hebraic Land* (Cambridge, New York: Cambridge University Press, 2012).

'Clashes During Maki-Demonstration', *Al Hamishmar*, 2 May 1969, p. 1 [Hebrew].

Claussen, Detlev, 'Terror in der Luft, Konterrevolution auf der Erde', *Links* 9 (1976), pp. 6–8.

Claussen, Detlev, 'Im Hause des Henkers', in Dietrich Wetzel (ed.), *Die Verlängerung von Geschichte: Deutsche, Juden und der Palästinakonflikt* (Frankfurt am Main: Neue Kritik, 1983), pp. 113–25.

Claussen, Detlev, 'Entréebillet Kommunismus. Eine Erinnerung an Isaac Deutscher', *Babylon. Beiträge zur jüdischen Gegenwart* 22 (2007), pp. 87–97.

Cliff, Tony, *A World to Win: Life of a Revolutionary* (London: Bookmarks, 2000).

Cohen, Aharon, *Israel and the Arab World* (Merhavia: Sifriyat Poalim, 1964).

Cohen, Aharon, *Israel and the Arab World* (London: W. H. Allen, 1970).
Cohen, Aharon, 'Portrait of a Helpless Revolutionary', *Emdah* 7 (1975), pp. 20–1, 25 [Hebrew].
Cohen, Michael, *Britain's Moment in Palestine: Retrospect and Perspectives, 1917–1948* (Abingdon: Routledge, 2015).
Cohen, Percy S., *Jewish Radicals and Radical Jews* (London: Academic Press, 1980).
Cohn-Bendit, Daniel, *Der grosse Basar: Gespräche mit Michel Lévy, Jean-Marc Salmon, Maren Sell* (München: Trikont-Verlag, 1975).
Cohn-Bendit, Daniel, *Wir haben sie so geliebt, die Revolution, Dt. Erstausg* (Frankfurt am Main: Athenäum, 1987).
'Concern over Ahmed Ben Bella's "Declaration of War" Against Israel', *Davar*, 12 April 1962, p. 1 [Hebrew].
'Conversation Between Etgar and the Founders of Semitic Action', *Etgar* 22, 11 January 1962, pp. 4–6 [Hebrew].
Cromer, Gerald, 'Udi Adiv', in Gerald Cromer, *The Writing Was On the Wall: Constructing Political Deviance in Israel* (Ramat-Gan: Bar-Ilan University Press, 1998), pp. 110–33.
Crusius, Reinhard, 'Einleitung', in Manfred Wilke and Reinhard Crusius (eds), *Entstalinisierung: Der XX. Parteitag der KPdSU und seine Folgen*, Edition Suhrkamp ([S. l.]: [s. n.]; Frankfurt am Main: Suhrkamp, 1977), pp. 9–20.
Crusius, Reinhard and Manfred Wilke, 'Polen und Ungarn 1956. Eine Dokumentation', in Manfred Wilke and Reinhard Crusius (eds), *Entstalinisierung: Der XX. Parteitag der KPdSU und seine Folgen*, Edition Suhrkamp ([S. l.]: [s. n.]; Frankfurt am Main: Suhrkamp, 1977), pp. 98–164.
Cypel, S., Email Communication with Sylvain Cypel, 15 July 2013 [English].
Dallasheh, Leena, 'Political Mobilization of Palestinians in Israel. The al-'Ard Movement', in Rhoda A. Kanaaneh and Isis Nusair (eds), *Displaced at Home: Ethnicity and Gender Among Palestinians in Israel* (New York: State University of New York Press, 2010), pp. 21–38.
Dan, Uri, '500 Arab Students Held a "Palestine Day" in Paris', *Ma'ariv*, 19 May 1967, p. 27 [Hebrew].
Dan, Uri, 'Danny the Red Calls for Overthrowing De Gaulle's "Police State"', *Ma'ariv*, 17 May 1968, p. 2 [Hebrew].
Danziger, Raphael, 'Algeria and the Palestinian Organisations', in Gabriel Ben-Dor (ed.), *The Palestinians and the Middle East Conflict: An International Conference Held at the Institute of Middle Eastern Studies, University of Haifa, April 1976* (Ramat Gan: Turtledove Publishing, 1976), pp. 347–73.
Dar, Yoel, 'Al-Ard: A Small but Dangerous Group', *Davar*, 30 July 1964, p. 3 [Hebrew].

Davis, M., *40Km into Lebanon: Israel's 1982 Invasion*, National Security Affairs Monograph (Washington: National Defense University Press, 1982).

Davis, Uri, *Crossing the Border: An Autobiography of an Anti-Zionist Palestinian of the Hebrew Language Group* (London: Books and Books, 1995).

Dayan, Aryeh, 'We Were "Stalin's Children" and We Have Nothing to Be Ashamed Of', *Haaretz*, 25 April 2000, pp. 4ב–5ב [Hebrew].

Dayan, Aryeh, 'Some Comrades Started to Complain about Strange Things that Happened around Ilan', *Haaretz*, 27 May 2001, pp. 8ב–9ב [Hebrew].

'Declaration of the Revolutionary Communist Alliance (16.12.1972)', *Israleft. News Service* 9, 15 January 1973, pp. 8–9.

'Der Krieg mit der Vergangenheit', in Israel-Palästina-Komitee Wien (ed.), *Libanon '82: Der israelisch-palästinensische Krieg. Eine Dokumentation* (Wien: Israel-Palästina Komitee, 1982), pp. 85–6 [first: *Frankfurt Rundschau*, 20 August 1982].

Deutscher, Isaac, 'Israel's Spiritual Climate [1954]', in Isaac Deutscher, *The Non-Jewish Jew and Other Essays* (London: Oxford University Press, 1968), pp. 91–117.

Deutscher, Isaac, 'The Russian Revolution and the Jewish Problem [1964]', in Isaac Deutscher, *The Non-Jewish Jew and Other Essays* (London: Oxford University Press, 1968), pp. 60–83.

Deutscher, Isaac, 'Who is a Jew? [1963/1966]', in Isaac Deutscher, *The Non-Jewish Jew and Other Essays* (London: Oxford University Press, 1968), pp. 42–9.

Deutscher, Isaac, *Die ungelöste Judenfrage*, ed. by Eike Geisel and Mario Offenberg (Berlin: Rotbuch-Verlag, 1977).

Deutschkron, Inge, 'Jerusalem in All its Colours at the Frankfurt Book Fair', *Ma'ariv*, 26 October 1969, p. 19 [Hebrew].

Devlin, Kevin, 'Communism in Israel. Anatomy of a Split', *Survey* 62: 1 (1967), pp. 141–51.

Diamond, James S., *Homeland or Holy Land?: The "Canaanite" Critique of Israel* (Bloomington: Indiana University Press, 1986).

Diner, Dan, 'Preface to The Foundations of Socialist Zionism by Ber Borochov' (The World Union of Jewish Students, 1969).

Diner, Dan, 'Vorwort', in Ber Borochov, *Die Grundlagen des Poalezionismus* (Frankfurt/M.: Borochov-Press, 1969), pp. 7–24.

Diner, Dan, 'Der Zionismus und die jüdische Frage heute', *Emuna. Horizonte zur Diskussion über Israel und das Judentum* 5: 3 (1970), pp. 153–9.

Diner, Dan, 'Panarabism, Zionism and the Palestinians', *Shalom Dialog. Magazine for Jewish European Youth* 20/21 (1972), pp. 93–9.

Diner, Dan, 'Zionism within the Context of Universalism and Particularism', *Shalom Dialog. Magazine for Jewish European Youth* 20/21 (1972), pp. 70–8.

Diner, Dan, 'Sozialdemokratie und koloniale Frage, dargestellt am Beispiel des Zionismus', *Die Dritte Welt* 3: 1/2 (1974), pp. 58–87.

Diner, Dan, 'Marché mondial, sionisme et violence. Thèses sur l'integration capitaliste du Mashreq et ses consequences politiques', *Khamsin. Revue des Socialistes Revolutionnaires du Proche-Orient* 4 (1977), pp. 66–87.

Diner, Dan, 'Zum Tod von Genossen', *Links* 116 (1979), p. 4.

Diner, Dan, 'Die Palästina-Frage im Vorderen Orient. Entwicklungen und Perspektiven', in John Bunzl (ed.), *Israel/Palästina: Klasse, Nation und Befreiung im Nahost-Konflikt* (Hamburg: Junius Verlag, 1980), pp. 169–82.

Diner, Dan, 'Fragments of an Uncompleted Journey. On Jewish Socialisation and Political Identity in Germany', *New German Critique* 8: 20 (1980), pp. 57–70.

Diner, Dan, *Israel in Palästina: Über Tausch und Gewalt im Vorderen Orient* (Königstein/Ts.: Athenäum, 1980).

Diner, Dan, 'Elemente einer Theorie der Bi-Nationalität in Palästina', in Friedhelm Ernst (ed.), *Nahost: Stimmen der Opposition, Palästina zwischen Krieg und Staatsgründung*, Der Schwierige Weg nach Palästina (Stuttgart: ESG-Geschäftsstelle – Bremen, 1981), pp. 67–72.

Diner, Dan, 'Israel. Nationalstaatsproblem und Nahostkonflikt', in Wolfgang Benz and Hermann Graml, *Weltprobleme zwischen den Machtblöcken: Das Zwanzigste Jahrhundert III*, Fischer-Weltgeschichte (Frankfurt: Fischer Taschenbuch Verlag, 1981), pp. 165–212.

Diner, Dan, 'Israels nukleare Option und das Trauma der Massenvernichtung', *Links* 136 ([July–August] 1981), pp. 8–9.

Diner, Dan, *Zur Kritik der zionistischen Struktur Israels: Für Bi-Nationalität in Palästina* (Wien: Israel-Palästina-Komitee, 1981).

Diner, Dan, 'Ich wäre glücklich wenn die USA und die UdSSR am Rande einer Konfrontation stünden. (Interview)', *Pflasterstrand* 134, 19 June 1982 – 2 July 1982, pp. 24–7.

Diner, Dan, *"Keine Zukunft auf den Gräbern der Palästinenser": Eine historisch-politische Bilanz der Palästinafrage* (Hamburg: VSA-Verlag, 1982).

Diner, Dan, 'Leserbrief [Letter to the Editor]', in Israel-Palästina-Komitee Wien (ed.), *Libanon '82: Der israelisch-palästinensische Krieg. Eine Dokumentation* (Wien: Israel-Palästina-Komitee, 1982), pp. 79–81 [first: *Die Tageszeitung*, 30 June 1982].

Diner, Dan, 'Zionismus und jüdisch-israelische Nation. Zur Begriffsbestimmung in der bundesrepublikanischen Debatte', in Friedhelm Ernst (ed.), *Palästina* (Kiel: Magazin-Verlag, 1982), pp. 22–4.

Diner, Dan, 'Israel and the Trauma of the Mass Extermination', *Telos. A Quarterly Journal of Critical Thought* 57 (1983), pp. 41–52.

Diner, Dan, 'Die jüdisch-israelische Nationalität. Über die Dialektik der Anerkennung', in Friedhelm Ernst (ed.), *Zionismus, Opposition und Bi-Nationalität*, Der Schwierige Weg nach Palästina (Stuttgart: Alektor-Verlag, 1984), pp. 21–6.

Diner, Dan, 'Bolschewismus ohne Kommunismus – Ben Gurion und der Holocaust. Zu dem Buch von Dina Porat über Yischuv und Holocaust', *Babylon. Beiträge zur jüdischen Gegenwart* 2 (1987), pp. 127–31.

Diner, Dan, 'Materialismus, Fortschritt und Utopie. Elemente europäischer Geistesgeschichte im Zionismus', in Karl-Heinz Schneider (ed.), *Der Zionismus und seine europäischen Wurzeln: Dokumentation einer Arbeitstagung in der Evangelischen Akademie Arnoldshain, November 1986*, Schriften / Deutsch-Israelischer Arbeitskreis für Frieden im Nahen Osten (Edenkoben: DIAK, 1987), pp. 37–53.

Diner, Dan, 'Der hebräische Mythos. Aus Anlass des Buches von Jacob Shavit', *Babylon. Beiträge zur jüdischen Gegenwart* 4 (1988), pp. 119–23.

Diner, Dan, 'Cumulative Contingency. Historicizing Legitimacy in Israeli Discourse', *History and Memory* 7: 1 (1995), pp. 147–70.

Diner, Dan, 'Hannah Arendt Reconsidered. On the Banal and the Evil in Her Holocaust Narrative', *New German Critique* 71 (1997), pp. 177–90.

Diner, Dan, 'Für ein Israel der Gegenwart. Eli Löbel oder Eine politische Gegenbiographie', *Blätter für deutsche und internationale Politik* 43: 5 (1998), pp. 613–17.

Diner, Dan, 'Täuschungen. Israel, die Linke und das Dilemma der Kritik', in Wolfgang Kraushaar (ed.), *Frankfurter Schule und Studentenbewegung: Von der Flaschenpost zum Molotowcocktail 1946-1995*, 3 vols (Hamburg: Rogner und Bernhard bei Zweitausendeins, 1998), vol. 3, pp. 187–94.

Diner, Dan, 'Man hat mit der Sache eigentlich nichts mehr zu tun', in Richard C. Schneider (ed.), *Wir sind da!: Die Geschichte der Juden in Deutschland von 1945 bis heute* (Berlin: Ullstein, 2000), pp. 233–52.

Diner, Dan, 'Sprachlos am Zaun. Israels Existenz hat drei Begründungen', *Die Zeit* 31 (2002), https://www.zeit.de/2002/31/200231_essay.diner.xml (accessed 28 July 2020).

Diner, Dan, 'Ambiguous Semantics. Reflections on Jewish Political Concepts', *The Jewish Quarterly Review* 98: 1 (2008), pp. 89–102.

Diner, Dan, 'Epistemics of the Holocaust. Considering the Question of "Why?" and of "How?"', *Naharaim. Zeitschrift für deutsch-jüdische Literatur und Kulturgeschichte/Journal of German-Jewish Literature and Cultural History* 1: 2 (2008), pp. 195–213.

Diner, Dan, *Lost in the Sacred: Why the Muslim World Stood Still* (Princeton: Princeton University Press, 2009).

Diner, Dan, 'Post-postkoloniale Flaschenpost', in Dan Diner, *Zeitenschwelle: Gegenwartsfragen an die Geschichte* (München: Pantheon, 2010), pp. 233–40 [first: *Die Welt*, 19 July 2008].

Diner, Dan, 'Banished. Jews in Germany after the Holocaust. An Interpretation', in Michael Brenner (ed.), *A History of Jews in Germany since 1945: Politics, Culture, and Society* (Bloomington: Indiana University Press, 2018), pp. 7–53.

Diner, Dan and Micha Brumlik, 'Libanon. Der reale und der imaginäre Krieg. Interview mit Dan Diner und Micha Brumlik', *Arbeiterkampf* 224, 25 August 1982, pp. 25–7.

Diner, Dan and Ella Weinstein, *Zur Situation im Nahen Osten* (Berlin: Bundesverband jüdisher Studenten in Deutschland, 1969).

'Discrimination, Suppression, Persecution', *Matzpen* 21 (1964), pp. 3–5 [Hebrew].

'Documents from the Trial of the Author and Publisher', in Sadik J Al-Azm, *Critique of Religious Thought* (Berlin: Gerlach Press, 2015), pp. 207–26.

Dotan, Shmuel, *Reds: The Communist Party in Eretz Yisrael* (Kfar Saba: Shevna Hasofer, 1991) [Hebrew].

'Dov Shas (1925–2006). Obituary', *Revolutionary History* 10: 1 (2006), https://www.marxists.org/history/etol/revhist/backiss/vol10/no1/prrg.html (accessed 28 July 2020).

Dror, Emmanuel, 'The Emergency Regulations', in Arie Bober (ed.), *The Other Israel: The Radical Case Against Zionism* (Garden City: Doubleday, 1972), pp. 134–44.

Dunkhase, Jan, 'Nimrod', in Dan Diner (ed.), *Enzyklopädie jüdischer Geschichte und Kultur*, 7 vols (Stuttgart, Weimar: Metzler, 2012–17), vol. 4, pp. 370–5.

Dunkhase, Jan, 'Hebräisch säkularisieren. Anverwandlungen einer heiligen Sprache', *Jahrbuch des Simon-Dubnow-Instituts/Simon Dubnow Institute Yearbook* 12 (2013), pp. 263–386.

Ebon, Martin, 'Communist Tactics in Palestine', *Middle East Journal* 2: 3 (1948), pp. 255–69.

'Editorial', *Khamsin* 8 (1981), pp. 2–4.

'Editorial: And Again – The Palestinian Question', *Matzpen* 71 (1974), p. 3 [Hebrew].

'Editorial: Apropos Sartre', *Matzpen* 34 (1967), pp. 2 and 10 [Hebrew].

'Educational Material about the Machover-Pilavsky Anti-Party Group', hdl.handle.net/10622/COLL00308%2E568?locatt=view:pdf (accessed 26 March 2020).

Edwards, C. D., 'Interview with Eli Lobel. Matzpen's Voice Abroad', 1972, Berkeley, audio recording.

Efrat, Gideon, 'The Last Sabra/Tzabar', *Iton 77* 325 ([August] 2007), pp. 18–21 [Hebrew].

Ehrlich, Avishai, 'The Crisis in Israel, Danger of Fascism?', *Khamsin. Journal of Revolutionary Socialists of the Middle East* 5 (1978), pp. 81–113.
Ehrlich, Avishai, 'Settler Societies', in Paola Cardullo, Rahila Gupta and Jamie Hakim (eds), *Sociology, Politics, Thinking and Acting: A Festschrift for Nira Yuval-Davies* (London: Centre for Research on Migration, Refugees and Belonging, University of East London, 2014), pp. 48–52.
Ein-Gil, Ehud, 'Religion, Zionism, and Secularism', *Khamsin. Journal of Revolutionary Socialists of the Middle East* 8 (1981), pp. 105–20.
Ein-Gil, Ehud, 'The Roots of Jihad', *Haaretz*, 16 March 2006, http://www.haaretz.com/the-roots-of-jihad-1.182958 (accessed 28 July 2020).
Ein-Gil, Ehud, 'In One Point We Will Remain the Same. In the Love for this Middle East. Ehud Ein-Gil Talks About Meetings with Arab Revolutionary Intellectuals', *Haaretz*, 1 March 2017, https://www.haaretz.co.il/magazine/.premium-1.3899423 (accessed 28 July 2020) [Hebrew].
Eisenstadt, Shmuel, *Israeli Society*, The Nature of Human Society Series (London: Weidenfeld and Nicolson, 1967).
Elam, Yigal, *An Introduction to a Different Zionist History* (Tel Aviv: Levin Epstein, 1972) [Hebrew].
El-Asmar, Fouzi, *To Be an Arab in Israel* (Beirut: The Institute for Palestine Studies, 1978).
El-Manssoury, F., 'Palestinians and Israelis', *Journal of Palestine Studies* 1/2: 5 (1975/6), pp. 115–26.
Elon, Amos, 'Our Youth Rebellion Lies Behind Us', *New Outlook* 11: 7 (1968), pp. 46–9.
Elon, Amos, *The Israelis: Founders and Sons*, 1st edn (New York: Holt, Rinehart and Winston, 1971).
Engelmann, Roger, 'Einleitung', in Roger Engelmann, Thomas Grossbölting and Hermann Wentker (eds), *Kommunismus in der Krise: Die Entstalinisierung 1956 und die Folgen*, Analysen und Dokumente (Göttingen: Vandenhoeck & Ruprecht, 2008), pp. 9–34.
Epstein, Helen, 'Danny's "Eight-Day-War"', *The Jerusalem Post*, 3 June 1970.
Epstein, Helen, 'New Arrivals on the Israeli Left', *Midstream* 16: 8 (1970), pp. 10–19.
Erel, Nitza, *Without Fear and Prejudice: Uri Avnery and Haolam Hazeh* (Jerusalem: Magnes Press, 2006) [Hebrew].
Erel, Nitza, *Matzpen: Conscience and Fantasy* (Tel Aviv: Resling, 2010) [Hebrew].
'Erklärung zum Bombenattentat auf das jüdische Gemeindehaus in Berlin', *SDS-Info* 25, 1 December 1969, pp. 29–30.
Ernst, F. (ed.), *Palästina* (Kiel: Magazin-Verlag, 1982).

Eshed, Eli, 'Yaakov Ashman: A Warrior for Hebrew. The Story of Gidi Geser and its Originator Yaakov Ashman', https://no666.wordpress.com/2006/05/05/ לוחם-על-עברי-עלילות-גידי-גזר-וייצרו-יע/ (accessed 11 April 2020) [Hebrew].

Eshel, Nimrod, *The Seamen's Strike* (Tel Aviv: Am Oved, 1994) [Hebrew].

Even-Zohar, Itamar, 'The Emergence of a Native Hebrew Culture in Palestine 1882–1948', in Jehudah Reinharz (ed.), *Essential Papers on Zionism* (New York: New York University Press, 1996), pp. 727–44.

Evron, Boas, 'Eichmann. The Monster in Captivity', *Etgar* 2 ([June] 1960), pp. 5–6 [Hebrew].

Evron, Boas, 'Sin and Punishment', *Etgar* 3: 55 (1963), pp. 2–3 [Hebrew].

Evron, Boas, 'Zionism without Mercy', in Boas Evron, *Jewish State or Israeli Nation?* (Bloomington: Indiana University Press, 1995), pp. 153–72.

Evron, Boas, 'Effective Methods to Stop Information. Why Hannah Arendts' "Eichmann in Jerusalem" Was Not Published in Hebrew Till this Year', *Haaretz*, 6 October 2000 [Hebrew].

Evron, Boas, 'Political Ideas and their Twists. "A Post-Zionist Autobiography"', http://hagada.org.il/2008/09/30/רעיונות-מדיניים-וגלגוליהם-אוטוביוג (accessed 6 September 2019) [Hebrew].

Fanon, Frantz, *The Wretched of the Earth* (London: Penguin Books, [1961] 2001).

Farah, Bulus, *From Ottoman Rule to a Hebrew State: The Life Story of a Communist and a Palestinian Patriot* (Haifa: Udi Adiv, 2009) [Hebrew].

Farouk-Sluglett, Marion and Peter Sluglett, *Iraq Since 1958: From Revolution to Dictatorship* (London, New York: I. B. Tauris Publishers, 2001).

Feinberg, Anat, 'Two Different Worlds and a Cemetery Between Them. Dahn Ben-Amotz's Novel "To Remember, To Forget"', *Trumah. Zeitschrift der Hochschule für Jüdische Studien Heidelberg* 21 (2013), pp. 69–80.

Feldman, Yotam, 'Pulp Fiction', *Haaretz*, 2 August 2007, http://www.haaretz.com/weekend/magazine/pulp-fiction-1.226748 (accessed 28 July 2020).

Ferron, Benjamin, 'La transnationalisation de "Matzpen". L'organisation socialiste israélienne (1962-2006)', *Pôle Sud* 30 (2009), pp. 67–84.

Fiedler, Lutz, 'Kommunistische Dissidenz und antisemitische Stimmung. Kuroń, Modzelewski und die Vorgeschichte des polnischen März '68', *Jahrbuch des Simon-Dubnow-Instituts* 9 (2010), pp. 165–85 [German].

Fiedler, Lutz, 'Akiva Orr (1931–2013)', *inamo (Informationsprojekt Naher und Mittlerer Osten)* 73 (2013), pp. 82–5.

Findley, Paul, *They Dare to Speak Out: People and Institutions Confront Israel's Lobby*, 3rd edn (Chicago: Chicago Review Press, 2003).

Finkelstone, Joseph, 'Arafat Ready to Make Peace. Exclusive Interview with PLO-Leader', *Jewish Chronicle*, 5 April 1974, p. 2.

Fisch, Harold, *The Zionist Revolution: A New Perspective* (London: Weidenfeld and Nicolson, 1978).

Fish, Rachel, 'Configurations of Bi-Nationalism. The Transformation of Bi-Nationalism in Palestine/Israel 1920's-Present' (PhD thesis, Brandeis University, 2013).

Flapan, Simcha, *5. Juni 1967. Der israelisch-arabische Krieg: Antwort an Isaac Deutscher* (Frankfurt a.M.: Borochov-Press, 1969).

Flores, Alexander, *Nationalismus und Sozialismus im arabischen Osten: Kommunistische Partei und arabische Nationalbewegung in Palästina, 1919-1948, Reihe Dissertationen zur Politik und Ökonomie in der Dritten Welt* (Münster: Periferia Verlag, 1980).

Flores, Alexander, *Die arabische Welt: Ein kleines Sachlexikon* (Stuttgart: Philipp Reclam, 2008).

Flores, Alexander, *Der Palästinakonflikt* (Freiburg im Breisgau: Herder, 2009).

Foitzik, Jan, *Zwischen den Fronten: Zur Politik, Organisation und Funktion linker politischer Kleinorganisationen im Widerstand 1933 bis 1939/40 unter besonderer Berücksichtigung des Exils, Politik- und Gesellschaftsgeschichte* (Bonn: Verl. Neue Gesellschaft, 1986), Bd. 16.

Foxlee, Neil, *Albert Camus's "The New Mediterranean Culture": A Text and its Contexts*, Modern French Identities (Bern: Peter Lang, 2010), v. 38.

Frangi, Abdallah, *Der Gesandte: Mein Leben für Palästina; Hinter den Kulissen der Nahost-Politik* (München: Heyne HC, 2011).

Freimüller, Tobias, 'Mehr als eine Religionsgemeinschaft. Jüdisches Leben in Frankfurt am Main nach 1945', *Zeithistorische Forschungen / Zentrum für Zeithistorische Forschung, Redaktion Zeitgeschichte-online* 7 (2010), https://zeithistorische-forschungen.de/3-2010/4475 (accessed 28 July 2020).

Friedländer, Saul, 'The Shoah between Memory and History', *Jewish Quarterly* 37: 1 (1990), pp. 5–11.

Friedmann, Georges, *The End of the Jewish People?* (Garden City: Doubleday, 1967).

'From Petty-Bourgeois Radicalism to the Building a Revolutionary Party of the Working Class', *Matzpen* 57 (1971), p. 13 [Hebrew].

Fuks, Sarit, 'Yaakov is Emanuel is Eli', *Ma'ariv. Weekend Supplement*, 16 July 1993, pp. 20–4 [Hebrew].

'Full Report of the Conversation between a Matzpen Member and a PLO Representative in London' (Tel Aviv: Matzpen Publications, 1975) [Hebrew].

GAL Hamburg, *Krieg im Libanon – Frieden in Europa?: Dokumentation einer Diskussionsveranstaltung der GAL Hamburg* (Hamburg: GAL Hamburg, 1982).

Geisel, Eike, 'Ein Gespräch mit Hanna Levy-Hass (1978)', in Eike Geisel (ed.), *Vielleicht war das alles erst der Anfang: Tagebuch aus dem KZ Bergen-Belsen; 1944–1945* (Berlin: Rotbuch Verlag, 1979), pp. 61–100.

Geisel, Eike, 'Narziß am Abgrund. Eike Geisel über Alain Finkielkraut: "Der eingebildete Jude"', *Der Spiegel* 17, 26 April 1982, pp. 228–32.

Geisel, Eike, 'Alle sind Sieger', in Eike Geisel, *Lastenausgleich, Umschuldung – Die Wiedergutwerdung der Deutschen: Essays, Polemiken, Stichworte* (Berlin: Edition TIAMAT, 1984), pp. 9–34.

Geisel, Eike, 'Um wieviel die Welt ärmer geworden ist. "Erinnerungen eines jüdischen Revolutionärs"', in Eike Geisel, *Lastenausgleich, Umschuldung – Die Wiedergutwerdung der Deutschen: Essays, Polemiken, Stichworte* (Berlin: Edition TIAMAT, 1984), pp. 107–15.

Geisel, Eike, Jakob Moneta and Jakob Taut, 'Die Judenfalle. Hersch Mendel – wie ostjüdische Arbeiter Zionisten wurden', *Forum (Wien)* 27 (1980), pp. 18–24.

Gelber, Yoav, 'Zionist Policy and the Fate of European Jewry (1939-1942)', *Yad Vashem Studies* 13 (1979), pp. 169–210.

Gelber, Yoav, 'El-Alamein', in Dan Diner (ed.), *Enzyklopädie jüdischer Geschichte und Kultur*, 7 vols (Stuttgart: Metzler, 2012–17), vol. 2, pp. 211–15.

Gerber, Jan, *Verborgene Präsenzen: Gedächtnisgeschichte des Holocaust in der deutschsprachigen Arbeiter – und Gewerkschaftsbewegung, Böckler Forschungsmonitoring* (Düsseldorf: Hans-Böckler-Stiftung, 2009), vol. 9.

Geries, Sabri, *Les Arabes en Israël: Précédé de Les juifs et la Palestine par Eli Lobel* (Paris: François Maspero, 1969).

Geries, Sabri, *Gli Arabi in Israele: Con un Saggio di Eli Lobel* (Roma: Editori Riuniti, 1970).

Geries, Sabri and Eli Lobel, *Die Araber in Israel* (München: Trikont-Verlag, 1970).

Germain, Ernest (Mandel, Ernest), 'A Biographical Sketch of Abram Leon', in *The Jewish Question: A Marxist Interpretation*, 2nd edn (New York: Pathfinder Press, 1970), pp. 15–31.

Gertz, Nurith, *Unrepentant: Four Chapters in the Life of Amos Kenan* (Tel Aviv: Am Oved, 2009).

'Gesprächsrunde über jüdisches Leben im Nachkriegsdeutschland', *Münchner Beiträge zur jüdischen Geschichte und Kultur* 6: 1 (2012), pp. 41–60.

Ghilan, Maxim, *How Israel Lost its Soul* (Harmondsworth: Penguin, 1974).

Ghoussoub, Mai, *Leaving Beirut: Women and the Wars Within* (London: SAQI, 2007).

Ginossar, Pinhas, 'From Zionism to Communism and Back. The Case of Moshe Sneh (1948–1967)', in Jonathan Frankel and Dan Diner (eds), *Dark Times,*

Dire Decisions: Jews and Communism, Studies in Contemporary Jewry: An Annual (Oxford: Oxford University Press, 2004), pp. 236–54.

Glasner-Heled, Galia, 'Displaced. The Memoir of Eliezer Gruenbaum, Kapo at Birkenau – Translation and Commentary', *Shofar* 27: 2 (2009), pp. 1–23.

Glass, Charlie, 'Jews Against Zion. Israeli Jewish Anti-Zionism', *Journal of Palestine Studies* 5: 1/2 (1975/6), pp. 56–81.

Glezerman, Avraham, '"Der Ring". Über die innerisraelische Opposition gegen den Libanonkrieg', in Dietrich Wetzel (ed.), *Die Verlängerung von Geschichte: Deutsche, Juden und der Palästinakonflikt* (Frankfurt am Main: Neue Kritik, 1983), pp. 126–35.

Gloy, Thomas, 'Fritz Bernsteins Soziologie des Judenhasses', in Hans-Joachim Hahn and Olaf Kistenmacher (eds), *Beschreibungsversuche der Judenfeindschaft* (Berlin: De Gruyter, 2015), pp. 286–313.

'Go in Peace!', *Matzpen-Marxisti* 62 (1972), p. 3 [Hebrew].

'Golda Meir gegen Verbot von Rakach und Matzpen', *Jedioth Chadashot*, 7 June 1970, p. 4.

Goldmann, Nahum, *The Jewish Paradox* (New York: Grosset & Dunlap, 1978).

Gordon, Adi, 'Orient: Exile of the Last Europeans', *Mediterraneans / Méditerranéennes* 14 (2000), pp. 62–8.

Gordon, Adi, *Brith Shalom and Bi-National Zionism: "The Arab Question" as a Jewish Question* (Jerusalem: Carmel, 2008) [Hebrew].

Gorenberg, Gershom, *The Accidental Empire: Israel and the Birth of Settlements, 1967–1977* (New York, Godalming: Owl, 2007).

Gouldman, M., *Israel Nationality Law* (Jerusalem: Institute for Legislative Research and Comparative Law, 1970).

Government of Israel, 'The Land-for-Peace Principle, 19. Juni 1967', in Itamar Rabinovich and Jehudah Reinharz (eds), *Israel in the Middle East: Documents and Readings on Society, Politics, and Foreign Relations, Pre-1948 to the Present*, 2nd edn (Waltham: Brandeis University Press, 2008), pp. 238–9.

Grab, Walter, *Meine vier Leben: Gedächtniskünstler – Emigrant Jakobinerforscher – Demokrat* (Köln: PapyRossa, 1999).

Grabski, August, '"Matzpen" and the State of Israel (1962–1973)', *Kwartalnik Historii Żydów* 219 (2006), pp. 354–65.

Greenstein, Ran, 'Palestinian Revolutionary. Jabra Nicola and the Radical Left', *The Jerusalem Quarterly* 46 (2011), pp. 32–48.

Greenstein, Ran, *Zionism and its Discontents: A Century of Radical Dissent in Israel/Palestine* (London: Pluto Press, 2014).

Greilsammer, Alain, 'Communism in Israel. 13 Years After the Split', *Survey* 23 (1977–8), pp. 172–92.

Gresh, Alain, *The PLO: The Struggle Within: Towards an Independent Palestinian State*, rev. and updated edn (London: Zed Books, 1988) [Translation of: *OLP*].

Grodzenski, Shlomo, 'Against Racist Discrimination. For the Forging of the Revolutionary Character', *Davar*, 24 July 1970, pp. 13 and 17 [Hebrew].

Grossbölting, Thomas, 'Entstalinisierungskrisen im Westen. Die kommunistischen Bewegungen Westeuropas und das Jahr 1956', in Roger Engelmann, Thomas Grossbölting and Hermann Wentker (eds), *Kommunismus in der Krise: Die Entstalinisierung 1956 und die Folgen*, Analysen und Dokumente (Göttingen: Vandenhoeck & Ruprecht, 2008), pp. 233–49.

Grossman, Hagit, 'Memoir. Writing for the Exiles and the Dispossessed', *Haaretz*, 27 May 2010, https://www.haaretz.com/life/books/1.5125846 (accessed 28 July 2020).

Gruener, Frank, 'Jüdisches Antifaschistisches Komitee', in Dan Diner (ed.), *Enzyklopädie jüdischer Geschichte und Kultur*, 7 vols (Stuttgart: Metzler, 2012–17), vol. 3, pp. 268–73.

Gur, Ben-Ami (Ben-Ami, G.), 'The Canaanite "Scapegoat"', *BaMaavak* ([May] 1947), pp. 13–14 [Hebrew].

Gvirtz, Yael, 'Stuck For Already 26 Years', *Yediot Aharonot*, 14 August 1992, pp. 12–13 [Hebrew].

Haber, Eitan and Yossi Melman, *The Spies: Israel's Counter-Espionage Wars* (Tel Aviv: Yediot Ahronot, 2002) [Hebrew].

Hadari-Ramage, Yona, 'War and Religiosity. The Sinai Campaign in Public Thought', in S. I. Troen and Noah Lucas (eds), *Israel: The First Decade of Independence*, SUNY Series in Israeli Studies (Albany: State University of New York Press, 1995), pp. 355–74.

Haelion, Yaacov, 'Rami Livneh's Trial as "Inspiration" For a Play', *Ma'ariv*, 23 July 1973, p. 2 [Hebrew].

Halevi, Ilan, *Allers-retours* (Paris: Flammarion, 2005).

Hammami, Said, 'The Palestinian Way to Middle East Peace', *The Times*, 16 November 1973, p. 20.

Hammami, Said, 'Making the First Move Towards Peace in Palestine', *The Times*, 17 December 1973, p. 14.

Hammami, Said, 'Middle East Terrorism (Letter to the Editor)', *The Times*, 17 April 1974, p. 15.

Hammami, Said, 'A Palestinian Strategy', *Intercontinental Press* 13: 34 (1975), pp. 1308–10.

Hanegbi, H., Interview with the Author, Ramat Aviv, 26 August 2008 [Hebrew].

Hanegbi, H., Interview with the Author, Ramat Aviv, 11 December 2008 [Hebrew].

Hanegbi, H., Interview with the Author (via phone), 20 June 2012 [Hebrew].

Hanegbi, Haim, 'Profil. Who is Uri Avnery', *Israel Imperial News* 2: 6 ([March] 1970), p. 8 [Hebrew].

Hanegbi, Haim, 'Ilan Halevi. From Udi Adiv until Sartawi', *Koteret Rashit*, 14 April 1983, pp. 18 and 39 [Hebrew].

Hanegbi, Haim, 'My Hebron. A Story of a Different Love', *Koteret Rashit*, 20 July 1983, pp. 20–3 [Hebrew].

Hanegbi, Haim, 'Udi, Ran and Uri. All From the Same Village', *Koteret Rashit* 129, 22 May 1985, pp. 16–17 [Hebrew].

Hanegbi, Haim, 'A Royal Visit', *Koteret Rashit*, 25 May 1988, p. 23 [Hebrew].

Hanegbi, Haim, 'Raif Chana Elias', *Chadashot. Shavuot Supplement*, 29 May 1990, pp. 8–9 [Hebrew].

Hanegbi, Haim, 'The Honey We Stole. Memories from the Naqba in Jerusalem', *Mita'am* 13 (2008) [Hebrew], http://www.mitaam.co.il/mit13hanegbi.htm (accessed 28 July 2020).

Harbi, Mohammed, 'Bauern und Revolution', in Bassam Tibi (ed.), *Die arabische Linke: Hrsg. u. eingel. von Bassam Tibi. (Aus d. Arab. von Bassam Tibi)*, (Dritte Welt) (Frankfurt a.M.: Europäische Verlags-Anstalt, 1969), pp. 123–37.

Har-Gil, Schraga, '"Danny the Red" Travelled Israel', *Ma'ariv*, 7 June 1968, p. 13 [Hebrew].

Har-Gil, Schraga, '"Danny the Red" Gives Advice to Israel', *Ma'ariv*, 31 May 1970, pp. 12 and 16 [Hebrew].

Har-Gil, Schraga, 'Der rote Danny im Kibbuz', *Jedioth Chadashot*, 4 June 1970, p. 3.

Harshav, Benjamin, *Language in Time of Revolution* (Berkeley, Los Angeles, London: University of California Press, 1993).

Hattis, Susan, *The Bi-National Idea in Palestine During Mandatory Times* (Haïfa: Shikmona Publishing, 1970).

Hawatmeh, Nayef, 'A Democratic Solution for the Palestine Problem', in Leila S. Kadi (ed.), *Basic Political Documents of the Armed Palestinian Resistance Movement* (Beirut: Palestine Liberation Organization, Research Center, 1969), pp. 175–8 [first: *Al-Hurriya*, 12 January 1970].

Hawatmeh, Nayef, 'A Democratic Solution for the Palestine Problem', *Al-Hurriya*, 12 January 1970 [Arabic].

Hawatmeh, Nayef, 'For a Democratic Solution to the Palestinian Problem and the Israeli Problem', *Matzpen* 52 (1970), p. 5 [Hebrew].

Hazan, Eliahu, 'The Paper as a Mean of Political Taunting. The Mockery of Mapai in the Opposition Press on the Occasion of the Kasztner Trial' (Master's thesis, The Hebrew University of Jerusalem, 2007) [Hebrew].

Hazaz, Haim, 'The Sermon', in Haim Hazaz, *The Sermon & Other Stories* (New Milford, Godalming: Toby; Melia [distributor], 2005), pp. 233–49 [first: *Luah Haaretz* 5703 [1942/3], pp. 82–96 [Hebrew].].

'Head of the "Popular Democratic Front for the Liberation of Palestine" Claims: We Have a Dialogue with "Matzpen"', *Haolam Hazeh* 1681, 19 November 1969, p. 14 [Hebrew].

Heenen, Susan, 'Deutsche Linke, linke Juden und der Zionismus', in Dietrich Wetzel (ed.), *Die Verlängerung von Geschichte: Deutsche, Juden und der Palästinakonflikt* (Frankfurt am Main: Neue Kritik, 1983), pp. 103–12.

Heller, Joseph, *Stern Gang: Ideology, Politics and Terror, 1940–49* (London: F. Cass, 1995).

Herf, Jeffrey, *Undeclared Wars with Israel: East Germany and the West German Far Left, 1967–1989* (New York: Cambridge University Press, 2016).

'History of Zionism', *Matzpen* 54 (1970), pp. 6–7 [Hebrew].

Holzer, Jerzy, 'Die Geheimrede Chruschtschows und ihre Rezeption in Ostmitteleuropa', in Hans H. Hahn and Heinrich Olschowsky (eds), *Das Jahr 1956 in Ostmitteleuropa* (Berlin: Akademie Vlg, 1996), pp. 13–20.

Honig-Parnass, T., 'On the Apartheid Nature of Israel, Matzpen and the Contradictions of the Zionist Left: The Flying Carpet Institute Interviews Israeli Socialist Tikva Honig-Parnass', https://theflyingcarpetinstitute.wordpress.com/2010/04/30/on-the-apartheid-nature-of-israel-matzpen-and-the-contradictions-of-the-zionist-left-the-flying-carpet-institute-interviews-israeli-socialist-tikva-honig-parnass/ (accessed 7 October 2019).

Honig-Parnass, Tikva, *False Prophets of Peace: Liberal Zionism and the Struggle for Palestine* (Chicago: Haymarket Books, 2011).

'Hostilities and Clashes at the Maki-demonstration in Tel-Aviv', *Ma'ariv*, 2 May 1969, p. 3 [Hebrew].

Hussein, A., 'Farewell to Lafif', http://almuslih.com/index.php?option=com_content&view=article&id=253:farewell-to-lafif&catid=38:obstacles-to-reform&Itemid=207 (accessed 7 October 2019).

Inbar, Efraim, 'The "No Choice War" Debate in Israel', *Journal of Strategic Studies* 12: 1 (1989), pp. 22–37.

International Secretariat of the Fourth International, 'Draft Theses on the Jewish Question Today', *Fourth International* 9: 1 (83) (1948), pp. 18–24.

Isaac, Rael, *Israel Divided: Ideological Politics in the Jewish State* (Baltimore: Johns Hopkins University Press, 1976).

Ismael, Tareq, *The Arab Left* (Syracuse: Syracuse University, 1976).

ISRACA, *Der Palästinastaat* (Frankfurt am Main: Israca, 1974).

Israeli, N., 'Zionism and Anti-Semitism', in Arie Bober (ed.), *The Other Israel: The Radical Case Against Zionism* (Garden City: Doubleday, 1972), pp. 167–75.

'Israeli Communist Party Backs Israel's Aggression', *World Outlook* 25, 30 June 1967, p. 644.

'Israeli Editors Given Prison Terms for Security Issue "Fabrication"', *Jewish Telegraphic Agency* 35, 20 February 1967, https://www.jta.org/1967/04/27/archive/two-israeli-journalists-quietly-released-from-tel-aviv-prison (accessed 29 July 2020).

Israeli Socialist Organization (Matzpen), 'Preface to the Declaration on the Palestine Problem and the Israeli-Arab Conflict', *Matzpen* 36 (1967), p. 2 [Hebrew].

Israeli Socialist Organization (Matzpen), 'General Declaration by the ISO, 22 March 1968', in Arie Bober (ed.), *The Other Israel: The Radical Case Against Zionism* (Garden City: Doubleday, 1972), pp. 226–30.

Israeli Socialist Organization (Matzpen), 'The Left in Israel', in Arie Bober (ed.), *The Other Israel: The Radical Case Against Zionism* (Garden City: Doubleday, 1972), pp. 102–22.

Israeli Socialist Organization (Matzpen), 'The Palestine Problem. Thesis Submitted for Discussion in August 1966', in Arie Bober (ed.), *The Other Israel: The Radical Case Against Zionism* (Garden City: Doubleday, 1972), pp. 35–53 [first: The Israeli Socialist Organization, *The Other Israel. Israeli Critique of Zionist History and Policy*, Tel Aviv, [July] 1948, pp. 1–8].

Israeli Socialist Organization (Matzpen), 'The Palestine-Problem and the Israeli-Arab Dispute, 18 May 1967', in Arie Bober (ed.), *The Other Israel: The Radical Case Against Zionism* (Garden City: Doubleday, 1972), pp. 208–13 [first: *World Outlook* 22: 5, 2 June 1967; *Matzpen* 36 (1967) [Hebrew]].

Israeli Socialist Organization (Matzpen), 'The Third Round', in Arie Bober (ed.), *The Other Israel: The Radical Case Against Zionism* (Garden City: Doubleday, 1972), pp. 214–25 [first: *Matzpen* 36 (1967)].

Israeli Socialist Organization (Matzpen), 'They All Promise Peace. October ISO Statement on 1969 General Elections', in Arie Bober (ed.), *The Other Israel: The Radical Case Against Zionism* (Garden City: Doubleday, 1972), pp. 243–5.

Ja'far, Mohammed (Makiya, Kanan) and Afsaneh Najmabadi (Tabari, Azar), 'Iran. Islam and the Struggle for Socialism', in Jon Rothschild (ed.), *Forbidden Agendas: Intolerance and Defiance in the Middle East* (London: Saqi Books, 1984), pp. 322–48 [first: *Khamsin* 8 (1981), pp. 83–104].

Jabotinsky, V. (Z.'e.), 'The Iron Wall', http://en.jabotinsky.org/media/9747/the-iron-wall.pdf (accessed 30 March 2020).

Jasse, Richard L., 'The Baghdad Pact. Cold War or Colonialism?', *Middle Eastern Studies* 27: 1 (1991), pp. 140–56.

Jeismann, Michael, 'Abenteurer. Historiker aus zwei Welten. Dan Diner zum Sechzigsten', *Frankfurter Allgemeine Zeitung*, 19 May 2006, p. 41.

Jockusch, Laura and Tamar Lewinsky, 'Paradise Lost? Postwar Memory of Polish Jewish Survival in the Soviet Union', *Holocaust and Genocide Studies* 24: 3 (2010), pp. 373–99.

Johnson, Alan, 'Putting Cruelty First. An Interview with Kanan Makiya', in Alan Johnson (ed.), *Global Politics after 9/11: The Democratiya Interviews* (London: Foreign Policy Centre, 2007), pp. 93–137.

'Joint Israeli-Arab Statement on the Middle East Crisis', *The Times*, 8 June 1967, p. 5, https://matzpen.org/english/1967-06-03/joint-israeli-arab-statement-june-3-1967/ (accessed 29 July 2020).

Jones, Rachel, *Advocate. Lea Tsemel*, 2019, Israel, 108 min, documentary.

'Juden für die Rechte der Palästinenser', *Die Tageszeitung*, 14 June 1982, p. 4.

Judt, Tony, *Postwar: A History of Europe since 1945* (New York: Penguin Books, 2006).

Kadi, L. S. (ed.), *Arab Summit Conferences and the Palestine Problem: 1936–1950* (Beirut: Research Center, 1966).

Kadi, L. S. (ed.), *Basic Political Documents of the Armed Palestinian Resistance Movement* (Beirut: Palestine Liberation Organization, Research Center, 1969 [1970]).

Kadi, Leila, *Histadrut* (Beirut: Palestine Liberation Organization, Research Center, 1967) [Arabic].

Kadi, Leila, *A Survey of American-Israeli Relations* (Beirut: Palestine Liberation Organization, Research Center, 1969).

Kadi, Leila, Letter to Moshé Machover, 27 August 1969, Private Archive of Moshé Machover, London.

Kadi, Leila, *The Israeli Socialist Organization (Matzpen)* (Beirut: Palestine Liberation Organization, Research Center, 1971) [Arabic].

Kadi, Leila, Letter to Moshé Machover, 1 August 1971, Private Archive of Moshé Machover, London.

Kadi, Leila, Letter to Moshé Machover, 23 February 1972, Private Archive of Moshé Machover, London.

Kadi, Leila, Letter to Moshé Machover, 22 May 1974, Private Archive of Moshé Machover, London.

Kadir, Nada, 'In the Maelstrom of Confessionalism', in Jon Rothschild (ed.), *Forbidden Agendas: Intolerance and Defiance in the Middle East* (London: Saqi Books, 1984), pp. 237–59 [first: *Khamsin* 3 (1976), pp. 101–23].

Kafkafi, Eyal, 'Turning to the Left as a Justification for Breaking a Strike. The Case of the Seamen's Strike', *Tura* 3 (1994), pp. 221–47 [Hebrew].

Kafri, Judith, *Zosha: From the Jezreel Valley to the Red Orchestra* (Toruń: Wydawn. Adam Marszałek, 2009).

Kahwaji, H., '"El Ard" Movement on the "Red Front"', https://hdl.handle.net/10622/90A6C004-BF1A-11E7-ADF4-6FB495D231EF?locatt=view:master (accessed 20 April 2020).

Kalter, Christoph, *Discovery of the Third World: Decolonization and the Rise of the New Left in France, c.1950–1976* (Cambridge: Cambridge University Press, 2016).

Kamil, Omar, *Die Araber und der Holocaust: Eine Diskursgeschichte* (Göttingen: Vandenhoeck & Ruprecht, 2012).

Kaplan, Eran, 'A Rebel With a Cause. Hillel Kook, Begin and Jabotinsky's Ideological Legacy', *Israel Studies* 10: 3 (2005), pp. 87–103.

Kaplan, Yirmiyahu (Kfir, Y.), 'Concerning the Debate of the Refugee Question', *Matzpen* 1 (1962), p. 4 [Hebrew].

Kauders, Anthony, *Unmögliche Heimat: Eine deutsch-jüdische Geschichte der Bundesrepublik*, 1. Aufl. (München: Deutsche Verlags-Anstalt, 2007).

Kauders, Anthony, 'West German Jewry: Guilt, Power and Pluralism', *Quest. Issues in Contemporary Jewish History. Journal of Fondazione CDEC* 1: 1 (2010), http://www.quest-cdecjournal.it/focus.php?issue=1&id=213 (accessed 28 July 2020).

Kenan, Amos, *With Whips and Scorpions* (Tel Aviv: Yisrael, 1952) [Hebrew].

Kenan, Amos, 'Required in the Country: A Left', *Matzpen* 1 (1962), p. 3 [Hebrew].

Kenan, Amos, 'The Use of the Report: A Detrimental Service to the Nation', *Ma'ariv*, 25 June 1967, p. 19 [Hebrew].

Kenan, Amos, 'A Letter to All Good People. To Fidel Castro, Sartre, Russell and All the Rest', in Amos Kenan, *Israel: A Wasted Victory* (Tel Aviv: Amikam, 1970), pp. 56–69 [first: *Yediot Aharonot*, 22 March 1968].

Kenan, Amos, 'A Short Trip to the Hermon', in Amos Kenan, *Israel: A Wasted Victory* (Tel Aviv: Amikam, 1970), pp. 152–4 [first: *Yediot Aharonot*, 19 June 1969].

Kenan, Amos, '"Matzpen" Seeks Admission Cheaply', in Amos Kenan, *Israel: A Wasted Victory* (Tel Aviv: Amikam, 1970), pp. 118–21 [first: *Yediot Aharonot*, 20 March 1969].

Kenan, Amos, 'New Left, Go Home!', in Amos Kenan, *Israel: A Wasted Victory* (Tel Aviv: Amikam, 1970), pp. 122–9 [first: *Yediot Aharonot*, 21 March 1969].

Kenan, Amos, '. . . and the Canaanite Was Then In the Land. Dan Omer Talks to Amos Kenan', *Proza* 17–18 (1977), pp. 4–11 [Hebrew].

Kenan, Amos, 'Who is Afraid of Joe Golan?', *Yediot Aharonot*, 8 September 1978, pp. 12–14 [Hebrew].

Kenan, Amos, 'These are the Annals of Shaaltiel', in Amos Kenan, *Your Land, Your Country* (Jerusalem: Yediot Aharonot, 1981), pp. 62–78 [Hebrew].

Kenan, Amos, 'Hubris', *Yediot Aharonot*, 4 June 1982, p. 9 [Hebrew].

Kenan, Amos, 'The Dark Years. Interview', *Koteret Rashit*, 26 December 1984, pp. 29–32 [Hebrew].

Kenan, Amos, 'Meeting Palestinians', *Yediot Aharonot*, 13 September 1985, pp. 16–17 [Hebrew].

Kenan, Amos, 'He Was and Existed and Happened', *Yediot Aharonot. Weekend Supplement*, 28 October 1988, p. 17 [Hebrew].

Keren, Michael, *Zichroni v. State of Israel: The Biography of a Civil Rights Lawyer* (Lanham, Boulder, New York: Lexington Books, 2002).

Keshet, Sylvie, 'Spring 1970. Or: McCarthy is Alive and Hiding in Israel!', *Haaretz*, 15 May 1970, p. 10 [Hebrew].

Keßler, Mario, 'Die Augustereignisse 1929 in Palästina, die KP Palästinas und die Kommunistische Internationale', in Mario Keßler, *Antisemitismus, Zionismus und Sozialismus: Arbeiterbewegung und jüdische Frage im 20. Jahrhundert*, 2. Aufl. (Mainz: Decaton-Verl., 1994), pp. 66–80.

Keßler, Mario, 'Joseph Berger. Communist Activist in Palestine and Victim of Stalinism (1904-1978)', *Moving the Social. Journal of Social History and the History of Social Movements* 51 (2014), pp. 159–78.

Kfir, Ilan, 'The Conscientious Objector Continues to Play the Role of a Martyr', *Yediot Aharonot*, 12 June 1972, p. 15 [Hebrew].

Khalidi, Walid, 'Plan Dalet. Master Plan for the Conquest of Palestine', *Journal of Palestine Studies* 18: 1 (1988), pp. 4–33.

Khasani, Shila, 'Minderheit in der Minderheit. Das politische Engagement der linksorientierten Juden in der Frankfurter "Jüdischen Gruppe"', *Trumah. Zeitschrift der Hochschule für Jüdische Studien Heidelberg* 14 (2005), pp. 55–74.

Khouri, Fred, *The Arab-Israeli Dilemma*, Contemporary Issues in the Middle East, 3rd edn (Syracuse: Syracuse University Press, 1985).

Kimmerling, Baruch, *Zionism and Territory: The Socio-Territorial Dimensions of Zionist Politics* (Berkeley: Institute of International Studies, University of California, 1983).

Kimmerling, Baruch and Joel Migdal, *Palestinians: The Making of a People* (New York, Toronto: Free Press; Maxwell Macmillan Canada; Maxwell Macmillan International, 1993).

Klehr, Harvey, *Far Left of Center: The American Radical Left Today* (New Brunswick: Transaction, 1988).

Klein, Yossi, 'Exile in His Country', *Haaretz*, 31 July 2003, https://www.haaretz.com/1.5353475 (accessed 29 July 2020).

Klein Halevi, Yossi, *Like Dreamers: The Story of the Israeli Paratroopers who Reunited Jerusalem and Divided a Nation* (New York, London: Harper Perennial, 2013).

Kloke, Martin, *Israel und die deutsche Linke: Zur Geschichte eines schwierigen Verhältnisses*, Schriftenreihe des Deutsch-Israelischen Arbeitskreises für Frieden im Nahen Osten e. V, 2., erw. und aktualisierte Aufl. (Frankfurt am Main: Haag + Herchen, 1994), Bd. 20.

Kodsy, Ahmad and Eli Lobel, *The Arab World and Israel* (New York: Monthly Review, 1970).

Koestler, Arthur, *Thieves in the Night: Chronicle of an Experiment* (New York: Macmillan, 1946).

Koestler, Arthur, 'Epilogue', in Arthur Koestler, *Promise and Fulfilment: Palestine 1917–1949* (New York: Macmillan, 1949), pp. 332–5.

Koestler, Arthur, 'The Culture of the New State', in Arthur Koestler, *Promise and Fulfilment: Palestine 1917–1949* (New York: Macmillan, 1949), pp. 324–31.

Koestler, Arthur, 'The Rebirth of the Hebrew Language', in Arthur Koestler, *Promise and Fulfilment: Palestine 1917-1949* (New York: Macmillan, 1949), pp. 311–15.

Kohansky, Mendel, 'The Case of the Dispossessed Queen', *Midstream* 16: 7 (August/September 1970), pp. 75–8.

Kraushaar, Wolfgang, *Fischer in Frankfurt: Karriere eines Aussenseiters* (Hamburg: Hamburger Edition, 2001).

Kraushaar, Wolfgang, *Die Bombe im Jüdischen Gemeindehaus*, 1. Aufl. (Hamburg: Hamburger Ed, 2005) [German].

Krohn, Helga, *"Es war richtig, wieder anzufangen": Juden in Frankfurt am Main seit 1945*, 1. Aufl. (Frankfurt am Main: Brandes & Apsel, 2011).

Kugelmann, C. and H. Loewy (eds), *So einfach war das: Jüdische Kindheiten und Jugend seit 1945 in Österreich, der Schweiz und Deutschland* (Köln: DuMont, 2002).

Kugelmann, Cilly, 'Was heißt jüdische Identität? Aufzeichnung eines Gesprächs (Teil 2)', *Alternative* 140/141 (1981), pp. 234–40.

Kuroń, Jacek, *Glaube und Schuld: Einmal Kommunismus und zurück* (Berlin: Aufbau-Verlag, 1991).

Kurzweil, Baruch, 'The New "Canaanites" in Israel', *Judaism* 2 (1953), pp. 3–15.

Kurzweil, Baruch, 'The Young Hebrews', *Jewish Spectator* (1953), pp. 21–9.

Kuzar, Ron, *Hebrew and Zionism: A Discourse Analytic Cultural Study* (Berlin: De Gruyter Mouton, 2001).

'La tâche des révolutionnaires israéliens et palestiniens', *Khamsin. Revue des Socialistes Revolutionnaires du Proche-Orient* 1 (1975), pp. 50–69.

Lachman, G., Email Communication with Gabi Lachman, 25 June 2012 [Hebrew].

Lakhdar, L. (ed.), *Lenin: Texts on the Attitude towards Religion (New Anthology)* (Beirut: Dar al-Talia, 1972) [Arabic].

Lakhdar, L., Email from Lafif Lakhdar, via Kristin Couper, to the Author, 2 April 2009.

Lakhdar, Lafif, 'A Letter from 'Afif al-Akhdar to Al-'arabi Bu-Hali (12.12.1968)', in Al-Sherrara (Spark) (ed.), *The Arab Left and the Palestinian Revolution* (Durham: The Committee for the Support of the Popular Democratic Front for the Liberation of Palestine, 1969), pp. 1–11 [first: *Al-Hurria* 463, 12 Mai 1969].

Lakhdar, Lafif, 'Zur Situation in der palästinensischen Widerstandsbewegung', *Al-Djabha. Die Front* 3/4 (1969), pp. 11–15.

Lakhdar, Lafif, 'From the Critique of Heaven to the Critique of Earth', in Lafif Lakhdar (ed.), *Lenin: Texts on the Attitude towards Religion (New Anthology)* (Beirut: Dar al-Talia, 1972) [Arabic].

Lakhdar, Lafif, 'De la guerre à la réconciliation arabo-palestinienne. Entretien avec Lafif Lakhdar', *Khamsin. Revue des Socialistes Revolutionnaires du Proche-Orient* 4 (1977), pp. 6–24.

Lakhdar, Lafif, 'Why the Reversion of Islamic Archaism?', in Jon Rothschild (ed.), *Forbidden Agendas: Intolerance and Defiance in the Middle East* (London: Saqi Books, 1984), pp. 275–301 [first: *Khamsin* 8 (1981), pp. 62–82].

Lakhdar, Lafif and Mustapha Khayati, 'Waiting for the Massacre', *On Target. Socialist Journal Concerned with the Middle East* 1: Winter (1975/6), pp. 39–53.

Landau, Jacob, *The Arabs in Israel* (London: Oxford University Press, 1969).

Laor, Dan, 'The Last Chapter. Nathan Alterman and the Six-Day War', *Israel Studies* 4: 2 (1999), pp. 178–94.

Laor, Dan, 'American Literature and Israeli Culture. The Case of the Canaanites', *Israel Studies* 5: 1 (2000), pp. 287–300.

Lapierre, Nicole, *Causes communes: Des Juifs et des Noirs, Un ordre d'idées* (Paris: Stock, 2011).

Laqueur, Walter, *Communism and Nationalism in the Middle East*, 2nd edn (London: Routledge and Kegan Paul, 1961).

Laskier, Michael, 'Israel and Algeria amid French Colonialism and the Arab-Conflict. 1954-1978', *Israel Studies* 6: 2 (2001), pp. 1–31.

'Law Report', *Jerusalem Post*, 28 April 1970, p. 6.

'Le sionisme et Israël sont dénoncés au cours d'une réunion a la mutualité', *Le Monde*, 20 May 1967, https://www.lemonde.fr/archives/article/1967/05/20/le-sionisme-et-israel-sont-denonces-au-cours-d-une-reunion-a-la-mutualite_2627633_1819218.html (accessed 28 July 2020).

LeBor, Adam, *City of Oranges: Arabs and Jews in Jaffa* (London: Bloomsbury, 2006).

Leggewie, Claus, *Kofferträger: Das Algerien-Projekt der Linken im Adenauer-Deutschland* (Berlin: Rotbuch-Verl., 1984) [German].

Leibovitz-Dar, Sara, 'The Days of Matzpen', *Hadashot*, 20 November 1992, pp. 23–6, 60 [Hebrew].

Lendvai, Paul, *Anti-Semitism without Jews: Communist Eastern Europe* (Garden City: Doubleday, 1971).

Léon, Abraham, *Conception Matérialiste de la Question Juive* (Paris: Édition Pionniers, 1946).

Léon, Abraham, *Il Marxismo e la Questione Ebraica* (Roma: Samonà e Savelli, 1968).

Léon, Abraham, *Marxismen och judefrågan* (Mölndal: Coeckelberghs Partisanförlag, 1968).

Léon, Abraham, *The Jewish Question: A Marxist Interpretation*, 2nd edn (New York: Pathfinder Press, 1970).

Léon, Abraham, *Judenfrage und Kapitalismus* (München: Trikont-Verlag, 1971).

'Les Procès du Réseau Judéo-Arabe', *Le Monde*, 14 July 1973, https://www.lemonde.fr/archives/article/1973/07/14/les-proces-du-reseau-judeo-arabe_2566502_1819218.html (accessed 29 July 2020).

Letter to Moshé Machover, 12 October 1970, Private Archive of Moshé Machover, London [Hebrew].

Lev, Tali and Yehouda Shenhav, '"Don't Call a Worker – But a Panther. Israeli Black Panthers and the Politics of Identity in Israel in the 1970s', *Theory & Criticism* 35 (2009), pp. 141–64 [Hebrew].

Lev, Yair, *Uri Avnery: Warrior for Peace*, 2002, Israel, 75 min, film.

Levenbraun, Avraham, Letter to the Minister of Justice, the Minster of Police and the Speaker of the Knesset, 8 January 1973, The Israeli Left Archives, hdl.handle.net/10622/COLL00308%2E611?locatt=view:pdf (accessed 21 April 2020) [Hebrew].

Levy, Shimon, 'Queen of a Bathtub. Hanoch Levin's Political, Aesthetic and Ethical Metatheatricality', in Gerhard Fischer and Bernhard Greiner (eds), *The Play Within the Play: The Performance of Meta-Theatre and Self-Reflection* (Kenilworth: Rodopi, 2007), pp. 145–65.

Lewin, Moshe, 'Interview with Paul Buskovitch', in Henry Abelove (ed.), *Visions of History*, 1st edn (New York: Pantheon Books, 1984), pp. 279–308.

Liberated Territory, 'No to the War!', https://web.nli.org.il/sites/NLI/Hebrew/digitallibrary/pages/viewer.aspx?presenterid=NNL_Ephemera&DocID=NNL_Ephemera700260923 (accessed 29 July 2020) [Hebrew].

Liebman, Charles and Eliezer Don-Yehiya, 'The "Status-Quo" Agreement', in Charles Liebman and Eliezer Don-Yehiya, *Religion and Politics in Israel*, Jewish Political and Social Studies (Bloomington: Indiana University Press, 1984), pp. 31–40.

Limor, Yehiel, '"Israeli" Seminar for Students of the "New Left" in Paris. Among the Lecturers: Dr. Moshe Sneh and Amos Kenan', *Ma'ariv*, 20 February 1969, p. 7 [Hebrew].

Livneh, Ernst, 'Das Recht der unzüchtigen Veröffentlichungen in Israel', *Zeitschrift für die gesamte Strafrechtswissenschaft (Auslandsteil)* 83: 1 (1971), pp. 319–31.

Livneh, Neri, 'Bober the Second', *Haaretz*, 13 May 2003, https://www.haaretz.co.il/misc/1.882116 (accessed 17 July 2015) [Hebrew].

Livneh, Rami, 'For a Joint Programme in a Joint Struggle', *Matzpen* 53 (1970), pp. 4 and 15 [Hebrew].

Lobel, Eli, 'Amidst the Jews of Berlin', *Al Hamishmar*, 13 January 1950, p. 4 [Hebrew].

Lobel, Eli, Letter to Moshé Machover, 4 February 1969, Private Archiv of Moshé Machover, London [Hebrew].

Lobel, Eli, Letter to Haim Hanegbi, 5 August 1969 (provided by Haim Hanegbi) [Hebrew].

Lobel, Eli, 'Die Juden und Palästina', in Eli Lobel and Sabri Geries, *Die Araber in Israel* (München: Trikont-Verlag, 1970), pp. 4–91.

Lobel, Eli, 'Palestine and the Jews', in Ahmad el Kodsy and Eli Lobel, *The Arab World and Israel* (New York: Monthly Review, 1970), pp. 63–137.

Lobel, Eli, 'Military Escalation within Israeli Society', in Arie Bober (ed.), *The Other Israel: The Radical Case Against Zionism* (Garden City: Doubleday, 1972), pp. 65–78 [first: 'L'escalade à l'intérieur de la société israélienne', in: *Partisans* 52 (1970)].

Lobel, Eli, Letter to Moshé Machover, 8 June 1974, Private Archive of Moshé Machover, London [Hebrew].

Lobel, Eli, 'Maintain the Outcry. Letter to the Members of Matzpen (October 1976)', *Matzpen* 88 (1980), p. 7 [Hebrew].

Lobel, Eli, Maxime Rodinson and Israël Shahak, 'Judaïsme et sionisme', *Khamsin. Revue des Socialistes Revolutionnaires du Proche-Orient* 1 (1975), pp. 67–81.

Locker-Biletzki, Amir, 'The Settler, the Native and the Communist. Nationalism, Colonialism, and Imperialism in Moshe Sneh's and Emil Touma's Ideology, 1953–1973', in Frank Jacob and Sebastian Kunze (eds), *Jewish Radicalisms: Historical Perspectives on a Phenomenon of Global Modernity*, Europäisch-jüdische Studien – Beiträge (Berlin: De Gruyter Oldenbourg, 2019), pp. 129–52.

Lockman, Zachary, 'The Left in Israel. Zionism vs. Socialism', *Merip Reports* 49: July (1976), pp. 3–18.

Löwy, Michael, *Revolution ohne Grenzen: Die Theorie der permanenten Revolution* (Frankfurt/M.: Isp-Verlag, 1987).

Lustiger, Arno, 'Wider den Zionismus', in Reinhard Renger (ed.), *Die deutsche "Linke" und der Staat Israel*, 1. Aufl. (Leipzig: Forum Verlag, 1994), pp. 89–100.

Machover, M., 'The Parisian PLO Representative at a Matzpen Member's Funeral in Paris: "Eli Lobel was a Friend of the Palestinian People"', https://matzpen.org/1979-10-13/נציג-אשף-בפאריס-בהלוויית-איש-מצפן-אל/ (accessed 21 April 2020).

Machover, Moshé, 'Preface to "Discrimination, Suppression, Persecution"', *Matzpen* 21 (1964), p. 3 [Hebrew].

Machover, Moshé, 'The Jewish Affinity and the Aliah', *Matzpen* 32 (1967), p. 9 [Hebrew].

Machover, Moshé, 'The Social Identity of Haolam Hazeh', *Matzpen* 32 (1967), p. 3 [Hebrew].

Machover, Moshé, 'The Whitewashers', *Matzpen* 41 (1968), pp. 6–9 [Hebrew].

Machover, Moshé, Letter to Leila S. Kadi, 22 July 1971, Private Archive of Moshé Machover, London.

Machover, Moshé, 'The Case for Hebrew Self-Determination', in Arie Bober (ed.), *The Other Israel: The Radical Case Against Zionism* (Garden City: Doubleday, 1972), pp. 176–81.

Machover, Moshé, Letter to Leila S. Kadi, 6 February 1972, Private Archive of Moshé Machover, London.

Machover, Moshé, Interview with Arturo Schwarz, April 1972, Private Archive of Moshé Machover, London.

Machover, Moshé, Letter to Leila S. Kadi, 12 June 1974, Private Archive of Moshé Machover, London.

Machover, Moshé, Letter to Said Hammami, 4 December 1975, Private Archive of Moshé Machover, London.

Machover, Moshé, 'Matzpen. The Israeli Socialist Organisation. Interview with Arturo Schwarz', in Uri Davis, Andrew Mack and Mira Y. Davis (eds), *Israel and the Palestinians* (London: Ithaca Press, 1975), pp. 302–3.

Machover, Moshé, Interview of the Author with Moshé Machover, 6 November 2007, London.

Machover, Moshé, 'A Peace Activist on the Border', in Moshé Machover, *Israelis and Palestinians: Conflict and Resolutions* (Chicago: Haymarket Books, 2012), pp. 249–56.

Machover, Moshé, 'Comrade Jabra Nicola (1912-1974)', in Moshé Machover, *Israelis and Palestinians: Conflict and Resolutions* (Chicago: Haymarket Books, 2012), pp. 7–10.

Machover, Moshé, *Israelis and Palestinians: Conflict and Resolutions* (Chicago: Haymarket Books, 2012).

Machover, Moshé, 'Matzpen and Ha'olam Hazeh–New Force (December 1966)', in Moshé Machover, *Israelis and Palestinians: Conflict and Resolutions* (Chicago: Haymarket Books, 2012), pp. 61–8.
Machover, Moshé, 'New Premises for a False Conclusion (May 1967)', in Moshé Machover, *Israelis and Palestinians: Conflict and Resolutions* (Chicago: Haymarket Books, 2012), pp. 138–44 [first: *Matzpen* 35 (1967)].
Machover, Moshé, 'Resurrection of the Dead (October 1967)', in Moshé Machover, *Israelis and Palestinians: Conflict and Resolutions* (Chicago: Haymarket Books, 2012), pp. 145–50 [first: *Matzpen* 38 (1967)].
Machover, Moshé (Avital, M.), 'Go in Peace', *Matzpen* 56 (1970), pp. 6–8 and 15 [Hebrew].
Machover, Moshé (Mor, Israel), 'Peking – Moscow: 1926–1962', *Matzpen* 3 (1963), p. 4 [Hebrew].
Machover, Moshé (Mor, Israel), 'Refugees and Immigrants', *Matzpen* 29 (1966), p. 9 [Hebrew].
Machover, Moshé (Pe'er, Z.), 'An Old Story', *Matzpen* 37 (1967), pp. 2–3 [Hebrew].
Machover, Moshé (Tzemach), 'An Argument with the Zionist Left. On Zionism and its Scarecrows', *Matzpen* 68 (1973), pp. 19–21 [Hebrew].
Machover, Moshé and Said Hammami, 'To Live Together', in Jon Rothschild (ed.), *Forbidden Agendas: Intolerance and Defiance in the Middle East* (London: Saqi Books, 1984), pp. 382–400.
Machover, Moshé and Haim Hanegbi, 'Letter to All Those "Once-Good" Israelis', *Matzpen* 43 (1968), pp. 8–10 [Hebrew].
Machover, Moshé and Haim Hanegbi, 'From Generation to Generation They Rise Up to Destroy Us', in Arie Bober (ed.), *The Other Israel: The Radical Case Against Zionism* (Garden City: Doubleday, 1972), pp. 79–86 [first: *Matzpen* 45 (1968)].
Machover, Moshé and Jabra Nicola, 'The Middle East at the Crossroads (September 1969). A Position Paper on the Palestinian Movement by the ISO', in Arie Bober (ed.), *The Other Israel: The Radical Case Against Zionism* (Garden City: Doubleday, 1972), pp. 237–42 [first: *Matzpen* 50 (1969)].
Machover, Moshé and Mario Offenberg, 'Zionism and its Scarecrows', *Khamsin. Journal of Revolutionary Socialists of the Middle East* 6 (1978), pp. 33–59.
Machover, Moshé and Akiva Orr, Letter to the Members of Maki's Jerusalem Branch, 20 September 1962, The Israeli Left Archives, http://hdl.handle.net/10622/COLL00308%2E554?locatt=view:pdf (accessed 21 April 2020) [Hebrew].
Machover, Moshé and Akiva Orr (Israeli, N.), 'Israel-Arab Peace, How?', *Matzpen* 11 (1963), p. 4 [Hebrew].

Machover, Moshé and Akiva Orr (Israeli, N.), '"Double Misunderstanding". Review of Aharon Cohen's Book "Israel and the Arab World"', *Matzpen* 22 (1964), pp. 4–6.

Machover, Moshé and Akiva Orr (Israeli, N.), 'Nationalism and the Israeli-Arab Conflict', *Matzpen* 16 (1964), pp. 6–7 [Hebrew].

Machover, Moshé and Akiva Orr (Israeli, N.), 'Hold Me...', *Matzpen* 25 (1965), p. 2 [Hebrew].

Machover, Moshé and Akiva Orr, 'The Class Nature of Israeli Society', *Matzpen* 55 (1970), pp. 3–4 [Hebrew].

Machover, Moshé, Akiva Orr and Haim Hanegbi, 'The Class Nature of Israeli Society', in Moshé Machover, *Israelis and Palestinians: Conflict and Resolutions* (Chicago: Haymarket Books, 2012), pp. 76–98 [first: *Matzpen* 55 (1970); *New Left Review* 65 (1971)].

Machover, Moshé and Meir Smorodinksy, '"State of Israel" or "Jewish State"', *Matzpen* 14 (1964), p. 2 [Hebrew].

Mack, Merav, 'Orthodox and Communist. A History of a Christian Community in Mandate Palestine and Israel', *British Journal of Middle Eastern Studies* 42: 4 (2015), pp. 384–400.

'Maki-Leadership Worries about Intellectual Circles of their Former Members', *Haaretz*, 14 September 1962, http://hdl.handle.net/10622/COLL00308%2E645?locatt=view:pdf (accessed 29 July 2020) [Hebrew].

'Man of the Year', *Haolam Hazeh* 884, 30 September 1954, p. 15 [Hebrew].

Mandel, Ernest, *Revolutionary Marxism Today* (London, New York: NLB, 1979).

Mardam-Bey, Farouk, 'Ilan Halevi. Palestinian Jew and Citizen of the World, 1943–2013', *Journal of Palestine Studies* 43: 4 (2014), pp. 67–70.

Mares, Detlev, 'Der Bruch zwischen Sartre und Camus. Ein Beitrag zur politischen Kultur Frankreichs zur Zeit des Kalten Krieges', *Französisch heute* 26 (1995), pp. 38–51.

Margalit, Galit, 'Israel. 1968 and the "67 Generation"', *Bulletin of the German Historical Institute* 6 (Supplement) (2009), pp. 111–17.

Marrus, Michael, *Lessons of the Holocaust* (Toronto, Buffalo, London: University of Toronto Press, 2016).

Marsden, Eric, 'The Plight of Israel's Young Pacifists', *The Times*, 16 June 1972, p. 16.

'May 1st 1969', *Matzpen* 49 (1969), pp. 8–9 [Hebrew].

Mayer, Thomas, 'Daniel Cohn-Bendit im Interview', *Der Standard*, 23 April 2014, http://derstandard.at/2000001502553/Ich-bin-wie-Obelix-in-den-Zaubertrank-der-Freiheit-gefallen (accessed 29 July 2020).

Mazower, Mark, *No Enchanted Palace: The End of Empire and the Ideological Origins of the United Nations*, Lawrence Stone Lectures (Princeton, Oxford: Princeton University Press, 2009).

McCarthy, Patrick, *Camus: A Critical Study of His Life and Work* (London: Hamilton, 1982).

Meisels, Moshe, 'Maki Persons Demand the Rehabilitation of the Names of those Communists who "Disappeared" in Russia', *Ma'ariv*, 13 September 1956, p. 2 [Hebrew].

Meisels, Moshe, 'No Room in Maki for Critical Voices', *Ma'ariv*, 9 October 1962, p. 3 [Hebrew].

Memmi, Albert, 'Camus ou le colonisateur de bonne volonté', *La Nef*, 12 December 1957, pp. 95–96.

Memmi, Albert, *The Colonizer and the Colonized* (London: Earthscan, [1957] 2003).

Mendel, Hersh, *Memoirs of a Jewish Revolutionary* (London, Winchester, MA: Pluto Press; Distributed in the USA by Unwin Hyman, [1959] 1989).

Mendes, Philip, 'The Rise and Fall of the Jewish/Left Alliance. An Historical and Political Analysis', *Australian Journal of Politics and History* 45: 4 (1999), pp. 483–505.

Merhav, Peretz, 'The "Compass" Astray', *New Outlook* 8 ([October] 1969), pp. 49–52.

Meyers, Oren, 'Israeli Journalists as an Interpretive Memory Community. The Case of "Haolam Hazeh"' (PhD Thesis, University of Pennsylvania, 2003).

Milson, Menahem, 'Lafif Lakhdar. A European Muslim Reformist', *Memri. Inquiry and Analysis Series* 314, 5 January 2007, https://www.memri.org/reports/lafif-lakhdar-european-muslim-reformist (accessed 29 July 2020).

Minning, Silke N., *Der Dialog zwischen der israelischen Friedensbewegung und den palästinensischen Friedenskräften: Divergenzen und Konvergenzen 1973–1993* (Münster: Lit-Verl., 2005).

Mintz, Alan L., *Translating Israel: Contemporary Hebrew Literature and its Reception in America* (Syracuse: Syracuse University Press, 2001).

Miodwonik, Dan, 'The Democratic Newspaper and Its Editor Mordechai Stein', *Kesher* 22 (1997), pp. 95–108 [Hebrew].

Miron, Dan, *From Continuity to Contiguity: Toward a New Jewish Literary Thinking* (Stanford, London: Stanford University Press, 2010).

Moneta, Jakob, 'Selbstverfasster Lebenslauf (1977)', in Jakob Moneta, *Mehr Macht für die Ohnmächtigen: Reden und Aufsätze*, 1. Aufl. (Frankfurt am Main: ISP-Verl., 1991), pp. 133–5.

Moneta, Jakob, 'Nachwort zur deutschen Ausgabe', in Hersch Mendel, *Erinnerungen eines jüdischen Revolutionärs*, Aus der Reihe, 1.-4. Tausend (Berlin: Rotbuch Verlag, 1979), pp. 265–70.

Moneta, Jakob, 'Mehr Gewalt für die Ohnmächtigen', in Jakob Moneta, *Mehr Macht für die Ohnmächtigen: Reden und Aufsätze*, 1. Aufl. (Frankfurt am Main: ISP-Verl., 1991), pp. 111–26.

Moneta, Jakob, 'Jakob Moneta wird 85', *Avanti. Zeitung des RSB* 44 (1999), pp. 8–9.

Moneta, Jakob, 'Tony Cliff (1917–2000)', *SoZ – Sozialistische Zeitung*, 11 May 2000, p. 15, http://www.vsp-vernetzt.de/soz/0010152.htm (accessed 29 July 2020).

Moneta, Jakob, 'Jakob Taut (1913–2001)', *SoZ – Sozialistische Zeitung*, 8 November 2001, p. 15, http://www.vsp-vernetzt.de/soz/0123152.htm (accessed 29 July 2020).

Moneta, Jakob, 'Erinnerungen an die Algeriensolidarität. Ein Kofferträger', *SoZ – Sozialistische Zeitung*, February 2005, p. 20, http://www.vsp-vernetzt.de/sozd/0502201.htm (accessed 29 July 2020).

Moonshine, David, *Moonshines Stories: Short Stories for Young Adults* (Tel Aviv: Modan, 1990) [Hebrew].

Moonshine, David, 'The Egg', in David Moonshine, *Moonshines Stories: Short Stories for Young Adults* (Tel Aviv: Modan, 1990), pp. 53–6 [Hebrew].

Morris, Benny, *Righteous Victims: A History of the Zionist-Arab Conflict, 1881–2001*, 1. Vintage Books edn (New York: Vintage Books, 2001).

Morris, Benny, *The Birth of the Palestinian Refugee Problem Revisited*, 2nd edn (Cambridge: Cambridge University Press, 2004).

Nakdimon, Shlomo, 'A "Matzpen" Member Met with a PLO Representative in the UK. Transcript to Be Released', *Yediot Aharonot*, 16 December 1975, pp. 1 and 7 [Hebrew].

Naor, Arye, '"Behold, Rachel, Behold". The Six Day War as a Biblical Experience and its Impact on Israel's Political Mentality', *Journal of Israeli History* 24: 2 (2005), pp. 229–50.

Ne'eman, Judd, *Ja brechen!: Seamen's Strike*, 1981, Israel, 68 min, documentary [Hebrew].

Neumann, Israel, 'Ben-Gurion Rejects the Comparison Between the Algerian Problem and Eretz Israel', *Davar*, 7 January 1962, p. 1 [Hebrew].

Nicola, Jabra (Said, A.), 'Aden, Great Britain and Israel', *Matzpen* 19 (1964), p. 5 [Hebrew].

Nicola, Jabra (Said, A.) and Moshé Machover, 'Arab Revolution and National Problems in the Arab East (Summer 1973)', in Moshé Machover, *Israelis and Palestinians: Conflict and Resolutions* (Chicago: Haymarket Books, 2012), pp. 19–25 [first: *Matzpen* 64 (1972)].

Noack, Hans-Joachim, 'Ferienlager bei El Fatah', *Die Zeit*, 15 August 1969, p. 7, https://www.zeit.de/1969/33/ferienlager-bei-el-fatah (accessed 29 July 2020).

Offenberg, Mario, *Kommunismus in Palästina: Nation und Klasse in der antikolonialen Revolution, Marburger Abhandlungen zur politischen Wissenschaft* (Meisenheim am Glan: Hain, 1975), vol. 29 [German].

Ohana, David, *The Origins of Israeli Mythology: Neither Canaanites Nor Crusaders* (Cambridge: Cambridge University Press, 2014).

Omer, D. (ed.), *Dapim Zehubim* (Jerusalem: Davka, 1968) [Hebrew].

Omer, Dan, *On the Way* (Jerusalem: Golgotha, 1966) [Hebrew].

Omer, Dan (ed. and trans.), *Howl! An Anthology of American Beat Poetry* (Jerusalem: Marcus, 1967) [Hebrew].

Omer, Dan, 'Quo Vadis Israel?', *The International Times* 3: 39 (1968), p. 17.

'On the Meeting Between Matzpen Members and PLO-Representatives', *Matzpen* 80 (1977), p. 4 [Hebrew].

'On the Palestinian Question – Here and Now', *Matzpen* 72 (1974), pp. 8–9 [Hebrew].

'On the Split', *Matzpen* 62 (1972), p. 2 [Hebrew].

'Open Letter to the Democratic Front for the Liberation of Palestine (June 1974)', *Matzpen* 72 (1974), p. 18 [Hebrew].

Ophir, A. (ed.), *50 to 48: Critical Moments in the History of the State of Israel* (Jerusalem: Hakibbutz Hameuchad, 1999) [Hebrew].

Orr, A., Interview with the Author, Tenuvot, 10 April 2008 [Hebrew].

Orr, A., 'How I Came to Politics, to Maki, and to Matzpen', https://matzpen.org/2008-09-01/איך-הגעתי-לפוליטיקה-למקי-ולמצפן-עקי/] (accessed 15 April 2020).

Orr, A., Email Communication with the Author, 24 December 2009 [English].

Orr, A., Email Communication with the Author, 17 May 2012 [English].

Orr, A., Interview with the Author, Tel Aviv, 1 November 2012 [English].

Orr, Akiva, 'Changing the Histadrut: How?', *Matzpen* 2 (1962), p. 4 [Hebrew].

Orr, Akiva, 'The Lesson of October and the "Old Bolsheviks"', *Matzpen* 1 (1962), p. 5 [Hebrew].

Orr, Akiva, 'Outside or Inside the Histadrut?', *Matzpen* 8 (1963), p. 4 [Hebrew].

Orr, Akiva, 'The Seamen's Strike', *Matzpen* 3 (1963), p. 5 [Hebrew].

Orr, Akiva, 'Replys to Readers Questions', *Matzpen* 14 (1964), p. 2 [Hebrew].

Orr, Akiva, 'Zionism. Theory and Practice', *Matzpen* 24 (1965), p. 8 [Hebrew].

Orr, Akiva, 'An Unfinished Struggle. Insights from the Seamen's Strike', *Matzpen* 35 (1967), pp. 5–6 [Hebrew].

Orr, Akiva, 'Socialism – What Is It? Clarification on the Events in France and Czechoslovakia', *Matzpen* 45 (1968), p. 7 [Hebrew].

Orr, Akiva, 'He Was No Teacher, But We Learned a Lot From Him', *Matzpen* 73 (1975), pp. 12–13 [Hebrew].

Orr, Akiva, *The UnJewish State: The Politics of Jewish Identity in Israel* (London: Ithaca Press, 1983).

Orr, Akiva, *Israel: Politics, Myths and Identity Crises*, Pluto Middle Eastern Series (London: Pluto Press, 1994).

Orr, Akiva, 'Israeliness', in Akiva Orr, *Israel: Politics, Myths and Identity Crises*, Pluto Middle Eastern Series (London: Pluto Press, 1994), pp. 44–52.

Orr, Akiva, 'Motives for Writing a Book on Jewish Identity', in Akiva Orr, *Israel: Politics, Myths and Identity Crises*, Pluto Middle Eastern Series (London: Pluto Press, 1994), pp. 4–7.

Orr, Akiva, 'The Kastner Case. Jerusalem 1955', in Akiva Orr, *Israel: Politics, Myths and Identity Crises*, Pluto Middle Eastern Series (London: Pluto Press, 1994), pp. 81–116.

Orr, Akiva, 'A Brutal Revolution', in Akiva Orr, *Enlightening Disillusionments* (Tel Aviv, 2011), pp. 124–9, http://www.akiorrbooks.com/files/Enlightening.pdf (accessed 29 July 2020).

Orr, Akiva, *Enlightening Disillusionments* (Tel Aviv, 2011), http://www.akiorrbooks.com/files/Enlightening.pdf (accessed 29 July 2020]

Orr, Akiva, 'Enlightening Disillusionment (Stage 1)', in Akiva Orr, *Enlightening Disillusionments* (Tel Aviv, 2011), pp. 4–16, http://www.akiorrbooks.com/files/Enlightening.pdf (accessed 29 July 2020).

Orr, Akiva, 'More Enlightening Disillusionment (Stage 2)', in Akiva Orr, *Enlightening Disillusionments* (Tel Aviv, 2011), pp. 17–29, http://www.akiorrbooks.com/files/Enlightening.pdf (accessed 29 July 2020).

Orr, Akiva, 'Peace, Peace, Yet There is No Peace', in Akiva Orr, *Enlightening Disillusionments* (Tel Aviv, 2011), pp. 36–48, http://www.akiorrbooks.com/files/Enlightening.pdf (accessed 29 July 2020).

Orr, Akiva and Moshé Machover, 'The Zionist Left and the Palestinian Resistance', in Arie Bober (ed.), *The Other Israel: The Radical Case Against Zionism* (Garden City: Doubleday, 1972), pp. 182–90.

Orr, Akiva and Moshé Machover (Israeli, N.), *Peace, Peace, When There is No Peace: Israel and the Arabs 1948–1961* (Jerusalem: Bokhan, 1961) [Hebrew].

Orr, Akiva and Moshé Machover (Israeli, N.), '"The Peula" and the Israeli–Arab Conflict', *Matzpen* 15 (1964), pp. 4 and 7, at p. 7 [Hebrew].

Orr, Akiva and Moshé Machover (Israeli, N.), *Peace, Peace, When There is No Peace: Israel and the Arabs 1948–1961* (Toronto, 2009), http://www.akiorrbooks.com/files/PEACE.pdf (accessed 29 July 2020).

Oz, Amos, 'Minister for Defence/Lebensraum', *Davar*, 22 August 1967, p. 4 [Hebrew].

Pagirsky, Ruth, *Memoirs* (New York: Pagirsky Family Press, 2013).

Palestinai, Yehuda (Adiv, Udi), 'Matzpen and the Palestinian Resistance Organizations', *Hazit Adumah* 3 ([April–May] 1972), pp. 15–17 [Hebrew].

Palestine Liberation Organization, 'The Palestinian National Charter. Resolution of the Palestine National Council July 1-17, 1968', in Leila S. Kadi (ed.), *Basic Political Documents of the Armed Palestinian Resistance Movement* (Beirut: Palestine Liberation Organization, Research Center, 1969 [1970]), pp. 137–42.

Palestine Liberation Organization, 'Political Program (June 9, 1974)', in Itamar Rabinovich and Jehudah Reinharz (eds), *Israel in the Middle East: Documents and Readings on Society, Politics, and Foreign Relations, Pre-1948 to the Present*, 2nd edn (Waltham: Brandeis University Press, 2008), pp. 344–6.

Perrault, Gilles, *The Red Orchestra* (London: Barker, 1968).

Perrault, Gilles, *A Man Apart: The Life of Henri Curiel* (London, Atlantic Highlands: Zed Books, 1987).

Persiko, O., 'Without Red Lines', https://www.the7eye.org.il/51989 (accessed 13 April 2020) [Hebrew].

Philipp, Thomas, 'In Memoriam: Gabriel Baer 1919–1982', *Middle Eastern Studies* 19: 3 (1983), pp. 275–6.

Pilavsky, Oded, 'How I Arrived at Matzpen', https://matzpen.org/2008-09-29/כיצד-הגעתי-למצפן-עודד-פילבסקי-י/ (accessed 29 July 2020) [Hebrew].

Pilavsky, Oded, 'A Front to Promote the Worker in the Histadrut', *Matzpen* 18 (1964), p. 8 [Hebrew].

Pilavsky, Oded, 'Easternization', *Matzpen* 23 (1964), p. 6 [Hebrew].

Pilavsky, Oded, 'On the Zionist Movement', *Matzpen* 14 (1964), p. 5 [Hebrew].

Pilavsky, Oded, 'Zionism's Most Valuable Fund', *Matzpen* 30 (1966), p. 5 [Hebrew].

Pilavsky, Oded, 'National Ethics', *Matzpen* 39 (1967), p. 8 [Hebrew].

Pilavsky, Oded, 'Left-Wing Slogans with a Right-Wing Meaning', *Matzpen* 56 (1970), pp. 5–6 [Hebrew].

Pilavsky, Oded, 'Palestinian–Israeli Dialogue. Controversy and Debate', *Matzpen* 53 (1970), pp. 3–4 [Hebrew].

Pilavsky, Oded, 'Judaism versus Humanism', *Matzpen* 58 (1971), p. 6 [Hebrew].

'Pioneer Palestinian Revolutionist. Jabra Nicola (1912–1974)', *Intercontinental Press* 13: 3 (1975), pp. 95–6.

Pohrt, Wolfgang, 'Erinnerung an Eike Geisel', in Wolfgang Pohrt, *Gewalt und Politik: Ausgewählte Reden & Schriften; 1979-1993*, Critica Diabolis (Berlin: Ed. Tiamat, 2010), pp. 378–82.

Popular Democratic Front for the Liberation of Palestine, 'A Democratic Solution to the Palestine Question', in Leila S. Kadi (ed.), *Basic Political Documents of the Armed Palestinian Resistance Movement* (Beirut: Palestine Liberation Organization, Research Center, 1969 [1970]), pp. 173–4.

Porat, Dina, 'Ben Gurion and the Holocaust', in Ronald W. Zweig (ed.), *David Ben-Gurion: Politics and Leadership in Israel* (London: Cass, 1991), pp. 145–70.

Portugez, Adi, 'Siah. The Case of a New Left Movement in Israel', *Israel. Studies in Zionism and the State of Israel* 21 (2013), pp. 225–51 [Hebrew].

'Possibly a New Communist Party will Emerge in this Country', *Haolam Hazeh*, 12 September 1962, p. 4 [Hebrew].

'Public Statement', *Matzpen-Marxisti* 73 (1973), p. 3 [Hebrew].

Ram, Uri, 'The Colonization Perspective in Israeli Sociology. Internal and External Comparisons', *Journal of Historical Sociology* 6: 3 (1993), pp. 327–50.

Rapoport, Meron, 'One Day, Two Declarations', *Haaretz*, 7 June 2007, https://www.haaretz.com/1.4824451 (accessed 29 July 2020).

Ratner, David, 'A Yesteryear's Tiger', *Haaretz*, 3 January 2010, p. 10 [Hebrew].

Ratosh, Yonathan, 'The New Hebrew Nation (The Canaanite Outlook). Interview July 1970', in Ehud Ben Ezer (ed.), *Unease in Zion* (New York: Quadrangle/ New York Times Book Co., 1974), pp. 201–34.

Ratosh, Yonathan, 'Epistle to the Hebrew Youth', in Yonathan Ratosh, *The First Days* (Tel Aviv: Hadar, 1982), pp. 32–8 [Hebrew].

Ratosh, Yonathan, 'Opening Speech at the Meeting of the Committee with Representatives of the Cells', in Yonathan Ratosh, *The First Days* (Tel Aviv: Hadar, 1982), pp. 149–203 [Hebrew].

Rauchwerger, D., 'A Life in Painting', *Haaretz*, 30 May 2001, http://www.haaretz.com/israel-news/culture/leisure/a-life-in-painting-1.364867 (accessed 11 April 2020).

Regev, Yoel, 'Pney Elohim. On Itamar Ben-Avi's Failed Project to Latinize Hebrew', *Mita'am* 22 (2010), pp. 49–61 [Hebrew].

Reime, H., *Century as a Fate. The Life and Times of Eli Lobel*, 31 December 2002, Finnish Broadcasting Company (Channel 1), radio documentary.

Rejwan, Nissim, 'A Dissenting Voice in the Arab World', *Midstream* ([April] 1971), pp. 71–80.

Renan, Ariel, 'The "Hallucinating a Myth" Has a Meaning', *Davar*, 14 September 1967, p. 3 [Hebrew].

Renken, Frank, 'Kleine Geschichte des Algerienkriegs', in Christiane Kohser-Spohn and Frank Renken (eds), *Trauma Algerienkrieg: Zur Geschichte und Aufarbeitung eines tabuisierten Konflikts* (Frankfurt am Main, New York: Campus, 2006), pp. 25–50.

'Representatives of Matzpen and the Revolutionary Communist Alliance Prepare a List Headed by Ramil Livneh', *Ma'ariv*, 3 July 1973, p. 9 [Hebrew].

Revolutionary Communist Alliance, 'On Kiryat Shmona, Ma'alot and All Similar Upcoming Operations', May 1974, The Israeli Left Archives, http://hdl.handle.net/10622/COLL00308%2E679?locatt=view:pdf (accessed 21 April 2020) [Hebrew].

Revolutionary Communist Alliance, *The Palestinian Question and the Right to Self-Determination* (Jerusalem: Ma'avak Publishing, 1974) [Hebrew].

Revolutionary Communist League, 'Against Partition!', *Kol Hamaamad* 31 (1947) [Hebrew], http://www.marxists.de/middleast/misc/partition.htm (accessed 29 July 2020) [English translation].

Revolutionary Communist League, 'Against the Stream. The Trotskyist Position in Palestine', *Fourth International* 9: 3 (85) (1948), pp. 86–9.

Richardson, David, 'Personal Protest', *The Jerusalem Post*, 13 August 1982, p. 7.

Richter, Horst and Horst Schiefelbein, 'Manifestation brüderlicher Solidarität', *Neues Deutschland*, 26 November 1977, p. 12.

Rocker, Simon, 'Meet the Trotskyist anti-Zionist Who Saw the Errors of His Ways', *The Jewish Chronicle*, 4 December 2014, https://www.thejc.com/news/uk/meet-the-trotskyist-anti-zionist-who-saw-the-errors-of-his-ways-1.62661 (accessed 30 July 2020).

Rodinson, Maxime, *Israel: A Colonial-Settler State?* (New York: Monad Press; distributed by Pathfinder Press, 1973).

Rodinson, Maxime, 'Islam Resurgent?', in Janet Afary and Kevin Anderson (eds), *Foucault and the Iranian Revolution: Gender and the Seductions of Islamism* (Chicago: University of Chicago Press, 2005), pp. 223–38 [first: *Le Monde*, 6.–8. December 1978].

Ro'i, Yaacov, *The Struggle for Soviet Jewish Emigration, 1948–1967* (Cambridge: Cambridge University Press, 1991).

Ron, I., 'Shameful Politics', *Matzpen* 24 (1965), p. 2 [Hebrew].

Rosen, Roli, 'Eli Lobel Committed Suicide in Fall of '79', *Kol Ha'Ir*, 11 June 1993, pp. 65–70, https://matzpen.org/1993-06-11/the-life-and-death-of-eli-lobel/ (accessed 28 July 2020) [Hebrew].

Rosenblum, Doron, 'The Exile Option in Paris and London. Part 2: London', *Hadashot*, 28 September 1999, pp. 22–9 [Hebrew].

Rothchild, Alice, *Broken Promises, Broken Dreams: Stories of Jewish and Palestinian Trauma and Resilience* (London: Pluto Press, 2010).

Rothschild, Jon, 'Civil War in Lebanon', in Jon Rothschild (ed.), *Forbidden Agendas: Intolerance and Defiance in the Middle East* (London: Saqi Books, 1984), pp. 233–5.

Rouleau, Eric, 'Die französische Nahost-Politik', *Europa-Archiv* 23: 5 (1968), pp. 149–70.

Rouleau, Eric, *Truths and Lies in the Middle East: Memoirs of a Veteran Journalist, 1952–2012* (Cairo, New York: The American University in Cairo Press, 2019).

Rowland, Robert, *The Rhetoric of Menachem Begin: The Myth of Redemption Through Return* (Lanham: University Press of America, 1985).

Rubenstein, Sondra M., *The Communist Movement in Palestine and Israel, 1919–1984*, Westview Special Studies (Boulder: Westview Press, 1985).

Sahish, Yaron, 'The Myth of Matzpen', *Iton Yerushalayim*, 20 November 1992, pp. 10–14 [Hebrew].

Salman, Magida, 'The Lebanese Communities and Their Little Wars', in Jon Rothschild (ed.), *Forbidden Agendas: Intolerance and Defiance in the Middle East* (London: Saqi Books, 1984), pp. 260–8 [first: *Khamsin* 10 (1983), pp. 13–20].

Sand, Shlomo, *The Invention of the Jewish People* (London: Verso, 2009).

Sand, Shlomo, *The Invention of the Land of Israel* (London: Verso, 2012).

Sand, Shlomo, *How I Stopped Being a Jew* (London: Verso, 2014).

Sarneh, Ygal, 'In Nahalal They Think He is a Traitor', *Yediot Aharonot*, 7 February 1992, pp. 22–3 and 54 [Hebrew].

Sarneh, Ygal, 'Olive Grove Ploughed the Final Time by Lawyer Mohammed Kiwan', *Yediot Aharonot*, 16 February 1996, pp. 10–11 [Hebrew].

Sarneh, Ygal, 'A Revolutionary Life', *International Socialism Journal* 87 (2000), http://www.marxists.de/intsoctend/cliff-bio/sarneh.htm (accessed 29 July 2020) [first: *Yediot Aharonot*, 4 October 1991].

Sartre, Jean-Paul, 'Preface', in Frantz Fanon, *The Wretched of the Earth* (London: Penguin Books, [1961] 2001), pp. 7–26.

Sayigh, Yezid, *Armed Struggle and the Search for State: The Palestinian National Movement 1949–1993* (Oxford, New York: Oxford University Press, 2011).

Schiff, Zeev and Ehud Ya'ari, *Israel's Lebanon War* (New York: Simon and Schuster, 1984).

Schnall, David, 'Notes on the Political Thought of Dr. Moshe Sneh', *Middle East Journal* 27: 3 (1973), pp. 342–52.

Schnall, David, 'Organized Communism in Israel', *Midstream* 24: 7 (1978), pp. 26–36.

Schnall, David, *Radical Dissent in Contemporary Israeli Politics: Cracks in the Wall*, Preager Special Studies (New York: Praeger, 1979).

Scholem, Gershom, 'Zionism – Dialectic of Continuity and Rebellion. Interview, April/Juli 1970', in Ehud Ben Ezer (ed.), *Unease in Zion* (New York: Quadrangle/New York Times Book Co., 1974), pp. 263–96.

Scholem, Gershom, 'On Our Language. A Confession [1926]', *History and Memory* 2: 2 (1990), pp. 97–9.

Scholem, Gershom, 'Reflections on Modern Jewish Studies [1944]', in Gershom Scholem, *On the Possibility of Jewish Mysticism in Our Time & Other Essays*, 1st edn (Philadelphia: Jewish Publication Society, 1997), pp. 51–71.

Scholem, Gershom, 'Israel and the Diaspora', in Gershom Scholem, *On Jews and Judaism in Crisis: Selected Essays*, edited by Werner J. Dannhauser (Philadelphia: Paul Dry Books, Inc., 2012), pp. 244–60.

Scholem, Gershom, *From Berlin to Jerusalem: Memories of My Youth*, Autobiography Jewish Studies, 1st Paul Dry Books edn (Philadelphia: Paul Dry Books, [1977] 2012).

Scholem, Gershom and Muki Tsur, 'An Interview with Gershom Scholem', in Gershom Scholem, *On Jews and Judaism in Crisis: Selected Essays*, edited by Werner J. Dannhauser (Philadelphia: Paul Dry Books, Inc., 2012), pp. 1–48.

Schröder, Mandred, 'Spionage-Prozess in Israel', *Süddeutsche Zeitung*, 10 March 1973.

Schwartz, A., 'Point of No Return: Jewish Refugees from Arab and Muslim Countries (Part II)', http://jewishrefugees.blogspot.com/2014/05/weinstock-mass-jewish-flight-was.html (accessed 9 April 2020).

Schwartz, Adi, 'The Inconvenient Truth about Jews from Arab Lands. Interview with Nathan Weinstock', *Haaretz*, 29 May 2014, https://www.haaretz.com/jewish/.premium-the-inconvenient-truth-about-jews-from-arab-lands-1.5250159 (accessed 29 July 2020).

Segall, Rudolf, 'Cyrano von Bergerac und die Geduld des Revolutionärs. Ein Gespräch mit Rudolf Segall (II)', *Inprekorr* 416/17 (2006), pp. 23–9.

Segev, Shmuel, '"Al-Ard". A Solution to the Palestine Problem in Nasser's Style', *Ma'ariv*, 14 July 1964, p. 10 [Hebrew].

Segev, Shmuel, 'Could There Be an Israeli "Algeria"?', *Ma'ariv*, 24 November 1964, p. 7 [Hebrew].

Segev, Tom, 'Dear Reader', *Koteret Rashit* 232 (1987), pp. 20–5 [Hebrew].

Segev, Tom, *The Seventh Million: The Israelis and the Holocaust* (New York: Hill and Wang, 1993).

Segev, Tom, *1949: The First Israelis* (New York: Henry Holt and Company, Inc. [First Owl Books Edition], 1998).

Segev, Tom, *Elvis in Jerusalem: Post-Zionism and the Americanization of Israel*, 1st American edn (New York: Metropolitan Books, 2002).

Segev, Tom, *1967: Israel, the War, and the Year that Transformed the Middle East* (New York: Metropolitan Books, 2007).

Semitic Action, *The Hebrew Manifesto: Principles of Semitic Action*, 2nd and complete edn (Tel Aviv: Central Committee, Semitic Action, 1959) [Hebrew].

'Sentences Reduced for Two Jewish Security Prisoners', *Jewish Telegraphic Agency* 138, 19 July 1974, p. 2.

Shafir, Gershon, *Land, Labor, and the Origins of the Israeli-Palestinian Conflict, 1882–1914* (Berkeley: University of California Press, 1996).

Shafir, Gershon, 'Settler Citizenship in the Jewish Colonization of Palestine', in Caroline Elkins and Susan Pedersen (eds), *Settler Colonialism in the Twentieth Century: Projects, Practices, Legacies* (New York: Routledge, 2005), pp. 41–57.

Shaked, Gershon, 'Fat Haim, Uzi & Co, and Ervinka', *Yediot Aharonot*, 13 December 1985, pp. 20–3 [Hebrew].

Shaked, Gershon, 'Watch the Facts!', *Yediot Aharonot*, 26 September 1986, p. 20 [Hebrew].

Shaked, Gershon, *Modern Hebrew Fiction* (New Milford: Toby Press, 2008).

Shalev, Michael, *Labour and the Political Economy in Israel*, Library of Political Economy (Oxford: Oxford University Press, 1992).

Shalev, Michael, 'The Labor Movement in Israel. Ideology and Political Economy', in Ellis Goldberg (ed.), *The Social History of Labor in the Middle East (The Social History of the Modern Middle East)* (Boulder: Westview Press, 1996), pp. 131–61.

'Shalom + Napalm', *Agit 883* 40, 13 November 1969, p. 9, http://www.trend. infopartisan.net/litlisten/aufruhr/aufruhr14.html (accessed 29 July 2020).

Shamgar, Shlomo, 'An Israeli Lecturer at Frankfurt University Preaches the Liquidation of the State', *Yediot Aharonot*, 16 October 1980, p. 21 [Hebrew].

Shapira, Anita, 'The Origins of "Jewish Labor" Ideology', *Studies in Zionism* 3: 1 (1982), pp. 93–112.

Shapira, Anita, 'Ben-Gurion and the Bible. The Forging of an Historical Narrative?', *Middle Eastern Studies* 33: 4 (1997), pp. 645–74.

Shapira, Anita, 'The Eichmann Trial. Changing Perspectives', *Journal of Israeli History* 23: 1 (2004), pp. 18–39.

Shapira, Anita, 'Whatever Became of "Negating Exile"?', in Anita Shapira (ed.), *Israeli Identity in Transition* (Westport: Praeger, 2004), pp. 69–108.

Shapira, Anita, 'Hirbet Hizah. Between Remembrance and Forgetting', in Benny Morris (ed.), *Making Israel* (Ann Arbor: University of Michigan Press, 2007), pp. 81–123.

Shavit, Ari, 'Cry, the Beloved Two-State Solution', *Haaretz*, 6 August 2003, https:// www.haaretz.com/1.5356751 (accessed 29 July 2020).

Shavit, Yaacov, *The New Hebrew Nation: A Study in Israeli Heresy and Fantasy* (London, Totowa: F. Cass, 1987).

Sheizaf, Noam, 'Matzpen and the Story of Two Ads', https://www.972mag.com/ matzpen-and-the-story-of-two-ads/65842/ (accessed 29 July 2020).

Shemesh, Moshe, 'Did Shuqayri Call For "Throwing the Jews into the Sea"?', *Israel Studies* 8: 2 (2003), pp. 70–81.
Shilon, Avi, *Menachem Begin: A Life* (New Haven: Yale University Press, 2012).
Shinar, Pessah, 'Ulama, Marabouts and Government. An Overview of their Relationships in the French Colonial Maghrib', *Israel Oriental Studies* 10 (1980), pp. 211–29.
Shlaim, Avi, 'The Debate about 1948', *International Journal of Middle East Studies* 27: 3 (1995), pp. 287–302.
Shlaim, Avi, 'Israel Between East and West, 1948–56', *International Journal of Middle East Studies* 36: 4 (2004), pp. 657–73.
Shlaim, Avi, 'The Iron Wall Revisited', *Journal of Palestine Studies* 41: 2 (2012), pp. 80–98.
'Signs for 1968', *Matzpen* 40 (1968), p. 1 [Hebrew].
Silberstein, Laurence, *The Postzionism Debates: Knowledge and Power in Israeli Culture* (New York: Routledge, 1999).
Sing, Manfred, 'Brothers in Arms. How Palestinian Maoists Turned Jihadists', *Die Welt des Islams* 51: 1 (2011), pp. 1–44.
Singer, Zvi, 'An Israeli in the PLO', *Yediot Aharonot*, 18 April 1983, pp. 1 and 7 [Hebrew].
Sivan, Emmanuel, 'Arab Revisionist Historians', in Emmanuel Sivan, *Interpretations of Islam: Past and Present* (Princeton: Darwin Press, 1985), pp. 45–72.
Slann, Martin W., 'Ideology and Ethnicity in Israel's Two Communist Parties. The Conflict between Maki and Rakah', *Studies in Comparative Communism: An International Interdisciplinary Journal* 7: 4 (1974), pp. 359–74.
Slezkine, Yuri, *The Jewish Century* (Princeton, Woodstock: Princeton University Press, 2006).
Slonim, Shlomo, 'Origins of the 1950 Tripartite Declaration on the Middle East', *Middle Eastern Studies* 23: 2 (1987), pp. 135–49.
Smith, Lilian, 'From Nowhere to the End of Night', *The Saturday Review*, 4 April 1964, pp. 39–40.
Smorodinsky, Meir (S. Meir), 'On Principles that Became Infertile', *Matzpen* 1 (1962), p. 2 [Hebrew].
Smorodinsky, Meir (S. Meir), 'Al-Ard and Us', *Matzpen* 21 (1964), p. 5 [Hebrew].
Smorodinsky, Meir (S. Meir), 'Religion. Who Coerces', *Matzpen* 20 (1964), p. 3 [Hebrew].
Smorodinsky, Meir (S. Meir), 'The Root of the Conflict. Zionism versus Arab Nationalism', *Matzpen* 23 (1964), p. 6 [Hebrew].
Smorodinsky, Meir (S. Meir), 'The Lesson of Nazareth Illit', *Matzpen* 24 (1965), p. 5 [Hebrew].

Sneh, Moshe, *On the National Question: Conclusions in the Light of Marxism-Leninism* (Tel Aviv: The Left Socialist Party, 1954) [Hebrew].

'Sneh's Comrades Leave Maki', *Ma'ariv*, 26 August 1958, p. 8 [Hebrew].

Somekh, Sasson, '"Reconciling Two Great Loves". The First Jewish-Arab Literary Encounter in Israel', *Israel Studies* 4: 1 (1999), pp. 1–21.

Speier, Moshe, Interview with the Author, Frankfurt am Main, 20 February 2008 [German].

Sprinzak, Ehud, 'The Emergence of the Politics of Delegitimization in Israel, 1967–72' (Doctoral dissertation, Hebrew University of Jerusalem, 1973) [Hebrew].

Sprinzak, Ehud, *Brother Against Brother: Violence and Extremism in Israeli Politics from Altalena to the Rabin Assassination* (New York: Free Press, 1999).

Stamer, Sabine, *Cohn-Bendit: Die Biografie* (Hamburg: Europa-Verlag, 2001).

'Statement of Banished Maki Members from Haifa', *Matzpen* 14 (1964), p. 7 [Hebrew].

Stein, Dina, 'Zwischen allen Stühlen', in Cilly Kugelmann and Hanno Loewy (eds), *So einfach war das: Jüdische Kindheiten und Jugend seit 1945 in Österreich, der Schweiz und Deutschland* (Köln: DuMont, 2002), pp. 82–8.

Stendel, Ori, *Arabs in Israel* (Brighton: Sussex Academic, 1996).

Sternhell, Zeev, *The Founding Myths of Israel: Nationalism, Socialism, and the Making of the Jewish State* (Princeton: Princeton University Press, 1998).

Stora, Benjamin, *Algeria, 1830–2000: A Short History* (Ithaca: Cornell University Press, 2004).

Strassman, Gabriel, 'The "New Left" and its "War on the Jews"', *Maariv*, 5 December 1969, p. 18 [Hebrew].

'Sur la conception matérialiste de la question juive', *ISRAC* 5 ([January–February] 1971), pp. 17–62.

Tadjer, Allyson, 'Triangulating Racism. French and Francophone African Reactions to the African American Freedom Movement (1954-1968)' (Dissertation, Georgia State University, 2015).

Tal, David, 'The American-Israeli Security Treaty. Sequel or Means to the Relief of Israeli-Arab Tension', *Middle Eastern Studies* 31: 4 (1995), pp. 828–48.

Talhami, Ghada, 'An Interview with Sadik Al-Azm', *Arab Studies Quarterly* 19: 3 (1997), pp. 113–26.

Taut, Jakob, 'On the History of Trotskyism in Palestine. Interview with John Bunzl', *Intercontinental Press* 10: 38 (1972), pp. 1155–7.

Taut, Jakob, *Judenfrage und Zionismus*, 1. Aufl. (Frankfurt/M.: Isp-Verlag, 1986).

Tessler, Mark, *A History of the Israeli-Palestinian Conflict* (Bloomington: Indiana University Press, 1994).

'The Café Herlinger Underground in the Trial of "Haolam Hazeh" Against "Davar HaShavua"', *Davar*, 8 May 1958, p. 4 [Hebrew].
The League of Arab States, 'Seventh Arab Summit Conference (October 1974)', in Itamar Rabinovich and Jehudah Reinharz (eds), *Israel in the Middle East: Documents and Readings on Society, Politics, and Foreign Relations, Pre-1948 to the Present*, 2nd edn (Waltham: Brandeis University Press, 2008), pp. 342–4.
'The Letter from an Anonymous Woman was Read During the Trial of the Editors of "Bul"', *Al Hamishmar*, 21 November 1967, p. 5 [Hebrew].
'The Parisian PLO Representative at a Matzpen Member's Funeral in Paris', *Haaretz*, 14 October 1979 [Hebrew].
'The Red Front Trial. The Depositions of Turki and Adiv', *Journal of Palestine Studies* 2: 4 (1973), pp. 144–50.
'The Spy Ring Story', *Israleft. News Service* 8, 15 December 1972, pp. 1–7.
'The Suppression of "Al-Ard"', *Matzpen* 23 (1964), p. 8 [Hebrew].
The Times Diary, 'Tzabar and Israel Imperial News', *The Times*, 7 March 1968, p. 8.
'The Week of "Danny the Red"', *Al Hamishmar*, 7 June 1970 [Hebrew].
'This Strike Is Justified!', *Matzpen* 3 (1963), p. 8 [Hebrew].
Tibi, Bassam, 'Einführung. Skizze einer Geschichte des Sozialismus in den arabischen Ländern', in Bassam Tibi (ed.), *Die arabische Linke: Hrsg. u. eingel. von Bassam Tibi. (Aus d. Arab. von Bassam Tibi)* (Dritte Welt) (Frankfurt a.M.: Europäische Verlags-Anstalt, 1969), pp. 7–41.
Tibi, Bassam, 'Vorbemerkung des Herausgebers', in Bassam Tibi (ed.), *Die arabische Linke: Hrsg. u. eingel. von Bassam Tibi. (Aus d. Arab. von Bassam Tibi)* (Dritte Welt) (Frankfurt a.M.: Europäische Verlags-Anstalt, 1969), pp. 119–22.
Tilman, David, *From the Cave of Decay to the Anonymous Soldiers. Memories of a Fighter* (Tel Aviv: Yair – Avraham Stern, 1993) [Hebrew].
'To Change the Face of the Histadrut [Program]', *Matzpen* 12 (1963), p. 8 [Hebrew].
'To the Jewish Public', *Matzpen* 19 (1964), p. 8 [Hebrew].
'To the Reader', *Matzpen* 72 (1974), p. 2 [Hebrew].
Toama, K., 'Zusammenleben in Würde, Gleichheit und Gleichberechtigung: Gespräch von Sophia Deeg mit Khalil Toama', https://www.neuerispverlag.de/aushang/deeg_id124_toama.pdf (accessed 15 April 2020).
Torbiner, Eran, *Matzpen. Anti-Zionist Israelis*, 2003, Tel Aviv, Israel, 54 min, film.
Torbiner, Eran, *Hebron in my Heart*, 2012, Israel, 21 min, film, https://www.youtube.com/watch?v=8HVz4YtHkJA (accessed 19 April 2020).
'Toward a New Perspective', *Ma'avak* 1 (1970), pp. 2–6 [Hebrew].

'Toward a New Perspective', The Israeli Left Archives, https://hdl.handle.net/10622/5D4051EE-BF1A-11E7-A02F-E355B54FC576?locatt=view:master (accessed 14 April 2020).

Trepper, Leopold, *The Great Game: The Story of the Red Orchestra* (London: Michael Joseph, 1977).

Troen, S. I., 'The Sinai Campaign as a "War of No Alternative": Ben Gurion's View of the Israel-Egyptian Conflict', in S. I. Troen and Moshe Shemesh (eds), *The Suez Sinai Crisis 1956: Retrospective and Reappraisal* (London: Cass, 1990), pp. 180–95.

Tsemel, Lea, 'Notes on the History of Torture in Israel', in Adalah – The Legal Center for Arab Minority Rights in Israel (ed.), *On Torture* (Haifa: Adalah, 2012), pp. 7–11.

Tsemel, Lea and Michel Warschawski (Mikado), 'Democratic Centralism is Not the Problem', *Israeli Socialist Organisation: Discussions on the Question of the Organisation* (1971), pp. 9–15 [Hebrew].

Tzabar, Shimon, *A Prickly Pear Thorn: Born in Palestine, Growing Up in Israel (An Unauthorised Autobiography)* (London [Private Printing of Shimon Tzabar], n. d.).

Tzabar, Shimon, 'Two Questions', *Haaretz*, 20 July 1967, p. 2 [Hebrew].

Tzabar, Shimon, *The White Flag Principle: How to Lose a War (and Why)* (New York: Simon & Schuster, 1972).

Tzur, Eli, '"To Be a Free People". The History of the "League for the Prevention of Religious Coercion"', in Anita Shapira (ed.), *A State in the Making: Israeli Society in the First Decades* (Jerusalem: Zalman Shazar Center, 2001), pp. 205–38 [Hebrew].

Vater, Roman, '"A Hebrew From Samaria, Not a Jew From Yavneh". Adya Gur Horon (1907-1972) and the Articulation of Hebrew Nationalism' (Doctoral dissertation, University of Manchester, 2015).

Vater, Roman, 'Hebrew as a Political Instrument. Language-Planning by the "Canaanites"', *Journal of Semitic Studies* 62: 2 (2017), pp. 485–511.

Vidal, Dominique, 'If I Forget Thee, O Zion. Could Israel's Kibbutz Experiment Finally Fail?', *Le Monde Diplomatique* (August 2000), https://mondediplo.com/2000/08/10kibbutz (accessed 29 July 2020).

'"Voice of America": Israel Officially Joins the West[ern Block]', *Ma'ariv*, 5 November 1951, p. 1 [Hebrew].

Voigt, Sebastian, *Der jüdische Mai '68: Pierre Goldman, Daniel Cohn-Bendit und André Glucksmann im Nachkriegsfrankreich* (Göttingen: Vandenhoeck & Ruprecht, 2015).

Vowinckel, Annette, 'Der kurze Weg nach Entebbe oder die Verlängerung der deutschen Geschichte in den Nahen Osten', *Zeithistorische Forschungen/Studies in Contemporary History* 1: 2 (2004), pp. 236–54.

Warschawski, Michel, 'Arafat Wants to be President', *Matzpen-Marxisti* 71 (1973), p. 17 [Hebrew].
Warschawski, Michel, 'Who Will Benefit From a Palestinian Ministate?', *Intercontinental Press* 12: 22 (1974), pp. 736–7.
Warschawski, Michel, *On the Border* (London: Pluto, 2005).
Warschawski, Michel (Mikado), Letter to Jabra Nicola and Moshé Machover, 1 October 1970, Private Archive of Moshé Machover, London [Hebrew].
Warschawski, Michel (Mikado), 'Open Letter to Our Former Anti-Zionist Comrades (?)', *Matzpen-Marxisti* 74 (1974), pp. 4 and 15 [Hebrew].
Weidner, Daniel, *Gershom Scholem: Politisches, esoterisches und historiographisches Schreiben* (München: Fink, 2003).
Weinstock, N., 'Das Bekenntnis eines ehemaligen Antizionisten', https://www.hagalil.com/archiv/2006/09/weinstock.htm (accessed 9 April 2020).
Weinstock, Nathan, *Le sionisme contre Israël* (Paris: F. Maspero, 1969).
Weinstock, Nathan, 'Introduction', in Abraham Léon, *The Jewish Question: A Marxist Interpretation*, 2nd edn (New York: Pathfinder Press, 1970), pp. 33–70.
Weinstock, Nathan, *Das Ende Israels?: Nahostkonflikt und Geschichte des Zionismus*, ed. by Eike Geisel and Mario Offenberg (Berlin: Wagenbach, 1975).
Weinstock, Nathan, *Zionism: False Messiah* (London: Ink Links Ltd, 1979).
Weinstock, Nathan, *Der zerrissene Faden: Wie die arabische Welt ihre Juden verlor: 1947–1967* (Freiburg: ça-ira-Verlag, 2019).
Weiss, P., 'Among the Refugees in Gaza (Series of Four Parts)', *Al Hamishmar*, 4 April 1952; 7 April 1952; 11 April 1952; 13 April 1952 [Hebrew].
Weiss, P., 'Among the Refugees in Gaza. Part 4: The City Cut Off from its Homefront', *Al Hamishmar*, 13 April 1952, p. 2 [Hebrew].
Weiss, Yfaat, *A Confiscated Memory: Wadi Salib and Haifa's Lost Heritage* (New York: Columbia University Press, 2011).
Weitz, Yechiam, 'Political Dimensions of Holocaust Memory', in Robert S. Wistrich and David Ohana (eds), *The Shaping of Israeli Identity: Myth, Memory, and Trauma*, Israel Affairs (London, Portland: F. Cass, 1995), pp. 129–45.
Weitz, Yechiam, *The Man Who Was Murdered Twice: The Life, Trial and Death of Israel Kasztner* (Jerusalem: Yad Vashem, the International Institute for Holocaust Research, 2011).
Wetzel, Dietrich, '"Die Verlängerung von Geschichte". Anstatt einer Einleitung', in Dietrich Wetzel (ed.), *Die Verlängerung von Geschichte: Deutsche, Juden und der Palästinakonflikt* (Frankfurt am Main: Neue Kritik, 1983), pp. 7–14.
Wieviorka, Annette, *The Era of the Witness* (Ithaca: Cornell University Press, 2006).

Wild, Stefan, 'Gott und Mensch im Libanon', *Der Islam: Journal of the History and Culture of the Middle East* 48: 2 (1971), pp. 206–53.

Wolfensohn, Avraham, 'The Conscience of Matzpen: Part I', *Davar*, 27 May 1970, p. 3 [Hebrew].

Wolfensohn, Avraham, 'The Conscience of Matzpen: Part II. The Fate of the Jewish People', *Davar*, 28 May 1970, p. 4 [Hebrew].

Wolfensohn, Avraham, 'The Conscience of Matzpen: Part III. The Objective. The Extermination of Israel', *Davar*, 31 May 1970, p. 4 [Hebrew].

Wolfensohn, Avraham, 'The Conscience of Matzpen: Part IV. The Slanderers of the Land', *Davar*, 2 June 1970, p. 6 [Hebrew].

Wolter, Udo, 'Die Arbeit des Global Theorist', *Jungle World* 51, 12 December 2001, http://www.trend.infopartisan.net/trd0102/t400102.html (accessed 29 July 2020).

Yaffe, Arnon, 'A PLO Representative Grieves for Eli Lobel', *Al Hamishmar*, 9 October 1979 [Hebrew].

Yavin, Jonathan, 'Danny the Red in the Land of White and Blue', *Haaretz*, 3 December 2000, https://www.haaretz.com/1.4777426 (accessed 29 July 2020).

Yerushalmi, Yosef, *Zakhor: Jewish History and Jewish Memory* (Seattle: University of Washington Press, 1996).

Yizhar, S., *Khirbet Khizeh* (New York: Farrar, Straus and Giroux, 2014).

Yoran, Noam, 'Haolam Hazeh', in Adi Ophir (ed.), *50 to 48: Critical Moments in the History of the State of Israel* (Jerusalem: Hakibbutz Hameuchad, 1999), pp. 137–47.

Yuval-Davis, Nira, 'Matzpen. The Israeli Socialist Organisation' (Master's thesis, Hebrew University of Jerusalem, 1977) [Hebrew].

Yuval-Davis, Nira, 'Avishai Ehrlich', in Nea Ehrlich, Lesley Marks and Nira Yuval-Davis (eds), *The Work of Avishai Ehrlich: Political Sociologist, Activist and Public Intellectual* (Newcastle upon Tyne: Cambridge Scholars, 2013), pp. 171–7.

Zahavi, Natan, 'Zahavi on the Ground: Stupid Palestinians', https://www.makorrishon.co.il/nrg/online/1/ART/984/472.html (accessed 29 July 2020).

Zertal, Idith, *Lords of the Land: The War Over Israel's Settlements in the Occupied Territories: 1967-2007* (New York: Nation Books, 2009).

Zertal, Idith, *Israel's Holocaust and the Politics of Nationhood*, Cambridge Middle East Studies (Cambridge: Cambridge University Press, 2011).

Zohar, David and Gil Keisari, 'Who Are You, Ilan Halevi?', *Ma'ariv*, 15 April 1983, p. 26 [Hebrew].

Zuckermann, Ghil'ad, *Israeli, a Beautiful Language: Hebrew as Myth* (Tel Aviv: Am Oved, 2008) [Hebrew].

Index of Persons

Abbas, Ferhat, 182
Abu-Khalil, Nicola, 375
Achcar, Gilbert, 262
Adiv, Ehud (Udi), 5, 235, 237–8, 240–9
Agnon, Shmuel Yosef, 142
Ali, Salem Rubaya, 299
Almogi, Yosef, 46
Alterman, Nathan, 141–2, 174, 189
Amichai, Yehuda, 174, 177, 347, 401
Amin, Samir, 292, 296, 318
Aminov, Eli, 145, 147, 149, 166, 185, 260
Amir, Aharon, 153, 171, 189–90, 307
Amitai, Yossi, 257
Arafat, Yasser, 221, 223, 256–8, 305–6, 309, 377, 385
Arendt, Hannah, 21, 120, 132, 312, 327, 331, 333, 344, 346
Argov, Shlomo, 368
Arif, 'Abd al-Salam, 38
Ashman, Yaakov, 159, 165, 167
Ashour, Shaykh Ibn, 297
El-Asmar, Fouzi, 80, 190, 192

Atatürk *see* Mustafa Kemal
Averbuch, Wolf, 354
Avidan, David, 177
Avineri, Shlomo, 350
Avnery, Uri (Helmut Ostermann), 20, 47, 111, 146, 149–50, 157, 159–65, 169–75, 180–1, 183–5, 187–91, 194, 196–7, 207, 222, 246, 257, 292, 342–3, 346–7, 349–50, 385–6
Al-Azm, Sadik J., 21, 281, 284, 286, 297, 300–3, 305–6, 308, 312–13, 356, 374

Bachar, Aharon, 16, 184–5, 241, 243
Baer, Gabriel, 86, 93, 99–100
Bajajo-Hanegbi, Haim *see* Haim Hanegbi
Ballas, Gila, 290
al-Banna, Sabri Chalil (Abu Nidal), 267
Baransi, Saleh, 80
Bartov, Hanoch, 347

Begin, Menachem, 235, 267, 339, 375–6, 383, 386
Ben-Akiva, Yossi, 260, 263
Ben-Amotz, Dan (Moshe Tehilimzeiger), 146, 165, 170–2, 175, 326, 341, 347–9
Ben-Avi, Itamar, 169
Ben Barka, Mehdi, 114, 175
Ben Bella, Ahmed, 298–9
Ben-Chorin, Shalom, 176
Ben Dov, Chana, 92
Ben-Ezer, Ehud, 201
Ben-Gurion, David, 2, 9, 46–50, 55, 61, 91, 102–4, 110, 145, 155, 160, 162–3, 165–6, 185, 332–3, 335, 339, 342, 345, 376
Ben-Nathan, Asher, 14, 294
Ben-Yair, Shaaltiel, 166, 171
Ben-Yehuda, Eliezer, 151, 169
Ben-Yehuda, Netiva, 170, 341
Berdyczewski, Micha Josef, 155
Berger-Barzilai, Joseph (Joseph Berger), 37, 354, 361, 364
Berlin, Isaiah, 312
Berman, Adolf (Abraham), 33
Berman, Jakob, 33
Bettelheim, Charles, 250, 292–3
Blauweiss, Hava, 94
Blauweiss, Theodor, 94, 101
Bluem, Burkhard, 366
Blum, Bernhard, 383
Bober, Arie, 145, 147, 149, 184–5, 192–3, 196, 260, 399
Bothmer, Lenelotte von, 379
Boumédiène, Houari, 298–9
Bourguiba, Habib, 297
Brahimi, Lakhdar, 292

Brenner, Josef Chaim, 155
Brumlik, Micha, 367, 370–2, 387, 399
Buber, Martin, 107
Buhali, Larbi, 303
Bunzl, John, 308, 313, 401, 403
Burg, Avraham, 385
Burg, Josef, 385
Bzozah, Hanoch, 33, 60

Camus, Albert 20, 113, 119–21, 123
Canaan, Haviv, 16
Carmi, Danielle, 228
Carmi, Menachem, 226–31
Castro, Fidel, 39, 293
Césaire, Aimé, 233
Claussen, Detlev, 366, 382–3
Cliff, Tony *see* Yigal Gluckstein
Cohen, Aharon, 107
Cohen, Shalom, 149, 161, 164, 183, 190
Cohen, Yehezkel, 240, 245
Cohn, Haim, 342
Cohn-Bendit, Daniel 1–6, 8, 11, 13–14, 16, 296, 325–8, 366–7, 371, 377, 383
Curiel, Henri, 183, 292, 294
Cygelmann, Viktor, 184
Cypel, Sylvain, 228–9

El-Dani, Fadel, 258
Dankner, Amnon, 164
Danziger, Itzhak, 146, 158, 177, 194
Darwin, Charles, 297
Davis, Uri, 146, 250
Dayan, Moshe, 141, 192, 216, 221, 241, 294, 350

Deutscher, Isaac, 308, 327, 331, 354, 357, 384
Diner, Dan, 20–1, 65, 308, 313, 365, 367, 370–4, 377–82, 387
Dinur, Nina, 192
Dolchin, Aryeh, 15
Domb, Leib *see* Leopold Trepper

Eban, Abba, 190, 329
Ehrenfeld, David, 143, 149
Ehrlich, Avishai, 307
Ehrlich, Paul (Meir), 89
Eichmann, Adolf, 341, 343–9
Ein-Gil, Aviva, 217
Ein-Gil, Ehud, 307
Einstein, Arik, 146
Eldad, Israel, 142, 159
Elias, Raif Chana, 143–5, 147, 149
Elon, Amos, 14
Eshel, Nimrod, 46–7, 49
Eshkol, Levi, 17, 141, 191, 293
Evron, Boaz, 159–60, 181, 346

Fanon, Frantz, 119, 121, 233–5, 298–9, 372
Farah, Bulus, 86
Farah, Farid, 86
Farjoun, Emmanuel, 281, 306, 309, 313
Farouk I., 294
Feld, Israel (Sroulik-le-Rouge), 354
Fisher, Yona, 177
Flores, Alexander, 308, 313, 375
Fogel, Max, 167
Foucault, Michel, 311
Frangi, Abdallah, 295, 373, 381–2
Fried, Erich, 13, 382
Fröhlich, Ali, 89

Gabay, Yaakov, 160
Gaspar, André, 323
Gaulle, Charles de, 1, 102
Geisel, Eike, 115, 308, 360, 364, 375, 382–4, 403–4
Geries, Sabri (Sabri Jiryis), 80, 294
Gemayel, Pierre, 309
Ghilan, Maxim, 55, 159, 174–5, 181, 183–4
Ghoussoub, Mai (Magida Salman), 323
Ginsberg, Allen, 178
Ginzburg, Shaul, 34
Givoli, Shaul, 288
Gluckstein, Akiva, 91
Gluckstein, Chanie, 98
Gluckstein, Esther, 91
Gluckstein, Yigal (Tony Cliff, Leo Rock), 86, 91–4, 98–9
Golan, Joe, 292
Golandsky, Moshe, 45
Goldmann, Nahum, 15, 110, 292, 361, 369
Gomulka, Wladyslaw, 32
Gordon, Judah Leib, 155
Goren, Shlomo, 140
Gouri, Haim, 177, 347
Grab, Walter, 32–3
Greenberg, Uri Zvi, 142
Grodzensky, Shlomo, 329
Gruenbaum, Benjamin 'Benio', 3, 241, 326
Gruenbaum, Eliezer, 4
Gruenbaum, Jitzchak, 4, 166
Gruenwald, Malchiel, 343
Guevara, Che, 221, 293, 298
Guez, Mathilda, 16
Gur, Ben-Ami, 160

Habash, George, 223, 256
Habibi, Emil, 60
Haddad, Simon, 248
Halev, Mohammed Ali, 238
Halevi, Benjamin, 343
Halevi, Ilan (Georges Alain Levin, Ilan Albert), 5, 226–7, 231–9, 244, 258–9, 262, 265, 318, 372
Halperin, Uriel *see* Yonatan Ratosh
Halperin, Uziel *see* Uzzi Ornan
Halperin, Yehiel, 151
Hammami, Said, 251–5, 257, 260–1, 264–7
Hanegbi, Haim (Haim Bajajo-Hanegbi), 2–3, 5, 10–13, 41, 66, 87, 142–3, 145–50, 184–5, 191, 193, 229, 236, 243–4, 260, 266, 294–5, 325, 350–2, 364–5, 374
Harari, Chaya, 290
Harbi, Mohammed, 298
Hassan II., 296, 318
Hatib, Shauki, 238
Hawatmeh, Nayef, 224–5, 255, 261, 264, 282
Hazan, Yaakov, 290
Hazaz, Haim, 142, 158
Hecht, Ben, 343
Hecht, Dina, 307
Heenen, Susann, 367, 401
Hefer, Haim, 146, 170
Herlinger, Oskar (Oskar Mareni), 177
Hercberg, Shimon *see* Shimon Tzabar
Herzl, Theodor, 107, 336, 344, 384
Hesse, Reinhard, 379
Hindi, Khalil, 224
Hobbes, Thomas, 312
Honig-Parnass, Tikva, 17, 217

Horon, A. G. (Adolphe [Edya] Gourevitch), 151–2, 154, 157, 160
Horovitz, David, 293
Hussein, Saddam, 312
Hussein, Taha, 297

Ilan, Uri, 242

Jabotinsky, Eri, 142, 151–2, 166
Jabotinsky, Vladimir, 109, 142, 151, 169
Ja'far, Mohammad *see* Kanan Makiya
Jeanson, Francis, 183, 292
Jibril, Ahmed, 256, 263
Jiryis, Sabri *see* Sabri Geries
Jumblatt, Kamal, 309–10, 314

Kadi, Leila S., 281–2, 284–6, 296–7, 306
Kadir, Nada, 310, 323
Kahwaji, Habib (Abu Kamel), 80, 246, 248
Kalvarisky, Haim, 91
Kanafani, Ghassan, 284, 315
Kaniuk, Yoram, 347
Kapeliuk, Amnon, 218
Kaplan, Yirmiyahu, 7, 29, 33, 35, 40, 54, 67
Kar'awi, Anis, 238, 248
Kardush, Mansour, 80
Kasztner, Rudolf (Reszö), 341–5
Katz, Moi, 94
Katzir, Vivi, 289
Keisary, Uri, 149, 161
Keita, Modibo, 234, 292
Kemal, Mustafa (Atatürk), 169

INDEX OF PERSONS | 459

Kenan, Amos, 146–50, 158–60, 164–7, 170–2, 177, 179, 181, 183, 185, 190–2, 194–6, 257, 288, 291–2, 346–7, 349–50, 352
Kenan, Eli, 147
Kerouac, Jack, 178
Kessous, Aziz, 121
Khaladi, Ahmed, 249
Khalifa, Ahmed, 13
Al-Khalil, Samir *see* Kanan Makiya
Khomeini, Ruhollah, 310
Khrushchev, Nikita Sergeyevich, 30, 32–3, 37–8, 40
Khushi, Abba, 91
Kishon, Ephraim, 170
Kleinbaum, Moshe *see* Moshe Sneh
Klingberg, Marcus, 260
Klingberg, Sylvia, 219, 260
Klutznick, Philip, 369
Koestler, Arthur, 269
Kook, Hillel (Peter Bergson), 152, 343
Kopp, Mordechai, 147
Kraus, Shmulik, 146
Krivine, Alain, 296
Kugelmann, Cilly, 367, 369–70
Kunzelmann, Dieter, 379
Kupfer, David, 240, 245
Kuroń, Jacek, 36, 42, 69
Kurzweil, Baruch, 155–6, 158

Lachman, Gabriel (Gabi), 184–6
Lakhdar, Lafif, 21, 284, 286, 296–300, 303–5, 308, 311–12, 314
Lambert, Pierre, 227
Landau, Moshe, 177
Langer, Felicitas, 250
Lavon, Pinhas, 49

Lenin, Vladimir Ilyich Ulyanov, 38, 40–1, 354
Léon, Abraham, 355–7
Lerman, Debby, 238
Lerman, Meli, 249–50
Levenbraun, Avraham, 225, 250
Levin, Hanoch, 15, 250
Levy-Hass, Hanna, 384
Levin, Moshe (Mishka), 35
Lifshitz, Uri, 143, 146, 193
Livneh, Eliezer, 50
Livneh, Rami, 174, 225, 235, 238, 249–50, 294
Lobel, Eli, 14, 20, 122, 183, 227–9, 235, 281, 285–97, 306–8, 313–14, 317–18, 352–3, 356, 373
Lobel, Solomon, 287
Loewy, Ronny, 366, 383, 401
Lustiger, Arno, 371

Machover, Ilana, 281, 306
Machover, Moshé, 7, 27, 29–30, 33–42, 54–8, 61–7, 84–5, 101–2, 104–5, 107–8, 110, 112, 115, 117, 124, 145, 185–6, 188, 196, 199, 216–17, 220, 222–4, 226–7, 229, 237–9, 251–4, 257, 260–1, 266, 281–2, 284–7, 293, 306, 318, 331, 334, 350–1
Magdi, Cherifa, 375
Makiya, Kanan (Mohammad Ja'far, Samir Al-Khalil), 309–13
Malcolm X, 234
Mao *see* Mao Tse-tung
Maor, Harry, 373
Masrawa, Ahmad, 12
Martí, José, 39

Marx, Karl, 49, 355
Maspero, François, 286
McCarthy, Joseph, 15
Meir, Golda, 6–7, 14–15, 242, 293
Memmi, Albert, 20, 113, 119
Mendel, Hersh (Mendel Stockfish), 354, 358–61, 363–4, 384
Mendes-France, Pierre, 369
Merlin, Shmuel, 152, 343
Mikunis, Shmuel, 59–60, 344
Mill, John Stuart, 312
Milo, Ruth (Trude), 89, 100–1
Moczar, Mieczyslaw, 363
Modzelewski, Karol, 36, 42
Moked, Gabriel, 149, 174, 184
Moneta, Jakob, 86, 89–94, 97–8, 100, 358–60, 364, 373, 382, 401, 403
Moonshine, David, 147
Moos, Alfred, 330, 401
Mor, Shmuel, 174–5
Murqus, Elias, 356
Mussolini, Benito, 50

Na'arani, Subhi, 240, 248–9
Najmabadi, Afsaneh (Azar Tabari), 310–12
Nasser, Gamal Abdel, 42, 80, 124, 180, 215, 300–1, 303, 328, 336
Nehru, Jawaharlal, 292
Neumann, Giora, 16, 294
Nicola, Alisa (Alisa Novick), 86, 100
Nicola, Jabra (Abu Said), 83, 86–7, 93–4, 100–2, 115, 223, 226, 237–8, 244, 358

Offenberg, Mario, 115, 308, 313, 384
Omer, Dan, 143, 147, 149–50, 175–7, 179, 184, 190, 192–3, 196
Omry, Benjamin, 181
Oren, Mordechai, 290
Ornan, Uzzi (Uziel Halperin) 153, 166
Orr, Akiva (Karl Sebastian Sonnenberg), 7, 11, 14, 29, 33–5, 37, 39–42, 44–6, 49–51, 53–8, 61–7, 74, 104–5, 107–8, 118, 129, 148, 158, 185–6, 194, 196, 214, 217, 222, 229, 290–1, 293, 313, 336–9, 343–4
Ostermann, Helmut *see* Uri Avnery
Oz, Amos, 218, 220, 386

Pahlavi, Muhammed Reza Shah, 310
Pail, Meir, 51
Peres, Shimon, 111
Peters, Lilia, 289
Pilavsky, Nachum, 51
Pilavsky, Oded (Odik), 7, 29, 33–5, 40, 51–4, 67, 111–13, 217, 222, 224–5, 237–9, 244, 260, 290, 331, 362
Pinkas, David, 165–6
Pira, Giorgio de la, 183
Plehve, Vyacheslav Konstantinovich von, 344
Pohrt, Wolfgang, 384
Pontecorvo, Gillo, 374
Postone, Moishe, 367, 401

Qasim, 'Abd al-Karim, 38

Rabin, Yitzhak, 257
Ratosh, Yonatan (Uriel Halperin, Uriel Shelach), 150–4, 157–60, 166–7, 177, 189, 340, 345
Riftin, Yaakov, 48
Rilov, Nissan, 294

Rimon, Avraham, 153, 170
Robinson, Joan, 292
Rock, Leo *see* Yigal Gluckstein
Rodinson, Maxime, 250, 290, 294, 303, 311, 356, 369, 374, 396
Roetz, Heiner, 366
Rommel, Erwin, 333–4
Rosenblum, Herzl, 171
Rosenstrauch, Yehuda, 143
Rosenzweig, Franz, 168
Rothschild, Sigi, 94
Rouleau, Eric, 115, 294, 318
Rürup, Klaus, 295, 318
Rürup-Braun, Ruth, 295, 318, 401
Russell, Bertrand, 13

as-Sadat, Anwar, 251, 254, 266, 386
Said, Abu *see* Jabra Nicola
Said, Edward, 312
Sand, Shlomo, 24, 217
Sartawi, Issam, 259
Sartre, Jean-Paul, 13, 118–19, 234, 250, 294, 372
Sayegh, Fayez Abdullah, 284
Schami, Rafik, 375
Schattner, Marius, 5, 238, 296
Scheib, Israel (Eldad), 159
Scheller, Bertold (Dov), 94, 373
Scheller, Susi, 94
Schmelzman, Shlomo, 386
Schmidt, Helmut, 383
Schocken, Gershom, 170
Scholem, Gershom, 156, 167–8, 188–9
Segall, Rudolf, 86, 90–1, 97–8, 358
Segev, Shmuel, 84
Selby, Tamar, 217
Senghor, Leopold, 293
Shahak, Israel, 250, 307

Shaked, Gershon, 172
Shalif, Ilan, 13, 244
Shamir, Itzhak (Michael), 159
Shammas, Anton, 149
Shapira, Rachel, 177
Sharett, Moshe (Shertok), 91, 332–3, 342
Sharon, Ariel, 368
Shas, Dov, 95, 101
Shazar, Salman, 175
Shelach, Uriel *see* Yonatan Ratosh
Shem-Tov, Shmuel, 15
Sheni, Theodor (Seidschnur), 35
Shereshevsky, Shimon, 184
Sherman, Shneur, 143, 147
Shiff, Meidad, 170
Shlonsky, Avraham, 153, 167
Shohat, Ana, 94
Shukeiri, Ahmad, 215, 222, 235, 303, 328
Slansky, Rudolf, 33–4, 290
Smilansky Yizhar (S. Yishar), 8–9, 62
Smorodinsky, Meir, 34, 41, 81–4, 106, 111–13, 121, 145
Sneh, Moshe (Moshe Kleinbaum), 34–5, 40, 49, 54, 57, 59–60, 83, 191, 290, 329–30, 350
Souss, Ibrahim, 258, 287, 296
Speier, Moshe, 370, 401
Speier, Sammy, 370, 401
Sprinzak, Ehud, 13, 17, 242
Stalin, Josef W., 32, 35–9, 60, 69, 93, 290, 329, 359, 362–4
Stein, Dina, 367, 370–1
Stein, Mordechai, 85, 94, 111, 192
Stern, Avraham (Yair), 151–2, 159
Sternhell, Zeev, 72
Stockfisch, Mendel *see* Hersh Mendel

Tabari, Azar *see* Afsaneh Najmabadi
Talmi, Alon, 92
Tamir, Shmuel, 342–3
Tammuz, Benjamin, 153, 157, 166, 170
Taut, Jakob, 83, 86–9, 91–5, 97, 100–1, 261, 358, 360, 364
Tchernichovsky, Shaul, 155
Tehilimzeiger, Moshe *see* Dan Ben-Amotz
Thälmann, Ernst, 88
Toama, Khalil, 12–13, 308, 339, 371, 375
Togliatti, Palmiro, 32
Tolstoy, Leo, 108
Trepper, Leopold (Leib Domb), 36–7, 354–5, 363–4
Trotsky, Leo, 19, 38–9, 88, 92, 101
Tsemel, Lea, 217, 250
Tse-tung, Mao, 221, 366
Tubi, Tawfiq, 60
Tumarkin, Yigal, 146, 194
Turki, Daud, 86, 187, 240, 242, 245–6, 248–9
Tzabar, Shimon (Shimon Hercberg), 139–43, 146–50, 160, 170–2, 177–9, 184, 190, 192–6, 293–4, 338, 341, 347, 350

Ussischkin, Menahem, 133, 177

Vered, Dan, 238, 240, 245, 247–9
Vidal-Naquet, Pierre, 250, 294
Vilenska, Esther, 40, 59–60
Vilner, Meir, 32, 40, 59–60

Warschawski, Michel, 24, 218–19, 226, 230–1, 238–9, 244, 260–2, 354, 369, 403–4
al-Wazir, Khalil (Abu Jihad), 298
Weigler, Otto, 94
Weinstein, Ella, 373
Weinstock, Nathan, 114–18, 121, 123–5, 308, 318, 357, 384
Weizmann, Chaim, 333, 339
Wetzel, Dietrich, 382–3
Wigoder, Shimshon, 217
Wolfensohn, Avraham, 8, 16, 222, 329

Ya'ari, Meir, 290
Yellin-Mor, Nathan (Gera), 159, 180–1, 183–5, 190, 349–50
Yerdor, Yaakov, 183
Yuval, Yochanan, 228
Yuval-Davis, Nira, 17, 307

Zach, Nathan, 149, 174
Zahavi, Nathan, 143
Zerubavel, Yaakov, 335
Zichroni, Amnon, 149
Zichroni, Rafi, 143, 149

EU representative:
Easy Access System Europe
Mustamäe tee 50, 10621 Tallinn, Estonia
Gpsr.requests@easproject.com

www.ingramcontent.com/pod-product-compliance
Lightning Source LLC
Chambersburg PA
CBHW052053300426
44117CB00013B/2107